THE
AMAZING
COLOSSAL
APOSTLE

THE
AMAZING
COLOSSAL
APOSTLE

The Search for the
Historical Paul

ROBERT M. PRICE

Signature Books | Salt Lake City | 2012

For more information, consult www.signaturebooks.com.

Cover design by Ron Stucki

16   15   14   13   12   5   4   3   2   1

Library of Congress Cataloging-in-Publication Data
Price, Robert M., 1954-, author.
   The amazing colossal apostle : the search for the historical Paul / by Robert M. Price.
      pages cm
   Includes bibliographical references and index.
   ISBN 978-1-56085-216-2 (alk. paper)
1. Paul, the Apostle, Saint. 2. Bible. N.T. Epistles of Paul—Criticism, interpretation, etc. I. Title.
   BS2506.3.P75 2012
   225.9'2—dc23
                              2012011325

CONTENTS

DECONSTRUCTING PAUL
A Short Introduction to What Follows

The Perils of Pauline Studies

At the dawn of the twenty-first century, it is a strange time for Pauline studies. After seemingly having run out of other ideas to beat to death, the academy has ventured into new territory. One might even say that, on analogy with the intrepid Netherlanders of old, Pauline scholars have *created* new territory to settle. A visit to the seminary book store or the religion aisle at Barnes & Noble will acquaint the reader with books arguing that Paul was a culture critic of Hellenistic Judaism, that he was a Jew and remained a Jew, that he wrote against U.S. foreign policy, and so on. Indeed, more than ever, he seems like a new Oracle of Delphi whose equivocal utterances may be read as conveying whatever message one most wants to hear. Like the infamous "historical Jesus," Paul has become a reflection of the scholars studying him.

Part of the reason for this state of affairs is that Jesus has recently been unavailable for these uses. As scholars have become more skeptical about recovering the goods on the historical Jesus (as witness the Jesus Seminar's claim that only 18 percent of the sayings database was reliable), the less plausible it has seemed to make him the poster boy for green politics, feminism, whatever. Granted, this hasn't stopped a number of scholars who still write books manufacturing and manicuring Jesus to look like them, since the less evidence there is, the more room is left for speculation; but some have retreated to Paul instead. Perhaps he can be the bulwark theologians once thought they had in Jesus. But great ironies lie this way.

First, the closer scrutiny the Pauline texts receive, the clearer it becomes (and by now it seems mighty clear indeed) that the epistles present us with many of the same challenges the Gospels did. They appear to be filled with the same variety of redactional seams, non-sequiturs, and double-audience rhetorical tricks we find in the Gospels. In short, the historical Jesus problem replicates itself in the case of Paul. The epistles reveal themselves to the discerning reader to have exactly the same sort of limitations as the Gospels do: both are collections of fragments and pericopae contributed and fabricated by authors and communities of very different theological leanings. Both present barriers to the access of the individuals under whose names they appear, not open doors.

Confronting the Protestant Christ

Second, scholars are more reluctant to recognize the data surrounding Paul and their implications. In short, Protestants of whatever vestigial degree have long ago elevated Paul over Jesus as their dogmatic master. Conservative evangelical Edward J. Carnell[1] was forthright about this: the epistles interpret or, in other words, trump the Gospels, and Romans and Galatians interpret (or trump) all the other epistles. I find a certain analogy from religious history helpful at this point. In esoteric Ismail'i Islam,[2] there is a belief that Allah sends pairs of incarnations of himself. First comes the "proclaimer" who gives as much of the gospel to the masses as they can understand: the milk, not meat. Shortly after him the "foundation" arrives, the master of esoteric meaning of what was preached by the proclaimer, truth that may sound quite strange to the run-of-the-mill believer and may indeed be rejected by them as heresy. But this is the meat. Rudolf Bultmann[3] understood the Gospel of John to be cognizant of something like this when it has Jesus predict the advent of the paraclete who will unveil new truths to the disciples, for which they were not yet ready during Jesus's earthly sojourn. The Beloved Disciple implicitly filled the role of the paraclete, and this is why the Gospel of John differs so much as to content and style from the Synoptics. It embodies the advanced course provided by the paraclete. Some Marcionites believed Paul was the paraclete, seeing in him the definitive interpreter of Jesus Christ's significance. Marcionites liked to depict Jesus sitting on a central throne with Paul to his right hand and Marcion to his left, and I would say that Protestants believe that too. Jesus gets reduced to "the Christ event," the naked and mute act of God which means nothing until some prophetic voice (Paul's) comes along to tell us what it means.

In the wake of the Protestant Reformation, the so-called magisterial reformers made Paul their figurehead and the source of their theology. It is he, not Jesus, who speaks in terms of justification by faith. It is Jesus who threatens to unravel the whole thing by enumerating commandments of the Torah and telling inquirers, "Do this and you will live." Ahem, enough of *that*, if you please! On the other hand, it is the Anabaptist Hutterites, Amish, and Mennonites who take their marching orders from Jesus: turn the other cheek, do not swear oaths. Three centuries later, liberal Protestants of the Harnack stripe discarded Paul for Jesus. "Paul" meant Protestant orthodoxy. And it was the ostensible historical Jesus they sought as a substitute for him, a Jesus who could be assumed to have preached a kind of Reform Judaism. This was a relief: no more Nicene Creed, no more worship of Christ, no more theology at all, just individual piety and the social gospel. Liberals wanted the religion of Jesus, the one he himself practiced, and no longer the religion *about* Jesus. They held Paul responsible for the changeover from one to the other. They dubbed Paul the "second founder of Christianity."[4]

Post World War I neo-orthodox theology went back to Reformation-era Paulinism, relieved at the seeming failure of the historical Jesus enterprise. As Albert Schweitzer showed, most of the historical Jesus models proposed by scholars reflected only their own biases. Schweitzer felt keenly Jesus's moral demands and famously obeyed them by founding a hospital in French Equatorial Africa but did not feel obliged to agree with Jesus theologically. He was able to see Jesus preaching a message of apocalypticism that sounded fanatical to modern ears, his own included, but categorized it as somewhat irrelevant theology. The neo-orthodox seized the distinction and reinterpreted the apocalyptic discourse of Schweitzer's Jesus in a different key. Jesus had come to bring, not the literal end of the world, but the end of the Jewish dispensation, to be followed by the Christian Church, not by the sky-descending kingdom of God. It was a bit of a shell game, but it provided passage back from Jesus to Paul. Indeed, it was surprising to see theologians willing to admit that Jesus had been wrong about the end of the world. But then, that only meant one could more easily put Jesus on the shelf and have recourse to Paul as one's chief theological oracle.

One receives the impression that Protestants, however liberal, have retreated from the perimeter wall—Jesus Christ—and taken refuge in the castle keep—namely Paul. The same moves made in the case of Jesus (refitting him as a post-colonialist, a feminist, an Orthodox Jew, and a green activist) have been made in the case of Paul. After this, there is nowhere to run. That is why scholars, so critical about the historical Jesus, have proven reluctant to accept significant higher criticism of the Pauline epistles. Just as an earlier generation of theological moderates surrendered John as unhistorical but retained the Synoptics for their picture of the historical Jesus, so Pauline scholars have cut off the Pastorals (1 and 2 Timothy and Titus) and relegated Colossians, Ephesians, and 2 Thessalonians to deutero-canonical status, products of the "Pauline school." Having done so, they nevertheless insist on the inviolable Pauline corpus containing the magic number seven: Romans, 1 and 2 Corinthians, Galatians, Philippians, 1 Thessalonians, and Philemon. Ferdinand C. Baur already debunked all but the first four as spurious, but even Bultmann dared not follow Baur that far. Bultmann needed enough of Paul's writings to build a theology on. Is the will to believe corrupting scientific criticism—again? I think so.

Paul and Sisyphus

I have been privileged to study with some outstanding New Testament scholars, including J. Ramsey Michaels, Andrew T. Lincoln, Gordon D. Fee, David M. Scholer, Donald Juel, Helmut Koester, Howard Clark Kee, Darrell J. Doughty, William Stroker, and Kalyan Dey. Lucky for me, they expressed a wide range of viewpoints, and all were seemingly omniscient. I recall Gordon Fee[5] bringing 2 Corinthians to life almost as if he were channeling the writer! I remember how he would hoist himself from one mighty peak of 1 Corinthians to the next, trying to demonstrate what one passage had to do with another, how text B was an answer to the question brought up in text A. There must have been some connection, but what was it? But then I recall several years later listening as Darrell Doughty pointed out that such reasoning was essentially *harmonization*, the kind of thing critics had long since stopped doing in the case of the Gospels. When we notice that a chapter of the Gospels is jumping from one topic to the next with no real connection except broad topics or catchwords, we learn to read this as a collection of originally separate sayings, stories, and aphorisms and do not insist that a single individual said all these things, much less that he did it in just that order and on that occasion. However, when reading the epistles, we see the same sort of rough edges and we want to make sense of them as moments of a single, spontaneous discourse set to paper. What is stopping us from recognizing, precisely on the basis of such phenomena, that we have been barking up the wrong tree? We have been harmonizing instead of exegeting. Doughty commented that virtually all commentaries on the epistles, including Fee's erudite tome on 1 Corinthians, are largely exercises in harmonization: *What would the text have to mean if it were a unitary discourse?* But it *isn't* one, and therefore such an approach bids us construct elaborate theological latticeworks, giving every verse a place in the structure that makes a synthetic whole much greater than its parts.

Doughty and I began to look into the neglected work of the Dutch Radical Critics who denied that the historical Paul had written any of the letters ascribed to him. On second thought, for instance, Walter Schmithals's brilliant book *Gnosticism in Corinth* explains many puzzles in the first letter to the Corinthians by reference to Gnostic trends that are attested only for the second century. It would make much more sense if he had placed 1 Corinthians in the second century. I began to weigh Willem van Manen's claim that the epistles made no lasting impact on any of the church communities to which they were ostensibly sent. From this, Van Manen inferred that the letters had not in fact been written or sent within the lifetime of the historical Paul but later. The Pauline letters were the favorites of Gnostics, Encratites, and Marcionites. Tertullian called Paul "the apostle of Marcion and the apostle of the heretics," and indeed it was Gnostics and Marcionites who wrote the first commentaries on the Pauline epistles and on the Gospel of John. Elaine Pagels's book *The Gnostic Paul*[6] demonstrated how much sense hitherto strange Pauline texts made when inserted into a Gnostic framework. By contrast, one looks in vain for any real Pauline influence on second-century writers. I began to frame a most unaccustomed question: *What if there were no Pauline communities, no Paulinists, until the late first and early second centuries?* The earliest Pauline Christians we know of were Marcionites and Gnostics. We have always inferred the existence of a Pauline wing of the early church from reading the epistles as products of the mid-first century. But what if their narrator was not the same as their author? What if their narratees were not the same as their actual readers? The Corinthians, for instance, may have been fictive characters like the Pharisees and the disciples whom Jesus addresses in the Gospels. Jesus is really talking over their heads to the reader.[7] So is Paul in the epistles, or so I am beginning to think. Just as in the Gospels, Jesus is really dispensing the views of the evangelists and other early Christians, so why not admit that the writers of these epistles were not Paul?

The deeper I have penetrated into the work of the Dutch Radicals and other critics, the more humbled I have become in finding the inevitable; what I thought were new insights I had found were discoveries already elaborated on by the old critics. It was a comfort, a corroboration of sorts, but I couldn't help feeling a certain sense of futility and frustration. The great Pauline scholar Winsome Munro, who nominated me for the Westar Institute Paul Seminar, told me once after looking at some of the work of Doughty, myself, and a couple of others, that she had begun to wonder whether we were not merely reinventing the wheel. That's okay. It's necessary since most people seem to have forgotten the wheel and its use. As I view it, the field of Pauline studies has been largely moribund for many years. It is high time we extricate ourselves from the Sargasso Sea of traditionalism and reclaim what our critical forebears achieved.

The Colossus of Tarsus

Now, as to the plan of the present book, the figure of the Apostle Paul looms, dwarfs everything, and towers over all. It is not easy to take it all in with a single glance. We must approach the subject of our study from various angles. Accordingly, I have tried to cover sections of the great figure in individual studies in these chapters.

Eventually I dropped out of the Paul Seminar because I didn't care for the direction it was taking. Instead I joined the Acts Seminar, where I felt more at home. Arthur J. Dewey, Chris Shea, Joseph B. Tyson, Dennis Smith, Richard I. Pervo, Gerd Lüdemann and others all agreed that Acts was pretty much an historical novel, much like the so-called Apocryphal Acts, and that it was written in the second century. There is virtually no historical value to it, but it is rich in edifying propaganda, its author having extensively rewritten sources that seem to include Homer, Virgil, Euripides, Josephus, and the Septuagint, creating a revisionist version of early Christianity in the golden age of its origin. Papering over bitter schisms and disputes known to us from the Pauline letters, Acts is a catholicizing document that wants to reconcile, as Baur thought, two factions: the Jewish-Torah Christians led by Peter and the Law-free gentile and Hellenistic Jewish believers led by Paul. It may be that Acts seeks to reconcile the Catholics who wanted to retain the Old Testament, symbolized by Peter, with the Marcionites who wanted to cut it loose and were symbolized by Paul. In either case, Acts draws extensive and contrived parallels between its two chief heroes, showing that the partisans of one can hardly discount the divine imprimatur on the other. Peter and Paul both raise someone from the dead (Acts 9:36-40; 20:9-12); heal a paralytic (3:1-8; 14:8-10); heal by extraordinary, magical means (5:15; 19:11-12); vanquish a magician (8:18-23; 13:6-11); and miraculously escape prison (12:6-10; 16:25-26). Paul is made over into a clone of Peter, keeping the Torah and circumcising the occasional convert, while Peter is given Paul's traditional role as the pioneer preacher to the gentiles, arguing that they needn't be circumcised or keep the Torah.[8]

In short, we should not look optimistically at Acts as a source for reconstructing the historical Paul. In "The Legend of Paul's Conversion," I show the probable literary sources of Luke's stories of Saul's conversion on the road to Damascus. Either the author of Acts did not know how Paul came to Christianity or thought the facts too mundane, replacing them with something much more exciting.

The second chapter introduces and summarizes the research

that led scholars to abandon some or all of the Pauline letters as spurious. This means that the quest for the historical Paul becomes more difficult: neither Acts nor the epistles will be much help to us. On the other hand, the epistles are fascinating and important in their own right. Where did we get them? Who preserved them, collected them, and perhaps edited them? How sure can we be that we have what their original authors wrote? Chapter two deals with these issues.

Scholars are agreed that there was at least a hiatus during most of the second century when the Pauline epistles were ignored or suppressed by the early Catholic Church because of their appeal to heretics or because they were actually heretical in character. I deal with that question a bit in chapter 3 but return to it in greater detail in chapter 4, where I review the *Acts* and *Apocalypses of Paul* current in the second century, asking who did and didn't quote the epistles and why.

Chapter 5 sets aside the letters for a moment to ask after the apostles. What did it mean to be an apostle? Exactly what was at stake when some affirmed that Paul was an apostle and others denied it? Did the historical Paul have disputes over such matters? Was it perhaps a later debate that was unknown in the first century? I examine the most important of the apocryphal Acts, the *Acts of Paul, Peter, Andrew, and Thomas*, together with their mythic or novelistic sources. We will see how originally wide-open and flexible the category of wandering preachers was until it was eventually shrunk down to twelve men who functioned as guarantors for an official Jesus for a single faction of Christians. Such a dispute can never have taken place in the lifetime of the historical Paul.

In chapter 6, I examine an additional strategy employed by the Catholic Church to suppress Paul's heretical legacy. Not only did they discourage the use of the Pauline writings, they began to squeeze him out of the history of the founding of the churches, crediting his accomplishments to other, safer apostolic names.

Walter Bauer, in his *Orthodoxy and Heresy in Earliest Christianity*, called attention to the mysterious replacement of Paul by John, son of Zebedee, as the founder of the Ephesian church.[9] I examine that theory, comparing legends attached variously to Paul or John in Ephesus. This anti-Pauline turf war wound up prompting a good bit of discussion in the Pauline epistles, whose authors stoutly defended Paul's historic role against others who retroactively claimed glory for themselves.

The Lion of Pontus

Chapter 7 approaches the identity of the historical Paul from a different angle to propose, with Hermann Detering,[10] that Paul was actually the same man remembered as Simon Magus, which may be why both men are said to have been the father of all heresy. There were other historical Pauls, namely the writers of the epistles. Marcion was one of these, having authored at least portions of Galatians and Ephesians and perhaps more. He must have used extant Simonian writings or at least teachings, modifying them in his own more socially conservative direction.

The remaining chapters of *The Amazing Colossal Apostle* venture analyses of each of the canonical Pauline epistles. I seek to distinguish various earlier and later layers within the texts, corresponding to Simonian, Marcionite, and early Catholic elements, plus interpolations from various sources. Interesting surprises await!

As I have pursued this research over many years, I have reached more and more radical and far-reaching conclusions. I began with fairly mainstream critical assumptions, and as the years passed I learned to appreciate, more and more, what Paul de Man called the dialectic of blindness and insight.[11] I realized that there were many big things I could never see until I had seen all of the little ones first. Small keys began to open bigger doors to larger rooms within. I began to have bigger and bigger suspicions, the larger ones made possible by the smaller ones. I have preserved this progression in the following chapters. Early on, I don't disabuse readers of their assumptions but begin by assuming that the epistles are substantially Pauline until we find reason to believe differently. Once we do, the puzzle pieces start fitting into unsuspected, much broader patterns. At first, my arguments may seem to strain at a gnat, whereas later on I will be swallowing whole camels or squeezing them through the eye of a needle. I will seem more conservative in both assumptions and conclusions in the beginning, partly because I was more conservative when I did my initial research, but equally because I know I must meet you readers where you are if I hope to convince you to come with me to where I end up. Feel free to jump off the train at any point if you are afraid we might crash. Especially when the train runs out of track.

NOTES

[1]Edward John Carnell, *The Case for Orthodox Theology* (Philadelphia: Westminster Press, 1959), 57-58.

[2]Sami Nasib Makarem, *The Doctrine of the Ismailis* (Beirut: Arab Institute for Research and Publishing, 1972), chapter 3, "Prophethood and Imamate," 35-47.

[3]Rudolf Bultmann, *The Gospel of John: A Commentary,* trans. George R. Beasley-Murray, et al. (Philadelphia: Westminster Press, 1975), 566-67.

[4]William Wrede, *Paul,* trans. Edward Lummis (London: Philip Green, 1907), 179: "It follows then conclusively from all this that Paul is to be regarded as *the second founder of Christianity.*"

[5]Gordon D. Fee, *The First Epistle to the Corinthians,* New International Commentary on the New Testament Series (Grand Rapids: Eerdmans, 1987).

[6]Elaine Pagels, *The Gnostic Paul: Gnostic Exegesis of the Pauline Letters* (Philadelphia: Fortress Press, 1975).

[7]Robert M. Fowler, *Let the Reader Understand: Reader-Response Criticism and the Gospel of Mark* (Minneapolis: Augsburg Fortress, 1991).

[8]Ferdinand Christian Baur, *Paul, the Apostle of Jesus Christ: His Life and Works, His Epistles and Teachings*, trans. Allan Menzies, 2 vols. (1873; Peabody, MA: Hendrickson Publishers, 2003), 1:5-11.

[9]Walter Bauer, *Orthodoxy and Heresy in Earliest Christianity*, eds. Robert Kraft and Gerhard Krodel, trans. Paul J. Achtemeier, et al. (Philadelphia: Fortress Press, 1971).

[10]Hermann Detering, "The Falsified Paul: Early Christianity in the Twilight," trans. Darrell J. Doughty, *Journal of Higher Criticism* 10 (Fall 2003).

[11]Paul de Man, *Blindness and Insight: Essays in the Rhetoric of Contemporary Criticism*, Theory and History of Literature Series, 2d. ed. (Minneapolis: University of Minnesota Press, 1983), chap. 7, "The Rhetoric of Blindness: Jacques Derrida's Reading of Rousseau," 102-41.

1.

The Legend of Paul's Conversion

We have ways of making you talk

One reason it is often difficult to tell whether a particular piece of biblical narrative we are dealing with is history or fiction is that stories in the Bible appear for their edifying or theological value. Since the stories are not there to satisfy idle curiosity, we cannot readily determine whether a given story has been remembered or fabricated, or is a bit of both. And in the nature of the case, it is always easier to show the unhistorical nature of a narrative than to verify it as historical. Historical criticism scrutinizes; it doubts and holds the text's feet to the fire, rather like the evil interrogator in the movies who assumes his captive has information but is lying when the accused pretends to know nothing. Even though the poor prisoner may, like Dustin Hoffman in *The Marathon Man*, really know nothing, the interrogator must nonetheless assume he is lying ("I'll ask you one more time ... "). Even so, the biblical critic may never be convinced his story is true even if God knows it to be a factual account. It is the futility of trying to prove a negative—in this case, that the text is not a piece of fiction. At any rate, the story of Paul's conversion (Acts 9, 22, 26) has been for many hundreds

1

of years both edifying (as a paradigm case of God's forgiving grace even to the chief of sinners) and apologetically important (miraculously proving the reality of the risen Christ). As such, it naturally calls forth our suspicions, and if the critic is like a merciless interrogator of texts, we may compare him with the picture of Paul as a persecutor[1] of the saints in the very story we intend to subject to such cross-examination here.

Seeing double

To suspect or reject the historical basis of the story of Paul's conversion as we read it in Acts is certainly nothing new in the history of scholarship. Indeed, one might conclude that the issue was settled long ago with a negative verdict by Baur, Zeller, and Ernst Haenchen.[2] The contradictions and implausibilities of the three linked episodes (Paul's persecution after Stephen's stoning, his vision of the risen Jesus on the Damascus road, and his catechism and baptism by Ananias) are well known. To review just a few of them, the Stephen martyrdom (as Hans-Joachim Schoeps,[3] followed by Robert Eisenman,[4] suggests) is a fictionalization of the martyrdom of James the Just, who found himself in similar circumstances, as one can still glimpse in Acts 7:52: "the Just One, whom you have now betrayed and murdered"[5]). Luke's reduction of the Jewish Sanhedrin to a howling lynch mob is not to be dignified with learned discussion. Worse yet, Saul has been appended to the narrative by means of a typical Lukan blunder. The law mandated casting aside clothes of the one executed, not those of his executioners, but Luke has Saul play coat-check for the mob (Acts 7:54). Then Saul does not spearhead the persecution so much as personify it. As Haenchen notes,[6] this is primarily a piece of "darkness before the dawn" hagiography anticipating the impending conversion of the enemy of the faith. The whole church is supposedly dispersed and jailed and has been tortured into blaspheming Jesus, but surprisingly, the apostles and myriads of their followers remain unmolested all the way into chapter 21. Saul obtains a hunting license from the high priest to persecute Jesus believers in Damascus, though in fact the jurisdiction of this ruler extended no further into Damascus than did that of Quirinius into Bethlehem.

The Damascus road Christophany is the creation of Luke, as is evident for several reasons. First, Luke quite properly (for artistry's sake) varied the details between his three accounts, even as he had with his two accounts of the Ascension, putting them a full forty days apart. As James Barr said regarding the latter, a writer who is so little concerned for consistency cannot very well have been striving for historical accuracy.[7] Second, as Gerhard Lohfink notes, Luke's stories copy standard scriptural type-scenes, to borrow Robert Alter's phrase.[8] The scenes "work" because they prompt the reader to recall the biblical prototypes. Since Luke offers them as transparent literary allusions, he cannot have expected his readers to take such scenes as historical reportage. The Damascus road episode certainly embodies such a type-scene, the kind Lohfink calls the "double vision." In such a sequence, a heavenly visitant grants the protagonist a revelation, adding that at the very same moment he or she is appearing to someone elsewhere with instructions to meet/help the protagonist.[9] A third reason, and the strongest of all, is that while Paul's epistles provide nary a historical peg from which to hang the Lukan tale, there are strikingly close literary prototypes on which Luke seems to have drawn.

Paul's con/version

Lohfink is willing to allow that "probably a real narrative lies at the bottom of it, but that is really not certain."[10] He is thinking of some oral-traditional story depicting Paul having a vision of Christ on the road to Damascus, but why should we assume this? Lohfink himself admits that Galatians 1:22-23, where Paul reminds his readers that their former persecutor was now preaching the Christian message, gives little to build on. And it is not uncommon for exegetes to note how the writings attributed to Paul really provide no parallel to the Damascus road account. Paul claims in 1 Corinthians 9:1 to "have seen the Lord" and says in 15:8 that "he appeared also unto me," but nothing about the circumstances or a connection to a religious conversion. The account in Acts runs together Paul's conversion to Christ and his being named the Apostle to the gentiles; therefore, one cannot assume that any Pauline reference to either must imply both. All Galatians 1:15-16 says on the matter is that "he who had set me apart before I was born, and had called me through his grace, was pleased to reveal his son in me, in order that I might preach him among the gentiles." Is there any echo or hint of the Damascus road story here? It is astonishing that Lüdemann can use the Lukan-derived term "the Damascus experience" for this or any other Pauline text.[11] On the contrary, unless we are determined to find the Damascus business there, Galatians will naturally be read as speaking of no conversion at all but of a lifelong religious commitment secured by divine fiat before his birth. At a subsequent point he was then "called by the grace" of God to some form of ministry, which later coincided in the showing forth to others the power of Christ's life within his mortal frame, precisely as in 2 Corinthians 4:10 and Galatians 3:1; 4:14.[12]

Does not the famous soliloquy in Romans 7 attest to something like a transformative experience on the apostle's part? Here Paul laments his tendency to choose evil over good and sin over righteousness. As is well known, this text is susceptible to too many viable interpretations, some of which will rule out the use of the passage as autobiography. Paul may rather be using "I" like the rhetorical "one." The same difficulty attaches to two other passages (Rom. 6:3; 1 Cor. 12:13) which may also be taken as instances of Paul rhetorically associating himself with his audience. If they are read as references to Paul's own baptism, he would seem to be presupposing anything but a unique mode of entrance into the Christian community.[13] Instead, he can speak of sharing his readers' baptismal experience just as he identifies by experience with the tongue-talking of the Corinthians (1 Cor. 14:18). One other bit of evidence pointing in this direction is spotlighted by Anthony J. Blasi:

> The conversion account in the Acts of the Apostles presents a dramatic scene in which the risen Jesus knocks Paul off his horse[14] on the road to Damascus and talks to Paul. None of this appears in the Pauline letters, however. Rather, we learn that "kinsmen" of Paul's were also apostles. In a letter of recommendation for the deaconess [sic; actually "deacon"], Phoebe, which is attached to the end of Romans, Paul notes that his kinsmen, Andronicus and Junias [sic: Junia], "are ... of note among the apostles, and they were in Christ before me" (Rom. 16.7).[15]

Here we overhear Pauline table talk to the effect that, like many present-day ministers, he is proud to hale from a family of previous ministers, and this hardly comports with the traditional picture of Paul radically turned about in his tracks, rescued like a brand from the burning by the miraculous intervention of Christ.

I suggest a comparison here between the case of Paul and his legend and that of Gautama Buddha. Later hagiographical texts tell the edifying tale of the Great Renunciation of Prince Siddhartha, who abandoned the opulence of his father's imperial palace to seek the solution to mankind's ills. It came about in this wise: Miraculous portents revealed to King Suddhodana that his newborn son should grow up to be either the world's redeemer or its conqueror. Being a mighty man of war, the king set about to make sure his son would follow in his bloody footsteps. He did so by shielding the boy from the knowledge that the world needed redemption. Prince Siddhartha lived a happy life roaming the extensive grounds and game preserves of the royal estate, never gaining a glimpse of human misery, never suspecting the woeful truths of pain, old age, infirmity, and death. This way, his father reasoned, he should know nothing of the world's need till irrevocably committed to the warrior's path. But it was not to be. The gods themselves saw to it that the prince's eyes should be opened: they took turns dropping down to earth in human form, one each day, disguised as a sufferer of illness, an old man, a fly-buzzing corpse, and at last as a mendicant monk. Each day the prince saw one, to the great consternation of his guardians. Thus he learned of sickness, old age, and death, and he meditated on this until the fourth day, when he beheld the monk in whom he saw his own way pointed. Abandoning sleeping wife and children, leaving a stricken father shaking his crown-heavy head, Siddhartha Gautama launched into the jungle and began his search for enlightenment. The story is rich in symbolism and implications, much like the story of Paul's conversion when the scales of unbelief fell from his eyes. But the judgment of Edward J. Thomas[16] is that the story is groundless and secondary. Now it may seem that this is stating the obvious, but that is only because we are used to taking New Testament supernaturalism for granted, and it does not occur to us to take Buddhist miracle stories seriously.

One might seek to historicize the Great Renunciation by rationalizing and demythologizing it. One might envision the prince rudely awakening from a pampered life, though without the fairy-tale luxury of the full-blown myth, by the unexpected sight of a genuine sufferer undertaking an ascetic life himself. Some historians of Buddhism have made these adjustments to salvage some of the story as historical. We may trace a striking parallel in the case of the legend of Paul's conversion. Many have been willing to rationalize the story by striking a deal between the historian and the believer within themselves.[17] Perhaps Paul had a hallucination, yes, a hallucination brought on by a deep crisis of conscience over his participation in the death of Stephen. Perhaps he even secretly coveted the freedom from the law that Stephen stood for. He was "persecuting" his own secret desire to be a Christian. And on the Damascus road his conscience and desire erupted from his subconscious in the form of the risen Christ to assure him his sin was forgiven and his desire granted. Despite the fact that this reconstruction ignores all the problems attending the Stephen and the Damascus road stories, it has not lost its popularity. For instance, Gerd Lüdemann dusted it off in his recent book on the resurrection.[18]

But rationalizing either story is only a stopgap. We need to invoke the fundamental historical-critical axiom that in any choice between a more or less spectacular version of the same event, the less spectacular is preferred since if the more colorful were first available we cannot account for the fabrication of the more mundane. But if only the less spectacular was available at first, we can well imagine someone replacing it with a more dramatic one. Accordingly, Thomas shows that any hypothesized version of the Great Renunciation story collapses when placed next to this passage from scripture:

> Thus, O monks, before my enlightenment, while yet a Bodhisattva and not fully enlightened, being myself subject to birth I sought out the nature of birth, being subject to old age I sought out the nature of old age, of sickness, of death, of sorrow, of impurity. Then I thought, "What if I being myself subject to birth were to seek out the nature of birth [etc.] and having seen the wretchedness of the nature of birth, were to seek out the unborn, the supreme peace of Nirvana?" ("The Sutta of the Noble Search," Majjhima Nikaya, i. 163)

Thomas concludes, "In these accounts we have no definite historical circumstances mentioned, nor any trace of the legend as we find it in the commentaries and later works. These have elaborated a story ... based upon the abstract statements of the earlier texts."[19] It seems to me that exactly the same relationship obtains between the more general language of passages like Galatians 1:15-16 and 2 Corinthians 4:6 and the miracle-mongering narrative of Paul's conversion as we read it in Acts.

Similarly, the canonical account of Mormonism founder Joseph Smith's "First Vision"—the appearance of Jesus and the heavenly Father in the Sacred Grove at Palmyra, New York—seems to be a secondary mythologization of an earlier process of introspective contemplation. According to the official version, in 1820 the four-teen-year-old Joseph found himself confused by the strife among local Baptists, Methodists, and Presbyterians. Which church should he join? Retreating to the woods to think and pray, he beheld an epiphany of the Father and the Son, who had come to tell him that his suspicions were well-founded: none of the competing sects was right, and he himself had been chosen to restore true Christianity to the world. Three years later, the angel Moroni appeared to Joseph, directing him to unearth the gold plates of the Book of Mormon. Strangely, this account of the revelation was unknown to Mormons and non-Mormon polemicists alike until Smith first recounted it in 1838. But according to Joseph's mother Lucy, it was at a time when the Smith family had been discussing the merits of the competing sects that Joseph went to bed one night and was awakened by an angel. The heavenly messenger told him that a great work would begin and he would start a new church, that all the other churches were wrong. It is apparent that Joseph later split this version of the story into two for greater effect. But in an 1832 account by Smith, he claimed that well before he had beheld a vision, it had been his own study of the Bible that had convinced him that none of the churches was scripturally authentic.[20] It is apparent that his own inner theological musings gradually became externalized, with the help of legendary embellishment, and the result was a legendary conversion narrative.

The story of Paul's Damascus road conversion can no more be salvaged by rationalizing historicization than that of the Great Renunciation of the Buddha or the visions of Joseph Smith. All alike are midrashic narratizations of earlier, less spectacular, auto-biographical musings.

Damascus covenant

I have noted the tendency, even among critical scholars (as witness Lüdemann), who ought to know better and who indeed do know better, to discount Luke's story of Paul's conversion in Acts as myth or even fiction and yet in effect to continue presupposing the substance of it to be historically true. Chronologies are based on the conversion of Paul despite the dearth of evidence for it. It is simply too much trouble to think through the implications, the redrawing of the rules that might become necessary. It is quite as unthinkable for them to let go the Big Bang model of Pauline origins as it is for them to dispense with what Burton Mack[21] calls the "Big Bang model" of Christian origins in general. If, as Mack suggests, the Big Bang of cross-and-resurrection is merely one version of a multiform myth of Jesus, we must shake off its spell and try to get behind the Easter morning faith of the disciples.[22] Similarly, the need is just as serious to get behind the legend of Paul's conversion if we wish to come to a better understanding of the evolution of the Pauline movement.

James D. G. Dunn's discussion[23] of various theories seeking to derive Paul's theology directly from his conversion experience on the Damascus road is instructive in ways he may not intend. Some have proposed that Paul drew primarily a Christological inference from his vision. Jesus was a transgressor of the Torah, yet he was resurrected; so it turns out that he was the messiah after all. Others suggest that Paul drew a legal inference: if the Torah (shorthand for works of righteousness) condemned the likes of the now-vindicated Jesus, then so much for the Torah. Dunn himself settles upon the nuance that Paul inferred the need for a gentile mission. If a law-transgressing Jesus was vindicated by the resurrection, then God had exercised his preferential option for the scofflaws—the gentiles. In all this, Dunn is worried about how Paul could have inferred either God's saving grace or Jesus's messiahship or the gentile mission from the Damascus road encounter, that is, *on the spot.* Dunn complains that previous theories do not comport with Paul's supposed claim in Galatians 1:15-16 of his calling and setting apart before birth, which Dunn, needless to say, interprets à la Acts 25:17-18 as a reference to the Damascus road, since he received his commission "the hour I first believed."[24] Never mind that Dunn's theory is the lamest of the lot, but what has he shown? Mainly, that exegetes can take such historical reconstructions and not notice that they have passed, with Luke, from the domain of historical explanation to that of midrash.[25] It is not that they miss Luke's point. No, they are on precisely his wavelength. It just isn't history. Dunn's "historical" reconstruction, even more than those he criticizes, leaves no room for a man hammering out his theology as new questions arose. Luke's picture of Paul receiving his gospel in one gulp on the road to Damascus is the same sort of theological cameo as the story of Moses getting the whole Torah on Mount Sinai. This is narratized theology, not history.

From Paul's biography to Luke's bibliography

If there is no graft point in the Pauline epistles for Luke's account of Paul's conversion, where did Luke derive his inspiration and why did he feel the need to include such a scene? First, it seems plain, as soon as one reads the texts in question, that Luke borrowed freely from two well-known literary sources, Euripides's *Bacchae*[26] and the story in 2 Maccabees of the conversion of Heliodorus. From 2 Maccabees, Luke has borrowed the basic story of a persecutor of the people of God being stopped by a vision of heavenly beings (3:24-26), thrown to the ground in a faint, blinded (3:27), and cared for by righteous Jews who pray for his recovery (3:31-33), whereupon the ex-persecutor converts to the faith he once tried to destroy (3:35) and begins witnessing to its truth (3:36). Given Luke's propensity of rewriting the Septuagint,[27] it seems special pleading to deny that he has done the same in the present case, the most blatant of them all.[28]

From the *Bacchae*,[29] Luke has derived the core of the Damascus road epiphany, the basic idea of a persecutor being converted despite himself by direct fiat from the god whose followers he has been abusing. Pentheus has done his best to expel the enthusiastic maenads of Dionysus from Thebes, against the counsel of Cadmus, Teiresias, and other level heads who warn him not to be found fighting against a god (Teiresias: "Reckless fool, you do not know the consequences of your words. You talked madness before, but this is raving lunacy!" 357-60; Dionysus: "I warn you once again: do not take arms against a god," 788-89; "A man, a man, and nothing more, yet he presumed to wage war with a god," 636-37; cf. Acts 5:33-39). The maenads, though they seem to be filled with wine, are really filled with divine ecstasy ("not, as you think, drunk with wine," 686-87; cf. Acts 2:15), as witnessed by the old and young among them prophesying ("all as one, the old women and the young and the unmarried girls," 693-94; cf. Acts 2:17-18) and the tongues of fire harmlessly resting upon their heads ("flames flickered in their curls and did not burn them," 757-58; "tongues of fire," 623-24; cf. Acts 2:3)! Pentheus remains stubborn in his opposition, arresting the newly-arrived apostle of the cult, who turns out to be Dionysus himself, the very son of god in mortal disguise. After an earthquake frees him from Pentheus's prison (585-603; cf. Acts 16:25-34), Dionysus strolls into Pentheus's throne room and mocks him ("If I were you, I would ... not rage and kick against necessity, a man defying god." 793-96; cf. Acts 26:14), offering Pentheus the chance to find the outlaw disciples in their secret hideaway. He may watch them at their sport, but he must go in drag, wearing their distinctive doeskin costume (912-16; cf. Acts 9:26-30). He mesmerizes Pentheus into agreeing to the plan (922-24; cf. Acts 9:17-18), and no sooner does Pentheus prettify himself than he has become a true believer despite himself (929-30). Still, the joke's on him, since Dionysus sends him to his doom—he knows Pentheus will be detected and torn limb from limb by the maenads. Poetic justice! The poor fool could dish it out but could not take it, even from the ladies! He wanted to persecute the maenads? Let him! He'll see how it feels from the standpoint of the persecuted! He becomes a true believer only to suffer the fate of one. And so does Paul. In light of the parallels with the *Bacchae* (Dionysus to Pentheus: "You and you alone shall suffer for your city. A great ordeal awaits you. But you are worthy of your fate," 963-64), we can at long last catch the awful irony of Acts 9:16: "I will show him how much he must suffer for the sake of my name!" Paul, a conscript despite himself, will find his punishment fitting his crime. He will suffer as a member of the same persecuted community against whom he himself had unleashed the persecution.

Another Jesus

We do not have far to seek to understand Luke's motive for the story. As is well known, Luke borrows from stories of Peter, and Jesus as well, in portraying Paul going about doing good, anointed with the Spirit, and healing the sick, raising the dead, casting out demons, and preaching in synagogues until he finally makes his way to Jerusalem like a moth to the flame. Passion predictions suggest what will happen there, and after a tumult at the temple, he is taken into custody, tried before the Sanhedrin and then by Herodian and Roman officials who all declare him innocent, and it is implied that he is killed (Acts 20:25; also cf. Acts 21:11 with Luke 18:31-33). Lest there be a missing piece, Luke felt it needful to include a scene corresponding to Jesus's baptism by John as the starting point of his ministry (Luke 3:21-22). This is the function of the Damascus road and Ananias sequence. The idea of Paul meeting the Risen One while traveling along a road comes from Luke's Emmaus story (Luke 24:13-33), and the encounter with "the Just One" (Acts 22:14) "whom you are persecuting" (Acts 22:8 and parallels) probably derives from an old story, echoed in the Clementine *Recognitions*, in which Paul ambushes James the Just in the temple.[30] But the sequence as a whole parallels the baptism of Jesus by John. Why does Luke bother to tell us that Paul was staying on the well-known "street called Straight" (Acts 9:11), if not to hint at John the Baptist's urging to "prepare the way of the Lord and make his paths straight" (Luke 3:4)? Paul's vision of Jesus reflects Jesus's own vision of the descending Spirit (Luke 3:22). As Jesus receives the Spirit at his baptism, so does Paul at the hands of Ananias (Acts 9:17). And Ananias even administers a baptismal rite aimed at washing away sins (Acts 22:16), just as John does (Luke 3:3). Finally, the very name Ananias (Hananiah, Hananyahu) is the merest disguise for John (Yah-hannon), the theophoric suffix replacing the identical prefix.

It is worth speculating whether Luke may have had some *Grundschrift* (underlying story) for the account of Ananias healing and baptizing Saul of Tarsus, though an unexpected one. As James Louis Martyn pointed out, the story in John chapter 9 of the blind man healed by Jesus and being excommunicated from the synagogue very likely reflected Jewish controversies over whether Jews might accept the help of Christian healers when all else failed. Martyn adduced two rabbinical anecdotes.[31]

> It happened with Rabbi Elazar ben Damah, whom a serpent bit, that Jacob, a man of Kefar Soma, came to heal him in the name of Yeshua ben Pantera; but Rabbi Ishmael did not let him. He said, "You are not permitted, Ben Damah." He answered, "I will bring you proof that he may heal me." But he had no opportunity to bring proof, for he died. (Tosefta Hullin 2, 22)[32]

> The grandson [of Rabbi Jehoshua ben Levi] had something stuck in his throat. Then came a man and whispered to him in the name of Jeshu Pandera, and he recovered. When he [the healer] came out, he [Rabbi Jehoshua] said to him, "What didst thou whisper to him?" He said to him, "A certain word [euphemistic for the Christian invocation of Jesus]." He said, "It had been better for him that he had died rather than this." And it happened thus to him. (J. Shabbath 14d)[33]

We see here the Jewish horror at the prospect of Jews being converted to the ranks of the Christian *minim* (heretics) by means of miracles. Why would it have been better to die than to receive healing in the name of Jesus Pandera? Because it would be to commit one of the three mortal sins: one ought to die before committing idolatry, and that is what conversion to the heathen demon Jesus would constitute. Note how the first of the two cautionary tales warns against even arguing the wrong side of the case lest disaster follow! Apparently there was some kind of ecumenical healing bridge between Jews and Jesus-sectarians, as witness also the striking inclusion of Yochanan ben Zabda (John, the son of Zebedee) alongside Asaph ben Berechiah as a pair of physicians who frame a kind of Hippocratic Oath in the Hebrew text *Sefer Refuot* (Book of Medicines), a text with Qumran affinities.[34]

Is it possible that Luke adapted a Jewish story which depicted a Jew, perhaps named Saul, beset with sunstroke and blindness, accepting the healing ministry of the Jewish Jesus-sectarian Ananias and, horror or horrors, becoming one of the *minim* as a result? Originally the Saul and Ananias story would have contained a slightly different cautionary message: look what will happen—it won't stop at healing!

Paul the persecutor

The reader has no doubt been asking whether the detail about Paul having previously persecuted the church does not require some sort of conversion episode. If Paul recalls his days of being a persecutor, does he need to make his conversion explicit? I believe that every single one of the apparent Pauline references to former persecution is secondary. As interpolations or parts of pseudepigrapha, such references, one and all, presuppose the same Pauline legend we read of in Acts.

First, John C. O'Neill marshals a number of considerations indicating that Galatians 1:13-14, 22-24 did not originally belong to the text of that epistle. "These verses have been interpolated into Paul's argument by a later writer who wished to glorify the apostle. The argument is irrelevant and anachronistic, the concepts differ from Paul's concepts, and the vocabulary and style are not his."[35] "The astounding reversal of roles he underwent, from a fierce persecutor of the Church to an evangelist of the faith, and from a precociously zealous Jew to an opponent of Jewish customs, is no argument in favour of Paul's position,"[36] which seems to be the thread of the passage otherwise.

The reference to "Judaism" is too late for Paul, since it implies that Christianity and Judaism are separate religions, a use analogous to speaking of "Judaism and paganism." Similarly, πιστις (pistis) as a reference to "the faith," that is, the Christian religion, would fit in Acts 6:7 and the Pastorals, but not in Paul. And Paul elsewhere uses the word εκκλησια (*ekklesia*) for local congregations. The use in 1:13 (cf. 23) smacks rather of the later Church Universal (or even the gnostic Church Aion) doctrine of Ephesians. The word αναστροφη (*anastrophe*) associated with Paul's name is elsewhere to be found only in Ephesians and 1 Timothy, while Ιου–δαισμος (*Ioudaismos*, or "Judaism"), πορθος (*porthos*), συνηλικι–ωτας, (*sunelikiotas* or "equals"), πατρικος (*patrikos* or "father's") do not occur even there. The frequency of the enclitic ποτε (*pote* or "when"), which occurs three times in these few verses, is closer to that in Ephesians and the Pastorals (seven) than the other Paulines (once more in Galatians 2:6, nine times elsewhere in the Corpus). Stylistically these verses are un-Pauline, the sentences even and regular, with 20, 19, 12, and 20 words respectively. And there is more.[37]

I have argued at some length elsewhere[38] that Winsome Munro, J. C. O'Neill, and others are quite correct in seeing 1 Corinthians 15:3-11, containing another reference to Paul's pre-conversion persecutions, as an interpolation. 1 Timothy 1:13 contains another reference to the mischief wrought by the pre-Christian Paul ("though

I formerly blasphemed and persecuted and insulted him; but I received mercy because I had acted ignorantly in unbelief"), but it is as spurious as the epistle which contains it. The same goes for Philippians 3:6, "as to zeal, a persecutor of the church." As Baur pointed out long ago, Philippians is virtually a fourth Pastoral Epistle, with its anachronistic references to bishops and deacons, the Gnosticizing kabbalism of the Kenosis Hymn in 2:6-11,[39] its unusual vocabulary, and most of all, its heavy hagiographic irony as it has Paul assure his readers that, though he would much rather wing his way to glory and finally attain his crown of perfection, he will continue to minister to them, which of course "he" does by means of this very pseudepigraph. The poignancy depends completely, as it does for the modern reader, on the implied reader knowing that Paul was in fact executed immediately after he wrote these sweet sentiments. It is another Acts 19, another 2 Timothy. It is no wonder that the writer knows the legend of Paul the persecutor. Note the anti-Semitism whereby it equates Jewish zeal with Christian-hunting. Paul could no more have written this than he can have regarded Judaism as a competing religion that he did not belong to (Gal. 1:14) or called fellow Jews the classic anti-Jewish jibe "haters of humanity" (1 Thess. 2:15—and here note yet another variation on the Pauline persecution legend where it was Palestinian Jews who persecuted Paul!).

Whence the Pauline persecution legend shared by Luke and his fellow Paulinists? I believe it is a late and garbled gentile Christian version, a turning to hagiographic advantage of an early and persistent Ebionite reproach of the Christian Paul as an "enemy of the faith," their faith, the Torah-gospel of James the Just and the Nasoreans.[40] In the Clementine *Recognitions*,[41] we read of attacks led by Paul ("the Enemy") on James and his flock. These are actual physical attacks upon James and the Jerusalem Ebionim, not unlike that attributed to Paul and the Sanhedrin in Acts. But in the Ebionite source underlying this episode of the *Recognitions*[42] it seems doubtful that Paul's attacks presaged a conversion; he is referred to uniformly as the Enemy of James throughout, as if nothing ever changed. Now, in fact, the historical Paul may never have mounted violent attacks on any group of rival religionists. "The legend of Paul's persecution of Christians ... may have been invented by the Petrine party, as the Paulinists invented the legend of Peter's denial of his Lord."[43]

Was it cut from whole cloth? Not exactly. Paul's reputation as one who, *as a non-Torah Christian*, opposed the "true" (Ebionite) faith and "fought" against it would have eventually crystallized into stories of his actually taking up "worldly weapons of warfare" (2 Corinthians 10:4). But the original point was simply that Paul as a Christian apostle strove, and polemicized, against the Nasorean Christianity of James and Peter. "They have heard concerning you that you teach all the Jews who are among the gentiles to forsake Moses, telling them not to circumcise their children or observe the customs" (Acts 21:21). Naturally, gentile Pauline Christians could never have interpreted his promulgation of the Law-free gospel as opposing the true faith, so when eventually they heard the charge that Paul had been an enemy of the faith they took it to mean he had once persecuted what *they* considered the true faith: their own Hellenized Christianity, which must, in turn, have meant he had previously been a non-Christian and then undergone a major about-face.[44]

Conquer by this

In suggesting that there never was any sort of dramatic conversion of Paul from a persecutor of Christians to a Christian apostle, I am floating a theory analogous to that of Thomas G. Elliott, who has recently argued that the famous story of Constantine converting to Christian faith as a result of a heavenly token seen in a vision before the Battle of the Milvian Bridge was a fabrication of Eusebius.[45] It seems much more likely that Constantine had simply been raised as a Christian. Originally the vision was supposed to have been no more than the origin of the symbolic battle standard, the *labarum*. Eusebius initially treated the story of the vision this way, as did all other early reporters of the vision. But eventually Eusebius introduced the notion that the event marked the miraculous conversion of Constantine to the Christian religion; subsequent writers who made the claim owed it to Eusebius. Elliott shows how, once we free ourselves of this bit of hagiographic propaganda about Constantine, we find ourselves in a better position to appreciate the mature, long-nourished convictions that led the emperor to involve himself in theological deliberations leading to Nicea. Constantine appears less the meddling amateur theologian, just as, without the Big Bang of the Pauline conversion, we can better understand the gradual, contextual development of his convictions without having to think that the risen Christ unscrewed Paul's cranium, dropped in a cassette, and pressed play.

The utility of the miraculous conversion legend is obvious in both cases: it served the same purpose as the common assertions that founder-prophets were unlettered. The eloquence of their revelations must then have come from God, not from the founder's own imagination, however gifted. Moses (Exod. 4:10-11), the prophet Muhammad ("But I cannot recite!"), the prophet Joseph Smith, Peter and John (Acts 4:13), and Jesus himself all are claimed never to have enjoyed formal schooling. "Where did he get all this? What is the wisdom given to him? Is not this the carpenter?" (Mark 6:2-3) "How is it that this man has learning, having never studied?" (John 7:15) The answer: "Flesh and blood has not revealed it to" him (Matt. 16:17). It must be good news from God, not good views from human beings.

Neither Paul nor Constantine could plausibly be depicted as uneducated, so the metaphor was just slightly different: what if each, albeit well-educated, was a non-Christian—in one case a pagan, in the other a Jew, converted to the faith by a miracle? This means the views subsequently propagated by them must be a gospel that is not of human origin (Gal. 1:1). "For I did not receive it from man, nor was I taught it, but it came through a revelation of Jesus Christ."

NOTES

[1]See Page duBois, *Torture and Truth* (New York: Routledge, 1991): "Is our very idea of truth ... entwined with the logic of torture?" Pass me the thumbscrews.

[2]F. C. Baur, *Paul the Apostle of Jesus Christ: His Life and Works, His Epistles and His Doctrine*, 2 vols., trans. Allan Menzies (London: Williams and Norgate, 1876), 2:42-89; Edward Zeller, *The Contents and Origin of the Acts of the Apostles, Critically Investigated*, trans. Joseph Dare (London: Williams and Norgate, 1875) 1:284ff; Ernst Haenchen, *The Acts of the Apostles: A Commentary*, trans. Bernard Noble, Gerald Shinn, and Robert McLachlan Wilson (Philadelphia: Westminster, 1971), 297-99, 318-29.

[3]Hans-Joachim Schoeps, *Theologie und Geschichte des Judenchristentums* (Tübingen: Mohr, 1949), 408-45. Having experienced audience reaction not unlike that accorded Stephen himself in the wake of his published hypothesis, Schoeps, in his 1969 popularization, *Das Judenchristentum* (*Jewish Christianity: Factional Disputes in the Early Church*, trans. Douglas R. A. Hare, [Philadelphia: Fortress, 1969]), decided only to hint at his theory "since all theologians immediately see red when the historicity of the alleged Hellenist deacon Stephen is questioned" (43). Little has changed in the interval, as the shocked and outraged reactions to Robert Eisenman's related conjectures in *The Dead Sea Scrolls and the First Christians: Essays and Translations* (Rockport: Element Books, 1996) have recently shown.

[4]Robert Eisenman, "Paul as Herodian," in Eisenman, *Dead Sea Scrolls*, 242-43; Eisenman, *James the Brother of Jesus: The Key to Unlocking the Secrets of Early Christianity and the Dead Sea Scrolls* (New York: Viking Penguin: 1996), 411-66.

[5]All Biblical quotations are from the Revised Standard Version.

[6]Haenchen, *Acts of the Apostles: Commentary*, 298.

[7]James Barr, *Fundamentalism* (Philadelphia: Westminster, 1978), 57.

[8]Gerhard Lohfink, *The Conversion of St. Paul: Narrative and History in Acts,*

trans. Bruce J. Malina (Chicago: Franciscan Herald Press, 1976), 80ff.; Lohfink, *The Bible: Now I Get It! A Form-Criticism Handbook* (Garden City: Doubleday, 1979), 123-24.

[9]Lohfink, *Conversion*, 73-77. In fact, one may note the presence of the same complex in Lucius Apuleius's *Metamorphosis*, also translated as *The Golden Ass*, in which poor Lucius, prototype for Francis the talking mule, beholds an epiphany of Isis, who instructs him to appear on the morrow in Rome to her priest Mithras, whom she is even now informing of the meeting. He will change Lucius back to human form in preparation for Lucius's initiation into her saving mysteries. This done, Mithras asks Lucius, "Why do you wait?" and initiates him (Book XI). Here, as in Luke's account of Paul, a blatantly metaphorical malady is healed preparatory to conversion-initiation, with the rhetorical prompt "Why do you wait?" (see Acts 22:16), which Oscar Cullmann long ago identified as a ritual cue, as also in Mark 10:14, "hinder them not"; Acts 10:47, "Can anyone forbid water for baptizing these people?" and Acts 8:36, "What doth hinder me to be baptized?" See Oscar Cullmann, *Baptism in the New Testament*, Studies in Biblical Literature No. 1, trans. J.K.S. Reid (London: SCM Press, 1952), 71-80.

[10]Lohfink, *Conversion*, 87.

[11]Gerd Lüdemann, *The Resurrection of Jesus: History, Experience, Theology* (Minneapolis: Augsburg Fortress, 1994), 50. He attempts to make the theological language of 2 Corinthians 4:6 an echo of a visionary experience on the way to Damascus. But if there is any relationship, the details of 2 Corinthians surely suggested the Damascus road story. Lüdemann's suggestion must be judged as an astonishing bit of nostalgic harmonization.

[12]It is always possible to read the Galatians passage in a way that would harmonize it with Luke's conversion tale, but this would be circular: the point is to see first what the Galatians text would seem to imply when read by itself. Only if it seemed problematical when read on its own would we be entitled to search elsewhere for some unspoken, missing premise. But if it makes sufficient sense as is, and obviously it does, then there is no need to read Luke's story into it. And if anyone wishes to nullify the natural implications of Galatians 1:15 by pointing out its allusion to Jeremiah 1:5, let me just note that the latter even more strongly envisions a continuous religious consciousness from early youth ("I am only a child."), not a drastic discontinuity or conversion.

[13]Reginald H. Fuller, "Was Paul Baptized?" in *Les Actes des Apôtres: Traditions, Rédaction, Théologie*, ed. Jacob Kremer, Bibliotheca Ephemeridum Theologicarum Lovaniensium vol. 48 (Gembloux: Leuven University

Press), 505. Fuller's article is pretty much a homiletical haze from which no real answer to the eponymous question ever emerges.

[14]Or better, on his ass.

[15]Anthony J. Blasi, *Making Charisma: The Social Construction of Paul's Public Image* (New Brunswick: Transaction Books, 1991), 26. One can always argue that "kinsmen" here merely means "fellow Jews," but other Jews are mentioned without such terminology. To distance him from his kinsmen is a leaf taken from those for whom the brothers and sisters of Jesus must be his cousins.

[16]Edward J. Thomas, *The Life of Buddha as Legend and History* (London: Routledge & Kegan Paul, 1927), 52.

[17]Van A. Harvey, *The Historian and the Believer: A Confrontation between the Modern Historian's Principles of Judgment and the Christian's Will-to-Believe* (New York: Macmillan, 1969).

[18]Gerd Lüdemann, *Resurrection of Jesus: History, Experience, Theology* (Minneapolis: Fortress Press, 1994), 81-84. This is only one respect in which Lüdemann has retreated into nineteenth-century rationalism and sentimentalism in this work, another being his Ernest Renan-like view that Jesus was resurrected into the nostalgia of the Twelve (97ff).

[19]Thomas, *Life of Buddha*, 52.

[20]David Persuitte, *Joseph Smith and the Origins of the Book of Mormon* (Jefferson, NC: McFarland & Co., 1991), 20-24.

[21]Burton L. Mack, *A Myth of Innocence: Mark and Christian Origins* (Philadelphia: Fortress Press, 1988), 7-9, 112-13, 368.

[22]Rudolf Bultmann, "New Testament and Mythology," trans. Reginald H. Fuller, in *Kerygma and Myth: A Theological Debate*, ed. Hans Werner Bartsch (New York: Harper Torchbooks, 1961), 42: "All that historical criticism can establish is the fact that the first disciples came to believe in the resurrection."

[23]See also James D. G. Dunn, "'A Light to the Gentiles' or 'The End of the Law'? The Significance of the Damascus Road Christophany for Paul," in Dunn, *Jesus, Paul, and the Law* (Louisville: Westminster/John Knox, 1990), 95.

[24]Dunn, "Light to Gentiles," 89-107.

[25]One finds a veritable cloud of witnesses to this point in the recent symposium collection, Richard N. Longenecker, ed., *The Road from Damascus: The Impact of Paul's Conversion on His Life, Thought, and Ministry* (Grand Rapids: Eerdmans, 1997). It would be closer to the truth, I am suggesting,

to speak of "the impact of Paul's life, thought, and ministry on the story of Paul's Damascus road conversion."

[26]Despite the pooh-poohing of Alfred Vögeli ("Lukas und Euripides," *Theologische Zeitschrift* 9 [1953]: 415-38), who held that Acts's parallels with the *Bacchae* are merely fortuitous and depend on dime-a-dozen literary motifs widespread in the Hellenistic world, it is plain that Luke has made extensive use of the *Bacchae*, as Lilian Portefaix has demonstrated in detail in *Sisters Rejoice: Paul's Letter to the Philippians and Luke-Acts as Received by First-Century Philippian Women* (Stockholm: Almqvist & Wiksell, 1988), 170. In fact, Luke has used the Pentheus versus Dionysus sequence twice, including the story of Paul and the Philippian jailer in Acts 16, though this time it is Paul who takes the role of Dionysus's apostle, while the jailer is the Pentheus analog.

[27]The Septuagint, or LXX, is the Greek translation of the Hebrew scriptures, or Old Testament, widely read by Hellenistic Jews and early Christians in New Testament times. Recent scholars have demonstrated how Luke seems to have gotten many of his own stories by adapting LXX prototypes. See Randel Helms, *Gospel Fictions* (Buffalo: Prometheus Books, 1988); Thomas L. Brodie, "Luke the Literary Interpreter: Luke-Acts as a Systematic Rewriting and Updating of the Elijah-Elisha Narrative in 1 and 2 Kings." Ph.D. dissertation, Pontifica Universita S. Tommaso d'Aquino, 1981(Ann Arbor: University Microfilms, 1992); Brodie, "Reopening the Quest for Proto-Luke: The Systematic Use of Judges 6-12 in Luke 16:1-18:8," *Journal of Higher Criticism* 2 (Spring 1995): 68-101.

[28]To return to the parallel with the legend of the Buddha's Great Renunciation, we might point out that, just as Luke appropriated the 2 Maccabees story of Heliodorus's blindness and conversion to embellish Paul's story, so the Buddhist tradition seems to have borrowed the legend of the Great Renunciation from the story of the Buddha's predecessor and near-contemporary Mahavira (Vardhamana), founder of Jainism (Maurice Bloomfield, *The Life and Stories of the Jaina Savior Parcvanatha* [Baltimore: Johns Hopkins Press, 1919], 114-15).

[29]I am using William Arrowsmith's translation in David Grene and Richard Lattimore, eds., *Greek Tragedies*, 23 vols. (Chicago: University of Chicago Press, 1972), 3:189-260.

[30]The *Recognitions*, attributed to St. Clement of Rome and quoted by Origen, are written in the form of a letter to James, the bishop of Jerusalem. Since James died long before the work was composed, its structure is a literary contrivance to convey historical and theological ideas, but nevertheless an important early Christian work.

[31]Reproduced here, with slight variations, from James Louis Martyn, *History and Theology in the Fourth Gospel* (New York: Harper & Row, 1968), 11.

[32]The Tosefta is a compilation of oral law complementing the Mishnah. One of the topical divisions, comprising several chapters, is called "Hullin," which means "unsanctified objects."

[33]This is a reference to the Mishnah, in this case as preserved in the Babylonian (as opposed to the Jerusalem) Talmud.

[34]Cited in Hugh J. Schonfield, *The Essene Odyssey* (Dorset, Eng.: Element Books, 1984), 51-52.

[35]John C. O'Neill, *The Recovery of Paul's Letter to the Galatians* (London: Society for Promoting Christian Knowledge, 1972), 24.

[36]Ibid., 24-26.

[37]Ibid.

[38]Robert M. Price, "Apocryphal Apparitions: 1 Corinthians 15:3-11 as a Post-Pauline Interpolation," in Price and Jeffery J. Lowder, eds., *The Empty Tomb: Jesus beyond the Grave* (Amherst: Prometheus Books, 2005), 69-104.

[39]The word *kenosis*, "emptying," here denotes the Savior's setting aside his divine status and prerogatives to undertake his earthly mission.

[40]The Ebionites were the ascetic Jewish Christians who followed James and denounced Paul, also known as, or at least closely associated with, the Nazarenes.

[41]Richard I. Pervo, *Profit with Delight: The Literary Genre of the Acts of the Apostles* (Philadelphia: Fortress, 1987), shows both the novelistic character of Acts and how traditional attempts to denigrate its "apocryphal" relatives have more to do with orthodox canon polemics than with historical judgment.

[42]For different estimates of the extent and worth of underlying Clementine sources, see F. Stanley Jones, *An Ancient Jewish Christian Source on the History of Christianity: Pseudo-Clementine Recognitions 1.27-71*, Christian Apocrypha Series (Atlanta: Scholars Press, 1995); Robert E. Van Voorst, *The Ascents of James: History and Theology of a Jewish-Christian Community*, Society of Biblical Literature Dissertation Series (Atlanta: Scholars Press, 1989); Robert Eisenman, *James the Brother of Jesus: The Key to Unlocking the Secrets of Early Christianity and the Dead Sea Scrolls* (New York: Viking, 1996).

[43]L. Gordon Rylands, *A Critical Analysis of the Four Chief Pauline Epistles: Romans, First and Second Corinthians, and Galatians* (London: Watts, 1929), 353.

[44]As Francis Watson ably shows in *Paul, Judaism and the Gentiles: A Sociological Approach*, Society for New Testament Studies Monograph Series (New York: Cambridge University Press, 1986), 26-38, there may well have been a Pauline "conversion," of sorts, from one type of Christian mission to another. Paul may have begun preaching a gospel compatible with circumcision among Jews, found only meager results, and turned to the wider gentile world, trimming back the stringent demands of the Law to make it easier for gentiles to convert, precisely as his foes alleged.

[45]Thomas G. Elliott, *The Christianity of Constantine the Great* (Scranton: University of Scranton Press, 1996).

2.

By Posthumous Post

Who wrote the "Pauline Letters"?

For nearly two millennia, no one questioned the authorship of the epistles attributed to Paul. Thirteen of them in the official New Testament canon bear his name, not to mention a number of other letters outside the canon. Origen of Alexandria understood that Paul could not have been the author of the Epistle to the Hebrews, but Paul's name wasn't on it; in fact, no name accompanied it. Nonetheless, most of the ancients were pleased to consider it Pauline because it had compatible theology and its inclusion provided a total of fourteen letters, two groups of seven, the lucky number in scripture. The first to deny Pauline authorship to one of the other thirteen was nineteenth-century theologian and critic Friedrich Schleiermacher (1768-1834).[1] Although he accepted 2 Timothy and Titus as Pauline, he rejected what he termed "the so-called First Epistle of Timothy." In an 1807 essay, he showed how this epistle contradicted all other Pauline materials in the New Testament, including the speeches in Acts and the other dozen epistles, as to vocabulary, theological conceptuality, and a presupposed ecclesiastical situation. He found points at which it appeared to be based on either 2 Timothy, Titus, or both; in some cases,

1 Timothy's author seems to have misunderstood what was borrowed. It was not long before other scholars widened the scope of
the investigation and discovered many of the same relations and
contrasts between the Pastoral Epistles (1 and 2 Timothy and
Titus) on the one hand and the remainder of the Pauline letters on
the other. Today, virtually all critical scholars agree that the Pastoral
Epistles are not the work of the historical Paul.

The Tübingen School

Another great nineteenth-century figure, Ferdinand Christian
Baur (1792-1860), the founder of the Tübingen School of New
Testament criticism,[2] whittled down the Pauline canon even further, finding himself left with only the four *Hauptbriefe* ("principal
epistles"), 1 and 2 Corinthians, Galatians, and Romans, as authentic and unassailable, minus a few questionable passages here and
there. Beyond the *Hauptbriefe*, Baur dismissed the letters as dis-
jointed, colorless, impersonal, and lacking specific occasion. Colossians, for instance, is awash in the terminology of later Gnosticism,
with Christ as the *pleroma*, or embodied divine fullness, as well as
the final goal of cosmic evolution, precisely as in Valentinianism,
one of the most influential of the Gnostic movements,[3] with everything finally imploding into oneness.

Gnostic influence is also evident in the notion of the cross as the
defeat of the principalities and powers, the archons and authorities,
which are angelic entities. And like the heretics condemned in the
Pastorals, the author of Colossians says the resurrection has already
happened at baptism (Col. 3:1; cf. Rom. 6, which stops on a dime,
just short of this).[4] Conservatives like to pretend that the author is
the historical Paul and that he was merely using the terminology of
Gnostic opponents ironically to refute them—a strange and obscuring tactic if ever there was one! No, the language and conceptuality
are the author's all right, just not from the author we know as Paul.

For Baur, Ephesians seems to be the work of the same author as

Colossians, just a different version of it. Later scholars would point out that although the vocabulary is Pauline, the sentence structure is not. The sentences are long chains of genitives with no end in sight. The first chapter comprises only two sentences in the original Greek! Edgar J. Goodspeed[5] would demonstrate by use of a table chart, much like a gospel synopsis, that every single verse of Ephesians comes straight out of, or at least closely parallels, material from Colossians, most of the other Pauline epistles, and the Septuagint, with nothing left over. No wonder it sounds like Paul—though without being by him.

Philippians presents Paul with fond hopes of one day being raised from the dead (3:10-11), whereas in his authentic epistles, his theology gives him absolute confidence in Christ. We are witnessing a shading off to Catholic "works piety," especially when believers are told to "work out your own salvation with fear and trembling" (2:12). What is the "perfection" Paul says he has yet to attain (3:12)? The real Paul would never have spoken this way, since in his view, one either lays hold on Christ or does not. In fact, readers receive the impression that the perfection the author aims at is actually martyrdom, which he plainly "anticipates" in nearly the same masochistic spirit as the author of the Ignatian Corpus.[6] Furthermore, Philippians is connected not by any sustained argument but rather by catchwords ("rejoice"). There is also uncharacteristic vocabulary. The author uses the adversative *plan* (πλην) three times, for example, whereas in all other Pauline letters it appears but once.

Note also the testamentary character of Philippians. It is filled with heavy irony, presupposing that the reader knows what finally happened to Paul. He didn't escape death as anticipated, but continued to edify his beloved Philippians nonetheless with posthumous letters like this one! This, plus the mention at the beginning of "bishops and deacons," makes Philippians almost a fourth Pastoral Epistle. And why does "Paul" promise to send Timothy with all the latest news when he is sending this present letter back to them via Epaphroditus? Couldn't Epaphroditus have filled them in? It is all artificial.

Nor is Philippians without a distinct Gnostic flavor.[7] Specifically, the Kenosis Hymn in 2:6-11 bears the marks of Valentinian theology. Just as Colossians had the *pleroma* embodied in Christ, Philippians has him exit the godhead (the *pleroma*) to sojourn in the extra-pleromatic sphere, the *kenoma* ("emptiness"). In thus disdaining an undeserved equality with God, he succeeds where Sophia failed, having trespassed from her perch on "the Limit" (what Jack Kirby called "the Source Wall") to seize the deep things of the Father. These are not mere seeds of Gnostic ideas that might one day grow into real Gnosticism; it is the real thing, met in passing allusions that will mean something to those familiar with the second-century system.

Both Thessalonian epistles are false, written perhaps by the same hand. The writer of 2 Thessalonians might have been embarrassed into correcting his own initial apocalyptic enthusiasm by dismissing his earlier work as that of some crank and not his own. The referent of 1 Thessalonians 2:16 must be the fall of Jerusalem in 70 CE. The writer must therefore have lived after this event. Once one stops insisting the text is the work of a man who died in 62 CE (Paul), it begins to make more sense. Most scholars today nervously attempt to pry this verse out of its context as a later interpolation, leaving the rest as genuinely Pauline. But this stratagem reminds one of fundamentalists' suggestions that Moses wrote the whole Pentateuch except for the account of his own death and burial (Deut. 34:5-8), which they suppose Joshua to have added. But in fact, it is just one more clue among many.

As with Galatians (6:11) and others (1 Cor. 16:21; Col. 4:18), the Thessalonian letters imply a contemporary cottage industry of spurious Pauline documents, against which one must learn to carefully guard (2 Thess. 2:15; 3:17). These are surely markers of a

time, long after Paul, when collections of his letters were considered authoritative, just like the reference in 2 Peter 3:15-16 that
"our beloved brother Paul wrote to you with the wisdom given him,"
just like he said in all his epistles when he discussed these things.
Granted, there are some difficult passages, "which the uneducated
and unstable twist." The author of 1 Thessalonians wants his letter to be read publicly to the congregation. What does this mean?
How *else* would it be read? It is, after all, ostensibly a letter to a congregation! Actually, the writer presupposes a situation in which the
Pauline letters have achieved at least quasi-canonical status and are
read in the liturgical cycle. It is this sanctity and authority that he
seeks to win for his own work.[8]

Once there came to be emphasis on apostolic writings, the
church at length grew understandably suspicious of the living voice
of prophecy (cf. 2 Thess. 2:2). Many were tempted to do away with
the whole thing, though our writer counsels evaluation on a case-by-
case basis first (1 Thess. 5:19-20), lest the Spirit's flame be entirely
quenched. Surely these concerns bespeak a common date of writing or a shared *Sitz-im-Leben* ("setting in life") with the *Didache*,[9]
with its similar suspicions against wandering prophets. We are by
no means in the time of Paul. In fact, the readers are urged to keep
safely to the venerable traditions Paul anciently imparted to them
(2 Thess. 2:15). This is like the fibbing author of 2 Peter 3:2 who
forgot he styled himself as one of the long-dead apostles whose old
predictions (3:4) were now coming true!

Baur's observations should have settled the matter, but just as
the majority of Martin Luther's followers lacked the daring to go
with their master's relegation of Hebrews, James, Jude, and Revelation to a canonical appendix, so most critical scholars quailed
in the face of Baur's challenge. Even the supposed arch-skeptic
Rudolf Bultmann quietly assumed the authenticity of seven Pauline epistles, restoring the haloes to 1 Thessalonians, Philippians,
and Philemon. One hates to think that the magic number seven

had anything to do with it. However, there were a few scholars who studied Baur's results and took off in the opposite direction, believing that he had not gone far enough.

The Dutch Radical Critics

Willem C. van Manen (1842-1905), Professor of Old Christian Literature and New Testament Exegesis at the University of Leiden, was identified with the school of Dutch Radicals who sought to go beyond F. C. Baur and carry his investigations into the Pauline epistles to their logical conclusions. In a series of articles and books,[10] he pressed his case that Paul had not written even the four *Hauptbriefe* (Romans, Galatians, 1 & 2 Corinthians) that Baur had left him. Though Van Manen confessed his debt to the pioneering work of Baur and saw his own work as the natural continuation of it, he reproached Baur for not having gone far enough. Baur had simply assumed that some of the "Pauline" epistles must be the work of the historical Paul. Closer examination of the *Hauptbriefe*, however, led Van Manen and his immediate predecessors to the conclusion that these, too, were pseudepigraphical.

Van Manen acknowledged his predecessors Edward Evanson (who wrote in 1792), Bruno Bauer, Allard Pierson, Samuel A. Naber, and Abraham D. Loman. These men wrote in the nineteenth century, and Van Manen considered Loman to have begun a new period of strictly scientific study of the question. Loman had attracted colleagues such as Rudolf Steck, Daniel E. J. Völter, and Van Manen himself. Van Manen first met Loman's theories with vigorous opposition, but his objections soon evaporated, the more closely he scrutinized his opponent's case. At length, Van Manen assumed the mantle of leadership of the new school of criticism because of the volume of work he devoted to the subject. No doubt, he was quite correct. The work of only one of these scholars has appeared in English, but thankfully, that one is Van Manen. Even then, however, we must be content with his articles in the *Encyclopaedia Biblica*.

Van Manen pointed out that external, or patristic, attestation of any epistle is worthless for establishing authorship. As Baur discovered, it provides nothing more than the opinion of some in the early church and proves nothing as to whether any ascriptions of the writings were actually justified. Internal evidence alone can settle the issue. For example, Papias thought Judas Iscariot's head swelled up like a parade balloon; why believe him when he says Mark was dictated by Simon Peter? On the one hand, tradition does not support the authenticity of the *Hauptbriefe* any more than that of the Prison Epistles (Philippians, Ephesians, Colossians, Philemon) or the Pastorals. Van Manen pointed out the inconsistency of those critics who supported the authenticity of Romans or Galatians by appealing to early patristic citation but who also counted such citations as irrelevant when they felt there were adequate internal grounds for rejecting the authenticity of epistles such as Ephesians. If it means nothing in one case, it can mean nothing in the other. An overarching unity among the Pauline epistles means only that there is the general conformity of a school of thought, not that of a single authorship.

Internal indications can demonstrate the fact of different authors but not, of course, whether Paul was ultimately the author of any one of them. To show that 1 Timothy is not the product of the same author as Romans implies nothing as to whether Romans was the work of Paul. All we can say is that they are not by the same Paulinist. Even within the *Hauptbriefe*, we find similar differences between the Corinthian epistles and Romans as exist between Romans and Philippians. The differences are linguistic, stylistic, ethical, and theological. The grounds for maintaining the pseudepigraphical character of all the epistles are as follows.

1. The question of their form

   a. They are *treatises, not letters*, whether to an individual or a group.

The matter of the epistle is destined for publicity. If the letter is always more or less private and confidential, the epistle is meant for the market-place ... All that is in the letter—address and so forth—[and] is of primary importance, becomes in the epistle ornamental detail, merely added to maintain the illusion of this literary form. A real letter is seldom wholly intelligible to us until we know to whom it is addressed and the special circumstances for which it was written. To the understanding of most epistles this is by no means essential.[11]

b. They cannot have been written to the ancient churches whose names they bear since they have *left no trace* on the history of those churches.

c. The imaginary nature of the letters is evident from *catholiciz-ing phrases* like "to all that are in Rome, called to be saints," "to the church of God which is at Corinth, them that are sanctified in Jesus Christ, called to be saints, with all who invoke the name of our Lord Jesus Christ in all places, etc.," "to the church of God which is at Corinth with all the saints in the whole of Achaia," "to all the churches of Galatia." Admittedly, one can reply that these phrases represent later, post-Pauline additions to make it easier to circulate the letter far beyond its originally intended readership. But again, how is this different from the desperate fundamentalist attempt to ascribe the Deuteronomic account of Moses's death to a later writer in order to attribute the rest of the Pentateuch to Moses himself?

d. They have been redacted. They teem with *discontinuities and internal contradictions* indicating, for example, that the epistles to the Corinthians and Romans are patchwork quilts in the style of a Synoptic Gospel, while Galatians seems to have been a Marcion-ite[12] document overlaid with a corrective series of orthodox inter-polations. As Darrell J. Doughty[13] points out, when we see such anomalies and anacoluthas in the Gospels, we readily recognize them as redactional seams, but when they arise in the epistles we brush the dust off our rusty harmonizations and go to work! It is just the sort of "blindness and insight" (Paul de Man)[14] evident in the earliest days of the Higher Criticism when it simply did not occur to scalpel-wielding Old Testament critics to subject the New Testament to the same surgery.

2. Their contents

a. There is *confusion over the nature of the churches* and Paul's implied relations with them. In Romans, "Paul" writes to a church ostensibly unknown to him, yet he does so with great presumption. In Galatians and Corinthians he is portrayed as writing to old friends and having to cajole, then threaten, after first boasting and flattering—none of which must be necessary if he is the authoritative oracle Romans makes him out to be. Which is the real Paul? Perhaps neither!

b. We can draw *no coherent picture of the opponents* Paul faces in his epistles. It seems rather that a pseudepigraphist or redactor is aiming scattershot at various heretical options current in his day, much like the later works of Irenaeus and Epiphanius who wrote "against all heresies." This is why scholars assuming Pauline authorship have repeatedly come up with implausible chimeras combining elements of Gnostics, Judaizers, apocalyptic enthusiasts, and charismatic triumphalists as candidates for Paul's opponents. This is like a police artist's conception of a crook created by combining features from this and that page of the standard sketchbooks.

c. The complexity and depth of the *theology and ethics* betoken a time long after the days of the historical Paul, who must have lived only a few years subsequent to the crucifixion. Apologists argue that we can trace a process of development between earlier and later epistles, reflecting a deepening of Paul's thought. Paul himself, as he is presented in these very same epistles, would hardly countenance such a view since he represents himself everywhere simply as the recipient of a prepackaged revelation from heaven, a "gospel not from man."

d. The kind of virulent advocacy, *opposition, and reinterpretation* of Pauline doctrine evidenced in these writings really is more appropriate if their subject is an authority *of the past*. We seem to be witnessing a debate over Paulinism by the Christians of a subsequent generation, much as we see in James 2:14-26 and 2 Peter 3:15-16, only here the writers are all posing as Paul in order to correct things authoritatively from within the Paulinist ranks. Paul's "previous" teaching to these churches ("Do you not remember that when I was with you I told you?") smacks of intrascholastic controversy, like Lutherans arguing over Luther. Imagine the peasants and proletarians of Corinth or Iconium scratching their heads over Paul's ratiocinations on the subtleties of justification and the Law. "How could the unphilosophic Galatians understand this letter? Loman compares it with Hegel lecturing to the aborigines of the East Indies," says Gustaaf van den Bergh.[15] What we actually seem to have are rebuttals of one Paulinist's interpretations by another, pulling rank by assuming the pose of Paul himself: "And why not do evil that good may come?—as some people slanderously charge us with saying. Their condemnation is just" (Rom. 3:8; cf. Gal. 5:11).

e. Is it really conceivable that the *pronounced post-Jewish Christianity* of Paulinism, which had utterly abandoned the authority of the twelve apostles, the Jewish Torah, and the nationalistic conception of the messiah for a spiritualized and internationalized religion, could have arisen only a matter of a few short years after the death of Jesus? Why do the Synoptic Gospels seem to attest a more primitive Christology than Paul? If Van Manen is right, it is because they are earlier than the Pauline epistles.

f. Insofar as the epistles address issues of concern to their intended readers (even if these are not the imagined readers in the Corinthian churches of 50 CE but the implied or actual readers of the next century), the concerns addressed are *anachronistic for the mid-first century*; they are really later concerns over celibacy (encratism) and the criteria of true apostleship.

g. There is a *historical retrospective tone* to the epistles.[16] They look back on the work of the apostles as something now in the past. Note, for instance, 1 Corinthians 3:6ff, where Paul is the revered founder of the Corinthian Church and Apollos is his successor; the whole thing is now in the hands of the post-apostolic generation, which is addressed with the warning: "Let each take care how he builds!" Paul's work is over. The writer can already assess that *Saint Paul* did more than the other apostles (15:8-10).

h. An advanced, *post-apostolic gnosis* is in view in 1 Corinthians 1:17-31; 2:6, 16 (cf. Baur on Colossians and Ephesians), though again, apologists desperately posit that Paul liked to turn his opponents' terminology and conceptuality against them. This would surely be the strangest and most muddying of polemical techniques, distorting the clear notes of the bugle into a confusing din: if Paul sounds so much like Corinthian Gnostics, does he agree or disagree with them?

i. Romans 9-11 speaks of the rejection of Israel in a manner impossible before the *fall of Jerusalem* in 70 C.E. Baur made the same point in the case of 1 Thessalonians 2:14-16, though, as we have seen, apologists claim these verses are a later interpolation in an otherwise genuine epistle. What event can have decisively signaled that God had written off the Jewish people? What, besides the disaster of 70 C.E. (or even that of 132 C.E.), could be the event to which Romans refers? Why has their "table" (temple altar) become their downfall and a "retribution" (Rom. 11:9)? Why is a parallel drawn with Elijah lamenting, "Lord ... they have demolished thy altars" (Rom. 11:3)?

j. There were apparently *no persecutions in the early period* in which Paul would have lived; these were the phenomena of a later period. Yet they are mentioned as a matter of present experience in the writer's day (Rom. 5:3-5; 8:17-39; 12:12, 14; 2 Cor. 1:3-7).

k. The epistles come from a time when "traditions" can be said (by Paul!) to derive from Paul (2 Thess. 2:15). Would he have spoken in this way of his own teachings, with the palpable *air of venerable antiquity*? Not likely. Again, what we have here is like 2 Peter 3:2, where the writer, passing himself off as "Simeon Peter," momentarily lets the mask slip and mentions how "your apostles" prophesied in the past of events that have now come present. Where is Peter writing this from? Heaven? Likewise, how old would Paul have to be for his teachings to be known as traditions? In 2 Thessalonians 2:5, Paul recalls the days of long ago: "when I was with you, I told you." What makes this any different from Luke 24:44, "These are my words which I spoke to you when I was still with you"? In each case, do we not have a writer clumsily putting his own words into the mouth of an authority of the past, having him speak as if from the Great Beyond in the present, forgetting to have him speak as from his own time? He is still with them in "story time," though someone seems to have forgotten it. "In a word," writes Van Manen, "the church has existed for not a few years merely. The historical background of the epistles, even of the principle epistles, is a later age. ... Everything points to later days—at least the close of the first or the beginning of the second century."[17]

The historical Paul

With the so-called Pauline epistles removed from consideration as sources for Paul's life, what evidence is left? Van Manen believed that Luke, in writing Acts, had made use of an earlier book of the Acts of Paul (not our apocryphal *Acts of Paul*), which was the source of Luke's Pauline episodes. Of this material, Van Manen judged that only some of the travel notes were authentic, as well as some details of the supposed "we source," the sections of the Acts written in the first person plural, as if by a companion of Paul. These data yield the minimal picture of a Paul somehow converted to a Christian faith of a still-Judaic type (no other type had yet made an appearance). Paul was a Hellenistic Jew and may have been one of those who first preached to gentiles after the martyrdom of Stephen. However, he remained within the bounds of Judaic Christianity, as witnessed by the various notes in Acts 18:18; 20:16; 21:23-26 about his undertaking vows and attending Jerusalem festivals. He differed in no essential respect from the twelve apostles and there is no reason to doubt that he preached among the gentiles.

Somewhere between 100 and 150 CE, Paulinism as a theological system arose out of a mystical and speculative circle. Van Manen speaks of the Paulinist movement and Gnosticism arising from the same circles.[18] As already noted, Van Manen read the original of Galatians as Marcionite. Tertullian called Paul "the apostle of Marcion and the apostle of the heretics," and both Irenaeus and Tertullian noted how much the heretics cherished Paul's writings. The first commentators on the epistles were the Gnostics Valentinus, Heracleon, and Basilides.

It is likely, according to Van Manen, that some very early pseudo-Pauline epistles did not survive except perhaps in the form of fragments incorporated in our own Paulines. Second Corinthians 10:9ff, with its reference to a known set of "his letters," may refer to this earliest group of epistles, but at least it betrays the writer of 2 Corinthians as a later Paulinist referring back to the corpus as in the equally spurious 2 Peter 3:15-16. The epistles we possess have passed through the hands of Catholic redactors who attempted to domesticate and sanitize the writings for the use of the orthodox, just as Bultmann later demonstrated a subsequent Catholic padding out and bowdlerizing of an originally Gnostic Gospel of John.

Luke was writing in the second quarter of the second century and saw himself as the heir of this catholicized Paul, contra Baur who argued that Luke was creating this Catholicized Paul in order to heal (or paper over) long-standing divisions between Jewish and gentile Christians, factions loyal to the memories of Peter and Paul respectively. Van Manen judged that Luke was by no means initiating the catholicizing; it was already an accomplished fact for him. The resulting picture is that of a great Pauline innovator of a new era in the development of Christian thought but hardly in a Gnostic direction.

How did the historical Paul come to be the figurehead of the second-century Paulinist school? We cannot say, but then neither can we say how the anonymous fourth Gospel and the three epistles were ascribed to the Galilean fisherman John bar-Zebedee. Similarly, how outlandish is it to call all Pauline epistles pseudepigraphical when we already think the same thing about all the Petrine epistles, gospels, apocalypses, and apocryphal acts? We already dismiss the authenticity of the *Acts of Paul*, the Nag Hammadi text *The Prayer of the Apostle Paul*, the two or three *Apocalypses of Paul*, and the apocryphal *Epistles to the Laodiceans, Alexandrians*, etc., as well as a good half of the canonical epistles anyway. It should occasion no great surprise if the name of an ancient apostle should have attracted to itself a larger or smaller number of pseudonymous epistles.

The structure of exegetical revolutions

No doubt, many readers of the present summary of Van Manen's approach have had no trouble in finding alternative, orthodox ways to account for many or all of the anomalies cited, hoping to preserve Pauline authorship. Harmonization is as popular today as it was anciently, and it is an apologetical strategy. It is not a tool of historical criticism. To the apologist's mind, if there is a way to believe the traditional view might possibly still be true, then it is true.[19] Thus any contrivance that seems to salvage the familiar, consensus position will seem to be *ipso facto* true since consonance with tradition is such a convincing piece of apologetics.

As Thomas S. Kuhn tells the tale, "when confronted by anomaly," the guardians of tradition will "devise numerous articulations and *ad hoc* modifications of their theory in order to eliminate any apparent conflict."[20] "The source of resistance is the assurance that the older paradigm will ultimately solve all its problems, that nature can be shoved into the box the paradigm provides. Inevitably, at times of revolution, that assurance seems stubborn and pig-headed as indeed it sometimes becomes."[21] But, says Kuhn, there is a real utility to the stubborn adherence to the old paradigm since only if it is played out as far as it can possibly go will we find its limits as well as discern precisely where a competing paradigm must show its strength. It therefore establishes itself by making intelligible those anomalies upon which the old paradigm ran aground. It is just as it is in the *Enuma Elish*, where we discover it is time for old Ea, the ancient of days, to abdicate his throne to a more vigorous young god who can do what Ea could not, defeat the dragons of Chaos, Tiamat and Apsu.[22] Marduk is successful in putting these distressing anomalies in their place and imposing order, thus transforming chaos into cosmos. He then becomes the reigning paradigm.

But what if that point never comes, if the adherents of the old way of looking at things simply determine that no one will ever unseat them, as on the *National Lampoon* cover where the bearded and wickedly grinning Old Year is holding aloft a condom instead of a diapered New Year baby? This is the case with scriptural inerrantists whose byzantine jury-rigging against all intruding phenomena threatens to turn the eroding dike into a honeycomb of corked-up leaks, weaker than ever. A paradigm which finally turns out to be nothing but a mass of meshed epicycles is doomed because before long it will have turned itself into a self-sealing premise invulnerable to attack but, by the same token, compatible with any and every state of affairs—and thus meaningless. A paradigm and its defenders must, unlike Muhammad Ali, know when to quit unless they want to wind up permanently punch-drunk.

Notoriously, such guardians of the reigning paradigm are like the protagonist of *The Testament of Abraham*, who simply will not pack it in even when God sends the death angel to fetch him. This may seem like senility or worse—see Robert Bloch's hilarious tale "A Case of the Stubborns,"[23] in which old Gramps refuses to admit he's dead and keeps on shambling into the kitchen for breakfast till one day his nose falls off into the cereal bowl in front of him! Ermanno Bencivenga[24] explains the politics of apologetical responses which seem to their authors to have refuted a new idea when they have only shown that the old idea is still possibly true but mostly desirable in upholding the "tenets of faith." To prove their necessity is too tall an order for even the most adept apologist, for "at most he can uphold the *possibility* that some things are [true]." And "in all cases [rationalizers] are fighting a credibility gap that threatens the status quo, and hence in all cases [their job is] to make this structure look plausible again."

This explains why Hans Conzelmann and others could route the enemy (to their own satisfaction, anyway) simply by meeting a new theory with the rebuttal of "Speculative!" as if any theory could be anything else. For a perfect example of this strategy of haughty dismissal, see C. S. Lewis, "Modern Theology and Biblical Criticism," in which Lewis[25] discounts all critical hypotheses as a series of merely probable chains forged from weak links, as opposed to the rock-solid credibility of traditional beliefs. In reality, those pre-critical positions seem immovable simply because of inertia. Their defenses are and can be nothing else than probabilistic chains of weak links. Baur, Strauss and others were never refuted but were simply given the cold shoulder by apologists who gave people permission to disregard the disturbing new ideas. Apologists are always preaching to the converted, just as smokers are the only people to whom the wild harmonizations of the tobacco industry sound convincing.

I am, of course, suggesting that the revolutionary hypotheses of Van Manen were never given a chance, and at second glance, they look appealing to me. To paraphrase Chesterton, it is not that the Dutch Radical critical paradigm[26] was tried and found wanting; it was found distasteful and not tried. But the rationalizations of our vested interests lose some of their hold on us if we come to recognize them for what they are. If this book can help produce such recognition, it will be because the time is finally ripe for Van Manen, once dismissed with scorn like Nietzsche's mad prophet, to receive his due and a sympathetic hearing. Like light from the farthest stars, his shocking tidings have taken a long time to reach us, but perhaps now we are ready to see and comprehend.

NOTES

[1] Friedrich Schleiermacher, "Über den sogenannten ersten Brief des Paulos an den Timotheos: Eine kritische Sendscreibung an J. C. Gass" ("Concerning the So-called First Letter of Paul to Timothy: A Critical Open Letter to J. C. Gass"), rpt. in *Friedrich Schleiermacher's sämmtliche Werke*, 30 vols., 1835-64 (Berlin: G. Reimer) 1:221-320.

[2] The Tübingen School, besides maintaining a late date for the composition of the New Testament epistles, also argued that Christianity in the second century was an amalgamation of two ideas: Jewish (Petrine) and gentile (Pauline) Christianity. The Dutch Radicals subsequently suggested that Acts meant to smooth over the once-raging conflict between Paulinist Marcionism and the "Petrine" Catholic Church in the second century.

[3] Tertullian says Valentinus became a heretic after he was passed over for bishop of Rome (Tertullian, *Adversus Valentinianos*, 4).

[4] Ferdinand C. Baur, *Paul, the Apostle of Jesus Christ: His Life and Work, His Epistles and His Doctrine; a Contribution to the Critical History of Primitive Christianity*, 2nd ed., 2 vols., trans. Edward Zeller, rev. Allan Menzies (London: Williams and Norgate, 1875-76) 2:7-14.

[5] Edgar J. Goodspeed, *The Key to Ephesians: A Provocative Solution to a Problem in the Pauline Literature* (Chicago: University of Chicago Press, 1956).

[6] Ignatius, *To the Romans*, chapters 5-8.

[7] Baur, *Paul, Apostle of Jesus Christ*, 2:45-54.

[8] Ibid., 95-96.

[9] The *Didache* was a church manual ascribed to the Apostolic Fathers of the first or second century CE but that probably originated in Egypt or Syria in a later century. In any case, it was regularly updated with the most recently accepted instructions on how to baptize (by immersion), fast (on

Wednesday and Friday), pray (the Lord's Prayer daily), and elect bishops and deacons, among other sensible rules. See Everett Ferguson, ed., *Encyclopedia of Early Christianity*, 2nd ed. (New York: Garland, 1998), s.v. "Didache."

[10]Willem C. van Manen, *Paulus*, 3 vols. (Leiden: L. van Nifterik, 1890-96); Van Manen, "Old Christian Literature," "Paul," "Philemon, Epistle to," and "Romans, (Epistle)," in Thomas Kelly Cheyne and J. Sutherland Black, eds., *Encyclopaedia Biblica: A Critical Dictionary of the Bible*, 4 vols. (New York: Macmillan, 1899-1903).

[11]Adolf Deissmann, "Epistolary Literature," *Encyclopaedia Biblica*.

[12]Marcion was an early Christian bishop in Asia Minor who clashed with the Roman bishops and was excommunicated in the second century CE.

[13]"In principle, the techniques and criteria for identifying redactional discontinuities and redactional material in the Pauline writings are not different from those employed in the study of the Gospels or Acts. Indeed, my own view is that the Pauline writings, which mediate the teachings of the great 'apostle to the gentiles' in literary form, are very similar to the Gospels, which mediate the 'teachings of the Lord' in narrative form" (Darrell J. Doughty, "Pauline Paradigms and Pauline Authority," *Journal of Higher Criticism* 1 [Fall 1994]: 104).

[14]"I spoke above of the blindness of critics with regard to their own insights, of the discrepancy, hidden to them, between their stated method and their perceptions" (Paul de Man, *Blindness and Insight: Essays in the Rhetoric of Contemporary Criticism*, 2nd rev. ed. [Minneapolis: University of Minnesota Press, 1983], 7:111).

[15]Gustaaf Adolf van den Bergh van Eysinga, *Radical Views about the New Testament*, trans. Samuel Benjamin Slack (London: Watts, 1912), 81.

[16]Van Manen, "Paul."

[17]Ibid.

[18]Ibid.

[19]James Barr, *Fundamentalism* (London: SCM [Student Christian Movement] Press, 1976), 85, 98, 126, 127.

[20]Thomas S. Kuhn, *The Structure of Scientific Revolutions* (Chicago: Chicago University Press, 1969), 78.

[21]Ibid., 151.

[22]The Babylonian creation narrative, *Enuma Elish*, was written on seven clay tablets and was found in the ruins of Nineveh at Mosul, Iraq. It tells of a young generation of gods, including Marduk, challenging an older genera-

tion of deities, including Ea, who feared to fight against the Chaos dragons Apsu and Tiamat, parents of the gods. The original "dragon of chaos" was the Egyptian deity Apep, who ruled the night with powers of destruction and death.

[23]Robert Bloch, "A Case of the Stubborns," in Mitchell Galin and Tom Allen, eds., *Tales from the Darkside* (New York: Berkley Books, 1988), 1:37-54.

[24]Ermanno Bencivenga, *Logic and Other Nonsense: The Case of Anselm and His God* (Princeton: Princeton University Press, 1993), 61.

[25]C. S. Lewis, "Modern Theology and Biblical Criticism," in Walter Hooper, ed., *Christian Reflections* (Grand Rapids: Eerdmans, 1967), 152-66.

[26]Hermann Detering, *Paulusbriefe ohne Paulus? Die Paulusbriefe in der holländischen Radikalkritik* (New York: Peter Lang, 1992); Richard John Knowling, *The Witness of the Epistles: A Study in Modern Criticism* (London: Longmans, Green, 1892), 133-243; Louis Gordon Rylands, *A Critical Analysis of the Four Chief Pauline Epistles: Romans, First and Second Corinthians, and Galatians* (London: Watts, 1929); Thomas Whittaker, *The Origins of Christianity, with an Outline of Van Manen's Analysis of the Pauline Literature*, 4th ed. (London: Watts, 1933).

3.

The Evolution of the Pauline Canon

Introduction

When considering the letters ascribed to the Apostle Paul, we are accustomed to speaking of *justification*. When we seek to tunnel beneath the theological ground we stand on, to deconstruct the notion of Pauline theological authority (that is, to take it apart and find out better how it works), we might better speak of *reification*, that process whereby a thing contrived by human beings like ourselves comes to assume an aura of inviolable sacredness, an autonomous reality, a wholeness greater than the sum of its parts. The Sabbath is reified when we begin to forget that it was made for men and women, not the other way around. The biblical canon is a classic case of reification. Most students and laypersons are both surprised and dismayed to discover that the Bible's contents are not self-evident, that a choice between accepting or rejecting certain writings was made at all, and this by mere mortals like themselves at a particular time in history. How can the eternal Word of God be subjected to such things?

The canon of holy scripture is like the holy place in the temple at Jerusalem: it is shielded from prying mortal eyes by a veil of sanctity. One is curious to peer inside yet fearful of being disappointed should one dare steal a glimpse like the profane usurper Titus who was startled to find an empty chamber. Or, worse yet, will one find a stammering man behind the curtain at the controls of a hidden booth as in *The Wizard of Oz*?

If the biblical canon is the holy place, perhaps the Pauline corpus can be likened to the Holy of Holies; for even among those for whom the outer veil has long ago been rent, this inner zone of canonicity retains its numinous inviolability. For Christian scholars, whether apologists or supposed critics, the Pauline epistles are like the metaphysical Presence of traditional ontotheology.[1] We are reluctant to have someone come along and play Jacques Derrida's[2] trick of showing us where the seams and junctures are.

Yet the game is afoot already, and profane feet have trodden the sacred courts. For the better part of a century, scholars have crossed swords, or at least pens (which are mightier), over the question of the collected Pauline epistles: who first collected them, when, where, and why? It will be our task to sift through a pile of these speculations, which, as Walter Schmithals[3] reminds us, is all such reconstructions can ever be. In the process, we may feel like we are sitting in the poorly-lit attic, exploring the confusing souvenirs of our ancestors as they emerge, one by one, from a neglected old steamer trunk. Let's get started.

Four approaches

I believe we can distinguish four clear lines of thought in approaching the question before us, and it will be useful to list our theories according to the distance they posit between Paul's career and his epistolary collection. Admittedly, this taxonomy violates the chronology of the history of scholarship in favor of a different sort of chronology. I believe little will be lost, however, as each major group of theories seems to have evolved autonomously. Though one may have arisen in reaction to another, that is seldom crucial to the logic of each theory. When it is important, it will be easy enough to note the fact. Within each family of theories, I will trace historical development. Furthermore, by arranging the theories in a timeline from minimal to maximal intervals between the apostle and the collection, we may come to see something important about the theories, their tendencies, and motives.

"Pauline Testament" theories

The first type of collection theory to consider may be called the "Pauline Testament" approach. Here there is virtually no interval at all between the apostle and the collection of his writings; as these scholars posit it, Paul himself collected them. The earliest exponent of this theory appears to be R. L. Archer,[4] who reasoned that Paul had kept copies of his epistles and that sometime after his death the Christians who inherited them hit upon the scheme of publishing them. They derived this notion from reading Seneca, a great publisher of collected letters. While Seneca frowned upon publication of strictly personal letters, Cicero, as is well known, found value in publishing even personal correspondence. Paul's posthumous admirers agreed with Cicero, and thus the Pauline writings, both literary epistles and personal letters, were published.

Donald Guthrie thinks Archer did well to look to the contemporary practice of letter collection and publication but remains skeptical whether early Pauline Christians would have been much interested in or influenced by the likes of Cicero and Seneca.[5] Against Guthrie's criticism, one may question whether he is influenced too heavily by Adolf Deissmann's[6] belief, based on 1 Corinthians 1:26, that the early church was a pedestrian, plebeian, and proletarian movement. Abraham Malherbe's more recent studies[7] might persuade us differently, but Guthrie still might have noticed that if "not many" of the Corinthians or Pauline Christians were to be numbered among the educated elite generally, the very wording of the verse in question implies that a few were. We need think only of the householders Stephanas, who "delivered the formal, written questions or statements of the community," and Chloe, who "supplied the oral information, hearsay, and gossip" mentioned by Paul.[8]

As for early Christian interest in the literary luminaries Seneca and Cicero, let us not forget the apocryphal *Epistles of Paul and Seneca*. Someone before Archer certainly envisioned early Christians as interested in Seneca; remember also St. Jerome's famous dream in which his Christian conscience rebuked his classical inclinations. An angel like the one who appeared to Hermas cast this in Jerome's teeth: "Thou art not a follower of Christ, but of Cicero!"

A more recent theory along similar lines is that of David Trobisch.[9] Trobisch, like Archer, deserves praise for exploring the contemporary practices of collecting and publishing letters, having studied many hundreds of epistles and letter collections from several centuries adjacent to the Pauline period on either side (300 BCE to 400 CE). He notes that in many cases the initial collection of an author's letters was made by the author himself with a view to publishing "selected" rather than "collected" letters. These might have been arranged in chronological order, but as Trobisch observes, when others undertook to publish more correspondence after the author's death, the additional letters were simply appended to the original set, not placed among them according to the original chronological sequence principle. The new letters would observe the same order among themselves, but they would follow the original corpus as a new block of correspondence. Trobisch calls an author's own selection of letters the "authorized recension." Posthumous additional collections might be published as separate volumes or, if thematically related to the authorized recension, they might be appended to the original volume and published together as what Trobisch calls an "expanded edition." Finally, scribes may try to unearth and publish all known letters together in a single manuscript in what Trobisch calls a "comprehensive edition." And in all expanded and comprehensive editions, Trobisch says, the added material starts over, recapitulating the sequential order of the originals but not intermingling with the letters of the author's own collection, leaving the integrity of the original collection intact. It would be comparable to a current-day author merely adding a new preface, an introduction to a new edition, or some appendices to the original text of a reprinted early work, rather than revising and updating it: "What I have written, I have written."

Trobisch calls attention to the fact that, with very few exceptions, the mass of ancient manuscripts arranges Paul's letters the same way, in an almost perfect order flowing from the longest to the shortest except that Ephesians is longer than Galatians and yet follows it. The descending length principle starts over once we reach the Pastorals, but no one seems surprised by this since we have reached a new category of, ostensibly, personal letters to individuals. However, what of Ephesians? After considering previous theories, Trobisch suggests it would make the most sense if Ephesians represented the point where a new expanded edition had been added. Of what did this expanded edition consist? Here Trobisch tips his hat to Edgar J. Goodspeed. One expects Trobisch to say, as did Schmithals,[10] that Ephesians led off a second, posthumous collection of a few letters, perhaps containing Ephesians, Colossians, and Philemon. Goodspeed, as we will see below, had suggested that Ephesians had once begun the whole corpus and was written by the Colossian freedman Onesimus for that purpose. Schmithals was willing to let Goodspeed be right only about the threefold corpus of Ephesians-Colossians-Philemon, but Trobisch is more generous, though less consistent. He explains: "If my analysis is correct, the letter to the Ephesians functioned as an introduction to the expanded edition of the thirteen letters because it is the first letter of the appendix."[11] However, it is difficult to see how Ephesians might serve as an introduction to the whole corpus of thirteen letters if it comes fifth! This, of course, is why Goodspeed posited a lead-off position for Ephesians, even without any manuscript evidence to back him up.

This is not the only problem with Trobisch's reconstruction. For one thing, while there is no *prima facie* unreasonableness in the suggestion that the initial four letters (Romans, 1 and 2 Corinthians, Galatians) were Paul's own choice for a letters volume, with Ephesians beginning a posthumous appendix, Trobisch seems merely to have shown that such a scenario, if true, would fit the analogy of a widespread practice of an author publishing his own letters. It seems that this is a viable form-critical argument, but Trobisch leaves it unclear whether the initial letter collections to which expansions were appended were always or usually collections by the author himself. We have in the case of Howard Phillips Lovecraft's letters something that at first seems to parallel the ancient practice as Trobisch describes it. Shortly following Lovecraft's death in 1937, two of his correspondents, August Derleth and Donald Wandrei, decided to collect and publish their late friend's letters. Lovecraft wrote innumerable epistles of fantastic length, so Derleth and Wandrei knew they must make a selection. At first they planned on a single volume of *Selected Letters*, but as the years went by and the sifting process continued, the project expanded to three, then four volumes. Following the deaths of Derleth and Wandrei, James Turner took up the task and compiled a fifth volume. All letters, edited and condensed for publication, were presented in chronological order from Arkham House Publishers.

Many Lovecraft aficionados were not satisfied, however, as their appetites had been merely whetted. So a couple of them, S. T. Joshi and David E. Schultz, scoured the archives of Brown University and contacted various obscure Lovecraft correspondents, seeking even more letters. Their labors produced several more volumes, *A Means to Freedom: The Letters of H. P. Lovecraft and Robert E. Howard*, to Richard Searight, to Robert Bloch, etc. And chronological order is observed within each such volume of Tosefta.[12] Finally, these editors hope one day to compile a definitive *Collected Letters of H. P. Lovecraft*.

It all sounds very much like Trobisch's assumptions about Paul—except that Lovecraft was dead when it all began. Do we know that first collections were always put together by the epistolarian himself? Trobisch does not tell us, and yet his reconstruction is considerably weakened if it is not so.

One suspects the underlying motive of the Pauline Testament theories is an apologetical one: it would seem to secure a set of texts with both authenticity and integrity guaranteed. After all, the inference goes, Paul himself wrote and edited them. And here one is reminded of the fundamentalist apologetic for the New Testament canon list as a whole. John Warwick Montgomery[12] and others assert that in John 16:12-14, Jesus authorized in advance the entire New Testament canon just as he put his imprimatur on the whole Old Testament canon in John 10:35. Think of Vincent Taylor's argument[13] that the synoptic tradition must be basically sound since the apostles were still around to oversee the progress of the oral tradition. Are not Archer and especially Trobisch trying to make it seem that Paul collected the Pauline corpus, or at least the *Hauptbriefe*, to rescue us from text-critical anxieties?

Such a purpose would not seem alien to Trobisch, who explicitly wants to return to a harmonizing reading not only of Paul but of the entire New Testament.[14] This would appear to be a move to neo-conservative hermeneutics, *a la* Brevard Childs. Trobisch surprises us, however, for what he gains in authenticity, he squanders in textual integrity. We are surprised to discover that he takes a leaf from Schmithals's codex and subdivides the Corinthian correspondence into no less than seven mini-letters. He discerns the seams in between, much as Schmithals does, in vestigial letter openings and closings; he maps out digressive passages, labeling them as Pauline redactional notes. Why Paul would have done this, especially since Trobisch has him leave the basic letter forms of Galatians and

Romans intact, is a puzzle. "Behold, I show you a mystery," but not, alas, a solution. Schmithals's controversial surgery on the epistles is at least supplied with a motive: the redactor needed to conflate his fragmentary sources into the catholicizing seven-fold form. Whether this is judged persuasive is one thing; whether it is better than no reason at all is another.

What is strikingly ironic is that Trobisch offers as his theory's chief merit that it makes possible a harmonizing reading of the Pauline corpus, or at least the *Hauptbriefe*, though he seems to want to go farther. Is this purpose served by breaking up the Corinthian letters? Or does he mean that Paul wanted the letters to be re-read as if they formed one or two longer texts? It seems Trobisch does not intend this, but in any case, he has undermined his own goal. To borrow another analogy from Lovecraft, Trobisch's reconstruction reminds us of the editing of Lovecraft's serialized story, "Herbert West—Reanimator." Each of his six installments began with a capsule résumé of the previous one(s). In book form, these capsules seemed redundant. Eventually, when Jeffery Combs prepared an audiotape version, he decided to trim away the summaries reasoning that, once the six episodes were read continuously, the summaries became counterproductive: first intended to reinforce continuity of reading, they now tended to interrupt it. Fair enough, but why would Paul trim away the beginning and end of most of the Corinthian mini-letters? This would make sense only if what Paul pared away was a set of "Now where are we's" and "More next time's." That is not the character of most of the Pauline greetings and closings, however. According to Schmithals and Knox, openings and closings may have been added to make a heap of random fragments into letters to begin with, and it is difficult to understand the procedure proposed by Trobisch.

Perhaps the most intriguing aspect of Trobisch's version of the Pauline Testament approach is his connection of the two Pauline collections, i.e., Paul's own collection of alms for the Jerusalem saints and the collection of Paul's epistles. Typically, though, Trobisch casts this potent seed on rocky ground and continues on his way. He notes that 1 and 2 Corinthians, Romans, and Galatians all mention the alms collection and that the thread of continuity seems to be that Paul agreed to the chore in the first place to conciliate the pillar saints of Jerusalem who had since, like Cephas in Antioch, betrayed their accord. As a result, he feared that the fruits of his harvest on their behalf might be rejected and become a bone of contention rather than an olive branch of peace. One purpose in Paul collecting letters and sending them to Ephesus would be to put his side of the story on file in view of the conflict anticipated in Jerusalem. I view this as a brilliant suggestion, though not compelling. Why wouldn't Paul simply write it out in a single new letter, using the same kind of plain talk he had used in Galatians? It is significant that, at the close of Trobisch's book, *Paul's Letter Collection*, there is a "fictive cover letter" in which Paul explains his object in compiling the corpus. Trobisch thus admits that some such word of explanation is necessary if his theory is to carry conviction—and yet, Paul did not supply one.

If one found the collection theory persuasive, one need not count it as evidence that Paul himself collected the *Hauptbriefe* (Romans, Galatians, 1 and 2 Corinthians). Paul's motive in collecting the money remained an issue between the Pauline communities and Jewish Jesus-sectarians who cast Paul in the role of Simon Magus crassly trying to purchase an apostolate with filthy lucre, as F. C. Baur argued. One can easily imagine (and that is all one may do) Paul's friends collecting the letters as a defense against Ebionite detractors, much as later Catholics would fabricate the Pastorals to distance Paul from the blasphemies of the Encratites.[15]

Paper-apostle theories

Our second group of theories calls to mind Rudolf Bultmann's dictum that Jesus "rose into the kerygma," the gospel preaching of the early church. These theories, to some of which Guthrie[16] applied the rubric "theories of immediate value," in effect have Paul die and immediately rise in the form of a collection of his writings which replaced the irreplaceable apostle. I dub this the paper-apostle approach, the person who emerges in the writings becoming more important than any biographical realities. The scenario envisioned here is much like that described in Islamic tradition following the death of the Prophet Muhammad when the voice of prophecy fell forever silent. Just the opposite of the Deuteronomic Moses, Muhammad was the definitive seal of the prophets: no "prophet like unto me" would be expected to succeed him. Thus, the Muslim faithful began to cherish and trade remembered *surahs* of revelation, recording these on whatever materials came to hand: scraps of leather, papyrus leaves, parchments, potsherds, even shoulder blades of sheep. At length the first caliph, Abu-bekr, decreed that the *surahs* should be collected, and the corpus of the Koran (Qur'an) was the eventual result. Thus the book of the prophet was the only successor to the prophet.

Adolf Harnack[17] reasoned that Paul's letters were treasured by enthusiastic readers who could not wait for further installments. "Did not our hearts burn within us as he opened the scriptures unto us?" Not content to wait for the apostle to post another missive to their own church, Pauline Christians would check through a network of scribes in other locations and copy each other's epistles till each church had a complete set, much like avid fans of an author today. The keen longing for more of Paul did not arise only after his death. His absence during his life, when working elsewhere far away, already led his fans to make up collections of his letters to serve as substitutes for his presence, like a treasured photograph of an absent lover. Thus, the groundwork for the Pauline canon was already in place when Paul himself passed away. One might say the Pauline corpus was already warming up even as the Pauline corpse was cooling off. Indeed, his death was a mere formality; as Roland Barthes[18] and Jacques Derrida[19] tell us, the author was dead as soon as he produced his text, which as a "dangerous supplement" took on a prodigal life of its own.

Harnack was persuaded of the immediate impact of the letters by four factors. First, we perceive Paul's letters as rhetorically and theologically powerful, and Harnack assumes ancient readers must have been just as astute. Yet we should not be too hasty in identifying our tastes with ancient predilections. For instance, someone, somewhere must have thought the Upanishads or the Saddharma Pundarika sounded good even though Max Müller[20] didn't. Mormon missionaries grow teary-eyed about the heart-warming experience of reading the Book of Mormon, but Mark Twain found it "chloroform in print." Wasn't Harnack reading the text through a haze of eighteen centuries of Christian piety? One thinks of the scene in Cecil B. DeMille's *King of Kings*, when thousands assemble to hear Jesus as if they realize that this is their chance to hear the soon-to-be-famous Sermon on the Mount.

Harnack took 2 Corinthians 10:10 ("His letters are weighty and strong, but his bodily presence is weak, his speech of no account") as denoting that even Paul's opponents had to admit his letters were powerful. However, isn't the point rather that Paul merely talks a good fight and can't back it up? As Paul himself says elsewhere: "The kingdom of God is not talk, but power" (1 Cor. 4:20). First Corinthians 7:17 ("And so I ordain in all the churches") meant to Harnack that what Paul had written here, he had written in epistles to all his churches, implying a large volume of letters. Not only is this an arbitrary reading of the verse, which might simply refer to oral instructions in person, but it had not occurred to Harnack that such a verse was likely a post-Pauline catholicizing gloss, added to facilitate the use of 1 Corinthians as an encyclical. "What I say to you, I say to all."

Finally, Harnack inferred from 2 Thessalonians 2:2 and 3:17 that in Paul's day, his letters were already numerous and authoritative enough to have called forth cheap imitations. In both his third and fourth arguments, however, Harnack gets himself into trouble. He seemed to realize that if Paul had written as many letters as his arguments implied, we must be missing most of them. Therefore, Harnack reasoned that a selection was made and that our Pauline corpus represents the cream of the crop. However, doesn't this notion undercut Harnack's whole reconstruction? For the true fan, there is no such thing as an embarrassment of riches. Rather, one seeks to preserve every scrap, just as P. N. Harrison pictured a redactor of Pauline fragments in 2 Timothy doing.[21]

As F. C. Baur pointed out long ago, as he felled another tree in a forest empty of anyone listening, the references to pseudepigraphy in 2 Thessalonians, like the request to have 1 Thessalonians read in church (1 Thess. 5:27), is a case of my four fingers pointing back at me when I point one at you. First and Second Thessalonians presuppose an earlier paper-apostle. As is well known, Harnack was a foe of Baur and Tübingen, and his apologetical tendency is no more difficult to spot here than in his early dating of Acts.

Donald Guthrie also wanted to close the gap between Paul and his letters to ensure the authenticity and integrity of the corpus. It is no surprise to see him favoring the Vincent Taylor/F. F. Bruce theory of oral transmission to shorten a dark and frightening tunnel period. Guthrie imagines that just after Paul's death, one of his associates—probably Timothy—saw to the collection of his master's literary remains.[22] After all, Timothy would have been present to hear Galatians read in his home church of Lystra. And years later he himself had brought Paul his suitcase full of parchments and scrolls, which might well have been a file of copies of his own epistles *a la* Archer. It is clear that for Guthrie, the Timothy character continues to play the guarantor role assigned him by the Pastoral author (2 Tim. 2:2). Guthrie's theory requires Acts to be historically accurate and the Pastorals to be genuinely Paul's.

We find ourselves in familiar territory with C.F.D. Moule's version of the paper apostle. For Moule, it was Luke, serving as Paul's amanuensis with a very long leash, who both wrote the Pastorals and collected the genuine Paulines after penning Luke and Acts.[23] A few subsequent scholars have also affirmed common authorship for Luke-Acts and the Pastorals, such as Stephen G. Wilson[24] and Jerome D. Quinn,[25] but unlike them, Moule pictured the author as being Luke the beloved physician and companion of Paul.

After developing suggestions from Hans Conzelmann[26] and Eduard Lohse,[27] Hans-Martin Schenke[28] allowed the pendulum to settle down in the middle of the paper-apostle options. Eschewing both Harnack's faceless "creative Volk community" approach, and Moule's and Guthrie's nomination of a single Pauline disciple, Schenke ascribed both the collection of the corpus and the writing of some deutero-Pauline epistles to a Pauline School, disciples of Paul who, like the anonymous sons of the prophets who passed on the traditions of Elijah, Elisha, and Isaiah, took on both the task of continuing Paul's work and the mantle of his authority as they made his voice sound forth again to meet new challenges and answer new questions. Harry Gamble[29] approves this notion since it avoids "the dubious idea of one particular collector." Yet we may ask, what is so dubious about the notion of a single collector? Perhaps Gamble, who shows himself elsewhere to be shy of all but the most cautious speculation, is willing, in his *Textual History of the Letter to the Romans*, to take but a carefully circumscribed Sabbath day's journey from the data and disdain the "scandal of particularity" involved in picking a single name like Luke, Timothy, or Onesimus. More likely, he finds theologically distasteful the lurking idea of a Marcion-like "second founder of Paulinism" (see below).

The image of Paul resurrected in his letters is especially apt for Schenke's[30] theory: "They were concerned with the living Paul, his work and word in the present, with the memory of him and his continuing work among them, with the work and teaching of the itinerant, fully-authorized representatives of Paul, with the work of those in the church who could serve as the extended arm of Paul, and with everything that was related concerning Paul." And though Schenke himself does not invoke the analogy of the schools of the Old Testament prophets, I believe the comparison is a helpful one. It invites us to understand the Pauline corpus, as Marcion did, as the private canon, the sectarian scripture, of a particular Christian body, the Pauline School in this case. This is much like the composite book of Isaiah, which contains not only the oracles of the original Isaiah of Jerusalem but also the deutero- and trito-Isaianic supplements of his latter-day heirs. As in the case of the Isaiah canon where (*a la* Paul D. Hanson[31]) we find intra-canonical collisions (cf. Ernst Käsemann[32]), so we find Pauline versus deutero-Pauline clashes here and there.

The living Paul who continues, as it were, to write through the pens of the Pauline School, is obviously the twin of the risen Christ to whose self-appointed prophets Bultmann[33] (and many others on down to M. Eugene Boring)[34] had ascribed many of the inauthentic sayings of Jesus. However, at least Schenke's "risen Paul" who thus lives on in *Geschichte* had lived a previous life in *Histoire*. ("If once we knew [Paul] after the flesh we know him so no longer.")[35] Next, however, we come to a much older theory of a Pauline School which surely fulfills the name "paper apostle" to the letter. Willem Christiaan van Manen was the greatest of the Dutch Radical Critics who sought to carry to their logical conclusion (some would say their *reductio ad absurdum*, but not me) the critical insights of Baur and the Tübingen School. Van Manen, Allard Pierson, Samuel Naber, Abraham Loman, and their predecessor Bruno Bauer denied the authenticity of every single Pauline letter despite the attempts of F. C. Baur to swat them away, much as Luther had dismissed the Radical Reformer Caspar von Schwenkfeld.[36] Van Manen saw no reason to doubt the existence of Paul as an early Christian preacher, whose genuine itinerary he thought had been preserved in Acts, but he judged the so-called Pauline epistles to have as little direct connection to this early apostle as the so-called Johannine and

Petrine writings have with their historically obscure namesakes. The epistles, Van Manen argued, display a universalizing and philosophizing tenor unthinkable for the apocalyptic sect pictured in Acts or the Gospels. Their greatest affinity was with Syrian Gnosticism. Nor did they represent the thinking of one theologian (the "Paulus Episcopus" of Pierson and Naber). Rather, in the Pauline epistles, we overhear intra-scholastic debates between different wings of Paulinism. Has God finally cast off the Jewish people or not? Does grace imply libertinism, as some hold? Do some preach circumcision in Paul's name? Can women prophesy or not?

Van Manen locates the home of Paulinism at Antioch or perhaps Asia Minor beginning at the end of the first century or the start of the second and thriving by 150 CE.[37] Fragments from this Gnostic Pauline circle were later compiled into the familiar epistles, each and all of which are in their present form redactional compositions, finally receiving a catholicizing overlay. "We do not know by whom the collection was made, nor yet what influence his work had upon the traditional text. Perhaps we may suppose that it led to some changes. Probably the collection was not wholly the work of one person, but arose gradually through additions."[38] Van Manen's theory belongs with the others we have lumped together under the paper-apostle approach in that it tends to minimize the interval between the writing of the letters and their collection. In this case, both the writing and the collecting are seen as occurring early in the second century.

"Snowball theories"

We find much less diversity among the theories Guthrie groups under the heading "theories of partial collections." I, however, prefer Moule's nomenclature of

> the slow, anonymous process of accretion, the snowball theory. We have to suppose ... that the intercourse between one Pauline

centre and another gradually led to the exchange of copies of letters, until, at any given centre, there came to be not only the letter
or letters originally sent to it, but also copies of certain others
collected from other Pauline churches. Thus in each centre there
would come to be little nests of letters, and gradually these would
move into wider circulation and would be augmented, until the full
number, as we know it, was reached. Then all that remained to be
done was the making of a careful "edition" of the whole corpus.[39]

Kirsopp Lake[40] had said the same in 1911: "Small and partial collections came into existence in various centers, before the Corpus in its completed form fully replaced them." Similarly Günther
Zuntz[41] suggests that "smaller collections may have been made in
and around Ephesus."

P. N. Harrison[42] thought the Corinthian correspondence was
something of a collection of fragments, to which was then added
Romans and later a Macedonian collection of Philippians and Thessalonians. Together these formed a European corpus, while an Asia
Minor collection of Galatians, Colossians, the Letter for Phoebe
(Romans 16), and Philemon developed. Once the latter had been
added to the European corpus, some Asian Christian penned Ephesians on the basis of all the others.

Lucetta Mowry[43] saw it the same way: "We can distinguish
three such regions each with its own body of material, the Asian
hinterland, with Galatians, Colossians and Philemon; Macedonia,
with 1 Thessalonians and Philippians; and Achaia with I Corinthians and Romans." I will return later to Walter Schmithals,[44] but I
should probably include him here since he understands Ephesians,
Colossians, and Philemon to have constituted a separate Asian collection, joined subsequently with a seven-letter collection (1 and 2
Corinthians, Galatians, Philippians, l and 2 Thessalonians, Romans).

What is the difference between a paper-apostle theory like
Harnack's and the snowball theory? It is simply a question of time
intervals. Snowball theories cannot credit so early a collection as

Harnack posits nor such a later one, *ex nihilo*, as does Goodspeed (see below). The collection came to fruition late, says the snowball theory, but we can supply the missing link by positing partial collections, like small multicellular creatures joining to form a more complex jellyfish. Yet, come to think of it, how did we get the multicellular creatures? How did they evolve from unicellular beasties? A development of the snowball theory supplies an answer.

Mowry, Nils Dahl and others have gathered evidence that various Pauline epistles must have circulated between the time of their initial appearance and that of the formation of local collections of encyclicals and hitherto uncirculated local letters. There are copies of Romans with no addressee and manuscripts lacking the last two chapters. Lightfoot, Dahl reports,[45] had already sought to account for this textual data by suggesting that Paul had sent out earlier copies, omitting personal and local concerns, to some of his churches. Lake put the shoe on the other foot and proposed that Paul had added the specifics to an earlier encyclical letter, making it into our Romans.

The famous catholicizing gloss of 1 Corinthians 1:2b ("together with all who in every place invoke the name of our Lord Jesus Christ, their Lord as well as ours") was seen by Schmithals, following Johannes Weiss, as evidence that 1 Corinthians once led off the Pauline corpus. However, Dahl reasoned that it might be more naturally understood (along with other glosses like 7:17; 11:16; 14:33) as the tool that made 1 Corinthians itself an encyclical letter. I would go further in the same direction pursued by those who view the letter as a set of fragments and compare 1 Corinthians and its "now concerning" transitions with the *Didache*, where such phrases are clearly mechanical introductions like Mark's redactional "immediately"s to begin discussion of new topics in a generic church manual, which I consider 1 Corinthians to be.

The grand epilogue to Romans (16:25-27) also makes better sense as a way of refitting Romans for a wider audience. Schmithals,[46] like Weiss, thinks Romans was adapted to close the sevenfold corpus. Mowry notes that since Galatians is addressed to "the churches of Galatia," then even if original it was more than a local possession. She sees 2 Thessalonians as a later pseudonymous encyclical aimed at dampening the premature apocalyptic fervor ignited by 1 Thessalonians. In fact, the fabrication of 2 Thessalonians would be symptomatic of the whole situation as Mowry sees it: as the living voice of charismatic prophecy fell more and more silent, the written word was needed to fill the gap. Ephesians, also without an addressee in the earliest manuscripts, is obviously another ideal candidate for an encyclical, a universalizing redaction of Colossians.

Walter Bauer[47] had long ago contended that the only Pauline epistle we have definite allusions to among the Apostolic Fathers is 1 Corinthians: "Whenever we come from the marshy ground of 'reminiscences' and 'allusions' to firmer territory, again and again we confront I Corinthians." Why? Because, as *1 Clement* makes plain, the epistle was useful to combat heretics and schismatics, foes of emerging Roman orthodoxy. The encyclical use of 1 Corinthians for which Dahl and Mowry argue fits Walter Bauer's thesis perfectly.

Whence 2 Corinthians, then? Mowry[48] sees it as a second collection of scraps intended to supplement its predecessor, explaining that "II Corinthians owes its composite character to the desire to produce something analogous in scope to I Corinthians. If any weight attaches to this suggestion, the inference would seem to be that I Corinthians, at least, had already circulated locally before the collector began his work." Mowry insinuates that the fragments used to compile 2 Corinthians came from the archives of the Corinthian church. It need not be so, however. Second Corinthians might simply denote a sequel to 1 Corinthians, just as 2 Thessalonians, on her theory, is a pseudonymous sequel.

Depending on what sort of Gnosticism, proto-Gnosticism, or gnosticizing Paulinism one sniffs out in 1 Corinthians (and I, for one, think Schmithals's case is a pretty good one), one might even want to reconsider one of Simone Petrement's fascinating guesses[49] that there is some connection between "Corinthians" and "Cerinthians." She thinks Cerinthus was like Ebion, an unhistorical eponymous founder, posited by heresiologists, in this case, of a gnosis originally associated with the Corinthians. I would turn it around, rehabilitate Cerinthus and ask if the antiheretical Corinthian epistles punningly refer to Cerinthian Jewish Gnostics. Knowing that the historical Paul lived before Cerinthus, he could not be made to address him directly, but some readers would take the hint, just as they did with the winking reference to Marcion's *Antitheses* and heretical gnosis in 1 Timothy 6:20.

We can also use Mowry's thinking on 1 and 2 Corinthians to shed light on the origin of the apocryphal *Third Corinthians*. The writer of the *Acts of Paul* obligingly constructed a fictive *Sitz-im-Leben* for the letter when he included it in his narrative, but in its previous, independent circulation, how had it justified its name? What was its connection with Corinth? Most likely none, but it was an attempt at a third antiheretical treatise and thus "Corinthian." In fact, as the *Acts of Paul* is singularly bereft of definite allusions to any canonical Pauline epistles at all (even the Iconium Beatitudes are an independent reflection of the paraenetic material shared with 1 Corinthians, as I attempt to show in Chapter Four), I suspect that *Third Corinthians* was the only Pauline letter available to the author of the *Acts of Paul*. This was no accident. *Third Corinthians*, which reads much like the short apocryphal Laodiceans, is a cento of phrases filched from canonical Pauline texts. My guess is that *Third Corinthians* was a local attempt to supplant and replace the Pauline collection which had become, as Walter Bauer and Goodspeed suggest, guilty by association with the heretics who so loved it.

Second-coming theories

Edgar J. Goodspeed and Walter Bauer (together with Hans von

Campenhausen[50] and others) have maintained that there is a reason for the crushing silence throughout the second century regarding the Pauline epistles. For instance, Justin Martyr never mentions Paul in his voluminous writings. When he is mentioned by other writers, Paul has nothing distinctive to say: he is a pale shadow and obedient lackey of the Twelve, as in Acts. When Ignatius, Polycarp, and *1 Clement* (all too blithely taken for genuine as early second-century writings) make reference to Pauline letters, as Bauer noted, they sound like ill-prepared students faking their way through a discussion of a book they neglected to read. *First Clement* (47:1) appears to have thought there was but a single Pauline letter to Corinth. Ignatius, in his letter to the Ephesians (12:2), somehow imagined that Paul had eulogized the Ephesians in every one of his epistles. Polycarp thought there were several letters to the church at Philippi (Philippians 3:2) and that all Paul's letters mentioned the Philippian congregation (11:3). The special pleading of Andreas Lindemann,[51] attempting to reinterpret these peculiar references, as well as to supply some citations of Paul for these writings, only serves to underline the embarrassment of his position.

Goodspeed saw a period of neglect of Pauline literature but placed it between Paul's death and the collection of his letters about 90 CE. Bauer saw the church in the role of Peter, denying his Lord when the latter's popularity waned or, perhaps better, like the haughty scribes who shunned Jesus because they didn't like the riffraff he associated with. Goodspeed, on the other hand, might have likened the church, who neglected Paul, to that "wicked lazy servant" who buried a valuable talent in the ground. Bauer would not disagree with this. Implicit in his theory, as John Knox puts it, was that Paul had never had the centrality in his own lifetime that the publication of his letters gave him posthumously. In any case, that influence was a long time coming, according to Bauer, Goodspeed, Knox, and C. Leslie Mitton. Then, through the first collector of the Pauline epistles, says Albert E. Barnett, a disciple of

Goodspeed, "Paul becomes a literary influence." We may call this the "second coming" approach.

The essentials of Goodspeed's widely discussed theory are easily stated. Taking up an idea put forth earlier by Johannes Weiss,[52] that Ephesians was written by the first editor of the Pauline collection, Goodspeed argued that Paul's influence had sputtered out until publication of Luke's Acts, which reawakened interest in the great apostle. This would have happened about 90 CE. Someone in the Ephesian church (Goodspeed nominated Onesimus, the runaway slave mentioned in Philemon) read Acts and thrilled to the gospel exploits of the man to whom he owed so much. If the reader were indeed Onesimus, as John Knox[53] would subsequently argue with some ingenuity, he had Paul to thank both for his freedom and his Christian faith. In any case, Goodspeed pictured a man who cherished his church's copies of Colossians and Philemon. Reading Acts set him to wondering whether there might be more such epistolary gems in the various churches, so he set out to retrace Paul's steps and his hunch bore out.

Goodspeed imagines that the church clerks at Corinth, Galatia, Philippi, Rome, and Thessalonika did manage to retrieve copies of letters that had languished beneath old church ledgers, membership rolls, and Sunday School lessons. They blew the dust off and handed them over. Like the new owner of the treasure hidden in the field, Onesimus (or whoever) went on his way rejoicing. Back in his study, as he thought over the matter, he was both determined to share his discovery with the wider Christian world and uncertain as to the best way to do it. At length he hit upon the idea of publishing a collection and writing a kind of digest of Pauline sentiments, a new Colossians, beefed up with gems from the Septuagint and Paul's other letters, to serve as an introduction to the whole. This new epistle bore no title. However, because it was published in Ephesus and began circulating outward from there, people eventually took it for a genuine epistle and simply assumed it had been mailed by Paul to the city whence it had subsequently emerged. Thus it came to be known as the Epistle to the Ephesians.

Goodspeed had essentially cast Onesimus in Goodspeed's own role of reviving and noising abroad the neglected work of a noble predecessor, which in Goodspeed's case was Johannes Weiss's theory about Ephesians. What evidence led them to draw their conclusions? Goodspeed noticed that Christian writings dating before circa 90 CE betrayed no evidence of familiarity with Paul's letters or influence by him. Here Goodspeed thought mainly of the Synoptic Gospels. After 90 CE, however, Paul's shadow is long and falls across the whole literary landscape. His ideas echo in the pages of Hebrews, *1 Clement*, 1 Peter, and the Gospel of John. The sudden flood of epistles, and particularly of the sevenfold epistle collections (Revelation 1-3; Ignatius, Dionysius of Corinth), all attest to the great impact of Paul's letters organized as if written to seven churches, with the Corinthian letters being conflated or at least counted together, likewise the Thessalonians, and even Philemon riding the coattails of Colossians. What happened in or around 90 CE that could account for such an overnight change? Only one thing, according to Goodspeed, and that was the publication of the Acts of the Apostles. It was the catalyst for the publication of the Pauline corpus.

Those are the main lines of Goodspeed's argument. Several problems become evident at once, however, and critics were not slow in pointing them out. For one thing, the degree of Pauline influence on a document is largely in the eye of the beholder. Ralph P. Martin makes Mark, not unreasonably, a Paulinist Gospel.[54] Why is there talk in Luke of "justifying" oneself and of being "justified"? Is not Paul in view in Matthew 5:17-19? On the other hand, is John's Gospel so very Pauline?

The same problem arises with respect to Goodspeed's dates. Guthrie thinks Goodspeed dated everything too late, but I would have the opposite objection. Why not place the Gospels in the early to mid-second century? As for Acts itself, even Goodspeed's own disciple, Knox, places it just before 150 CE. Though otherwise he follows Goodspeed as loyally as Onesimus followed Paul, Knox does not think Onesimus would have needed to read Acts to be moved to collect the epistles.

Regarding the sevenfold collections, one has to cheat, as Schmithals points out,[55] to squeeze Philemon together with Colossians. Did the idea of seven letters from Paul have to come from John of Patmos? The Apocalypse is crawling with sevens, as Guthrie noted against Goodspeed, and not even Goodspeed dared claim John got all of them from Paul.

Mowry thinks Goodspeed made Onesimus into a first-century Tischendorf,[56] traveling to exotic locales, hot on the trail of rare manuscript finds. Apparently Tyrrell's quip about the nineteenth-century questers for the historical Jesus applied no less to questers for the origins of the Pauline collection: they looked down a deep well and saw only their own faces reflected. No doubt, F. F. Bruce[57] is correct when he dismisses the whole thing as "a romantic embellishment." Specifically, it is cut from the same bolt as the patristic fictions of Mark the evangelist being Peter's major domo or Luke playing Bones to Paul's Kirk ("Damn it, Paul, I'm a doctor, not an ecclesiastical historian!").

Goodspeed, Knox, and Mitton are happy to point to Walter Bauer's thesis to strengthen their own about a period of Pauline neglect, but Bauer[58] had a rather different candidate in mind for the herald of Paul's second coming: Marcion of Pontus, the second founder of Pauline Christianity. Says Bauer: "I would regard him as the first systematic collector of the Pauline heritage." This opinion, like Goodspeed's, was hardly unprecedented. F. C. Burkitt[59] had hazarded the same educated guess.

When ... we consider Marcion's special interest in S[aint] Paul, he being, according to Marcion, the only one who understood the doctrine that Jesus came to deliver to mankind; and when, further, we remember that Marcion was perhaps more of a traveler than any other Christian in the second century, and therefore had opportunities for collection above most of his contemporaries; when we consider these things, we may be permitted to wonder whether Marcion may not have been the first to make a regular collection of the Pauline Epistles.

Incidentally, both Bauer and Burkitt thought that at least 1 Corinthians must have circulated widely before Marcion's collection.

John Knox, an advocate of Goodspeed's Onesimus as the first collector, seems to realize he should follow Bauer's lead instead. After all, in Knox's *Marcion and the New Testament* (1942), he demonstrates the soundness of the view—defended by Baur, Ritschl, Volkmar, and Hilgenfeld—that Marcion's Gospel was not an abridgment of canonical Luke but rather a more modest abridgment of a shorter Ur-Lukas, which was also subsequently used by the writer/redactor of canonical Luke-Acts in the second century.[60] Lukan themes and favorite vocabulary are thickly concentrated in special Lukan material not shared with Marcion's text (patristic writings list what was "missing" from Marcion's versions), but are largely absent from material present in both Marcion and canonical Luke. Sometimes mundane non-Lukan synonyms appear where canonical Luke has favorite Lukan words, and none of these has any conceivable theological-polemical relevance; that is, Marcion would not have switched them, whereas they are just the sort of stylistic changes Luke regularly makes in his copying from Mark.

To make a long story short, Knox argues persuasively along many lines that Luke-Acts was a second-century Catholic response to Marcion's Sputnik, the *Apostolicon*. Canonical Luke was a catholicizing expansion of the same Ur-Lukas Marcion had slightly abbreviated, while Acts was a sanitized substitute for Marcion's Pauline corpus. Thus it presents a Paul who, though glorified, is co-opted, made the merest narcissistic reflection of the Twelve—and who writes no epistles but only *delivers* an epistle from the Jerusalem apostles! Knox sees the restoration of the Pauline letters—domesticated by the "dangerous supplement" of the Pastorals—and the addition of three other Gospels and several non-Pauline epistles, in short the whole formation of the New Testament canon, as a response to the challenge of Marcion and the Marcionite Church.

In light of all this, why does not Knox abandon Goodspeed, as Andrew and his friends did John the Baptist, and attach himself to Bauer instead? There are four reasons. First, he believes the Catholic Pauline collection reflects a different text than Marcion's, so it must be based on another version of the corpus already available before Marcion. On the one hand, Knox himself admits we cannot know for sure how Marcion's text read since we read it through the thick lenses of the Catholic apologists. They, in turn, may have read an already evolved post-Marcion text from the Marcionite Church or the splinter-sect of Apelles. On the other hand, why not assume that Marcion's opponents simply reacted to Marcion's collection by making their own collection of Pauline letters from different sources? As we have already seen, it is likely enough that, if one looked hard enough, one could find one's own texts of 1 Corinthians, Romans, and perhaps any of the others. Even Bauer does not ask us to believe that no one had access to the Pauline epistles before Marcion, as if Marcion had discovered them in a cave at Qumran. If the Catholic Pauline corpus was a counter-collection (not just the same collection of texts, but an attempt to restore Marcion's "omissions"), then the question of a variant textual tradition need not worry us too much. Knox imagines Bauer's theory to require, so to speak, a Catholic edition of the Revised Standard Version when it could just as easily have entailed a fresh Catholic corpus like the Jerusalem Bible.

Knox's second reason for rejecting Marcion as the first collector is that he believes, contra Bauer, that the Apostolic Fathers do show familiarity with various Pauline letters. The only way to settle this is to compare each supposed allusion with the corresponding Pauline text and to ask whether we are dealing only with a similar turn of phrase or a piece of common ecclesiastical jargon. Admittedly, we do still find Polycarp to be filled with Paulinisms, but in this case the allusions suggest too much. The epistle of Polycarp, *To the Philippians*, reveals itself upon close inspection to be little more than a clumsy and pointless pastiche composed of Pauline and Pastoral formulas. Anyone might have written it, and one would certainly have expected the great Polycarp to have had a bit more of his own to say. It is only acquiescence to tradition that causes "critical" scholars, weary with debates over Pauline authenticity, to accept Polycarp's *To the Philippians*, at face value. (And think of *1 Clement*, as anonymous as Hebrews!) Knox, then, ought to have thought twice before banishing Bauer by invoking Polycarp. On the other hand, it may be that Polycarp was the author of the epistle *To the Philippians* and also of the Pastoral Epistles, which is why Pastoral material is "reflected" in his epistle.

Knox cannot imagine the collection taking form as late as Marcion's time, since Ephesians already presupposes the other nine letters. However, R. Joseph Hoffmann argues cogently that "Laodiceans" was not merely Marcion's name for our familiar Ephesians, it was an earlier Marcionite version. Just as canonical Luke is a catholicized, anti-Marcionite version of Ur-Lukas, so, according to Hoffmann[61] (a latter-day admirer of Knox's book on Marcion), canonical Ephesians is a catholicized reworking of an original Marcionite Laodiceans. This Laodiceans was the work of Marcion himself. As with Knox's argument on these texts (Luke, Marcion's Gospel, and the Ur-Lukas), one must engage Hoffmann's extensive exegesis before reaching a judgment. It is impossible to present it adequately here.

Van Manen[62] had made almost exactly the same diagnosis of Galatians, in which we read of an encounter between Paul and the Jerusalem pillars, strikingly reminiscent of Marcion's clash with the Roman Church hierarchy: it was at first a Marcionite text, later catholicized by his opponents, who then covered their tracks by accusing Marcion of abbreviating it.

The identification of Marcion as possibly the first collector is now generally considered to be dead in the water, though, ironically, for almost the opposite reason to one of Knox's arguments. Knox felt the difference between Marcion's text and that of the Catholic edition of Paul implied Marcion had chosen one of perhaps several editions of the corpus already available. However, Nils Dahl, John J. Clabeaux,[63] and other scholars think they have found evidence of a widespread textual tradition to which Marcion's text appears to have belonged. In other words, now it is Marcion's textual *similarity* to other texts of Paul that eliminates him as the first collector. How have things turned about? It is no longer solely a question of textual relatedness or difference. We have already suggested that the availability of several copies of various individual Pauline letters would have allowed different collections of the same documents to reflect different streams of textual transmission. By far, most of Clabeaux's valuable study reinforces this conclusion; not surprisingly, other editions of Paul had drawn on some of the same textual streams that Marcion's did.

The new factor is the possibility that Marcion's collection was an edited version of a collection already arranged in the same distinctive order, one that had always been considered Marcion's innovation: Galatians first (no surprise if Marcion himself wrote it!), then 1 Corinthians, 2 Corinthians, Romans, 1 Thessalonians, 2 Thessalonians, Laodiceans/Ephesians, Colossians, Philippians, and Philemon. This order, or something like it, is attested in two other places: in the so-called Marcionite Prologues and in the Old Syriac canon, as attested in Ephraim and in a canon list from the late third century. If these instances could be shown not to derive from Marcion's *Apostolicon*, we would see them instead as evidence of a more widely current edition of the corpus with this arrangement. Dahl, building upon the argument of Hermann Josef Frede,[64] tries to disassociate both sources from Marcion. His argument centers on the theological slant of the Prologues.

Dahl's two major arguments are first, that the false apostles everywhere denounced in the prologues as Paul's opponents need not be the Judaizing Twelve of Marcionite polemic; second, that Paul is not pictured as the sole authentic apostle in the prologues. I think he is wrong, at least wholly unpersuasive, on both counts. First, the pseudo-apostles of Corinth are said to represent "the sect of the Jewish Law." This by itself could mean many things, but the Prologue to Romans speaks of the unwary being lured by the false apostles "into the Law and the Prophets" as opposed to "the true Evangelical faith." Dahl's attempt [65] to evade the force of the "Law and Prophets vs. Gospel" opposition is special pleading. If the author of the prologue was not a Marcionite, he had a funny way of showing it.

Dahl also thinks that the Corinthian Prologue depicts Paul fighting on two different fronts against two different groups of false apostles, one specializing in "Jewish Law," to be sure, while the other dealt in "the wordy eloquence of philosophy." This reflects the contents of the Corinthian letters themselves, to borrow Dahl's own observation on the Galatian Prologue, and in no way means the prologist did not view the Corinthian opponents of Paul as the Jerusalem pillars. After all, F. C. Baur thought the same thing.

And as for the possibility that the Prologue to Corinthians speaks favorably of other apostles besides Paul, there is some textual confusion here. Where Dahl reads that the Corinthians "heard the word of truth from the apostles," plural, *ab apostalis*, he is making a text-critical choice. A number of manuscripts do have this reading, but others have it the way Knox reads it, with the singular *ab apostolo*, "from the apostle." In view of the fact that the singular (*ab revocat apostolus*) occurs also at the conclusion of the Corinthian prologue, the most likely option is surely that the plural reading preferred by Dahl is an orthodox, catholicizing "correction." Dahl's[66] own motive in attempting to read the prologues as endorsing Cephas and Apollos alongside Paul is obviously the same.

If the prologues remain tilting to the Marcionite side, their order must be assumed to derive from the *Apostolicon* of Marcion. What about the Old Syriac? Of this, Dahl says,[67] "the arrangement of the letters in the Old Syriac version seems to be due to an amalgamation of an order like that of Marcion and the Prologues for the first four letters and an order more like that of our Greek manuscripts for the others. Textual affinities are not so striking that they suggest Marcionite influence upon the Old Syriac version of Paul." In other words, the textual evidence is inconclusive. In that case, why simply assume it was "an order like that of Marcion" and not Marcion's own?

Mowry[68] accepts most of Goodspeed's reconstruction, except that she fills in the emptiness of the tunnel period, as we have seen, with the circulation of individual epistles. As for Marcion, Mowry hypothesizes that he obtained a copy of Goodspeed's/Onesimus's ten-letter (or seven-church) corpus but, having learned of earlier versions of individual letters, he obtained them and undertook his own critical edition on that basis. This would explain Marcion's use of the short ending of Romans, the encyclical version. If there is good reason to accept Marcion as the first collector, however, why not simply turn Mowry's reconstruction on its head and suggest, as we have above, that it was the Catholic opposition who scrambled to assemble their own counter-collection from different textual sources? The one seems as likely as the other. Obviously, all such speculations remain educated guesses, unverifiable at present, as Burkitt admitted, but why is the identification of Marcion as the first collector so unthinkable even to someone like Knox, who comes so close to that conclusion? Again, we may only speculate that Guthrie[69] speaks for many: "It is highly improbable that a heretic should have been the first to appreciate the value of the

Pauline corpus." The hands are the hands of historical criticism, but the voice is that of Eusebian apologetics.

The archetype debate

Having reviewed several distinct theories of how the Pauline corpus first came to be, we must now give some attention to the disputed question whether all of our texts of the Pauline epistles descend and diverge from a particular, definitive edition of the Pauline corpus. This is not to ask whether there had ever been different Pauline collections or different ancient editions. Almost everyone agrees that there would have been, but did one of these supersede all the others to form the basis of all our extant manuscripts? Or do our manuscripts still reflect (because they descend from) several, albeit quite similar, Pauline corpus editions? Let us survey a handful of proposals regarding a definitive archetype.

Günther Zuntz decided that the best way to account for a Pauline textual tradition that differs so much in minor respects but hardly at all in major ones was to posit the compilation of a definitive variorum edition about a half-century after the original writings. In the meantime there would have been extensive copying of various individual letters, giving rise to the variants catalogued in the archetype. The only tradition of ancient scholarship capable of producing such a critical text was the Alexandrian school, and there seemed to Zuntz no particular reason to prevent our locating the operation in Alexandria itself. Zuntz believed he could identify several glosses introduced into the text by Alexandrian scholars. Later scribes who made copies on the basis of the resultant master text would not be so careful (pedantic?) as to bother noting variant readings but, like some modern Bible translators, would simply choose one of the alternatives in each case and go on. Thus the definitive edition provided a precedent for its own undoing. In broad outline, Bruce accepts Zuntz's reconstruction. As we will see, others think quite differently.

Walter Schmithals,[70] notorious for his division of most of the Pauline epistles into hypothetical earlier fragmentary letters, adopted the older theory of Johannes Weiss that the earliest collection of Paul's letters must have begun with 1 Corinthians, with the catholicizing gloss in 1:2 introducing the whole corpus to a wider readership. He thought it must have ended with Romans, the grand doxology of 16:25-27 ringing down the curtain on a broader ecumenical stage. Schmithals pictured an original seven-letter collection excluding Ephesians, Colossians, Philemon, and the later Pastorals; these may have been, *a la* Trobisch, two independent three-letter collections later appended to the original. The number seven was important to the compiler/collector, just as it was to John of Patmos, to Ignatius, and to Eusebius (collector of letters of Dionysius of Corinth) because it "expressed original and perfect unity."[71] The corpus was meant to stand for the truth of Catholic orthodoxy against Gnostic heresy.

It was this symbolic constraint, felt by various other letter collectors as well, that provides the motive for the compiler stitching together the various Pauline fragments as he did. He could not leave any of the precious text on the cutting room floor so, by hook or by crook, he got it all in. This scenario would also account for the anti-Gnostic polemic Schmithals finds in every letter. It is not so much that Schmithals thinks Paul was a first-century Joe McCarthy looking for a Gnostic under every bush. Rather, it was the concern of the redactor to include some of Paul's anti-Gnostic polemic in each of the seven letters.

Schmithals feels that Colossians, Ephesians, and Philemon do not show signs of the distinctive hand of the redactor and therefore cannot have belonged to the original collection. He knows that Goodspeed and Knox, who also invoke the analogy of other early seven-letter collections, try to squeeze in these three by combining the pairs of Corinthian and Thessalonian letters, but Schmithals says that to go on and make Philemon and Colossians count as one letter is to force a square peg into a round hole. Schmithals points out that the key thing is not *letters to seven churches* (neither the Ignatian nor the Dionysian collection fits that pattern—some letters being to individuals, others to more than one congregation), but rather *seven letters to churches*. Thus, Schmithals anticipated the criticism of Gamble that it had to be seven letters to seven churches for the symbolism to make any sense.[72] Perhaps so, but don't tell Schmithals; tell it to the compilers of the letters of Dionysius and Ignatius. As to place and time, Schmithals approves Harnack's suggestion that the letters were compiled at Corinth, and he thinks it happened already by 80 CE. The first collector was also the redactor, and he bequeathed us our archetype.

Winsome Munro argued with great ingenuity and attention both to general criteria and to specific detail that all our copies of Paul's epistles descend from a particular archetype, which she, unlike Zuntz and Schmithals, did not identify with the original collection. She demonstrated the existence of a comprehensive and systematic set of textual interpolations across the whole Pauline corpus as well as in 1 Peter, long recognized as something of a Paulinist adjunct anyway. These interpolations stand out because of their great affinity with the socio-political stance and pious quietism of the Pastorals and for their clash with the many elements of apocalyptic egalitarianism and sectarian radicalism in the other Pauline letters. Munro reviews a raft of previous critical treatments of these jarring "subjection texts" and notes that not infrequently scholars would peg this or that individual text (e.g., Rom. 13:1-7; Eph. 5:21-33; 1 Cor. 11:1-16; 14:34-38) as a possible interpolation. Munro draws all these suggestions together, isolates criteria for identifying what she calls a "Pastoral stratum," and uncovers several more passages of the same type. This stratum "does not come from the original collector and redactor of a Pauline letter corpus, but from different circles at a more advanced stage of Christian history. The later stratum, together with the Pastoral epistles, will therefore be characterized as 'Pastoral' or trito-Pauline ... its milieu is the Roman hellenism of the first half of the second century, when the Christian movement was prey to sporadic persecution, but was nevertheless hopeful that it might gain recognition and tolerance from the Roman authorities under the Antonine emperors."[73]

However, the Pastoral redactor couldn't have been either the first collector or one who reissued the corpus in a new edition after a period of neglect. In either of these cases, Munro felt sure, the Pastoral reviser would have been much freer to excise remaining elements of Pauline radicalism distasteful to him. "The inescapable conclusion is that the ten-letter collection was in circulation at the time of the Pastoral revision. That means it must have been taken over from an opposition group and revised in order to counteract its influence."[74] Dennis R. MacDonald made much the same case, though in brief outline, in *The Legend and the Apostle*.[75] He too saw the hand of the Pastor in the editing of what became our textual archetype, though in my opinion MacDonald's profile of the opponents is more convincing than Munro's. He makes them a motley collection of Encratite Christian radicals, whereas Munro has spoken more narrowly of Jewish-Christian ascetics.

Let us remind ourselves briefly of Trobisch, whose theory certainly entails an archetype corpus, since his method depends significantly on the study of the order of the Pauline letters in extant manuscripts. He notes that various canon lists have atypical orders but that virtually no extant manuscripts do. He ascribes the order, at least of Romans, 1 and 2 Corinthians, and Galatians, to Paul. Trobisch concludes that Paul himself edited this collection and provided the archetype. He leaves unanswered (even unasked) whether there were other collections made after Paul's death by people who were ignorant of the sheaf of copies he had sent to Ephesus. If so, they must have utilized copies of the unedited versions of Paul's letters. Then which edition would have been considered more authoritative?

If Bruce, MacDonald, Munro, Schmithals, Trobisch, and Zuntz believe a single archetype edition lies behind all extant manuscripts, their agreement is impressive but by no means unanimous. Significant voices taking the opposite view include Kurt Aland and Harry Gamble. Aland pronounces thusly on the matter:

> The opinion that a uniform "ur-Corpus" of seven Pauline Epistles had been collected by the close of the first century, from which all later witnesses have descended, is nothing but a "phantasy of wishful thinking" ... By about AD 90 several "Ur-Corpora" of Pauline Epistles began to be made available at various places, and ... these collections, of differing extent, could have included some or all of the following: 1 and 2 Corinthians, Hebrews, Romans, Galatians, Ephesians, Philippians. Eventually other traditional Pauline Epistles were added to the several collections and a more or less stabilized collection finally emerged.[76]

In several publications, Gamble voices essentially the same sentiments. Yet one should not imagine that Aland and Gamble envision a radically diverse textual tradition. Just the opposite. In general, they believe the stream of textual transmission flowed pure and without deviation. It was like the disciple of Rabbi Johannon ben Zakkai, a plastered cistern that lost not a drop. No archetypal ur-corpus was needed to ensure faithful transmission of the text, and none is needed to account theoretically for textual near-unanimity. Gamble says:

> If, then, the Pauline textual tradition goes back to multiple sources, it remains a matter of note in relation to redactional hypotheses [like Schmithals's] that the forms of the Pauline letters remain fundamentally the same in all known witnesses. Except in the case of Romans [with its longer and shorter endings], the tradition preserves no textual evidence that any of the letters ever had basically different forms than the forms in which we know them. The case of Romans offers the exception that proves the rule: when

textual revisions have taken place they have left their marks in the evidence.[77]

In other words, there is just enough textual variation to show that there was not a uniform and universal archetype, in which case all texts would agree completely, but there is by no means enough textual variation to indicate the existence of significantly different text forms. Earlier, shorter (non-interpolated) versions of Pauline letters might have existed without managing to leave any traces in the manuscript tradition. In fact, Aland and Gamble ignore the fact that when scribes compared longer and shorter versions of the same epistle, they naturally would have harmonized the two by choosing the longer reading. Mowry understood this: "The new collection came into immediate demand, and soon supplanted every other edition still in circulation. But copies of letters, in the form they had had when circulating individually and locally, survived here and there and left their mark either directly or indirectly in [the] manuscript tradition ... Their textual additions survived; their omissions tended to disappear."[78]

Similarly Knox:

Once a book came to be officially adopted in a particular form, older forms which lacked any such ecclesiastical approval tended to disappear. Manuscripts would gradually, and fairly rapidly, be conformed to the "correct" text. The process would never have become complete, and thus we have the various local texts, which emerge clearly enough in the early third century. These, however, differ relatively little from one another; and that is true not because the autographs were so faithfully followed in the late first and early second centuries but rather, on the contrary, because official editions and publications so completely drove the autographs (if there were any surviving) and their descendants from the field.[79]

William O. Walker, Jr., is not surprised that there should be no surviving manuscript evidence for literary interpolations: "Indeed, if a collector-editor's real goal was to include all available Pauline writings, as seems at least plausible, the tendency almost inevitably would have been to err on the side of inclusion, not of exclusion. In addition, deliberate or inadvertent interpolations may well have been introduced prior to the final editing of the letters. Also to be noted in this context, of course, is the well-documented practice of copying glosses into the texts of later manuscripts."[80] As John C. O'Neill anticipates:

> [The answer to] the objection ... that we might well expect more [consequential] texts than Marcion and D [without glosses] ... is that scribes would on the whole prefer to transcribe the longest text, being unwilling to lose anything precious. Every addition would tend to be recorded, even if the addition depended for its sense on an omission that the scribe was unwilling to adopt. That means that Vaticanus in fact bears traces of the whole history of the text. That history cannot, however, be read from Vaticanus, without evidence from other manuscripts which have gone a different way.[81]

The other consideration neglected by Aland and Gamble is the possibility of official ecclesiastical suppression of earlier or otherwise deviant text forms. Winsome Munro thinks of it in terms of more or less voluntary conformity within the orthodox plausibility structure: "Though episcopacy was probably not yet firmly established in the Aegean region [at the time of the Pastoral revision], it would have been possible to maintain a standard text within orthodox circles. Acceptance of this ecclesiastical authority would have involved adherence to the scriptures and revisions of scripture it authorized, and rejection or deviation therefore would have spelt expulsion."[82]

Think of the revulsion with which fundamentalists greeted the debut of the Revised Standard Version. Certainly none would be caught dead with anything but King James in church. Likewise sectarian heretics would not be eager to share their cherished scripture versions with their religious opponents, so neither side probably had much to fear in the way of textual infection. And when these sects expired, their scriptures were buried with them: witness, for example, the dearth of Bogomil or Catharist scriptures. Walker envisions a slightly later situation in which internalized authority might prove insufficient:

> We only know that the surviving text of the Pauline letters is the text promoted by the historical winners in the theological and ecclesiastical struggles of the second and third centuries. Marcion's text disappeared—another example, no doubt, of the well-documented practice of suppressing and even destroying what some Christians regarded as deficient, defective, deviant, or dangerous texts. In short, it appears likely that the emerging Catholic leadership in the Churches "standardized" the text of the Pauline corpus in the light of "orthodox" views and practices, suppressing and even destroying all deviant texts and manuscripts. Thus it is that we have no manuscripts dating from earlier than the third century; thus it is that all of the extant manuscripts are remarkably similar in most of their significant features.[83]

One cannot help but wonder if text-critical theories like those of Aland, Gordon D. Fee, Gamble, Harnack, and Bruce M. Metzger are simply contemporary attempts to safeguard the officially sanitized textual tradition in the interests of the same ecclesiastical establishment that produced the text they so jealously guard.

Conclusion

In composing a survey like this one, it is scarcely possible to avoid reaching some tentative conclusions of one's own. I will take the liberty of sharing them here. Most of them will by now come as no surprise. I can see some early use of Romans and 1 Corinthians, followed later by the sequel 2 Corinthians, all as encyclicals, as well as the local exchange and circulation of other letters. The question of authorship would have little bearing here one way or the other. No doubt, interpolations were made and gradually permeated the text of each letter until final canonization of the Pastoral edition and concurrent burning of its rivals.

The best candidate, if we want a name for the first collector of the Pauline epistles, remains Marcion. No one else we know of would be a good candidate, certainly not the essentially fictive Luke, Onesimus, or Timothy. Marcion, as Burkitt and Bauer show, fills the bill perfectly. Of the epistles themselves, he is probably the original author of Laodiceans, the *Vorlage* of Ephesians, and perhaps of at least part of Galatians, too. Like Muhammad in the Koran, he would have read his own struggles back into the careers of his biblical predecessors. Nonetheless, as our investigations proceed, we may find it more plausible to ascribe the formation of the Pauline corpus to a Marcionite successor than to Marcion himself.

Marcion, or Marcionites, adapted the now-lost Ur-Lukas and combined it with the ten-letter Pauline corpus to form the *Apostolicon*. As Knox perceived clearly, our canonical Luke tried to supplant the Marcionite Gospel, augmenting the pre-Marcionite Ur-Lukas with new, catholicizing, and anti-Marcionite material of various sorts. Canonical Luke succeeded in this effort (again, the longer displaces the shorter). And according to Knox, the Acts of the Apostles, which has Paul as a clone of Peter—someone who does not even write letters—replaced the dangerous corpus of "the apostle of the heretics." Like Jacob, however, it only managed to usurp priority over Esau, not to destroy him, even today subtly governing the way historical critics read the Pauline epistles. The Pauline corpus survived alongside it.

One modification I would make in Knox's reconstruction is to factor in Jerome D. Quinn's proposal that the author of Luke-Acts was the author of the Pastoral Epistles and that he intended a tripartite work on the pattern of contemporary collections of documents about or by a famous figure, concluding with a letter or collection of letters by the great man. Luke-Acts-Pastorals would then be a tripartite tractate to counter Marcion's scripture, the Pastorals intended to supplant the earlier letters. I suspect the redacted Ephesians and *Third Corinthians* were originally similar Pauline diatessarons aiming but failing to replace Marcion's Pauline corpus. I should note that Knox did, of course, regard the Pastoral Epistles as post-Marcion and anti-Marcion; he just didn't group them with Luke-Acts.

Since the corpus could not be eliminated, Plan B was to reissue them in a sanitized edition, domesticated by means of the Pastoral stratum. From there on in, it became easier to destroy rival versions of the Pauline letters. The Gospels of Mark and Matthew were added and so was John once it had undergone ecclesiastical redaction (Bultmann), just like Laodiceans and Ur-Lukas. How interesting that, just as Acts has Paul chained to a Roman guard on either side, so are the most heretical of New Testament writings escorted by watchful Catholic sentinels on both sides: John is bracketed between Luke and Acts, Paul's letters between Acts and the Pastorals. They shouldn't offer any trouble.

Eventually, the nondescript Catholic or General Epistles were spuriously ascribed to the pillar apostles so as to dilute Paul's voice yet further. There was even an attempt to fabricate an innocuous, one-page replacement for the Marcionite Laodiceans. It didn't catch on, but it managed to fool Harnack.

NOTES

[1]The term was coined by Immanuel Kant. It "was the type of transcendental theology characteristic of Anselm of Canterbury's ontological argument, which believes it can know the existence of an *Urwesen* [original being] through mere concepts, without the help of any experience whatso-

ever" (Iain Thomson, *Heidegger on Ontotheology: Technology and the Politics of Education* [New York: Cambridge University Press, 2005], 7).

[2]French philosopher Jacques Derrida (1930-2004) was one of the most influential Deconstructionists of the twentieth century.

[3]Walter Schmithals, *Paul and the Gnostics*, trans. John E. Steely (New York: Abingdon Press, 1972), 270.

[4]R. L. Archer, "The Epistolary Form in the New Testament," *Expository Times* 63 (1951-52), 296ff.

[5]Donald Guthrie, *New Testament Introduction* (Downers Grove, IL: Inter-Varsity Press, 1970), 657.

[6]Adolf Deissmann, *Paul: A Study in Social and Religious History*, 2nd ed., trans. William E. Wilson (New York: Harper Torchbooks, 1957), 5-6.

[7]Abraham J. Malherbe, *Paul and the Popular Philosophers* (Minneapolis: Fortress Press, 1989).

[8]Elizabeth Schüssler Fiorenza, "Rhetorical Situation and Historical Reconstruction in 1 Corinthians," in eds. Edward Adams and David G. Horrell, *Christianity at Corinth: The Quest for the Pauline Church* (Louisville, KY: Westminster John Knox Press, 2004), 153-54.

[9]David Trobisch, *Paul's Letter Collection: Tracing the Origins* (Minneapolis: Fortress Press, 1993).

[10]Schmithals, *Paul and the Gnostics*, 266.

[11]Trobisch, *Paul's Letter Collection*, 101.

[12]The actual Tosefta was a subsequent collection of materials left out of the Mishna by its scribal compilers.

[13]Vincent Taylor, *The Formation of the Gospel Tradition* (London: Macmillan, 1957), 41: "If the Form-Critics are right, the disciples must have been translated to heaven immediately after the Resurrection."

[14]Trobisch, *Paul's Letter Collection*, 97-98.

[15]Dennis Ronald MacDonald, *The Legend and the Apostle: The Battle for Paul in Story and Canon* (Philadelphia: Westminster Press, 1983). The Encratites were ascetics who, like the Shakers, rejected all sexuality as the price of salvation.

[16]Guthrie, *New Testament Introduction*, 646.

[17]Adolf Harnack, *Die Briefsammlung des Apostels Paulus* (Leipzig: Hinrichs, 1926).

[18]Roland Barthes, "The Death of the Author," in Barthes, *Image–Music–Text*, trans. Stephen Heath (New York: Noonday Press, 1988), 142-48.

[19]Jacques Derrida, *Of Grammatology*, trans. Gayatri Chakravorty Spivak (Baltimore: Johns Hopkins University Press, 1974), 145, 154, 157.

[20]Max Müller, "Preface to The Sacred Books of the East," in *The Upanisads*, Part I (Oxford: Clarendon Press, 1879), ix-xxxix. He writes, for example, of "the wild confusion of sublime truth with vulgar stupidity that meets us in the pages of the Veda, the Avesta, and the Tripitaka" (xv-xvi).

[21]Percy Neale Harrison, *The Problem of the Pastoral Epistles* (London: Oxford University Press, 1921), 87-137.

[22]Guthrie, *New Testament Introduction*, 655-57.

[23]Charles Francis Digby Moule, *The Birth of the New Testament* (New York: Harper & Row, 1962), 204; Moule, "The Problem of the Pastoral Epistles: A Reappraisal," *Bulletin of the John Rylands Library* 47 (1965): 430-52.

[24]Stephen G. Wilson, *Luke and the Pastoral Epistles* (London: Society for Promoting Christian Knowledge, 1979).

[25]Jerome D. Quinn, "The Last Volume of Luke: The Relation of Luke-Acts to the Pastoral Epistles," in Charles H. Talbert, ed., *Perspectives on Luke-Acts* (Danville, VA: Association of Baptist Professors of Religion, 1978), 62-75.

[26]Hans Conzelmann, "Paulus und die Weisheit," *New Testament Studies* 12 (1965): 321-44.

[27]Eduard Lohse, *Die Briefe an die Kolosser und an Philemon* (Göttingen: Vandenhoeck & Ruprecht, 1964), 14.

[28]Hans-Martin Schenke, "Das Weiterwirken des Paulus und die Pflege seines Erbs durch die Paulusschule," *New Testament Studies* 21, issue 4 (1975).

[29]Harry Gamble, *The New Testament Canon: Its Making and Meaning* (Philadelphia: Fortress Press, 1985), 39.

[30]Schenke, "Weiterwirken des Paulus," 511.

[31]Paul D. Hanson, *The Dawn of Apocalyptic: The Historical and Sociological Roots of Jewish Apocalyptic Eschatology* (Philadelphia: Fortress Press, 1975), 32-208.

[32]Ernst Käsemann, "The Canon of the New Testament and the Unity of the Church," in Käsemann, *Essays on New Testament Themes*, trans. W. J. Montague (London: SCM Press, 1964), 95-107.

[33]Rudolf Bultmann, *History of the Synoptic Tradition*, trans. John Marsh, 2nd ed. (New York: Harper & Row, 1968), 127.

[34]M. Eugene Boring, *Sayings of the Risen Jesus: Christian Prophecy in the Synoptic Tradition*. Society for New Testament Studies Monograph Series 46 (New York: Oxford University Press, 1982).

[35]It is unfortunate that in English we have two separate words for *story* and *history*, whereas in German and French, the same word, though different in the two languages, covers both concepts.

[36]Hermann Detering, *Paulusbriefe ohne Paulus? Die Paulusbriefe in der holländischen radikalkritik Kontexte* (Frankfurt am Main: Peter Lang, 1992).

[37]Willem Christiaan van Manen, "Paul," in T. K. Cheyne and J. Sutherland Black, eds., *Encyclopaedia Biblica* (New York: Macmillan, 1914).

[38]Willem Christiaan van Manen, "Old-Christian Literature," *Encyclopaedia Biblica*.

[39]Moule, *Birth of the New Testament*, 203.

[40]Kirsopp Lake, *The Earlier Epistles of St. Paul* (London: Rivingtons, 1911), cited in Leslie C. Mitton, *The Formation of the Pauline Corpus of Letters* (London: Epworth Press, 1955), 16: "Small and partial collections came into existence in various centers, before the Corpus in its completed form fully replaced them."

[41]Günther Zuntz, *The Text of the Epistles: A Disquisition upon the Corpus Paulinum* (Oxford: Oxford University Press, 1953), 279.

[42]Percy Neale Harrison, *Polycarp's Two Epistles to the Philippians* (Cambridge: Cambridge University Press, 1936), 239-40.

[43]Lucetta Mowry, "The Early Circulation of Paul's Letters," *Journal of Biblical Literature* 63 (June 1944), 73-86.

[44]Schmithals, *Paul and the Gnostics*, 239-74.

[45]Nils Dahl, "The Particularity of the Pauline Epistles as a Problem for the Ancient Church," in *Neotestamentica et Patristica: Eine Freundesgabe Herrn Professor Dr. Oscar Cullmann zu seinem 60 Geburtstag überreicht* (Leiden: Brill, 1962), 269.

[46]Schmithals, *Paul and the Gnostics*, 259.

[47]Walter Bauer, *Orthodoxy and Heresy in Earliest Christianity*, eds. Robert Kraft and Gerhard Krodel, trans. by a team from the Philadelphia Seminar on Christian Origins (Philadelphia: Fortress Press, 1971), 219.

[48]Mowry, "Early Circulation of Paul's Letters," 81.

[49]Simone Petremont, *A Separate God: The Christian Origins of Gnosticism*, trans. Carol Harrison (San Francisco: HarperSanFrancisco, 1990), 223.

[50]Hans von Campenhausen, *The Formation of the Christian Bible*, trans. J. A. Baker (Philadelphia: Fortress Press, 1972), 144-45.

[51]Andreas Lindemann, "Paul in the Writings of the Apostolic Fathers," in William S. Babcock, ed., *Paul and the Legacies of Paul* (Dallas: Southern Methodist University Press, 1990), 25-43. I shall deal with most of these supposed Pauline references in Chapter Four.

[52]Johannes Weiss, *Der erste Korintherbrief* (Göttingen: Vandenhoeck & Ruprecht, 1910); Weiss, *Earliest Christianity: A History of the Period AD 30-150*, 2 vols., trans. and ed. Frederick C. Grant (New York: Harper & Row, 1959), 2:684.

[53]John Knox, *Philemon among the Letters of Paul: A New View of Its Place and Importance* (New York: Abingdon Press, 1935; rev. ed. 1959).

[54]Ralph P. Martin, *Mark: Evangelist and Theologian* (Exeter: Paternoster Press, 1972), 161-62.

[55]Schmithals, *Paul and the Gnostics*, 264.

[56]The German scholar Lobegott Friedrich Konstantin von Tischendorf spent the mid-nineteenth century in the Middle East hunting for the oldest extant Bible manuscripts. In Palestine he discovered the fourth-century Codex Sinaiticus, which he presented to his benefactor, Tsar Alexander II of Russia.

[57]Frederick F. Bruce, qtd. in Arthur G. Patzia, "Canon," in *Dictionary of Paul and His Letters*, eds. Gerald F. Hawthorne, Ralph P. Martin, Daniel G. Reid (Downers Grove: Inter-Varsity Press, 1993), 88.

[58]Bauer, *Orthodoxy and Heresy*, 221.

[59]Francis C. Burkitt, *The Gospel History and Its Transmission* (Edinburgh: T&T Clark, 1906, rpt. 1925), 318-19.

[60]John Knox, *Marcion and the New Testament: An Essay in the Early History of the Canon* (Chicago: University of Chicago Press, 1942), 77-113.

[61]R. Joseph Hoffmann, *Marcion: On the Restitution of Christianity: An Essay on the Development of Radical Paulinist Theology in the Second Century*. AAR Academy Series 46 (Chico, CA: Scholars Press, 1984), 274-80.

[62]Van Manen, "Paul."

[63]John J. Clabeaux, *A Lost Edition of the Letters of Paul: A Reassessment of the Text of the Pauline Corpus Attested by Marcion*. Catholic Biblical Quarterly Monograph Series No. 21 (Washington, D.C.: The Catholic Biblical Association of America, 1989).

[64]Frede, *Altlateinische Paulus-Handschriften* (Freiburg im Breisgau: Verlag Herder, 1964).

[65]Nils Dahl, "The Origin of the Earliest Prologues to the Pauline Letters," *Semeia* 12 (1978): 260.

[66]Ibid., 259.

[67]Ibid., 254.

[68]Mowry, "Early Circulation of Paul's Letters," 80.

[69]Guthrie, *New Testament Introduction*, 644.

[70]Schmithals, *Paul and the Gnostics*, 259.

[71]Ibid., 261.

[72]Harry Y. Gamble, "The Redaction of the Pauline Letters and the Formation of the Pauline Corpus," *Journal of Biblical Literature* 94 (Sept. 1975).

[73]Winsome Munro, *Authority in Paul and Peter: The Identification of a Pastoral Stratum in the Pauline Corpus and I Peter*. Society for New Testament Studies Monograph Series 45 (New York: Cambridge University Press, 1983), 2.

[74]Ibid., 141-42.

[75]MacDonald, *Legend and the Apostle*, 85-89.

[76]Aland, qtd. in Patzia, "Canon," 89.

[77]Gamble, "Redaction of the Pauline Letters," 418.

[78]Mowry, "Early Circulation of Paul's Letters," 86.

[79]Knox, *Marcion*, 131.

[80]William O. Walker, Jr., "The Burden of Proof in Identifying Interpolations in the Pauline Letters," *New Testament Studies* 33 (Oct. 1987), 612.

[81]John C. O'Neill, *The Recovery of Paul's Letter to the Galatians*. (London: SPCK, 1972), 36.

[82]Munro, *Authority in Paul and Peter*, 143.

[83]Walker, "Burden of Proof," 614.

4.

The Apocalypses and Acts of Paul

Having examined in the previous chapter the possible circumstances behind the collection of Pauline epistles, I want to turn to another, quite large portion of writings ascribed to Paul. These are the major second-to-fifth-century Pauline apocrypha, consisting of a *Prayer of the Apostle Paul*, two surviving Pauline apocalypses, and the *Acts of Paul*. My goal is to assess the use of the Pauline epistles by these authors or redactors. If a presumed Pauline document seems unacquainted with Paul's other writings, is this because the author wished to distance Paul from the heretical associations his epistles had come to have? So-called Catholic documents from this period make little or no use of Paul's letters because they were tainted, through association with the heretics who used them, with subversion. Paul had become the "apostle of the heretics." Justin Martyr never mentioned Paul but must have known of him. What he knew was that Paul was sacred to Marcion, whose legacy Justin despised. This period of neglecting Paul ended with late second-century apologists Irenaeus, bishop of Lugdunum (Lyons) in Gaul, and Tertullian of Carthage. They both sought to rehabilitate the fascinating Pauline epistles that Polycarp and others had tried to sanitize to win Marcionite and Gnostic (that is, Pauline) Christians over to Catholicism. I find this approach completely convincing as a way of accounting for the evidence of who did and did not quote Paul and why.

There is a rival explanation that circumvents the issues of early Christian factionalism. On the one hand, Andreas Lindemann argues that various early documents do allude to Paul, and widely. I will examine these supposed allusions presently. As to the apocryphal *Acts of Paul*, Dennis R. MacDonald[1] thinks this document makes little use of Paul's epistles because it represents a declining deutero-Paulinism that dealt in visions and miracles. Against MacDonald, one may quickly invoke the chicken-and-egg question: how is it that such a non-Pauline or deutero-Pauline picture of the apostle came to prevail so thoroughly if not through the prior neglect of the letters? Even if MacDonald was judged correct in relation to the *Acts of Paul*, we would still have to account for the strange non-use of the Pauline epistles in the *Apocalypse of Paul* since the epistles were awash in apocalyptic mysteries and revelations. Why would a Catholic writer of the *Apocalypse of Paul* make no use of this juicy material? Again, I think it is because one had learned to stay away from the documents, favored as they were by the wrong Christians. One might have thought to create a safe, substitute Paul in their place.

The apocalypses

Before we examine the extant Pauline apocalypses, it may be worth asking the reason someone would have written such documents in the first place. If we were to begin from the standard explanation encountered in the study of the Jewish apocalypses,[2] we might expect that a later Christian had a revelation, or perhaps some good ideas, to announce and decided to secure a wider hearing by attaching to it the name of an apostolic worthy. The connection with the historical figure whose name he or she chose might be minimal, though if the figure, like Moses or Enoch, were already associated with visions and revelations, so much the better. In this case, if there were some cosmetic connection between the vision and the known visionary experiences of the pseudonym, then we would expect to see the writer plunge into blue skies, drawing on themes from the earlier material and then going on to say something new.

If we were to approach the Pauline apocalypses with these expectations in mind, however, we would be seriously disappointed. In fact, any connection to previous Pauline writings is tenuous, and the apocalypses are mostly indebted to items borrowed from other alleged authors from the traditional canon. There is also a surprising lack of originality, which may be due to the fact that the apocryphal writers were trying to fill a gap left by the loss of an ancient work, the title of which had alone survived to intrigue them. (To this cause, for instance, we seem to owe the unspectacular *Epistle to the Laodiceans*.)[3] Here we may suggest that Paul's account of his vision of the third heaven, together with his coyness in revealing precisely what he heard there, naturally proved too great a temptation for a later pseudepigraphist to resist.

For the most part, our Pauline apocalypses seem to conform to the urge to fill a gap; they are therefore not surprisingly derivative in content. They just don't borrow from the Pauline epistles. Why not? Surely there is abundant material of a visionary nature despite the fact that the apostle kept mum on his paradise revelation. Paul is forever vouchsafing mysteries (Rom. 11:25; 1 Cor. 2:7; 4:1; 15:51; Eph. 1:9; 3:3; 5:32; Col. 1:27) and divine commands (1 Cor. 14:37). He knows all manner of things about the coming of the Lord (1 Cor. 15:51-54; 1 Thess. 4:12-17), the appearance of the Man of Sin (2 Thess. 2:1-12), and so on. However, such nuggets as these are conspicuous by their absence in the Pauline apocalypses. That can't be a coincidence.

At least two pseudo-Pauline apocalypses have not survived the passage of the centuries. One of these is that mentioned by Origen as accepted by the church. This Apocalypse of Paul had certain points of contact with the better-known apocalypse to be discussed presently, but Hugo Duensing thinks it cannot be the same text because early Christian historian Salminius Sozomen says it was unknown until the reign of Theodosius. The apocalypse known to Origen may have been an ancestor of the later work since both speak of the postmortem fate of the damned, the topic mentioned by Origen in connection with his text.

From Epiphanius, we hear of a text called *The Ascension* (*Anabatikon*) *of Paul*, composed by the Cainite sect and disseminated among its Gnostic brethren.[4] It was an attempt, apparently, to supply the revelation hinted at in 2 Corinthians 12:1-10. Oh that this old text might turn up in a monastic trash bin somewhere! As Paul is made to lambaste the Cainite Christology in 1 Corinthians 12:3, it would be fascinating to read what the so-called Cainites might have had him say on their behalf.

What remains are two Pauline apocalypses proper and a third text, the *Prayer of the Apostle Paul* from the Nag Hammadi library, which is not strictly an apocalypse but is related in content, just not in form. Of the two formal apocalypses, the earlier *Apocalypse of Paul*, which I prefer to render as the *Revelation of Paul*, is also from the Nag Hammadi collection. Of this text, George W. MacRae and William R. Murdock judged that "nothing in [it] demands any later date than the second century."[5] The better-known document of the same title, *Apocalypse of Paul*, dates from "the last years of the fourth century," contends Montague R. James, or "the beginning of the fifth century," according to Hugo Duensing.[6] *The Prayer of the Apostle Paul*, because of its apparently Valentinian coloring, according to Dieter Mueller, would seem to stem from "between the second half of the second century and the end of the third century."[7]

The two Nag Hammadi texts are clearly Gnostic, which is evident by their content and not simply by the mere accident of their preservation at Nag Hammadi.[8] According to the "apostle of the heretics" model, we would expect to see some familiarity with the Pauline epistles in Gnostic sources. Do we find it here? Indeed we do.

The Revelation of Paul

Surprisingly, the *Revelation of Paul* makes only the shakiest allusion to 2 Corinthians. One passage (19:21-24) reads, "Then the Holy Spirit who was speaking with [him] caught him up on high to the third heaven." But immediately "he passed beyond to the fourth [heaven]," we are told, apparently not pausing at all in the third heaven for a revelation. MacRae and Murdock say, "The ascent builds on 2 Co[rinthians] 12:2-4,"[9] but we might rather say it bypasses this text just as Paul bypasses the third heaven. Instead, the revelation makes clear use, as MacRae and Murdock also recognize, of Galatians. On his way to Jerusalem, Paul is accosted by a "little child," apparently an angel or the polymorphic Risen Christ who appears in Christian apocrypha as a child (see the *Acts of John*). "I know who you are, Paul," the child says. "You are he who was blessed from his mother's womb" (18:14-17). Such a salutation need not be an allusion to Galatians 1:15 and could be a biblical-style honorific derived from Old Testament sources, but the allusion is made secure by the words that follow: "For I have come to you so that you may go up to Jerusalem to your fellow apostles" (18:17-19). Surely this sentence refers to Paul's account in Gal. 2:1-2, "I went up ... to Jerusalem ... I went up by revelation; and I laid before them (but privately [to] those who were of repute) the gospel which I preach among the gentiles." In the immediate context, these reputable ones are identified as the apostles (1:19). It is mundane enough; why would a journey up-country to Jerusalem imply a detour to heaven? Later in the epistle, we are told that Paul visits "the Jerusalem that is above" (4:26), so that by creative esoteric exegesis, the apocalyptist makes the revelation of Galatians 2 his jumping off point rather than the visionary journey of 2 Corinthians 12.

The rest of the vision is taken up with fairly standard features of apocalyptic, including glimpses of the judgment of damned souls accosted by tormenting angels, although the scene takes place in the fourth heaven rather than in hell as in later apocalypses and presents challenges which must be met to ascend to heaven without hindrance. Paul encounters someone who is apparently to be identified with Daniel's Ancient of Days or the cosmic demiurge who created the world out of chaos. This entity seeks to bar Paul's entrance to the Ogdoad, or eighth heaven, by unleashing upon him the principalities and authorities. But at the suggestion of the Holy Spirit, Paul presents an unnamed sign, before which the demiurge and his creatures cringe.

Strikingly, Paul himself is made a Gnostic redeemer figure in this brief text, recalling the atoning savior of Colossians 1:24. We learn that Paul is the one who will proceed to the lower parts of the earth and "lead captive the captivity that was led captive in the captivity of Babylon," that is, the sparks of pleromatic light. It is a nod to Ephesians 4:8-9, where it is Christ who descends and ascends to rescue the elect. Presumably, in this sense, we can see that Paul's own mission to the gentiles had been reinterpreted. It is this great destiny of redemption to which Paul was "set apart from his mother's womb" (23:3-4, alluding to Gal. 1:15) as even the demiurge himself acknowledges, much as the demons of the Synoptics recognize the great hidden truth about Jesus.

Paul meets his fellow apostles in the heavenly Jerusalem, but in this telling, they are merely a crowd of extras at the side of the stage. No one speaks a word, no one is named. The interesting thing is that the historical rivalry between Paul and the twelve is harmonized, just as the emerging Catholic Church would harmonize it, except that in neither case did anyone maintain the balance attained by Luke, who begrudged both Peter and Paul any miracle or apostolic feat not paralleled in the other's ministry.

As F. C. Baur pointed out, Jewish (Ebionite) Christianity tended to blacken Paul's memory by casting him in the role of Simon Magus, archenemy of the true gospel and its true apostle Peter, while Catholic Christianity tended to make Paul into the merest shadow and imitator of Peter. In this way, Paul could be domesticated and safely ignored, shunted into the shadow of Peter and the twelve who even usurped his role in church tradition as the Apostle to the gentiles. But the *Revelation of Paul* harmonized the story in the other direction: there Paul is central, as he was in his own conception, and the twelve have become sanctified superfluities. The *Revelation of Paul*, then, manifests some familiarity with Galatians and Ephesians. The apocalyptist may have known of more epistles, but his text is really quite short, and perhaps he had no occasion, given the brief compass of the work, to make further references.

The Prayer of the Apostle Paul

The *Prayer of the Apostle Paul* is even shorter than the *Revelation of Paul*, but it alludes much more freely to Pauline epistles. Christ is invoked as "the one who is and who preexisted in the name that is above every name," a reference to the kenosis hymn of Philippians 2:5-11. He is "[the Lord] of Lords, the King of Ages," an apparent reflection of 1 Timothy 1:17; 6:15, or related liturgical texts, as it was appropriated by the Pastorals' author. Paul prays, "Give me your gifts, of which you do not repent," a possible allusion to Romans 11:29. Christ is said to be "the First-born of the pleroma of grace," possibly harking back to the Gnosticizing language of Colossians 1:15, 19, although really it is the common parlance of Gnosticism and would not need to come directly from Colossians.

This document is familiar not only with Pauline texts but also with John's Gospel ("the Spirit, the paraclete of [truth]") and even the late doxology to the Lord's Prayer ("[for] yours is the power [and] the glory and praise and the greatness for ever and ever [amen]"). There is what seems to be an exegetical reflection on

Paul's quoted mystagogical formula in 1 Corinthians 2:9, interpreting it in light of the preceding verses 6-8. By itself, the verse, which also appears in *Thomas* 17, *Acts of Peter* 39, and the *Apocalypse of John the Lord's Brother* from a Coptic encomium on John the Baptist,[10] would seem to promise the initiate secrets which have hitherto remained hidden from human beings. This seems to be implied by the fact that these wonders are said never to have entered into the "human mind/heart of man."

But the sharp eye of the composer of the *Prayer of the Apostle Paul* noticed how, in 1 Corinthians 2:6, 8, we read that the esoteric wisdom was hidden also from the prying archons of the age; hence the version we read in the prayer: "Grant what no angel eye has [seen] and no archon ear (has) heard and what has not entered into the human heart" (A1.25-29). The best way to explain this modification of the traditional wording is by reference to the material surrounding the verse as it appears in 1 Corinthians but not in any other ancient sources containing it. Our author is working from 1 Corinthians. No stranger to the epistles generally, he nevertheless devoted his closest study of Pauline material to the text of 1 Corinthians. We find an entirely different situation when we come to the fourth-century *Apocalypse of Paul*.

The *Apocalypse of Paul*

The fourth-century *Apocalypse of Paul* is heavily dependent on earlier apocalyptic narratives. Duensing agrees with James on the influence from the Apocalypses of Peter, Elijah, and Zephaniah.[11] Not surprisingly, there are also frequent echoes of hellfire passages of Matthew and the Revelation of John. However, I venture to go further and suggest that our would-be Paul used the work of his anonymous predecessor, the writer of the Nag Hammadi *Revelation of Paul*. In chapter 13 of that text, Paul wishes to behold the fate of souls as they depart earthly life. He is bidden: "Look down at the earth ... And from heaven I looked down on earth, and I saw the whole world and it was as nothing in my sight. And I saw the children of men as if they were nothing and growing weaker; and I was amazed and I said to the angel: 'Is this the size of men?'" In the next chapter, Paul sees an angel greeting a righteous soul just as it is exiting its dead body. The angel urges it, "Soul, take knowledge of your body which you have left, for in the day of resurrection, you must return to the same body to receive what is promised to all the righteous." Is it possible that both visions are elaborations on what was said by the revealing spirit in the earlier *Revelation of Paul*: "'Look and see your [likeness] upon the earth.' And he looked down and saw those [who were upon] the earth" (19:26-31)?

The terrifying reception granted the damned is commonplace in apocalyptic works (see the Zoroastrian *Menog-i Khrad* 1.101-22),[12] but it may not be entirely coincidental that both our apocalypses of Paul have similar scenes of demonic retribution, a briefer one in the earlier text (20:5-22) and a more elaborate one in the later work (15-17). In both, the soul of the wicked is made to face the souls of the ones he had murdered or otherwise wronged on earth. The fourth-century apocalypse has a scene (chapter 20) in which Paul arrives in the third heaven and finds himself approached by "an old man whose face shone as the sun. And he embraced me and said, 'Hail, Paul, dearly beloved of God.'" This figure turns out to be the undying Enoch. Can the fourth-century apocalyptist have been inspired by this similar scene in the earlier Gnostic revelation: "[Then we went] up to the seventh [heaven and I saw] an old man [clothed in] light [and whose garment] was white. [His throne], which is in the seventh heaven, [was] brighter than the sun by [seven] times. The old man spoke, saying to [me], 'Where are you going, Paul, O blessed one'" (*Apocalypse of Paul*, 22:23-30; 23:1-3)?

As noted above, the old man in the Nag Hammadi *Revelation of Paul* seems to be the Danielic Ancient of Days, but there is no real contradiction, since the apocalyptic tradition had already identified Daniel's "one like a son of man" with Enoch (*1 Enoch* 71:14), and in Revelation 1:13-14, the figures of the Ancient of Days and the one like a son of man were combined. Thus, a later apocalyptist had only to shift his interpretative imagery within the existing exegetical range. The use of Danielic imagery and the possible use of the earlier revelation may suggest two interesting points for understanding the later apocalypse. First, the earlier text pointedly did not seize the literary opportunity generously provided by 2 Corinthians 12:1-10, instead curiously sinking its roots into the shallower soil of Galatians 2:2. The later apocalypse corrected this peculiarity, as the prologue makes explicit: "The revelation of the holy apostle Paul: the things which were revealed to him when he went up even to the third heaven and was caught up into Paradise and heard unspeakable words." Thus, the later apocalyptist succumbed to the temptation to supply the revelation which readers of 2 Corinthians had so long wondered after. In doing so, he shrewdly reinterpreted Paul's absolute refusal to utter what, after all, was said to surpass human speech, along the lines of a qualified prohibition drawing on Daniel 12:9: "Go your way, Daniel, for the words are shut up and sealed until the time of the end." Suppose Paul could not utter the secrets vouchsafed to him to his generation, but that the time had come for these things to be revealed in the late fourth century?

The earlier apocalyptist was a Gnostic; his successor was a churchman and apparently a monk.[13] Indeed, the only genuinely new element in the later work is a set of threats aimed at those who fail to keep monastic and liturgical duties as they ought to. Here we see the monkish hand of our would-be Paul revealed. We might suggest that the writer was an archivist and much read in the earlier apocalyptic texts. Perhaps he wanted to throw a holy scare into his lazy brethren but felt the barbs hurled by the *Apocalypse of Peter* were too easily shrugged off. At hand was the *Apocalypse of Paul*, itself a favorite of monastics. Recall that the Nag Hammadi collection may have been the library of the Saint Pachomias monastery. In any case, that apocalypse was dangerously Gnostic, so our ecclesiastical redactor set out to compile a new and orthodox *Apocalypse of Paul*, utilizing the best of previous works in the genre.

But strangely, except for the Corinthian letters, his sources do not seem to have included Pauline writings. Is this because the epistles shared the same heretical odium that disqualified the earlier *Revelation of Paul*? Our task is to examine the passages in the *Apocalypse of Paul* that might be taken as allusions to the epistles to see if the resemblances are strong enough to count them as such. Duensing discerns an allusion to 2 Thessalonians 1:7-10 in the words of the angel to Paul in chapter 21, "And then the Lord Jesus Christ, the eternal king, will be revealed and he will come with all his saints to dwell in [the restored earth] and he will reign over them for a thousand years." Contrary to Duensing, this passage might be a *cento* of apocalyptic phrases present in Jude 14, Revelation 20:6, and elsewhere. The only thing particularly reminiscent of 2 Thessalonians is the phrase, "the Lord Jesus Christ will be revealed," and this could as easily have come from the line in 1 Peter 1:13 to "set your hope fully on the grace that is coming to you at the revelation of Jesus Christ."

Two passages might possibly be taken as allusions to Romans. In chapter 15, a worldly man, about to discover the error of his ways on the other side of mortality, is characterized as saying, "I eat and drink and enjoy what is in the world. For who has gone down into the underworld and coming up has told us there is a judgment there?" Might this skeptical taunt be an allusion to Romans 10:7, "Who will descend into the abyss"? Possibly, but the verbal coincidence is far too slight to be sure. We might as easily seek an echo of Paul's alternative to the resurrection in 1 Corinthians 15:32, "If the dead are not raised [meaning there would be no future judgment], 'let us eat and drink, for tomorrow we die.'" Here we would seem to be on somewhat firmer ground, especially as there seem to be other, stronger allusions to 1 Corinthians 15, but still we cannot be sure we have more than a spontaneous parallel due to a similar theme. The parallel is equally similar to Luke 16:19-31, which may be the origin of this passage in the apocalypse.

In chapter 49, the beatified Job says to Paul, "For I know that the trials of this world are nothing in comparison to the consolation that comes afterwards." Duensing refers the reader to Romans 8:18, "I consider that the sufferings of the present time are not worth comparing with the glory that is to be revealed to us." This is indeed a close parallel, though I cannot help but wonder if the sentiment, and even the phrase, were not common in times of persecution. Consider, for instance, Acts 14:22: "Through many tribulations we must enter the kingdom of God."

Chapter 48 presents a rather detailed lament by the glorified Moses, who is anguished that his people have utterly and totally apostatized. Undoubtedly, the writer of this soliloquy paid no attention to the more complex and optimistic sketch of the Jews' final destiny laid out in Romans 9-11. Could he have had it in front of him and ignored it? Chapter 14 gives us what might be an allusion to Colossians 1:12. A saved soul is called "a fellow-heir with all the saints," recalling the phrase from Colossians about "giving thanks to the Father, who has qualified us to share in the inheritance of the saints in light." Yet we find the same language in 1 Peter 3:7, "you are joint heirs of the grace of life."

This leaves us with a small set of possible allusions to 1 and 2 Corinthians. First, there are repeated references to the journey to a third heaven. These occur in the prologue, in chapter 11 ("And he caught me up in the Holy Spirit and carried me up to the third part of heaven, which is the third heaven"), chapter 19 ("And he lifted me up to the third heaven"), and chapter 21 ("And the angel answered and said to me: 'Whatever I now show you here and whatever you will hear, do not make it known to anyone on earth.' And he brought me and showed me and I heard their words which it is not lawful for a man to speak. And again he said: 'Follow me further and I shall show you what you ought to tell openly and report'").

In this last case it is especially clear that we are dealing with the text of 2 Corinthians 12:1-10 since we can see the rationalizing footwork of an author presuming to divulge Paul's esoterica yet denying that he is doing so. In the Coptic recension, which is discussed further below, we find a possible allusion to 2 Corinthians 3, where the apostle ventures to compare himself with Moses, estimating himself the minister of a greater covenant. In the Coptic text, Christ greets Paul as "mediator of the covenant."

In chapter 42, Paul is shown a hell of ice and snow and told it is the assigned abode of "those who say that Christ has not risen from the dead and that this flesh does not rise." Duensing sees this as an allusion to 1 Corinthians 15:12ff., and with some justification. The two clauses juxtapose the specific denial of Christ's resurrection with that of the resurrection generally, precisely as Paul does in 1 Corinthians 15: "But if there is no resurrection of the dead, then Christ has not been raised" (v. 13). Of course, the same general-to-specific denial of the resurrection occurs throughout Acts,[14] but the verbal parallel in Acts is not nearly as close. It must be kept in mind that our apocalyptist is by no means shy of citing New Testament literature, with his numerous clear references to John's Revelation and the Gospels. Why are there hardly any unquestionable allusions to Paul's epistles in an apocalypse that is credited to Paul? And why are they almost all from the letters to the Corinthians?

Before we venture an explanation, it is important to know that virtually the same condition exists in the epistles of Polycarp, Ignatius, and 1 Clement. None of the writers are aware of Paul's reputation as a great epistolarian, and each makes strange statements implying an utter lack of familiarity with the Pauline corpus. For instance, Clement seems to know of only one Corinthian epistle (47:1). Ignatius has somewhere gotten the notion that Paul mentions the Ephesians in every letter (Ignatius, *To the Ephesians* 12:2). Polycarp thinks Paul brags on the Philippians in his letters to "all churches" (Polycarp, *To the Philippians* 11:3) and that he wrote several letters to the Philippians (3:2). Such statements betray a distant, hearsay knowledge of the letters. On the other hand, Polycarp, Ignatius, and 1 Clement can be shown to make allusions to the letters to the Corinthians. I remain unpersuaded by the attempts of Andreas Lindemann to secure other Pauline citations,[15] save for Polycarp's references to the Pastorals which are the exceptions to prove the general rule, since the Pastorals are pseudepigraphical attempts to supply more safe Pauline epistles to replace the ones used with such profit by heretics.

I believe we may look to Walter Bauer's theory about the early currency of 1 Corinthians to find the explanation of these phenomena. He suggests that, starting at least with 1 Clement, the Roman hierarchy found 1 Corinthians to be useful as a weapon against heresy and sectarianism. Because of this utility, 1 Corinthians was widely circulated, even as other Pauline letters were shunned and suppressed in the Roman-leaning circles.[16] This would explain a few things. Bauer spoke only of the ecclesiastical circulation of 1 Corinthians, but to include 2 Corinthians, as I do, is simply to extend the theory farther in the same direction. I see 2 Corinthians as a collection of Pauline fragments compiled by Roman authorities as a sequel to 1 Corinthians and a new weapon in their arsenal. The fictional letter to Corinth was created because in orthodox eyes, a Corinthian epistle had, by this time, come to mean a defense against heresy. The title of the letter alone was tantamount to a second treatise against heresy. I think this hypothesis serves us well in understanding the genesis of the apocryphal *Third Corinthians* when we later consider the *Acts of Paul*.

A Coptic appendix

A word should be said about the Coptic conclusion of the fourth-century *Apocalypse of Paul*. Duensing thinks it may represent the original ending, lost from all other manuscript traditions.[17] If he is right, we would have an even closer parallel with the pattern evident in the Apostolic Fathers because, in the Coptic conclusion, Christ greets Paul as an "honoured letter writer!" This acknowledgment is juxtaposed with a stunning ignorance of Paul's epistles. Yet, there is reason to doubt the originality of the Coptic text. Most manuscript traditions bring the apocalypse to an abrupt end with chapter fifty-one, in which Paul converses with the prophet Elijah. While I dissent from James's guess that the original conclusion was three chapters later where Paul wrings from God a Sabbath rest for the inmates of hell, I concur in his judgment, against Duensing, that the longer Coptic ending veritably crawls with traits specific to Coptic Gospel apocrypha. This is especially true regarding the appearance of the ascended Christ, who converses with the apostles atop the Mount of Olives. Here we are clearly in the neighborhood of the *Pistis Sophia*.[18]

Yet even this result is interesting. If the Coptic conclusion is a secondary embellishment, we can consider it virtually a separate document, and it is striking that it includes the same pattern of knowledge that Paul was a letter writer, coupled with the conspicuous absence of references to anything but the Corinthian correspondence. The Coptic text, as we have seen, seems to make reference to 2 Corinthians 3, and there is a reference to 2 Corinthians 12, Paul ascending twice to the third heaven, where the second time he is warned again against revealing anything of what he has beheld there. This re-ascent must be recognized as a redactional seam; in the original Coptic apocalypse, this trip to the third heaven was probably his initial and only trip to paradise, an independent revelation-journey. Eventually someone added it onto the longer *Apocalypse of Paul* by way of harmonization.

The *Acts of Paul*

The second-century *Acts of Paul* was widely known. In addition to the entire manuscript, people also circulated part of it separately as the *Acts of Paul and Thecla*. As MacDonald has shown,[19] some of what were traditionally taken for Patristic references to the *Acts of Paul* are more likely references to some of the stories that circulated orally before they were crystallized in writing. However, this fact does not appreciably change the picture. It remains apparent that the *Acts of Paul* was popular throughout the ancient church despite the qualms of Tertullian and the hierarchs in Asia Minor who defrocked the author of the work.

The popularity of the work is important for two reasons. First, its image of Paul was widespread and deeply ingrained in the period of concern to us. Here we see who Paul was in the minds and imaginations of many Christians in the second century. Second, we have another important sample of Pauline literature to use in assessing how widely the epistles were known to the second-century church.

The most striking feature of the apostle's teachings, according to the *Acts of Paul*, was his forthright advocacy of the encratite doctrine.[20] This Paul taught that one must embrace celibacy in order to enter the kingdom of heaven. "Blessed are the continent, for to them shall God speak" (chapter 5). His teaching connects with 1 Corinthians 7, a point to which we must return, for much hinges upon it. Does Paul's celibacy teaching presuppose 1 Corinthians 7 or vice versa? Or is there some third option? We will be in a better position to say after examining possible allusions to Paul's letters elsewhere in the *Acts of Paul*, to which we will now turn our attention.

In his *New Testament Apocrypha*, Wilhelm Schneemelcher is noncommittal, saying that "the author [of the *Acts of Paul*] perhaps takes … for granted" that readers were aware of Paul's letters and Luke's Acts of the Apostles.[21] This is curious since the apostle's itinerary in the *Acts of Paul* proceeds in sovereign disregard of the itinerary in the canonical Acts. It would make the most sense to assume that the *Acts of Paul* was an original, independent collection of oral tradition. Any allusions to the canonical Acts might have been later scribal assimilations to Luke's Acts, even inadvertent trivial redactions, during transmission of the *Acts of Paul*. As Schneemelcher's remark implies, there is little to go on in determining how much knowledge the author might have had of the letters attributed to Paul. Let us bracket for a moment the apparent use of 1 Corinthians 7 in the Iconium sermon (*Acts of Paul* 5),[22] as well as allusions to various Pauline letters in *Third Corinthians*. They are special cases we can look at later. Our conclusions with regard to the rest of the *Acts of Paul* will in fact help us make sense of the apparent allusions in the Iconium sermon and *Third Corinthians*.

In chapter 2 of Paul's *Acts*, we are told that the good Christian Anchares refused to "requite evil for evil." This phrase is found in Romans 12:17, but I am unpersuaded that the present instance denotes the use of Romans. The writer of Romans 12 was himself employing traditional material, which we also find in Matthew 5:39 and Luke 6:27-28.[23] It would be dangerous to insist that the phrasing of the sentiment, as we find it in Romans 12, is original to that context and equally dubious to suppose that the *Acts of Paul* is quoting from it. Probably the author has access to the same traditional maxim. Schneemelcher thinks we may have an allusion to 2 Thessalonians 1:7 in chapter 37, where Thecla assures the pagan governor that the Son of God is "to the oppressed relief." Surely these few words are too slim a basis to claim literary dependence.

In chapter 43, Hermocrates expresses the pious hope that he "may believe as thou [Paul] hast believed in the living God." Can we believe, as Schneemelcher believes, that this confession harbors an allusion to 1 Thessalonians 1:9? All that the two passages have in common is the phrase "the living God," repeated again when Paul exhorts Artimilla in Ephesus to "no longer serve idols and the steam of sacrifice, but the living God." Surely such terminology is the stock in trade of Hellenistic Jewish missionary preaching and need not have come from 1 Thessalonians.

In the same context, Paul refers to "the sonship that is given through him in whom men must be saved." Schneemelcher points us to Romans 8:15, 23; 9:4; Galatians 4:5; Ephesians 1:5. But this relative plenitude of possible references implies rather that the bare word *sonship* was known Paulinist terminology and does not denote a particular text. Nor is there enough in common with any of the passages Schneemelcher cites. I will have more to say about this question later. Schneemelcher suggests a reference to Philippians 4:22 in *Martyrdom of the Holy Apostle Paul*, another sometimes independently circulated portion of the conclusion to the *Acts of Paul*. The parallel consists solely of a notice that "a great number of believers came to him from the house of Caesar." If a historical Paul had indeed made converts from the imperial household, that item would not have needed a citation in Philippians to survive in Christian memory.

Paul promises Nero, "I will arise and appear to thee (in proof) that I am not dead, but alive to my Lord Christ Jesus." Schneemelcher thinks he sees here an allusion to Romans 14:8. One could be equally convincing in saying it came from Luke 20:38 ("all are alive unto him") or from nowhere at all. If it came from Luke, this would not be surprising. As in the *Apocalypse of Paul*, there are clear references to the Gospel of Matthew and other New Testament writings in the *Acts of Paul*. The author was by no means shy of making references to other Christian writings. We can only explain the dearth of specific Pauline references by the supposition that such writings were unknown to him or tainted by heresy and thus shunned.

The Iconium Sermon

We must now take up the question of the relationship between 1 Corinthians 7 and the Iconium sermon. The latter would, on first reading, seem to abound with literary echoes of the former. The sermon is set forth in the form of a series of beatitudes, clearly modeled upon those in the Sermon on the Mount. This fact itself is interesting, as it implies the writer did not know Luke's Acts, for if he had, models for apostolic sermonizing would have been plentiful. The closest model he could think of was the sermon of Jesus from Matthew's Gospel.

Several of the beatitudes of the encratite Paul recall 1 Corinthians. The second, "Blessed are they who have kept the flesh pure, for they shall become a temple of God," brings to mind Paul's reminder that the Corinthians were collectively (1 Cor. 3:16-17) and individually (6:19) God's temple, although the image was not unique to Paul (1 Pet. 2:4-5). The fifth beatitude, "Blessed are they that have wives as if they had them not," strikingly recalls Paul's words in 1 Corinthians 7:29, "from now on let those who have wives live as though they had none."

The eleventh beatitude, "Blessed are they who through love of God have departed from the form of this world, for they shall judge angels and at the right hand of the Father they shall be blessed," reflects 1 Corinthians 7:31, "For the form of this world is passing away," as well as 6:3, "Do you not know that we are to judge angels?" The last part of the beatitude would seem to reflect Psalm 16:11, "at thy right hand are pleasures forevermore." The thirteenth beatitude, "Blessed are the bodies of the virgins, for they shall be well pleasing to God, and shall not lose the reward of their purity," carries various echoes of 1 Corinthians 7:32-34: "I want you to be free from anxieties. The unmarried man is anxious about the affairs of the Lord, how to please the Lord; but the married man is anxious about worldly affairs, how to please his wife, and his interests are divided. And the unmarried woman or virgin is anxious about the affairs of the Lord, how to be holy in body and spirit; but the married woman is anxious about worldly affairs, how to please her husband."

There are not only several pronounced verbal similarities—all of them more pronounced than any of the other alleged allusions suggested by Schneemelcher—but they are compounded by the fact that most of them reflect the same complex of verses in 1 Corinthians 6-7. If anyone concludes that 1 Corinthians was one of the sources of the *Acts of Paul*, we cannot for the present gainsay him or her. And if this is true, let us note the repetition of the pattern discerned in the *Apocalypse of Paul*: a general ignorance of the Pauline letters with the conspicuous exception of 1 Corinthians. This is probably because that letter was circulated by the ecclesiastical authorities as a *panarion* (all-purpose remedy) against heresy. Of course, this observation, to some extent, anticipates my conclusions with regard to *Third Corinthians*, and I will have to beg the reader's patience.

Having granted for the moment the likelihood that the *Acts of Paul* employs 1 Corinthians as a source, we must now explore another possible way of accounting for the parallels, namely that portions of 1 Corinthians 7 are post-Pauline and stand in the same relationship to the *Acts of Paul* as do the Pastorals: perhaps both documents reflect traditions which claimed Paul as the great champion of encratism, the *Acts of Paul* embracing them, 1 Corinthians conscripting Paul in opposition to them.

First, we must decide what 1 Corinthians 7 is about. Here a great deal of confusion exists among translators and commentators, most of it probably because the chapter is unpalatable to modern sexual ethics and to apologetics for Pauline authorship. I will attempt, as briefly as possible, to review the case that it makes good sense when understood as a discussion of celibacy, within and without marriage, framed on encratite terms. Some translations place the statement of verse 1, "It is good for a man not to touch a woman," in quotation marks to make it seem like an eccentric opinion to be refuted. But in view of what follows, the sentiment is surely the writer's own. There is at least an approval of some kind of celibacy here, strengthened and widened if one translates it as, "It is good for a husband not to have sex with his wife," given the ambiguity of *aner* and *gune* and the contemporary use of *aptesthai* as a euphemism for "having sexual relations with." Thus the writer already seems to give at least a qualified endorsement of the practice of celibacy within marriage, a theme he will explore at greater length.

Traditionally, verse 2 ("But because of the temptation to immorality, each man should have his own wife and each woman her own husband") has been taken as a sober reckoning with the danger of embracing a celibate life instead of getting married: since the unmarried would-be celibate is bound sooner or later to give vent to his or her sexual urges, it would be morally more prudent to be married and so to ensure oneself a legitimate sexual outlet. But the larger context, as we will see, implies that we ought instead to translate it as follows: "But because of the temptation to immorality, let each husband have [sex with] his own wife and each wife her own husband." Precisely as in Elizabethan and modern English, *echo,* "to have," was a euphemism for sexual intercourse. In this case, the advice was to be realistic about the chances that sooner or later, one or the other partner would prove unable to keep the commitment to celibacy within marriage and, because the other would not break the encratite vow, the lusty one would have to seek satisfaction elsewhere in adultery or prostitution.

Note how this reading makes the next verses follow much more smoothly, whereas the traditional view makes the verses beginning with 3 seem to introduce a new subject out of thin air. Instead of an unrealistic commitment to permanent mutual continence or a stubborn unilateral holding to it by a partner when the other has reconsidered, "the husband should give to his wife her conjugal rights, and likewise the wife to her husband. For the wife does not rule over her own body, but the husband does [and she may not make a unilateral declaration of celibacy]; likewise the husband does not rule over his own body, but the wife does. [In contrast to unilateralism,] do not refuse one another except perhaps by agreement for a season that you may devote yourself to prayer."

Note the admission that sexuality and spirituality are incompatible: "But then come together again, lest Satan tempt you through lack of self-control," using the word *akrasian*, the opposite of *encrateia*. In verse 6 ("I say this by way of concession, not of command"), exactly what is the writer conceding? The suspension of celibacy for certain periods of time. How he wishes everyone could experience the glories of a sexless existence! He writes, "I wish that all were as I myself am. But each has his own special gift from God, one of one kind and one of another." Verse 8 advises singles and cloistered widows to maintain their celibacy. Marriage, says verse 9, is an option only for those unable to maintain the ideal of *encrateia* (*me enkrateuontai*).

Verse 10 considers a new wrinkle in encratite ethics. Suppose one spouse wishes to undertake the encratite discipline but knows good and well that the other spouse will have none of it. Again, one partner declares unilateral celibacy, but this time via the expedient of divorce. The writer will not countenance this, just as Marcion appears to have forbidden either the creation or dissolution of a marriage.[24] Then we have verses 12 through 16, which constitute a digression, about Christians with pagan spouses. The author says the couple is not living in sin and that the children are not illegitimate because one Christian partner in a union legitimizes the marriage in God's eyes. The Christian cannot initiate divorce, but if one's partner suggests it one would do best not to resist. Note the similar concern in the Pastorals (1 Tim. 5:4-14) that radical Christians not blacken the Christian name by antisocial behavior.

Verses 17 through 24 seem to be trying to put a damper on the social radicalism we associate with prophetic encratites of the second century.[25] The writer turns Paul's previous reasoning on its head: although the nearness of the end relativizes social structures, one should not bother trying to change anything. This would be like rearranging furniture aboard the *Titanic*. Verses 25 through 38 are in some ways an expression of the crux of the problem. Who are the virgins in view here, who are not so clearly in view due to translators who have modestly veiled them? Surely the New English Bible, with the renderings of James Moffatt and F. F. Bruce, is correct in detecting a reference to the practice of *virgines subintroductae*. The New English Bible renders verses 36 and 37 as follows: "But if a man has a partner in celibacy and feels that he is not behaving properly towards her, if, that is, his instincts are too strong for him, and something must be done, he may do as he pleases; there is nothing wrong in it; let them marry. But if a man is steadfast in his purpose, being under no compulsion, and has complete control of his own choice; and if he has decided in his own mind to preserve his partner in virginity, he will do well. Thus he who marries his partner does well, and he who does not will do better."

Against this interpretation, many translators have resorted to alternatives that are more quotable in church. One of the most popular is that Paul had reference to an engaged couple.[26] Here *parthenos* is taken to mean "fiancé" or "betrothed." But there are two insurmountable difficulties attached to this view. First, it is lexically impossible. *Parthenos* never means "fiancé," the only exception in the Bauer lexicon coming from a Byzantine erotic court poet of the twelfth century who is irrelevant for the New Testament period. Second, what sense can it possibly make for the writer to advise the man to "keep" the woman in question "as his fiancé" if his intent is never to marry her?

The other major alternative exegesis is the "father-daughter" view, which envisions an arranged marriage that a father may unconditionally veto.[27] Again, the use of *parthenos* to mean "virgin daughter" would be peculiar. Besides, this view would compel us to take *uperakmos* in verse 36 to mean "she is getting on past childbearing years." Indeed, it might mean this, but it would seem improbable in light of the next verse with the second half of a contrast ("... but if he is firmly established in his heart, being under no necessity, but having his desire under control ..."). The preceding half of the sentence forms the first half of the contrast only if *uperakmos* means "his passions are strong." In fact, otherwise the chiasmic structure is destroyed, in which "If anyone thinks he is not behaving properly toward his virgin" matches "has determined this in his heart, to keep her as his virgin"; "if his passions are strong" with "having his desire under control"; and "it has to be" with "being under no necessity."

In defense of the "father-daughter" view, it might be urged that *gamein* in verse 36 means "to give in marriage," but this is only certain in Luke 17:27 where *gamein* is coupled with *gamizein*. By itself, *gamein* can, and sometimes clearly does, mean "to marry." I therefore find it reasonable to read 1 Corinthians 7 as a treatment of encratite ethics. While accepting a preference for the celibate state, it attempts to moderate this radical stance, admitting that marriage "is no sin" (v. 36), that to marry is to "do well," even if only second best (v. 38). However, we must ask whether such a debate could have occurred during the lifetime of the Apostle Paul. It hardly seems likely. It presupposes an enthusiastic zeal for celibacy attested to only in the second century and beyond; it presupposes an ecclasiastical structure in which there exist celibate orders subsidized by the congregation. This freedom from worldly concerns, predicated on the *parthenoi*, implies individuals who are free as birds to pursue holiness in body and spirit (vv. 32-34). Can church structure have advanced so far already in the lifetime of the Apostle Paul?

I consider it likely that much of the material in 1 Corinthians 7 is a subsequent interpolation, as suggested by Winsome Munro in *Authority in Paul and Peter*.[28] It deals with issues Paul would not have recognized. We can say the author of chapter 7 is moderating and domesticating encratism but not trying to eradicate it.[29] At least for the sake of argument, we can take it as established that 1 Corinthians 7 and the *Acts of Paul* are both dealing with the question of asceticism and that both are using the memory of Paul to promote their viewpoints. Even on this understanding, it is possible to envision the writer of the *Acts of Paul* using 1 Corinthians as a guide, though we would have to picture him rejecting the verses that seek to moderate or confute the thoroughgoing encratite gospel he espoused. This is certainly not out of the question, if we only consider how today's Pentecostalists read 1 Corinthians 12-14 to promote their doctrine that all may simultaneously speak in tongues in public worship. Selective citation of only amenable texts is nothing new. But why bother? Is it possible to understand the parallels between 1 Corinthians and the Iconium sermon in another way? Might both writers have drawn on a common fund of traditional encratite terms and notions?

We have already noted the idea, encountered in the second beatitude, of keeping the body as pure as a temple of God. But let us now suggest that it may be seen to comport with something else in 1 Corinthians in a less obvious way. Does not the beatitude, "Blessed are they who have kept the flesh pure, for they shall become a temple of God," fit rather well with the logic of 1 Corinthians 6:13b, 19, which says "the body is not for *porneia*, but for the Lord, and the Lord for the body. ... Do you not know that your body is a temple of the holy spirit which you have within you, which you have from God?" I suggest that, especially in light of the admission in 7:5, 34, that sexuality is, strictly speaking, deemed incompatible with the highest path of spirituality. The rejection of *porneia* in 6:13b must naturally, and originally did, refer to sexual intercourse. The writer of 1 Corinthians no longer understood it so, and his use of it implies a reinterpretation of an encratite formula, according to which the one devoted in body and spirit to the Lord must refrain from being united to a mortal partner. On this understanding, any sexual union, even that with a legal spouse, must constitute adultery (cf. 1 Tim. 5:11-12). This, needless to say, was precisely why the people addressed in 1 Corinthians 7:1-5 were "refusing one another." I suggest, then, that the Iconium beatitude preserves the original sense of the formula, while 1 Corinthians 6:13b is secondary.

The third beatitude, "Blessed are the continent, for to them

God will speak," is interesting because it does not reflect the wording of any particular statement in 1 Corinthians. It supplies a missing link that enables us better to understand the particular situation being addressed in 1 Corinthians 11:2-16, where at first glance it is not quite clear who is to wear the veil while prophesying: all women or only wives. Probably the reference is to wives, due to the discussion of Eve having been created for Adam and being subordinate to him. The idea would be that wives must wear the veil as a token of modesty before and subordination to their husbands. The male-female relationship here is pictured solely in terms of the husband-wife relationship. Thus, wives are most likely in view. Then what of the Corinthian *parthenoi*? The argument seems to bypass them entirely. Why? I suggest it is because it is presupposed that their vow of celibacy lifts them above the customary male-female framework (cf. Gal. 3:28), and their sexual modesty no longer comes into question. They are, so to speak, off limits and no longer sex objects. Thus, they may go unveiled as they prophesy.

The principle underlying this state of affairs is nowhere stated in 1 Corinthians, but the beatitude supplies it: the continent have made themselves pure and proper vessels of the revelations of God, which they are to pass on to the community. Questions remain only in the case of the married Corinthian women. And sure enough, it is only their case that arises in 1 Corinthians 11.

A compromise is struck. They may prophesy, but they must still bear the marks of wifely submission. Again, the material in the *Acts of Paul* deals with the same topic as that in 1 Corinthians 7, but the former seems the more primitive.

On the face of it, the fifth beatitude would appear to be the clearest possible instance of straight borrowing from 1 Corinthians: "Blessed are they who have wives as if they had them not," compared to 1 Corinthians 7:29, "From now on let those who have wives live as though they had none." Closer examination reveals that, again, it is the beatitude which preserves the original sense of this striking phrase. In light of the discussion in the whole of chapter 7, what could the phrase possibly refer to but the formal, sexless marriages of the *virgines subintroductae*?[30] Indeed, it would be hard to think of a clearer and more succinct way to sum up the idea of a celibate marriage than as "having a spouse as though not." In the context of the Iconium sermon, this would be precisely what it would mean.

But in 1 Corinthians 7 this sense of it has been obscured, as can be seen from the author's attempt to apply it in blanket fashion to nearly everything: "And those who mourn as though they were not mourning, and those who rejoice as though they were not rejoicing, and those who buy as though they had no goods, and those who deal with the world as though they had no dealings with it" (1 Cor. 7:30). The writer has broadened the original encratite sense to include a nebulous Stoicizing about inner detachment. I suggest that the writer of 1 Corinthians 7:29-30 no longer understood the phrase or felt uncomfortable with it and therefore reinterpreted it. Since the Iconium beatitude still understands "having wives but living as not" in its straightforward sense, I judge it to be the more original, certainly not secondary to 1 Corinthians 7. In precisely the same fashion, Luke has reinterpreted or misinterpreted an encratite saying, "Blessed are the barren and the wombs that never bore, and the breasts that never gave suck" (23:29), while the *Gospel of Thomas* 79 has preserved the original sense of it.

Consider the line from the beatitudes, "Blessed are they who through love of God have departed from the form of this world, for they shall judge angels." The similarity with 1 Corinthians 7:31 and 6:3 may again be best explained if both documents had independent access to common encratite tradition. That 1 Corinthians 6:3 appeals explicitly to common knowledge is clear: "*Do you not know that* we are to judge angels?" Whence the connection between, of all things, judging angels and leaving behind the worldly schema? Keep in mind that in the Iconium sermon, the righteous encratite is always held as the Christian model. It is the sex-shunning encrat-ite, not the family man, who will sit in judgment over angels. Inter-esting to note is that Revelation 14:4; 20:4 makes clear this con-nection between celibacy and sharing the judgment seat of Christ, but 1 Corinthians does not. In failing to make it, the text severs the underlying link, without which the very notion becomes wholly arbitrary. It is not just any Christians whose privilege it would be to judge any angels. We must keep in mind just what form, accord-ing to contemporary belief, the fall of the angels took. Only celibate Christians can judge those notorious angels "who kept not their first estate" of chastity and lusted after the daughters of men (Jude 6; Gen. 6:1-4; *1 Enoch* VI and VII). The chaste encratites will have earned the right to judge the perverted "watchers" and condemn them, for unlike the latter, the former did not succumb to the lusts of the flesh. Who could have a better right to wield the gavel?

We have once again seen that the beatitude stands closer to the source and is not dependent on 1 Corinthians. All that now remains is to consider the eleventh beatitude— "Blessed are the virgins, for they shall be well pleasing to God and shall not lose the reward of their purity"—which is not, after all, so close to the wording of 1 Corinthians 7:32-34 that it demands an admission of dependence. It seems that we are dealing with common stock phrases exhorting abstinence.

So it may not be so clear that the author of the *Acts of Paul* knew or referred even to 1 Corinthians. As we have seen, the rest of the narrative evidences no certain knowledge of any of the Pauline epistles. The only remaining section of the *Acts of Paul* where we may yet encounter Pauline references is the apocryphal *Third Cor-inthians*. To it we now turn.

Third Corinthians

While it is not unnatural for an ancient narrator to interrupt his story with a real or fictitious letter, just as the author of the canonical Acts did (15:23-29; 23:26-30), scholars have doubted whether *3 Corinthians* and the material immediately surrounding it—a letter from Corinth which prompts a reply, as well as connective material between the letters—originally formed part of the *Acts of Paul* where it exists today. It also circulated independently and was considered canonical in some areas of the church. If the correspondence did not originate as part of the narrative, we face two possibilities. It might be that *Third Corinthians* pre-existed and the author of the *Acts of Paul* incorporated it into his book or that it was interpolated into the longer narrative by someone else at a later time.

Schneemelcher argues that the author of the *Acts* created *Third Corinthians*. Indeed he says, "it must ... be taken as certain that 3 Cor. was an original constituent part of the AP."[31] He bases his argument on the fact that in most of the manuscript tradition, even when they appear outside the larger *Acts of Paul* narrative, the two epistles from and to Corinth appear with some or all of the contextual (introductory and connective) material. That makes it look like they were excerpted. He seems to realize that if the two letters occurred in any manuscripts without the adjacent text, we might have to consider, as suggested by Michel Testuz, that the letters did originate independently.[32] But as it happens, there *are*, in fact, isolated instances where the letters stand alone, which Schneemelcher discounts, perhaps too hastily. The Bodmer Papyrus, our only Greek text of the letters, as well as some Latin manuscripts, contain no adjacent contextual material. Why does Schneemelcher dismiss the force of this evidence? All that is apparent from his discussion is that he feels the Bodmer Papyrus is an inferior witness due to some readings that are inferior compared to those of the later Latin manuscripts which include the contextual material.

However, the form of a text and the quality of its particular readings are two distinct text-critical questions. After all, may it not be that the letters began their literary life without the contextual material and, as they wended their way through the vicissitudes of scribal copying, suffered two different kinds of corruption or embellishment? They may have accumulated explanatory material along one path and suffered corrupt readings along another path. So, the Bodmer Papyrus and its Latin congeners might preserve the original form even though they are poorer readings of the text.

Against Schneemelcher, we may also point out a form-critical parallel, that of the *apophthegmata* of the Gospel tradition. It seems that certain aphorisms circulated for a while, puzzling their hearers since they contained insufficient clues as to their meaning (cf. Matt. 7:6). Eventually, unknown tradents sought to supply exegeses for these aphorisms in the form of narrative introductions. In this way, a brief account of what led Jesus to utter a saying provided the interpretation of it. We can readily picture something like this occurring in the case of the apocryphal Corinthian letters. Perhaps they did originate as we now find them in the Bodmer Papyrus. But as they continued to circulate, they attracted to themselves short narrative introductions, still independent of any larger narrative framework.

For this hypothetical state of affairs, we are able to supply ancient and close analogies. First, let us consider the apocryphal letters between King Abgarus of Edessa and Jesus. As James notes, these letters came to form the centerpiece of the legend of the Apostle Addai in Edessa.[33] But the first appearance of the letters is through their quotation by Eusebius. It is clear that Eusebius is not abstracting them from any larger narrative. Instead, he says, they come from the archives of Edessa. While Bauer is no doubt correct that their origin was not quite as Eusebius would have us believe (or would have believed himself),[34] there is no reason to doubt that Bishop Kune delivered them to Eusebius as discrete letters, not as part of a larger document. Yet the letters carry with them adjacent explanatory material: "A copy of a letter written by Abgarus the toparch to Jesus, and sent to him by means of Ananias the runner, to Jerusalem"; "The answer, written by Jesus, sent by Ananias the runner to Abgarus the toparch."

Next we may consider the *Letter of Lentulus*, which purports to be the eye-witness description of Jesus written down by a Roman official. This document began as a straight narrative, not a letter. Even in this form, it carried with it a brief introduction: "It is read in the annal books of the Romans that our Lord Jesus Christ, who was called by the Gentiles the prophet of truth, was of stature ..." and so on. In all other manuscripts, however, the report of Lentulus appears as a letter, and it, too, has an introduction: "A certain Lentulus, a Roman, being an official for the Romans in the province of Judaea in the time of Tiberius Caesar, upon seeing Christ, and noting his wonderful works, his preaching, his endless miracles, and other amazing things about him, wrote thus to the Roman senate." Thus, we have two cases of what Schneemelcher believed to be impossible: apocryphal letters which originated and circulated independently of any larger narrative, yet with brief introductory or connective narrative notes.

Given the possibility, do we have any evidence that the *Third Corinthians* complex did originate independently? We do, for it will become immediately apparent that whoever composed *Third Corinthians* made ample use of the Pauline epistles, whereas, as we have seen, it does not seem that the author of the rest of the *Acts of Paul* did so. It now remains to show that *Third Corinthians* used a set of Pauline letters. We read first that "the Corinthians were in [great] distress [over] Paul, because he was going out of the world before it was time." Though there is no strong verbal parallel here, it is not unlikely that we have an echo of Philippians 1:25, "I know that I shall remain and continue with you all, for your progress and joy in the faith."

One of the Corinthian presbyters who complains of the infiltration of Gnostic heretics is named Stephanus, apparently a reflection of the Stephanas mentioned in 1 Corinthians 1:16; 16:15. Paul's lamentation upon reading of Gnostic blasphemies disseminated at Corinth was, "Better were it for me to die and be with the Lord than to be in the flesh and hear such things!" which reminds us clearly of Philippians 1:23b-24, "My desire is to depart and be with Christ, for that is far better. But to remain in the flesh is more necessary on your account." The narrator reports that "Paul in affliction wrote the letter," apparently borrowing from 2 Corinthians 2:4, "For I wrote you out of much affliction."

The salutation of *Third Corinthians* 3:1, "Paul, the prisoner of Jesus Christ," appears to have been taken directly from the salutation of Philemon (verse 1). To be sure, the expression also occurs in Ephesians 3:1, but the writer would not have chosen it if he had not seen it used as a salutation in Philemon 1. This is important, for the use of Philemon demands the use of an entire Pauline collection; otherwise little Philemon would never have come to the writer's attention. In 3:2, Paul says, "I am in many tribulations," which looks like another reflection of 2 Corinthians 2:4. Chapter 3, verse 4, reads: "For I delivered unto you in the beginning what I received from the apostles who were before me" and is certainly a composite of 1 Corinthians 15:3, "For I delivered to you first what I also received," as well as Galatians 1:17, "to those who were apostles before me." Verse 7 contains a Pauline phrase, "adoption into sonship," which suggests borrowing from Romans 8:15, 23 or Galatians 4:5.

In close proximity, verses 19, 20, and 22 juxtapose the phrases "children of wrath" and "sons of disobedience," as we find in Ephesians 2:2, 3. The use of Ephesians also implies the use of a whole Pauline collection, if we accept the theory of Goodspeed and Knox that this epistle was composed to serve as an introduction to such a collection. In 3:21, Paul advises readers to steer clear of Gnostic troublemakers: "From them, turn ye away." We are reminded here of the admonition of the writer of the Pastorals in 2 Timothy 3:5 against "holding the form of religion but denying the power of it. From such people turn away." It is possible that 3:31 ("How much more, O ye of little faith, will he raise up you who have believed in Christ Jesus, as he himself rose up?") is, as Schneemelcher suggests, drawing on Romans 6:4 even though the wording is not particularly close.

We are on firmer ground suggesting that the polemic against the deniers of the resurrection in 3:24ff. comes straight from 1 Corinthians 15. For instance, in 3:26, we have a consideration of those who "do not know about the sowing of wheat or the other seeds, that they are cast naked into the ground and when they have perished below are raised again by the will of God in a body and clothed." This depends verbally, as well as conceptually, on 1 Corinthians 15:36-38, "You foolish man! What you sow does not come to life unless it dies. And what you sow is not the body which is to be, but a naked kernel, perhaps of wheat or of some other grain. But God gives it a body as he has chosen."

In *Third Corinthians* 3:34-35, we read: "But if you receive anything else, do not cause me trouble; for I have these fetters on my hands that I may gain Christ, and his marks on my body that I may attain to the resurrection of the dead," which is an obvious conflation of several Pauline texts, including 2 Corinthians 11:4 ("For if someone comes and preaches another Jesus from the one we preached, or if you receive a different spirit from the one you received, ..."), Galatians 6:17 ("Henceforth let no man trouble me; for I bear on my body the marks of Jesus"), 2 Timothy 2:9 ("the gospel for which I am suffering and wearing fetters like some criminal"), Philippians 3:8 ("in order that I may gain Christ"), and Philippians 3:11 ("that if possible I may attain the resurrection from the dead.")

Immediately we find in *Third Corinthians* 3:36-37, "And whoever abides by ... the holy Gospel, he shall receive a reward ... But he who turns aside therefrom—there is fire with him." This recollects 1 Corinthians 3:13, 15: "Each man's work will become manifest; for the Day will disclose it, because it will be revealed with fire ... If the work which any man has built survives, he will receive a reward. If any man's work is burned up ... he himself will be saved, but only as through fire."

What, then, are we to make of *Third Corinthians?* We can observe three things about it. First, it is aware of many Pauline letters, probably the whole corpus, but neglects to quote some of them. Second, it is clearly an epistle against heresy, explicitly against Gnosticism. Third, though it is heavily theological and markedly Pauline, it is rare that it is simultaneously theological *and* Pauline, the references to 1 Corinthians really constituting exceptions that prove the rule. The writer seems to have known the whole corpus but felt comfortable only with 1 Corinthians. We can infer that 1 Corinthians was not tainted by heresy in our writer's mind. No doubt, the Pastorals and 2 Corinthians were equally amenable to the writer, but in light of the easy utility of 1 Corinthians for his purposes, the use of the others seemed superfluous. References to the other epistles show the tendency to salvage from them only safe elements of vague exhortation or Pauline hagiography, precisely the elements of Paul that survived among the orthodox in the second and subsequent centuries.

I suggest that in *Third Corinthians*, the author was trying to produce a miniature substitute for the dubious Pauline corpus. His aim was somewhat similar to that of the writer of Ephesians, who also produced a digest of the Pauline epistles, depending mainly on one of them, but in his case Colossians.[35] Whereas Ephesians was intended to preface and to pre-interpret the Pauline corpus in a Gnosticizing direction, *Third Corinthians* was apparently to substitute for the others in the manner of a Pauline *diatessaron*.

The Pastorals were intended to co-opt Ephesians,[36] prefacing the Pauline corpus in an orthodox direction, but the heretical character of the epistles managed to penetrate the shield as heretics continued to read them through their own special spectacles. Our author decided that more radical measures were called for, hence *Third Corinthians*. From his standpoint, if you had *Third Corinthi-*

ans, you had all that was essential and safe from Paul.[37] Why did he designate it as another Corinthian epistle? Simply so it could supplement (or perhaps more likely replace) the old favorite weapon against heretics, 1 Corinthians. By this time, a Corinthian epistle simply meant an anti-heretical epistle.

Now can we decide whether *Third Corinthians*, which we have judged to be originally independent of the *Acts of Paul*, was taken over by the author of the *Acts of Paul* or by someone else. I believe the former possibility is closer to the truth. One might argue that if the former author had known of *Third Corinthians*, he would have borrowed some of its phraseology to pepper Paul's speeches throughout the letter. But I suspect the lone reference to "the sonship that is given through him" is an allusion not to Romans 8:15, 23, or Galatians 4:5 but rather to *Third Corinthians* 3:8. Note that the *Third Corinthians* reference seems to preserve a bit more of the phraseology of Romans and Galatians, whereas the reference earlier in the *Acts of Paul* retains the bare word "sonship." This is why, earlier on, we could not recognize this reference as an allusion to the Pauline letters. It may be an allusion to *Third Corinthians*.

Further, I would suggest that scholars have misconstrued what are actually other allusions to and borrowings from *Third Corinthians* elsewhere in the *Acts of Paul*. Schneemelcher cites as evidence that the author of the *Acts of Paul* also wrote *Third Corinthians*, that "the kinship in spirit and in tendency between the letters and the other parts of the AP" are striking.[38] Maybe this kinship is better explained by considering the influence *Third Corinthians* may have had upon the author of the *Acts of Paul*. Much of what he borrowed from *Third Corinthians* partook of the non-Pauline substance of it, but how was he to know? He thought he was lending Pauline color to his narrative.

If we have correctly assessed the similarities between *Third Corinthians* and the rest of the *Acts of Paul*, then another important conclusion follows. If the author of the *Acts of Paul* made such use

of the one epistle available to him, we can see that, contra Mac-
Donald, he did not find the content of an epistle to be be inappropriate to the Acts genre, and the fact that he used one single letter
surely means he had no others to use.

Conclusion

Our survey of the apocryphal Pauline literature of the second
to fifth centuries disclosed that we are dealing with no less than six
documents: the *Prayer of the Apostle Paul*, the Nag Hammadi *Revelation of Paul*, the *Apocalypse of Paul*, the Coptic appendix to the
Apocalypse of Paul, *Third Corinthians*, and the *Acts of Paul*. Of these,
we saw that the *Prayer* and the *Revelation* were Gnostic compositions. The *Prayer* made use of various Gnostic-sounding or Gnosticizing phrases from the Pauline epistles, while the *Revelation* was
apparently cognizant of Ephesians and Galatians and gave an esoteric interpretation to the latter. Both documents show the very
"twisting" of "all his letters" by "unstable persons" mentioned
in 2 Peter 3:16, which led, on Bauer's theory, to the shunning of
Paul's letters by the emerging orthodox authorities. Accordingly,
when we considered the later *Apocalypse of Paul*, we found that
the author was probably an "ecclesiastical redactor," specifically a
monk, who was not striving for originality; rather, he digested and
regurgitated the traditional sources, of which one was probably the
Revelation of Paul, even tainted as it was by Gnosticism. In sanitizing and rehabilitating the Pauline apocalyptic tradition, the author
might have been expected to make use of the other epistles which
brim with appropriate material. But in fact, he can be shown to
have used, and presumably therefore to have known of, only 1 and
2 Corinthians.

This fact is what I sought to explain with reference to Bauer's
theory that 1 Corinthians alone was promulgated by the orthodox
authorities. It was a kind of *panarion* against all heresies. I suggested
that 2 Corinthians was a subsequent compilation for the same pur-

pose and that a "Corinthian epistle" had come to denote precisely an anti-heretical epistle. The same situation held good for the Coptic apocalypse/appendix, really a separate Pauline apocalypse. Though it made explicit reference to Paul as a famous epistolarian, it, too, showed awareness only of the Corinthian correspondence. By contrast, *Third Corinthians* used phrases drawn from a variety of Pauline letters, but it used only innocuous, non-theological phrases, the only exception being quotes from the anti-heretical 1 Corinthians, with theological passages, ironically, derived from non-Pauline texts. I further suggested that *Third Corinthians* was an orthodox attempt to provide a substitute for the Pauline corpus, tainted as the epistles were by heretical use. It was to be a digest of safe material in the form of yet another Corinthian (anti-heretical) epistle.

The *Acts of Paul* used traditional materials throughout, as MacDonald has shown, but I could not agree with MacDonald's account of why the writer used no material from the Pauline letters. He thought the letters were probably considered inappropriate for the Acts genre. What I found was a writer who took the trouble to incorporate *Third Corinthians* into his *Acts* and even borrowed ideas and phrases from it to lend "Pauline" color to the rest of his work. Presumably, he would have used the other Pauline letters if they had been available to him. By contrast to the *Acts of Paul*, the author of the canonical Acts—whom I consider to be Polycarp of Smyrna—represents the later attempt to Catholicize and co-opt Paulinism. The *Acts of Paul* makes frequent use of the canonical epistles to supply information about his movements and to add minor color to the orthodox portrait of him, which however is still deutero-Pauline or nascent Catholic. The *Acts of Paul* still manages to avoid preaching the Pauline gospel despite the author's acquaintance with his letters.

NOTES

[1]For a summary of the theory of the orthodox neglect of Paul, see William S. Babcock's introduction in his anthology, *Paul and the Legacies of Paul* (Dallas: Southern Methodist University Press, 1990), xiii-xvii. For MacDonald's viewpoint, see his essay, "Apocryphal and Canonical Narratives about Paul," in the same collection, 55-69.

[2]R. H. Charles, *Eschatology, the Doctrine of a Future Life in Israel, Judaism, and Christianity: A Critical History* (New York: Schocken, 1963), 202-05; Walter Schmithals, *The Apocalyptic Movement: Introduction and Interpretation* (Nashville: Abingdon, 1975), 16; Christopher Rowland, *The Open Heaven: A Study of Apocalyptic in Judaism and Early Christianity* (New York: Crossroad, 1982), 69.

Harold Henry Rowley's explanation, that pseudonymity was a convention that began with the Book of Daniel where the author wished to identify with the stories of Daniel (*The Relevance of Apocalyptic* [London: Lutterworth, 1952], 37-39), is unconvincing. Little better is the conjecture of D. S. Russell, *The Method and Message of Jewish Apocalyptic* (Philadelphia: Westminster, 1964), 132ff., which invokes H. Wheeler Robinson's now much-disputed "corporate personality" theory. John J. Collins's explanation, that pseudepigraphy aimed to lend a note of remoteness and numinous mystery to the revelations (*The Apocalyptic Imagination: An Introduction to the Jewish Matrix of Christianity*, [New York: Crossroad, 1989], 4), is interesting but may be unduly influenced by modern literary theory. Would ancient writers have intentionally striven for such an effect with little to achieve by it?

[3]Montague Rhodes James, ed., *The Apocryphal New Testament* (Oxford: Clarendon Press, 1972), 478; Edgar J. Goodspeed, *Famous Biblical Hoaxes, or Modern Apocrypha* (Grand Rapids: Baker, 1956), 81.

[4]James, *Apocryphal New Testament*, 525.

[5]George W. MacRae and William R. Murdock, introduction to *The Apocalypse of Paul* in *The Nag Hammadi Library*, ed. James M. Robinson, rev. ed. (San Francisco: Harper & Row, 1988), 256-57.

[6]James, *Apocryphal New Testament*, 525; Hugo Duensing, introduction to *The Apocalypse of Paul*, in *New Testament Apocrypha*, eds. Edgar Hennecke & Wilhelm Schneemelcher (Philadelphia: Westminster, 1965), 756.

[7]Dieter Mueller, introduction to *The Prayer of the Apostle Paul*, in Robinson, ed., *Nag Hammadi Library*, 27.

[8]Until recently the *Gospel of Thomas* was assumed to be Gnostic on the

basis of the ancient library with which it was found. It is true that the Gospel is susceptible to Gnostic exposition, but so are the canonical four. For a different interpretation of *Thomas*, see Stevan L. Davies, *The Gospel of Thomas and Christian Wisdom* (New York: Seabury, 1983).

[9]MacRae and Murdock, in Robinson, ed., *The Nag Hammadi Library*, 256.

[10]Ernest A. Wallis Budge, trans. and ed., *Coptic Apocrypha in the Dialect of Upper Egypt* (1913; New York: AMS Press, 1977), 344-50.

[11]James, *Apocryphal New Testament*, 525; Duensing, in Hennecke and Schneemelcher, eds., *New Testament Apocrypha*, 757.

[12]"But when the man who is damned dies ... the demon Vizarsh comes and binds the soul of the damned in a most shameful wise ... And the soul of the damned cries out with a loud voice, makes moan, and in supplication makes many a hideous plea ... but the demon Vizarsh drags him off against his will into nethermost Hell. Then [an ugly girl] comes to meet him. And the soul of the damned says to that ill-favoured wench, 'Who art thou? for I have never seen an ill-favoured wench on earth more ill-favoured and hideous than thee.' [She replies:] 'I am thy deeds—hideous deeds, evil thoughts, evil words, evil deeds, and an evil religion.' There follows a list of the man's crimes and sins against the righteous," qtd. in Robert C. Zaehner, *The Teachings of the Magi: A Compendium of Zoroastrian Beliefs* (New York: Oxford University Press, 1975), 136-37.

Islam envisions the same scenario. We read in the Koran: "When the two angels meet together, sitting one on the right, and one on the left, not a word he utters, but by him an observer is ready. And death's agony comes in truth. ... And the Trumpet shall be blown. ... And every soul shall come, and with it a driver and a witness. 'Thou wast heedless of this; therefore We have now removed from thee thy covering, and so thy sight today is piercing.' [And God will say to the angels:] 'Cast, you twain, into Gehenna every froward unbeliever, every hinderer of the good, transgressor, disquieter, who set up with God another god; therefore, you twain, cast him into the terrible chastisement'" (50:17-26). This frightening postmortem encounter is graphically embellished by al-Ghazali in his twelfth-century work, *The Pearl Precious for Unveiling Knowledge of the World to Come* (see S.G.F. Brandon, *The Judgment of the Dead* [New York: Scribner's, 1967], 147).

[13]Duensing, 757.

[14]Acts 4:1-2; 17:31-32; 23:6-8; 24:21; 25:19; 26:8.

[15]Most recently, Andreas Lindemann, "Paul in the Writings of the Apostolic Fathers," in Babcock, *Paul and Legacies*, 25-43.

[16]Walter Bauer, *Orthodoxy and Heresy in Earliest Christianity*, eds. Robert A. Kraft and Gerhard Kroedel (Philadelphia: Fortress Press, 1971), 219ff.

[17]Duensing, 757, 795-796.

[18]James, *The Apocryphal New Testament*, 555. The *Pistis Sophia* was a second-century Gnostic text said to contain teachings of the resurrected Jesus to his disciples.

[19]Dennis R. MacDonald, *The Legend and the Apostle: The Battle for Paul in Story and Canon* (Philadelphia: Westminster Press, 1983), 17-33.

[20]I am using the term *encratite* to refer to more than the original sect of Tatian, just as MacDonald does, to mean all celibate, egalitarian, prophetic, rigorist, socially radical, family-rejecting, and vegetarian Christians in the second and third centuries. Harnack did the same thing with the word *adoptionist* to broaden its reference to a specific theological party to that of the same tendency wherever it occurred. Stevan L. Davies forbears using *encratite* in a broader sense in *The Revolt of the Widows: The Social World of the Apocryphal Acts* (Carbondale: Southern Illinois University Press, 1980), 12-13, but Schneemelcher uses it the way I do.

[21]Schneemelcher, in *New Testament Apocrypha*, 343.

[22]Iconium was in the Roman province of Galatia in what is now central Turkey.

[23]F. F. Bruce, *Paul and Jesus* (Grand Rapids: Baker, 1974), 77-78; J. C. O'Neill, *Paul's Letter to the Romans* (Baltimore: Penguin 1975), 205.

[24]R. Joseph Hoffmann, *Marcion: On the Restitution of Christianity: An Essay on the Development of Radical Paulinist Theology in the Second Century* (Chico: Scholars Press, 1984), 255-56, relying on Tertullian, Adversus Marcionem 4.34.1, 5f.

[25]MacDonald, *Legend and Apostle*, 34-53; Davies, *Revolt of Widows*, 11-16; Elaine Pagels, *Adam, Eve, and the Serpent* (New York: Random House, 1988), 78-97.

[26]This is the view found in the Good News Bible, New International Version, New Jerusalem Bible, Revised English Bible, Revised Standard Version, and translations by Edgar Goodspeed, Frank Laubach, Olaf Norlie, and John Bertram Phillips. Hans Conzelmann maintains this view, unconvincingly in my opinion, in *First Corinthians: A Commentary of the First Epistle to the Corinthians*. Hermeneia Series (Philadelphia: Fortress, 1975), 135-36. I owe much of the discussion of 1 Corinthians 7 to David M. Scholer's utterly fascinating lectures, though he would likely not endorse my views on the relation between 1 Corinthians and the Iconium sermon.

²⁷This view is promoted by the Easy-to-Read Version, Jerusalem Bible, New American Standard Bible, and translations by Heinz Cassirer, James Kleist and Joseph Lilly, Helen Barrett Montgomery, Richard Weymouth, Charles Williams, and Kenneth Wuest.

²⁸Winsome Munro, *Authority in Paul and Peter: The Identification of a Pastoral Stratum in the Pauline Corpus and 1 Peter,* Society for New Testament Studies Monograph Series, No. 45 (New York: Cambridge University Press, 1983).

²⁹This was precisely the approach of St. Augustine at a later time (Pagels, *Adam, Eve, and the Serpent,* 98-126).

³⁰See the classic treatment of the subject by Hans Achelis, *Virgines Subintroductae: Ein Beitrag zum siebenten Kapitel des ersten Korintherbriefs* (Leipzig: J. C. Hinrich, 1902). More recently, see Peter Brown, *The Body and Society: Men, Women, and Sexual Renunciation in Early Christianity* (New York: Columbia University Press, 1988); Susanna Elm, *"Virgins of God": The Making of Asceticism in Late Antiquity* (Oxford: Clarendon Press, 1996); Dyan Elliott, *Spiritual Marriage: Sexual Abstinence in Medieval Wedlock* (Princeton: Princeton University Press, 1993).

³¹Schneemelcher, in *New Testament Apocrypha,* 342. In the 1992 revised edition, Schneemelcher changes his opinion (228-29), convinced by A.F.J. Klijn ("The Apocryphal Correspondence between Paul and the Corinthians," *Vigiliae Christianae* 17 [Mar. 1963]: 2-23), and Willi Rordorf. I prefer to stand by my own, independent arguments here.

³²Schneemelcher, in *New Testament Apocrypha,* 341.

³³James, *Apocryphal New Testament,* 477.

³⁴Bauer, *Orthodoxy and Heresy,* 36.

³⁵Edgar J. Goodspeed, *New Chapters in New Testament Study* (New York: Macmillan, 1937), 29; Goodspeed, *The Key to Ephesians* (Chicago: University of Chicago Press, 1957), x; John Knox, *Philemon among the Letters of Paul: A New View of Its Place and Importance,* rev. ed. (1935; New York: Abingdon, 1959), 71-90. On the Gnosticizing character of Ephesians, F. C. Baur must still be reckoned with. I for one find it too convenient to explain away the Gnostic-sounding language as an opportunistic appropriation of the opponents' terminology in order better to refute them.

³⁶MacDonald, *Legend and Apostle,* 85-89.

³⁷Richard A. Norris Jr., "Irenaeus' Use of Paul in his Polemic against the Gnostics," and Robert D. Sider, "Literary Artifice and the Figure of Paul in the Writings of Tertullian," in Babcock, ed., *Paul and Legacies,* 79-98, 99-120,

argue for a wide use of Paul's letters by the orthodox and heretical alike in the second century on the basis of Irenaeus and Tertullian. This is by no means incompatible with Bauer's thesis, keeping in mind that Irenaeus and Tertullian were both heresiologists. Naturally, they would be acquainted with the Pauline letters, just as they were with other Marcionite and Gnostic writings. It would be far more revealing to know whether Irenaeus and Tertullian promoted the general reading of the Pauline letters among the faithful. The writer of *Third Corinthians*, too, had access to the Pauline Corpus, but on my reading he certainly did not want the rank-and-file reading it. Instead, he saw fit only to pass on to the Christian public a severely expurgated version in the form of *Third Corinthians* itself.

[38]Schneemelcher, in *New Testament Apocrypha*, 342.

5.

The Original Gnostic Apostles

Elusive epiphanies

Walter Schmithals argues[1] that the concept of an apostle was not native to either Judaism or Christianity but instead grew up in oriental Gnosticism. Gnosticism had a pessimistic world view[2] embraced by those who saw themselves as strangers in a strange land, isolated, and superior to the slobs and fools around them.[3] It had an ingenious answer to the perennial problem of theodicy, or how to get God off the hook for all the evil in the world. How could this world be the creation of a righteous God and be ruled by his justice? Whence all the tragedy and evil? Gnostics chose to resolve the dilemma by positing the idea that the true, unknown God, hidden away within the fullness or pleroma of unapproachable light (1 Tim. 6:16), did not create the world. Instead, he emanated from himself a whole series of paired divine beings, or syzygies. At the end of this process, there emerged a single divinity, Sophia, or Wisdom. She felt alienated from the godhead, from which, of all the divine entities, or aions, she was farthest removed. She was also frustrated about having no partner with whom to beget further aions.

However, the divine essence was running out by this point,

diminishing much like the picture quality of a tenth-generation videotape. So when Sophia contrived to bear offspring through a virgin conception and birth, the result was a brutish and malign entity called the demiurge (which means creator, carpenter, or craftsman). This character was borrowed from Plato, who had posited him as a mythic link between philosophical categories of eternal matter and eternal spirit. The celestial gods were too aloof to get involved in creation, leaving it to the demiurge, whose job it was to ceaselessly impose the likenesses of the eternal Forms, the spiritual prototypes of all things, onto hunks of unstable, shifting matter for as long as they could hold it.

The Gnostics, heavily influenced by the allegorical Hellenistic Judaism of Alexandria, interpreted the Genesis creation and fall in Platonic categories, the same as Philo of Alexandria did. But they went much further. Their shocking result was to identify the demiurge as evil, yet at the same time as Jehovah, or Yahweh, the Hebrew God. Religious modernists have made essentially the same move by saying that the Old Testament writers depicted God according to their limited, primitive conceptions, while the more abstract concept of the New Testament is superior. H. Wheeler Robinson comes close to a Gnostic position when he says that "the limitations of the Old Testament idea of God ... may be compared with those which attach to the Carpenter of Nazareth. As the Christian may see the manifestation of the Eternal Son of God within those limitations, so may be seen the manifestation of the Eternal God Himself through the limitations of 'Yahweh of Israel.'"[4] We just speak of different God concepts, where the Gnostics and Marcion spoke of different gods.

The demiurge, imitating the ultimate godhead, of whom he was nonetheless ignorant, proceeded to create matter and a series of material creations, a kind of mud-pie substitute for the pleroma of light. He created a world, but it was inert and chaotic, "without form and void." To get some action going, he managed to steal

some of the spiritual light from the pleroma. According to which-
ever Gnostic text you choose, this might have been accomplished
by waylaying and dismembering the Man of Light, the Son of Man,
Primal Man (*Fourth Ezra* 13:1-4), or another of the aions, or the
light might have been taken from the reflected image of Sophia. In
any case, the demiurge and his evil lieutenants, the archons (the
fallen sons of God or angels from Jewish apocryphal versions of
Genesis 6:1-6), used these sparks of alien light as something like
DNA to program self-replicating order into the otherwise stillborn
cosmos of matter.

The descendants of Adam and Eve from their son Seth possessed a divine spark of light inherited from the heavenly Eve,
while the offspring of Cain were the bastard spawn of the archons.
This is the version of events put forth by the Sethian sect, who
regarded Seth as a messianic revealer and redeemer. Later, upon
assimilation into Christianity, they reinterpreted Seth to be a previous incarnation of Christ; in other words, Christ was the second
coming of Seth. Others, like the Ophites or Naassenes, understood
Adam and Eve to be local variants of the myth of Attis and Cybele,[5]
and thus made Jesus a later incarnation of the slain-and-resurrected
Attis. Whatever name they might have used, the various Gnostic
sects believed their doctrine, or gnosis, had come to them from a
heavenly revealer who came to earth in human flesh or something
like it and awakened those possessing the divine spark to their true
origin and destiny. This enabled them to escape the vicious cycle of
rebirth and, upon death, to ascend once and for all to the pleroma
and rejoin the godhead.

As Schmithals[6] showed, pure, original Gnosticism would have
understood the fact of self-knowledge as sufficient to effect postmortem liberation. Later, more corrupt and superstitious forms of
the doctrine pictured Jesus or Seth or Melchizedek as providing
not only self-knowledge but also a set of magical formulae and passwords which would enable the elect soul to slip unnoticed through

the cosmic checkpoints in each of the crystal spheres concentrically encasing our world. At each sphere there waited a ruling archon, playing the role of the old Babylonian planetary gods who were ready to turn back any escaping soul like Cold War marksmen posted along the Berlin Wall.

Schmithals envisioned Gnostic apostles who did not preach a historical individual called Christ but rather an invisible cosmic Christ, a redeemer who had done his saving work among the aions and the archons far from the numb senses of men. This Christ was the universal Man of Light who dwelt in the souls of the elite among the human race, those whom the Gnostic apostles sought in their Diogenes-like quest.[7] This Christ spoke authoritatively through the Gnostic apostles because they were the very few in whom the Redeemer's light had awakened self-consciousness. Through this apostolic preaching, the inner Christ called out to other dormant sparks, desiring to awaken them as well. Seeing it the way Schmithals did, one might say that the Gnostic Christ had become incarnate for the first time in the preachers through whom Christ sought to seek and save what was lost.

Perhaps the earliest known form of Gnosticism, which Hippolytus of Rome believed existed before Simonianism (which others have said was the fountainhead of Gnosticism), is the Naassene sect, named for the Serpent, or *nahash* in Hebrew, who was probably understood in accord with the original intent of the Eden tale as the Promethean bringer of light and knowledge to the human race. The Naassenes drew upon various cognate Near Eastern myths and allegorized the resultant synthesis. They posited a supreme deity who animated the clay of which "Adamas" (Adam) was created. Adamas lay inert until he was suffused with the divine spirit. However, he and his descendants remained burdened and imprisoned by the dead weight of material flesh. Men were brutish and lacked all knowledge of God. The Naassenes taught that to remedy this predicament, a son of Adamas, or "son of man," tried to liberate the portion of the divine spirit that dwells in humans. In doing so, the Son of Man became burdened and contaminated by matter. Even so, some people are pneumatics ("spiritual ones") in whom the soul has been freed. Others are psychics ("natural ones") for whom the flesh prevails and the spark of divinity has been extinguished. In mythic-narrative terms, this means that the Son of Man is "put to death" in the psychics. If one of them repents and becomes a pneumatic, it is a kind of resurrection from the dead and ascension to heaven: "This also, they say, is the ascension which takes place through the gate of the heavens, through which all who do not enter remain dead."[8] The son of Adamas was also called Logos, symbolized in Hermes, the messenger of the gods, as well as in the dying and rising Attis. Eventually Jesus was added to the mix, but the inner Son of Man (not a historical being) had already been dubbed the Christ. The Logos was said to be what "enlightens every man coming into the world," as John's Gospel put it.

There had already been wandering Gnostic and Cynic apostles before the Christian apostles came onto the scene. As Thomas Whittaker pointed out,[9] the circle of apostles, so jealously restricted in the New Testament to the Twelve (plus, according to some, Paul), must at first have been a wide-open field. We can tell this from the discussion of apostles in the *Didache*, an early church manual from Syria which scholars believe stems from the first or early-second century. It seems to preserve very old traditions, including a primitive, pre-Gospel version of the eucharistic liturgy containing none of the features familiar to us from the Synoptic Gospels and Paul. The *Didache* outlines proper church conduct for anyone claiming to be an apostle while acknowledging his authority for regulating Sunday worship. These itinerant apostles who demanded food and shelter are the "wandering radicals" described so well by Gerd Theissen who drew on New Testament sources for a picture of these wing-and-a-prayer evangelists.[10] They were men who had heeded the call to "let goods and kindred go" for the gospel's sake, to tread dusty paths in imitation of the Son of Man, who had no floor on which to lay his head. They took no bag, no money belt, no staff or spare provisions, but trusted God to feed and house them through the charity of those they preached to. It worked because their hearers responded to the promise of a reward equal to the apostle's own for accommodating him (Matt. 10:41). These gospel vagabonds were *the* apostles, and their ministry continued for decades. The restriction of apostleship to twelve men portrayed in the four Gospels came later and was artificial.

At some point a concern developed for weeding out false apostles who were sponging off the church—the "gospel bums" as their modern-day counterparts were known in the 1970s Jesus Movement.[11] For example, the *Didache* warns that the apostle who stayed longer than three days without commencing to work should be asked to pay for his keep. If he says that the Holy Spirit wants the congregation to give him money, like a modern TV evangelist, he should be hounded out of town as a false prophet. Such self-serving "oracles" by these panhandling prophets perhaps underlie the passage Mark 14:7. The synoptic mission charge[12] seems to belong to this debate, as also the clashing beliefs in 1 Corinthians 8-9 about whether an apostle ought to accept money from clients.

As these free-lance apostles lost out to consolidating church institutions, history was rewritten to depict a limited number of twelve apostles who had been pupils of a historical Jesus of Nazareth (Acts 1:21-22) This was the work of what Käsemann called nascent Catholicism.[13] It was part of the same theological transformation whereby the myth of the slaying of the Man of Light by the archons before the foundation of the world was rewritten as the historical crucifixion of a human being, Jesus Christ, at the hands of the Sanhedrin and the Roman procurator. As the extraction and seeding of the spiritual photons of the Son of Man had enlivened the new-made earth, so the blood of Jesus was now said to redeem the souls of humanity. Elaine Pagels[14] discerns the agenda of the second-century orthodox bishops who sought to crush Gnostic mystagogues; it was an attempt to provide a tangible foundation for the church and its authority, beginning with the insistence that Jesus had been no divine phantom but had suffered due to his genuine incarnation. The Gnostic Christ, Pagels and Charles H. Talbert[15] observed, was a subjective and unverifiable inner voice. Nascent Catholics needed a more objective warrant for doctrinal and institutional claims. To say that the Jesus Spirit had appeared to a hermit in a trance and said such and such was uncontrollable. One soon found oneself at sea and paralyzed with indecision when basing one's life on such ephemeral authority, with no objective warrant for believing the inner-Christ's prophecy. The insistence of Luke-Acts on an official interpretation of scripture propounded by a risen, fleshly Christ to his disciples, thereafter hermetically sealed and passed on to bishop-successors, was a necessary step toward institutionalization. "The rest of you can go on having your visions," the bishops said, "but we have the real deposit of truth. Have fun with your oracles. We have the church. We have an objective Jesus who died and rose in the flesh and did not appear in different forms simultaneously to several people, telling them different things." Or so the hierarchy claimed.

Surely Pagels and Talbert are right, but so was Arthur Drews,[16] who had already taken the same thinking farther. He figured that it was no mere question of conflicting postmortem appearances of Jesus. There had not been a historical Jesus on earth. Jesus was a heavenly revealer *within* one's heart. A la Schmithals, true Gnostics would not be satisfied with a finite gospel; they would seek their own revelations. Irenaeus mocked the Gnostics for their visions and myth-making, saying that they denied the real, historical Jesus. The Gnostic approach was too vague to lend its factions much advantage. To claim that Jesus had actually appeared in recent history and passed the party line on to his chosen successors was comforting. Creating a historical Jesus, rather than believing in a purely spiritual one, became imperative. A limited number of apostles attesting to a historical being and his teachings became useful as a guarantee against uncontrollable future pronouncements from spiritual sources that would introduce chaos into the church. The historical Jesus was one on whom the emergent Catholics could bestow their doctrine; the twelve apostles, composites drawn from the original Gnostic apostles, were the guarantors of those doctrines.

Interestingly, the only reference to the Twelve in any of the Pauline literature is in a late interpolation, 1 Corinthians 15:5.[17] The Pauline epistles know of leaders in Jerusalem called "the pillars," including James, "the Lord's brother;" Cephas, who may be Peter; and John (the son of Zebedee? John Mark?). Paul mentions apostles but does not number them (1 Cor. 9:5). They seem to include the pillars (Gal. 1:19) as well as Paul himself! He has opponents in the apostolic guild, whom he vilifies as "super-apostles" (2 Cor. 11:5, 12:11), "false apostles" (2 Cor. 11:13), and apostles of Satan (2 Cor. 11:13-15). What makes Paul a genuine testifier of the Lord Jesus is his having seen him for himself (1 Cor. 9:1) and having thereafter brought converts to the church and performed miracles among them (2 Cor. 12:12). His vision of Jesus may have been private and interior: "It pleased God to reveal his Son *in me*" (Gal. 1:16).

What qualified the pillars to occupy their positions, Paul does not say. The title itself implies that these men formed a mediating axis between earth and heaven. We hear nothing of them having been close to a historical Jesus. Even James is called "the brother of *the Lord*," not "brother of Jesus of Nazareth." We usually do not imagine the claim made in 1 Corinthians 9:1 ("Am I not an apostle? Have I not seen the Lord?") to mean that Paul saw Jesus of Nazareth during the latter's earthly career. It is, rather, the divine heavenly Christ whom he sees. Consequently, that must have been enough to qualify the other apostles, too. One might say that there was not yet an earthly existence of Jesus to claim to have seen. The fabrication of such a character and such a career (created by rewriting stories from the Septuagint) is one with the fabrication of a group of twelve apostles to verify the account of him. That is why it is the pseudo-historical, narrative Gospels in which we first hear of the twelve disciples, not the epistles.

Mark knew of "disciples" and of "twelve" men but not yet the term "apostles" in reference to church officials. In Mark 6:30, where Jesus sent a few men out on errands, they are called the *apostoloi*, meaning "the ones he sent." Similarly, where twelve apostles are listed in Matthew 10:2, they are the ones who were "sent out," not necessarily called to office. It is Luke who creates the notion, unattested anywhere else, of "twelve apostles" (6:13, "he called his disciples and chose from them twelve, whom he named apostles"). In Acts 1:21-22, we learn the function of these newly defined ambassadors: "Therefore it is required that one of these men who accompanied us the whole time the Lord Jesus associated with us, starting with John's baptism until the day he was taken up from us, must become a witness along with us of his resurrection." A true apostle, therefore, must have witnessed the whole ministry of Jesus in order to be able to attest what Jesus did and did not do. The artificiality of the criterion is clear from the fact that even the twelve do not qualify, since none of them were ever said to have been present at Jesus's baptism. And of course the prerequisite was designed to exclude the late-comer Paul. It is on just this basis that Peter, in the Clementine *Recognitions*, derides Paul's claim to have been called as an apostle of Christ on no more basis than a subjective vision.

This again is the point of the forty-day cut-off in Acts 1:9. During that interval the risen Jesus is said to have vouchsafed his advanced teachings to the Twelve (none of which is shared with the reader since it is intended as a blank check for whatever may turn out to be called "apostolic tradition"). But after that, no mere vision of Jesus (consider Stephen's vision in 7:56, Ananias's in 9:10-16, Paul's in Corinth in 18:9-10, Paul's in the temple in 22:17-21) is going to count as a resurrection appearance. Significantly, even in Paul's decisive conversion experience (9:3-6; 22:6-11; 26:12-18), Saul does not *see* Jesus, 9:17 and 22:14 notwithstanding, because he is blinded by the light. The reader will scarcely need to be reminded that, although Acts lionizes Paul, it seems to withhold from him the title of apostle. Two apparent exceptions occur in Acts 14:4 where the term *apostle* is generic, with no specific names attached, and in 14:14 where *apostles* is absent altogether from the Western text.

The Twelve, whether one calls them disciples or apostles, appear to be fictive expansions from the list of the Jerusalem pillars: James the Just, Cephas (Peter), and John (Gal. 2:9).[18] These three obviously formed the basis of the inner circle of Simon Peter, James, and John bar-Zebedee in the Gospels (Mark 5:37; 9:2). A longer list of the pillars (or "Brotherhood of the Lord," 1 Cor. 9:5) appears in Mark 6:3, where the group has been historicized to the point that they are literal brothers of a fleshly Jesus. They are James, Joses, Judas, and Simon. It lists James but lacks John. Simon is, I will suggest, the same as Simon Peter. My guess is that "Joses" originally belonged in the previous line, when the townspeople ask themselves, "Isn't this the carpenter, the son of Mary?" It would have read, "Isn't this the carpenter, the son of Mary and Joses (Joseph)?" And the fourth name would have been John. It may have been on the basis of this reading that Luke got the idea of making John the Baptist Jesus's cousin.

In any case, when the twelve disciples, or apostles, appear at all, they do so as a bare list of names.[19] Basically, that is all they are. Consider their possible derivation from the pillars. From Simon bar-Cleophas, whom tradition makes the bishop of Jerusalem after his brother, James the Just, we derive both Simon Cephas/Peter and Simon Zelotes. Andrew, meaning "man" or "male," is a brother of Simon, which may be an extrapolation of "Simon the brother of the Man," or "brother of the Son of Man." John becomes John, son of Zebedee. Judas Thomas (as Syrian sources dub him, as in the *Gospel of Thomas*) refracts into Judas Iscariot and Judas *not* Iscariot (John 14:22), as well as Thaddaeus (Mark 3:18), Judas bar-Sabbas (Acts 15:22), and Theudas (Acts 5:36).[20] From James the Just, we get James, son of Zebedee, and James of Alphaeus,[21] and even Nathaniel, "a true Israelite in whom is no guile" (John 1:47). The reference here is to the Old Testament Jacob, making him a "true Jacob" or James. James is even Lebbaeus, an apostle appearing in some manuscripts of Mark, because "Lebbaeus" appears to be another spelling of "Oblias," the bulwark, an epithet of James the Just in Eusebius. If Joses was the original reading in Mark 6:3, he probably became Joseph Bar-Sabbas (Acts 1:23) and Joseph Barnabas (Acts 4:36). Philip is an interloper from the list of seven Hellenists in Acts 6:5. Matthew, though a real name, functions here as a pun on "disciple" (*mathetes*). The Matthias of Acts 1:23 is his double.

We can witness the process of their mitosis into disparate individuals in the second- and third-century apocryphal Acts of the Apostles, which we will consider shortly. As we will see, it is all legend. The beginning of the apostolic historicization appears to come from Mark, where Peter is given the literary role of Jesus's straight man, so to speak, who asks stupid questions.[22] This gives the evangelist the opportunity to explain things to the reader, making Peter the equivalent of Ananda, the Buddha's disciple, and Dr. Watson, Sherlock Holmes's sidekick. James and John fill the same role sometimes (Mark 9:38; 10:35 ff; Luke 9:54). The infamous story of Peter's cowardly denials, as Loisy saw,[23] must be a smear created by Paulinists who opposed the Peter faction. "Paulinists invented the legend of Peter's denial of his Lord," he concluded.[24]

Second Corinthians 3:1, as Dieter Georgi[25] saw, implies that the original itinerant apostles compiled growing resumes, including lists of miracles performed in each church as endorsements that opened doors for them. We know nothing of these nameless apostles except, as Stevan L. Davies suggests,[26] the tales of their miraculous exploits that wound up in the apocryphal Acts of the Apos-

tles. Their actual names were eventually forgotten, or more likely
suppressed, in favor of the names of the Twelve and Paul, once the
catholicization process in Acts had made all the apostles happy
teammates. This suppression came about for a simple reason I have
already suggested: the field of apostles had to be narrowed down so
that they would no longer function as loose canons who could pro-
mulgate new Jesuses and strange Gospels (2 Cor. 11:4; Gal. 1:6-9).
Instead, they took on the role of spokesmen who could attest to the
Catholic claims of an official Jesus.

Thus, the miracle occurred of anonymous apostles being given
names, then form and color, for the first time. It was a process not
unlike that by which the heavenly Jesus took on a history and form,
clothed with texts rewritten from the Septuagint.[27] In this chapter
we will examine some of the exploits of the apostles from the apocryphal books, demonstrating that the underlying role of an apostle
in each case was just what Schmithals said it was: they were virtually Christs in their own right, insofar as the light of Christ shone
through them, and taught an otherworldly asceticism characteristic
of the flesh-hating Gnostics.

A structuralist approach

One of the most inventive and fruitful tools for decoding the
meaning of myths is the structuralism of Claude Levi-Strauss. The
anthropologist sought to account for myths on a level deeper than
plot and characterization by examining important signals an author
leaves in a narrative like bits of masonry hinting at buried remains
of some primordial structure. Levi-Strauss postulated that all myths
are based on binary sets of oppositions, a configuration derived from
an assumption that the human mind is itself binary in structure. In
his schema, the mind will raise a question, ponder some dilemma,
and mediate the opposition between two alternatives. It is not done
logically by the means of philosophical scrutiny but mythologically
by how a resolution is reached within a literary narrative. To iden-

tify the question being resolved and the individual conceptual elements being opposed and mediated, Levi-Strauss suggested that the plot structure be disregarded, the order of events discarded, and the individual story elements classified according to similarity. One can separate out groups of like characters, events, and names and then strive to discern some implied relationships.

The classic example illustrating the method is the structuralist dissection of the Oedipus cycle. Levi-Strauss began with the observation that, as incredible as it may seem, ancient people agonized over whether human beings are "born from two" (from parents like themselves) or "born from one" (Mother Earth). Juvenal's Sixth Satire recalls ancient days when "men lived differently: ... clay-moulded, parentless." The model of "born from two parents" came to predominate, perhaps as the relationship between sexual intercourse and the birth of babies was more fully understood, yet the old belief that Mother Nature caused birth died hard. This conflict of beliefs, Levi-Strauss suggested, lay at the base of the Oedipus myth. He found that, if it was diagrammed as he suggested, the similar elements would group themselves into two sets of opposing notions. Family ties were overvalued in some instances and undervalued in others, First, there is a set of overvaluations of family ties, implying the unsuccessful preference for the "born from two" model. Second, there is a set of undervaluations of family ties, implying the failure or rejection of the "born from two" model. Third, there is a set of human conquests over earth-elementals, implying humanity's attempt to deny its earthly origin. Fourth, there is a set of lameness images, implying the inability to tread the earth, and one's earthly origins, underfoot.

The point of the myth is that when culture denies its earthly basis and character, relationships between human beings, as well as the relationship between humans and the earth, suffer due to an alienation from our true nature. Here are examples based on the analysis Levi-Strauss supplied:

Overrating blood relations
> Kadmos seeks his sister Europa, ravished by Zeus.
> Oedipus marries his mother, Jocasta.
> Antigone buries her brother Polynices despite a prohibition against it.

Underrating blood relations
> The Spartoi kill each other.
> Oedipus kills his father, Laios.
> Eteocles kills his brother Polynices.

Overcoming nature
> Kadmos kills the dragon.
> Oedipus kills the Sphynx.

Succumbing to nature
> Laios's father is lame.
> Laios is left-handed.
> Oedipus means "swollen foot."

Levi-Strauss added that the myth represented "the attempt to escape autochthony [birth from the earth]," while recognizing "the impossibility to succeed in it. Although experience contradicts theory, social life verifies the cosmology by its similarity of structure. Hence cosmology is true."[28]

I will attempt to bring the tool of structuralist analysis to bear on the apocryphal Acts of the Apostles, written for the most part in the second and third centuries CE. I will focus on a particular set of themes which invite such treatment. Before commencing the analysis, however, one more principle of structuralism requires comment.

> [Our] method eliminates a problem which has been so far one of the main obstacles to the progress of mythological studies, namely, the quest for the true version, or the earlier one. On the contrary, we define the myth as consisting of all its versions; to put it oth-

erwise, a myth remains the same as long as it is felt as such ... An important consequence follows. If a myth is made of all its variants, structuralist analysis should take all of them into account.[29]

It is possible to consider the variations of a myth even if the variations do not share all specific details. Even unrelated myths may be seen as variant versions of one another, as semioticist Charles Segal writes of so-called megatexts.

> To take a relatively simple instance of this [kind of] network, the youth at the transitional point between adolescence and manhood is a recurring figure in Greek myth: Theseus, Perseus, Telemachus, Orestes, Phaethon, Hippolytus, and Actaeon are familiar examples. Their importance reflects concern with the socialization of adolescent energies. ... From a semiotic point of view, however, what is interesting is the process of coding which interrelates all of these myths as common parts of the megatext ... Particularly interesting from a semiotic perspective is the way in which any one of these figures may serve as a paradigm for another. We are dealing here with a coded system of virtually interchangeable symbols.[30]

I hope to demonstrate that the same is true with the characters of the apostles in the various apocryphal narratives. And this ought to tell us some important things about the apostolic office as such. The extent of interdependence between the apocryphal Acts books is debated. Unlike Schneemelcher,[31] I cannot see sufficient evidence that the *Acts of Paul* makes use of the *Acts of Peter*, which I imagine to be the later of the two documents, though I accept MacDonald's case that the apocryphal *Philip* and *Thomas* seem to depend upon *Andrew and Matthias*.[32] In any event, the more independence we see between the various books, the more appropriate it will be to view them all as variants of the same myth.

Most scholars agree that in large measure the apocryphal Acts of the Apostles were inspired by the Hellenistic novels. Some would even say the stories are Christianized versions of existing novels.[33] In either case, this means we are probably justified in viewing Hellenistic fiction as variants of the same myths embodied in the apostolic Acts, their characters variants within the same megatext. Accordingly, I will supply examples from both branches of literature in the discussion that follows.

The collections of apostolic Acts, at least the major five books that were once attributed to Leucius, heretical disciple of John, and circulated as canon by the Manicheans, all stem from a Christianity that demanded celibacy, even within marriage, as the price for salvation. This ascetic tendency can be shown to have penetrated and become embodied in several forms of early Christian practice, including Montanism, Marcionism, Gnosticism, and Tatianist Encratism.[34] The apocryphal *Acts of Paul*, *Peter*, *John*, *Thomas*, and *Andrew* all promote such encratism plainly and repeatedly. The eponymous apostles are all faithful preachers of a celibacy gospel. But according to the persuasive argument of Stevan L. Davies, the title characters are more than mere mouthpieces for the favorite doctrines of the authors.[35] They are probably based on a group of influential itinerants who largely answered to Gerd Theissen's description of wandering charismatics.[36] This breed gradually died out under opposition from the emerging ecclesiasticism. Among their most ardent supporters were the communities of celibate charismatic women who organized themselves on the margins of the churches as orders of widows and virgins and shared with the itinerants a Cynic indifference to traditional social structures.

Davies argues forcefully that the apocryphal Acts, or at least many of the stories underlying them, arose from these circles of widows. In part, the stories were polemics on behalf of the ecclesiastically embattled itinerant apostles seeking to legitimate their kind of ministry by appeal to the original apostles, the disciples of Jesus, who formed the ostensible heroes of the books. In part, the books represented the celibate women's communities, which were also coming under attack in the church, as witnessed, for example, by the Pastoral Epistles' crippling restrictions on widows' monastic orders. Both the itinerant apostles and the orders of women taught encratite doctrine and held themselves aloof from ecclesiastical power structures. The widows, by writing and perhaps circulating these writings, sought to safeguard their own position by invoking the ancient solicitude of the original apostles. In other words, they were trying to beat the anti-charismatic claimants of apostolic succession, the bishops, at their own game.

Besides encratism, the other major theological preoccupation of the apocryphal Acts is docetism, the belief that Jesus did not have a physical body. Between encratism and docetism, something beyond a fortuitous connection has often been noted. Ascetics who deny the pleasures of the flesh in search of spirituality will understandably be reluctant to contemplate the Savior having taken on a coat of human flesh. All the major books of Acts are explicitly or implicitly docetic. In the *Acts of John*, we read the clearest account of a docetic Christ to be found anywhere in early Christian literature. In the *Acts of Thomas*, only vestigial traces of docetism remain, but they are clearly present. It may be that the more explicit docetic Christology was expunged by later orthodox censors.

It is striking that the incarnationism that finds its way into the apocryphal Acts is of the variety discussed by semiologist Roland Barthes in his essay, "The Writer on Holiday," in which he comments on a picture of André Gide rafting down a river reading a book. The photo exposes the cheat at the heart of incarnationism. The writer, a creature of more than human gifts, still condescends to go on vacation like the rest of us mere mortals. Yet, look: even on holiday he is engaged in literature! This juxtaposition of outward mundane form and inner divine drive to do the Muses' work only serves, Barthes says, to subvert the initial impression of the Great Man sharing the common human lot. The fact that, even sharing our apparent limitations (he needs, after all, to vacation like the

rest of us, no?), he continues in the godlike state of literary pro-
ductivity shows that his talent can have nothing to do with human
resources.

> Thus the function of the man of letters is to human labour rather
> as ambrosia is to bread: a miraculous, eternal substance, which
> condescends to take a social form so that its prestigious difference
> is better grasped. ... For I cannot but ascribe to some superhu-
> manity the existence of beings vast enough to wear blue pyjamas
> at the very moment when they manifest themselves as universal
> conscience.[37]

Every celebrity interview presupposes the same understanding of sham incarnation. The humanity of the celebrity, the star,
is merely an earthen vessel holding priceless treasure within. And
such is the humanity of Christ in the apocryphal Acts, even when
they are not explicitly docetist. Flesh merely serves as an occasion
to show forth a power that transcends the flesh and must therefore
come from the divine sphere.

The docetic epiphany of Christ

The notion of a divine being putting on the mere semblance of
humanity to communicate with human beings did not, of course,
begin with Christianity. In Heliodorus's *An Ethiopian Story*, the
Egyptian priest Kalasiris explains the rationale as well as the manner of the docetic epiphany of gods on earth.

> Kalasiris paused for a moment until he had achieved the exalted
> state of mind appropriate to the contemplation of holy mysteries.
> Then he said: "Knemon, when gods and spirits descend to earth
> or ascend from earth, they very occasionally assume the form of
> an animal, but generally they take on human shape: the resem-
> blance to ourselves makes their theophany more accessible to us.
> They might pass unperceived by the uninitiated, but they can-
> not avoid recognition by the wise, who will know them firstly by

their eyes, which have an extraordinary intensity and never blink, but more especially by their method of locomotion, which is not accomplished by the displacement or transposition of their feet, but by a sort of smooth, gliding motion and without touching the ground, so that they cleave rather than walk through the circumambient air. [38]

Iamblichus reports about Pythagoras that he "came ... for the purpose of remedying and benefiting the condition of mankind, and that on this account he had assumed a human form, lest men, being disturbed by the novelty of his transcendency, should avoid the discipline which he possessed."[39] Similarly, Apollonius's hagiographer, Philostratus, prefaces a recounting of several of his hero's adventures with the observation that "such episodes are comparable to the visits of mankind paid by the sons of Asclepius."[40] Later in the book, Philostratus depicts Apollonius, in prison awaiting his trial before Domitian, receiving a visit from his disciple Damis, who is ostensibly the main source of Philostratus's information. Damis is worried about the outcome of the trial. His master reassures him:

> "I shall be set at liberty this day, but so far as depends upon my own will, now and here." And with these words he took his leg out of the fetters and remarked to Damis: "Here is proof positive to you of my freedom, so cheer up." Damis says that it was then for the first time that he really and truly understood the nature of Apollonius, to wit that it was divine and superhuman, for ... he quietly laughed at the fetters, and then inserted his leg in them afresh, and behaved like a prisoner once more. (II, 257)

Once Apollonius appears before the tyrant and says his piece, he miraculously vanishes, quoting the *Iliad* 22:13, "For thou shalt not slay me, since I am not mortal" (II, 283). Thus "he left no one in ignorance of his true nature, but allowed it to be known to all to be such that he had it in him never to be taken prisoner against his own will" (II, 285). Of course, the reader has known since the beginning that Apollonius was born the incarnation of the shape-shifting god Proteus (I, 13).

The Christ of the canonical Gospels is similarly contemptuous of the measures employed by puny humans to detain him against his will (Matt. 26:53-54; John 18:6; 19:11). The docetic Christ of the apocryphal Acts fits the pattern even more closely. We hear that he took on a human semblance only because a direct vision of his glory would be too much for mere mortals to bear, who presumably could not see it and live. In his *Acts of John*, that apostle extols Christ's "greatness, which at present is invisible to us, but visible only to the pure as it is portrayed in thy manhood only" (256).[41]

Peter echoes this Christology: "The Lord in his mercy was moved to show himself in another shape and to be seen in the form of a man" (*Acts Pet.*, 302, Stead translation). Similarly, Thomas exults in the docetic condescension: "Glory to thy majesty which for our sakes was made small; glory to thy most exalted kingship which for our sakes was humbled; ... glory to thy Godhead which for our sakes was seen in the likeness of men" (*Acts Thom.*, 485-86, Wilson translation). If the gods of Kalasiris walked a few inches above the earth, so does the Jesus of the apocryphal Acts. In the *Acts of John*, the beloved disciple wistfully recalls how "his feet were whiter than snow, so that the ground there was lit up by his feet ... And I often wished, as I walked with him, to see his footprint in the earth, whether it appeared on the ground—for I saw him as it were raised up from the earth—and I never saw [footprints]" (*Acts John*, 226-27, Stead).

Kalasiris revealed that the gods on earth betray themselves by never blinking. So with the apocryphal Jesus; in the *Acts of John*, that disciple says, "I never saw his eyes closing, but always open" (225). In the *Acts of Peter*, we learn that "he was not born from the womb of a woman, but came down from a heavenly place" (307). John recalls how "sometimes when I meant to touch him I encountered a material, solid body; but at other times again when

I felt him, his substance was immaterial and incorporeal, and as
if it did not exist at all" (*Acts John*, 227). It is conceivable that
here we have the original meaning of the scene in John 20:27, that
Thomas would have passed his hand through the insubstantial
flesh of Jesus and learned, as John does in the *Acts of John*, that
Jesus never could have been crucified. To put his hand into Jesus's
side was not to insert it into a gaping wound but rather to see that
there was no real flesh to offer it any resistance! He was the one
"whom no human hand has grasped," (*Acts Pet.*, 302). At mealtime,
Jesus never ate. Instead, "he would bless his [portion] and divide
it among us" (*Acts John*, 227). Similarly, in the *Acts of Peter* we discover that "he ate and drank for our sakes, though himself without
hunger or thirst" (302).

Such a Jesus could not have suffered on the cross, and while the
crucifixion appeared to be taking place, John was called to a cave in
the Mount of Olives (an analogue to the empty tomb scene) and
told:

> "John, for the people below in Jerusalem, I am being crucified and
> pierced with lances ... But to you I am speaking ..." And I saw
> the Lord himself above the Cross, having no shape but only a kind
> of voice [cf. Acts 9:3-7] ... which said to me, "... I have suffered
> none of those things which they will say of me ... You hear that I
> suffered, yet I suffered not; ... and that I was pierced, yet I was
> not wounded; that I was hanged, yet I was not hanged; that blood
> flowed from me, yet it did not flow; and in a word, what they say of
> me, I did not endure." (232-34)

One of the most fascinating aspects of docetic Christology is the
implication that if Christ's human form was only an illusion, he
was not restricted to any single illusory form. Thus, he would have
appeared in several.

Let me note that the same notion is attested for the other Hellenistic deities, including the shape-shifting Proteus, who appeared

in the form of Apollonius of Tyana. In *The Golden Ass*, the narrator has a night vision of Osiris in which, contrary to his usual habit, Osiris appears "not disguised in any other form, but in his own essence and speaking to me with his own venerable voice" (282). Only in the crucifixion vision of John does the docetic Christ vouchsafe his real form, which is none at all, and his true voice, which was "not that voice which we knew, but one that was sweet and gentle and truly the voice of God" (*Acts John*, 233).

Elsewhere we hear that "each one of us saw him as he was able, as he had power to see" (*Acts Pet.*, 302), in forms appropriate to the beholders. John recalls the day Jesus called him and his brother to become disciples.

> And my brother said this to me, "John, what does he want, this child on the shore who called us?" And I said, "Which child? ... You are not seeing straight, brother James. Do you not see the man standing there who is handsome, fair and cheerful-looking?" And as we left the place, wishing to follow him, he appeared to me again as rather bald-headed but with a thick flowing beard, but to James as a young man whose beard was just beginning ... I tried to see him as he was, but ... sometimes he appeared to me as a small man with no good looks, and then again as looking up to heaven. (*Acts John*, 225)

They refer to Christ as the one with the "many-formed countenance" (252). Thomas, too, invokes what is probably the vestige of a stronger, unedited docetic text: a "Jesus of many forms, ... who dost appear in the guise of our poor manhood" (523).

As he appeared on earth, according to these narratives, so he continued to appear in visions. For instance, Peter led a group of widows in a vision of Christ and they "'saw an old man who had such a presence as we cannot describe to you,' but others said, 'We saw a growing lad'; and others said, 'We saw a boy ...' So Peter praised the Lord, saying, '... God is greater than our thoughts, as we have learnt from the aged widows, how they have seen the Lord in a variety of forms'" (*Acts Pet.*, 304). In the *Acts of Paul*, docetism is rejected as heresy. But as I argue elsewhere,[42] the portion of the text that does so is borrowed from *Third Corinthians*, which represented a different time and culture.

The semiotic significance of the docetic epiphany, already implied by Barthes, may be seen in terms of truth and falsehood, affirmation and negation. The divine being has a truth he wants to communicate to this world of darkness and error. How can he communicate truth to a world of falsehood? How can his light be understood in a world of blindness? In the manner of thinking of the ancient world, the redeemer must convey truth through the device of falsehood, for only so can he speak the language of those with whom he wants to communicate. Hence, he adopts the pretense of humanity. The first deception of the deity is to conceal his divinity, the second is to pretend to be human.

This stratagem is calculated as much to reveal something of himself as to conceal his true identity, for it is a false humanity he adopts, one that does not pass close scrutiny. It is a veil that the wise and pure can penetrate. After the ruse is detected, the original truth of the Savior's divinity is understood after all. It passes through the filtering lenses of the double deception, concealing the divinity to reveal it, to dilute the overly potent strength of truth for those with a low truth-tolerance. In the final sum, truth has been successfully communicated by the two mutually negating lies. A double negative equals a positive.

Interestingly, the whole picture is reproduced as a mirror image in the case of the Christ's opposite, Simon Magus, who sometimes appears as an Antichrist figure. First, we hear that his father, the devil, was a spirit who, like Christ, could appear in various guises, earning him the epithet "the many-formed Satan" (*Acts John*, 247). In the *Acts of Thomas*, a woman being harassed by Satan describes how "I said to the handmaid who was with me: 'Didst thou see the youth and his shamelessness, how without shame he spoke with me openly?' But she said to me: 'I saw an old man conversing with thee.'" Thomas laments the work of Satan: "O thou of many forms—he appears as he may wish, but his essence may not be altered" (467). Since the same was said of Christ, in this respect the two were similar.

Depicted as a false Christ who is semiotically the equivalent of Satan, it made sense to people that Simon Magus, too, was a shape-shifter. In the *Acts of Peter and Paul*, we read how "Simon transformed himself into various forms, the form of a youth, of an old man, yet another time, of a soldier. In such a fashion, through the assistance of the devil, he assumed many shapes."[43] Again, to have many shapes implies that the deity has no true form. We hear of the Antichrist Simon, just as we did of Christ Jesus, that his body was physically insubstantial. In the pseudo-Clementines, we read that once Simon's rival, Dositheus, took a swing at him with his staff and "the stick seemed to go through Simon's body as if it were smoke."[44] In the same way, John often found the flesh of Jesus to be immaterial. However, sometimes the beloved disciple was equally confounded to notice that the consistency of his Lord's body had become "hard like rock" (*Acts John*, 226).

At this juncture I cannot resist citing a parallel to this whole business from the lore of Hindu Shaivism. A twelfth-century Hindu saint, Allamaprabhu, teased a spiritual novice, Goraksa, by asking him to cut the saint with a sword.

> Goraksa, the leader of the Siddhas, had a magical body, invulnerable as diamond. Allama mocked at his body, his vanity. Legend says that he gave Allama a sword and invited him to try cutting his body in two. Allama swung the sword at him, but the sword clanged on the solid diamond-body of Goraksa; not a hair was severed. Goraksa laughed in pride. Allamaprabhu laughed at this show-off and returned the sword, saying, "Try it on me now." Goraksa came at Allama with all his strength. The sword swished through Alla-

ma's body as if it were mere space. Such were Allama's powers of self-emptying, his "achievement of Nothingness." Goraksa was stunned—he felt acutely the contrast between his own powers and Allama's true realization, between his own diamond-body in which the carnal body had become confirmed and Allama's body which was no body but all spirit. This revelation was the beginning of his enlightenment.[45]

Likewise, in the Simon story a conflict between rival mages, Dositheus and Simon, leads to Dositheus's acknowledgement of Simon's superiority. And note that both the smoke body and the adamantine body occur in the apocryphal tradition, both attributed there to Jesus.

If the divine redeemer employs two deceptions, which cancel each other out, in order to convey the truth to those sunk in error, his opposite Simon adds a third deception, namely that he is the Christ, and thus he negates the double negative and its affirmation. He seeks to keep people in the darkness of illusion.

The apostle mistaken for God

A second group of textual anomalies forms a binary opposite to that of the docetic epiphany of Christ. If Christ is mistaken for a man, so is the apostle mistaken for God, which is not surprising given the complete conformity of these characters to the stereotype of the *theios aner* (divine man). As we will see, the apostles are swift to deny such inflated dignity. It is worth noting that this kind of mistaken identity occurs frequently in Hellenistic novels. In *Chaereas and Callirhoe*, the heroine has been kidnapped and sold into slavery as the property of the nobleman Dionysius, a patron of the temple of Aphrodite, where he is introduced to her.

So Dionysius saw her. "Aphrodite," he cried, "be gracious to me!" He was in the act of prostrating himself when [his servant] Leonas caught him up and said: "Sir, this is the woman I bought—don't be alarmed. Woman, come to your master!" … Dionysius struck Leonas. "Impious man!" he cried. "Do you speak to gods as if they were human?" … At that Callirhoe replied: "Stop making fun of me! Stop calling me a goddess—I'm not even a happy mortal!" As she spoke, her voice seemed the voice of a god to Dionysius." (40-41, Reardon translation; cf. Acts 12:22)

Another example occurs in *An Ephesian Tale* wherein a young couple, Habrocomes and Anthia, are mistaken for gods because of their unusual beauty (135, Anderson translation; cf. Acts 14:11-13).

So the ship put into Rhodes, and the sailors disembarked; Habrocomes too came off, hand in hand with Anthia. All the Rhodians gathered, amazed at the young people's beauty, and no one who saw them passed by in silence; some said it was a visitation of auspicious gods; some offered them worship and adoration... [cf. Acts 14:11-13] (Anderson translation, p. 135).

In another novel, *An Ethiopian Story*, the heroine Charikleia is a priestess who, like Anthia, possesses divine beauty because her mother was looking at a tapestry depicting Andromeda when she conceived the child. Kalasiris tells the pirate Peloros, who was about to see Charikleia for the first time, "You will see Artemis herself sitting there!" (469). Later in the same novel, people see the arrival of King Hydaspes as "the epiphany of you, our god and savior" (553).

In the *Story of Apollonius King of Tyre*, the king has been separated many years from his wife and thinks her dead, but she has become the high priestess of Diana in Ephesus. Entering Diana's temple, Apollonius catches sight of her, not knowing her true identity. "When they saw her, Apollonius, his daughter, and son-in-law rushed to prostrate themselves at her feet, for she radiated so much glittering beauty that they thought that she was the goddess Diana" (770, Sandy translation). A miniature romantic novel, *The Story of Cupid and Psyche*, has been inserted in Apuleius's *The Golden Ass*. In it we meet yet another maiden whose beauty makes her appear to be divine. People "came daily by thousands to ... worship and reverence her ... as if she were the Lady Venus indeed ... [and] call[ed] upon the divinity of that great goddess in a human form" (108-109).[46]

In the apocryphal Acts, the apostles are regularly taken for gods walking the earth. John even mistakes himself for a deity! Unknown to him, someone has painted his portrait. When the artist unveils it, John does not at first recognize who it is. Seeing the image of a man surrounded by the accoutrements of a pagan altar, John exclaims, "Is it one of your gods that is painted here? Why, I see you are still living as a pagan!" Once persuaded with the aid of a mirror that the image is indeed his own, he nonetheless concludes, in the spirit of Platonic aesthetics, "What you have done is childish and imperfect; you have drawn a dead likeness of what is dead." That is, the real John is his inner man, not his fleshly shell (*Acts John*, 220-21).

Earlier, John had said to the same man, after raising his wife from the dead, "It is not my feet, man, that you should kiss, but those of God in whose power you have both been raised up" (219). The Ephesian priests of Artemis are astonished at John's miracles and cry out, "'This is one of the race of our lady Artemis.' But S[aint] John was crying out: 'I am a man subject to passions ... Do not worship me, ... but worship and praise Him, who formed us and created us.'" But all the nobles knelt down, saying that John's face glowed as if it were illuminated."[47] After drinking poison and not being harmed, he causes his Roman enemies to conclude in terror that "he is a god in a human body."[48]

An admirer of Peter, the sea captain Theon, says to him, "I hardly know you, whether you are God or man" (*Acts Pet.*, 284). Peter answers an admiring crowd, "You men of Rome, seeing that I too am one of you, wearing human flesh, and a sinner, but have obtained mercy, do not look at me, as though by my own power I were doing what I do" (310). Nonetheless, "they venerated him as a god" (313). After the death of a cup-bearer who had ill-advisedly slapped Thomas for his insolence, a flute girl comments that "this man is either a god or an apostle of God" (*Acts Thom.*, 447).

In all these cases, what we are seeing is another affirmation of true deity by means of a double negation. At first there seems to be a docetic epiphany: people think the miracle wrought (or in the case of the novels, a beauty displayed) denotes that what otherwise seems to be a mortal is really an immortal masquerading as a human. If they were correct, we would have another case of the double negative conveying divine truth. But in fact, what they are seeing is someone who is, in fact, a mere mortal, albeit one with unusual endowments. So the misapprehension on the part of the apostles' admirers must be counted as a third mistake that leaves them believing in a falsehood; the apostle is not the god they think he is. Fortunately, they are not left in the dark because the apostle, like Callirhoe, immediately denies what is not true about himself— his supposed divinity. His is a fourth negation, negating the falsehood created by the third negation, their false belief in his divinity. He has restored the balance of truth.

Before discussing the meaning of the two sides of the antinomy posed by the docetic epiphany of the divine savior and the denial of his own divinity by the human apostle, let us note that again the figure of Simon Magus serves to highlight the truth of the self-abnegating apostle by contrast. Simon is now to be considered as a false apostle, not so much a false Christ. This view of Simon is found among our sources in the Clementine *Homilies*, when Simon Peter explains that he and Simon Magus, the Anti-Simon, are opposing syzygies (545-546). They have been sent into the world, respectively, to preach truth and error. At any rate, Simon Magus, like the genuine apostles, is mistaken for divinity, but unlike them, he accepts the blasphemous acclamation. The devotees of Simon Magus proclaim, "Thou art god in Italy; thou art saviour of the Romans" (*Acts Pet.*, 283). "He then came forward claiming to be accepted as a mighty power of the very God who has created the world" (*Homilies*, 546). "They all gave heed to him, from the least to the greatest, saying, 'This man is that power of God which is called Great'" (Acts 8:10). The crowds proclaimed him God but did so in error, the same as they had with the true apostles. What confirmed the authenticity of Peter, Thomas, and John was that they all denied the belief in their divinity.

The crowds proclaim Simon Magus God in error, just as when they acclaimed the true apostles as gods they were in error. But what made the latter true apostles, and Simon a false one, is that John, Peter and Thomas all deny the false belief in their divinity, restoring the balance of truth by negating truth's negation. Simon, by contrast, affirms truth's negation. He follows the third negation with an affirmation of that negation to promote the lie of his own divinity, and in his case error is on balance the winner. But since the narrator knows Simon is lying in affirming the crowd's denial of truth, and so depicts it, the narrator is able to negate Simon's affirmation and so restore the balance of truth for the reader. The double negative, overriding Simon's affirmation of error, again brings out the truth of the matter.

Now what is the relation of the two poles of the first antinomy? What have the truly docetic epiphany of Christ and the admittedly false deification of the apostles to do with each other? Regardless of which side of the barrier of flesh one is on, the barrier may not be breached. The docetic epiphany poses the question, "Can God become flesh?" answering it negatively. The corollary, whether flesh can become divine, is answered equally in the negative, safeguarding the line between divinity and flesh: neither is able to penetrate to the other side. This is the connection between the falsely human epiphany of Christ and the admittedly false (or misleading) divine epiphany of the apostles.

The Christomorphic apostle

If the human, fleshly apostle cannot be identified as a god, he might be seen as a stand-in for Christ. The narrators expect the reader to know that when overenthusiastic crowds acclaim the divinity of an apostle, they are wrong. Yet it is no less clear that the narrators themselves mean to present the protagonists as Christ figures in the truest sense. Like Christ, John cannot be tempted. "Now I know that God dwells in you, blessed John! How happy is the man who has not tempted God in you; for the man who tempts you tempts the untemptable" (*Acts John*, 242). Earlier, Christ himself is called "him that cannot be tempted" (226). After John dies, his tomb is found empty, just as his master's tomb was, at least in the canonical Gospels. For in the *Acts of John* there can be no tomb of Christ, empty or otherwise, for he had no physical body to be placed in one. This is, I suspect, a significant point: the apostles conform to a Christological idea that the same texts reject in the case of Christ himself. I think this seeming contradiction can be made intelligible further on.

The pattern of Christ's martyrdom is overtly projected onto the apostle in the *Acts of Peter*, where Peter meets Jesus entering Rome:

> "Lord, whither goest thou here?" And the Lord said to him, "I am coming to Rome to be crucified." And Peter said to him, "Lord, art thou being crucified again?" He said to him, "Yes, Peter, I am being crucified again." And Peter came to himself; and he saw the Lord ascending into heaven; then he returned to Rome rejoicing and giving praise to the Lord, because he said, "I am being crucified"; since this was to happen to Peter. (*Acts Pet.*, 318)

His Roman follower Marcellus plays the role of Joseph of Arimathea, recovering Peter's body from the cross, liberally anointing it with spices, unguents, and honey and burying it "in his own burial-vault" (321). In a dream, Peter appears to Marcellus, scolding him for wasting all the rich substances on his worthless husk. Then "Marcellus awoke and told the brethren of Peter's appearing" (321). Peter's crucifixion could not be portrayed more explicitly as an antitype to that of Jesus. On Peter's cross Jesus himself is "being crucified again," so what wonder is it for Peter to make a Jesus-like postmortem appearance to a grieving disciple?

The same scenario is rehearsed in the *Acts of Paul* when the apostle to the gentiles takes on the role of Christ. The disciples Demas and Hermogenes deny knowing Paul, much as Peter once denied Jesus (356, Wilson translation): "Who this man is, we do not know." Later, Paul plays cowardly Peter for a moment in order to assist the Christomorphosis of another character, Thecla. Amazingly, the once-fearless apostle fairly clucks, "I do not know the woman" (260). But don't think ill of Paul; his momentary failure of nerve is simply a means whereby Thecla can become another Christ figure. As such, she needs to have a denier. This is an important point missed by Davies[49] and Elizabeth Hazelton Haight,[50] who interpret Paul's seeming cowardice in contrived ways.

Paul is arrested in a scene recalling Jesus's arrest in Gethsemane's groves: "He saw Hermippus coming with a sword drawn in his hand, and with him many other young men with their cudgels. Paul said to them: 'I am not a robber nor am I a murderer. The God of all things, the father of Christ, will turn your hands backwards, and your sword into its sheath'" (366). Again, Christ appears and tells the apostle that he will recapitulate Christ's own crucifixion: "'Paul, I am about to be crucified afresh.' And Paul said, 'God forbid, Lord, that I should see this!' But the Lord said to Paul: 'Paul, get thee up, go to Rome, and admonish the brethren, that they abide in the calling to the father'" (381). Of course, Paul's death will be a second crucifixion of Christ.

At this point, I must register my disagreement with Schneemelcher, who sees the occurrence of the *quo vadis* scene ("Where are you going?") in the *Acts of Paul* and *Acts of Peter* as indicating the literary dependence of the former on the latter.[51] This might be a reasonable conclusion if the texts were much more alike than they actually are, but as it is, I conclude that it is more likely that both texts employed the same tradition independently. Most probably the story was first told concerning Peter, since tradition held that Peter, but not Paul, was crucified. Given the widespread tendency in the second century to assimilate the two great apostles to one another, not least attested in Luke's canonical Acts, the *quo vadis* episode was probably already associated with Paul in oral tradition, perhaps on the strength of Galatians 2:20. From there, the story could have entered both apocryphal books independently.

The overall pattern of the Christomorphism of the apostles in these books also makes clear that the word of Jesus to Peter or to Paul does not denote, as one often hears, that Christ seeks to shame the faint-hearted apostle into taking the cup of martyrdom God has drawn for him (as if to say, "If you won't do it, I suppose I'll have to go through it all over again"), but rather that the fearless martyr-apostles in their deaths conform to Christ's image and share in his Passion (cf. Col. 1:24).

Paul's death comes with a sword stroke, not a cross, but his passion retains a vestige of Jesus's in that one of the Roman soldiers is named Longinus, the same as the soldier whose spear pierced the side of Christ according to a whole cycle of legends. Longinus is converted in both narratives. "It has been suggested more than once that the name Longinus was first connected with the soldier converted at the execution of Paul, and that it was afterwards transferred to the centurion (soldier) converted at the crucifixion of Christ."[52] I cannot accept this, though, for the simple reason that the name Longinus comes from the Latin word for *lance*, so the character must have originally been named for his role in the Christ story where a lance comes into play. There is no lance at the martyrdom of Paul, so the character of Longinus must have been borrowed for Paul's story. If he had no lance to wield, why would he have been brought over from Jesus's story? "But when the executioner struck off [Paul's] head, milk spurted upon the soldier's clothing. And when they saw it, the soldier and all who stood by were amazed, and glorified God" (386), just as the centurion at the cross was moved, despite himself, to exclaim, "Truly, this man was the Son of God!" (Mark 15:39). Paul then appears alive again in order to warn Nero and his sycophants of the doom to come. "'I am not dead, but alive in my God.' ... And when Paul had said this, he departed from him" (386). Paul is later observed standing before his empty tomb, where his disciples "were astounded" (387).

One would think it impossible to become more of an icon of Christ than Paul in the *Acts of Paul*, but Thomas outdoes him in his own Acts. As is well known, the Syrian church thought Thomas to be the twin brother of Jesus. In the *Gospel of Thomas*, the esoteric meaning of this designation is explained. "Thomas said to Him: Master, my mouth will not at all be capable of saying whom thou art like. Jesus said: I am not thy Master, because thou hast ... become drunk from the bubbling spring which I have measured out" (log. 13). "Jesus said: Whoever drinks from my mouth shall become as I am and I myself shall become he, and the hidden things shall be revealed to him" (log. 108).

It is in this sense that Thomas, and indeed all the apostles in the apocryphal books, is the "twin brother of Christ" (*Acts Thom.*, 459, 464), not a literal brother. The apostle harbors secret knowledge about Christ that other men do not share. At the beginning of the story, Thomas is more Jonah-morphic than Christomorphic because he flatly refuses to obey Christ's missionary charge to evangelize India. So the Risen One appears and strolls through a Jerusalem bazaar until he finds a merchant in need of a carpenter, which Thomas happens to be. Then Jesus sells Thomas into slavery! The sheer strangeness of the idea is bound to have been intended to poke the reader in the ribs to remind him that Christ, on entering our world, "took the form of a slave," in other words, a slave to death (Phil. 2:7).

Thomas wastes no time incurring the wrath of jealous Indian

husbands whose wives he persuades to adopt encratite celibacy. Thomas is eventually condemned to death for his home wrecking, for "deceiv[ing] many other women" (506), thereby mirroring the public charge made against the encratite Jesus, according to Marcion: "He leads our wives and children astray." About to die, Thomas assures his followers that his coming departure will be only an "apparent death, ... not [real] death, but deliverance and release from the body" (527). Again, I wonder if this is not another vestige of an original docetic view in which Thomas would have repeated the phantom death of a Jesus who never had a body. Despite the fact that Thomas dies, stay dead he does not. As his disciples mourn at his tomb, Thomas "appeared to them, and said: 'I am not here. Why do you sit here and watch over me? For I have gone up and received what was hoped for'" (530). Two more such appearances follow.

The Apostolomorphic Christ

While an apostle can be an earthly stand-in for Christ, the Savior can also appear on earth in the guise of one of his apostles, his many forms including the bodily shapes of his followers. We can adduce a few non-Christian examples of the same sort of phenomenon from the ancient novels, which of course may be the source from which the whole notion entered into the apocryphal Acts. For instance, in *An Ethiopian Story*, Theagenes tells Charikleia, "Be it Kalasiris or a god in Kalasiris's shape, he appeared to me and seemed to speak these words" (528). In *Joseph and Asenath*, the repentant Asenath "looked up and saw a man like Joseph in every respect, with a robe and a crown and a royal staff. But his face was like lightning and his eyes were like the light of the sun" (XIV:8-9).

Alexander the Great was a son of the god Amun. Although he was not a shape-shifter, he masqueraded as his own messenger behind enemy lines, pretending to be a courier or an official of his own court on a diplomatic mission.[53] This, too, is the semiotic equivalent of Jesus descending into the material world in the guise of an apostle. Here are Christ's apostolomorphic appearances:

> Drusiana had said, "The Lord appeared to me in the tomb in the form of John and in that of a young man" (*Acts John*, 224-25).

> And immediately a man who looked like yourself, Peter, [appeared] ... so that I gazed upon you both, both on you and on the one ... whose likeness [of you] caused me great amazement. And now I have awakened, and have told you these signs of Christ. (*Acts Pet.*, 305)

> But Thecla sought for Paul, as a lamb in the wilderness looks about for the shepherd. And when she looked upon the crowd, she saw the Lord sitting in the form of Paul (*Acts Paul*, 358).

> Maximilla, the Lord going before her in the form of Andrew, went with Iphidamia to the prison (*Acts Andr.*, 414, Best).

> And he saw the Lord Jesus in the likeness of the apostle Judas Thomas (*Acts Thom.*, 448).

The apostolomorphic Christ is the mirror reflection of the Christomorphic apostle. In a sense, they are one and the same, at least as semiological equivalents. For instance, in the *Acts of John*, we have the fascinating Round Dance of the Savior, who says: "I am a mirror to you who know me ... Now, if you follow my dance, see yourself in Me who am speaking" (230). Similarly, in the *Acts of Thomas* we have the Hymn of the Pearl, in which we read: "The splendid robe became like me, as my reflection in a mirror; I saw it wholly in me, and in it I saw myself quite apart from myself, so that we were two in distinction and again one in a single form" (502). The idea is that the enlightened soul can become united with its heavenly twin, who is the Savior.

Our first antinomy was that posed between the docetic Christ and the apostle who denies his own divinity. We saw that the line of flesh versus illusion may not be breached. Humanity remains on one side, divinity on the other. But now our second antinomy seems to contradict this. It is between the Christomorphic apostle and the apostolomorphic Christ, but the resolution is that it is possible for the two to merge. But is this not the opposite of the first antinomy's conclusion that human and divine may not interpenetrate? Thus a third antinomy forms between the conclusions of the first two.

The resolution of it is really rather simple, and it lies in recalling that the apostles of Christ in these Acts do not preach just Christianity in general, but specifically encratite Christianity, which involves the utter denial of the flesh. Whereas flesh constitutes the impenetrable barrier between humanity and divinity, encratism suggests that what may not be gotten through may yet be gotten out of the way. The barrier is removed for those who deny the flesh. Here we have a third antinomy, which is to become a docetic epiphany oneself, to mirror him who never took on flesh. Hence, we see the far from fortuitous connection between the docetic Christology and the encratite ethic of the apocryphal writings.

The Gnostic apostle

This study would tend to support Walter Schmithals's hypothesis in that the apocryphal Acts propose a paradox involving a docetic Christ becoming incarnate in his apostles, who suffer real crucifixion where Christ himself did not. We can draw no firm line between these apostles and their Lord. The Lord's appearance as Andrew or Peter or John is, in a sense, more of an incarnation than that of Jesus of Nazareth since the apostles are more fleshly than he ever was. I suggest that the apocryphal Acts actually preserved the original Gnostic apostle conception more faithfully than Luke and the church that followed his lead.

NOTES

[1]Walter Schmithals, *The Office of Apostle in the Early Church*, trans. John E. Steely (New York: Abingdon, 1969), 114-97.

[2]Eric Robertson Dodds, *Pagan and Christian in an Age of Anxiety: Some Aspects of Religious Experience from Marcus Aurelius to Constantine* (Cambridge: Cambridge University Press, 1965), 23-24.

[3]Hans Jonas, *The Gnostic Religion: The Message of the Alien God and the Beginnings of Christianity*, 2nd ed. (Boston: Beacon Press, 1963), 320-40.

[4]H. Wheeler Robinson, *The Religious Ideas of the Old Testament*, 2nd ed. (London: Duckworth, 1956), 75-76.

[5]The Cybele and Attis myth is a love story between a goddess and a mortal. Cybele rejects the sexual advances of Zeus, but Zeus impregnates her while she sleeps. Cybele then gives birth to the evil hermaphrodite, Agdistis. His strength is feared by the gods, but they manage to cut off his penis; the blood fertilizes an olive tree. A woman named Nana eats an almond from this tree and becomes pregnant herself. She gives birth to a boy, Attis. Unknown to Attis, Cybele falls in love with him, but when Attis falls in love with the daughter of the king of Pessinus, Cybele becomes jealous and barges into the lovers' wedding ceremony. Attis, now aggrieved at his infidelity, castrates himself and bleeds to death. His blood brings forth the first violets (just as the blood of the crucified Christ colors the blossoms of the dogwood tree). Zeus and Cybele then resurrect the deceased Attis.

[6]Walter Schmithals, *Gnosticism in Corinth*, trans. John E. Steely (New York: Abingdon, 1971), 27-28, 168, 248-49.

[7]Diogenes the Cynic was said to have been on a quest for one honest man, for which he carried a lamp during daylight hours in order to illustrate the impossibility of the task. He died in 323 BCE in Corinth.

[8]Hippolytus, *Refutation of All Heresies*, 5:8; L. Gordon Rylands, *The Beginnings of Gnostic Christianity* (London: Watts, 1940), 126-31.

[9]Thomas Whittaker, *The Origins of Christianity: With an Outline of Van Manen's Analysis of the Pauline Literature*, 4th ed. (London: Watts, 1933), 158-59.

[10]Gerd Theissen, "The Wandering Radicals," in Theissen, *Social Reality and the Early Christians: Theology, Ethics, and the World of the New Testament*, trans. Margaret Kohl (Minneapolis: Fortress Press, 1992), 33-59.

[11]"He is the person who travels around from one Christian [communal]

house to another sometimes getting saved at each, but always getting a free meal and a place to sleep. 'It's not a bad life,' one young man named Rich told me. 'I just go from place to place, and if the Christians think you're saved too, they don't bug you. If one comes up and starts to lay a rap on me, I just pick up a Bible or close my eyes to pray. Sometimes I even talk in tongues, and they really think that's heavy" (Michael McFadden, *The Jesus Revolution* [New York: Harper & Row, 1972], 173-74; cf. Lowell D. Streiker, *The Jesus Trip* [New York: Abingdon Press, 1971], 38; Jack Sparks, *God's Forever Family* [Grand Rapids: Zondervan, 1974], 62-64).

[12]Mark 6:7-13; Matt. 10:5-15; Luke 9:1-9; 10:1-12.

[13]Ernst Käsemann, "Paul and Early Catholicism," trans. Wilfred F. Bunge, in Käsemann, *New Testament Questions of Today* (Philadelphia: Fortress Press, 1969), 236-51.

[14]Elaine Pagels, *The Gnostic Gospels* (New York: Random House, 1979), 6-8, 10-11, 13-17.

[15]Charles H. Talbert, *Luke and the Gnostics: An Examination of the Lucan Purpose* (New York: Abingdon Press, 1966), 28-32.

[16]Arthur Drews, *The Christ Myth*, trans. C. Delisle Burns, 3rd ed. (Amherst: Prometheus Books, 1998), 288-89.

[17]Robert M. Price, "Apocryphal Apparitions: 1 Corinthians 15:3-8 as a Post-Pauline Interpolation," in Price and Jeffery J. Lowder, eds., *The Empty Tomb: Jesus beyond the Grave* (Amherst: Prometheus Books, 2005), 69-104.

[18]Robert Eisenman, *James the Brother of Jesus: The Key to Unlocking the Secrets of Early Christianity and the Dead Sea Scrolls* (New York: Viking, 1996), 770-816. See also Robert M. Price, "Eisenman's Gospel of James the Just: A Review," in Bruce Chilton and Jacob Neusner, eds., *The Brother of Jesus: James the Just and His Mission* (Louisville: Westminster, 2001), 186-97.

[19]Mark 3:16-19; Matt. 10:2-4; Luke 6:14-16; Acts 1:13; cf. John 21:2.

[20]Robert Eisenman, *The New Testament Code: The Cup of the Lord, The Damascus Covenant, and the Blood of Christ* (London: Watkins, 2006), 939-56. We might add to the list Addai (Thaddaeus in Edessan tradition), Bar-Ptolemy, and certain pre-Islamic prophets mentioned in the Koran (Eisenman, "Who Were the Koranic Prophets Ad, Thamud, Hud, and Salih?" *Journal of Higher Criticism* 11, no. 2 [Fall 2005], 96-107).

[21]The Koran has "Salih the Just" (cf. Acts 15:22). The early Christian writer Hegesippus refers to "Oblias the Bulwark." Some manuscripts of Mark mention a Lebbaeus.

[22]Mark 1:36-37; 8:32-33; 9:5; 10:28; 11:21; 14:29; Matt. 14:28; 17:24-25; 18:21.

[23]Alfred Loisy, *Birth of the Christian Religion*, trans. Lawrence P. Jacks (London: George Allen & Unwin, 1948), 102.

[24]L. Gordon Rylands, *A Critical Analysis of the Four Chief Pauline Epistles: Romans, First and Second Corinthians, and Galatians* (London: Watts, 1929), 353.

[25]Dieter Georgi, *The Opponents of Paul in Second Corinthians*, trans. Harold Attridge, Isabel and Thomas Best, Bernadette Brooten, Ron Cameron, Frank Fallon, Stephen Gero, Renate Rose, Herman Waetjen, and Michael Williams (Philadelphia: Fortress Press, 1986), 244.

[26]Stevan L. Davies, *The Revolt of the Widows: The Social World of the Apocryphal Acts* (Carbondale: Southern Illinois University Press, 1980), 30-31.

[27]Randel Helms, *Gospel Fictions* (Buffalo, NY: Prometheus Books, 1988); Robert M. Price, "New Testament Narrative as Old Testament Midrash," in *Encyclopaedia of Midrash: Biblical Interpretation in Formative Judaism*, eds. Jacob Neusner and Alan J. Avery-Peck, 2 vols. (Boston: Brill, 2005), 1:534-73.

[28]Claude Levi-Strauss, "The Structural Study of Myth," in Levi-Strauss, *Structural Anthropology*, trans. Claire Jacobson and Brooke Grundfest Schoepf (Garden City: Doubleday, 1967), 212.

[29]Levi-Strauss, *Structural Anthropology*, 213.

[30]Charles Segal, *Interpreting Greek Tragedy: Myth, Poetry, Text* (Ithaca: Cornell University Press, 1986), 56-57.

[31]Edgar Hennecke and Wilhelm Schneemelcher, eds., *New Testament Apocrypha*, 2 vols. (Philadelphia: Westminster Press, 1965), 2:266.

[32]Dennis R. MacDonald, *Acts of Andrew and the Acts of Andrew and Matthias in the City of the Cannibals* (Atlanta: Scholars Press, 1990), 31-44.

[33]Elizabeth Hazelton Haight, *More Essays on Greek Romances* (New York: Longmans, Green, 1945), 48; Ben Edward Perry, *The Ancient Romances, A Literary-Historical Account of Their Origins* (Berkeley: University of California Press, 1967), 31-32; Thomas Hagg, *The Novel in Antiquity* (Berkeley: University of California Press, 1983), 160-61 (both Perry and Hagg are loath to say that the books of apostolic Acts simply evolved from the novels or that they can be considered Christianized novels; still, neither denies some connection or influence); Arthur Heiserman, *The Novel before the Novel: Essays and Discussions about the Beginnings of Prose Fiction in the West* (Chicago: University of Chicago Press, 1977), 205; Bryan P. Reardon, ed., *Collected Ancient Greek Novels* (Berkeley: University of California Press, 1989), 3; Wilhelm

Schneemelcher and Knut Schaferdiek, "Second- and Third-Century Acts of Apostles," in Edgar Hennecke and Wilhelm Schneemelcher, *New Testament Apocrypha*, trans. A. Higgins, et al. (Philadelphia: Westminster Press: 1963-66), 2:176; Rosa Söder, *Die apokryphen Apostelgeschichten und die romanhafte Literatur der Antike* (Stüttgart: W. Kohlhammer Verlag, 1932), 148, qtd. in Davies, *Revolt of Widows*, 85; Virginia Burrus, *Chastity as Autonomy: Women in the Stories of Apocryphal Acts* (Lewiston: Edwin Mellon Press, 1987), 58, sees the connection as between common folklore sources, not direct literary dependence between the two genres.

[34]When referring to the celibacy gospel in general, not just the sect of Tatian, I follow the scholarly convention of referring to this movement with a lowercase "e."

[35]Davies, *Revolt of Widows*, 29-49.

[36]Gerd Theissen, *Sociology of Earliest Palestinian Christianity*, trans. John Bowden (Philadelphia: Fortress Press, 1978), 8-23.

[37]Roland Barthes, *Mythologies*, trans. Annette Lavers (New York: Hill & Wang, 1972), 28-29.

[38]Heliodorus, *An Ethiopian Story*, trans. J. R. Morgan, in *Collected Ancient Greek Novels*, ed. Bryan P. Reardon (Berkeley: University of California Press, 1989), 349-88, and for which pagination to other novels mentioned in this chapter will apply.

[39]Thomas Taylor, trans., *Iamblichus' Life of Pythagoras or Pythagoric Life* (1818; Rochester, VT: Inner Traditions, 1986), 50.

[40]Frederick Cornwallis Conybeare, trans., *The Life of Apollonius of Tyana* by Flavius Philostratus, Loeb Classical Library (1912; Cambridge: Harvard University Press, 2005), 125.

[41]References to the apocryphal Acts collected in volume two of Hennecke and Schneemelcher, *New Testament Apocrypha*, are supplied in the text by page number of that collection.

[42]See chapter four of the present book.

[43]Maire Herbert and Martin McNamara, eds., *Irish Biblical Apocrypha*, trans. Maire Herbert (Edinburgh: T & T Clark, 1989), 100-01.

[44]Hennecke and Schneemelcher, *New Testament Apocrypha*, 548.

[45]Attipat K. Ramanujan, *Speaking of Siva* (Baltimore: Penguin, 1985), 146.

[46]Lucius Apuleius, *The Golden Ass*, ed. Harry C. Schnur, trans. William

Adlington (New York: Collier, 1962). All further references to *The Golden Ass* are to this edition.

[47]*The History of John the Son of Zebedee*, as found in *Apocryphal Acts of the Apostles*, ed. William Wright (London: Williams & Norgate, 1871) 26, 27.

[48]"Episodes from the Life of John the Beloved Disciple," in Herbert and McNamara, *Irish Biblical Apocrypha*, 91.

[49]Davies, *Revolt of Widows*, 57.

[50]Haight, *More Essays on Ancient Fiction*, 57-58.

[51]Hennecke and Schneemelcher, *New Testament Apocrypha*, 2:266.

[52]Rose Jeffries Peebles, *The Legend of Longinus in Ecclesiastical Tradition and in English Literature, and Its Connection with the Grail*, Bryn Mawr College Monographs, 9 (Baltimore: J. H. Furst Co., 1911), 30.

[53]*The Alexander Romance*, trans. Ken Dowden, in Reardon, ed., *Collected Ancient Greek Novels*, 694, 722.

6.

Paulus Absconditus

In his great work, *Orthodoxy and Heresy in Earliest Christianity*,[1] Walter Bauer, the Eusebius of our time, has shown the extent to which early Christian historiography was essentially propagandistic in intent; in other words, it sought to show the providential and inevitable triumph of Constantinian and Catholic orthodoxy. This was hardly a surprise, but the early Christians were no more guilty than anybody else in doing this. As Bernard Lewis[2] has amply shown, virtually all ancient attempts to write history were of precisely the same character. The tendency of the biblical Acts of the Apostles to go in this direction is widely acknowledged, and has been at least since Ferdinand Christian Baur, that other farmer of the ancient field, came on the scene. His work has demonstrated how the extensive Peter-Paul parallels found throughout Acts must have been meant to symbolically reconcile the factions of Peter and Paul by juxtaposing their aretalogies rather than allowing competing narratives to fuel factionalism in the church.

The present chapter focuses on just one chapter of Acts, sniffing for tendencies like those disclosed by Baur and Bauer. I will argue that Paul's farewell speech, his last testament to the Ephesian elders in chapter 20 of Acts, provides a vital clue to understanding an otherwise puzzling narrative element in the previous chapter of Acts. Then I will invoke a complete set of parallels from slightly later Ephesian stories starring John, the son of Zebedee. I will go on to argue that this set of parallels is evidence of the same kind of competition between two apostolic traditions as Acts tries to iron out in the cases of Peter and Paul. Once this is established, I believe we will have arrived at a new framework for understanding much of the polemics in the Pauline epistles.

After me, the deluge

Walter Bauer reviews various lines of evidence indicating that the Christianity of second-century Ephesus did not meet the standards of emerging Catholic orthodoxy and that some who blamed Paul sought to replace him as Ephesus's patron saint with John, son of Zebedee. In precisely the same way, Mark would later be called on to provide a retroactive apostolic pedigree for orthodoxy in once-heretical Egypt, crediting Addai with bringing orthodoxy to Edessa to supplant the traditions of Marcion and Basilides there. Bauer understood that Acts 20:30 represented a harmonizing, catholicizing tendency that co-opted Paul for Catholic orthodoxy.

> Paul had laid the foundation in Ephesus and built up a church through several years of labor. If Romans 16 represents a letter to the Ephesians, then, on the basis of verses 17-20, we must conclude that already during the lifetime of the apostle, certain people had appeared there whose teaching caused offense and threatened division in the community. To this would correspond the complaint in 1 Corinthians 16:9, concerning "many adversaries" in Ephesus, if it refers to those who had been baptized. In any event, the book of Acts has Paul warning the Ephesian elders (*presbyteroi*) in his farewell to them at Miletus that *from their own midst* there will arise men speaking perverse things to draw away the Christians for themselves (20:30). This prediction actually

describes the situation in Ephesus at the time of the composition of Acts.[3]

Luke makes Paul look to the future and say, "Don't blame me!" But some did, as Bauer says:

> We find as we turn to the Apocalypse that in this book the recollection of the Pauline establishment of the church of Ephesus appears to have been completely lost, or perhaps even deliberately suppressed. ... In the Apocalypse, only the names of the twelve apostles are found ... (21:4); there is no room for Paul. And at the very least, it will be but a short time before the Apostle to the Gentiles will have been totally displaced in the consciousness of the church of Ephesus in favor of one of the twelve apostles, John.[4]

Sure enough, "in the second century, the [Roman] 'church' sought ... to appropriate Ephesus by means of John as one of the twelve apostles."[5]

I want to urge that the Leucian *Acts of John* embodies this apologetical supplantation of Paul with John, though the result will still be somewhat far from the eventual solidification of orthodoxy. The Lukan Acts of the Apostles presupposes this and attempts to substitute for it a rehabilitated Paulinism, as it does elsewhere over other issues. It is interesting that Acts turns Paul into a Torah-observant disciple among Petrine, or Jamesian, Christians, which sweetens the scent of Paul's memory at the same time it undercuts his message and makes him somewhat irrelevant.

Brand X

In John 3-4 Jesus is depicted baptizing recruits, or rather having his disciples baptize them, in friendly (?) competition with John the Baptist. It is generally acknowledged that we have here a symbolic comparison of early Christian baptism with its outmoded but still-offered prototype, the baptism of John and his ongoing sect.

The intent was, apparently, to appeal to John's followers to abandon their sinking ship and jump into the Christian lifeboat, in essence, to ask the question, "Don't you want to go with a winner?" Jesus did not actually baptize, nor did he oversee such activity in his own movement. The evangelist has retrojected church baptism from a later generation into the time of Jesus to place the figureheads of both sects on stage side by side. Luke has done the same thing in Acts 19:1-7, where Paul encounters some curiously reticent disciples of *someone*, but they won't say of whom, and Paul must play Twenty Questions to find out. The artificiality of the scene is clear. If we picture it happening in real life, it looks contrived: "You look like religious fellows! Er, just what religion do you follow?" Plus, how can they have been disciples of John and not known of the existence of the Holy Spirit? The very Spirit who was, according to Luke's own account of John's preaching, to refresh the baptized with his blessing (Luke 3:16)!

As we now read the passage, we can tell that the contrast is between the superannuated John the Baptist movement, represented by "about twelve men in all," and Catholic Christianity on the other. This represents a double obfuscation, however, since the "John" here in Ephesus must have originally referred to John bar-Zebedee, rather than John the Baptist. The number of disciples whose baptisms lag behind Paul's must represent the twelve apostles, including John, son of Zebedee. We are seeing an anachronistic contest between Ephesian apostle traditions: Paul versus John the apostle, the two fighting over the claim of priority. The story almost allows the claim of Johannine priority by having the twelve disciples already baptized when Paul gets there. However, it then yanks away the prayer rug from under John's knees by reducing the Ephesian disciples to spiritless pre-Christianity! The point could not be made unless John, son of Zebedee, were made into John the Baptist, wink, wink.

In Acts 20:29-30, we have Luke's acknowledgment that Ephesus had undergone a post-Pauline lapse into heresy and that this should not be blamed on Paul, whose warning, if heeded, could have averted the danger. In Acts 19:1-7, the beginning of the story of Paul's ministry in Ephesus, Luke spoofs and rejects the attempt to replace Paul with John as apostolic founder of the Ephesian church. Let us now see whether the rest of Acts 19 follows the same trajectory. Do the rest of the Pauline Ephesian episodes share a retrospective viewpoint? Are they more concerned with the legacy and good name of Paul and his place in history, and not simply with Paul himself? This may seem an odd and artificial distinction to draw, but I believe scrutiny of the stories will justify it.

The name of Paul

I will reserve Acts 19:8-10 until the consideration of the Demetrius episode (19:23-41), which it seems to anticipate and introduce, albeit at long distance. Verses 11-12 are traditionally, and correctly, read as attesting Paul's divine power as a human dynamo and as a warrant for relic-mongering, which Catholics and Oral Roberts can see but mainstream Protestants cannot. Much like the fans who ripped the clothes off Elvis, Ephesian admirers grabbed any work apron from Paul that was not tightly knotted around him, his *loincloths*, as Hugh J. Schonfield translates it, as well as his used handkerchiefs. They carried these to the infirm and demon-possessed, and the victims' maladies fled them. Similar thaumaturgy is predicated for people who stepped within Peter's shadow (Acts 5:15) or touched Jesus's prayer shawl (Mark 5:27-29).

What has not been equally evident to many readers is the symbolic device such stories share with other remote healings recounted in Mark 7:24-30, Matthew 15:21-18, and elsewhere.[6] In each of these, the point is to retroactively authorize the gentile mission by having Jesus dispense salvation and healing to those of the next generation (a daughter and a *pais*, a child or servant) and at a distance in space, standing for Asia Minor and Europe. In just the same way, the point in Ephesians 19:11-12 is to posit a continuing force of gospel healing in the last days, stemming from Paul's earlier activity in Ephesus. That is the precise logic of relics, whether Luke had them in mind or not—and he might have, no matter how distasteful we may find it. Shake the hand that shook the hand.

In Acts 19:13-17, Luke decides he doesn't quite agree with the lone wolf exorcist pericope from Mark 9:38 and Luke 9:49-50, where Jesus welcomed the efforts of an exorcist using his name but unaffiliated with him:

> And some of the itinerant Jewish exorcists also tried their hand at uttering the name of Jesus over those having evil spirits, saying, "I command you by the Jesus whom Paul preaches!" And there were seven men who billed themselves as sons of a certain Sceva, a Jewish high priest, who were doing this. And they came to see a demonized man and commenced invoking the name, saying, "We command you by Jesus whom Paul preaches, to come out!" And replying, the evil spirit said to them, "Jesus, I know, and I have heard of Paul, but who are you?" And the man in whom the evil spirit lurked leaped on the men and overpowered both, so that they barely managed to escape, naked and wounded, from that house.

In Mark and Luke, successful independent exorcists received Jesus's endorsement: "Whoever is not against us is for us." Here we have a pair of Jewish exorcists who appear to be based on Jannes and Jambres, who withstood Moses (2 Timothy 3:8).[7] As Schonfield surmises, there is confusion over the word *sheva*, which means seven, and *Sceva*, a proper name, the demoniac being based on the Gerasene demoniac in Mark and Luke.[8] The point of the tale is that no one but the hero himself can successfully accomplish the feat in question. It is not sufficient to simply invoke the hero's authority. Gehazi cannot raise the son of the Shunnamite, even using Elisha's wand: only Elisha himself can (cf. 2 Kings 4:31). In the same

way, no one can exorcise the deaf-mute epileptic in Mark 9—not
Judas, Andrew, Thomas, Bartholomew, Simon Zelotes, Matthew,
Lebbaeus, James of Alphaeus, or Philip (9:17-18). Only Jesus. Thus
we might expect to see Paul come on stage to succeed where the
pair of *fakirs* failed—but he doesn't! When the conventions of the
form are thus conspicuously violated, some point is surely being
made, as when Mark cuts off the customary acclamation of the
crowd after Jesus heals the daughter of Jairus in Mark 5, reinforcing
the messianic secret (v. 43). The point in this case is that Paul is
not present and we are dealing with the legacy of Paul—the proper
and improper use of it by those who, in subsequent generations,
would invoke his name (cf. Matthew 7:22-23).

Chock full o' gods

The New Testament book of Acts allows Paul two years and
three months to preach in Ephesus (19:8, 10), sufficient time, the
author reckons, for Christianity to permeate Asia Minor. This is
a source of anxiety for Demetrius, president of the idol mongers
local. He sees his profits and those of his colleagues rapidly vanish-
ing because of the wildfire success of Paul's gospel. Before long, no
one will want chintzy replicas of Artemis's temple anymore, which
is historically as likely as Peter managing to convert and baptize
three thousand people in a single day (Acts 2:41). It is as difficult
to take seriously this picture painted for us of the success of Christianity as it is to accept the spurious (actually Christian) epistle of
Pliny the Younger (Book 10, no. 96), who claims the meat markets
were closing up because so many pagans had converted to Christianity that no one was buying beef for sacrifices anymore! That the
author of Acts is himself aware of the anachronism is evident from
Demetrius's boast (27) that "all Asia [Minor] and the whole inhabited earth worship" Artemis. That being the case, what was the
problem? Who's abandoning Artemis?

Clearly, Luke took the long view and imported into what purported to be a story set in Paul's own day a narrative that could only have happened decades later. If this were not already clear enough, consider Paul's absence from the story's action. A riot is brewing and *Paul's colleagues* are being manhandled by the mob, but Paul himself cannot be permitted on to show his face. Here is a good example of Martin Noth's redundancy principle: Gaius and Aristarchus are suffering for the gospel while Paul waits in the wings and never emerges. Originally the two colleagues of Paul, actually *successors* of Paul in Ephesus, were the real stars of the show. An attempt was made to replace them redactionally, but just barely.[9]

In sum, Paul is hardly even present in Acts 19. Rather, he is shown to have been powerful in spreading the gospel in times past. His legacy consists of his name, his colleagues, his relics, and according to Acts 20:20 his teachings. The Book of Acts tries to stymie attempts to replace Paul with John as the patron saint and founder of the Ephesian church. Rather than replace Paul, the favorite of heretics, Luke seeks to rehabilitate him. Why? Because Luke has not given up on the various Marcionite, Gnostic, Encratite, or other sectarians who consider Paul their founder. Luke wants to reconcile them with the nascent Catholic Church. So he cannot simply drop Paul and replace him with John as others, content to jettison Paul along with his "heretical" followers, have been trying to do.

In a glass darkly

In the *Acts of John* 26-29, there is a scene in which Lycomedes commissions a painter to render a portrait of John, and when the apostle is startled at the sight of his own image, Lycomedes fetches a mirror. At that point, the disciple learns that John has never seen his reflection in a mirror before! Let this serve as an allegory of reading for the *Acts of John* itself, which presents a set of Johannine wonders that recalls those of Paul generally and in Acts 19 so specifically that we might call John and Paul mirror images of one another. Like John, we may never have noticed the likeness before. And it is up to us to judge which is the original face, which is the reflection.

Let us review Paul's exploits in Acts 19, comparing them with their Johannine counterparts. First, of course, both Paul and John spend considerable time ministering in Ephesus, gathering converts and followers, and as Demetrius foresaw the eclipse of his religion by Christianity, so did John, but as a *fait accompli*. He thanks God that "You have abrogated every form of worship through conversion to you. In your name every idol, every demon, and every unclean spirit is banished" (*Acts John*, 41).

The two apostles both have a showdown with worshippers of Artemis, only unlike Paul, John is on the scene like Elijah confronting the prophets of Baal. John causes the altar of the goddess to break into pieces, seven of the divine images to fall, and half the temple structure to collapse (42)! Again, he accepts the challenge of the chief priest Artemidorus to drink poison under the protection of Christ and survives it.[10] Paul is able to heal Ephesians at a distance (Acts 19:11-12), but John's disciples raise people from the dead (19-24, 47). If Paul heals many Ephesians at a distance (Acts 19:11-12), John personally raises a good number from death itself, besides lesser healings. He does have disciples handle a couple of the resurrections second-hand. Lycomedes, an Ephesian commander who recalls both the Q centurion (Matt. 8:5; Luke 7:1-10) and Cornelius (Acts 10:1-8), sends for John, who raises his wife Cleopatra from the dead but not before Lycomedes himself has prematurely succumbed to grief. Then John has Cleopatra resurrect her husband (19-24)! A relative of a priest of Artemis who died in the temple collapse brings the corpse to John, but John has the man, a new believer, perform the resurrection himself (47). Here is our historical distancing device: in their miracles, the successors of John continue his own ministry.

The Ephesians seek bits of Paul's clothing, hoping his charisma will rub off (Acts 19:11-12), and likewise in the *Acts of John*: "After this we came to Ephesus. And when the brethren who lived there had learned that John had returned after this long time, they met in the house of Andronicus, where he was also staying, grasped his feet, put his hands to their faces, and kissed them because they had touched his clothes" (62).

We have seen that Paul's name and authority are known to a demoniac who would have yielded had Paul himself confronted him instead of his would-be imitators. In Smyrna (56-57), John does actually cast out demons from a pair of brothers, sons of Antipatros (these brothers are victims, not rival exorcists as in Acts 19), but in Ephesus, we hear only that demons sensed John's approach and "confessed to Verus the deacon as to the coming of John ... 'Many will come to us in the last times to turn us out of our vessels,'" that is, our possessed human bodies (*Epistle of Titus*, quoting a lost portion of the *Acts of John*). Like Paul, John's apostolic reputation among demons precedes him.[11]

The *Acts of John* has tales much taller than the canonical Acts, which I take to imply that they are "improved" copies of the Pauline tales preserved in Luke's Acts. Both sets of stories employ similar historical distancing devices, though Acts 19 uses this technique more consistently than the *Acts of John*, where John is actually on stage, which is itself a way to strengthen the Johannine versions. I am not suggesting Leucius (the ostensible author of the *Acts of John*) knew Luke's Acts. He may have but known the traditional miracle stories that Luke used. Again, he very likely used inflated Johannine stories he himself did not create but which had already been based on the Pauline episodes.

When Luke compiled Acts, he gathered what Paul Achtemeier called parallel "miracle catenae"[12] ascribed to both Peter and Paul. That similar deeds should have been interchangeably attributed to more than one rival hero is natural, and we see it in stories shared between Jesus, Pythagoras, and Apollonius. Luke paralleled the two sets of deeds in Acts so followers of each apostle would realize that the other apostle, attested by his works, was just as valid. My guess is that Luke also found ready-to-hand parallel sets of miracle traditions featuring Paul and John at Ephesus (the latter, copying and inflating the former and surviving in the *Acts of John*). But this time his strategy was different. He knew that to posit a Johannine pioneer apostolate in Ephesus would exclude the comparable but competing (and older) tradition of the Pauline mission there. Paul and Peter did not overlap in this way, so their miracle-catenae could be placed side by side. But Luke had to choose between Pauline and Johannine Ephesian traditions, and he chose Paul, the only way not to alienate the Pauline faction in Ephesus. Since the Johannine version was a fictive imposition, like making Mark the founder of the Alexandrian church, there were no specifically "Johannine" Christians in Ephesus. It wasn't an indigenous tradition. There were only Paulinist heretics and early Catholics. And there was an alternate way of mollifying the Catholics in the Lukan fold: remaking Paul into a Catholic Christian like them instead of the prototype of Ephesian heresy as history had made him.

In the chapters that follow, we are going to see instance after instance of the retrospective struggle over the Pauline legacy, the contest for various churches' allegiance to Paul's name and successors or the alien action of ecclesiastical spheres of influence. The clear implication of debates over Paul's authority and proper scope of influence in epistles written after his death is that the issue did not die with him. Traditions clash, too. Successors mount turf wars, and we will see them again and again in the Pauline letters.

NOTES

[1]Walter Bauer, *Orthodoxy and Heresy in Earliest Christianity*, ed. Robert A. Kraft, trans. Gerhard Krodel (Philadelphia: Fortress Press, 1971).

[2]Bernard Lewis, *History: Remembered, Recovered, Invented* (Princeton: Princeton University Press, 1975).

[3]Bauer, *Orthodoxy and Heresy*, 82-83.

[4]Ibid., 83-84.

[5]Ibid., 233.

[6]Matt. 15:21-28; Mark 7:24-30; cf. Matt. 8:5; Luke 7:1-10.

[7]Luke wrote at least 2 Timothy and Titus, in my opinion. See Jerome D. Quinn, "The Last Volume of Luke: The Relation of Luke to the Pastoral Epistles," in *Perspectives on Luke-Acts*, ed. Charles L. Talbert (Danville, VA: Association of Baptist Professors of Religion, 1978), 62-67, for Lukan authorship of the Pastorals.

[8]Mark 5:1-20; Luke 8:26-37; Hugh J. Schonfield, trans., *The Authentic New Testament* (New York: New American Library, 1958), 228. See also Dennis R. MacDonald, *The Homeric Epics and the Gospel of Mark* (New Haven: Yale University Press, 2000), 67-74.

[9]Martin Noth, *A History of Pentateuchal Traditions*, trans., Bernhard W. Anderson (Englewood Cliffs, NJ: Prentice-Hall, 1972), 175-88. Noth shows how the sidelining of Moses and Aaron on the bench while the Israelite elders are petitioning Pharaoh in Exodus 5:20 indicates that Moses and Aaron are late additions to all these stories, but have, in most of the stories, supplanted the original protagonists at center stage.

[10]This comes from the Latin work, *Virtutes Iohannis*, presumably once part of the *Acts of John*, which survives in Latin and Greek fragments.

[11]John K. Elliott, ed. and trans., *The Apocryphal New Testament* (New York: Oxford University Press, 1993), 346. All quotations from the *Acts of John* are from Elliott's translation. The anecdote about the demons turning tail and running comes from the apocryphal *Epistle of Titus*, quoting a lost portion of the *Acts of John*.

[12]Paul J. Achtemeier, "Toward the Isolation of Pre-Markan Miracle Catenae," *Journal of Biblical Literature* 89 (Sept. 1970), 265-91; "The Origin and Function of the Pre-Markan Miracle Catenae," *Journal of Biblical Literature* 91 (June 1972), 198-221.

7.
The Secret of Simon Magus

Simon and Samaria

Simon appears on the scene as an already notorious figure in a number of second-century documents, including the Acts of the Apostles, the writings of Justin Martyr, and the Clementine *Homilies* and *Recognitions*. Later heresiologists make him the father of the so-called Gnostic heresy. Simon is depicted as being a Samaritan, meaning that his ancestors came from the northern Hebrew kingdom of Israel, the capital city of which was Samaria. Following the death of the tyrant Solomon, the northern tribes seceded from the Davidic confederation, leaving Judah in the south with Jerusalem, on the border, as its capital. The people of Israel grew tired of the dynasty of David and Solomon (1 Kings 12) and forever after had little use for the traditions of Judah. Their form of the Yahwist religion evolved parallel to the Judaism of the south, which was created by Ezra and the Pharisees and later rabbis.

Both the Samaritans and the Jews condemned each other as heretics. The Hasmonean kings, having won a century's worth of freedom from the Seleucid Empire of Antiochus IV Epiphanes, turned inward, converting the Galilee of the gentiles to Judaism at sword-point and bulldozing the Samaritan temple atop Mt. Gerizim. Jews claimed that after Israel had been absorbed by the Assyrian Empire in the seventh century BCE, the conquerors shipped in foreign colonists who intermarried with the Israelites, also mixing up their polytheistic religion with the local Yahweh worship. This provided an excuse to reject Samaritans as non-Jews, the same way the Orthodox rabbis in modern Israel deny that anyone belonging to the synagogues of Reform Judaism are real Jews. There was probably nothing to this cavil.[1] It is history written in hindsight, glossing over the fact that both Israel and Judah were predominantly polytheistic in the seventh century. Hebrew monotheism was a late development that appeared for the first time with Jeremiah and Second Isaiah in the sixth and fifth centuries BCE and remained a minority view for a long time thereafter.[2] Samaritan polytheism was insignificant. What is important is that the feuding sister faiths both eventually became genuinely monotheistic, probably around the same time in the late first century CE, leaving some isolated holdouts for that old-time, polytheistic religion.

How did Samaritans differ from emerging Judaism? One of the divergent points of belief had to do with the expected résumé of the coming deliverer. Many Jews, but not all, expected a king or messiah (royal "anointed one") to continue David's dynasty,[3] but no Samaritan did. They had repudiated the house of David, so they could not expect its resumption. No, but they awaited the Taheb, a prophet like Moses and "restorer" (see John 4:25), as predicted in Deuteronomy 18:15. In later centuries, this expectation would mutate into the hope for a second advent of the original Moses himself.[4] The two faiths also differed on the content of the canon. The Jewish list of approved writings eventually grew into the same number of books as the Protestant Old Testament. The Catholic and Orthodox Old Testaments are longer and reflect the contents of the Septuagint, the Greek translation of Jewish scriptures used by Hellenized Jews outside of Palestine. The Samaritans, on the other hand, accepted only the Pentateuch, the so-called books of Moses consisting of Genesis, Exodus, Leviticus, Numbers, and Deuteronomy. Joshua was almost as important to them, and some had a different book with the same title. Once you got beyond Joshua, most everything in the Old Testament stemmed in some way from the royal court and the temple hierarchy of Jerusalem— the southern stuff that was of no interest to Samaritans up north. The Samaritan sect still exists as a tiny group of a few hundred. To modern Israel, the Samaritans are a cherished living fossil of biblical ancestry. It took a long time, admittedly, but the old hatchet is buried deep underground.

The New Testament mentions the Samaritans in a few places, accounting for why most of us have heard of them. Matthew 10:5 warns missionaries not to set foot on Samaritan territory. Luke, on the other hand, has the splendid parable of the Good Samaritan (10:29-37), the positive portrayal that single-handedly made *Samaritan* synonymous with someone who goes out of his way for someone else. Luke adds the episode of the Grateful Samaritan (17:11-19) about a leper who returns to thank Jesus for curing him. John the Evangelist lampoons the childish spite that separated Jews and Samaritans so that they considered each other's dinnerware to be ritually unclean (4:7-9, 20-24).

The sequel to Luke's Gospel, the Acts of the Apostles, has Philip, one of the Seven who led the Hellenistic Christians, preach in Samaria and convert the whole capital city to faith in Jesus (Acts 8:5-8ff). This is where Simon Magus comes in. Luke, the narrator of Acts, says that when Philip came to town, he found a revival of another sort already in progress. The whole place was captivated by a magician who claimed to be the Great Power, or Godhead, in the flesh. Simon validated this by producing astonishing miracles (Acts 8:9-11). Then Philip arrived, according to Luke; but Luke digresses from the legend preserved in other Christian sources and claims the whole Samaritan populace was swayed by Philip to become Christian, including Simon!

The Great Power and the First Thought

Various heresiologists tell us that Simon was like Travis Bickle in the movie *Taxi Driver* and had rescued a woman from a brothel and subsequently traveled with her. Named Helen, she was his eternal soul mate, having existed in the divine pleroma, the heavenly world of light and spirit, as the *Ennoia* or *Epinoia*, the First Thought. This was pretty much the same idea as the personified Lady Wisdom in Proverbs 8, Sirach 1, and Wisdom of Solomon 7, or the Logos of Philo, but female. As such, she and the Great Power formed a syzygy, or a yoked pair, reminiscent of the coupling of Shiva and his *shakti*, Kali, in Tantric mysticism. She had been lost in the swamp of the world of matter, the sinister creation of the pernicious archons, or rulers, since the beginning, and it was only her spiritual wisdom which, like Spock's kidnapped brain in the subterranean world of miniskirted Amazons on *Star Trek*,[5] kept the world running. It was to rescue her that the Great Power had condescended to enter the dark world of matter.

This salvation myth, quite typical of Gnosticism in general, implied that those who followed Simon and learned his secret knowledge (*gnosis*) would be saved after death. You see, his girlfriend's soul was the incarnation of the divine Light of Wisdom that had been shattered into a million sparks and scattered throughout the material world. One supposes that the ex-harlot Helen embodied the greatest single concentration of this wisdom. But many others possessed smaller shares of that light. And such a one would snap out of one's amnesia if one had ears to hear Simon's *gnosis*. The whole Gnostic schema, including the Simonian heresy, was strikingly parallel to the Kabbalah of Isaac Luria[6] in sixteenth-century Galilee. The pious Gnostics perceived in themselves a latent spark of divine glory and sought to liberate it from reincarnation by means of meditative exercises and asceticism, including the denial of fleshly pleasures. A few took the left-handed path and sought libertine antinomianism in keeping with Aleister Crowley's philosophy:

"Do as thou wilt shall be the whole of the law."[7] If the flesh was unimportant, then you could go either way and still find enlightenment. The crucial thing was to attain mental and spiritual independence from worldly laws and religion since they were the creations of evil archons, the unseen rulers of the world, one of whom was the Jehovah (Yahweh) of the Old Testament.

According to the Church Fathers, Simon Magus assumed the title of the Standing One, the divine entity who is reborn continually throughout the history of the world, and claimed he had recently appeared in Judea in the form of the Son of God, implicitly claiming to be the reincarnation of Jesus of Nazareth. The great Theosophist scholar George Mead, in his book on Simon, understood this claim to imply that Simon was appropriating the esoteric doctrines of Jesus, not that he was inhabited by the same spirit.[8] Since Acts has Simon Peter confronting Simon Magus (one has to pay attention to keep the names straight), this would make the magician a contemporary of Jesus. It was therefore similar to Elisha, a younger contemporary of Elijah, bearing the same spirit as his master (2 Kings 2:15). However, there remains another possibility, as we will see later on.

Luke did not adequately conceal the traces of the story he was borrowing and rewriting. The original story must have had Philip and Simon Magus engaging in a miracle contest. Luke omitted this battle because his sympathies were with Peter, so he deemed it unseemly for Philip to be depicted as the superhero. This left Luke with no account of why Simon suddenly retired from the field and allowed Philip to co-opt his whole movement without so much as a challenge. Luke presents it as a vaudeville act, with Simon as the opening number and Philip the main event on an evening's billing. Equally artificial is the claim that Philip baptized everyone but withheld the Holy Spirit until Simon Peter could dramatically arrive from Jerusalem and make it official (Acts 8:14-17). Simon Magus himself, cowed and repentant, is reduced to a Christian convert who sheepishly asks Peter to teach him, for money, the trick to making people speak in tongues and prophesy (Acts 8:18-19). Peter rebukes him, as translated by J. B. Phillips, saying: "To hell with you and your money!" Simon retreats with his arrow-pointed devil's tail between his legs.

It is evident that in Luke's source, the story would have originally featured Philip, not Simon Peter, and that after a duel of miracles, Simon Magus would have been forced to withdraw from Samaria, precisely as Simon Peter does in the post-Lukan Clementine writings, the *Acts of Peter*, and elsewhere. Again, what Luke did when he rewrote the story was to steal thunder from Philip and transfer it to Peter, a more important ecclesiastical symbol in those days, the same as someone did when he took the feat of slaying Goliath from the lesser-known hero Elhanan of Bethlehem (2 Sam. 21) and credited David instead (1 Sam. 17). Subsequent post-Lukan writers kept the on-stage miracle contest, retaining Peter as a rival magician and adding a rematch in Rome, where Simon Magus traveled to steal Peter's converts from him. Simon Magus is successful until Simon Peter challenges him to another demonstration of power, reminiscent of the contest between Elijah and the priests of Baal Melkarth in 1 Kings 18. Peter wins, regaining all of his gullible and fickle converts, when Simon Magus, having rigged up a special effects trick, seems to fly but soon crashes to the ground. Legend subsequently transferred this motif (pride going before a literal fall) to the folklore figures of the Antichrist and Dr. Faustus. The legends seem to reflect the real competition between competing sects of Simonians and Christians, who were represented in both Samaria and Rome. Justin Martyr, himself a Samaritan convert to Christianity and visitor to Rome, tells us that in his day Simonianism had swept all Samaria into its fold, while Rome had notable Simonian congregations.

An interesting question surrounding Simon Magus is why the Great Power would repeatedly incarnate himself? After all, in Gnosticism the soul returns to another incarnation if the person is ignorant of his or her true origin and destiny. When one becomes enlightened, the cycle of reincarnation is broken and the spirit sloughs off the defiling flesh in order to enter the pleroma. But Simon certainly did not share that ignorance. Voluntarily, in the manner of the Bodhisattvas of Mahayana Buddhism, he voluntarily undertook countless births in the world to seek out and to save that which was lost: Helen, the *Ennoia*, the symbol of the soul of the Elect Ones. It is out of compassion that the Standing One repeatedly descends into the flesh to show the world the true path. Helen is the bait.

Luke seems to know all this, as Gerd Lüdemann[9] points out, since he uses a special, rare Greek word in Peter's rebuke of the magus: "Pray to the Lord that this thought (*epinoia*) may be forgiven you" (Acts 8:22). It looks to be a spoof on the beliefs of the Simonians. John the Evangelist does the same thing when he depicts a Samaritan woman as having had five husbands and a live-in boyfriend (4:16-18). This is to say the Simonian Helen had appeared in some five previous incarnations and Simon was living openly with her in sin. If the insinuation was that Helen was still a whore, it was a common polemical vilification that the Church Fathers later stooped to when they portrayed Mary Magdalene as a demoniac and prostitute.[10]

Speaking of vilification, we may pause to note that the appellation *magus*, meaning *magician*, is another example. Anthropologists have shown that magic is not qualitatively different from what people call religious miracles. The difference is one of evaluation. My miracle is your magic, and vice versa.[11] "It is by Beelzebul the prince of devils that he casts out demons," Mark depicts Jesus's critics as having charged (Mark 3:33). To call Simon a magician was to discount his reputation for miracles without actually denying, as modern skeptics would do, that he had really performed them.[12] In the same way, Jesus is depicted as a magical trickster in the various *Toledoth Jeschu* Gospels produced by Jewish anti-Christians. Theudas, a messianic revolutionary king in the 40s CE, predicted he would part the Jordan River as Joshua had done. This would, of course, be a miracle. His opponents called him Theudas the Magician, as Josephus attests. Philostratus, in his *Life of Apollonius of Tyana*, dispels popular skepticism about whether Apollonius was a demigod or a charlatan.

If *magician* was an undercutting term of reproach, so was the epithet *Samaritan*, which had become synonymous with *heretic*. John has the opponents of Jesus insult him with the question, "Are we not justified in saying you are a Samaritan and that you have a demon?" (8:48). The implication is that the demon at his disposal was able to perform magic tricks. We sometimes mistake ancient metaphors for biographical data. That Simon was called a Samaritan might have implied that he was a heretic. What was his heresy? As we have already seen, he claimed to be the embodied Great Power or son of the Great Power. Michael D. Goulder accepts this and even argues that Christians borrowed from Simonianism the whole notion of God becoming incarnate.[13] One source, the Clementine writings, has Simon preaching that there are two Gods but that the world was created by angels. Though in some ways reminiscent of Gnosticism, there were features of Simonianism that seem to have more closely paralleled Marcionism.

Man of lawlessness

Marcion of Pontus, in today's northern Turkey, started a church in the early- to mid-second century. It was a Christian denomination, but Marcion held that the twelve apostles had misunderstood their master's intentions. It is a view plainly shared by the Gospel of Mark. Marcion taught that the twelve apostles mixed up Judaism with the new tenets of Christianity, as if trying to put new wine into worn-out wineskins. While Marcion was not an anti-Semite, and he respected Judaism as a separate faith, he believed Jesus was the son of a higher God than Jehovah. The Jewish God had created the material world and commanded the Mosaic Law. But Jesus came to reveal a different, more loving deity, the Father of Jesus, who punishes no one but only exercises love. The Father was willing to adopt the creations of the lesser God as his own children.

Marcion believed that Paul taught what Jesus intended—the birth of a new religion separate from Judaism. Thus, Christians should give the Old Testament back to the Jews and stop pretending it predicted Jesus. To replace this Jewish scripture, he suggested the adoption of the epistles of Paul and what he called "the gospel," which might have implied an earlier, shorter form of our Gospel of Luke, an *Apostolicon* ("book of an apostle") as a new Christian scripture. Though later Catholic writers accused Marcion of having censored and edited these New Testament books, it looks like they were holding up the mirror to their own underhanded shenanigans. Studies by John Knox and others[14] make it seem more likely that Marcion was not only the first to collect the Pauline epistles but also the first to propose the idea of a Christian testament. The Catholic bishops, alarmed at the success of Marcion's sputnik, hastened to follow suit, only they added several more books and sanitized Marcion's documents by padding them out with orthodox interpolations. The eventual result was today's familiar New Testament.

Marcion was Christianity's first great Paulinist.[15] He was followed by Valentinian and Basilidean Gnostics who wrote commentaries on Paul's epistles. So great was their interest, early Catholic writer Tertullian called Paul "the apostle of Marcion and the apostle of the heretics." This may have been quite true, and in a very literal sense. In fact, the great epistolarian was partly a creation of Gnostics and Marcionites. Willem Christiaan van Manen argued that Galatians was originally drafted by Marcion himself, writing pseudonymously under Paul's name. R. Joseph Hoffmann[16] argued cogently that Ephesians began as a Marcionite epistle to the Laodiceans. Of course, both texts were later padded and sanitized by the Catholics for their own use. The same was likely true for the other Pauline epistles, according to the Dutch Radical critics,[17] represented today by Hermann Detering,[18] Darrell J. Doughty,[19] and myself, among others. If there was a historical apostle Paul, which seems likely enough, his figure has retreated behind the pseudepigraphical epistles attributed to him by various Marcionite and Gnostic members of the Pauline School.

A number of documents—including the pseudonymous *Apocalypse of Paul* (not the one discovered at Nag Hammadi), *Acts of Paul,* canonical Acts of the Apostles, *Acts of Xanthippe and Polyxena,* and *Acts of Peter and Paul*—depict Paul as a missionary apostle but are unaware that he penned any letters or preached any distinctive doctrines. According to the theories of Ferdinand Christian Baur, Walter Bauer, and others, this was the result of an attempt to co-opt and catholicize the figure of Paul by ignoring the epistles (see chapter four of the present work) as well as the distinctive theology associated with his name. There seem to have been three or more attempts to replace the dangerously heretical-sounding epistles with safe substitutes. These would be the apocryphal *Third Corinthians* (again, see chapter four), the Pastorals (1 and 2 Timothy, Titus), and the Latin *Epistle to the Laodiceans.* As Winsome Munro demonstrates,[20] even the epistles we read today have suffered an extensive series of domesticating, catholicizing interpolations.

With all this redaction of the epistles, one feature of the Paulinist theology that seeps through is the very foundation stone of Protestantism, albeit distorted through the lens of Martin Luther's introspective psychologizing.[21] It is the nullification of the Jewish Torah. Paul says it has been made superfluous by faith in Christ, so gentile converts need not trouble themselves with adopting Jewish customs. This feature of Paul, as remembered by Catholics, Marcionites, and Gnostics alike, was enough to disqualify Paul as an apostle in the eyes of yet other ancient Jesus sectarians, the Nasoreans, Ebionites, and Elchasites—the so-called Jewish Christians. These devotees of the Torah wrote off Paul as a false apostle and an anti-Christ. The debates are reflected in just about all the Pauline literature of the early church, whether pro or con. And this brings us right back to the figure of Simon Magus. For, as F. C. Baur argued,[22] Simon Magus appears to have been a kind of satirical vilification of Paul.

Paul's "monstrous double"

The evidence for Paul's double comes from the canonical Acts of the Apostles and the Clementine writings. Acts was penned in the mid-second century, while the fourth-century Clementines preserve important textual sources from the second century. The *Homilies* and *Recognitions* by pseudo-Clement are two recensions of a novel starring Simon Peter, fictively narrated by the bishop of Rome. The actual author is unknown. The Clementine narratives feature confrontations between Simon Peter and his archrival, Simon Magus, and were probably borrowed from the earlier *Kerygmata Petrou*, or *Preachings of Peter*, an Ebionite document. In these sections we hear Peter speaking of Simon in terms that are unmistakably reminiscent of Paul. For instance, Simon Peter dismisses Simon Magus's claim to the apostleship on grounds that seeing the risen Christ in a vision was not sufficient to qualify one to be an apostle, the real apostles having known the earthly Jesus and taught his gospel. We also read there a condemnation of the doctrine that the Torah had been superseded by the coming of Christ. These are exactly the gripes Jewish Christians had against Paul.

> When Simon [Magus] heard this, he interrupted, saying, "You say you learned accurately your master's teaching by hearing and seeing him immediately, face to face, and that it is impossible for anyone else to experience the same thing by means of dreams or visions. Let me show you the fallacy of this: When one hears something directly, he is far from sure of what was said. He must ask himself if, given his human frailties, he has not been mistaken in what he thinks he heard. By contrast, a vision carries with it its

own intuitive certainty that one is seeing the divine. Answer me that, if you can."

And [Simon] Peter said, "Everyone knows that any number of idol-worshippers, adulterers, and other sinners have seen visions and dreams that predicted the future accurately, and also that some have had visions conjured by demons. For my position is that mortal eyes can never behold the disembodied existence of the Father or of the Son, because it is veiled in unbearable light. Thus it is a sign of God's mercy, not of peevishness, that he remains invisible to fleshly humans. For, if anyone sees him, he must die. No one is capable of seeing the disembodied might of the Son or even of an angel. No, whoever has a vision ought to recognize he is the dupe of an evil demon.

"For the truth dawns of itself to any pious, natural, and pure mind. It is not gained through dreams. No, it is granted to the righteous through simple discernment. For it was in this way that the Son was revealed even to me by the Father. Hence I know the power of revelation; I myself learned it from him. For on that occasion when the Lord asked us what people called him, although I was aware that others called him something different, it arose in my heart to reply, nor do I know how I got it out, 'You are the Son of the living God.' [Matt. 16:13-16] From this you can see that it is only announcements of divine wrath that are mediated by visions and dreams, while conversation between friends happens by word of mouth, plainly and without riddles, visions and dreams, which are appropriate to converse with an enemy.

"And if our Jesus did appear to you as well, becoming known in a vision, intercepting you with anger as an enemy, then so he has addressed you only with visions and dreams and superficial revelations. But who is rendered competent to teach through a mere vision? And if you think, 'It is quite possible,' then why did our teacher bother to spend a whole year with us, who were awake and not airily dreaming? How are we to believe you even if he did appear to you? And how can he have appeared to you if your goals are the opposite of what you must have learned from him? No, if you really were visited by him for a single hour so he might teach you and you have thus become an apostle, then preach his words! Expound his teachings! Befriend his apostles and stop arguing with me, who am his closest advisor. In fact, you have hostilely opposed me [see Gal. 2:11-21], a steadfast rock, the foundation stone of the church [Matt. 16:18 versus 1 Cor. 3:11]. If you were other than an enemy [Gal. 4:16], why would you slander me and insult my preaching, undermining the acceptance of my message when I preach what I heard with my own ears from the Lord? As if I were decidedly condemned and you were approved! And when you say I am condemned, it is God you are accusing, since it is he who revealed Christ to me [Matt. 16:17b]. You are belittling him who pronounced me blessed because of the revelation vouchsafed me [Matt. 16:17a]. Look, if you really want to further the truth, then start by learning from us what we learned from him, and as a student of the truth, join us as a colleague." (*Recognitions* 17-19)

This is also where we hear Simon Magus described in theological terms curiously recalling Marcion, implying that the version of Paul that Jewish Christians rejected was fashioned by Marcionite and Gnostic Paulinist theologians.

Peter: "But if, as you say, there be some God more benignant than all, it is certain that he will not be angry with us... we have not been drawn by vain imaginations to forsake our own Father and follow him..."

Simon: "But the good God bestows salvation if he is only acknowledged; but the creator of the world demands also that the law be fulfilled."

Simon Magus sounds even more like a polemical caricature of Paul in the canonical Acts of the Apostles when he tries to bribe Simon Peter, as mentioned above. This is reminiscent of Paul's attempt to bring charitable aid to Jerusalem and the hope that Peter, James, and John would appreciate the effort and recognize him as a fellow apostle, although to no avail. The relief effort is mentioned throughout Paul's epistles, but the Book of Acts never mentions it. In Acts we read that Paul was associated with an earlier relief

fund during a famine.[23] This probably indicates that the author of
Acts knew the outcome of Paul's offer to the church in Jerusalem
and disguised the episode, transferring Paul's failure to a narrative
double, Simon Magus, who is portrayed trying to buy the apostleship outright. It looks like an invidious version of Paul's taking up
a collection and may even be an episode from Marcion's career,
inserted retrospectively into the life of his master, Paul. Marcion
journeyed to Rome with a donation for the church there and to
present his views, hoping to be made a bishop. At first they welcomed his money, but when they had considered his theology they
returned the funds and declared him a heretic. This episode, then,
would be reflected in both Paul's visit to the Jerusalem pillars and
the attempt of Simon Magus to buy the apostolic authority to dispense the Holy Spirit.

Why would the narrator choose to cloak an incident involving Paul in an episode involving someone named Simon? Perhaps
because Jewish Christians viewed Paul as the opposite of Simon
Peter, making him the anti-Simon. We have seen that calling someone a *magician* might have suggested a medicine show charlatan.
The acts of Simon Magus could be considered a satire on the claim
made by Paul that he had performed "all the signs of an apostle
... marvels, demonstrations of power."[24] There was no love lost on
Paul among the Jewish Christians. The Ebionites spread a rumor
that he was not even Jewish. He was a gentile who was infatuated
with a daughter of the high priest in Jerusalem and had gone to
some lengths to prove himself a keeper of Jewish law, although he
secretly despised it. When he was rejected by the high priest, it
set him on the war path against Judaism, creating a perverted version of a religion that would overthrow the very Torah at which, as
a gentile outsider, he had chafed. The attempt to portray Paul as a
scorned lover was not a particularly novel idea. It was used as a slur
against both Marcion and the prophet Muhammad; it is a metaphor
for the reformer who has "seduced the pure virgin of the church,"

a charge also leveled against Jewish-Christian apostles in 2 Corinthians 11.

When Justin Martyr and others make Simon Magus the father of Gnosticism, do we not see a reflection of the fact that Gnostics hailed *Paul* as the founder of their faith? Valentinus claimed he received his Gnostic teachings straight from Theodas, an original disciple of Paul. It looks to me like Paul, in order to be given a place at the Catholic table at all, had everything stripped from him, whoever he may have been, including the qualities given to him by the Marcionites and Gnostics; these qualities were consigned to a scapegoat double, the evil twin. As René Girard said, only by means of a chosen scapegoat could order be established in the face of factional strife. [25] The claim was made in *First Clement* that both Peter and Paul were delivered to the authorities for martyrdom "out of envy" on the part of each other's disciples, according to Oscar Cullmann.[26] Once the two apostles were said to have been executed, their followers closed ranks and accepted the saintly character of each other's figurehead. In order still to have someone to blame for all the strife, they created a body double on which they could heap all the opprobrium the Petrine faction had once focused on Paul himself. This scarecrow substitute was Simon Magus.

Simon Magus's double

Hermann Detering, in *The Falsified Paul,* carries F. C. Baur's hypothesis a step further to turn the theory on its head. What if Simon Magus was the historical figure, and instead of Simon being the fun-house mirror reflection, *Paul* was the fictive character? What if Paul is a theological rendering of *Simon?* It appears that there actually was a Simon Magus, about whom some information survives in Josephus's *Antiquities of the Jews.* As Acts appears to have used Josephus's chronicles more than once, it is especially interesting to see the possible borrowing in this case. Josephus depicted Simon as a pretend sorcerer from Cyprus, something of a Rasputin in the household of the Roman procurator Felix and his wife Drusilla.

> But for the marriage of Drusilla with Azizus [King of Emesa, who had become circumcised in order to marry Drusilla], it was in no long time afterward dissolved upon the following occasion: While Felix was procurator of Judea, he saw this Drusilla, and fell in love with her; for she did indeed exceed all other women in beauty; and he sent to her a person whose name was Simon [some manuscripts read: Atomus], one of his friends; a Jew he was, and by birth a Cypriot, and one who pretended to be a magician, and endeavored to persuade her to forsake her present husband, and marry him; and promised, that if she would not refuse him, he would make her a happy woman. Accordingly she acted ill, and because she was desirous to avoid her sister Bernice's envy, for she was very ill treated by her on account of her beauty, was prevailed upon to transgress the laws of her forefathers, and to marry Felix; and when he had had a son by her, he named him Agrippa. But after what manner that young man, with his wife, perished at the conflagration of the mountain Vesuvius, in the days of Titus Caesar, shall be related hereafter. (Josephus, *Antiquities of the Jews* 20.7.2, Whiston trans.)

Simon Magus is said by later writers to have come from Gitta, which is in Samaria but could have been confused with *Kittim*, the sea peoples of Cyprus. Josephus characterized the Samaritans in one instance as "Sidonians [Phoenicians] in Shechem" (12.4.5), which pretty much closes the gap. And, remember, Gitta was originally the Philistine city called Gath, the home town of Goliath.[27] There is a closer link still, one that connects with the episode of Saul and Barnabas preaching the gospel in Cyprus. Here the author of Acts created the episode of Paul squaring off against Elymas the sorcerer (13:8 ff), much like Peter's contest with Simon Magus. So Elymas looks like a reworking of Simon Magus.[28]

In fact, Acts 13 looks like a clumsy attempt to untangle Paul from someone closer to Simon, a Catholicizing attempt to exorcize all that was later perceived as unorthodox in Paul in order to sanitize him for popular consumption. Our author may have known quite well that the two characters, Simon and Saul, were related, as one can see from the fact that in a repeat of Saul's conversion story, Elymas goes blind after hindering the gospel. As for the missionary hero Saul, he is transformed into Paul, a Roman citizen with connections. Contrary to popular devotional twaddle, there is nothing here at all about Saul having proved himself worthy of henceforth being known as Paul. Pious readers tend to jump the gun and read the story as a match for Genesis 17, where Abram is renamed Abraham, and Genesis 32, where Jacob is renamed Israel, not to mention, nearer at hand, Mark 3 and John 1, where Jesus gives Simon the nickname Peter. No, Acts 13:9 says simply, "But Saul, who is also Paul" and leaves it ambiguous whether Saul received a second name, Paul, to be used henceforth, or whether he, like Sergius Paul (proconsul of Cyprus), was already generally called Paul. The Saul character literally morphs into Paul before the reader's eyes in a demonstration that the author has probably created a fictional opponent for Simon Magus, Paul's alter ago.

At the same time, in a narrative game of musical chairs, Acts's author drives a wedge between Paul, the ideal orthodox hero, and Simon Magus, the hero's shadow and Saul's historical prototype. The story drops an important hint by telling us that the name Paul was secondary. I think his name may have been Simon, and when the Paul persona was spun off into a separate character, the redactor preserved the original consonant. In musical chairs, the whistle blows and the players drop into place, Saul sitting in Sergius Paul's chair and henceforth bearing his name, and Elymas, or Simon Magus, sitting in a chair he had been sharing with Saul. Sergius may be sitting in a chair that was originally engraved with the name of Felix.

Or perhaps it would be better to say that Felix is sitting in Sergius's chair to conceal the particulars of the story of Simon, Felix, and Drusilla. Josephus intimates that Simon was originally a myst-agogical guru. The scene of Paul's audience before Felix and Drusilla in Acts 24 is a doublet of his appearance before Herod Agrippa II (Marcus Julius Agrippa) and sister-wife Berenice in Acts 25-26. Drusilla was Berenice's sister. Behold how the author of Acts has rewritten Josephus here to make Drusilla her literary double. When Simon advises Drusilla to leave the newly circumcised Azizus for the foreskin-sporting Felix, we catch a note of the familiar Pauline hostility (or at least indifference) toward circumcision. But as Detering says, the rest, as we now read it, is another Lukan attempt to disguise the apostle by making Felix hope for a bribe, rather than being a confidant like Elymas was with Sergius, and having Paul preach continence instead of advising adultery, as Simon did with Drusilla.

Paul and Queen Helena

From where did Acts draw the raw material for the prophecy of Agabus forecasting famine during Claudius's reign, setting up the need for Paul's trip from Antioch to deliver famine relief funds in Jerusalem? What about the earlier tale of Philip and the Ethiopian eunuch? From our old friend Josephus. The credit for this discovery goes to Robert Eisenman.[29] It all stems, by hook and crook, from the story of Helena, Queen of Adiabene, a realm contiguous with Edessa, whose king was Agbar or Abgarus. Some texts make Abgarus Helena's husband. Helena and her son Izates converted to Judaism, though initially Izates was not circumcised because his Jewish teacher, a merchant named Ananias, told him that it was more important simply to worship God than to be circumcised. His mother similarly advised against it since his subjects might resent him for embracing such an alien custom. Soon another Jewish teacher arrived from Jerusalem, one Eleazar, and found Izates poring over the Genesis 17 passage on Abraham's covenant of circumcision. Eleazar asked him if he understood the implications of what he was reading. If he did, then why did he not see the importance of being circumcised? The prince was persuaded. Among other philanthropies, Helena and Izates sent agents to Egypt and Cyprus to buy grain during a famine under Claudius and distribute it to the poor in Jerusalem. Don't take my word for it. I beg your leave to reproduce the important Josephus passage in full so you will have the same evidence in front of you that I have.

> About this time it was that Helena, queen of Adiabene [a region of Assyria] and her son Izates, changed their course of life, and embraced the Jewish customs, and this on the occasion following: Monobazus, the king of Adiabene, who had also the name of Bazeus, fell in love with his sister Helena, and took her to be his wife, and begat her with child. But as he was in bed with her one night, he laid his hand upon his wife's belly, and fell asleep, and seemed to hear a voice, which bid him take his hand off his wife's belly, and not hurt the infant that was therein, which, by God's providence, would be safely born, and have a happy end. This voice put him into disorder; so he awaked immediately, and told the story to his wife; and when his son was born, he called him Izates. He had indeed Monobazus, his elder brother, by Helena also, as he had other sons by other wives besides. Yet did he openly place all his affections upon Izates, [as upon an] only begotten son, which was the origin of that envy which his other brethren, by the same father, bore to him; while on this account they hated him more and more, and were all under great affliction that their father should prefer Izates before them. Now although their father was very sensible of these their passions, yet did he forgive them, as not indulging those passions out of an ill disposition, but out of a desire each of them had to be beloved by their father. However, he sent Izates, with many presents, to Abennerig, the king of Charax-Spasini [at the northwest tip of the Persian Gulf], and that out of the great dread he was in about him, lest he should come to some misfortune by the hatred his brethren bore him; and he committed his son's preservation to him. Upon which Abennerig gladly received the young man, and had a great affection for him, and married him to his own daughter, whose name was Samacha:

He also bestowed a country upon him, from which he received large revenues.

But when Monobazus was grown old, and saw that he had but a little time to live, he had a mind to come to the sight of his son before he died. So he sent for him, and embraced him after the most affectionate manner, and bestowed on him the country called Carrae; it was a soil that bare amomum [cardamom] in great plenty: there are also in it the remains of that ark, wherein it is related that Noah escaped the deluge, and where [it is] still shown to such as are desirous to see [it]. Accordingly, Izates abode in that country until his father's death. But the very day that Monobazus died, Queen Helena sent for all the grandees, and governors of the kingdom, and for those that had the armies committed to their command; and when they were come, she made the following speech to them: "I believe you are not unacquainted that my husband was desirous Izates should succeed him in the government, and thought him worthy so to do. However, I wait your determination; for happy is he who receives a kingdom, not from a single person only, but from the willing suffrages of a great many." This she said, in order to try those that were invited, and to discover their sentiments. Upon the hearing of which, they first of all paid their homage to the queen, as their custom was, and then they said that they confirmed the king's determination, and would submit to it; and they rejoiced that Izates's father had preferred him before the rest of his brethren, as being agreeable to all their wishes: But that they were desirous first of all to slay his brethren and kinsmen, that so the government might come securely to Izates; because if they were once destroyed, all that fear would be over which might arise from their hatred and envy to him. Helena replied to this, that she returned them her thanks for their kindness to herself and to Izates; but desired that they would however defer the execution of this slaughter of Izates's brethren till he should be there himself, and give his approbation to it. So since these men had not prevailed with her, when they advised her to slay them, they exhorted her at least to keep them in bonds till he should come, and that for their own security; they also gave her counsel to set up someone whom she could put the greatest trust in, as a governor of the kingdom in the meantime. So queen

Helena complied with this counsel of theirs, and set up Monobazus, the eldest son, to be king, and put the diadem upon his head,
and gave him his father's ring, with its signet; as also the orna-
ment which they call Sampser, and exhorted him to administer
the affairs of the kingdom till his brother should come; who came
suddenly upon hearing that his father was dead, and succeeded
his brother Monobazus, who resigned up the government to him.

Now, during the time Izates abode at Charax-Spasini, a certain
Jewish merchant, whose name was Ananias, got among the women
that belonged to the king, and taught them to worship God according to the Jewish religion. He, moreover, by their means, became
known to Izates, and persuaded him, in like manner, to embrace
that religion; he also, at the earnest entreaty of Izates, accompanied him when he was sent for by his father to come to Adiabene;
it also happened that Helena, about the same time, was instructed
by a certain other Jew and went over to them. But when Izates had
taken the kingdom, and was come to Adiabene, and there saw his
brethren and other kinsmen in bonds, he was displeased at it; and
as he thought it an instance of impiety either to slay or imprison
them, but still thought it a hazardous thing for [him] to let them
have their liberty, with the remembrance of the injuries that had
been offered [by] them, he sent some of them and their children
for hostages to Rome, to Claudius Caesar, and sent the others to
Artabanus, the king of Parthia, with the like intentions.

And when he perceived that his mother was highly pleased
with the Jewish customs, he made haste to change, and to embrace
them entirely; and as he supposed that he could not be thoroughly
a Jew unless he were circumcised, he was ready to have it done.
But when his mother understood what he was about, she endeav-
ored to hinder him from doing it, and said to him that this thing
would bring him into danger; and that, as he was a king, he would
thereby bring himself into great odium among his subjects, when
they should understand that he was so fond of rites that were to
them strange and foreign; and that they would never bear to be
ruled over by a Jew. This it was that she said to him, and for the
present persuaded him to forbear. And when he had related what
she had said to Ananias, he confirmed what his mother had said;
and when [Ananias] had also threatened to leave him, unless he

complied with him, [Ananias] went away from [Izates], and said that he was afraid lest such an action being once made public to all, he should himself be in danger of punishment for having been the occasion of it, and having been the king's instructor in actions that were of ill reputation; and he said that [Izates] might worship God without being circumcised, even though [Izates] did resolve to follow the Jewish law entirely, which worship of God was of a superior nature to circumcision. [Ananias] added, that God would forgive [Izates], though he did not perform the operation, while it was omitted out of necessity, and for fear of his subjects. So the king at that time complied with these persuasions of Ananias. But afterwards, as he had not quite left off his desire of doing this thing, a certain other Jew that came out of Galilee, whose name was Eleazar, and who was esteemed very skillful in the learning of his country, persuaded him to do the thing; for as he entered into his palace to salute him, and found him reading the law of Moses, he said to him, "Thou dost not consider, O king! that thou unjustly breakest the principal of those laws, and art injurious to God himself; for thou oughtest not only to read them, but chiefly to practice what they enjoin thee. How long wilt thou continue uncircumcised? But if thou hast not yet read the law about circumcision, and dost not know how great impiety thou art guilty of by neglecting it, read it now." When the king had heard what [Eleazar] said, he delayed the thing no longer, but retired to another room, and sent for a surgeon, and did what he was commanded to do. He then sent for his mother, and Ananias his tutor, and informed them that he had done the thing; upon which they were presently struck with astonishment and fear, and that to a great degree, lest the thing should be openly discovered and censured, and the king should hazard the loss of his kingdom, while his subjects would not bear to be governed by a man who was so zealous in another religion; and lest they should themselves run some hazard, because they would be supposed the occasion of his so doing. But it was God himself who hindered what they feared from taking effect; for he preserved both Izates himself and his sons when they fell into many dangers, and procured their deliverance when it seemed to be impossible, and demonstrated thereby that the fruit of piety does not perish as to those that have regard to him, and fix their faith upon him only. But these events we shall relate hereafter.

But as to Helena, the king's mother, when she saw that the affairs of Izates's kingdom were in peace, and that her son was a happy man, and admired among all men, and even among foreigners, by the means of God's providence over him, she had a mind to go to the city of Jerusalem, in order to worship at that temple of God which was so very famous among all men, and to offer her thank-offerings there. So she desired her son to give her leave to go thither; upon which he gave his consent to what she desired very willingly, and made great preparations for her dismission, and gave her a great deal of money, and she went down to the city Jerusalem, her son conducting her on her journey a great way. Now her coming was of very great advantage to the people of Jerusalem; for whereas a famine did oppress them at that time, and many people died for want of what was necessary to procure food withal, queen Helena sent some of her servants to Alexandria with money to buy a great quantity of corn, and others of them to Cyprus, to bring a cargo of dried figs. And as soon as they were come back, and had brought those provisions, which was done very quickly, she distributed food to those that were in want of it, and left a most excellent memorial behind her of this benefaction, which she bestowed on our whole nation. And when her son Izates was informed of this famine, he sent great sums of money to the principal men in Jerusalem. However, what favors this queen and king conferred upon our city Jerusalem shall be further related hereafter. (2.2.1-4)

These events left their mark in the New Testament as follows. Eisenman observes, as others do, that there is no place for this famine relief visit in the Galatians 1:15-2:2 itinerary of Paul's trips to Jerusalem. If anything, it would have had to be during Paul's sojourn in Arabia (Gal. 1:17), which in the parlance of the time could have included Adiabene. The Book of Acts mentions two Antiochs, those in Pisidia and Syria, but there were others, including Edessa, as it was also called. Eisenman identifies Paul as the unnamed partner of the Jewish merchant Ananias who tells Izates he need not be circumcised. It certainly sounds like Paul! This episode seems to lie at the basis of the Antioch episode recounted in Galatians 2, wherein the "men from James," which is to say from the circumcision party, sound like Josephus's Eleazar of Galilee. They arrive in Antioch to tell Paul's converts they need to be circumcised after all, as also mentioned in Acts 15: "But some men came down from Judea and were teaching the brethren, 'Unless you are circumcised according to the custom of Moses, you cannot be saved.'"

Finally, Paul was one of the delegates who brought famine relief to Jerusalem from Antioch in Acts 11:27. Helena, too, Josephus tells us, made a pilgrimage to Jerusalem from Antioch and caused relief supplies to be sent there. Eisenman deduces that the two relief missions are one and the same.[30] This makes Paul an advisor to Queen Helena. While Eisenman does not identify Saul with Simon Magus, I do, and from that perspective this association of Paul with Queen Helena makes a lot of sense, for it is identical to the implied relationship Simon had with Drusilla and Felix (likewise Elymas with Sergius Paul), a servant and mystagogue among their retinue, no doubt a counselor and advisor. And as I have already noted, Simon Magus is paired in the ancient sources with one Helen (from Tyre) who had once reigned as Queen of Troy. Here they are together again: Simon Magus and Queen Helen, this time, of Adiabene.

We pick up the theme of the Helena story again in Acts 8, only this time with Philip substituting for Eleazar. Philip accosts the financial officer of a foreign queen traveling from Jerusalem through Egypt by way of Gaza. This is, of course, the story of the Ethiopian eunuch, and this time Acts transforms Helena into a New Testament Queen of Sheba, having come to Jerusalem to hear the wisdom of Solomon. There is also a pun on the root *saba*, denoting baptism, a la the Essenes, Sampsaeans, Sabeans, Masbutheans, and Mandaeans, the type of Judaism Helena would have converted to (given the later Zealot involvements of her sons and her own reputed 21 years of Nazirite asceticism). Henry Cadbury pointed out long ago that Luke fell into the trap of thinking that Candace was a personal name when it was really *kandake*,[31] the title of all Ethiopian queens. What Cadbury did not know was that there were no Ethiopian queens at this time. Acts has, then, derived the queen character from Helena.

When Acts has the prophet Agabus predict famine, the author has derived the name from Helena's husband, sometimes rendered Agbarus. When the eunuch invites Philip to step up into his chariot, we have an echo of Jehu welcoming Jonadab into his chariot in 2 Kings 10. When Philip asks the Ethiopian if he understands what he is reading, Acts seems to borrow from the story of Izates and Eleazar where the question also presages a ritual conversion. This time the passage in question is Isaiah's prophecy of Jesus, and the initiatory ritual is baptism, not circumcision. However, the original circumcision may survive in the form of the Ethiopian being a eunuch, having been fully castrated (cf. Gal. 5:11-12). Even the location of the Acts episode is dictated by the Helena story, as the Ethiopian travels into Egypt via Gaza as Helena's agents must have in order to buy grain from Alexandria. The substituted motivation for the trip in Acts, by contrast, is absurd because a eunuch could not go to Jerusalem to worship, where eunuchs were barred from the Temple.[32]

The Standing One

Again, Eisenman does not equate the colleague of the Jewish teacher Ananias with Simon Magus, though he does make him the same as Paul. It is I who am making the connection with Simon, tying Eisenman's work together, as seems inevitable to me, with that of Detering, who shows the identity of Saul and Simon. But Eisenman adds other important data concerning Paul, arguing that in the Dead Sea Scrolls, particularly the *Habakkuk Pesher*, Paul may be thinly veiled as the "spouter of lies" and "man of the lie" because of his stand against the Torah. In the same way, James the Just, whom Galatians implicitly pits against Paul, may be the Qumran guru, the anonymous Teacher of Righteousness. The pesher's mysterious "wicked priest" could have been the high priest Ananus ben Ananus, who Josephus says had James beaten to death for heresy. The Man of the Lie began as a member of the Qumran sect, which I believe would put him in proximity with the sect of John the Baptist, that is, the Mandaeans and Nasoreans who were ascetical baptizers. Of the untruthful charlatan said to have been active in Qumran, we read that he "repudiated the Torah in the midst of the congregation" and went on to found a rival sect, largely composed of "the simple ones of Ephraim," naïve gentile "God-fearers" and proselytes whom the dissenter promised need not keep the Torah. They are those whom the *Habakkuk Pesher* called "traitors with the Man of the Lie, because they have not [obeyed the words of] the Teacher of Righteousness from the mouth of God." He is "the Man of the Lie, who had rejected the Law in the presence of their entire company ... the Spreader of Lies, who deceived many, building a worthless city by bloodshed and forming a community by lies for his own glory, making many toil at useless labor, teaching them to do false deeds."[33]

This does sound like Paul. It also sounds like Simon Magus in his bitter dispute with Dositheus amid the sect of the Baptist after their master's death. This is the story as we find it in the pseudo-Clementine *Recognitions*:

> Meantime, at the outset, as soon as [Simon] was reckoned among the thirty disciples of Dositheus, he began to depreciate Dositheus himself, saying that he did not teach purely or perfectly, and that this was the result not of ill intention, but of ignorance. But Dositheus, when he perceived that Simon was depreciating him, fearing lest his reputation among men might be obscured (for he was supposed to be the Standing One), [was] moved with rage, when they met as usual at the school, [and] seized a rod,

and began to beat Simon; but suddenly the rod seemed to pass through his body, as if it had been smoke. On which Dositheus, being astonished, says to him, 'Tell me if thou art the Standing One, that I may adore thee.'

And when Simon answered that he was, then Dositheus, perceiving that he himself was not the Standing One, fell down and worshipped him, and gave up his own place as chief to Simon, ordering all the rank of thirty men to obey him; himself taking the inferior place which Simon formerly occupied. Not long after this he died.

Therefore, after the death of Dositheus[,] Simon took Luna [Helen] to himself; and with her he still goes about, as you see, deceiving multitudes, and asserting that he himself is a certain power which is above God the Creator, while Luna, who is with him, has been brought down from the higher heavens, and that she is Wisdom, the mother of all things, for whom, says he, the Greeks and barbarians contending [at Troy], were able in some measure to see an image of her; but of herself, as she is, as the dweller with the first and only God, they were wholly ignorant.

Propounding these and other things of the same sort, he has deceived many. But I ought also to state this, which I remember that I myself saw. Once, when this Luna of his was in a certain tower, a great multitude had assembled to see her, and were standing around the tower on all sides; but she was seen by all the people to lean forward, and to look out through all the windows of that tower. Many other wonderful things he did[,] and does; so that men, being astonished at them, think that he himself is the great God. (2:11-12)[34]

In all these retellings, I believe we are catching glimpses of an historical individual, distorted as Simon Magus, or vice versa. If we assemble the pieces of the puzzle, the picture that emerges is of a sect in crisis after the death of its beloved prophet, whom we may identify as the Essene Teacher of Righteousness or perhaps as John the Baptist, slain at the command of Herod Antipas. Assuming one or the other, or varying epithets for the same individual, we can identify among this leader's principle disciples Dositheus and Simon, both Samaritans—to which we might add Jesus the Nasorean. There may have been other factions (Ebionites, Mandaeans, Sabeans) and other prominent leaders who faced similar confusion over the role of the Torah in the impending new age. Ebionism, Gnosticism, and Marcionism all stemmed ultimately from the sects that existed near the Jordan River, surviving today as Mandaeans and Nasoreans, that baptized acolytes and came to reject the Torah. As one scholar summarized: "In the Mandaean *Book of John* it is written that Adonai (Jehovah) called the [evil] Spirit and said to him, 'Let us write a book of abomination and imposture' (the Pentateuch). Then the Spirit uttered a command and Mercury and the Seven (Planets) composed and wrote the Law."[35] Ebionites blamed the heretical words and unworthy deeds of Jehovah in the Old Testament on scribes who were inspired by the wicked one, Satan. They said that Jesus, the True Prophet, had entered into the world to weed out "false pericopes" so that the true Torah might be preserved in purity for the first time since Moses.

The Gnostic Ptolemy's *Epistle to Flora* assigns some passages of the Hebrew Bible to men, some to angels, and some to the demiurge:

> First, you must learn that the entire Law contained in the Pentateuch of Moses was not ordained by one legislator—I mean, not by God alone[.] Some commandments are Moses's, and some were given by other men. The words of the Savior teach us this triple division. The first part must be attributed to God alone, and his legislation; the second to Moses—not in the sense that God legislates through him, but in the sense that Moses gave some legislation under the influence of his own ideas; and the third to the elders of the people, who seem to have ordained some commandments of their own at the beginning. (qtd. in Epiphanius of Salamis, *Panarion*, 33.3.1-33.7.10)

Marcion relegates the whole Old Testament to Jehovah. Like

the Gnostics, he rejected the idea that Jehovah was the Christian God. Dositheus reportedly substituted an entirely new Torah of his own creation in place of the traditional text. All these appear to have been evolving options within a single school of thought. Hans-Joachim Schoeps traces the whole Simon-versus-Peter disputation concerning unedifying passages of scripture (below) to the Ebionite response to the Marcionites; Peter stands for the Ebionites and Simon for the Marcionites.[36]

The Ebionites (meaning literally "the poor")[37] claimed that Paul was not a Jew by birth, that he tried to convert to Judaism and wound up renouncing it to create a rival faith. The Mandaeans remember the dispute over the Torah as having its origin in the much-regretted baptism of "Messiah Paul," that is, a false messiah. The Dead Sea Scrolls recall a dust-up over a spouter of lies who repudiated the covenant within the sect. What did Simon Magus conclude on the question of the Torah? According to Irenaeus, "Simon Magus said that men are saved by grace and not by just works. For actions are not just by nature, but by accident; according as they were laid down by the angels who made the world, and who desired by commandments of this kind to bring men into servitude to themselves."[38] Unless I am mistaken, that is exactly the teaching of the Epistle to the Galatians.

The Sect of Simon

The first to comprehend that the New Testament is straining at the seams with factional polemic was F. C. Baur, his point of departure being the enigmatic denominational slogans from Corinth:

> My brothers, some from Chloe's household have informed me that there are quarrels among you. What I mean is this: One of you says, "I follow Paul"; another, "I follow Apollos"; another, "I follow Cephas"; still another, "I follow Christ." Is Christ divided? Was Paul crucified for you? Were you baptized into the name of Paul? (1 Cor. 1:11-14)

Baur saw in this puzzling text evidence that Corinth, and the early church in general, was divided along Pauline and Petrine lines, Peter being Cephas. The former comprised a membership of Hellenistic Jewish and gentile converts who were indifferent to Jewish law and custom. The latter demanded circumcision and Torah-piety from all who took on the name of Jesus, Jew or gentile. Baur didn't really know what to do with the Christ and Apollos parties, so he subordinated them to the others, surmising that the Christ slogan denoted Jewish messianism, while the Apollos faction was another flavor of Paulinism. He went on to trace the sectarian fault lines running through the New Testament, classifying individual books as either Petrine Jewish writings (Matthew, Revelation, possibly James), Paulinist writings (most of the epistles, plus Mark and John), and the conciliatory, catholicizing books that either sought to heal the wounds or presupposed a subsequent reconciliation (Luke-Acts, 1 Peter, the Pastorals). His work still stands, modified by the addition of even more distinctions, slicing the New Testament pie into more and thinner slices for the Gnostics, Encratites, and other factions. Burton L. Mack has balkanized the early Christian map with even more colors and borders.[39]

What if the 1 Corinthians passage goes deeper than Baur imagined? I think the passage is a fossil inserted into its present context, presupposing an early, virtually pre-Christian period in which Paul, Apollos, Cephas, and Christ were rivals, distinct saviors, avatars, gurus, or gods. The competition created a kind of apostolic pantheon in which Christ eventually found the top spot, with Paul, Apollos (perhaps the same as Apollonius of Tyana), and Simon Peter (Cephas) being reinterpreted as subordinates of Christ. The Gospel saying, "Don't forget: the disciple is not superior to his master," may have been coined in order to curb the hero-worshipping proclivities of some who were still loyal to the also-rans.

Ever since David Friedrich Strauss,[40] we are used to reading accounts of John the Baptist as the vestiges of sectarian competition between emerging Jesus and John cults. Each regarded its slain founder as a resurrected messiah. Each had its holy nativity. Each claimed prophetic fulfillments.[41] Eventually the Jesus sect won out, and one of its stratagems was to assimilate the adherents of its rival by giving their figurehead an honorable mention in its own pantheon. John became the forerunner for Jesus, the cousin of Jesus who revered him already in the womb. But John was not the Christ and was not even worthy to shine the man's shoes. Even the most inconspicuous member of the new order outweighed John in importance. The old animus lurked beneath the surface, but John had been co-opted, and by the time the Gospel of John was written, John could be depicted as freely recommending to his disciples that they leave him and follow Jesus instead.[42] And just as the Baptist had been made the forerunner of the victorious Christ, I think Cephas, Paul, and Apollos were made into his apostles and proclaimers after the fact. This is certainly the point of Acts 8 where Simon Magus is shown converting to faith in Christ, albeit with ulterior motives. He loses out to Philip, then to Peter, tries to buy apostolic power, and is sternly warned to straighten up and fly right, a warning, in truth, to Simonian recruits to Christianity.

I have implied that there were partisans who revered Paul as their figurehead in his own right, with no reference at all to Jesus. To such people, hinted at in the early verses of 1 Corinthians, it was not necessarily absurd to suggest that Paul had been crucified for them, that they owed their salvation to baptism in his name. We can trace the broad outlines of such a cult in the *Acts of Paul* where the subject of the book is a hero in his own right. We glimpse this group of exclusively Paul-worshiping people in the Nag Hammadi *Revelation of Paul,* in which the name of Jesus is never once mentioned. It is Paul who is commissioned to bring Gnostic illumination to mortals. What do we know of the pre-Christian cult of Paul? *It was the Simonian cult!* It is his devotees who are in view in 1 Corinthians 1:11-14 when we hear the shout, "I am of Paul!" Call him what you will, but call on his name by all means. He is Simon Magus, who claimed to be a savior, the Great Power. Justin Martyr tells us that the Magus was widely worshipped for decades. He had not converted to Christianity any more than the historical Baptist had endorsed Jesus as the one who was to come. It means, too, that Christianity failed to co-opt and absorb Simonianism. But it tried.

It will come as no surprise that the followers of Simon Magus returned the favor, trying their best to assimilate Christianity. Simonianism sought to co-opt the competing Jesus movement by claiming it was someone named Simon who was crucified, albeit only seemingly. We see this depicted, for those who have eyes to see, in Mark, Matthew, and Luke. These Gospel writers, with no discernible narrative motivation, claimed that Simon of Cyrene was pressed into service to carry the cross in Jesus's stead.[43] I do not mean to say that the Gospel writers would have recognized the significance of this oral tradition, but the Gnostics did. In Samaria, Simon said he had been worshipped as Jehovah ("the Father") in Old Testament times. Now he was being *manifest to the gentiles* as the Holy Spirit. Bingo! There is the Pauline mission to the gentiles. But among Jews he had gone to the cross where he appeared to be crucified, that is, as Jesus. By the way, we need not suppose chicanery on Simon's part. He may well have believed himself to be the reincarnation of Jesus Christ, just as the third-century Apostle Mani, as we have seen, claimed he was the latest vessel of the spirit that had embodied itself in Zoroaster, the Buddha, and Jesus Christ.

Desperately seeking Helen

When Simon Magus claimed to have been the divine Son[44] and the reappearance of a historical figure, who did he have in mind? crucified albeit only in appearance, what historical frame did he have in mind? ?

Jewish sources included some Talmudic references to a Jesus who was a disciple of second-century BCE Rabbi Jeschu ben-Perechiah.

Epiphanius of Salamis reported on heretical accounts of Jesus that placed his death at about 100 BCE. There was a Jewish Gospel satire called the *Toledoth Jeschu* (*Generations of Jesus*) that put the Jesus story at about the same time, a hundred years prior to the conventional dating. I think the Simonian claim that Simon had suffered as the Son (Jesus) fits this time frame best. In claiming to have appeared among the Jews as the Son, Simon must have been referring back to the scenario presupposed in the *Toledoth Jeschu*. There the revolutionist and magician Jeschu sought audience with Queen Helena, widow of Alexander Jannaeus, and in fact did win her over to faith in him. She was somewhat fickle, too ready to listen to the warnings of the Sanhedrin against Jeschu, but sympathetic in the end. No one can miss the pattern: again we would have the transmigrating Magus seeking out and finding his soul-mate, Queen Helen, this time Queen of the Jews.

The climax to the *Toledoth* features an aerial dogfight, the soaring magician Jeschu battling his erstwhile disciple Judah, a secret agent for the Sanhedrin and hero of the story for its intended audience. Jeschu owed his powers to the forbidden knowledge of the Tetragramaton (divine name) which he had obtained in the temple. Judah gained it too, in order to be able to defeat the false prophet, and he did, sending Jeschu plummeting earthward, where his foes arrested him. It can be no accident that the *Acts of Peter* has Simon Magus perform the same spectacle of flying, only to be sent crashing to the ground in response to Peter's prayer. The same feat, with its ensuing downfall, is ascribed to the Antichrist in Christian literature where the apocalyptic figure is acknowledged by most scholars to have been inspired by Simon Magus.

Perhaps the most astonishing piece of evidence from that neglected legend-trove, the *Toledoth Jeschu*, comes in the aftermath of Jeschu's execution. Years go by, and the Jeschu-cultists are making a terrible nuisance of themselves, harassing Jews and blaming them for killing God's anointed. What to do?

Now when the sages of Israel saw the state of things, they said, "It has been thirty years since that villain was killed, and from that day to this we have had no peace with these impious fellows. This has surely happened to us because of the great number of our sins, as it is written, 'They have goaded me into a jealous rage with their false god; they have provoked me to fury with their idols! So I am going to goad them to jealously over a false people,' namely the Nazarenes, who are false, 'and I will provoke them to anger with a nation of fools,' namely the Ishmaelites."[45]

And the sages said, "How long are the radicals to desecrate the sabbath and the feasts, and kill each other? Let us find a man wise enough to remove these impious louts from the community of Israel! Today marks thirty years we have warned them, and they have not returned to the Lord. Instead, the notion has entered their heads that Jesus is the Messiah. If this plan works, they may go to perdition, and we will have rest at last."

And the sages shared their knowledge and agreed on a greatly erudite man named Simeon son of Cleophas. And they said to him, "We have agreed to pray for you, and (despite the deception we ask of you,) you shall surely be numbered among the company of Israel who will share in the age to come. Go and do a great service of mercy to Israel: Remove the radicals from our midst, so they may pursue their own path to destruction." So Simeon went from the council at Tiberias to Antioch, principle city of the Nazarenes, and he sent word through the whole territory of Israel: "Let every believer in Jeschu join me!"

When they had assembled to hear him, he announced, "I am the apostle of Jeschu! He has sent me to you, and I will give you a sign just as Jeschu did!" They brought him a leper, and he placed his hand on him, and he was healed. Then they brought him a lame man, and he uttered the Tetragrammaton and placed his hand upon him, and he was healed and stood to his feet. At once they bowed before him, saying, "Truly you are the apostle of Jeschu, for you show us signs just as he did!"

And he said, "Therefore Jeschu greets you, saying, 'I am at my Father's side in heaven, yes, at his right hand until he avenges himself upon the Jews, as David says, "The Lord said to my lord, 'Sit here on my right till I make your enemies your footstool!'"

In that hour they all wept, adding folly to their foolishness. Simeon addressed them: "Jeschu says to you, 'Whoever would join me in the age to come, let him leave the community of Israel behind and do not associate with them, for my Father in heaven despises them and from now on he rejects their sacrifices. For he says as much by the pen of Isaiah: 'Your new moon observances and your scheduled feasts, I hate from the center of my being! They are a nuisance to me, and I am sick of enduring them!' But Jesus says to you, 'Whoever would belong to my company, let him desecrate the sabbath, for the Holy One, blessed be he, hates it and observes the first day of the week instead, since on it the Holy One, blessed be he, gave light to his world. And instead of the Passover celebrated by Israel, you shall observe the commemoration of the resurrection, for in that day he rose from the grave. And in place of the Feast of Weeks, celebrate the day of his ascension. And instead of New Year, observe the Finding of the Cross. And instead of the Day of Atonement, keep the feast of his circumcision. And in place of the Feast of Lights, celebrate the Calends.[46]

"'The foreskin is nothing; circumcision is nothing. Whoever wishes to be circumcised, let him be circumcised. Whoever wishes it not, let him not be circumcised.

"'Furthermore, whatever the Holy One, blessed be he, created in his world, from the tiniest gnat to the largest elephant, butcher it and eat it; for so it is written: "Just as I gave you the green plants, I have given you all things ...'"[47]

And so he preached until he had separated them from Israel. And this Simeon, who "gave them statutes that were not good,"[48] did it in order to restore peace to Israel. And the Nazarenes called him Paul. After Paul had established these statutes and commandments, the impious separated themselves from Israel, and the strife stopped. (8:7-41)

Lo and behold: here is a passage which explicitly says Paul had first been known as Simeon. Some manuscripts specify "Simeon bar Cleophas," the epithet of one of the so-called heirs of Jesus, also known as the pillars of the Jerusalem church (Gal. 2:9). This is even more interesting, because James Tabor argues that the names

"Cleophas" and "Alphaeus" are variants of the same epithet, denoting "the replacer, the successor."[49] It is difficult to resist the temptation to connect this epithet with the Arabic *khalifa* ("caliph"), the vicar on earth of an absent (deified or dead) ruler. Of course that is the title of the caretakers of the Islamic community after Muhammad. It must have meant the same thing in the Gospels before being historicized (fictionalized) as a personal name. "James of Alphaeus" originally referred to James the Just, brother of the Lord and his caliph. "Simeon bar Cleophas" meant Simeon the Caliph of the Lord. But that is not the nuance in the *Toledoth Jeschu*, where the epithet as connected with "Simeon" must denote Simon Magus, who we may say, if we connect the dots, was the namesake of the one who had *substituted* for Jesus on the cross. Simon led people away from Judaism, which was also Paul's mission, when seen from a Jewish perspective. Note that the *Toledoth Jeschu* depicts Simeon as a miracle worker who produces wonders to lead the gullible astray. That is Simon Magus. And that is Paul.

Marcionism and early Simonianism

The anti-heretical writers of the early church tell us that Marcion "descended" from Simon Magus through a kind of anti-apostolic succession. The link between the two men was said to be a teacher named Cerdo, although Stephan Hermann Huller makes Marcion the immediate successor of Simon. Huller identifies Marcion ("Little Mark") with Marcos the Magician, elsewhere attested as Simon's immediate disciple. Irenaeus pictured Marcos as something of a Svengali and gigolo, converting wealthy women who had nothing better to do. Anyone familiar with the apocryphal Acts of the Apostles will hear an echo in this accusation of the pejorative portrayals of Paul and the Twelve. Preaching an anti-family gospel of celibacy, the apostles were condemned as seducers, exploiters, and home-wreckers—again, distorted by the fun-house mirror of polemical slander. But even without the links supplied by Irenaeus, we would be able to tag Marcion as a Simonian simply because of the identity of their basic doctrine. Marcion, like Simon Magus, rejected the Creator and law-giver of the Old Testament as an alien god, distinct from Jesus Christ's father. Jesus revealed another God who wanted to gather in the hapless creatures of Jehovah and welcome the poor wretches as his adopted sons and daughters, once Jesus had paid the Creator for them by his redemptive death on the cross.

Paul would have been, like Simon, an itinerant radical preacher who circulated among communities of followers, perhaps clandestine circles of admirers within synagogues or churches. As a Gnostic, he would have taught sexual radicalism, which may have amounted to either total celibacy or libertinism—or both! Oddly, once one abolishes conventional marriage, as the history of sectarianism shows, sexuality loses the authority of regulation or even definition. Religious law extends a grid of order over otherwise raw, "profane" behavior, rendering it sacred insofar as the law is obeyed. In this way, actions become meaningful. But if the law is done away with, behavior lapses into profanity, that is, meaninglessness, anomie. And that is what happens in antinomian Gnosticism, which repudiates the law as the imposition of false Powers. Sometimes, "free" of regulation, as in the film *Suddenly Last Summer*, one even begins to perceive sexual license as celibacy. Similarly, the Gnostic concentration on the inner rather than the outer caused conventional social and economic relations to languish. As with all new and radical sects, the followers of Paul would have felt themselves increasingly alienated from a worldly society full of temptation to unbelief and assimilation, including especially the utter inability of unsaved relatives to understand one's new salvation. Such a group has no future in a world which refuses to accommodate it. This is why they so often lean toward apocalyptic orientation, hoping to rocket directly to the end of the present order and divide the sheep from the goats once and for all.

All this must have sounded fine as it was pitched to individuals who had little to lose anyway and were already alienated from socially adjusted maturity or who fancied themselves elite strangers in a strange land. Some of the affluent—ever seeking new modes of superiority over rivals—might have found the Gnostic preaching appealing. Certain members of the ruling class certainly did, as witness the jet-set circles in which Josephus says Simon the Magician moved. But essentially it was a worldview for the lone wolf, except insofar as such groups were just mutual admiration societies. They were the kind of group that anthropologist Mary Douglas characterizes as a community possessing "high grid, weak group" characteristics.[50] This means one had to overcome a high hurdle to get inside, such as mastering Gnostic complexities and undergoing initiations; but once in, the members were essentially one-man cults with little real use for the others. They were like individual cars parked in the same garage.

Radical sects have a habit of quickly evolving: settling in, losing zeal, and beginning to re-assimilate conventional norms of society that they formerly left behind. This happens because energy lags and one seeks or creates new family ties. One begins to need ethics to define family, group, and social behavior. One needs to theorize half-way covenants and B plans. When the sect begins to morph into a church, the original circuit-riding lone wolves find they have less to say to such groups. As per Stevan L. Davies, itinerant apostles found their individualist teachings increasingly inapplicable to social life in a community.[51] Their appeals to "let goods and kindred go," to give wealth to the poor, etc., began to fall on deaf ears. Their formerly eager parishioners have returned to the real world, and the religion they left behind no longer sounds so corrupt and worldly. "All those Day-glo freaks who used to paint the face, they've joined the human race. Some things will never change."[52] They are like hippies who grow up and take the kind of corporate jobs they criticized their parents over.

My theory is that this is the very point at which Simonianism may have become Marcionism. Marcion represents the second phase, the domestication of Simonianism. Strange to say, but
Marcion I think marks the first step back to the mainstream, the
first move toward nascent Catholicism. Once upon a time, spontaneous prophecy sufficed, but now a canon of authoritative writings replaces it. The canonical letters themselves were emended
and updated. The texts we inherited are full of hints of spiritual
decline, the loss of the first love and fervency. We find even in the
Pauline letters the idea that believers are now enjoying merely the
"earnest of the Spirit," "the first fruits of the Spirit." This represents a disillusionment, a decline from a period of initial sectarian enthusiasm. When we discover this in the epistles, we ought
not regard it as Paul's own attempt to dampen down fanaticism
(as Ernst Käsemann would have it) but rather a piece of Marcionite dampening down of Paulinism (Simonian Gnosticism). It is like
the Buddhist transference of hope for liberation from the present toward a future advent of Maitreya when living, present salvation would again seem possible. Once Gnostics forbade marriage,
or at least sex between already married spouses; now Marcion will
allow it, grudgingly. Divorce used to be moot, but Marcion forbids
it since he tolerates marriage.

Why Jesus?

If Marcion was a Simonian, why does he speak about Jesus as
much as he does? Why does he not talk about the salvation wrought
by Simon? We have to infer that the Simonian enfolding of Jesus
into its salvation history scheme was not merely a propaganda tactic. That may have been part of the motivation, as when Christians
drafted John the Baptist as Jesus's forerunner, after the fact. Subsequent Christians took the whole thing seriously, as Christians still
do today, venerating "St. John the Baptist." We can envision the
same thing happening in the faith of Simonians. If the suffering of

the Son in Judea mattered enough for Simonians to lasso it and draw it into their orbit, they must have thought it important enough to use once they had borrowed it. It is not difficult to surmise the way in which they did so. They held Simon himself as the Great Power who came to redeem all souls possessing a spark of the divine Epinoia, scattered in the material world. He had for ages sought out her essence, ever re-embodied in his syzygy-counterpart Helen, and he had found her. He had suffered in Judea, too, and this must have been construed as some other needful act of salvation. We might guess that, a la Valentinus (disciple of Theodas, disciple of Paul), the crucifixion was on behalf of the *psuchikoi*, the well-meaning creatures of the demiurge who were not proper children of the Heavenly Father but who might be adopted into his family.

Marcion and the Gospel story

We always read that Marcion came armed to the theological fray with a sheaf of Pauline letters plus a single Gospel, a shorter version of canonical Luke. Church apologists said Marcion's version was shorter than Luke because Marcion abbreviated it, removing what he deemed "false pericopes." This is not implausible and it would just mean that Marcion used the same critical methodology his contemporaries, the Ebionites, applied to their copies of the Old Testament. Others believe Marcion possessed an original, shorter Gospel, which he tampered with only minimally, an early version of Luke. Paul-Louis Couchoud[53] argued that Marcion's Gospel was very nearly what other scholars have called proto-Luke or ur-Lukas. G.R.S. Mead hypothesized that Marcion did not have such a Gospel narrative but rather a collection of sayings, something like the hypothetical Q source.[54] This diversity of opinion translates into the uncertainty as to whether we are dealing with Marcion's own canon or whether we are hearing what Marcionites would later compile and ascribe to Marcion. They were not hidebound traditionalists, after all. It is my opinion that Marcion's scripture contained only epistles, and no Gospel. His followers added proto-Luke (or ur-Lukas) later on.

First, it appears to me both that Marcion is responsible for significant portions of the epistolary text and that the epistles are quite innocent of the Gospel tradition of sayings and deeds by an earthly Jesus. Therefore, Marcion not only possessed no Gospel but knew nothing of our Jesus tradition. All he would have gleaned from Simonianism was the belief that someone had seemingly undergone crucifixion among the Jews. Isn't that close enough? Wouldn't he at least have taken for granted a recent historical Jesus? No, I think not, and for two reasons. First, our oldest narrative Gospel, that of Mark, already contains not only the episode of Simon substituting for Jesus, but it is a version that has been historicized, implying an earlier version in which Simon of Cyrene's identity was that of Simon Magus. Second, as we have already seen, the Jesus story in the *Toledoth Jeschu* is a much better candidate for the Jesus story to which Simon would have appealed in that it has a magus seeking out another Helen. This is not to say that the *Toledoth Jeschu* was available to Simon, but elements of it may have been.

The second reason for doubting that Marcion knew any written Gospel is the attractiveness of a different accounting of Gospel origins suggested by our earlier discussion of the fertile sectarian debate over how to treat unworthy passages of scripture. Some dispensed with the Old Testament altogether, while others picked out and eliminated (on the ostensible authority of Jesus) the offensive "false pericopae." And so forth. As Hans-Joachim Schoeps observed, the Ebionites' "false pericopae" theory was certainly their reaction to the Marcionite approach of discarding scripture. Why not cut one's losses? Just give up the disputed ground and keep the rest? I believe the composition of the Gospels, beginning very late in the first century, but mainly in the second, was another such response to the crisis of scripture. A raft of scholars, including Randel Helms, Thomas L. Brodie, and John Dominic Crossan have shown again and again how this and that Gospel passage probably originated as a Christian rewrite of this or that Old Testament passage. What one testament had Moses do, the other had Jesus do. Fill in the name. What did David do? Joshua? Elijah? Elisha? Turns out Jesus did it, too, and even in the same descriptive words! When one assembles the best and most convincing of these studies,[33] the results are startling indeed: one can make a compelling argument for virtually every Gospel story's derivation from Old Testament sources.

How do we account for this? Why the sudden interest in rewriting the Jewish scripture as a book about Jesus? The Catholic policy was to retain the Old Testament but to reread it as a book about (that is, predicting) Jesus and Christianity. If this procedure were cut off, as Marcion did, what remained? One had to rewrite the Old Testament to make it explicitly about Jesus! In this way, even the Old Testament of the Jews became, as Martin Luther would say, *was Christum treibt* ("what conveys Christ"). This had not happened by Marcion's time. There were no Gospels for him to include in his new scripture, only epistles which showed no sign of acquaintance with any Gospels. On the other hand, Marcionites seem to have had a role in the production of the Gospels. Mark's Gospel, for instance, holds what can hardly be called other than a Marcionite view of the buffoonish twelve disciples and a Gnostic view of secret teachings which, despite their privileged position, the twelve simply do not grasp. Think of the Transfiguration (Mark 9:1-8): how can one miss the Marcionite implications of Mark's setting up Jesus, Moses (the Torah), and Elijah (the Prophets) as in a police line-up, followed by the Father's urging that, of the three, Jesus alone is to be heard and heeded? Mark, of course, refers to Jesus giving his life as a ransom for many (Mark 10:45). Though Mark fails to tell us to whom Jesus would be paying this ransom, Marcion tells us. He paid it to the Creator, and no non-Marcionite theologian has produced a better candidate.

One wonders if even the name of the Gospel of Mark reflects

awareness of the fundamentally Marcionite character of the book. Mark, the secretary of Peter, the John Mark of Acts, would be too early for us to identify with Marcion, but it is quite possible that Mark, the secretary of Peter, is an unhistorical safe version of Marcion, manufactured to be an author of the Gospel, much as Eusebius posited a "John the Elder" as author of Revelation once he no longer wanted to ascribe it to John, son of Zebedee.

The Gospel of John is heavily Marcionite: Moses and the Jews knew nothing of God. Despite all that Deuteronomy says about Moses seeing God face to face, John denies that any mortal has ever seen the true God (John 1:18). Jesus's Father is not the same God the Jews worship (8:54-55). All who came to the Jews before Jesus, presumably the Old Testament prophets, were mere despoilers (10:8). The Father is unknown to the world (17:25). The Torah had nothing to do with grace and truth (1:17). Jesus raised himself from the dead (10:17-18). Papias of Hierapolis, writing about 125-150 CE, wants us to believe that young Marcion had worked as John's secretary, taking dictation as the old evangelist composed his Gospel, but secretly inserting his own heresies. Once John read over the proofs, however, he sent Marcion packing with a severance check and a boot in the behind.

> The Gospel of John was revealed and given to the Churches by John whilst he was still in the body, as Papias, called the Hierapolitan, the beloved disciple of John, has reported in his five books of Exegetics. But he who wrote down the Gospel, John dictating correctly the true evangel [Gospel], was Marcion the heretic. Having been disapproved by him for holding contrary views, he was expelled by John. (Bishop Fortunatus's preface to the Gospel of John)

Of course, the story, as with all Papias's "traditions," is a tall tale. Plainly, the point of telling it is to admit and to apologize for the perceived Marcionite element in the Gospel when it was too late to redact it further. Too many people already had copies. Had John actually discovered that his Gospel had been corrupted, he would have burnt the errant manuscript and started over again. But he didn't, and the marks of Marcionism are plain to see. Joseph Turmel,[55] on the basis of such data as these, suggested in 1925 that John was originally a Marcionite Gospel, subsequently redacted by a Catholic.

The Q Document has Jesus exclaim that no one knows his Father but him (Matt. 11:27; Lk.10:22). What? Not Israel? Not Moses? Not John the Baptist? It would take quite a lot of ingenuity to come up with some other interpretation of this one. "No one knows the Father except for the Son and any to whom the Son may deign to reveal him." That's straight Marcionism, isn't it?

Thomas 52 reads: "His disciples say to him, 'Twenty-four prophets spoke in Israel, and every one of them predicted you!' He said to them, 'You have disregarded the Living, who is right in front of you, to prattle on about the dead!'" Augustine found half of the saying, Jesus's reply, quoted in an explicitly Marcionite pamphlet handed him on the street in Carthage. The first half of the saying, the set-up remark of the disciples, was unknown until 1945 when the *Gospel of Thomas* was discovered. Looking at the truncated version, Joachim Jeremias[56] surmised that the Marcionites must have taken "the dead" to refer to the prophets, while Jesus was actually refuting rabbinic arguments that the messiah to come would be a returned Old Testament personality, perhaps Joshua or Hezekiah. No, here he is, right in front of you; I fear Jeremias's theory must be judged an extreme harmonization, an attempt to preserve an attractive saying by scrubbing away the Marcionite tint. And the discovery of *Thomas* confirmed the Marcionite intent of the passage.

So the composition of Gospels, being rewrites of the Old Testament, was a counterblast to the Marcionite rejection of the Old Testament. Once the trend began, Marcionites made their own contributions to it, and thus to the process of historicizing an originally mythic Jesus.[57] Marcion himself, then, had no Gospel. It must have been subsequent Marcionites who ascribed the choice of one to him. Even the invidious contrast, always attributed to Marcion, between the Twelve and Paul must be a later apologetic since it presupposes a late redefinition of the originally unrestricted apostolate to an exclusive dozen.

NOTES

[1]Richard J. Coggins, *Samaritans and Jews: The Origins of Samaritanism Reconsidered* (Atlanta: John Knox Press, 1975).

[2]Margaret Barker, *The Great Angel: A Study of Israel's Second God* (Louisville: Westminster/John Knox Press, 1992).

[3]James H. Charlesworth, ed., *The Messiah: Developments in Earliest Judaism and Christianity* (Princeton: Princeton University Press, 1987); Jacob Neusner, William S. Green, and Ernest Frerichs, eds., *Judaisms and Their Messiahs at the Turn of the Christian Era* (New York: Cambridge University Press, 1987).

[4]John MacDonald, *The Theology of the Samaritans* (London: SCM Press, 1964), 443-44.

[5]The episode was "Spock's Brain," written by "Lee Cronin" (Gene L. Coon), and first aired September 20, 1968.

[6]Gershom G. Scholem, *Major Trends in Jewish Mysticism*, 3rd ed., trans. George Lichtheim (New York: Schocken Books, 1960), 244-86.

[7]Aleister Crowley, *The Book of the Law* (Montreal: 93 Publishing, 1974), 18-19.

[8]George R. S. Mead, *Simon Magus: An Essay on the Founder of Simonianism, Based on the Ancient Sources, with a Re-evaluation of His Philosophy and Teachings* (1892; Chicago: Ares Publishers, 1978), 40.

[9]Gerd Lüdemann, "The Acts of the Apostles and the Beginnings of Simonian Gnosis," *New Testament Studies* 33 (1987), 420-26.

[10]Robert M. Price, "Mary Magdalene: Gnostic Apostle?" *Grail*, 6, no. 2 (June 1990): 54-76.

[11]There is a good discussion of this double standard in Susan R. Garrett, *The Demise of the Devil: Magic and the Demonic in Luke's Writings* (Minneapolis: Fortress Press, 1989), 4ff.

[12]See ibid., 61-78. I believe Garrett errs in trying to subsume all of Acts's anti-magic episodes in a consistent campaign against Satan. Where is Satan in the episode of the Philippian pythoness, for instance? On the other hand, Stephen Haar, in *Simon Magus: The First Gnostic?* (Berlin and New York: Walter de Gruyter, 2003), engages in special pleading in order to disentangle Simon from a rogues gallery of charlatans and rehabilitate him as an expatriate Persian astrologer. Give it up.

[13]Michael D. Goulder, "The Two Roots of the Christian Myth," in John Hick, ed., *The Myth of God Incarnate* (Philadelphia: Westminster Press, 1977), 64-86. See also his "Samaritan Hypothesis," in Goulder, ed., *Incarnation and Myth: The Debate Continued* (London: SCM Press, 1979), 247-50.

[14]John Knox, *Marcion and the New Testament: An Essay in the Early History of the Canon* (Chicago: University of Chicago Press, 1942); Joseph B. Tyson, *Marcion and Luke-Acts: A Defining Struggle* (Columbia: University of South Carolina Press, 2006).

[15]Adolf von Harnack, *Marcion: The Gospel of the Alien God*, trans. John E. Steely and Lyle D. Bierma (Durham, NC: Labyrinth Press, 1990), 21-24.

[16]R. Joseph Hoffmann, *Marcion: On the Restitution of Christianity: An Essay on the Development of Radical Paulinist Theology in the Second Century*, AAR Academy Series 46 (Chico: Scholars Press, 1984), 242-80.

[17]See chapter 2 of the present book; Hermann Detering, "The Dutch Radical Approach to the Pauline Epistles," *Journal of Higher Criticism* 3, no. 2 (Fall 1996): 163-93.

[18]Hermann Detering, "The Falsified Paul: Early Christianity in the Twilight," trans. Darrell J. Doughty, *Journal of Higher Criticism* 10, no. 2 (Fall, 2003): passim.

[19]Darrell J. Doughty, "Pauline Paradigms and Pauline Authenticity," *Journal of Higher Criticism* 1, no. 1 (Fall, 1994): 95-128.

[20]Winsome Munro, *Authority in Paul and Peter: The Identification of a Pastoral Stratum in the Pauline Corpus and I Peter*, Society for New Testament Studies Monograph Series 45 (New York: Cambridge University Press, 1983).

[21]Krister Stendahl, "The Apostle Paul and the Introspective Conscience of the West," in Stendahl, *Paul among Jews and Gentiles and Other Essays* (Philadelphia: Fortress Press, 1976), 78-96.

[22]Ferdinand C. Baur, *Paul, the Apostle of Jesus Christ: His Life and Work, His Epistles and Doctrine,* trans. Edward Zeller, rev. Allan Menzies (London: Williams and Norgate, 1876), 88-92, 232.

[23]Rom. 15:25-28; 2 Cor. 8, 9; Acts 11:27-30. For the assumption that when he met Peter, James, and John, they would recognize his apostleship, see Gal. 2:7-10; for the hope that the aid would be accepted as a good-will gesture, implying an awareness that his beneficence might be misunderstood, see Rom. 15:25-28, 31.

[24]See 1 Cor. 14:18; 2 Cor. 12:1-12; Gal. 3:2.

[25]René Girard, *Violence and the Sacred,* trans. Patrick Gregory (Baltimore: Johns Hopkins University Press, 1977; Girard, *The Scapegoat,* trans. Yvonne Freccero (Baltimore: Johns Hopkins University Press, 1986).

[26]Oscar Cullmann, *Peter: Disciple, Apostle, Martyr,* trans. Floyd V. Filson (New York: Meridian Books, 1958), 101-02.

[27]As Eisenman notes, some of Josephus's manuscripts name the magician Atomus, which sounds like Adamas, the Gnostic Primal Man, and could be a link to the reincarnated Standing One (Robert Eisenman, *James, the Brother of Jesus: The Key to Unlocking the Secrets of Early Christianity and the Dead Sea Scrolls* [New York: Viking, 1996], 894).

[28]Elymas's patronymic was "bar-Jesus," meaning "son of Jesus." The Western Text of Acts gives the name as Etoimas or Etomas instead of Elymas, and this is pretty close to Josephus's "Atomus."

[29]Ibid., 883-922.

[30]Ibid., 903.

[31]Henry J. Cadbury, *The Book of Acts in History* (New York: Harper and Brothers, 1955), 17.

[32]Deut. 23:1; cf. Gal. 5:12

[33]See the Habakkuk Pesher in Michael Wise, Martin Abegg Jr., and Edward Cook, *The Dead Sea Scrolls: A New Translation* (San Francisco: Harper San Francisco, 1996), 116, 118, 121.

[34]*ANF,* 199, Roberts and Donaldson.

[35]L. Gordon Ryands, *Did Jesus Ever Live?* (London: Watts, 1935), 80.

[36]Hans-Joachim Schoeps, *Jewish Christianity: Factional Disputes in the Early Church,* trans. Douglas R. A. Hare (Philadelphia: Fortress Press, 1969), 92, 122-26.

[37]Notice that this was also a self-designation of the Jerusalem Christians (Gal. 2:10) and of the Dead Sea Scrolls sect.

[38]*Against Heresies* 1.23:3.

[39]Burton L. Mack, *A Myth of Innocence: Mark and Christian Origins* (Minneapolis: Fortress Press, 1988), 78-123. See my friendly critique and proposed elaboration of Mack's taxonomy of early Christianities in Price, *Deconstructing Jesus* (Amherst: Prometheus Books, 2000), 47-96.

[40]David Friedrich Strauss, *The Life of Jesus Critically Examined*, 2nd ed., trans. George Eliot (1892; Philadelphia: Fortress Press, 1972), 209-36.

[41]See Mark 6:14; Luke 1:5-2:52; 16:16a.

[42]See Luke 1:44; Mark 1:7; Matt. 11:11; John 1:35-37.

[43]Matt. 27:32-35; Mark 15:21-25; Luke 23:26. This is probably the incident that inspired the gospel story of Barabbas, in which Jesus bar-Abbas ("Jesus, son of the father") escapes crucifixion, while "Jesus called the Christ" goes to the cross instead.

[44]Justin Martyr said that a statue on an island in the Tiber River bore the inscription, "To Simon, the Holy God," and was erected out of respect for the Simonians. The statue was found in the modern era and shown to be dedicated to Semo Sancus, an old Italian deity. Even so, one sees in the assumption of Justin Martyr the status Simon Magus must have held in the Levant (cf. *Against Heresies*, i.23.1; Hippolytus, *Refutation of All Heresies*, vi.20; Epiphanius of Salamis, *Panarion*).

[45]Deut. 32:21.

[46]Calends was the Roman New Year holiday, which came to be loosely associated with Christmas.

[47]The characterization of Christian teachings is supported by 1 Cor. 7:18-19; Gal. 5:6; Acts 10:12-13.

[48]Ezek. 20:25.

[49]James D. Tabor, *The Jesus Dynasty: The Hidden History of Jesus, His Royal Family, and the Birth of Christianity* (New York: Simon and Schuster, 2006); Tabor, "Getting Our Jameses Straight," Taborblog, www.jamestabor. com.

[50]Mary Douglas, *Natural Symbols: Explorations in Cosmology* (New York: Pantheon Books, 1982), 58-61.

[51]Stevan L. Davies, *The Revolt of the Widows: The Social World of the Apocryphal Acts of the Apostles* (Carbondale: Southern Illinois University Press, 1980), 36.

[52]Walter Becker and Donald Fagan, "Kid Charlemagne," *The Royal Scam*, recorded by Steely Dan, 1976, ABC Records.

[53]Paul-Louis Couchoud, "Is Marcion's Gospel One of the Synoptics?" *The Hibbert Journal: A Quarterly Review of Religion, Theology, and Philosophy* 34, no. 2 (1936): 265-77.

[54]G.R.S. Mead, *Fragments of a Faith Forgotten: The Gnostics, a Contribution to the Study of the Origins of Christianity* (New Hyde Park: University Books, n.d.), 244.

[55]Joseph Turmel, *Le Puatrieme Évangile* (Paris: F. Rieder et cie, 1925).

[56]Joachim Jermais, *Unknown Sayings of Jesus*, trans. Reginald H. Fuller (New York: MacMillan, 1957), 74-77.

[57]Does not the phenomenon of the Ebionites demand that there had been an historical Jesus? They speak of Jesus as the True Prophet, lately come to reveal the false pericopae of the Torah. Was he not, then, a recent figure? It is always possible that they envisioned him as speaking prophetically through their own teacher of righteousness, not incarnate as a separate individual. But essentially, "Jesus" functioned for them as a personification of the "law-reviser," the new exegesis of their sect, just as Moses had long functioned (fictively) as Law personified for other Jews. Why the name "Jesus," then? I cannot help suspecting that their "Jesus" was originally supposed to be Joshua, immediate successor of Moses, whom the Book of Joshua shows making a covenant for Israel, not merely making a copy of the old one (24:25-26). He would have made his own Torah shortly after Moses. The "Jesus" of the Ebionites would, then, have been the Old Testament Joshua, successor to Moses. Subsequently, at the point of federating with the other sects of the Gnostic Jordan *Schwärmerei*, they simply identified their "Jesus" with that of their Christian brethren. In fact, what the heresiologists say of the ostensible/inferred founder, "Ebion," may have been true of the one they claimed as their founder, Jesus! He didn't exist but was just a name for a new set of scriptural exegeses.

8.

Salvation and Stratification

In order to gain the necessary perspective for distinguishing earlier and later strata in the epistles attributed to Paul, we require some sort of working model of the evolution of Paulinist thought. If we can isolate one particular theological trajectory, we may be able to use it as a measuring rod to tell which piece of text represents what likely stage of development along the Simonian-Pauline-Marcionite and Gnostic axes of development. The best candidate for this theological trajectory, as it strikes me, is *soteriology*, the doctrine of salvation. Let us briefly trace its evolution, reconstructed from a broad range of sources.

Primitive sacramentalism

The mystery cults began as culture-wide agricultural religions which featured a seasonal ritual for the recovery of nature's vigor as well as the mandate of heaven for the god-king. The land would share the fate of the slain and resurrected god-king, who re-enacted the primordial battle of the young warrior god (Zeus, Marduk, Baal, Yahwe, Indra) against the chaos-monsters. His victory entitled him to the throne, and he created (or replenished) the world from the carcass of the vanquished monster(s). Eventually, as we see in

Egypt, this immortality by identification with the god was democ-
ratized, and any layman might be divinized by ritual initiation, tem-
porarily becoming one with the god and his victory. The identification originally established between the deity and the ruler was now
established with any initiate. For him or her, it denoted a personal,
spiritual renewal.

The same democratization occurred elsewhere as well, seemingly under the influence of population migration and the many
ethno-religious diasporas of peoples throughout the Roman Empire.
Since, under such circumstances, the cultural dimension and agricultural basis of the old faiths were gone, the rituals were reinterpreted in order to reinforce the subcultural identity of the ethnic
group, to which outsiders eventually came to be added. The various mystery cults, transplanted into new, urban soil, performed the
same function as ethnic enclaves do today, such as a Slavonic Hall
and Black Student Union. The new rootage in a pluralistic society, alongside similar cults from other lands, led to syncretism and
henotheism: an individual might join any number of such groups,
in which, because of their basic similarity, he felt at home. And
once he did join, it is obvious the beliefs of each would readily rub
off onto the others to which the initiate belonged. He probably
couldn't keep them all straight! They started out as analogous and
similar; they wound up looking more and more alike. Finally, many
regarded them as mere variations on a common theme, or even as
different names for the same thing.

But how did an originally agricultural fertility rite turn into a
ritual of rebirth? The old, native societies, like all societies everywhere, had possessed rites of passage[1] for individual maturation
as full members of the social group. Puberty rites were the most
important, leading to adulthood. There were intra-adult rites like
marriage and occupational ordination, but puberty rituals were
the most important, since they initiated the common person into
adulthood. But what if there were a further, even more esoteric rite

in which godhood and ultramundane salvation were to be attained? Such was an echo of the divinization once predicated of the long-vanished king. Adulthood already brought hitherto-secret knowledge of what adults knew that children did not. Now deification brought the secrets of the gods which, it used to be, were restricted to kings only. True, there were no more kings over one's own people, but as in ancient wedding ceremonies (and Greek Orthodox weddings still today), every man became king. Each person symbolically died and rose, becoming mystically identified with the savior deity in the latter's death and resurrection. As the king had been one with the land, now the land was far away so the god became one with his people instead.

Sworn to secrecy, an initiate dared not blab the contents of the ritual to outsiders, though some did, and it turned out the *mysterium* was often an unimpressive symbolic relic or common object like an ear of corn. By this time, one could not admit that the revered ritual was mundane. Cognitive dissonance reduction demanded that the *mysterium* be profound. Otherwise, one's ancestors and current colleagues would not have granted it such reverence. The new initiate would have to admit he had been suckered into banality and wasted his time if he confessed to the vacuous content of the ceremony, so more often than not, people assumed that there must be some hidden knowledge in the secret rites that they themselves did not comprehend.

In all this, the presupposition was Aristotelian: entities that were naturally and hitherto strange to one another were brought together. This note will sound again in Marcionism where they believed in adoption by an alien, hitherto unknown God. The initiate began an inner transformation so that he could manifest a *doxa* (glory) body in the heavenly world, much as in Vajrayana Buddhism where the adept cultivates the growth of an internal, invisible *vajra*, or adamantine, body. Such a creature sloughs off the mortal cocoon at death and ascends through the gauntlet of planetary rulers.[2] What the devout seek, in both cases, is transcendence of mere humanity.

Gnosticism

Gnosticism must have begun as a form of Platonism by which one looked within to realize one's own deity. Gnostic teachers promulgated the doctrine and assumed that fellow latent pneumatics would find the spark of scattered divine light within themselves. When someone awakened to a realization of it, his task was to awaken others. Here was the original and natural context of the Redeemed Redeemer myth.[3] This myth depicted the heavenly revealer entering the material world only to become besotted and confused by its sensations, finally forgetting who he was and why he was there. Eventually he comes to his senses (much like the character in the parable of the Prodigal Son), and thus reawakened, the redeemer is better able to help others escape the very predicament he has shared. This awakening marked the reunion of what had been separated, not of strangers but of the estranged. As in Shankara's teaching in the Advaita Vedanta tradition,[4] the simple understanding of one's true nature is supposed to produce a liberated state of consciousness as one's blinders fall away. Initially such sudden revelations are common, especially under the immediate, personal influence of the revealer. But as time goes by, religious experience is not as dramatic or produced so simply. One begins to look back on that far-off beginning stage (if it ever really happened that way!) as a golden age of spiritual receptivity, whereas one's own period must be one of spiritual declension and befuddlement. One seeks techniques to midwife the longed-for transformation: stages of initiations, passwords to use with the archons who seek to prevent one's heavenly ascent, rites of baptism and of the bridal chamber.[5]

The same thing happened among adherents of the Samkhya philosophy in India. Samkhya taught that all pain arises from a confusion over the psycho-mental self with the true spirit within. The psychological self you think of as "me" is not the real you. No, the real self is an immortal, impassive spark of the divine deep inside you. It never suffers, but it is like the battery in a flashlight. The battery does not illumine anything, but it causes the flashlight bulb to illumine them. Thus, the spiritual spark, the *purusha*, causes the psycho-mental self (*prakriti*) to suffer. We can end the pain by recognizing the difference between the *prakriti* self and the *purusha* self. That will disentangle them. Merely realizing the difference was supposed to do the trick. As this did not seem to work for many, who were nonetheless pretty darn sure they understood the theory, they sought refuge in Patanjali's yoga, which added techniques to the doctrine: meditations for prying loose the spirit from the self.[6]

Again, think of how the failure of the Parousia (Second Coming of Christ) resulted in a chastened reduction of expectations on the part of the earlier apocalyptic enthusiasts (see below). In just the same way, many Gnostic converts must have been disappointed when acceptance of the secret truth seemingly did nothing to bring on-the-spot enlightenment, so they resorted to spiritual exercises. In case you don't recognize this, all these fall-back strategies would seem well described as a decline from salvation by faith to a gospel of works.

Max Scheler[7] explained this evolution or, if you prefer, declension. In any sect's second generation, the initial perfectionism fades, and instead of imitating the pioneer teacher-prophet (Gnostic revealer, Buddha, Jesus, and so forth), one comes to transfer the burden of salvation to him, making him into a savior who did the work for us so we would not have to do it for ourselves. The revealer becomes a redeemer. We can understand this shift as part of the move from sect to church, the process of assimilation and accommodation whereby a charismatic movement gradually backslides to the norms of the society from which it once withdrew. In like manner, its disappointed yet still committed members resign themselves to mundane mediocrity for the long haul.

Apocalyptic theology

Believers in the soon-coming end of the age anticipate a cosmic renewal and try to either bring it closer still or just to be ready for it when it happens. This they do by means of individual repentance and baptism. This was just like the mystery cults, where moral purification was necessary as a preliminary condition for one's salvation. We can even speak of a kind of elite *gnosis* for apocalyptic believers in that one knows how to discern the signs of the times, the ominous meaning of events leading up to the eschaton, ignored by the heedless worldlings who blithely go about their business even as the doomed contemporaries of Lot and Noah. "This calls for wisdom. Let him who is wise calculate the number of the Beast, for it is the number of a man." Again, as in the mysteries, the baptized apocalyptic believer anticipated a glorified body, stored in heaven, to be donned at the resurrection (2 Cor. 5:1-4).

The eager belief in an imminent coming brings enthusiasm and a feeling that we are already receiving a foretaste of the eschatological glory. We might call this "inaugurated eschatology."[8] The air seems thick with visions and revelations, apparitions, and the energy of miracles or their likelihood. Features of such enthusiasm include perfectionism (we "can't" sin, so we don't) and/or libertinism (we "can't" sin, so what I do must not *count* as a sin!). Apocalyptic zealots often also abandon family structure and gender roles because fleshly categories are rendered obsolete, along with the fallen age which is now over for us. Do you need parental roles and responsibilities when there is to be no future procreation? There may be expectations of perfect health since the "demons" of death and sickness are defeated. Believers may expect exaggerated longevity in order to survive till the End comes. The Blackstone Valley, Massachusetts, Immortalist sect believed they would attain immortality in the flesh, as did, two centuries later, Charles Fillmore, founder of the Unity School of Christianity.[9]

There are also claims of eschatological invulnerability: "O

Death, where is thy sting?" Poison-drinking and snake-handling Pentecostals are familiar in America. Again and again, we read of the total faith of this or that millenarian group, persuaded that the bullets of the enemy would turn to water or otherwise harmlessly impact them. The fate of such eschatological shock troops is well known, as in the most famous cases, such as the Boxer Rebellion in China (1899-1901) and the Maji-maji Rebellion in Tanganyika (1905-06). Peter Worsley[10] provides numerous tragic examples from the Cargo Cults. Papuans heeded "propaganda about the magical efficacy of a holy-water drink of invulnerability. This would effectively protect the user if certain taboos were observed. Bullets striking the user's body would turn to water." Japanese invaders proved them wrong. Thus perished also the ostensibly bullet-proof minions of the "Father of the World" in Indian Bihar.[11] Such was also the promise of the doomed prophets of the Tana Bhagat movement in the same region in 1915. And let's not forget the bullet-proof promises of the Lakota Sioux prophet Kicking Bear and their sad failure at Wounded Knee.

Nor, in light of the now-dawning kingdom, should one waste one's time in holding down a job. Why not let God provide, like for the birds that spend their time endlessly praising him in song? Thus, the fishermen leave their nets and toll-collectors their booths. Concerning the Tuka movement that was started in 1882 by the Fiji prophet Navosavakandua, Worsley tells us: "His lieutenants traveled far and wide urging people to abandon everything."[12] Regarding the Milne Bay Prophet movement (1893): "Since food would be so abundant, all pigs were to be killed and eaten, and food in the gardens consumed. The people heeded his message. No work was done, and some 300-400 pigs were killed and eaten."[13] Amid the Vailala Madness (1919-31): "Confident in the arrival of the Cargo, villagers spent their time seated with their backs towards the tables, abandoned gardening and ceased their traditional trade."[14] And of the followers of Marafi, prophet of Satan (1932), we read,

"Owing to the expectation of the imminent cataclysm, gardens were abandoned; deserters from employment hid in the villages."[15] The prophet Mambu (1930s) "encouraged them to eat up all their food."[16] In the early 1930s, the Melanesian prophet Sanop, on one of the Solomon Islands, "stressed that the Cargo ship would bring tinned food for those who lacked it, and that those owning large gardens or many pigs should give their food away in feasts if they wished to qualify for a share in the Cargo."[17] "Gardens were harvested and pigs slaughtered; if this were not done, the *Koreri* [utopia] would never come, manna would not fall, and the people would be condemned to a life of toil in the gardens."[18] Stephen Fuchs[19] provided more information on the 1895 Father of the World, otherwise known as Birsa Munda, who predicted an imminent catastrophe from which only his believers should survive. It "was wasted labour, therefore, to weed the crops; and as the people would have no further use for ploughing, they should turn all the cattle loose."

Ernst Käsemann[20] applied a distinction to New Testament passages, based on a suggestion by Martin Luther, that depended on whether the crucifixion or the resurrection was emphasized ("cross or glory"). In one category he described the perceived teaching of Mark and Paul to the effect that, during our earthly sojourn, we are treading the way of the cross, a path of suffering and humility, in which the glory of Christ manifests itself in our endurance of suffering and persecution (2 Cor. 4:7-11). If the centurion could recognize in Jesus the son of God while he was on the cross (Mk. 15:39), we too should properly see the glory of Christ in contemplation of the crucifixion. We ought to see even the risen Christ as the crucified one now exalted. Jesus was "lifted up," as John 12:32 has it, *on the cross*. The power of God is perceived by the eye of faith in the midst of an ambiguous world that still looks pretty much unredeemed (2 Cor. 4:18). We approach God, even as baptized Christians, as penitents knowing that God gives grace to the humble and spurns the proud (1 Pet. 5:5). It is easy to stray from this path and to imagine ourselves to be living already in the fullness of divine glory as promised for the millennial kingdom, or heaven. The passage in 1 Corinthians 4:8, Käsemann says, rebukes this tendency.

To be sure, believers "have tasted the goodness of the word of God and the powers of the age to come" (Heb. 6:5)—but how much? The more of the future eschatological glory we claim to have experienced, the more we operate on the theology of glory. And here is that other category. We become charismatics, enthusiasts, even fanatics, erasing any line between faith and sight (2 Cor. 5:7), between present and future, even between human and divine (prematurely, since this, too, is scheduled for the future, 1 Cor. 15:28).

But the more we defer such triumphalism, the more we abide by the theology of the cross. We are pessimistic but willing to shoulder our own crosses. The glory of the resurrection will one day be ours, but in the meantime we must not jump the gun. When we hear or read such admonitions, we can be sure eschatological fervor is dwindling, and that those doing the admonishing, seeking to soften the blow most, do not yet see it coming. This is the whole point of Gospel parables like Matthew's parable of the Wise and Foolish Virgins (Matt. 25:1-13).

Suppose a messiah announces himself. What do you know? The world does not change outwardly after all, so the eschatological hope becomes "realized."[21] "It's here!" But only secretly or in figurative form. This heady feeling lasts only so long, since the mundane world stubbornly refuses to give way to the Millennium. The messiah cannot live forever, and his death, whether at the hands of his enemies or from old age, marks a return to history and a revision of theology. The routinization of charisma[22] leads to institutionalization, re-assimilation, and a redefinition of the messiah as a religious founder. He becomes no longer the embodiment of a living future but a monument of a holy past. Now his believers posit a *second* coming, which becomes the new focus of expectation, and the cycle begins again.

Or he may be relegated to the role of a forerunner, with a new figure slated to come to fulfill the forerunner's mission. This happened when the Messiah Simon bar-Kochba ("Son of the Star," Num. 24:17), endorsed by the great Rabbi Akiba, fell in battle against the Romans in 135 CE. Was he then a false messiah? Not at all, just a preliminary messiah, messiah ben-Joseph, who had to die in battle to expunge Israel's sins and prepare the way for the sure-to-be-victorious Messiah ben-David, soon to come.[23]

Sooner or later, "realized" eschatology declines into mere "inaugurated" eschatology, and our modest spiritual experiences get reduced to the level of "first fruits" (Rom. 8:23) or "earnest money" (2 Cor. 1:22; 5:5) toward the real thing, which will be delivered with the *eschaton*. The game is cognitive dissonance reduction:[24] "Well, it wasn't exactly a mistake. It wasn't just a false start. No, the event turned out to be more of a process. It did begin; it just hasn't come to consummation." That's the ticket.

The same thing happened when frustrated Buddhists who could not seem to attain nirvana began to defer their hopes to the imagined future arrival of a new Buddha, Maitreya, in whose far-off era salvation and enlightenment would flow as freely as a river. They hoped to be lucky enough to be reborn in that distant day and achieve the liberation that eluded them here and now. Likewise, Cargo cultists did not renounce their faith when the treasure-laden ships failed to arrive. "Morale was ... boosted in the face of failure by concrete 'evidence' of success: cartridges from wrecked planes, newspaper, calico and other trade goods were often shown as magical first fruits of the harvest to come."[25]

Another way of dealing with the disappointment of the predicted end is to swallow hard and insist that the new world has in fact come, despite all appearances. This is to stretch the notion of realized eschatology as far as it can possibly go. The sect's cherished *gnosis* may include knowledge that, despite all appearances, the kingdom is all around us.[26] The kingdom may remain a purely interior reality, a devotional fantasy, or it may be actualized in secret group behavior such as glossolalia meetings or, at the other extreme, libertine orgies as in the fourth-century Phibionite sect and seventeenth-century Jakob Frank cult.[27] Either way, the saved souls flout the old law, saying that "sin was in the world before the law was given, but sin is not charged against anyone's account where there is no law" (Rom. 5:13). Marcion had no truck with libertinism because he still accommodated family structures among the less than perfect, second-class membership. By contrast, Gnostics were lone wolves, although most functioned secretly within churches where it was safer to be ultra-moral, a la the Sermon on the Mount, a higher righteousness that pretty much makes the Law moot: "Against such there is no law" (Gal. 5:23).

Libertinism and asceticism are equally at home in Gnosticism and apocalyptic. In the first case, one disdains the code of the demiurge, knowing oneself to be superior to him and to it. In the second, antinomianism may be legitimized as liminal behavior on the boundary of the ages. In an "interim ethic," the old laws just don't apply, having been designed to meet the needs of a world now passing away. Or it may be an anticipation of the eschatological abolition or reinterpretation of the Torah, so that what was once forbidden is now permitted. But even this, a la Jakob Frank, represents an accommodation to deferral: one day the kingdom will come outwardly, and until it does, we behave as we do in secret.

Worsley provides a number of examples of millenarian Cargo Cults abolishing traditional marriage and sexual arrangements, having in common the notion that "all things are become new" in the face of impending eschatological fulfillment. One New Guinea prophet "called for the abolition of the old exogamous restrictions and for the amendment of marriage customs."[28] "If we examine the many cases of 'sexual excess,' 'erotic communism,' 'morbid asceticism,' and all the other labels pinned to ritual obscenity and sacrilege, it becomes clear that we are not dealing with unbridled lust or

with ascetic perversion. We are dealing with the deliberate enact-
ment of the overthrow of cramping bonds of the past, not in order
to throw overboard all morality, but in order to create a new brotherhood with a completely new morality … Sexual communism and
sexual asceticism, both so common in millenarian movements, are
thus two sides of the same coin—the rejection of outworn creeds."[29]

There was also the practice of "spiritual wifery" among the radical sect of the Separates in eighteenth-century Blackstone Valley,
Massachusetts. Wives discarded their husbands, choosing new partners within the sect who were considered more spiritual. This led
to accusations of antinomianism.[30] As radical as it may seem, even
the notion that the Torah, which once had value, had been superseded as part of the plan of God, sounds like the back-pedaling
compromise of an even more radical, Gnostic, and ascetic Paulinism
in which the Law was the creation of the demiurge, the serpent,
angels (Gal. 3:19-20), or even the devil. Depending on one's viewpoint, the change represents either mitigation or vilification.

Marcionism

Marcionite soteriology posits Jesus's crucifixion as a ransom
to purchase the Creator's creatures, which will free them so they
can be adopted by the Father, the alien God. It is not a death for
sin. It is not a sacrifice. It is not an atonement or expiation. Marcion taught this openly, not as a privately held secret that would be
known only to a few chosen ones. His intent was to found a public
institution. By contrast, Valentinians, Frankists, and others existed
as secret groups within Catholic congregations. Therefore, as suggested by *Thomas* 13,[31] the true believers had to maintain secrecy.
In Marcionite churches, there was no need for such tact and strategy. The Marcionite baptism was a rite of passage rather than the
initiation into greater *gnosis*. It indicated a full embrace of the ethical implications of membership. People who believed in the ascetical ideal delayed baptism until they were ready to put it into prac-

tice, in which they were not alone. Many contemporary Christians did the very same thing.[32]

Catholicism

Where does Catholic Christianity begin to diverge from Paulinism? As Adolf Harnack said, Catholicism perpetuated the originally Gnostic notion of an earthly Jesus as a temporary manifestation of the heavenly Christ, though without the docetic denial of a fleshly incarnation.[33] It merged this with a mystery religion sacramentalism. Thus, Catholic Christianity was not even one of the earliest types of Christianity, but a secondary mixture of elements from the Christianities its bishops despised and condemned. Where along the line did it become a separate species? I think it was occasioned by the split between the original Gnosticism, which expected instantaneous enlightenment upon understanding the secret doctrine, and the subsequent version which introduced various exercises to cultivate the enlightenment gradually. What were those exercises? Moral "good works" of salvation. In the general Hellenistic Christian context, "works" no longer suggested Jewish Torah observance ("works of the Law"), to most Christians. Originally, moral discipline had been, as for Socrates and the mystery religions, a preliminary training exercise to get the soul ready for greater things. As the Gnostic goal of higher, mystical aspiration fell away, as it did also in Buddhism as the generations passed, "good works" themselves became the way of salvation. The goal that had been penultimate now became ultimate. And of course, the sacramental mysteries themselves became central to salvation in the same unstable combination with moral preparation which we still see in today's forms of Christianity.

. . . . .

In the chapters that follow, I want to place each section of the text of the Pauline epistles against the most plausible of the theological backgrounds outlined here to see if it sounds more Gnostic, libertine, enthusiastic, Marcionite, Catholicizing, or something else. It seems that each bit of material belongs to the stage of soteriology it sounds the most like. I want to discern the most plausible *Sitz-im-Leben* (life context) for each. In this way we will be able to deconstruct the texts, tracing each segment back to its probable origin. Only in this manner can we take up Darrell Doughty's challenge to Pauline studies, namely, to treat individual pericopae in the epistles as we do in the Gospels. We need, for the moment, to ignore the present context and ask instead what is the best sense that can be made of each passage from internal clues. Only then do we have the right to begin redaction criticism: discerning what the redactor has done with his mosaic tiles in forming them into a larger picture. But that endeavor I leave to others. Unlike L. Gordon Rylands, Walter Schmithals, J. C. O'Neill, and others, I make no attempt here to get back to the original Romans, Galatians, Ephesians, or other missive. That would be like the numerous attempts to peel away inauthentic Jesus materials to get back to those which are authentic to Jesus. I think both goals are equally futile. All I feel confident in doing is laying bare the composite character of each epistle, tracing each jigsaw piece to its likely origin. My goal is to make a running start at doing for the Pauline epistles what Rudolf Bultmann did in his *History of the Synoptic Tradition*. I am no more sure about restoring pristine, original autograph versions of the epistles, whether by Marcion, Simon Magus, Paul, or anyone else, than I am that the Jesus traditions took their rise from a single historical figure. These texts we now read as epistles may have been patchwork quilts from the start. We see the historical Paul come in and out of focus like the projection of a flickering hologram.

In the remaining chapters, I provide my own translation of and commentary on the letters that have been traditionally ascribed to Paul, and if someone objects that the whole procedure is subjective and circular, I deny it. Right or wrong, I have laid out my criteria, derived from a paradigm of widely attested religious evolution. If someone charges that my endeavor here is wholly speculative, I congratulate him on his grasp of the obvious.

NOTES

[1]Arnold van Gennep, *The Rites of Passage*. Trans. Monika B. Vizedom and Gabrielle L. Caffee (Chicago: University of Chicago Press, 1960).

[2]Richard Reitzenstein, *Hellenistic Mystery-Religions: Their Basic Ideas and Significance*, trans. John E. Steely, Pittsburgh Theological Monograph Series 15 (1926; Pittsburgh: Pickwick Press, 1978), 325-30, 334-36, 440-41, 444, 450, 454-55.

[3]This is the concept that the redeemer himself needs redemption, usually in the sense that there are sparks of divinity in everything, including plants and animals, and that by being part of the physical world, God suffers. These divine elements need to be gathered up and re-united with God through some act of redemption.

[4]Agehananda Bharati, *The Tantric Tradition* (Garden City: Doubleday Anchor Books, 1970), 19-20; Mircea Eliade, *Yoga: Immortality and Freedom*, 2nd ed., trans. Willard R. Trask, Bollingen Series 57 (Princeton: Princeton University Press, 1969), 144-45; Eliot Deutsch, *Advaita Vedanta: A Philosophical Reconstruction* (Honolulu: East-West Center Press, 1969).

[5]Walter Schmithals, *Gnosticism in Corinth*, trans. John E. Steely (New York: Abingdon Press, 1971), 27-28, 168, 258-59.

[6]On Samkhya and Yoga, see Eliade, *Yoga: Immortality*, 7, 15.

[7]Max Scheler, *Problems of a Sociology of Knowledge*, trans. Manfred S. Frings, International Library of Sociology (London: Routledge & Keegan Paul, 1980), 84-85.

[8]Ernst Haenchen and Joachim Jeremias spoke for many scholars when they described the future-expectation of Jesus, based on his own experience of the presence and power of God, as "eschatology in the process of realization." Haenchen suggested the term to Jeremias in a letter. Jeremias popularized it in his classic work *The Parables of Jesus*, trans, S. H. Hooke (Lon-

don: SCM Press, 1954), 159. Jeremias expounded on the notion by refering to various Gospel materials in his *New Testament Theology: Part One, The Proclamation of Jesus*, trans. John Bowden, New Testament Library (London: SCM Press, 1971), 103-08. The point of the unwieldy nomenclature is to distinguish the position from "realized eschatology," which denotes that the Kingdom of God has fully arrived, albeit figuratively or spiritually, and with no future remainder to be expected. See Norman Perrin, *The Kingdom of God in the Teaching of Jesus* (London: SCM Press, 1963), 87-89, who provides a succinct taxonomy of various related theories on the subject, distinguishing their nuances nicely.

Gershom G. Scholem describes the fervor among the believers in seventeenth-century messiah Sabbatai Sevi in terms that strikingly parallel Jeremias's sketch of "eschatology in the process of realization": "Before redemption had actually come, it was felt by many to have become reality" (*Major Trends in Jewish Mysticism*, trans. George Lichtheim. [New York: Schocken Books, 1973], eighth lecture: "Sabbatianism and Mystical Heresy," 288). See also Scholem, *Sabbatai Sevi: The Mystical Messiah*, trans. R. J. Zwi Werblowsky, Bollingen Series XCIII (Princeton: Princeton University Press, 1973), 512.

[9]John L. Brooke, *The Refiner's Fire: The Making of Mormon Cosmology, 1644-1844* (New York: Cambridge University Press, 1994), 56.

[10]Peter Worsley, *The Trumpet Shall Sound: A Study of "Cargo" Cults in Melanesia*, 2nd ed. (New York: Schocken Books, 1968), 141.

[11]Stephen Fuchs, *Rebellious Prophets: A Study of Messianic Movements in Indian Religions* (New York: Asia House Publishing, 1965), 29-30, 32, 41, 96, 98, 123, 149, 220.

[12]Worsley, *Trumpet Shall Sound*, 23.

[13]Ibid., 52-53.

[14]Ibid., 84.

[15]Ibid., 103.

[16]Ibid., 107.

[17]Ibid., 116-17.

[18]Ibid., 139.

[19]Fuchs, *Rebellious Prophets*, 29; see also Felicitas D. Goodman, *Ecstasy, Ritual, and Alternate Reality: Religion in a Pluralistic World* (Bloomington and Indianapolis: Indiana University Press, 1988), 40.

[20]Ernst Käsemann, *Perspectives on Paul*, trans. Margaret Kohl (Philadelphia: Fortress Press, 1971), 1-2.

[21]John 5:24-25; 11:22-26; 14:22-23.

[22]Max Weber, *The Theory of Social and Economic Organization*, trans. Anketell Matthew Henderson and Talcott Parsons (New York: Oxford University Press, 1947), 363-73.

[23]Geza Vermes, *Jesus the Jew: A Historian's Reading of the Gospels* (London: Fontana/Collins, 1976), 140.

[24]Leon Festinger, Henry W. Riecken, and Stanley Schachter, *When Prophecy Fails: A Social and Psychological Study of a Modern Group that Predicted the Destruction of the World* (NY: Harper & Row Torchbooks, 1956).

[25]Worsley, *Trumpet Shall Sound*, 203.

[26]Luke 17:20-21; Thom. 51, 113.

[27]Gershom Scholem, "Redemption through Sin," trans. Hillel Halkin [Michael A. Meyer translated the rest of the book], in Scholem, *The Messianic Idea in Judaism and Other Essays on Jewish Spirituality* (New York: Schocken Books, 1971), 78-141.

[28]Worsley, *Trumpet Shall Sound*, 109; also 150-51 ("Husbands should show no jealousy, for this would disturb the state of harmony which the cult was trying to establish."), 167, 202; Victor Turner, *The Ritual Process: Structure and Anti-Structure*, Lewis Morgan Henry Lectures for 1966 (Ithaca: Cornell University Press, 1977), 94-130; Albert Schweitzer, *The Mystery of the Kingdom of God: The Secret of Jesus' Messiahship and Passion*, trans. Walter Lowrie (1914; New York: Schocken Books, 1964), 97, 103; Gershom G. Scholem, *On the Kabbalah and Its Symbolism*, trans. Ralph Manheim (New York: Schocken Books, 1974), 32-86.

[29]Worsley, *Trumpet Shall Sound*, 250-51.

[30]Brooke, *Refiner's Fire*, 56.

[31]"Jesus says to his disciples, 'Compare me and tell me what I am like.' Simon Peter says to him, 'You are like a righteous angel.' Matthew says to him, 'You are like a philosopher possessed of understanding.' Thomas says to him, 'Master, my mouth can scarcely frame the words of what you are like!' Jesus says, 'I am not your master, because you have drunk, you have become filled, from the bubbling spring which I have measured out.' He took him aside privately and said three things to him. So when Thomas rejoined his companions, they pressed him, saying, 'What did Jesus say to you?' Thomas said to them, 'If I tell you even one of the things he said to me, you will pick up stones and hurl them at me—and fire will erupt from the stones and consume you!'" (*Thomas*, Saying 13)

[32]Steven Runciman, *The Medieval Manichee: A Study of the Christian Dualist Heresy* (NewYork: Viking/Compass Books, 1961), 164.

[33]Adolf von Harnack, *History of Dogma*, 7 vols., trans. Neil Buchanan (Boston: Little, Brown, 1901), 1:258-59.

9.

The Epistle to the Romans

Upon very close examination, the Epistle to the Romans, with its numerous contradictions and anachronisms, starts to look like a patchwork quilt stitched together by the hands of various Paulinists with competing views. What might be the historical occasion for the nucleus to which all the rest was eventually added? What if the trip to Rome anticipated by the writer is that of Marcion when he brought a contribution to the church at Rome and set forth his gospel before its elders? He was rejected, as was his monetary gift. Perhaps the basis of Romans was written by (or for) Marcion to be submitted as a statement of his theology. The deliberations over the Torah and the Jews would then reflect the dispute over the Marcionite belief that Jews had a separate religion from Christianity, and that the two had nothing in common. Arguments from scripture in the original Marcionite text would have to be understood as circumstantial *ad hominem* arguments, embarrassing the Catholic leaders who were committed to retaining the Old Testament as Christian scripture.

Subsequent Marcionite redactors and Gnostic interpolators would have interposed their own opinions here and there in the text, "correcting" views they thought erroneous or deficient, as is the way with ancient copyists. Compare the case of the Hindu Upanishads, heavily overlaid with clashing metaphysics and mythology. Once Catholics decided to co-opt the Marcionite canon, they would have padded the text with new material in order to domesticate and sanitize Romans for their own use. This is surely the origin, for instance, of the tortuous treatment of the Old Testament law, both condemning and defending it in a manner that has always baffled exegetes. A comparison of modern commentaries reveals that scholars, trying to fit all the jigsaw pieces into a single coherent puzzle, cannot agree on so basic a point as whether "Paul" believed the Jewish Law was still in force! No wonder.

1

[1]Paul, slave of Christ-Jesus, called as apostle, devoted exclusively to the news of God, [2]which he had already promised through his prophets in Holy Scripture, [3]about his Son, "sprung from the line of David according to flesh, [4]miraculously appointed Son of God according to the Spirit of Holiness by a resurrection of the dead, Jesus-Christ, our Lord."

We start off with a Catholic interpolation, piling on anti-Marcionite features, namely Old Testament prophecy, adoptionistic Christology, and Davidic Messianism. Marcion did not believe the Jewish scripture predicted the Christian Jesus. He did believe a Jewish messianic king, descended from King David, would appear and satisfy Jewish expectation, but this was not Jesus Christ. Nor did Marcion accept the Jewish-Christian notion that Jesus had become God's son by adoption. For Marcion, Jesus simply appeared on earth one day, already an adult and with a celestial body. A Catholic redactor has tried to counteract all these features of Marcionism to sanitize the epistle for Catholic use, and he wastes no time in doing so: right at the beginning!

All commentators recognize that verses 3 and 4 are foreign material, partly because of the non-Pauline adoptionism. But mainstream critics suggest Paul himself has inserted, that is, quoted, a fragment of a Jewish-Christian creedal affirmation cherished by the faction of Roman Jewish Christians to whom, in part, the epistle is directed. Paul wants to win them over, and right off the bat. The trouble with this theory is that it envisions an utter lack of sincerity on the author's part, imagining Paul in effect signing on to a creed, a pretty serious matter, to which he does not in fact subscribe. That is a bit more than "doing as the Romans do." Besides, can we really envision normative creeds belonging to different Christian denominations this early in Christian history? That is, if the author is the historical Paul? It is almost like having Paul comment on the *filioque* clause of the Nicene Creed.

One might point out, however, that it would be equally dishonest for an interpolator to smuggle into the text a creedal bit he had no reason to believe Paul would have affirmed. But that is not quite right. In such a case, what we have to envision is a scribe thinking how best to improve or amend a regulative *text*, not whether to misrepresent the opinions of an historical *individual*. As 2 Peter 1:21 says, "prophecy was never brought by human initiative, but mortals spoke from God as the Holy Spirit carried them along in a passive state."

[7b]May God, our Father and that of the Lord, Jesus-Christ, grant you his favor and his blessing of peace.

As often elsewhere, the emphasis on God *the Father*, which we have learned over the centuries to take for granted, emphasizes Marcionite theology in which we have abandoned the Creator God to be adopted as the children of the Father of Jesus Christ.

[8]First of all, let me thank my God, invoking Jesus-Christ, for all of you! Your faith is being made known worldwide, [9]since, as God is my witness, whom I serve at the core of my being in service of the news of his Son, I never omit mention of you [10]in my prayers wherever I happen to be, requesting if perhaps by the will of God I may be granted a propitious journey to come to you. [11]For I yearn to see you in order to present you with some spiritual charisma so you may be established as greatest among the churches of God, [12]and in order that we may be mutually encouraged by means of the faith you and I have in one another. [13]But brothers, I do not want you to be unaware

that I have several times resolved to come see you, only to be hindered till now, wanting to harvest a crop from you as I have among the other nations. [14]I am in debt to both Greeks and uncouth barbarians, to both the wise and the savage. [15]Consequently, insofar as it is up to me, I am eager to preach to you *in Rome.* [16]My long absence is by no means due to some reluctance I might have about the news of Christ. How could it be? It is divine power to save everyone who believes, first of course the Jew, and also the Greek. [17]For in it there is revealed a salvation beginning and ending in faith, just as it is written: "The righteous man will live off faith."

This makes more sense as a fragment of an actual letter from Marcion himself announcing his intention to visit Rome, which he did. In Paul's day there was no church there, according to Acts. But in our epistle, there is already an established congregation before Paul visits. The text seems confused: Paul is pictured as the pioneer missionary to gentiles, so he wants to exercise this ministry in Rome (verses 13-15). That would seem to mean he wants to found a church in Rome as he has done elsewhere—but then whom is he addressing? Are we to imagine him writing this to a Roman church that does not yet exist? If there *is* one for him to write to, then it is a bit too late for him to found the church, isn't it? It all makes more sense as the announcement of Marcion to preach among them a version of the gospel they may not have heard. We know he did, in fact, "audition" his gospel in Rome, hoping to be acclaimed bishop there.

[18]For the heavens declare the wrath of God on all the impiety and unrighteousness of mankind who hide away the truth in unrighteousness [19]because what is known about God is no secret to them: God has revealed it to them [20]simply by creating the world. For anyone can clearly see his invisible attributes in the things he made, notably both his everlasting power and divinity, and this leaves human beings without excuse; [21]because even though they knew God, they did not worship him as God nor render him due thanks, but instead, their thinking became an exercise in futility, their obtuse minds blinded. [22]Claiming a reputation for wisdom, they only became more foolish [23]and refashioned the sublimity of the immutable Godhead into something like the image of ephemeral humanity and birds and

quadrupeds and reptiles. [24]Accordingly, God abandoned them to pursue their hearts' desire for impurity, to the mutual defilement of each other's bodies, [25]these who twisted the truth of God into a tissue of lies, offering worship and sacrifice to the creature rather than to the creator, blessed may be he through the ages! [26]Because of all this, God surrendered them to degrading passions, for even their females, of whom better might have been expected, traded the natural function for the unnatural, [27]and in the same way, the males, too, disdaining the natural vessel for their seed, the female, burned with their desire for one another, males on males, enacting the perversion and unable to evade the inevitable repercussions of their error on their consciences. [28]And as they did not judge it best to retain God in their awareness, God allowed them to fall victim to a substandard mind, inclined to the worst thoughts, to do whatever is improper, [29]bloated with all manner of injustice, evil, covetousness, maliciousness, full of murderous envy, deceitful strife, ill-will, conspiratorial whisperers, [30]detractors, God-haters, over-weening pride, the arrogant, braggarts, evil schemers, defiant of parental authority, [31]obtuse, welchers, without love of family, unrelenting; [32]those who know full well the edict of God, that people doing these things deserve death, and not only still do them but approve others who do the same.

2

[1]So what excuse can you possibly offer, O man, when you presume to judge everyone else? For whenever you condemn another, you yourself are equally guilty. [2]But we know the verdict that God renders on people who practice such things is objective. [3]And you who condemn those who practice these things while doing them yourself, do you imagine you will escape the judgment of God? [4]Or is it perhaps that you disdain the wealth of his goodness and his tolerance and patience, oblivious of the fact that the kindness of God ought to lead you to repent? [5]But as your stubborn, impenitent heart deserves, you have amassed yourself a tidy sum of wrath to be inherited on the Day of Wrath when the righteous judgment of God will be declared—[6]he who will repay every individual as his deeds deserve: [7]on the one hand, age-long life to those who seek to be glorified and honored with immortality by persisting in good deeds;

[8]on the other, wrath and anger to those who are self-seeking, disobeying the demands of truth but obeying the dictates of unrighteousness. [9]There will be tribulation and anguish upon every human soul who does evil, both to Jew, firstly, and to Greek; [10]but glory, reward, and respite upon every one doing good, both to Jew, firstly, and to Greek. [11]For no partiality is to be found with God. [12]Every one who sinned outside the reach of the Torah will also perish without reference to the Torah; and every one who sinned, having the Torah, will be condemned from the Torah. [13]For it is not those who merely hear the Torah readings who will be declared just before God, but those who practice the commandments will be accepted. [14]For whenever nations without the Torah nonetheless obey the dictates of the Torah, these without the Torah are nonetheless a law unto themselves; [15]they evidence the requirement of the Torah inscribed on their hearts, their conscience vouching for them when their inner thoughts either accuse or excuse them [16]*on that day when God judges the secrets of mortals, as my preaching has it, by means of Jesus-Christ.* [17]But suppose you bear the designation "Jew" and rely on the Torah, boasting of your God, [18]knowing the divine will and approving the things that excel, having been instructed in the Torah, [19]having convinced yourself you are a guide to the blind, a beacon for the benighted, [20]an instructor of the simple, a trainer of infants, possessing in the Torah the very standard for knowledge and truth. [21]You who teach another, do you not bother teaching yourself? You who preach not to steal: do you steal? [22]The one saying not to commit adultery: do you commit adultery? The one who hates idols: do you rob temples? [23]You who brag about the Torah: do you disgrace the name of God by violating the Torah? [24]For indeed the name of God is ridiculed among the nations because of you, as it is written. [25]While circumcision is worthwhile if you keep the Torah, if you are a violator of the Torah, your circumcision has reverted to uncircumcised paganism. [26]Equally, then, if an uncircumcised man keeps the provisions of the Torah, will not his lack of circumcision be waived, with him being considered as if circumcised? [27]The one who is uncircumcised but keeps the Torah spontaneously will judge you who, despite possessing the written text and circumcision, violate the Torah. [28]For he is not the Jew externally, nor is the real circumcision external in the

flesh. [29]But Jewish identity is an invisible thing and the circumcision is of the heart, by spirit, not by letter, and it calls forth the admiration not of one's fellows, but of God.

This section is the text of a Hellenistic Jewish synagogue sermon.[1] L. Gordon Rylands[2] understood this section as originally a part of a Gnostic epistle, precisely because of its affinity with Philonic, philosophical Judaism, from which he thought Gnosticism grew. He may have been quite right about the affinity to Philo, but that hardly makes it Gnostic. There is absolutely nothing Gnostic about this section in its own right. I regard it as a Jewish text, following J. C. O'Neill. It would have been added by a Catholic redactor who liked the positive evaluation of Jewish Law. All the better that gentiles are not required to keep the Jewish code, despite its divine authority.

But take a close look at the sermon's doctrine of the Torah, and of just *why* Jews and gentiles are equal before it. It has nothing to do with what we think of as the Pauline gospel. Pauline doctrine has it that all are *equally guilty* and thus in need of some other, extra-legal path of salvation, and that this has been provided by God's grace. This sermon, by contrast, teaches that Jews and gentiles may prove themselves *equally worthy* of salvation by their good deeds, whether these are defined by the Mosaic Torah or by the inner moral compass common to all human beings.

Verse 2:16 superficially Christianizes the sermon text. It is thus a redactional tack serving to attach the sermon to the larger context. It is just like Genesis 6:3, which tacks the pericope of Genesis 6:1-2, 4, about gods mating with mortals, into the story of the flood, with which it originally had nothing to do.

Verse 2:24 refers to passages like Psalms 74:10, 18; 79:9-10a; Exodus 32:12. The implication is that God's name comes into disrepute at times of national tragedy for Jews, since gentiles scoff at the Jews' much-vaunted trust in God. If they are his chosen people, why didn't he deliver them? The appearance of this theme here implies a recent national disaster, which must be the Roman defeat of Jewish uprisings in CE 73 or 136. We will see other evidence of a post-70 CE date for Romans.

3

[1]In that case, what is the advantage in being a Jew? Why is it better to have been circumcised? [2]Actually, its value is quite considerable by any standard! First and foremost, they were vouchsafed the revelations of God. [3]What do you think? Just because some of them failed to believe, will their unbelief nullify the fidelity of God? [4]Never! No, let God be true and every human being a liar! So it is written: "Thus you are proven right in your assertions and will prevail when you come before the bar of judgment." [5]Now if our unrighteousness accentuates God's righteousness, what are we to infer? Is God in the wrong to inflict wrath? I am just playing devil's advocate, you understand. [6]Never! If that were so, how could God judge the world? And we know he will, so your reasoning has gone off track somewhere. [7]But if by means of my lying, God's truth is magnified, glorifying him all the more, then why am I also condemned as a sinner? [8]Indeed, why not say, as we are slanderously misrepresented by some as saying, "Let us do evil deeds to bring about good results." These people deserve every bit of the judgment awaiting them!

[9]What, then? Are we Jews better? Not at all! We have already demonstrated both Jews and Greeks to be equally under sin, [10]exactly as it is written: "There is not a single righteous man! Not one! There is no man of understanding! [11]There is no one seeking God! [12]All turned away from him, *en masse* they have become worthless; there is not a one engaging in kindness—not even one!" [13]"From their throats rise the loathsome exhalations of a violated grave." "They deceive with their tongues like asps with their venom sacks." [14]"Their mouth overflows with bitterness and execration." [15]"They run swiftly to violent crime. [16]Behind them stretches a wake of ruin and woe. [17]They are total strangers to the ways of peace." [18]"They reckon without the fear of God." [19]Now it stands to reason that whatever the Torah says to those mentioned in the text it says not to them alone, but in order to silence every mouth and place the whole human race under judgment before God, [20]for the simple reason that all flesh will not be vindicated before him by means of deeds of Torah. No, the role of the Torah is to document the full extent of sin, as we have just seen. [21]But now, apart from the Torah a way of salvation sent from God has been revealed in full view of the Torah and the Prophets, [22]a salva-

tion that comes from God by means of belief in Jesus-Christ for all those who believe. For there is no difference; [23]for all sinned and forfeit the vision of God, [24]being vindicated for free by token of his beneficence, their freedom purchased by means of Jesus-Christ. [25]*By virtue of his fidelity even to the point of shedding of blood, God deigned to accept him as a propitiation to vindicate his righteousness since he had patiently overlooked sins previously committed, [26]showing forth his plan of salvation now in the present time, himself being just and the one who accepts those with the belief in Jesus-Christ.*

This section is Catholic-retooled Paulinism, genuine Pauline insights harmonized with the Old Testament. The prerogative of the Christian God to judge is affirmed, as well as documented from Jewish scripture. The Marcionite opposition of Torah and Gospel is retained, but in the Lutheran manner, dialectically, so that the Torah is no mere sham but is a needful preliminary stage. Verse 8 is a Catholic repudiation of Paulinist/Gnostic libertinism (whether real or merely imagined as the supposedly inevitable implication of the law-free theology). The verse is exactly parallel to 2 Peter 3:15b-16: "So also our beloved brother Paul wrote to you according to the wisdom given him, speaking of this in all his letters. There are some things in them hard to understand, which the ignorant and unstable twist to their own destruction, as they do the other scriptures." Here, too, Paul is welcomed into the club, while his earlier, heretical admirers are written off as cranks who don't know what he meant. So don't blame Paul for what some of his fans claim he taught.

Verses 25-26 appear to be a later interpolation or an earlier bit of text stitched in here by the Catholic scribe who composed the present context.[3] It makes sense as part of a Catholic gloss, making the crucifixion a way of patching the gentiles into the salvation history of Israel, not exactly a Marcionite concern.

[27]What room is left for bragging? It is ruled out. But by what rule? The Torah of deeds? No, through a principle of faith. [28]We have to conclude thusly: a person without the Torah is accepted by God through belief. [29]Or does God belong to Jews only? Does he not belong to the nations, too? Yes, to the nations, too, [30]since there is a single God who will accept circumcision by faith and uncircumci-

sion through faith. [31]Do we in this way nullify the Torah through this faith? Never! Instead, we set the Torah on a whole new footing.

Here and in 7:7 we have accommodating attempts by Catholic Paulinists to back away from the thoroughgoing anti-Torah position of original Marcionite and Gnostic Paulinism, seeking to retain the Torah nominally by domesticating it with theological euphemism, while still setting it aside as essentially irrelevant and obsolete. One might call it a case of damning with faint praise, but that is just the goal: the Catholic Paulinist wishes only to secure a secondary position for the Torah, insultingly lesser and lower than that claimed for it in Judaism. It reminds us of the kid-gloves treatment of former rival John the Baptist in the Gospels: better to co-opt his heritage and followers than to vilify their figurehead outright (as some Christian sectarians, however, did, calling John the fountainhead of all heresies).

Note how, in the ensuing chapter, the Torah does not, in fact, play the role assigned here. Rather, it seems to pose the danger of obscuring the better promise to come. That is because we are comparing the work of two different writers.

4

[1]How shall we characterize the achievement of Abraham, our father according to the flesh? [2]For if it was by deeds of Torah that Abraham was saved, then he has reason to brag, but not as far as God is concerned! [3]After all, look what Scripture says: "And Abraham believed God, and it was counted for him as merit." [4]So the wages paid the workman are not weighed up by gratuitous kindness but by what he is owed by contract. But as for the one without deeds of Torah, [5]while counting on the one who accepts the irreligious, his belief is counted as merit, [6]even as David says, too, describing the bliss of the one to whom God ascribes merit without deeds of Torah: [7]"Blessed are they whose deeds of lawlessness were forgiven, and whose sins were covered up! [8]Blessed be a man to whom Adonai may in no respect ascribe sin!" [9]Is this beatitude pronounced only upon the circumcised? Or not also upon the uncircumcised? For our position is that it is the faith of Abraham that was ascribed to him as merit. [10]And precisely how was it ascribed? With him in a state of circumcision? Or in a state of uncircumcision? Not in circumcision, but

in uncircumcision! [11]He received circumcision only subsequently as a token of the merit of the faith he exercised while uncircumcised so he could be a fit father to all who believe, despite not being circumcised, so merit might be ascribed to them, [12]as well as a father of a covenant with those, not only of the circumcision, but also those following in the steps of the uncircumcised faith of our father Abraham. [13]For the promise to Abraham or to his descendants that he should inherit the world did not come to him via the Torah but by the merit of his faith. [14]For if the heirs owe their position to Torah, faith has been vitiated and the promise destroyed. [15]For the Torah effects wrath, and where Torah is absent, neither can there be transgression! [16]That is why it is a matter of faith, so it might come by God's gratuitous will, so that the promise will continue to be firm for all the descendants, not only to those who observe the Torah, but also to those marked by the faith of Abraham, who is thus the father of all of us equally, [17]as it is written: "I have appointed you a father to many nations."

He stands as our father in the sight of him whom he believed, namely God, the one who resuscitates the dead and calls the nonexistent into being, [18]as he did with Abraham, who, long past all hope, nonetheless staked everything on hope in order to become a father to many nations, in accord with the promise made to him: "So shall your descendants be." [19]And without weakening in faith, he wrote off his body as already moribund, being about a century old, and Sarah's womb just as dead. [20]But he did not give up on the promise of God by unbelief, but was strengthened by faith, worshipping God, [21]and being fully convinced that what he has promised he will also be able to deliver. [22]This is why it was ascribed to him as merit. [23]Understand that it was written that it was ascribed to him not just to memorialize him, [24]but also because of us, to whom it is soon to be ascribed, those counting on the one who raised Jesus our Lord from the dead, [25]he who was yielded up, thanks to our offenses, and was raised through our salvation.

Here we have, or so I venture to guess, part of an epistle to Queen Helena and Prince Izates of Adiabene, part of Abraham's Chaldea. In chapter 7, I suggested that, a la Robert Eisenman, Paul was the unnamed partner of Ananias, who assured Helen's son Izates that he might convert to Judaism without undergoing circumcision since this might alienate him from his subjects who would feel he had abandoned his heritage for an alien one. I take this passage to be a sample of that persuasion: like his countryman Abraham, Izates may please God by believing in him, just as Abraham did, lacking circumcision.

5

[1]Therefore, being accepted by faith, we enjoy peace with God, thanks to our Lord, Jesus-Christ, [2]who has also arranged access for us, by the password of faith into this position of favor we now occupy, bragging of our hope of sharing the divine splendor. [3]Not only that, but we even brag amid our tribulations, remembering that tribulations breed patience, [4]and patience leads to approval, and approval to hope. [5]And this hope will not disappoint, because the love of God has been poured out into our hearts with the Holy Spirit given us. [6]Indeed, while we were past help, just in time, Christ died on behalf of the irreligious. [7]Hardly anyone will die on behalf of a righteous man, though admittedly someone might venture to die on behalf of a good man. [8]But it bespeaks the love God had for us that Christ died on our behalf while we were still sinners. [9]Now that we have been accepted by his blood, by how much more shall we be rescued by him from the coming wrath! [10]For if, being enemies, we were reconciled to God by the death of his son, having now been reconciled, we shall much more be saved by his life. [11]And not only that, but we are also bragging on God thanks to our Lord, Jesus *Christ*, through whose agency we have the reconciliation we now enjoy.

This section reads like part of some Gnostic treatise or letter. It sets forth the absolutely basic Gnostic theme that Christ has won access for us to the hitherto-inaccessible deity. We had been separated from him by mighty archons, angels, principalities, and powers, who created the world and entrapped our spirits to energize it. But Christ infiltrated their cosmos to bring glad tidings of escape to the pneumatic elect, who now know the hidden way to the Father. Marcionite soteriology was a good bit simpler, as we have seen. But Gnostics equally regarded themselves the theological heirs of Paul.

The passage in 5:3-10 starts out with what reads like a comment by yet another writer who thinks to improve upon the point made by someone else before him in the text. It represents a retreat from the triumphalism of Gnostic realized eschatology, where the elation of salvation is a present possession, to the chastened hope of a deferred eschatology. In the interval there will be tribulations to face. Accordingly, verse 5 remarks that an eschatological hope based on the endurance of suffering will not disappoint, implying that some previous expectation had been both premature and facile.

Verse 6 leaps to another subject, disguising the discontinuity with the bluffing transition "indeed" (*gar*).[4] The new topic is an assertion of Christ's sacrifice in order to secure the inclusion of "sinners," the irreligious, which implied gentiles. That the writer is not Paul is apparent from his self-inclusion among these barely-saved gentiles (unless, of course, this piece of text stems from someone who shared the Ebionite belief that Paul was not born a Jew).

Verse 7a sets up a contrast between most people's reluctance to lay down their lives for a righteous person and Christ's heroic willingness to give his life even for undesirables (v. 8). But 7b adds a Marcionite quip about their own martyrs' well-known willingness to die for Chrestos, as they called him, "the good one," here alluded to by a synonym, "*agathos*," literally a worthy person.

The phrase "and not only that" (v. 11) reproduces the beginning of the insertion in verse 5. The same interpolator has introduced it here in verse 11 to go out the same way he came in, returning to the original text. It is a redactional seam.

[12]Therefore, just as sin gained entry into the world through a single individual, with death arriving on sin's coat tails, death permeated all mankind since all sinned. [13]Before the Torah, of course, there was sin in the world, but sin is not counted as such when there is no law to condemn it. [14]Nonetheless, death prevailed from Adam till Moses even among those not sinning the same way Adam did, he who reflects the mirror-image of the Coming One. [15]But the offense is not quite like the gift; for if it was by means of the one man's offense that the many died, how much more fully did the gratuitous gift of God become abundant for the many by one individual! [16]And the gift is not as with the one individual sinning; for on the one hand, the judgment starts from a single offense and ends in condemna-

tion, while on the other, the free gift starts from many offenses and ends in salvation. [17]For if it was by the one individual's offense that death prevailed through an individual, how much more will those who accept the abundance of kindness and the gift of salvation prevail in life through the one individual Christ-Jesus! [18]So therefore, as through one single offense all humanity came to condemnation, even so through one single righteous act, all humanity came to salvation and life. [19]For as through the disobedience of the one man the many were made sinners, so also through the obedience of one man the many will be made righteous. [20]But law entered the picture so that the offense might be magnified; but where sin became abundant, divine favor became more abundant still, [21]in order that in the same way that sin prevailed by means of death, so too divine favor might prevail through salvation to age-long life by means of Jesus-Christ, our Lord.

With all the talk of original sin, this passage must be a Catholic interpolation. It seeks to mitigate the Marcionite rejection of the Jewish scripture, for which the Torah is a synecdoche, a part standing for the whole thing. All right, it increased sin, but this was a clever part of the plan of redemption! We are so used to this sequence, as it now reads, that it is difficult at first to recognize what an outrageous harmonization we are being offered. In any case, the point is made succinctly if we jump from the end of verse 13 all the way to verse 20. Verses 15-19 are so repetitive and redundant that we must ask if perhaps some copyist has rounded up all known variant readings to provide a variorum edition of this passage. At any rate, the point of the insertion appears to be a pedantic correction of the analogies between Adam's sin and all subsequent sins in verse 12 and between the implications of Adam's sin on one hand and of Christ's obedience on the other. It seems more natural to think of one writer's proposed analogy critiqued by a skeptical scribe than to picture a single man writing the whole thing, suddenly hedging and half-withdrawing his suggestion in the same breath with which he ventured it.

6

[1]What can we infer from this? May we continue sinning to make the divine forgiveness the more abundant? [2]Never! How can those

who died in respect to sin continue to live in it? ³Or don't you realize
what baptism means? Every one baptized into Christ-Jesus was baptized, specifically, into his death. ⁴Thus we shared a common grave
with him by virtue of baptism into death, in order that, as Christ was
raised from the dead by the splendor of the Father, we too might
live a new quality of life. ⁵It only stands to reason that, if we have
become one with him in the symbol of his death, so we will also be
with regard to the resurrection, ⁶mindful of this: that our old humanity was crucified along with him so this incarnation of sin might be
destroyed so we should obey sin's orders no more. ⁷For anyone who
has died has been delivered from sin. ⁸But if we died with Christ, we
believe that we shall also live with him, ⁹keeping in mind that Christ,
having been raised from the dead, is henceforth immune to death, so
that death has no further claim on him. ¹⁰For insofar as he died, he
died one single time, leaving behind the world of sin, but insofar as
he still lives, he lives anew in the world of God.

This whole passage, representing a mystery-religion sacramentalism, cannot be the product of the same Paulinist who said, "Christ
did not send me to baptize, but to evangelize" (1 Cor. 1:17a). Nor
does it comport with the many passages in Romans where *belief* is
made the sole criterion of salvation. Thus, I make it more Paulino-
Catholicism. Such sacramentalism goes well beyond the instantaneous enlightenment approach of the early Gnostics as well as the
arcane disciplines of the second-stage Gnostics. The retreat to par-
ticipatory salvation through the sacraments was the logical next step:
shifting from an internal, Zen-like salvation technique to an external transaction by token of rituals and physical substances. That's
Catholicism: the mystical sanctification of matter, turning it into a
channel of saving grace.

¹¹The same goes for you: consider yourself dead in respect to sin,
but alive with respect to God, newly awakened from the dead with
your members as veritable weapons of righteousness at God's disposal. ¹²Therefore, do not allow sin to rule your mortal bodies, obeying its impulses, ¹³nor put your members at sin's disposal as an arsenal of unrighteousness, but instead put yourselves at God's disposal
as newly awakened from the dead with your members as weapons of

righteousness. [14]For sin's dominion over you is finished since you are no longer under obligation to the Torah, but to divine favor.

The mental exercises recommended here are an attempt at a technique to help bring about the enlightenment the Gnostic had first imagined would be instantaneous upon his understanding the *gnosis*, the correct doctrine. We might make this section either a Marcionite attempt to curb raw Simonian enthusiasm or the product of a second-stage phase of some other emerging Gnostic branch.

[15]What is the implication? Are we at liberty to sin because we are out from under the Torah but under the umbrella of divine favor? Never! [16]Isn't it obvious that you become enslaved to whomever you decide you are going to obey, whether it is sin leading to death or obedience leading to salvation? [17]But thank God, though you were slaves of sin, you swore heart-felt fealty to the type of religion to which you were consigned. [18]And having been liberated from sin, you became slaves of righteousness. [19]I am resorting to a worldly analogy by way of accommodation to your human way of thinking. So as you used to offer your members as slaves to impurity and lawlessness, leading to lawlessness, in the same way you must now offer your members as tools of righteousness leading to sanctification. [20]For when you were slaves to sin, you were free of righteousness. [21]And what benefit did you reap from that? Now you find yourselves chagrined at those things, for they led in the end to death. [22]But having now been liberated from sin and enslaved to God, you harvest fruit ripening to sanctification, the ultimate end being age-long life. [23]For the wage paid by sin is death, but the anointing of God brings age-long life in union with Christ-Jesus, our Lord.

The Marcionite answer to libertinism is not threats of judgment but simply pointing to a sanctification presently enjoyed. Tertullian just could not grasp such thinking: "Come, then, if you do not fear God as being good, why do you not boil over into every kind of lust, and so realize that which is, I believe, the main enjoyment of life to all who fear not God? Why do you not frequent the customary pleasures of the maddening circus, the bloodthirsty arena, and the lascivious theatre?" (*Against Marcion*, chapter 27) Again, in his *Apology*, 38:

"Why in persecutions also do you not, when the censer is presented, at once redeem your life by the denial of your faith? 'God forbid!' you say with redoubled emphasis."

Though Marcion did not exactly condemn the Hebrew Creator God as sinful or evil, he did consider him a steel general,[5] ruthless and responsible for genocidal atrocities. And it is tempting to understand as Marcionite this passage's contrast between slavery to sin, law, and the lawlessness it defines, versus righteousness with no mention of law. It is a clear choice one is free to make: against the Creator/Legislator and for the Father.

Notice the redactional seam in verse 15, which pretty much reiterates verses 1-2, marking all that lies between them as interpolations.

7

[1]Can you be unaware, brothers, for I address myself to those familiar with the Torah, that the Torah governs a man's conduct only as long as he is alive? [2]For example, the married woman has been bound to the living husband by law; but once the husband dies, she has been released from the law of the husband. [3]Therefore, with the husband yet alive, she will be considered an adulteress if she becomes wife to another; but if the husband dies, she is free from the law of the husband and is not to be considered an adulteress for marrying a new husband. [4]So my brothers, you too were put to death vis-à-vis the Torah by means of the body of Christ so that you might belong to someone else, the one who has been raised from the dead, in order for us to bear fruit for God. [5]For when we were hostage to the flesh, sinful urges animated our members through the Torah to bring forth fruit ripening to death. [6]But since what held us fast has died, we have now been released from the Torah, so we might serve in a new freedom of spirit, no longer in the old slavery to a written text.

This much sounds like pure Marcionism with its characterization of the Torah as a back-firing failure at making its adherents righteous. Thanks to the ransom paid by Christ to the Creator, we are well rid of the Torah. The widowhood analogy, betokening that we are no longer bound to the Law, is aimed at converts (one might say refugees) from Judaism. Unlike Galatians's *inheritance* analogy (Gal. 4:1-7), that of *widowhood and remarriage* implies leaving behind the Old Testament God for another deity, the Father, to whom one has no natural relation. The metaphor here would be *adoption*.

[7]So what are we to say? The Torah must be synonymous with sin, no? Never! Yet it has to be admitted that I would have been innocent of sin if not for the Torah. Likewise, I should never have become acquainted with lust had the Torah not commanded, "You shall not lust after your neighbor's goods." [8]But sin seized the opportunity afforded by the commandment and produced in me every kind of lust! For without the Torah, sin is moot. [9]Once I was living without the Torah, but when the commandment arrived, sin revived, [10]and I died. And the commandment to choose life turned out to spell death for me. [11]For sin, seizing the opportunity afforded by the commandment, deceived me and used it to kill me! [12]So the Torah *per se* is holy, and the commandment is holy and just and good.

[13]So did that which is good spell death for me? Never! And yet sin, in order that it might be exposed in its true colors as sin, by using the good to kill me—that is, in order that it might become odiously sinful by means of the commandment—[14]look, we know that the Torah is spiritual. The problem is that I, on the other hand, am carnal, sold into the slavery of sin. [15]For my own behavior is a mystery to me! For it is not what I wish that I practice, but what I hate, I do. [16]But if I do what I do not wish, I agree with the Torah: it is good! [17]But now it is no longer I who act, but the sin that lurks within me. [18]For I know that no goodness lives in me, I mean, in my flesh; for to wish the good is easy for me, but not to do it. [19]For I do not perform the good I wish, but the evil which I wish not to do—that I do! [20]But if what I do not wish is what I actually do, then it can no longer in any meaningful sense be I who am doing it! The real culprit is the sin that lives inside me. [21]So then, I discover a law of human behavior: whenever I wish to do the good, [22]the evil is closer to hand. For I delight in the divine Torah in the inner being, [23]but I can see a very different law governing my members, struggling against the law my mind embraces and taking me prisoner using the Torah. [24]Miserable wretch that I am! Can anyone rescue me from this living corpse? [25]I thank God, invoking Jesus-Christ our Lord. To sum up, then: on the

one hand, as the real me, I serve the divine Torah, while on the other, with the flesh, I obey the commands of sin.

This section is a mitigating, mediating pro-Catholic gloss on the Law. Though admittedly the Torah only magnifies sin, this is part of the divine economy. Again, what a Herculean effort at joining opposites! To turn one thing into its opposite! A simple, unequivocal Judaism would honor the Torah and place the blame squarely on the weakness of the flesh. Plain, unclouded Gnosticism would deride the Torah as the scheme of the angels and archons, the "universal obsessional neurosis of humanity" (Freud).[6] But here is a bald-faced attempt to make the Torah holy precisely insofar as it whispers temptation to the heart, making known the seductions of sins hitherto unknown.

The unstable mix of Judaism and its opposite winds up, not surprisingly, as quite pessimistic, characterized by disappointment and lowered expectations: *one day* Christ will deliver us from this living death, but in the meantime we are stuck with this frustration because we are stuck with the Law! Earlier eschatological triumphalism has been left behind, and this is a prime feature of early Catholicism, distancing itself from the embarrassments of premature apocalyptic enthusiasm.

8

[1]Thus no condemnation is due those joined to Christ-Jesus. [2]For the rule of the vivifying Spirit in Christ-Jesus liberated you from the rule of sin and consequently of death. [3]For what remained impossible to the Torah, the weakness of the flesh being its Achilles' heel, God supplied by sending his own Son in the semblance of flesh and of sin to deal with sin, condemning it in its very seat of power, the flesh, [4]and this in order that the dictates of the Torah might be kept by us, insofar as we conduct ourselves, not by the influence of the flesh, but under the influence of the Spirit. [5]For the fleshly ones concern themselves with materialistic matters, but those who are spiritually oriented concern themselves with matters of the Spirit. [6]For the worldly mind is death, but the spiritual mind enjoys life and peace. [7]This is why the worldly mind is automatically set against God, for it is not submissive to God's sovereignty, nor in the nature

of the case can it be. [8]Nor can the materialistic please God. [9]But you are not mired in the flesh, but rather soaring free in the Spirit, provided God's Spirit lives within you. But should anyone lack the Spirit of Christ, such a one does not belong to him. [10]But assuming Christ is inside you, the body is dead to sin, while the spirit is alive through practicing righteousness. [11]But if the Spirit of the One who raised Jesus from the dead lives in you, the One who raised Jesus from the dead will also vivify your mortal bodies by means of his Spirit living inside you.

[12]So then, brothers, this makes us debtors, but not to the flesh, as if we were obliged to live by its dictates. [13]Because if you do that, you are soon going to die! But if by the Spirit you atrophy the practices of the body, you will live. [14]For every one responsive to the leading of the divine Spirit is a son of God. [15]For it was no spirit of slavery you received, to fear all over again. No, you received a spirit of adoption, which prompts us to cry out, "*Abba*! Father!" [16]The Spirit itself agrees with our spirit that we are children of God. [17]And if children, that means heirs as well, in one respect direct beneficiaries of God, in another, co-beneficiaries with Christ, since we share his suffering to share his glory. [18]And the way I look at it, the sufferings of the present time amount to nothing compared to the future splendor to be revealed from within us! [19]For the eager anticipation of all rational creatures is to behold their unveiling as the sons of God. [20]Why was the world subjected to futility in the first place? It was not voluntary, but rather the decision of the one who did the subjugation. The hope is that [21]all beings will themselves be liberated from their bondage to corruption to share the freedom of the immortal bliss of the sons of God! [22]For it is readily apparent that all beings groan in unison and suffer labor pains till the present hour.

[23]Not only that, but even we who observe the first flowering of the Spirit inside us nevertheless groan inside, desperately waiting for the adoption papers to be signed, that is, the salvaging of our bodies at the resurrection. [24]For we staked our salvation on this hope, but remember, a visible object of hope is not hoped for at all! After all, who would say he "hopes for" the thing he can see? [25]But if we hope for something we do not see, we have to wait for it patiently. [26]The Spirit, too, takes a hand in our weakness: while we do not

know our own good well enough to ask for it, the Spirit itself intercedes on our behalf with inarticulate groanings; [27]with the result that the searcher of hearts knows the thinking of the Spirit because he is able to ask on behalf of the saints from God's perspective. [28]Equally, we know that in the eyes of those who love God, everything is seen to work together for their good, the good of those called to participate in his grand plan: [29]namely, those he chose beforehand were also destined to be transformed into the image of his Son, so to make him the firstborn of many likewise resurrected brothers. [30]The ones thus destined would also be summoned, and those he summoned would also be saved. In turn, those saved must also receive the divine splendor. [31]All one can say is: "If God is for us, what matter who is arrayed against us?" If he did not spare even his own Son, [32]but on all our behalf gave him up, how will he not, with his Son, freely give us everything else? [33]Who do you picture leveling a charge against God's chosen ones? God is vindicating, [34]so who is condemning? Certainly not Christ-Jesus, the very one, after all, who died, or should I say who was raised, who is at the right of God and intercedes on our behalf! [35]Who could possibly separate us from the love of Christ? Tribulation? Distress, maybe? How about persecution? Famine? Abject poverty? Danger? Sword? [36]It is not as if we are immune to these things, as it is written: "For your sake, we are being butchered all day long; we were considered no more than sheep for slaughtering." [37]But in all these seeming defeats we are superconquerors, thanks to the One who loved us! [38]For I have become convinced that neither death nor the vicissitudes of this life; neither angels nor archons, nothing in either the present or the future, nor the powers; neither Hypsos nor Bathos nor anything in all creation will succeed in isolating us from the love God has for those united with Christ-Jesus our Lord.

This chapter is a splendid display of Marcionism, sharing a few kindred notions with Gnosticism. Both were brain-children of Paul, according to Marcion and Valentinus, the latter claiming to have been taught by Paul's disciple Theodas. In the very first verse we find the hallmark of Marcionism: no condemnation! Removed from the sphere of the demiurge, the Christian has no grounds for fear of future judgment. The Marcionite Christian has henceforth to deal only with the

Father and the Son, both of whom are committed to man's salvation, neither of whom has any truck with judgment (vv. 33-34).

The ensuing verses delineate a severe dichotomy of spirit and flesh. Without twentieth-century Protestant psychologizing, we can see the same ascetical understanding on display here as in the flesh-hating Desert Fathers, the Nag Hammadi monks, and any Sufi, Jainist, or Hindu anchorite you care to name. Verses 3 and 4 discount the Torah as any kind of solution to the predicament of the sinful flesh since it comes from the same sphere from which one needs to be saved. This was the advantage of the Gnostic Redeemer Jesus, who engaged sin on its own ground by disguising himself in the semblance of flesh, yet without being truly incarnate. In that case he, too, should have been subject to the flesh's domination. Verses 6 and 7 remind us of the utter incompatibility between spirit and flesh because of an utter alienage of nature between them. God and man do not need to be *re*conciled, as if they were once together. No, man needs to break with the God who created him and turn to the Father who will adopt him and bestow divine Spirit upon him. Once this happens, the Spirit of Sonship floods the hearts of those adopted, who have henceforth washed their hands of the flesh, the Law, and the sins spawned by the lusts of the first and defined by the stipulations of the second.

Here, too, is classic Gnostic soteriology: the Redeemer blazes a trail for us back to the pleroma, the Godhead, past the ranks of archons and angels who would bar our way. Our condition of lostness is essentially this separation from the Godhead, so redemption is a matter of clearing the path for the soul's ascension. We can locate the self-consciousness of the Paulinist writer as occupying the second stage of dampened-down enthusiasm: the daunting disappointment of the one who believes himself to grasp the *gnosis* theoretically, yet for whom the gates of perception have not yet swung wide. So, for the present, he cultivates the knowledge that will assure his safe passage after death, admitting that for now there is only hope, not sight.

Verse 15 offers the key term of Marcionite soteriology: the Father of Jesus Christ has offered adoption to the creatures of the Hebrew God. Originally subjects of the one, they may now transfer themselves to the loving fatherhood of the other. And because of this, all will one day be liberated from the corruption and frustration to which the world's Creator, the demiurge, subjugated, against its will, that which he had created.

The scripture quote (Psalm 44:22) in verse 36 properly calls on the Old Testament Psalmist as a gloomy witness of the fate the Creator holds in store for his hapless creatures. It is a circumstantial *ad hominem* argument akin to that in Titus 1:12, "A certain one of them, a prophet of their own, said..."

9

¹Despite my reputation, I swear before Christ I am telling the truth! I am not lying! My conscience vouches for me, inspired by the Holy Spirit; ²I suffer deep sorrow and unremitting emotional pain. ³I was even invoking a curse from Christ on my own head on behalf of my brothers, my natural kinsmen, ⁴who bear the distinction of being Israelites, to whom belong the adoption as God's children, the leading of the Shekinah, the covenants with Abraham, Moses, and David, the promulgation of the Torah, and the temple service, and the messianic promises, ⁵and the patriarchs, and from whose physical line Christ descends. May God, who reigns over all, be blessed through the ages! Amen.

⁶But then, what has happened? It is not that the message of God has failed to gain its object. For not all descended from Israel are true Israel; ⁷neither does mere descent from Abraham make all of them his children; but "Isaac's line will be called your descendants." ⁸This means, it is not the natural children who are children of God, but rather only the children of the promise are counted as his descendants. ⁹And this is the promise in question: "About this time, I will come by, and Sarah will have a son." ¹⁰Not only this, but Rebecca, too, having conceived by one man, namely our father Isaac, was told, "The older will serve the younger," ¹¹though neither had yet been born, much less done anything good or bad, in order that the plan of God might continue according to divine choice—¹²not based on deeds, but on the decision of the one who issues the call. ¹³This is just what is written: "Jacob I loved, but Esau I hated."

¹⁴What are we to say to that? Is God unfair? Never! ¹⁵For he says to Moses, "It is for me to decide whom I will show mercy and whom

I will pity!" [16]So therefore, it is not up to the one who wishes or the one who competes, but to God the merciful. [17]For scripture says to Pharaoh, "I brought you to the throne for one purpose only: so I might use you to demonstrate my power, and so my reputation might spread throughout the earth!" [18]From this we can see that he shows mercy to whomever he wishes, and equally he makes whomever he wants obstinate. [19]I know what you're going to say: "Then how can he still find fault with us? It all happens just as he wishes, and who can gainsay him?" [20]But I turn the question around. Who are you, a mere mortal, to be telling God his business? [21]Does the artifact ever call the artificer to account, "Hey! Why did you make me this way?" [22]Doesn't the potter have every right to use half the lump of clay for a wine goblet and the other for a bed pan? So suppose God wanted to demonstrate his anger as well as his endurance and so patiently put up with those who were created long ago as targets of his anger [23]and that he wanted to demonstrate his heavenly splendor in vessels of mercy, previously made to hold the splendor and set aside for that purpose. [24]And these latter are we ourselves, not only Jews, but also those he summoned from the nations. [25]He says the same in Hosea: "I will call 'my people' that nation hitherto foreign to me; and those not beloved heretofore, them I will love." [26]"And it shall come to pass that in the very place they had been told, 'You are no people of mine!' there they will be called 'sons of a living God!'" [27]Nonetheless, Isaiah cries out concerning Israel, "Should the number of the sons of Israel be the same as the grains of sand on the seashore, still only a remnant shall be delivered! [28]For Adonai will wrap up his inventory of all the earth and even cut it short." [29]And as Isaiah had said in advance: "If Adonai Sabaoth had not left us seed, we should have perished completely like Sodom and would have been likened to Gomorrah!"

[30]What is the upshot of all this? That nations not even pursuing salvation nonetheless found it, a salvation by means of belief, [31]while Israel, seeking to follow a law of salvation, failed to arrive at salvation. [32]Why? Because they pursued it not as a matter of faith, but as a matter of deeds. They tripped over the hidden stumbling stone, [33]as it had been written: "Watch as I place someone in Zion for a stone for stumbling and a rock of offense, and whoever believes in him will not be sorry he did."

10

[1]Brothers, from my heart I request on their behalf that God grant them the boon of salvation. [2]For I can testify what zeal they have for God, albeit misdirected by ignorance. [3]Ignorant of God's salvation and trying to achieve their own, they failed to accept the saving message of God. [4]For everyone who believes can see that Christ is the goal to which the Torah points. [5]For Moses writes: "The one who performs the righteous deeds of Torah will gain life thereby." [6]But the salvation that comes from faith says not, "Who can ascend into the sky?" which is to reject Christ's ascension to the right hand of God. [7]Nor does it say, "Who will descend into the abyss?" which is to disbelieve the death of Christ. [8]But what does it say? "The word is near you, on the tip of your tongue, already in your heart." This is the very message of faith which we preach! [9]Because if you swear fealty to Jesus and you believe sincerely that God raised him from the dead, you will be saved. [10]For it is with the sincere heart that one believes, gaining merit, and it is by public confession that one gains salvation. [11]For again, scripture says, "Every one who believes in him will not be reluctant to admit it." [12]For there is no distinction between Jew and Greek. For the same Lord of all alike is bountiful toward all those invoking him. [13]For "whoever calls on the name of Adonai shall be delivered."

[14]But you will say, how are they supposed to call on one in whom they do not believe? And how are they supposed to believe in one they have never heard of? And how are they supposed to hear if no one serves as herald? [15]And how is a herald to preach if he is not sent? As it is written: "How welcome are the footsteps of the bearer of good tidings!" [16]But not everyone so welcomed the news. For Isaiah says, "Lord, did anyone believe what they heard us preach?" [17]This tells us that faith comes from hearing, and hearing requires some communication about Christ.

[18]But I say in answer to this: Are you so sure they did not hear? Surely they did! For "their speech went out to all the earth, and their words to the far reaches of the inhabited earth." [19]And further, I ask, did not Israel know? In the first place, Moses says, "I will provoke you to jealousy over those who are 'no-people' to me; over an ignorant nation I will anger you!" [20]But Isaiah is bolder still when he says,

"I was found by those who were not looking for me; I revealed myself to those not asking after me." [21]Meanwhile, to Israel he says, "The whole day long I motioned with my hands, beckoning to a people who only disobeyed and contradicted me!"

11

[1]So I must ask: has God not rejected his people? Never! After all, even I am an Israelite, descended from Abraham, of the tribe of Benjamin. [2]God did not reject his people whom he chose in advance. Or don't you remember what scripture tells of Elijah, when he actually prays for judgment on Israel? [3]"Adonai, they killed your prophets, they dismantled your altars, and I alone am left—and now they are after me!" [4]But what does the divine response say to him? "I kept back for myself some seven thousand men who never swore fealty to Baal." [5]In exactly the same way in our day, there has emerged a remnant according to the divine choice to make God's favor the criterion. [6]And if the criterion is divine favor, it is no longer decided by deeds since, if it were, divine favor would be so in name only. [7]So where are we? What Israel sought after, he did not gain, but the chosen remnant gained it, while the rest were reinforced in their obtuseness, [8]as it is written: "God stupefied them with a soporific draught, eyes not seeing, ears not hearing," which still prevails. [9]And David says, "May their table become a death trap, a means of capture, to offend them and to recompense them. [10]May their vision fade to blindness and their backs ever bend to the burden!"

[11]I have to ask, then, did they take a fatal misstep from which they can never recover? Never! Rather, by means of their transgression, salvation came to the nations in order to goad them to jealousy! [12]But if their transgression spells riches for the world, and their impoverishment means the wealth of the nations, how much greater bounty shall come from their eventual repentance?

[13]Now let me speak to you gentiles. Naturally, since I am the apostle to the nations, I glorify my ministry—for the sake of Jews! [14]I hope to goad my natural kinfolk to jealousy and in this way save some of them. [15]I mean, if their expulsion occasions the reconciliation of the nations, what would it have to mean if God received them back? Resurrection of the dead! [16]And if the first fruits of the

showbread are holy, the rest must be, too. And if the root is holy, so must be the branches. [17]And what if some of the branches were broken off and you, a wild olive branch, were grafted in among them, becoming fellow sharers in the nutrition that rises from the root? [18]That is certainly no reason for you to brag about your own position at the expense of the natural branches! If you are inclined to brag, just remember this: it is the root that bears your weight, not the other way around! [19]You might reply: "Branches were broken off to make room for me to be grafted in! That must mean something!" [20]Good point! They were broken off because of unbelief, true, and because of faith you maintain your position in God's favor. Don't be conceited, but fear! [21]For if God had no scruples about chopping off the natural branches, he is not likely to be any more reluctant to dispense with you. [22]Picture, then, both the kindness and the severity of God: on the one hand, severity upon those who have fallen, and on the other, the kindness of God toward you, provided you continue in his kindness, since otherwise you too will be cut off. [23]Equally, if they do not continue in unbelief, they will be grafted back in, for it is no great feat for God to restore them. [24]After all, you were cut from the wild olive, where you naturally belong, to be grafted against nature onto a cultivated olive; how much simpler a task it will be to graft the branches back onto an olive to which they naturally belong!

[25]Brothers, I do not want you to remain ignorant of this hitherto-hidden plan of God, lest you become conceited, namely, that obstinacy has afflicted Israel in part only until the full predetermined number of converts from the nations come in, [26]and in this way all Israel will at last be saved, as it is written, "The deliverer will emerge from Zion, and he will turn away impiety from Jacob. [27]And this is my covenant with them when I take their sins away." [28]On the one hand, when it comes to preaching the news, they are your opponents; on the other, when it comes to the ancient election, they are God's beloved because of the patriarchs. [29]For the spiritual endowments and the vocation from God are irrevocable. [30]Keep in mind how once you disobeyed God and now you have obtained mercy because of the disobedience of these others. [31]In the same way, these have now disobeyed because of the mercy shown you, in order that now they may

obtain mercy, too. ³²This way, God finds all alike guilty of disobedience so he may show mercy upon all.

³³How deep, how abundant are the wisdom and the knowledge of God! How mysterious are his decisions, how far beyond human ken the courses he plots! ³⁴For who could know the thinking of Adonai? Has he ever sought the advice of mortal man? ³⁵Who has given anything to God, so that he owes him anything? ³⁶No, from him and by means of him, and unto him all things proceed! All worship to him throughout the ages! Amen!

With Van Manen,[7] we must ask why the author of chapters 9-11 almost never refers to "Jews," only to "Israel," the exact opposite of the usage up to chapter 9. His answer: chapters 9-11 are not the work of the same author. Chapters 9-11 represent various post-Marcionite, Catholicizing attempts to formulate a framework of salvation history encompassing both Christians and Jews. The chapters were not present in Marcion's version of Romans, as his critics tell us, nor did he entertain any of these theories. For him, as for today's ecumenical "double covenant" theologians, Jews have their own salvation history with its own integrity and its own *dramatis personae*. Christians have another, independent salvation history, under the aegis of a different deity, the Father. How different might the long, bloody history of Christian-Jewish relations have been if only Marcion's theology had prevailed!

The parallel of 9:1-3 with Exodus 32:32 implies that the faithless Israelites are damned, since it is their damnation Paul would vicariously bear if possible. This is not the impression we will receive in chapter 11, where a rather different fate is projected for Israel—final redemption. But in chapter 9 through 10:13, the idea is that it is nothing new for the lion's share of Israelites to reject God's will and weed themselves out of the "true Israel." Like poor bemused Gideon's army, Israel had always been subject to a narrowing-down process. Who said that saved Israel would be any different? It will be a righteous remnant, nothing new in Israel. This all functions as a Jewish-Christian rejoinder to critics who wrote off Christianity as one more failed messianic enthusiasm such as Jews had already beheld many times since Herod the Great's death. If only some marginalized clique of heretics believed it, what were the chances that they were right and all other Jews were wrong? So said the skeptics. The Jewish-Christian rejoinder? "O ye of little faith! Don't you see it's always been this way?"

Chapter 9, verses 14-23, constitute a patch by a scribe who misunderstood the talk of election in context and, by means of catchwords, inserted this section on individual, personal predestination. In terms that have changed little ever since, the interpolation wrestles with the apparent injustice of unconditional election, finally evading the question by condemning the effrontery of mortals who would dare ask it. The rest of the chapter represents a Catholic- (and Reformed-) style co-optation of Israel, understanding Christianity to supercede it completely. Yet another Catholic scribe will sharply repudiate this in 11:17-32.

In 10:14-17, which seems to pop up out of nowhere, "Paul" argues for the necessity of sending and financially supporting foreign missionaries. The section is not a straw man statement, posed merely for the sake of argument and intended to be refuted. No, we can tell this from the scripture citations meant to reinforce the argument. You start citing scripture only when you want to prove the point. What follows, then, in verses 18-20 is not a *continuation* but rather a genuine *refutation* of these thoughts by yet another Paulinist, added here to correct the preceding.

Chapter 11 represents a still later reflection on the problem of Jewish rejection of Jesus, positing an eventual reconciliation. In this chapter we meet with a very different notion of predestination. In this case God is said to cast a spell on whole nations, one at a time, in order to direct traffic into his kingdom of salvation. He will divide and conquer the human race. First, he causes Jews (with what they naively think is their free will) to give the Christian gospel a miss, which frees it up for gentile consumption. But then Jews, watching from the sidelines, will behold with astonishment the success of Christianity in winning pagans from their degenerate superstitions. At this point the Jews will find themselves strangely warmed to the Jesus sect which once seemed so repugnant. They, too, will jump aboard and, with all the reserved seats filled, the plane to heaven will take off.

In what sense are the approaches of chapters 9-10 and 11 Catholic? It is not merely that they are post-Marcionite and non-Gnostic. No, the distinctively Catholic nature of the two discussions is evident from the fact that, while both writers seek to preserve the Jewish scriptures for the Christian canon (which Gnostics and Marcionites did not), their goal in this is not to preserve the privileges of Israel for Jews (as Jewish-Christian Ebionites would), but rather to claim the old promises made to Israel *for themselves.* For Marcionites and Gnostics, by contrast, the Old Testament scriptures had nothing to say to Christians. For Catholics, and the more recent Reformed Protestants, the Jewish scriptures speak only to Christians, no longer to Jews. This is true even for the author of chapter 11, since he anticipates that Jews will be saved *as Christians* in the Christian way, and with no reference to any Israelite theocracy.

Romans 11:1-10 concerns the fall of Jerusalem. The allusions in verses 3 and 9 to the destruction of the temple and its altar ("table") are anachronistic, given the usual dates for Paul. But then, so is the whole condition, presupposed in chapters 9-11, that there has already been a definitive split between Jews and Christians. Could this really have been apparent within the lifetime of the historical Paul? Such a judgment would seem to require a good bit more water to have passed under the bridge.

12

[1]In view of this, brothers, I urge you by the compassion of God to present your very bodies as a sacrifice while yet alive, one that is holy and meeting with God's approval, which is the fit worship of a rational creature. [2]And do not let yourselves be assimilated to this present world system, but be transformed by renewing the intellect, enabling you to determine what the will of God is, what is good, what meets his approval, what is perfect.

In view of *what?* The transition fits better coming directly off the end of chapter 8. It was probably added to 8 before someone else added 9-11. But on the other hand, there being no shadow of distinctly Christian motivation in view, one might be tempted to read 12:1b as a bit of Hellenistic Judaism, a Stoic-style appeal for rational, ethical religion as a replacement for temple-sacrifice religion, rendered impossible with the fall of Jerusalem in 70 CE. The warning not to conform to the ways of the surrounding world rings true as a warning by one Hellenistic Jew to others of his kind, already so attracted to Greek ways and thus tempted to go all the way and let Judaism go. Could this be another fragment of the synagogue sermon on display in Romans 1:18-2:29?

³For by the prophetic inspiration given me, I say to all present: Do not cultivate an overly high estimate of yourself, but rather reckon realistically just what portion of faith God has assigned to each one. ⁴For just as in a single body we have many distinct members, each with its special function, ⁵so we, being many, constitute a single body in Christ-Jesus, all being members of one another. ⁶And having gifts that differ according to the varying endowments allotted us, let us exercise them appropriately; if it is prophecy, prophesy within the formula of the faith; ⁷if it is to serve, serve in the diaconate; if to teach, teach within the doctrine; ⁸if in exhortation, as a paraclete; if sharing, in material simplicity; if leadership, then lead diligently, gladly lenient in assigning penance.

These ecclesiastical offices and formulae of teaching are anachronistic for Paul, as is the idea that faith could be a quantifiable charisma not shared in common by all believers. Spiritual endowments are on their way to becoming fixed offices. Some have thought this section to be a précis of 1 Corinthians 12-14, blurring over the fine points. For instance, "not to cultivate an overly high estimate of yourself" (v. 1) sounds like a short-hand reference to 1 Corinthians's Gnostic *pneumatikoi* who supposedly disdained their ungifted brethren. Here it has become simple pride in office.

Notice, too, that the first thing said about the once dangerous gift of prophecy (verse 7), as liable as it is to upset the apple cart, is to remove its barb: don't prophesy anything not already contained within the accepted doctrinal system. Needless to say, the same went for teaching (verse 7), lest anything new be said for the next two thousand years.

⁹Let love be non-hypocritical. Recoil from evil and stick closely to the good. ¹⁰Love one another like family, with brotherly love, deferring in order to show one another the greater honor. ¹¹Be zeal-

ous, not slothful, burning in spirit to serve the Lord. [12]Rejoice at the sure prospect of eventual deliverance, enduring amidst affliction, doggedly persisting in prayer. [13]Give for the needs of the saints and pursue a policy of hospitality to itinerant preachers. [14]Bless persecutors! Bless them instead of cursing them. [15]Share the joy of the fortunate and the tears of the mournful. [16]Hold one another in equal regard, showing no preference to the rich nor patronizing the humble. Do not be too confident of your own wisdom. [17]Do not repay anyone evil for evil; be a source of noble deeds in the sight of all. [18]If possible, insofar as you have any control in the matter, try to live at peace with everyone. [19]Beloved ones, do not avenge yourselves, but just let it go. For it is written, "Vengeance is my prerogative: leave it to me, says Adonai." [20]Instead, "if your adversary is hungry, feed him; if he is thirsty, give him a drink; for in this way you will be heaping live coals on his head!" [21]Do not be vanquished by the Evil One, but conquer the Evil One by doing good!

It is not merely the absence from the epistles of sayings familiar to us from the Gospels that makes us think the Gospels had not yet been written, or that the sayings we now read in the Gospels had not yet been credited to Jesus. Equally important is the presence in the epistles of many Gospel-sounding maxims that are, however, not attributed to Jesus. If they had been, no one would have been content to pass them on without his name attached. Granted, the wisdom of a saying ought to give it whatever power it possesses, no matter who coined it. But there is no one even today who will neglect to mention that so-and-so Gospel saying is not merely his own bright idea but rather the word of Jesus Christ. Thus we may recognize here the anonymous raw material that would soon wind up in the Gospels but had not yet been pressed into that service.

13

[1]Let every immortal soul be humble before the authorities arrayed above him! For there is no authority except under God, and the existing ones have been ordained under God. [2]So whoever resists the authorities has opposed himself to the order established by God, and such opponents will receive condemnation. [3]For the archons do not frighten people away from good deeds, only from evil! Do you

want to be free from fear of the authorities? Do only the good, and you will have its praise! [4]For it is God's servant assigned you for good. But if you are doing evil, then you are right to be afraid; for he is not afraid to use the sword God has supplied him, being God's servant, an avenger of wrath to whomever practices evil. [5]This is why it is necessary to submit—not just for fear of wrath, if I have given that impression, but for conscience's sake. [6]This is also why you pay them tribute, for they are constantly engaged in worshipping God. [7]So render to all their due, to human leaders taxes and tolls; to the authorities honor, and to God holy fear.

Many scholars take this section to inculcate servile obedience to secular government in the interest of bourgeois Christianity. This interpretation is based on understanding "archons" and "authorities" as earthly governments, and "every soul" to denote "every individual." Read this way, the passage does seem Catholicizing in vocabulary and conception and would be later than its context. There is nothing particularly implausible in such a reading. But if one translates it as I do, then what we are dealing with is a Gnostic text, a preface to secret information such as is attributed to the Risen Jesus in numerous works like the *Pistis Sophia*. There Jesus tells the initiate what to say during one's heavenly ascent (at death) to successfully pass by the vigilant archons manning the ramparts of the spheres separating the world of God from this sublunar mudball. As for verse 6, in Gnosticism one pays the successive planetary archons, in the course of one's journey back to the Godhead, upon exiting their respective spheres. One does so by setting aside the elements originally derived from each sphere (physical, ectoplasmic, astral, etheric, psychical). Such preparatory exercises represent, in Schmithals's view, which I am adopting here, a decadent, second-stage Gnosticism. In the real thing, the simple realization of one's divine selfhood was enough to catalyze instantaneous *satori*. One had no need of secret handshakes and magic words.

[8]Owe nothing to anyone, except to love each other, for whoever loves the other has carried out the Torah. [9]For "you shall not commit adultery," "you shall not kill," "you shall not steal," "you shall not covet," and whatever other commandments you can name, can

be reduced to one byword: "You shall love your neighbor as yourself." [10]Love does no evil to the neighbor; thus love is the carrying out of the Torah.

Verses 8-10 must originally have been an independent statement on love and the Torah. The statement means to reduce true Torah obedience to the deeds of the natural conscience, much as in the Hellenistic synagogue sermon (Rom. 1:18-2:29), of which it may constitute yet another fragment. That is a likely candidate for the origin of this patch because of the positive yet minimizing estimate of the Torah. Lip-service must be paid it, but obedience to it is really no different from everyday decent behavior. Accordingly, such a text would fit well into the Catholic agenda, where the Torah has the same venerable "out to pasture" status. A Catholic redactor has seen fit to add it here.

[11]And be mindful of the times we are in: it is high time for you to wake up from sleep, for now the day of salvation is nearer than when we first believed. [12]The night is waning, and dawn has drawn near! So let us cast away the deeds done in darkness, and let us don the armor of daylight! [13]Specifically, let us behave appropriately for the daytime, not in revels and drinking binges, not in profligate sex and gluttony, not in strife and jealousy. [14]Instead, don the Lord Jesus-Christ like a second skin and eliminate any opportunity down the line to give in to the impulses of the flesh.

Occasioned by the motivation-sapping delay of the Parousia of Jesus, this exhortation seeks to jostle to wakefulness a readership or congregation that has thoroughly backslidden into crass, sensual behavior. Their heedlessness is well described in Matthew 24:48-51: "But suppose the slave is wicked and says to himself, 'My lord is late!' and begins to beat his fellow slaves for minor infractions and eats and drinks with the drunks. The lord of that slave will show up on a day when he does not expect and at an hour of which he had no warning, and he will dismember him and will assign him a place with the hypocrites" (cf. Psalm 73:11, "And they say, 'How can God know? Is there knowledge in the Most High?'"). Just as such preachments attributed to Jesus must be unhistorical, stemming from long after the initial eschatological tension has slackened and the nerve of expectation has been cut. Such sentiments mark this section of Romans as post-Pauline. The implicit threat of judgment at the smashing hands of a judging Christ marks the passage as Catholic.

14

[1]Welcome anyone who is weak in the faith, but do not subject him to judgments over debatable matters. [2]One has the confidence to eat all foods, but the weak one eats herbs. [3]The one eating meat should not look down on the one abstaining, nor let the abstainer condemn the meat-eater, for after all, God welcomed him. [4]Who are you to judge the performance of someone else's domestic servant? It will be in the eyes of his own master that he succeeds or fails, and in this case he will succeed, for the Lord is able to make him succeed! [5]One observes this day as more holy than that, while another considers every day equally holy; let each one come to his own conclusion. [6]The one observing the special day dedicates it to the Lord. The one who eats meat gives thanks to God for it. [7]For not a single one of us lives his life in isolation, nor does anyone die in isolation. [8]For while we live, we live for the Lord; and when we die, we die for the Lord. Thus either way, dead or alive, we belong to the Lord, [9]for this is why Christ died and lived, in order for him to become judge both of the dead and of the living. [10]So what are you doing judging your brother? Or how dare you look down on your brother. For all of us are going to appear before the judgment throne of God. [11]For it is written: "As I live, says Adonai, every knee will bend before me, and every tongue will swear fealty to God!" [12]Thus each one of us will have to explain himself before God. [13]So let us resolve not to judge one another any more.

The second-century Encratite sect of Asia Minor, and many kindred spirits elsewhere, sought to effect a symbolic return to Edenic innocence. They believed, thanks to an admirably literal reading of Genesis 2-3, shared by Gnostics, that the original sin was sexual intercourse and that the divisions subsequently introduced into mankind (male vs. female; slave vs. free, ruler vs. subject, Israelite vs. gentile) would all fall away if we repudiated sex and the family structure. "Encratism" comes from the Greek *encrateo* ("self-control"), denoting sexual continence. The Spirit could indwell and empower all alike without regard to worldly and physical distinctions which were henceforth to be ignored by God and mortals alike. The practical results included vegetarianism, teetotalism, universal celibacy, anarchism, egalitarianism, pacifism, communal ownership, and so on. As we saw in chapters 4 and 5, the popular apocryphal Acts embodied this perspective, which was therefore widely influential. Encratism was understandably viewed by outsiders as fanaticism. But as its theology and ethos were not far from those of emerging Catholicism, encratites eventually found themselves brought on board by the Catholic Church. The church would honor them as long as they conceded that the path of chastity and poverty was not for the common run of Christians, but only for an elite. The celibacy gospel became "counsels of perfection." Encratites became monks and nuns.

What we are reading in Romans 14:1-12 is an attempt to facilitate the assimilation of encratites. We glimpse reflections of them in the 144,000 males who had not defiled themselves with women in Revelation 14:4 and the prophesying virgins of Acts 21:9. They were about to be received into what they had formerly viewed as the worldly, compromising church, the Harlot Babylon. The encratites held their noses at the worldly stench of meat-eating, sexually active, wine-drinking Christians whom they now had to accept as brothers and sisters. Likewise, the Catholics could not help viewing their new co-religionists as neurotics cringing inside a cocoon of ultra-piety, a retreat from a world God created (not the demiurge!) for the enjoyment of the saints. Both sides had to learn to tolerate each other. "Imagine!" our Catholic fragmentist seems to urge: "Though genuinely different from you, they too are pleasing God!" Might the Q saying in Matthew 11:16-19 and Luke 7:31-35 have originated in this climate? It looks like Romans 14:1-13 did.

[13b]Except for this: make up your mind never again to scandalize or offend your brother. [14]I know and am convinced that in the code of Jesus-Christ, no food is inherently profane, except that it remains profane for the poor soul who still considers it so. For him nothing has changed: it is profane. [15]So if your brother is affronted by what you eat, you are no longer behaving in love. Do not destroy, by your food,

this man for whom Christ died! [16]Do not cause what you consider good to be spoken ill of because it tempts a brother to violate his tender conscience. [17]For God's order is not concerned with dietary rules, but with righteousness, peace, and holy ecstasy of the spirit! [18]For the one who serves Christ in this respect will win both God's warm approval and the esteem of other people. [19]So therefore, let us pursue objectives conducive to peace, and those which strengthen each other. [20]Do not unravel the work of God for the sake of food. All foods indeed are ritually clean but are nonetheless evil for the one who eats them, invited against his conscience. [21]It is good not to eat meat or to drink wine or to do anything else that trips up your brother. [22]The faith you have: keep it between yourself and God. Blessed is the one who does not condemn himself by virtue of the very action he approves! [23]But the man who is unsure of the rightness of his act and goes ahead and eats meat, he has condemned himself! All that does not proceed from the confidence of faith, it is sin.

15

[1]So then, we, the strong, ought to shoulder the burdens of the weak, and not act just to please ourselves. [2]Let each one of us behave so as to please his neighbor for his good, his strengthening.

In Romans 14:3b-23; 15:1-2, I believe we can detect a subtle difference from what precedes it. Acts 15:19-29 depicts Jewish-Torah Christians extending a special dispensation to newly converted pagans. But Acts 21:23-26, recalling the same decision, spins it in the direction of defending Jewish-Christians' right to keep the Torah, over and against the practice of a gentile majority. In much the same way, I suggest, Romans 14:3b-23; 15:1-2 tries to tip the ecumenical balance to the side of the encratites: even if one dismisses their scruples as excessive ("weak in faith"), one ought nonetheless keep to the same standards for fear of offending them. Otherwise, the fact that you are treading the wider, more generous path may strike them as a temptation to sin (see the Q saying in Matthew 7:13-14; Luke 13:23-24). Do not try to educate them, for in so doing, you might be tempting one of the brethren to let his behavior exceed his convictions, and his sin, however neurotic in origin, will be your fault. You will have "destroyed" him! Here, despite the matted hair of Esau, we can tell we are listening to crafty Isaac, a clever legalist trying to manipulate things in his own direction. The result is like that in Acts 21's charade of Paul undertaking the motions of a Nazirite vow to prove his Jewishness—or, really, to keep up such appearances, lest any zealot for the Law get his nose out of joint. No more of the live-and-let-live policy advocated in 14:1-13a. This is the triumph of legalism.

Since verses 17-23 seem to paraphrase and repeat verses 14-16, one wonders whether the redactor of Romans has here harmonized two variant versions of the same source-text.

³For even Christ did not endeavor to please himself, but as it is written: "The insults of those who insulted you rebounded on me." ⁴For whatever scripture records from ancient times, the intention was to teach subsequent readers that through patience and the encouragement of the scriptures we might have hope. ⁵And may the God of patience and of comfort bless you with unanimity in this attitude toward one another, as is the way of Christ-Jesus, ⁶in order that, united in peace, you may with one voice worship the God and Father of our Lord Jesus-Christ.

Verse 3, recalling the theme of the previous verses, is a redactional seam leading into verse 4, an exact equivalent to 2 Timothy 3:16-17 ("Every passage of Scripture is the very exhalation of God, advantageous for teaching, for reproving, for correcting, for schooling in righteousness, in order that the servant of God may be equipped for every good deed that may be required of him."). Both are specifically aimed at countering the Marcionite erasure of the Old Testament from the Christian canon.

Verse 6 looks like a benediction closing the epistle. If so, it turned out someone else wanted the last word. The epistle kept growing as it circulated, even as the Gospels of Mark and John did. Each of them has been saddled with postscripts, too.

⁷That being the case, welcome one another, just as Christ welcomed us into the glorious presence of God. ⁸For I tell you this: Christ became a servant of the circumcised on behalf of the trustwor-

thiness of God, to give substance to the promises made to the patriarchs, [9]and a servant to the nations to lead them to worship God for his mercy, as it is written: "Therefore I will testify about you before nations, and I will sing praise to your name." [10]And elsewhere he says, "Rejoice, O nations, along with his people!" [11]And yet again: "All nations, praise the Lord, and may all the peoples praise him!" [12]And again, Isaiah says, "One will sprout from Jesse's root to rule the nations; on him will the nations set their hope." [13]Now may the God of hope fill you with all joy and peace as you believe, so you may enjoy a wealth of hope by the power of the Holy Spirit.

A subsequent Catholic scribe seeks here to demonstrate just how handy the Old Testament scriptures are for Christian use. But for his subject matter, he returns to the terms of chapters 9 through 11, Jews and gentiles together in the plan of God. He may have thought this was still the issue, even as many modern commentators do, in chapter 15.

The interpolator of verses 7-13 tries his hand at concluding the Epistle to the Romans with 15:13, but again someone else is waiting to have his say.

[14]But I, even I myself, have been convinced, my brothers, concerning you, that you yourselves are full of goodness, having been filled with all knowledge, also capable of admonishing one another; you don't need my intervention. [15]But I took the liberty of writing you, partly by way of reminder, using the inspiration granted me by God [16]as a servant of Christ-Jesus to the nations, performing the priestly task of preaching the news of God, in order that the offering of the nations may prove acceptable, having been made holy by the Holy Spirit.

Here we seem to connect back up with the fragment of Marcion's preparatory letter (Rom. 1:7b-17). Is it genuine or a pastiche?

[17]I have therefore grounds to boast, thanks to Christ-Jesus, in the things pertaining to God. [18]I will, however, not presume to say anything about the things Christ did not accomplish through my own hands for securing the submission of the nations in word and deed,

¹⁹by the power of signs and wonders, by the power of Spirit, so that I should have fulfilled the commandment of the news of Christ from Jerusalem and adjacent parts to Illyricum. ²⁰So therefore, I have been doing my best not to evangelize where Christ was already invoked, so as to avoid building on someone else's foundation, ²¹but rather, as it is written, "They shall see, they to whom nothing about him had hitherto been announced, and those who have not heard of him will understand."

A defender of the boundaries of the traditional Pauline sphere of influence here tries to discourage recent attempts to revise history and replace the heretical Paul with a less controversial apostolic founder, as we saw in chapter 6. Do not think to steal Paul's legacy, his converts, his churches, from him. They will be his offerings to Christ at the End (Phil. 2:17; 4:1; 2 Cor. 1:14). "The controversy, therefore, was not between Paul and Cephas and James, but between their successors at the close of the first or the beginning of the second century."[8]

²²This is also why I was repeatedly hindered from coming to you. ²³But now, having finished the work in this area, and having desired to visit you for many years now, ²⁴whenever I make my trip to Spain I hope, on my journey, to see you and to have you send me on my way to Spain if only I may first be somewhat replenished by you.

But does not Paul's announced intention to go to Rome to reap some harvest (1:13-15), *even though he did not found the Roman church*, directly contradict his supposed scruples about working in someone else's assigned field of service (15:20)? It is difficult to see how the apostle himself, if we picture him in the situation here described, could be so confused. It makes more sense to imagine a pseudepigraphical writer unable to keep the details of his fictive premise straight.

²⁵But right now I am off for Jerusalem to serve the saints. ²⁶For Macedonia and Achaia deemed it good to make some contribution for the poor among the saints in Jerusalem. ²⁷For they deemed it only proper, being indebted to them; for if the nations shared in their spiritual riches, they ought also to return the favor when it comes

to material things. [28]So once I have wrapped up this task and signed over this harvest to them, [29]I will go on by way of you to Spain. And I know that when I do come to you, it will be with the complete approval of Christ. [30]I plead with you, *brothers*, by our Lord Jesus-Christ and by the love of the Spirit to agonize with me in prayer to God on my behalf, [31]that I may be delivered from those disobedient to the faith in Judea, and that my service to Jerusalem may prove acceptable to the saints, [32]so that coming to you, by God's will, rejoicing, I may at last fall asleep there among you. [33]And may the God of peace be with you all. Amen.

This chapter has Catholicized and Judaized Paul entirely in the spirit of the Acts of the Apostles. The writer has also possibly confused Marcion's crucial visit to Rome with Paul's to Jerusalem. Both are said to have headed to their goal with a large monetary gift in tow, and neither was warmly received. Our writer may know the Acts narrative, anticipating as he does the disastrous reaction of the Jerusalem zealots to Paul's planned offering. In Acts 21 Paul is advised to save his skin by using the money, not for poor relief or for supplementing the Jerusalem church treasury, but merely for paying off the Nazirite vow for himself and others, as if this will deceive his enemies (Acts 21:20-24). It does not, and they seek to lynch him (21:27-30). Romans 15:31 surely betrays knowledge of this outcome. That Romans does not know a pre-Acts version of the story is clear from the fact that Romans 15:31 agrees with Acts 21:27 on identifying Paul's assailants as non-Christian Jews, whereas, as F. C. Baur detected,[9] originally, that if there is any historical nucleus to the story, the assailants must have been Torah-zealous Jewish *Christians* (Acts 21:20). So this late portion of Romans shares the Catholicizing agenda of Acts.

Verse 32 anticipates Paul's death. J. C. O'Neill[10] recognizes this as the meaning of *sunanapausomai*, a reference to the legend of Paul's martyrdom in Rome. The writer looks back on the death of Paul, as he knows his readers will. The prospect of a further journey to Spain is meant to tantalize the reader and make him muse over what might have been. The effect sought is exactly the same as in Philippians 1:23-26, where Paul entertains the possibility of going to his well-deserved rest but cannot stop himself from planning further apostolic work. In both cases the writer knows the reader also knows that the indefatigable Paul did not, in fact, get to carry out those plans. That's how Paul would *have* to die: in mid-stride, preaching his gospel. Who can think of him spending his last years watching *Jeopardy* in a Corinthian nursing home?

16

[1]Now I recommend to you our sister Phoebe, a deacon of the community at Cenchrea, [2]in order that you may welcome her in the name of the Lord in a manner befitting the saints and support her in whatever manner she may require of you, for truly she became a benefactress of many, myself included. [3]Greet Prisca and Aquila, my colleagues in Christ-Jesus, who risked their necks to save my life. [4]It is not only I, but also all our communities among the nations, who owe them a great debt. [5]Greet also the congregation that gathers in their home. Greet Epaetnus, my beloved, one of the first generation for Christ in Asia. [6]Greet Maria, who has labored much for you. [7]Greet Andronicus and Junia, my relatives and fellow prisoners, who are notable among the ranks of apostles and who indeed were my predecessors in the service of Christ. [8]Greet Ampliatus, my beloved in the Lord, as well as my beloved Stachys. [9]Greet Urbanus, our colleague in the service of Christ. [10]Greet Apelles, approved in Christ's service. Greet those of the house of Aristobulus. [11]Greet Herodion, my relative. Greet those of the house of Narcissus who are believers in the Lord. [12]Greet Tryphaena and Tryphosa, who labor in the Lord's vineyard. Greet the beloved Persis, who labored long in the Lord's ranks. [13]Greet Rufus, chosen of the Lord, and his mother, who is like a mother to me, too. [14]Greet Asyncritus, Phlegon, Hermes, Patrobas, Hermas, and the brothers associated with them. [15]Greet Philologus and Julia, Nereus and his sister, even Olympas, and all the saints associated with them. [16]Greet one another with a ritual kiss. All the communities of Christ greet you.

[17]Now I urge you, brothers, to watch out for those who foment divisions and scandals alien to the teaching which you learned, and to turn away from them. [18]For such people are serving not our Lord Christ but merely their own belly; they use eloquence and flattery

to deceive the minds of the innocent. [19]For the report of your submission to the faith came to everyone; therefore I rejoice over you. I want you to be wise in the good, innocent of the bad. [20]For then the God of peace will trample the accuser under your feet soon! May the favor of our Lord Jesus-Christ be with you!

[21]Timothy, my colleague, greets you, and so do Lucius and Jason and Sosipater, my relatives. [22]I, Tertius, the one writing this epistle, greet you in the name of the Lord. [23]Gaius, my host, greets you, along with the whole community. Erastus, the municipal treasurer, greets you, as does Quartus, a brother. *May the favor of our Lord Jesus-Christ be with you all. Amen.*

[25]So too the one who is capable of making you stand firm in allegiance to my message, even the proclamation of Jesus-Christ, part of the process of revealing the mystery kept secret for long ages, [26]but now being made manifest *through the prophetic writings*, as commanded by the everlasting God, made known to all nations to secure their submission to the faith. [27]To God, who alone is wise, let all worship be directed, age after age, through the invocation of Jesus Christ! Amen.

Chapter 16 is a separate letter on behalf of one Phoebe. Is the letter of recommendation for Phoebe fictive? Why would anyone create such a writing and attribute it to Paul? They would do it simply because it establishes an apostolic link between Paul and the church leaders and workers named in it. The letter is equivalent in function to the resurrection appearance list in 1 Corinthians 15:3-11, providing apostolic credentials for those named. It is also equivalent in purpose to the genealogies in 1 Chronicles, which served as credentials for the priestly houses whose representatives wrote the book and administered the Second Temple. It is also possible that this one-chapter epistle has the same intended function Tertullian attributed to the *Acts of Paul and Thecla*: to authorize the leadership role of women in heretical Paulinist sects. That, after all, is pretty much the same use made of it by Christian feminists today.

Verse 3 mentions Priscilla and Aquila, elsewhere referred to as associates of Paul (Acts 18:2, 18, 26; 1 Cor. 16:19; 2 Tim. 4:19). It is striking that Simon Magus, too, had a disciple named Aquila, as mentioned in the Clementine *Recognitions*. There Aquila breaks with Simon and becomes a follower of Peter. One could not ask for a nicer instance of "Tübingenism" (the schema set forth by F. C. Baur and his students). Again, Simon is Paul, and like Acts's "John Mark" (Acts 12:12; 15:36-40; 1 Peter 5:13), Aquila leaves the Pauline circle to wind up in the Petrine circle instead. Disciples of each apostle are (fictively) traded like ambassadors of two hitherto hostile countries. And why should we not take verse 10's reference to Apelles as a mention of the Marcionite Apelles?

Verses 17-20, which interrupt the sequence, sound strikingly like the Pastoral Epistles and are likely interpolated by a Pastoral redactor. Without the phrase "through the prophetic writings," which thus may be a secondary addition, the concluding doxology in 16:25-27 sounds Marcionite. Note that the gospel has been hidden for ages and is only now revealed, something one would never say if one regarded the Old Testament as full of messianic predictions and typologies. This concluding doxology seems to have been formulated by a redactor to end Romans as a whole and was not part of the letter for Phoebe.

NOTES

[1] J. C. O'Neill, *Paul's Letter to the Romans*, Pelican New Testament Commentaries (Baltimore: Penguin Books, 1975), 40-56.

[2] L. Gordon Rylands, *A Critical Analysis of the Four Chief Pauline Epistles: Romans, First and Second Corinthians, and Galatians* (London: Watts, 1929), 29.

[3] For the interpretation given here, see Sam K. Williams, *Jesus' Death as Saving Event: The Background and Origin of a Concept*, Harvard Dissertations in Religion 2 (Missoula: Scholars Press, 1975), 19-51. Williams, however, believes the relevant verses to be Paul's own insertion of earlier material. Hellenistic Jews, as we can see in the books of 2 and 4 Maccabees, had already come to understand the martyrdoms of faithful Jews as expiation sacrifices accepted by God on behalf of sinful Jews. Williams surmises, quite persuasively, that Hellenistic Jewish Christians, once they saw

gentiles converting to Christianity, had to consider how Christian gentiles might be grafted onto the olive tree of Israel (Rom. 11:17, 24). And they adapted the doctrine of expiatory martyrdom, concluding that God had accepted the heroic death of Jesus as washing away the impurity of the gentiles who believed in Jesus. Jewish Christians did not require it, since the Levitical sacrifices had kept them ritually clean in God's sight. gentiles had never been held responsible for keeping Jewish purity laws, which was all right as long as they remained "righteous gentiles" or "God fearers" (like Cornelius in Acts 10). Morality was one thing, ceremonial purity quite another. The pious gentiles were already morally approved by God, but in order for them to be considered part of the chosen people, they had to be ritually purified. Other than becoming full converts, proselytes, who would henceforth keep all the provisions of the Torah (something they were unwilling to do), how might gentiles be purified? That is where the expiatory sacrifice of Jesus came in: it cleansed them in the sight of God, placing them on a par with Israel. This seems to be the point of Ephesians 2:11-19 and 1 Peter 1:14-19.

[4]Rylands, *Critical Analysis*, 156: "That conjunction "for" [*gar*, "for," "indeed," etc.] is a valuable mark of interpolation, being inserted to give an appearance of continuity; and when there is no continuity the artifice betrays itself." See also 118.

[5]"As for the Christian theology, can you imagine anything more appallingly idiotic than the Christian idea of heaven? What kind of deity is it that would be capable of creating angels and men to sing his praises day and night to all eternity? It is, of course, the figure of an Oriental despot, with his inane and barbaric vanity." *Dialogues of Alfred North Whitehead, as Recorded by Lucien Price*, an Atlantic Monthly Press Book (Boston: Little, Brown and Company, 1954), 277.

[6]Sigmund Freud, *The Future of an Illusion*, trans. W. D. Robson-Scott, rev. and ed. James Strachey (Garden City: Doubleday Anchor Books, 1964), 71.

[7]W. C. van Manen, "Romans (Epistle)," *Encyclopaedia Biblica*, ed. T. K. Cheyne and J. Sutherland Black (New York: Macmillan, 1914), col. 4135.

[8]Rylands, *Critical Analysis*, 285.

[9]F. C. Baur, *Paul the Apostle of Jesus Christ: His Life and Work, His Epistles and Doctrine*, 2 vols, trans. A. Menzies (London: Williams and Norgate, 1876), 1: 212-213.

[10]O'Neill, *Paul's Letter*, 250.

10.

1 Corinthians

First Corinthians is the earliest of the Pauline epistles to have left clear and definite quotations in early Christian writings. The document was employed by the Roman church, hub of emerging Catholicism, to suppress rival varieties of Christianity and to pull other churches into its sphere of influence, suggesting that it was written (or compiled) for that specific purpose in a post-Pauline generation. Though it is a patchwork quilt drawn from many sources and has suffered numerous interpolations and redactional glosses, the book as a whole is an attempt to provide a church order, much like the *Didache*, or *Teaching of the Twelve Apostles to the Nations*. Titus and 2 Timothy are likewise not real letters but church manuals with Paul's name attached.

Walter Schmithals (*Gnosticism in Corinth*, 1971) observed how virtually everything in the document would make sense if the unifying thread of the issues addressed in 1 Corinthians was Gnosticism. Christian Gnosticism was a second-century phenomenon, but Schmithals argued that it must have begun already in Paul's day, since 1 Corinthians seems to refer to it. But it seems more likely to me that 1 Corinthians itself stems from the late first or early second centuries.

1

¹Paul, an apostle of Christ-Jesus, summoned to the task by the will of God, and Sosthenes, the brother, ²to the assembly of God at Corinth, to those who have been consecrated to Christ-Jesus, *made saints, and to all those in every place who invoke the name of our Lord Jesus-Christ, likewise their Lord and ours:*

³May God our Father and the Lord Jesus-Christ grant you favor and peace! ⁴I ever thank my God for you on account of God's favor shown you by Christ-Jesus, ⁵because you were enriched by him in every respect, in all manner of inspired speech and gnosis, ⁶just as the testimony about Christ was corroborated by you, ⁷so that you lack not one of the charismas, awaiting revelations from our Lord Jesus-Christ, ⁸who in turn will certify you as blameless when you reach perfection when the day of our Lord Jesus-*Christ* dawns. ⁹God is faithful, who summoned you into the mystic sharing in his Son, Jesus-Christ our Lord.

Verse 2 reads, "And to all … in every place," and so on. This material might be, as some think, a later insertion into an epistle that was originally directed to a single church, the goal being to make it speak to all. Or else, as I think, it is original to the text, indicating the fictive character of the addressees. It is, in fact, intended for the widest possible audience, with no particular focus on Corinth, and was published as an encyclical against heresy from the beginning.

¹⁰Let me charge you, brothers, by the name of our Lord, Jesus-Christ, that you all teach the same thing, that there be no schisms among you, but that you may be unified in the same thinking and the same opinion. ¹¹You see, my brothers, those who follow Chloe demonstrated this to me about you: that there are contentions raging among you. ¹²This is what I am talking about: one individual announces, "As for me, I belong to Paul!" while another says, "For my part, I belong to Apollo!" Or "I belong to Cephas!" Or "I belong to Christ!" ¹³Since when was Christ divided up? Was Paul crucified for you? Or was it Paul's name into which you were baptized?

Verse 10 shows a typically second-century Catholicizing concern for orthodox unanimity. It is the sort of thing we should expect to find in the Ignatian epistles. It is an attempt to press a lid down onto the fertile chaos of Pandora's box. The goal is to undercut the variety of Christian faith in the writer's day by having Paul bemoan it, so to speak, in advance, precisely as Acts 20:29-30: "I know good and well that after I leave, bloodthirsty wolves will attack your flock, sparing no one, and men will emerge from your own ranks, speaking perverse things to siphon off disciples for themselves."

Verses 11-12, the Chloe fragment, reveal that the sectarian rivalry implicates the names of Paul, Cephas, Apollo(s), and Christ, as if they were all current objects of Corinthian devotion. But to imagine Paul himself addressing this problem this way is anachronistic. It is not that a Christian leader in any age might not regret factional bickering with his name on it. The trouble, rather, is that Paul is made to pull rank on everyone else when ostensibly the point is to urge co-existence and tolerance among those committed to various leaders. The rank hypocrisy entailed in the historical Paul presuming to order everyone around, when he is supposed to be rejecting the exaltation of any one apostle over the rest, cannot be ignored. It would amount to Paul saying: "Okay, everybody, get this straight: no more difference of opinion. From now on you accept my views, not those of my colleagues and rivals, got it? And to hell with your Apollos and your Cephases!" But there is no hypocrisy involved (unless perhaps one deems pseudepigraphy itself underhanded) in a later Catholic admirer using the revered name of Paul to call for feuding theological tribes to come together in genuine compromise.[1] That, after all, was the whole point of "nascent Catholicism," which sought to rehabilitate or dilute the legacy of Paul, which was so important to the heretical rivals it hoped to absorb.

On the other hand, we can readily imagine Paulinists rejecting the proposal, since they wanted (as reflected in Romans and 2 Corinthians) to safeguard the boundaries of the Pauline sphere of influence, that is, the clout of the successor bishops in the Pauline churches. This clout would vanish if Catholics were able to foist rival foundation legends, in which John or someone else was retroactively declared the founder of the Pauline churches. (See chapter 6 in the present book.)

[14]I am glad now that I baptized none of you—except for Crispus

and Gaius; [15]otherwise someone might charge I was baptizing you in my own name! [16]But I also baptized Stephanas's family and slaves; as for the rest of the congregation, to tell the truth, I can no longer remember whom I may have baptized.

One might read this as simply apostolic small talk. In fact, it is fictive window-dressing to achieve the impression of a spontaneous letter from Paul. That sort of thing was common in pseudepigraphical letters. Oddly enough, that would actually lend at least some functionality to what would otherwise seem irrelevant trivia. Islamic savants showed genuine insight when they denied that epistles could qualify as scripture, since they are communications from one human being to another, not direct bulletins from God to human beings, like in the Koran.[2] It does seem odd to think of apparent trivia, especially involving a lapse of memory, as somehow the word of God, the product of inspiration. Surely scripture cannot feature such occasional and ephemeral elements? But that would be naive. These names appear here for a definite reason, as form criticism bids us recognize: nothing got passed on without some concrete utility. Verse 14 looks like an attempt to establish or to reinforce episcopal succession claims in the names of Crispus and Gaius, excluding all others. The afterthought in verse 16a, a still later insertion added by another hand, pushes the door open still wider: Stephanas and his sons or successors are added to the Pauline succession genealogy. Then 16b stops up the fountain lest such claims become inflated and devalued. Otherwise, the result would be like that in Romans 16, where the list of Pauline lieutenants and protégés goes on and on 'til there is little of the apostolic goose left to carve up.

[17a]After all, Christ did not send me to baptize, but to evangelize,

Paul, like Gautama Buddha, was remembered as one of those virtuosi who, back in the hazy dawn of the faith, had been able to spread liberation and illumination to all he encountered. The Holy Spirit accompanied his legendary preaching, with miracles as corroboration, and his hearers' lives were radically converted. Would that we might go back to those times when an apostolic word was sufficient to douse the hearer with the Spirit (Acts 10:44) and a touch with the apostolic bandana was enough to bring healing (Acts 19:11-12)! But we do not, and now we must try *techniques* to get to the same, once-spontaneous results. One such is baptism, well known from the mystery cults. Verse 17a reminds us of John 4:2, "Jesus himself did not baptize, but only his disciples." In both cases, there is the admission that the prevalent baptismal practice developed subsequent to the founder, whether Jesus or Paul.

[17b]and that not with subtle rhetoric; otherwise the cross of Christ is rendered moot. [18]You see, on the one hand, the message of the cross is utter nonsense to those who are perishing. On the other, for us who are being saved by it, it is the very power of God. [19]For it is written: "I will destroy the wisdom of the sophisticates, and the prudence of the judicious I will nullify!" [20]And hasn't he done it? Find me a sophist! Find me a scribe! Find me one of the debaters of this worldly age! Has any joined us from their ranks? Has not God in fact exposed the wisdom of the world for nonsense? [21]For since, by the hidden plan of God, the world in its vaunted wisdom failed to arrive at knowledge of God, God thought it good sport to use the nonsense of the proclamation to save the ones believing in it. [22]Seeing that Jews demand signs from heaven and Greeks seek after wisdom, [23]we still proclaim "Christ crucified"—a scandal on one hand to Jews, and on the other to the nations mere nonsense; [24]but to the ones summoned from the ranks of both Jews and Greeks, Christ is God's power and God's wisdom. [25]Because God's most foolish scheme is yet wiser than mortals, and God's weakest link is yet stronger than mortals. [26]It is evident in your own case, brothers! There are among you not many wise by mortal standards, not many powerful, not many high-born. [27]It was precisely the nonsense of the world that God chose in order to shame the sophisticate; God chose the unimpressive things in order to put the strongest ones to shame, [28]and the most common and contemptible things—God chose the nothings in order to abolish the some-things. [29]All this in order to prevent mortals bragging in the presence of God. [30]And thanks to him, you are included in Christ-Jesus, who was himself a revelation to us of God's wisdom, namely righteousness and sanctification and redemption, [31]so as to bring about the state described in scripture: "Let the braggart brag on Adonai."

2

[1]I, too, brothers, when I came to you, I did not come armed with excellent rhetoric or wisdom as I announced to you the witness to God. [2]I had decided that while among you, I should offer no other answer to any question, but Jesus-Christ, and him crucified. [3]And it was in weakness and fear and much trembling that I was with you, I freely admit, [4]and my speaking and my proclamation were not marked by sophistical rhetoric, but by a definitive display of spirit and power. [5]Otherwise you should have placed your faith in human wisdom, not in divine power.

On the assumptions that the letter is genuinely Paul's and that the sequence of events in Acts 17 and 18 is correct, many infer that these ruminations reflect Paul's post-game analysis of his relative failure preaching the gospel to the Stoics and Epicureans at the Athenian Areopagus. He received only a smattering of interest when he tried to play philosophical apologist, so from now on he will get out of the way and let the Spirit do the preaching through him. But, in fact, we are by no means reading the aftermath of a single experience of a single man. No, this passage reflects a considered policy that has grown from a number of attempts by Christian preachers to win over philosophers—people like Plotinus and Celsus. It must not have gone well. And what follows here is classic sour grapes theology. Why did Christians lose the argument again and again? It must have been God's way of showing the futility of pagan intellectualism. If you know you're right, yet you are soundly beaten by intellectual opponents, what can you conclude? It must be the wrong approach. One finds oneself in short supply of either authenticating miracles (a vacuum the miracle stories about Jesus would soon try to fill) or compelling arguments such as Philo once attempted and which apologists like Justin Martyr would try again. What does the Christian preacher have left? Why, the crucified Christ! Might as well not try to gild the message or to gussy it up. Might as well not try to make it sound good. It will only sound good, and without your help, if the hearer is open to God and predisposed to it anyway. Expect ridicule, then. But expect converts, too.

We find exactly the same sort of wound-licking rationalization in Matthew 11:25-26a: "And at that time, Jesus replied to certain scribes, saying, 'I applaud you, Father, Lord of the sky and the earth, because you concealed these things from the wise men and the intellectuals, revealing them instead to infants. Yes, Father, because so it seemed good sport to you!'" Here, too, we discern failed apologetics, in this case against Jewish scribes, turning into stewing, smug know-nothingism. A certificate from a fundamentalist diploma mill is worth more than a doctorate from Harvard—in the sight of God! What those stuffed-shirt professors call stupidity, we in the sect call wisdom. No, human reason cannot uncover divine truth. It has to be revealed by God and received by faith.

Before us lies an open textbook of sectarian fanaticism. Paul is on record as eschewing the very sort of rhetoric in which he is at the very same time engaging, which has not been uncommon in antiquity and today. And he argues that a so-called faith that might result from a hearer being convinced by a cogent argument is still potentially vulnerable to a better argument from some wandering philosopher who might show up next week, out of nowhere, even as Paul and the itinerants in his tradition did. But if the convert's faith is anchored instead in some emotional conversion experience, his faith is more deeply rooted, being no mere intellectual opinion, as tentative as all such must be.

The content of a faith based on a feeling of conviction is inevitably going to be second-hand and derivative, dependent upon the beliefs of one's catechist. It was his stirring delivery that won you over, not some cogent line of reasoning, so you have a great interest in simply accepting everything else he may say. Why? If you do not, if you get curious and begin to question him on theoretical points of doctrine, you may start to wonder if he was right about the gospel, either. Here is Catholic "implicit faith," attained by simplified preaching of the baptismal-redemptive mystery: the lowest common denomination. Here is the origin of "proto-orthodoxy" or "nascent Catholicism."

⁶In fact, however, we do utter wisdom among the perfect, though hardly a wisdom of this temporal world, nor of the archons who rule it and who are rapidly being brought to nothing. ⁷But

we speak a wisdom of God known in a mystery and hidden away, preordained by God before the ages to result in our transfiguration into the divine splendor; [8]one which none of the archons ruling this worldly age so much as suspected. Had they known, they never would have crucified the Lord of splendor. But as it is written, "Things which eye saw not and ear heard not and never arose in the human mind"—how many such revelations has God prepared for those who love him! [10]For God revealed them to us through the Spirit. You see, the Spirit scrutinizes all things, even the depths of God! [11]After all, among human beings, who knows the truth of a person except that person's own inner spirit? Just so, no one has come to know the truth of God except for God's Spirit. [12]And we did not receive the spirit of the cosmos but the Spirit that comes from God so we may grasp the secrets freely given us by God, [13]the very secrets we relate not in terms of learned rhetoric, but of that taught by the Spirit, conveying spiritual matters to those who have the Spirit. [14]But the natural man can make nothing of the truths of the Spirit of God since to him they appear nonsense. Indeed, he is simply incapable of grasping them, for they can be understood only by means of the Spirit. [15]But the pneumatic, on the one hand, understands everything, but on the other, is understood by no one. [16]For who knew the Lord's thoughts, to be able to instruct him? But we do have the mind of Christ.

A different writer here stakes a claim for Gnostic mystagogy. The preceding verses, 1:17b-2:5, present the Christian response to worldly wisdom in an entirely different way from what appears here. In the earlier section, the "wisdom of God" is reduced to "dogmatic Christian preaching." It was a free act of God to send Christ to save humanity. This act could not have been derived from general premises. It is not the function of a theoretical system, but rather a free act of a person intervening in history. Thus, it has nothing to do with philosophy, whose task it is to understand the axioms of the universe. Things are very different when we come to verses 6 and following. Here we read of a type of theosophy, a higher wisdom. Not a complex system like Plato's but rather revelations of unguessable divine truths, the character and content of which even the planetary archons did not know. As we read in the *Ascension of Isaiah*, 1 Corinthians 2:8 hints that Christ descended to the earth through the concentric planetary spheres, stopping at each to clothe himself in the outward likeness appropriate to each sphere, the various concentric astral, ectoplasmic, psychic, ghostly-appetitive, and physical bodies[3] possessed by the archons and their subjects on each level. In this way he could descend to earth incognito, slipping past the guardian archons.[4]

Here we breathe the atmosphere of Valentinian Gnosticism. Humanity is parceled out among three categories: first, the pneumatics or spirituals who possess a spark of the divine Spirit awakened by the preaching of the gospel; second, the *psuchikoi* or "soulish" ("natural") ones who are not divine by nature but may still be saved through faith in the death of Jesus; and third, the doomed *sarkikoi* or "carnal" ones, two-legged animals driven by lust. The higher truths are for the first group only, for only they are equipped to understand them. If one could effectively preach esoteric wisdom to all and sundry, it would make the cross moot; no one would need it. But the *psuchikoi* do need it. The crucifixion happened for their benefit as a way of salvation for the natural ones unable to discern the Gnostic call (1 Cor. 1:17; 2:14). It should not surprise us to find this schema hinted at here in 1 Corinthians. After all, Valentinus claimed to be the student of Theodas, a disciple of Paul. Valentinians were the first to write commentaries on the Pauline letters. Thus, along with Marcionites, Valentinians are the earliest Paulinist Christians we know of.

3

[1]The trouble is, brothers, that when I first came among you, I could not speak to you as to pneumatics, but as to carnal beings, as to mere infants, new initiates in Christ. [2]It was milk I gave you to drink, not solid food, because that's all you were ready for. But you are still not capable of more even now! [3]For you are still carnal! For insofar as jealousy and strife flourish among you, are you not carnal, conducting yourself in a merely human manner? [4]For whenever anyone says, "I myself belong to Paul!" and another replies, "Well, I belong to Apollo!" are you not mere mortals? [5]After all, what is Apollo, and what is Paul? Merely servants through whom you came to

believe, each as the Lord assigned. [6]I planted, Apollo watered, true, but it was God who made it grow! [7]Just as in agriculture: who did the planting and who did the watering is quite immaterial. [8]So the one who plants and the one who waters—it's all the same and each will receive the appropriate reward his particular labors have earned. [9]For we are fellow laborers for God; you are God's farm, God's building project. [10]Like an architect, I used the skill given me by God to lay the foundation, leaving it to another to do the actual building. Just let each subsequent builder watch how he does the construction! [11]Let none imagine he may start over from a different foundation than the one I laid down: Jesus-Christ! [12]Now whether anyone builds on this foundation using gold, silver, and precious stones on the one hand or wood, hay, and stubble on the other, [13]the quality of each one's work will be revealed for all to see. It is the Day of Judgment that will reveal it because fire will make it clear, and the fire will test the work of each to see what quality it has. [14]If anyone's construction work survives the ordeal, he will receive a reward. [15]If anyone's construction is burnt up, he will be left empty-handed. He himself will be saved, like a burned-out homeowner grateful just to be alive.[16]Don't you understand that together you are a shrine of God, that God's Spirit lives among you? [17]Well, whoever defiles the shrine of God, God will render him profane, for God's shrine is holy, and you are that shrine.

The Valentinian section continues. It restricts the list of legitimate apostles to Paul and Apollos, leaving out the Jewish-Christian (or Catholic) Cephas, understood as Peter. He is under suspicion in verse 11 as the claimed but false foundation of the church a la Matthew 16:17-18.

"Apollo" (Greek Apollos), who is often mentioned as a Pauline colleague (Acts 18:24; 19:1; 1 Cor. 1:12; 3:4, 5, 6, 22; 4:6; 16:12; Titus 3:13), may be a transparent disguise for Apelles, a disciple of Marcion who, however, struck out on his own, revising Marcionite theology in some respects.

As W. C. van Manen noted, the discussion in verse 6 assumes Paul and Apollo are figures of the past, whose distinct church-building careers can be looked back upon and compared.

It is important to note the distinction carefully drawn by the author between the final judgment of apostolic, or ministerial, *works* on the one hand and the fate of the one who performs them on the other. While wasted efforts will be burnt off, there is no need to worry for the sake of those who contributed them, for the Father of Marcion and of Valentinus is no vindictive tyrant, such as we see evaluating his underlings' work in Matthew 25:14-31.

[18]Let no one kid himself: if anyone among you considers himself wise by worldly standards, let him become a moron: that way he really will be wise. [19]Because the wisdom of this cosmos is nonsense to God. We know this, for it is written: "The One who apprehends the wise in their cleverest moment." [20]And again: "Adonai is well aware of the reasonings of the sophists, that they are moot." [21]In view of this, let no one brag about mortal men, for all things belong to you; you do not "belong to" them, [22]whether Paul or Apollo or Cephas, or the cosmos or life or death, either the present order or that which is coming—all these belong to you, [23]just as you belong to Christ and Christ belongs to God.

These verses form a continuation of the Catholic anti-wisdom section of 1:14-16, democratizing and dumbing down the faith. Once again, the opposite of wisdom is not esotericism but simplicity. The pious attitude is that which regrets the sampling of the knowledge tree in Eden, the erection of the Babel tower. Such a one is happy to mortgage his faith to the Grand Inquisitor.

The author is happy to pepper his exhortations with Old Testament citations, unlike the Marcionites and Gnostics. It is, however, odd that the writer thinks nothing of approvingly citing the Polonius-like Eliphaz of Teman in Job 5:13. It reminds us of the practice of some Gnostics who lionized the villains of the Old Testament as Gnostic heroes. But in view of the entirely conventional citation of Psalm 94:11 in the same context, we are probably just dealing with the atomistic, out of context, exegesis of the ancient world and not a distinctive Gnostic hermeneutic. The author appears for other reasons to be a Catholic, not least that "Cephas" appears once again in the list of apostolic names.

4

¹Thus, people ought to think of us as Christ's retainers and stewards in charge of doling out the mysteries of God. ²More than anything else, it is demanded of stewards that one be found reliable. ³And to me, it is insignificant if you judge me as unreliable, or if I am judged on some court date before a mortal tribunal, but neither do I judge myself. ⁴For I am not aware of any strike against me but that does not vindicate me; no, the one to judge me is the Lord. ⁵So do not rush to judgment ahead of time until the Lord arrives. It is he who will both expose to the light the things hidden in darkness and reveal the inner will. ⁶Now all this, brothers, I have ventured to apply to myself and Apollo because of you so that in our case you might learn not to read between the lines, so that you do not make too much of either one at the expense of the other.

This Marcionite section forestalls lay criticism, pulling rank, as Marcion and Apelles (Apollos) were divine mystagogues such as mere mortals are in no position to critique. Paul says that even if God were to judge, he would be handing out positive commendations. He says he has written this concerning himself and his colleague so that readers can learn to live according to "what is written," which is to say, the Marcionite scripture they are reading right now. But more broadly, when the Lord comes, he will not unleash plagues and flames but rather unflinching self-knowledge. This is what we should expect from the non-judgmental deity of the Marcionites. Note how Cephas, the Catholic favorite, is again absent, and not by accident.

Verse 4 is strikingly reminiscent of John 8:15-16 where the same is said of Jesus, though supposedly *by* Jesus. It is equally pseudonymous here: the kind of apologetical statement more likely to be made on a great founder's behalf by a latter-day admirer. Out of the man's own mouth, it sounds unbearably defensive, or even megalomaniacal.

⁷For what makes you so great? And what do you have that you did not receive? And if indeed you did receive it, why do you brag as if you hadn't? ⁸Now you are sated! Now you are rich! Without us, you reign unopposed! But in fact, it is to our advantage that you reign, because

perhaps we might be your co-regents! ⁹For sometimes I think God has assigned us apostles to bring up the rear in the triumphal procession, prisoners condemned to death. Why? Because we were made a gladiatorial spectacle to the world, both to evil angels and to mortals alike. ¹⁰We are thus stage buffoons on account of Christ, but you are "realistic" in Christ! We are "weak," but you are "strong"! You are held in high esteem, while we are dishonored. ¹¹Even now we both hunger and thirst, go naked and get beaten up, flee from place to place, ¹²*and are reduced to working with our hands. Insulted, we bless; persecuted, we endure;* ¹³though slandered, we act the Paraclete. *We became the very filth of the world, scrubbed-off rust and dirt—and still are!*

As per Ernst Käsemann,⁵ this is an attempt to curb enthusiasm that insists the new world is here already. Some of the symptoms of such unbridled enthusiasm might include sexual libertinism, as with the later Frankist sect;⁶ leaving off working for a living (the Cargo Cults jeered at any who didn't knock off work and slaughter all livestock for a feast as having no faith);⁷ heedless glossolalia (no matter the public reaction); poison drinking, snake-handling, and braving gunfire to demonstrate eschatological invulnerability.⁸ The danger is in believing that one has already transcended all norms of the mundane world, which one may indeed have done inwardly, while still abiding in a world that has not outwardly changed. As long as one must live in it while waiting for the consummation of the new age, one must still follow the old rules in order to function. The illuminatus is, for now, just as vulnerable to physical harm and social repercussions as anyone else.

¹⁴My motive in writing these things [cf. 3:23] is not to shame you, but rather to admonish my beloved children. ¹⁵For while you might have ten thousand pedagogues in the things of Christ, you can have only one father, and in the religion of Christ-Jesus I have fathered you by means of the news. ¹⁶Thus I urge you: become imitators of me. ¹⁷Indeed, this is precisely why I sent you Timothy, my beloved and reliable child in the Lord's family, whose conduct will remind you of my own in the way of Christ-Jesus, *that which I teach everywhere in every assembly.*

[18]So when I failed to visit you, some egos became inflated. [19]But I will come quickly to you, if the Lord allows, and I will ascertain the truth of the matter: not just the talk of those inflated egos, but whether there is any power behind it. [20]For the kingdom of God does not come by mere talk, but in power. [21]Which would you prefer? That I come to you with a rod, ready to punish, or in love and a gentle spirit?

Was the historical Paul an insufferable egotist who held himself up as an ethical paragon for all to emulate? Does not such self-exaltation in verses 16-17 make more sense as a Paulinist's praise of his favorite apostle long after the fact?

But then we must ask again: what could be the point, in a pseudepigraphon, of having Paul assert and reassert his fatherhood of the congregation addressed? It is part and parcel of the apostolic turf war taking place in the second century when tradition fabricators were busy rewriting history to ascribe the founding of this and that episcopal see to this and that "safe" apostle, covering over the original heretical foundation. Against such efforts, our Marcionite Paulinist is waving the banner of Pauline foundation and authority in Achaia, lest some other apostle's ostensible successors move in.

The discussion in verses 8-21 sounds much like a prophecy of the Risen Christ warning of imminent apocalyptic judgment, only in this case it is supposed to be the savior Paul. In verse 18 there is even the problem of the delay of Paul's expected Parousia, just as in Matthew 24:48-51. The passage may have originated as an oracle of the Risen Christ and was then transferred here, ascribed to Paul, who was taking on ever more Christlike proportions.

5

[1]One actually hears of a kind of whoredom among you that even the pagans do not tolerate: that a man should have sex with his stepmother! [2]And your reaction is to be inflated with pride—instead of mourning for the one who committed this deed because he has been expelled from your company? [3]For I myself, indeed, albeit absent in body, am nonetheless present in spirit, and [4]assembled with you in the name of the Lord Jesus and of my spirit, with the power of our Lord Jesus. [3b]I have already passed judgment on the one who com-

mitted this deed, ⁵*that he be handed over to the accuser for the destruction of the flesh in order that the spirit may be saved in the day of the Lord Jesus.*

One must suspect that the sexual scandal referred to here was an overflow of the sort of either eschatological (Käsemann) or Gnostic (Schmithals) libertinism resulting from the transcendence of the law, albeit prematurely, while the strictures of this world yet linger. Our Marcionite writer continues, invoking the hovering presence of *Kurios Paulos* in judgment now, to preserve the rigorous standards of the Marcionite community. Even here, however, the goal is that the excommunicated brother be *saved* in the end. As we will see again in 2 Corinthians, for Marcionites, suffering is educative, not punitive.

Verses 3 and 4 are exactly parallel to Matthew 18:18-20, only here it is Paul himself who hovers like the divine Shekinah (*Pirke Aboth* 3:7)⁹ over the assembly of his followers, empowering them with the keys of the kingdom. As we will shortly see, the Paulinist and the Matthean measures of communal justice are practically identical, stemming, no doubt, from their common origin in the sectarian jurisprudence of Qumran and the Baptist community.

⁶This bragging of yours is not healthy! Don't you realize that it takes only a pinch of yeast to permeate the whole mass? ⁷Expurgate the old yeast in order to become a new unleavened loaf, which ostensibly you are. ⁸For Christ, our counterpart to the paschal lamb, has been sacrificed. So let us celebrate the feast, neither with the old yeast of Judaism nor with the insidious corruption of malice and wickedness, but with the pure matzoh of sincerity and truth.

I take this section to be a Catholic gloss, with its Judaizing metaphors. In accord with the two-step maneuver of Catholic co-optation of the Old Testament, the text claims for its own a Jewish heritage, but only to denigrate it as an inferior preliminary stage. Consider the denigration of the literal Passover meal of historic Judaism. *Judaism itself* is the contaminating yeast, as seems implied in the strange reference to "the old yeast." The image is equivalent to that of the Cana miracle in John 2:1-11, where Judaism *per se* is symbolized by the water jars consecrated for use in ritual ablutions. By changing their contents into wine, the Johannine Jesus has rejected traditional

Jewish usage. The sacredness of the original use has been jettisoned in favor of something formerly mundane, festive wine drinking, now made sacred through its role in the Christian eucharist. The talk of the Lord's Supper as a Christian Passover represents the Catholic attempt to paper over the manifest origins of the eucharist in the Mystery cults of Dionysus and Osiris, something syncretist Gnostics did not mind admitting.

⁹In the epistle I wrote you not to patronize prostitutes, ¹⁰but not to avoid completely the prostitutes, or for that matter, the covetous, the greedy, and the idolaters among the worldly—in that case, you should have to leave the planet! ¹¹But now I wrote you to shun the company of any reputed brother who is a prostitute or a coveter or an idolater or an abusive drunk or greedy, not even to share a meal with such a one! ¹²For what business is it of mine to judge outsiders? Don't you judge those inside the fold? ¹³Those outside, God will judge. Expel the evil one from your company!

In some ways, remember, Marcionism was already Käsemann's "nascent Catholicism" in that it marked the transition from free-wheeling, lone-wolf, weak-group Gnosticism into a strong-group structure on its way to institutionalism. Our Marcionite writer here rebukes Simonian libertinism, the mention of prostitutes perhaps referring specifically to Simon's consorting with Helen, whom he rescued from a Tyrian brothel. Of course, our writer may not have grasped the symbolic nature of that legend, which intended that Simon, the redeemer, had saved Helen, us, the Bride of Christ, from this whore-house of a sinful world.

When the writer says, "I wrote to you *in my letter* not to associate with prostitutes" or the immoral, he is most likely talking about the earlier verses of this very chapter. Thus, this verse may be a subsequent clarification by the same or another hand. And note that, for him, it is God who will judge those outside, whereas for the author of chapter 6, Christians will judge the world. But would a Marcionite writer conceive of God judging anyone at all? Ah, but he doesn't say *which* God he means. Marcion allowed that the angry Jehovah would indeed judge the wicked. Christians, however, thanks to the sacrifice of Christ, now fell outside that deity's jurisdiction.

Christians would have to exit the planet in order to avoid all influence of sin (verse 10). But is that so silly? The writer of 1 Corinthians 15:22-24 envisioned just this happening eventually, but the writer here seems to introduce the prospect of leaving the world to escape the wicked as a *reductio ad absurdum*. It is not absurd, except from a position of bourgeois religiosity which can no longer conceive of a Qumran-style, communal-monastic withdrawal from the sinful world. Here we witness a put-down of an earlier, more radical stage of Paulinism in the name of a later, more domesticated one.

The contrast formula (verse 11), setting aside previous exegesis and practice in favor of new ones, reminds one of the famous antitheses of Matthew 5:21-22, 27-28, 31-32, 33-34, 38-39, 43-44. And yet the strategy can hardly be called Matthean. We seem to have here the strategy rejected in Matthew 13:14-30, 36-43 and in 1 Corinthians 4:5: if pious separatists try to purify the religious community already in this world, they will only succeed in destroying the common life of all. Matthew has learned this lesson, perhaps the hard way, having thus reached more of a post-sectarian compromise, at least in this respect. And yet, Matthew has his own version of shunning (Matt. 18:17—"Treat him as you would a pagan or a toll collector").

6

¹Does any one of you who has some complaint against a brother dare take it before the unrighteous rather than the saints? ²Or can it be you don't know the saints will one day judge the world? And if the world is one day to be judged by you, don't tell me you are not equal to adjudicating trivial matters! ³Are you unaware that we shall judge angels? So why not matters of this life? If then you do in fact have disputes over matters of this life, do you take them before those despised in the assembly? ⁵I say this to shame you! Don't tell me you cannot find a single wise man among you equal to the task of trying his brother's case! ⁶But instead, brother hauls brother to judgment, and that before unbelievers? ⁷As it is, the fact of your mutual lawsuits signals a complete collapse. Wouldn't it be better simply to suffer the original wrong? Wouldn't it be better just to suffer deprivation? ⁸But you act unjustly and deprive, and you do it to brothers! ⁹Surely you cannot be unaware that the unrighteous shall not receive the kingdom of God when they die. Don't kid yourselves! No prostitutes, no

idolaters, no adulterers, no call-boys, no men who lie with men, [10]no thieves, no coveters, no drunken loudmouths, no greedy will receive the kingdom of God when they die. [11]And some of you used to be on this list, but you were washed by the Spirit of our God, you were made holy, you were set right invoking the name of the Lord Jesus-Christ.

The section lays down the law of a sectarian community. Because of its stringent standards of membership and the close bond between its members, anthropologists refer to such a community as a "high-grid/strong-group" community.[10] Diaspora Jews had access to Roman courts, but they maintained their own ethnic courts, too. If a Jew skipped the judgment of his own people, preferring secular justice, he earned the scorn of his compatriots.[11] This section of 1 Corinthians, exactly as in Matthew 18:15-20, presupposes a parallel system of Christian sectarian courts, with Christian elders handing down the verdict. This can hardly come from the time of Paul. Yet this is a substantially earlier stage than we glimpse in 2 Corinthians 8:21, where it is assumed that Christians will share moral standards with the rest of mankind ("do what is right ... in the sight of all"). Here, in 1 Corinthians 6, by contrast, we have a Qumran-type vilification of all outsiders simply as "the unrighteous," while Christians are simply to be equated with "the saints." The 2 Corinthians 8:21 stance is well on the way to a second-generation rapprochement with wider society, while the one here in 1 Corinthians 6 is a piece of pure sectarianism.

With verse 3, contrast 5:12 where the saints have no business judging the world! These two passages, from different sources, owe their juxtaposition to simple catchword repetition: "judging those without/of the world," regardless of the respective contexts. Are they on the same topic? Good enough.

Verse 11 is awash in baptismal language, stemming from a secondary stage of Paulinism with its sacramentalism, whether Marcionite or Catholic. It must have been the original Simonians who rejected water baptism, believing themselves the heirs of John the Baptist, Simon Magus's teacher: "I baptize you in water, but the Coming One will baptize in spirit." But again, as maverick sectarians, after withdrawing from institutions, grow and mature, they too, sooner or later, form their own communities, and these require rites of passage such as baptism.

¹²All things are permitted me! But not everything is expedient. Nothing is forbidden me, but neither will I mortgage my liberty. ¹³Food is for the belly and the belly is for food, but in the end, God will destroy both, won't he? The body, on the other hand, is not for prostitution but is set aside for the Lord, and the Lord satisfies the body. ¹⁴And God both raised up the Lord and will raise us up by his power. ¹⁵Can you be ignorant of the fact that your bodies are members of the cosmic body of Christ? So how about if I take the members of Christ's body and make them the members of a prostitute? Never! ¹⁶You know, of course, that whoever joins himself with a prostitute is a single body with her, for it says, "the two shall be one flesh." ¹⁷But whoever joins himself to the Lord becomes one spirit with him. ¹⁸Abandon prostitution! Whatever sin one may commit is external to the body, but the one prostituting himself actually sins against his own body! ¹⁹Or perhaps it has escaped you that your body is a shrine of the Holy Spirit in you, which you have received from God, so that you are no longer your own property. ²⁰For you were bought at considerable cost. So use your body *and your spirit, which belong to God*, to worship God.

Verses 12-13 remind us at once of Mark 7:18-19, where we read that food "enters not the heart, but only the mouth and thence passes on into the latrine, which purges all foods." The point in Mark would seem to be the futility of kosher laws. The writer of this passage of 1 Corinthians, a Marcionite, brings up similar antinomian slogans, presumably from the libertine wing of Simonianism. He agrees with them in principle but qualifies the affirmations of freedom, as we have come to expect, by a sense of realism regarding the stubborn perseverance of the mundane world. It is still a world in which one requires rules of behavior which are analogous to a map, since there is a real danger otherwise of getting lost. The prostitution element, again, may reflect the Simonian theme of Helen as a Tyrian harlot.

Verse 14 speaks of the resurrection as yet future. This reflects the simmering down of the radical "realized eschatology" that had been characteristic of the primitive stage when Paulinists imagined the Kingdom of God had already arrived.

Verse 16 quotes the Old Testament, initially surprising for a Marcionite, but in fact it is quite appropriate to quote the demiurge's scripture about the demiurge's invention of marriage. And what a disdainful view of marriage! It is little more than prostitution. This is the view of Marcionites, most Gnostics, and encratites. We should expect nothing from these quarters about the sanctity of holy matrimony, though Marcion grudgingly tolerated it.

Verse 20 states clearly the central Marcionite doctrine of the atonement: Jesus's death was the ransom paid by his Father to the demiurge to purchase the freedom and adoption of his creatures. "You were bought with a price" from the demiurge, Marcion believed.

7

[1]Now concerning the things you wrote about. It is good for a husband not to have sex with his wife. [2]But because of the temptation of prostitution, let each husband have sex with his wife, and let each woman have sex with her own husband. [3]Let the husband pay what he owes his wife, and likewise the wife her husband. [4]The wife does not possess exclusive rights to her own body, but the husband has rights to it, too. In the same way, the husband does not have exclusive rights to his body, but his wife has rights, too. [5]Do not deprive one another, unless you mutually agree to abstinence for an opportune period so as to use the time for prayer instead, and then you may come together again in case the accuser tempt you due to a lack of self-control. [6]Now I say this by way of permission, not as a command. [7]In fact, I wish everyone was celibate like I am myself, but each one has his own particular calling from God, one this way, one that.

Verse 1 presents the first of several subject-heading introductions (1 Corinthians 7:1, 25; 8:1; 12:1; 16:1). The notion of some Corinthians having written to ask Paul's advice on these matters is a fictive device. The point is really just to produce a "church order" manual like the topically divided Gospel according to Matthew, the Qumran *Manual of Discipline*, and the numerous second-, third-, and fourth-century church orders like the *Didache* (which has the same sort of subject-section dividers, *peri de*, "now concerning"), the *Didascalia*

Apostolorum, and the *Apostolic Constitutions*. All these Christian texts pass themselves off as having been composed by the apostles so as to claim their authority, just as the Old Testament contains several successive law codes attributed to Moses.

The verse contains an anachronistic (for Paul) reference to the second- and third-century phenomenon of the *agapetae* or *virgines subintroductae*, partners in celibate marriage, which was much debated by Tertullian, Chrysostom,[12] and others. Pious second-century Christians imagined Mary and Joseph had shared such an arrangement; thus, though legally married, Mary was perpetually a virgin. Though Marcionites are said to have been ascetics and to have advocated "spiritual" or celibate marriage, we know they were not the most radical of encratites. They forbade divorce despite the fact that they deemed marriage the device of the demiurge to keep his material pond well-stocked with trapped souls. Also, since Marcion allowed members to defer baptism till they felt fully ready to embrace his rigorous standards, he must have tolerated conventional marital relations for many of his congregants. His stance might very well have been nuanced exactly as we read here. Again, we can see how Marcionite Christianity is already "nascent Catholicism" compared to its parent Simonianism, which was more radical still. The point throughout chapter 7 is to mitigate the radicalism of Pauline encratism like that celebrated in the *Acts of Paul and Thecla*. First Corinthians 7 represents an attempt by later Paulinists to adjust the movement's lifestyle closer to the mainstream. The Pauline sect (Simonianism) is on its way to becoming the Pauline church (Marcionism).

Why was the effort necessary? Many Paulinists (Valentinians, Marcionites, encratites) still walked the straight and narrow path of gospel celibacy traditionally ascribed to Paul, but after a while their zeal flagged, and they needed some sort of fall-back position. We see the same thing happening in Matthew's modification of the Markan prohibition of divorce. Mark, followed by Luke, had Jesus ban divorce (Mark 10:2-12; Luke 16:18). Matthew, by contrast, allows divorce in the special case of *porneia* (adultery, consanguineous marriage, prostitution? Matt. 5:31-32; 19:3-9). He has ameliorated both the Markan and the Q versions of the saying. Apparently his community found the rule too rigid in practice: the human heart had not, after all, changed that much since Moses, despite gospel claims to cardiac renewal.

Verse 2 grudgingly admits that conventional marital relations are preferable to taking a vow of celibacy prematurely if one is liable to wind up tempted to have sex with another's spouse on the sly.

Verse 5 accepts the Gnostic-ascetic assumption that spirituality and sexuality are totally incompatible. If one wants to undertake a season of prayer, one will naturally abstain from sex for the duration.[13] That would be a good first step; don't jump all the way to a full celibacy commitment too soon or you may rue the consequences.

Verse 7 confirms what we knew from Patristic sources: though Marcion urged complete celibacy, he allowed the lay folk to put off this degree of initiation till later. It was for the hardness of their hearts. Had he insisted upon it, he'd have had as few members as the Shakers. (What? You say they're extinct?)

[8]Now I say to the unmarried men and to the widows, it is good for them to remain as I am, too. [9]But if they lack self-mastery, let them marry; it is better to marry than to burn.

Presumably, the "burning" is the flame of lust. I am taking the reference in verse 8 as simply to men who have not yet gotten married and to women whose husbands have died and left them alone. On the other hand, the latter might instead refer to consecrated women, precursors of Roman Catholic nuns, who are pining away for their absent "husband," Jesus Christ, especially since secular, literal widows come in for mention in 7:39-40.

[10]But to those who have married, I charge you—actually not I but the Lord—a wife not to be separated from her husband. [11]But if, in fact, she is already separated, she must remain single or else reconcile with her husband. Equally, I charge a husband not to leave his wife.

Here is the famous Marcionite prohibition of divorce. Interestingly, children of unions with even one Christian parent seem to escape the taint of the demiurge. ("Otherwise they would be unclean.") But what might be the motive of the Christian spouse who weighs whether or not to leave the marriage (verse14)? In the apocryphal Acts, which promote the encratite celibacy gospel, the believing spouse repudiates the unbelieving spouse as a matter of course. Sex itself is the original sin, and no one who indulges can be saved. Such rigorism may have characterized Simonianism, or some faction of it. Already couples who convert together in the apocryphal Acts swear off sex forever. Rigid restrictions of this kind are as social as they are sexual in nature. In all sectarian groups, access to bodily orifices is as strictly guarded as the social openings to the body politic, which they symbolize. Such, for example, is the function of kosher laws, as in Acts 10:10-28; 11:3. To shut off the non-Christian spouse from sex is to isolate the inner circle of believers from all those outside, to minimize sinful influences. "Outside are male prostitutes, drug-dealers, whoremongers, murderers, idolaters, and everyone who loves lies and invents them" (Rev. 22:15).

To what source does the author appeal in verse 10? It is not his own judgment, he avers, but that of "the Lord," presumably Christ. But where has he derived this command? Some think the writer has access to a set of sayings attributed to Jesus of Nazareth.[14] But this seems to me to be reading too much into the text, namely an alien apologetic agenda. In light of 14:37 ("If anyone deems himself a prophet or a pneumatic, then let him prove it and admit that what I write to you is a commandment of the Lord!") it seems more likely that he sometimes receives prophetic bulletins, and this is one of them.[15] For such revelations from the heavenly Christ to Paul, see 2 Corinthians 12:9.

[12]And to the rest, it is not the Lord but I who say if any brother has an unbelieving wife and she is content to live with him, he must not leave her. [13]And if a woman has an unbelieving husband who agrees to live with her, she must not leave her husband. [14]For the unbelieving husband has been made holy by virtue of his connection to his wife, and the unbelieving wife has been made holy by her connection to her husband. Otherwise the children of such unions would be considered profane, but as it is, they are considered holy.

[15]But if the unbeliever is the one who separates, let the spouse go; the brother or sister is not bound to the marriage in such circum-

stances, for God has called you to live in peace. [16]After all, O wife, you cannot be sure you will save your husband. And husband, how can you be sure you would save your wife?

Verse 12 seems to introduce a later, compromising, conventional morality like that of the Pastoral Epistles (1 Tim. 2:22). Common sense replaces revelation, and comfortable living is the goal of those who are prudential or realistic in Christ (1 Cor. 4:10). For one thing, the subject changes: now it is simply a question of religiously mixed marriages and of how to raise the children. It is imagined that a pagan spouse might find the Christian affiliation of the other to be intolerable. (Plutarch: "It becomes the wife to worship the gods her husband believes in and to recognize none other. Her house door should be closed to exotic rites and alien superstitions.") [16]And if the break-up comes, well, the believer is not bound, that is, to the marriage. Think of the saying of Jesus in the Gospels (Mark 10:10-12; Matt. 5:31-32; Luke 16:18) that any man who divorces his wife, causing her to marry another, *ipso facto* forces her into adultery since in the eyes of God the first marriage has not been dissolved. This means both divorced spouses are still bound to the marriage even though they are not behaving like it. A different view prevails here. The spurned Christian spouse may indeed remarry with a clear conscience. We are no longer listening to a Marcionite.

[17]Only let each one live the life to which God called him when he distributed our respective lots. *And this I command in all the assemblies.* [18]Was anyone circumcised when God called him? He must not seek the procedure to undo it. Was anyone uncircumcised when God called him? He must not be circumcised. [19]Circumcision is nothing to brag about, nor is uncircumcision; what matters is keeping the commandments of God. [20]So let each one remain in the niche he occupied when God called him. [21]Were you a slave when God called you, my friend? Don't let it bother you, but if in fact you are able to become free, by all means avail yourself of the opportunity! [22]For the slave called by the Lord is henceforth the Lord's freedman. Conversely, the free man called by Christ is henceforth the slave of Christ. [23]You were brought at considerable cost; don't sell yourself

into slavery to pay your debts. [24]Whatever niche one occupied, brothers, let him remain there—God will be with him there.

Verses 17-24 might be another Catholicizing gloss designed to apply the text to a wider audience. Or verse 17, if original here, may be a signal that the text was originally written for the general reader, the Corinthians being fictive addressees, as in Luke 12:41 and Mark 13:37. Verses 18-24 constitute an off-topic insertion, swerving away from the announced topic of sexual relations and treating broader topics characteristic of the *Haustafeln*, or household codes, sprinkled into the epistles (Eph. 5:21-6:9; Col. 3:18-22; 1 Pet. 2:13-3:7) by the Pastoral redactor.[17] These more comprehensive topics include slavery and relations between Jews and gentiles. The occasion for the insertion was that the original discussion treated male-female relations, as do the household codes. But the rest of the domestic agenda was lacking, so the Pastoral redactor thought it wise to supplement the original here. The interpolated section is neatly set off by redactional seams. Verse 24 reproduces verse 17, which in context summarized the preceding discussion that men and women should not change the marital status they occupied when they converted to Christianity. Verse 24 seeks to restore the peg from which the subsequent verses originally depended.

Verse 19 seems oddly paradoxical: circumcision does not matter as long as one keeps the commandments of God. Isn't circumcision one of the most important Torah commandments (Gen. 17:9-14)? And yet gentile Christians are told not to bother. Thus, the commandments in view here may be the so-called Noachide commands of Genesis 9:4-6, the only ones Jews believed God expected gentiles to obey. These are adapted for gentile Christian converts in Acts 15:29. The point here in 1 Corinthians 7:19 would be for the circumcised Jew and the uncircumcised pious gentile to keep the commandments appropriate to each. But no Marcionite would draw such distinctions. The laws of Jehovah are passé for Christians, period. Again, this is Catholicizing material, though from a different pen than the one from which the Catholic verses 12-16 came.

The *dharma* doctrine[18] of verses 20-24 could as easily result from either a bourgeois concern to squelch revolutionary unrest (Col. 3:22-

25; 1 Tim. 6:6-10) or from an apocalyptic fatalism that sees no use in rearranging the furniture aboard a sinking ship (Rev. 22:10-11).

[25]Now concerning consecrated virgins: I admit I lack any commandment from the Lord, but I give a legal opinion as one who is reliable, thanks to the mercy Adonai has shown me. [26]I think that, given the present distress, this virginal state is good— that it is good for a man to be so. [27]Have you been joined to a wife? Do not seek to be released. Have you been released from a marriage? Do not seek another one. [28]But if indeed you do marry, you have not sinned, and if a consecrated virgin marries, no sin has occurred, but such individuals are asking for the troubles besetting this natural life, and I mean to spare you that.

[29]But I will say this, brothers: the remaining time has grown short. As for everyone else, I could wish for those who have wives to be the same as those who do not; [30]for those who weep to be the same as those who are not weeping; the one rejoicing the same as the ones not rejoicing; the ones buying the same as those with no property; [31]and the ones manipulating this world as those who don't abuse it. For the system of this cosmos is passing away. [32]But I want you to be free of care. The unmarried man is at liberty to care only for the Lord's concerns, [33]considering how he may please the Lord. But the married man of necessity occupies himself with worldly affairs, considering how he may please his wife. [34]Thus his attention has been divided. And the unmarried woman, that is to say, the consecrated virgin, is mindful only of the concerns of the Lord, in order to be holy both in the body and in the spirit. But the married woman is properly mindful of worldly concerns, planning how to please her husband. [35]All this I say for your own advantage, not in order to hinder your freedom but for good order and for you to be attentive servants of the Lord without distraction.

Our author has no command from the Lord, but as the context shows, this seems to be because no absolute directive is possible, given the circumstances. It's not the kind of thing a command covers. You have to look at the whole situation with its shades of gray and take your best shot. So, the writer is not so much saying that his words have less authority than they might, but rather that only a nuanced, conditional position is possible.

The subject of this section is eschatological celibacy, part of what Albert Schweitzer called an "interim ethic."[19] The practical application of the absolute is made more acute by the impending end of the world as we know it. Just as the daylight is bent at a sharper angle and so changes color at sunset, so the light of eschatological ethics outlines things more starkly. What would ordinarily be quite wholesome, at least excusable, may now be ill-advised—though still not wrong, just tricky: the Creator's world is on the point of passing away. Notice how, in verse 28, the motivation for celibacy has nothing to do with Marcionite and encratite teaching, which made sex the original sin. The thinking is precisely that of the Essene monks, as Josephus describes it: "There are about four thousand men that live in this way, and neither marry wives, nor are desirous to keep servants; as thinking the latter tempts men to be unjust, and the former gives the handle to domestic quarrels" (*Antiquities of the Jews*, 18.1.5, Whiston trans.).[20] It is a matter of distraction from total focus on God and divine service. There's nothing really wrong with marriage, but uninterrupted worship is better.

But neither do we find here the early Catholic stance of the Pastoral redactor. First Timothy 5:11-12 directly contradicts 1 Corinthians 7:28. First Timothy maintains that the consecrated virgin who later decides she'd rather get married after all has broken her prior pledge of marriage exclusively to Christ, and this is a serious sin. Given this danger, 1 Timothy warns, younger women ought not even consider joining the Order of Widows, which included once married, now celibate women and young virgins. I judge this section of 1 Corinthians 7 to derive from traditional Essenism, handed down from the common Jordan Valley sectarian milieu shared by Essenes, Mandaeans, Simonians, and Dositheans. Another such fragment occurs in 2 Corinthians 6:14-7:1.

In verses 29-31, we see an insertion, as indicated by the repetitious redactional seams beginning and ending the passage. The instructions smack both of Stoicism, with its prescription of inner detachment, and of encratism, with its purely formal, nonsexual marriage arrangement. It aims to fill in the specifics behind the references to worldly duties and cares in verses 28 and 33, but from a different religious perspective.

> [36] But if anyone thinks he is behaving inappropriately toward his virgin partner, and he is sexually frustrated and it seems inevitable, let him do what he wants; he does not sin. Let them marry. [37] But he who stands firm in his heart, not feeling the inevitable urge but having authority over his own will, and has decided in his own heart to keep his virgin partner at arm's length, he will do a fine thing. [38] Thus the one who marries his virgin partner does a fine thing, and the one who does not marry will do better!

Most translations, as we saw in chapter 4 of the present volume, do not know what to do with this passage, the original New English Bible being one of the few exceptions. It deals rather clearly with the controversial question of the *virgines subintroductae*, or spiritual marriage partners. The commitment one may have made to celibate marriage is not quite so urgent here as in the pure encratism on display in the apocryphal Acts. It is, rather, consistent with the Marcionite adjustment of such standards in a more comprehensive community setting, one ever so gradually drifting from being the camp of the saints (like Qumran) to being a school for sinners (as Cyprian called the church).

> [39] A wife has been bound for as long a time as her husband lives; but if the husband falls asleep in death, she is free to be married to whomever she pleases, only within the household of the Lord. [40] But she is sure to be happier if she remains as she is, at least in my opinion, and I think I, too, have the wisdom of the Spirit of God.

Why is the advice given back in verses 8-9 reproduced, barely paraphrased, here at the close of the discussion of celibacy and sex? It might well indicate that all that falls between these matching sets of verses is a later addition, which has, as we have seen, suffered its own further additions. This possibility might make it easier for some readers to accept my suggestion in chapter 4 that the material in 1 Corinthians 7 on celibate marriage is actually later than the Iconium Sermon in the *Acts of Paul*.

8

¹Now concerning the meat of idol sacrifices: we are agreed that we all possess gnosis. Gnosis tends to ego-inflation, while love leads to edification. ²If anyone thinks he knows something, he only shows that he does not yet know as he ought to know. ³But if anyone loves God, God is ipso facto known by him. ⁴Thus concerning idol sacrifice meat, we know that no deity depicted by an idol exists outside the imagination, and that there is no God except one. ⁵For even if there are so-called gods, either in heaven or on earth, as in fact there are many gods and many lords ⁶still, as far as we are concerned, there is one God, the Father, from whom all things are, and we in him, and one Lord, Jesus-Christ, through whom are all things, and we through him. ⁷But not all men possess this gnosis, and some by habit cannot help thinking of the meat as an idol sacrifice as they eat it, and their conscience, weak as it is, is defiled. ⁸But food will not make us pleasing to God; we are at no disadvantage if we do not eat it, nor are we superior if we do eat it. ⁹But watch out that this authority of yours does not degenerate into a scandal to trip up the weak ones! ¹⁰For if anyone sees the gnostic sitting down to a meal in an idol's temple, won't his weak conscience be encouraged to eat the idol sacrifice as an act of devotion to an alien deity? ¹¹Thus the weak one is destroyed by your gnosis, this brother for whom Christ died! ¹²And so sinning against the weak brothers and wounding their consciences, you are sinning against Christ. ¹³This is why, if food trips up my brother, I will never eat meat again so that I do not trip up my brother!

Verses 1 and 7 seem to contradict one another. Do all of us possess superior knowledge? Or only those of us who realize the indifferent character of idols? My guess is that verse 1 intends to identify with the Simonian-Gnostic elite: "Sure, you and I know better. But old Stupidicus isn't as enlightened as you and I. Let's go easy on the poor fellow." Basically we have here another instance of Marcionite institutionalism trying to mitigate the increasingly offensive character of the original Simonianism, especially their practice of brazenly eating meat offered to idols. Verses 1, 4, and 10:23 recall the slogans of Simonian Gnostic libertinism, and the rest of the chapter, plus 10:23-11:1, tries to mitigate it for the sake of stable Marcionite church life, where strong group harmony is valued, not just the high grid of the earlier Gnostic virtuosi who were essentially lone wolves. As for the specific infraction, "We are told that Simonians did not hesitate to burn sacrifices to idols."[21]

What exactly is the danger implied in verse 12? Who is going to be misled into what error? It has something to do with false worship, worship of false gods. But what? The underlying issue is whether Christians may attend dinners given in the fellowship halls of pagan temples or where a host serves meat originally offered to pagan gods. Temple priests often sold leftover sacrificial meat to the local market. Would sitting down to such a meal implicate a Christian in idol worship? Gnostics said no and happily attended. To them it was just meat. The pagan deities were fakes, so what's the problem? It's as if someone offered you cookies left for Santa but still on the plate Christmas morning. We might call the Gnostic a *monotheist* (or possibly a God-Christ *binitarian*), since he knows the Greek gods to be mere figments, their altars nothing more than buffet tables. But the easily confused recent convert is a mere *monolater*, imagining that the other deities exist but are not his to worship. And the danger, from the writer's point of view, is that the Gnostic's example, misunderstood as participation in pagan religion, may encourage monolaters to become instead *henotheists*, worshipping Christ and other gods serially. Henotheism, also called "kathenotheism," means, literally, "one-god-at-a-time-ism." Stephen Fuchs describes what looks like the same situation among the Faraizi sect, a Wahabi-style Muslim fundamentalist movement in late nineteenth-century Bengal, today's Bangladesh:

> There can be no doubt that the vast majority of Muslims in the delta of the Ganges and Brahmaputra are descendants of the low Hindu castes and the aborigines who willingly embraced Islam at the time of the Mohammedan conquest in preference to remaining outcastes beyond the pale of exclusive Hinduism. But though they became converts in outward profession, they still retained many of the superstitious customs and beliefs of their former life, and joined in social merry-makings with their Hindu fellow villag-

ers. In particular, they used to observe the Durga *puja* festivities and worshipped other deities and spirits of the Hindus.[22]

But our writer summons us to lock the barn door long after the horse has escaped. The easy flow of religious seekers between and among Mystery Cults, including that of the Kyrios Jesus, had already resulted in a syncretistic exchange of mythemes and soteriologies,[23] as the shape of Christianity in this epistle readily attests.

I would identify the writer of this section as a Marcionite, not a Catholic. Catholics, of course, would not relish their members dabbling in other religions, either. But it is hard to believe they would brook the amount of agreement with Gnostics that we are finding in the chapter so far. The Catholic view is more solidly theological and takes demonolatry much more seriously, as we will see in chapter 10.

If chapter 8 does represent Marcionism, it raises a very interesting possibility for understanding 8:5-6. We know that Marcion was unabashedly monolatrous, freely acknowledging the existence of the Creator God, the Hebrew God of the Old Testament. It was just that Christians had no business worshipping him, any more than Elijah thought Israel had any business worshipping Baal when Yahve was their rightful deity. He didn't deny Baal existed, which he might easily have done if that was what he thought. So when a Marcionite says, "There are indeed many gods and many lords, but for us there is only one of each," is it possible he means pagan gods are real deities, albeit irrelevant to Christians?

I propose going straight to the discussion of chapter 10 and then returning to chapter 9, most of which I regard as an interpolation interrupting the discussion of eating idol sacrifice meat. The original discussion from chapter 8 continues in 9:23-33. Why so clumsy an insertion? Not so clumsy, perhaps: the point was to wait 'til the discussion in 8 had faded a bit from the reader's mind. That way he might not notice the blatant contradiction between the two treatments of the single theme. It is just like the separation of three versions of the legend in Genesis 12:10-20; 20:1-18; 26:1-16 about the patriarch and his beautiful wife in a foreign land. The redactor placed many stories between them, hoping the reader would not notice they were simply three versions of the same original tale.

10

¹For I do not want you to ignore the fact that our Jewish ancestors were all sheltered beneath the pillar of cloud and all passed through the sea, ²and all were committed to Moses through baptism in the cloud and in the sea, ³and all alike ate the same spiritual food, ⁴and all drank the same spiritual drink, for they all drank from the same spiritual rock that pursued them, and the rock was the counterpart to Christ. ⁵Still, with the majority of them, God was not pleased, as can be seen from the fact that their bones were left scattered in the wilderness. ⁶So these things were precedents, to warn us not to yearn for evil things as those people did. ⁷And you must refuse to be idolaters as some of them were, as it is written: "The people sat to eat and to drink and got up to revel." ⁸Neither let us indulge in prostitution, as some of them indulged in cult-prostitution, where twenty-three thousand fell in a single day! ⁹Neither let us push the Lord's patience over the limit as some of them did—and were destroyed by serpents! ¹⁰Neither must you grouse as some of them groused and were destroyed by the destroyer. ¹¹Now these things befell these people paradigmatically and were recorded to provide admonition for future readers like us, whom the cusp of the ages has overtaken. ¹²So whoever thinks he stands, let him watch out that he does not fall! ¹³No trial has beset you that is beyond human capacity. No, God is reliable: he will not allow you to be tested beyond the breaking point; with every test, he will also provide an escape route so you will be able to endure it.

¹⁴For this reason, my beloved ones, abandon idolatry! ¹⁵I assume I am writing to people with some sense; draw your own conclusion. ¹⁶The sacred cup that we consecrate, is it not a sharing in the blood of Christ? The bread we break, is it not a sharing in the body of Christ? ¹⁷Because the bread is a single loaf, we the many are made one body because we all share in the one loaf of bread. ¹⁸Consider ethnic Israel: are not those who eat the sacrifice sharers in the altar? ¹⁹So what am I trying to say? That it is anything more than a charade when a sacrifice is offered to idols? Or that there is any reality to an idol? ²⁰Rather, that what the poor fools sacrifice, they are offering to demons, not to God. And I do not want you to become table companions with demons! ²¹You cannot drink a cup of the Lord and a cup

of demons; you cannot partake of a table of the Lord and a table of demons. ²²Or do we propose to make the Lord jealous? Can we possibly manipulate him?

Verses 10:1-22 represent the Catholic point of view on eating idol sacrifice meat. These verses are a corrective inserted by someone with a weaker theological conscience, someone who could not believe the act of participation in idol-feasts was really so neutral as Gnostic pneumatics would like to make it. It must be shunned, not merely because of unintended collateral damage to third parties, but because it is blasphemous in its own right: such sacrifices are really being consecrated to devils! As of verse 23, however, we find the original continuation of the argument offered by one who believes the practice is morally neutral but advises against it for the sake of the weaker brethren, the *psuchikoi.*

²³*All things are permitted me, but not everything is smart to do. Everything is permitted, but not everything is constructive.* ²⁴*Let no one look out for his own interests alone, but also to the good of others.* ²⁵*For conscience's sake, eat whatever is sold in the marketplace without asking questions about where it came from. For ultimately, it comes from the Lord in any case, as he owns the whole earth and its bounty.* ²⁷*If any unbelievers invite some of you to dinner and you want to go, feel free to eat everything they serve you without asking the questions of an over-scrupulous conscience.* ²⁸*But if anyone remarks, "This is sacrificial meat, you know," decline to eat it, both because of the man who pointed it out and for the sake of conscience.* ²⁹*Not one's own conscience, mind you, but that of the other. But why should my freedom be condemned by the conscience of another?* ³⁰*If I partake, offering thanks, why should what I am giving thanks for expose me to false charges of doing evil? I'm free to do it, all right, but it's hardly worth it.*
³¹*So whether you are eating or drinking, whatever you may do, do everything as worship offered to God.* ³²*Learn not to give needless offense either to Jews or to Greeks or to the congregation of God,* ³³*just as I also try to get along with everyone in every matter, by not pursuing my own advantage, but that of the many, in order that they may be saved.*

11
¹*Imitate me in this policy as I am imitating Christ.*

These verses conclude the Marcionite discussion of eating idol meat. *Whose* conscience is in view in verse 29? Is it the pagan host, who must not be allowed to think Christians participate in any way in idolatrous feasts? Or is it one's Christian companion, also invited, whose tender conscience may be confused? Probably the latter is intended, as the pagan host is taken care of in the previous verse as a separate matter. In any case, as long as no one says anything, it is just meat, just a meal, without complications. If you don't actually know the steak came from the Mithras temple, you need not assume the worst. But suppose your host brags, "You won't believe the deal I got on these steaks! Fresh from sacrifice!" You'll have to make do with the dinner rolls.

Why all the concern with sensitivity in verses 32-33? It is another, less controversial way of issuing the traditional Gnostic advice not to throw one's doctrinal pearls before unenlightened swine, since they will surely misunderstand higher truth as blasphemy and feel obliged to punish the blasphemer. Some Gnostics advised "dissimulation" (what the Moonies used to call "heavenly deception"), keeping one's controversial beliefs under one's vest even under interrogation. ("If they ask you, 'Where are you from?' say to them ..." *Gospel of Thomas*, saying 50.) They don't have the right to know; you don't have the right to tell them, since it would only goad them into violence.[24]

9

[1]Am I not free to do as I please? Am I not an apostle? Have I not seen Jesus our Lord? In fact, are you not my work in the Lord's service? [2]If to others I do not count as an apostle, still indeed I count as one as far as you are concerned! For you are the authenticating mark of my apostleship. [3]To anyone cross-examining me, this is my defense: [4]Haven't we the right to eat and to drink at our converts' expense? [5]Haven't we the right to be accompanied by a sister-wife like the rest of the apostles and the brothers of the Lord and Cephas? [6]Or is it only I and Bar-Nabas who lack the right not to engage in secular work? [7]Who ever goes off to serve in wartime at his own expense? Who plants a vineyard without receiving a share of the grapes from it? Who shepherds a flock without receiving some of the milk from it? [8]I am not speaking merely from common sense; does not the Torah

itself say these things? [9]As a matter of fact, in the Law of Moses it is written: "You shall not muzzle an ox while threshing." Do oxen matter to God? [10]Of course not. The whole reason he says it is for our sake! It was written because of us. The ploughman ought to plow with some incentive. The thresher should thresh in hope of partaking of the wheat! [11]If we did the spiritual sowing among you, is it asking too much for us to reap some material return from you? [12]If others have a right to expect some share of support from you, surely it should be we who have that right! But we did not avail ourselves of this right, but we would rather put up with anything than place an obstacle in the path to the news of Christ. [13]Don't you know that those who work at priestly duties get their living from the holy place and that those who wait on the altar share in what is offered there? [14]In the same way, the Lord ordained that those who proclaim the news should live by the news. [15]Yet I have not availed myself of any of these precedents. Nor have I written these things in order to do so now. For I should prefer to die rather than to have anyone nullify my boast!

[16]It is not the preaching of the news of which I boast. No, I have to do that, and woe is me if I do not preach the news! [17]If I did this on my own initiative, I might be due a reward, but as it is a matter of obedience, I am more of a slave entrusted with the stewardship. [18]What reward could I desire? Simply that in preaching the news without charge I may offer the news in such a way as to refrain from using my full rights as an apostle of the news. [19]Being free of everyone, I became enslaved to everyone in order that I might gain the more. [20]And among the Jews I comported myself like a Jew so as to win Jews. Among those under the Torah, I comported myself like one under the Torah, so as to gain the confidence of the Torah-observant. [21]Among those without Torah, I became as one without Torah—not, you understand, actually being without the Law of God, but still abiding by the law of Christ!—so I might gain the confidence of those without the Torah. [22]Among the weak in faith, I observed their scruples, so as to gain the confidence of the weak. I have become everything to everyone in order that, by whatever means, I might gain the confidence of some.

[23]But all this I do because of the news in order that I may come to share in the salvation promised by it. [24]Don't you know that of all

who compete in the stadium race, only one receives the prize? Run fast enough to win! [25]And everyone who agonizes in any sport exercises self-mastery, and they do it for the sake of receiving a fading laurel wreath. But we seek one that will never fade. [26]That is why I run as I do in no random direction, and why I box as I do, not wasting my punches on thin air. [27]I subject my body to a severe regimen, making it my slave so I will never find myself, having preached to others, in the end disqualified.

Chapter 9 is an interpolation, occasioned by the occurrence of the catchwords "food and drink." Verses 1-3 form an isolated fragment defending Pauline apostolic authority (in other words, Marcionite clout) in the province of Achaia, of which Corinth was a part.

Another section, verses 4-12a, and 13-14, argues for congregational support for missioners. I am not quite ready to make the section Catholic on the basis of the appeal to the Torah. The blatantly allegorical interpretation, which utterly dispenses with the original sense, reminds one of the *Epistle of Barnabas* or even of Philo's opponents who were fellow Jewish allegorizers and, unlike him, went on to disregard the literal sense of the commandments. On display here is the sort of experimental hermeneutics from Alexandrian circles that eventually gave rise to Gnostic exegesis.

Verse 5 speaks again of virginal partners traveling to evangelize, as Chrysostom and Tertullian debated. Simon Magus traveled thus with Helen, too. In all cases, the practice generated scandal and criticism, though in all likelihood it was innocent enough, like a spinster housekeeper living under the same roof as a Catholic priest.

Note the anachronistic reference to Barnabas, who does not appear alongside Paul as a colleague elsewhere in the epistle, as if the interpolator did not recall which apostolic associate had been mentioned earlier and just thought of them, as modern readers tend to do, in one big lump. But then, is it possible, in view of the brand of exegesis for sale in verses 9-10, that this writer is actually thinking of the *Epistle of Barnabas*?

Up to 12b we have been reading a defense against critics who regard itinerant apostles as flim-flam artists bilking the gullible out of their money, as in Lucian's satire *Alexander the Quack Prophet*. Paul is said to have received such support in Philippians 4:10-19 and in 2 Corinthians 11:8. A subsequent scribe's correction in verses 12b and 16-18 retroactively attributes a more recent missionary practice to Paul in order to legitimize it. This view of Paul, declining congregational support, appears in 2 Corinthians 11:7, 9, 12. We can see similar differences among the various versions of the Synoptic Mission Charge texts (Mark 6:7-11; Matt. 10; Luke 9:1-5; 10:1-16), reflecting changes in missionary practices, with Jesus updating them in successive redactions.

Modern harmonizers plead that the first argument is Paul's statement of agreement on basics with his critics regarding an apostle's right to receive compensation, whereas the second argument presents his extenuating reasons for, nonetheless, not exercising the rights for which he has so eloquently argued. But no one takes such trouble to establish the other fellow's argument, only to dismiss it and establish one's own position in a few words, as we would have to read Paul as doing here if he wrote the whole thing. No, we are reading an initial plea for recognition of the apostolic rights of missioners to receive love offerings; then someone else's brief for a different, "above-board" approach which avoids all suspicion of financial exploitation.

The notion in 9:20-22 that Paul "became a Jew to Jews, a Greek to Greeks, law-abiding to the one, free of Law to the other" sounds like a latter-day attempt to reconcile variant polemical traditions, pro and con, about Paul. If there was "another Jesus" (2 Cor.11:4), there also had been "another Paul" (cf. Gal. 5:11). Compare with this the Ebionite claim "that he was a pagan, with a pagan mother and father, that he went up to Jerusalem [from Tarsus] and stayed there a while, that he desired to marry the priest's daughter and therefore became a proselyte and was circumcised but then did not obtain the girl who was of such high station, and in his anger wrote against circumcision, the Sabbath, and the law."[25] While this catalogue of motives is obviously a catty smear, the notion of a pre-Jewish gentile identity for Paul is not so silly. After all, the epistles certainly convey a gentile outsider's view of the Torah as an intolerable burden, which is the way it must seem to someone imagining what it would be like to assume the burden of an alien culture's mores. By contrast, Jews who had grown up amid the Torah com-mandments took them for granted like a fish in water. If 9:20-22 is a harmonization, it is an unfortunate one, for it makes room for all the divers pictures of Paul by making them different, deceptive faces of a chameleon-like con man.

On the other hand, one wonders if there may not, after all, be more to 9:19-22. Is it possible that it preserves elements of Simo-nianism? Is it perhaps a statement of Paul's own divine incarnation? "For though I am free from all, I have made myself a slave to all, that I might win the more." Compare the hymn-lyric of Philippians 2:6 ff., "Though he was in the form of God, ... [he] emptied himself, tak-ing the form of a slave, being made in the likeness of men." This he did to save others, of course, as did Paul.

"And among the Jews I comported myself like a Jew so as to win Jews. Among those under the Torah, I comported myself like one under the Torah so as to gain the confidence of the Torah-observant. Among those without Torah, I became as one without Torah ... so I might gain the confidence of those without the Torah. Among the weak in faith, I observed their scruples so as to gain the confidence of the weak. I have become everything to everyone in order that, by whatever means, I might gain the confidence of some." (1 Cor. 9:20-22). This sounds like a statement of the redeemer's docetic appearance among humanity in order to save them. He took on, not just the form of humanity (though it *is* just the outward like-ness), but various *different* forms to save different classes of people. In the same way, the *Acts of John* has Jesus appear on earth in ever-changing forms (again, see the passages reproduced in chapter 4 of this volume). Likewise, Origen (*Conta Celsum*, II:67) says that the risen "Jesus, then, wanted to show forth his divine power to each of those able to see it, and according to the measure of his individual capacity."[26] The point is to save various groups of people by match-ing the revealer's appearance to theirs. Only lying beneath 1 Corin-thians 9:19 ff. is a redeemer myth starring Paul, not Jesus. What we have in this passage is no mere missionary strategy (and if we do, it is a bad one, full of hypocrisy), but rather a doctrine of polymor-phous "incarnation."

Verses 9:24-27 look like a displaced fragment from the discussion in chapter 7. Verses 24-27 would make more sense in that context, since "to exercise self-mastery" (*encrateuetai*) is a key term in encratite spirituality and the origin of its name, the celibacy gospel.

11

²But I take my hat off to you, that you have remembered me in every detail, and that you have held firmly to the traditions in the same form I originally committed them to you. ³But I should add something you didn't know: that of every male, the chief is Christ, and of a wife the chief is the husband, and of Christ, the chief is God. ⁴Thus every male praying or prophesying with something drawn down over his head is hiding his head in shame. ⁵But every female praying or prophesying without a veil covering her head shamelessly exposes her head, for it is one and the same with the case of the woman with a shaved head. ⁶For if a woman is not veiled, let her hair be cut off! But if a shaved or shorn head is a mark of shame for a woman, then let her follow the same instinct for propriety and go veiled. ⁷For while a male ought not to veil his head, being the image and the delight of God, the female is the delight of a male. ⁸For male does not originate from female, but female from male. ⁹For indeed it was not the male who was created for the sake of the female, but the female for the sake of the male! ¹⁰That is why a woman ought to have an authority over the head, because of the angels. ¹¹Nevertheless, there is neither female apart from male nor male apart from female in the Lord's order of things.

¹²For just as the female is from the male, even so the male now comes from the female, so there is parity after all. ¹³Judge for yourselves: is it fitting for a woman to pray to God unveiled? ¹⁴Doesn't nature herself teach you that if a man wears his hair long, it is dishonorable for him? ¹⁵But if a woman has long hair, it is her boast; for she was created with long hair as a natural veil. ¹⁶But if anyone seems to be argumentative on the point, we have no such custom as allowing women to prophesy unveiled, nor do the assemblies of God.

As W. C. Van Manen[27] noted, these references (11:2, 16) by "Paul" to traditions and customs (not merely, say, instructions) must imply a post-Pauline authorship looking back over a great many years. The tone is the same as the exhortations of the author of Revelation 2-3 (especially 2:13), speaking fictively for the Risen Jesus to congregations decades after the death of Jesus of Nazareth.

This chain of command (verses 3-5) is intended to supplant the initial state of gender equality typical of a sect, which had hitherto prevailed. This correction is a second-generation accommodation to the surrounding social mores, a case of being "conformed to this worldly age" (Rom. 12:2a). That it is a subsequent interpolation meant to introduce what follows is evident from the different senses in which the word *kephale*, or "head," is used, first as "chief" (as in the Septuagint), then as "cranium."

This is Marcionite decorum for *prophesying wives*, demanding veiling, on the basis of the Genesis 2 account, which Marcionites admitted governed married couples since marriage was the invention of the demiurge and marriage lingered among those who attended Marcionite congregations prior to full initiation. The Catholic position, by contrast, was to silence female participation altogether, as in 1 Cor. 14:33b-35. Our Marcionite writer criticizes Simonian and Gnostic Marcosian practice whereby, appealing (as Moses-adoring Samaritans would) to Moses's practice of removing his veil to speak to God, the prophetesses went unveiled (cf 2 Cor. 3:18).

Verse 10 appeals to a Gnostic-style midrash on Eve and the archons. As depicted in the *Hypostasis of the Archons*, another version of the Eden myth—older in some respects than the one in Genesis—lustful archons[28] (angels of the demiurge) sought to rape Eve, though she had been prepared for Adam. She was herself a mighty power (angel) and escaped their clutches, turning into a tree, presumably the Tree of Life, as Daphne did when fleeing the lust of Apollo. She left behind a docetic, phantom likeness of herself which the angels proceeded to gang-rape. How is all this relevant to female decorum in worship? If married women wear the veil, it will somehow provide the angelic presence of the Spiritual Eve, who will protect her earthly sisters from the depredations of the evil angels, still feared in Jewish apocalyptic and Gnosticism. What a different world!

Verse 11 is a still later correction of the preceding discussion[29] by a Marcionite ill-disposed to sacrifice the movement's early egalitarianism, suggesting that the New Testament order rendered the Old Testament order superfluous. (We find the same understanding in Galatians 3:28: in Christ, male and female are on a par.) Or the verse may be an interpolation presenting an appeal to the priestly creation account (Gen. 1:27) in which men and women are created simultaneously, excluding any ranking by priority.

Verse 12 constitutes yet another liberal Marcionite correction based on today's order of things, where men are born to women, regardless of Eve coming from Adam once upon a time. This correction seeks to refute the order-of-creation argument on its own grounds, unlike the strategy in verse 11.

Unless one adopts an analysis at least somewhat along these lines, one is stuck with either a dithering waverer, who writes (or dictates) before he is done thinking his ideas through, or perhaps a multiple personality.

[17]*But in this admonition, I cannot praise you, because it is not for the better that you assemble, but for the worse.* [18]*For first of all, when you gather in the assembly, I hear there are schisms among you, and to some degree I am inclined to believe it.* [19]*For there must be heresies among you in order that the ones with God's approval may become manifest for all to see.* [20]*The result is that when you come together, it is not to eat a supper dedicated to the Lord.* [21]*No, each one takes his own meal first, leaving one hungry while another is drunk!* [22]*Don't you have houses in which to eat and drink? Or is it perhaps that you disdain the assembly of God and humiliate the needy? I am at a loss as to what to say to you! Shall I praise you? No, on this score, I cannot praise.*

[23]*For I myself received directly from the Lord what I in turn delivered to you, that the Lord Jesus, on the night he was delivered up, took bread* [24]*and, having given thanks, he broke it and said, "This is my body, on your behalf. Do this as my memorial."* [25]*In the same fashion he took the cup after dining, saying, "This cup is the new covenant written in my blood. Do this every time you drink it, as my memorial."* [26]*For every time you eat this bread and drink the cup, you portray the death of the Lord until he comes.* [27]*In view of this, whoever eats the bread or drinks the cup of the Lord unworthily will be guilty of the body and the blood of the Lord.* [28]*But let a person undergo self-examination and only then eat of the bread and drink of the cup.* [29]*For anyone eating and drinking his own condemnation is eating and drinking oblivious of the body.* [30]This is why many of you are weak and sickly and a number sleep in death. [31]But if we only engaged in introspection, we should avoid condemnation. [32]But judged by the

Lord, we are chastened, so that we do not face the judgment with the rest of the world. [33]*And so, my brothers, coming together to eat, wait for one another!* [34]*If anyone is especially hungry, let him eat something at home beforehand so that you don't risk coming together to incur judgment. As for the rest of your concerns, I will set everything in order when I come.*

Verses 11:17-19 read like a Catholic's grudging recognition (it sounds like *First Clement*) of the inevitability of heresies; at least, the true faith may become evident by contrast, as in John: "By this they will know that you are my true disciples, that you love one another." The passage is inconsistent with 1 Corinthians 1:10-12, where Paul says he knows too well that factions are wracking the Body of Christ in Corinth. Factionalism is introduced here as if a new topic. How can the writer of 1 Corinthians 1:11-13ff. have written this?[30] Has he only vaguely heard of Corinthian factional strife? He is not quite sure whether to believe it? "Heresies" (vv. 18-19, literally "factions") denotes "false doctrines" in second-century usage. We are reading a Catholic scribal note. Verse 15 appeals to the universal, ecumenical custom of the Catholic Church, the flip side of which is to make deviation into heresy, and this seems anachronistic for Paul, the pioneer missionary.

Verse 17 sounds like a direct continuation of verse 2 and probably was. This marks the whole intervening treatment of women and veils as a subsequent interpolation. It seemed to the redactor to fit well enough there, as it is also a question of church decorum, like what follows.

Verses 23-32 are a later insertion and deal with a different subject, the eucharistic meal, a secondary ritualization of the earlier, simple communal meal or *agape* feast. Verse 33 connects back up with verse 22 as the proper conclusion of the discussion of decorum at the *agape*. Introducing the new understanding of the meal, verse 23 employs the same device as in John 16:12-14: the text professes merely to remind the community of important information once given them, when actually it is a new teaching, unveiled here for the first time, offered fictively in the name of the founder. "Paul" is correcting a messy situation which probably would not have existed if anyone had actually explained the eucharistic meal in these terms to begin with.

Loisy saw this: "It is strange that Paul, if he had really told all this to the Corinthians before, should here be obliged to recall it."[31]

We should not be surprised to find Paul acknowledging receipt of this bit of tradition from his blessed predecessors in Jerusalem. We do find such a claim in 15:3, after all, where it is the mark of a Catholic origin. But here the point is quite the opposite, just like his gospel itself in Galatians 1:1, 11-12, the brief sketch of the institution of the sacred meal is ascribed to immediate revelation from the Lord Jesus. Scholars rightly invoke the similar terminology of rabbinic tradition which has it that this or that precept was received by Rabbi A and passed on by him to Abba B. On this basis they think that Paul means he received the Last Supper pericope from the earlier apostles. But they do not have it quite right. The true parallel is with *Pirke Aboth* 1:1, "Moses received the Torah on Sinai, and handed it down to Joshua; Joshua to the elders; the elders to the prophets; and the prophets handed it down to the Men of the Great Assembly." Then afterward, for example, "Antigonus of Socho received the tradition from Simon the Just" (1:3).[32] Paul is not like Antigonus, but like Moses. He stands at square one. He is the first mortal recipient of the tradition. He is not a subsequent link in the chain, as he would be on the Catholic model, where he would have received sacred tradition from the apostles before him.[33]

Loisy also notes the layering of the passage, reflecting theological-liturgical evolution:

There is ground ... for saying that mystic commemoration of the saving death, the mystic communion with the crucified Christ, is superimposed on a form of the Supper as an anticipation of the banquet of the elect in the Kingdom of God, a form clearly indicated in a saying embedded in the oldest tradition of the Synoptic Gospels:

Verily, verily, I tell you
that I will drink no more
of the fruit of the vine,
Until that day
When I drink it new
In the Kingdom of God.

The account of the mystic Supper, in First Corinthians, belongs to the evolution of the Christian Mystery at a stage of that mystery earlier than Justin, earlier even than the canonical edition of the first three Gospels but notably later than Paul and the apostolic age. It must be dated in the period when the common meal was in process of transformation into a simple liturgical act. The passage in question is a conscious attempt to further the transformation by giving it the apostolical authority of Paul. ... In Marcion's time it was a thing of the recent past ... We conclude that this lesson on the good ordering of the Supper was drawn up towards 140 in some circle where the memory of Paul was held in honour.[34]

Verses 11:23-32, then, are a Marcionite rebuke of radical Simonian disdain for the eucharist as a sacred meal, treating it simply as an all-you-can-eat buffet. Simonians regarded it as they did idol feasts: just food.[35] As such, it is an intra-Pauline dispute. Our Marcionite writer posits that the words of institution were delivered directly to Paul from Christ, not from anyone's historical memory. Note that the text refers to "a cup," not necessarily of wine, since Marcionites used water in holy communion.

The eucharistic section may easily be read as an even later insertion than I have suggested, depending on how we understand the sacramentalism of it. Marcion was notoriously docetic, and yet Marcionites celebrated the eucharist. They believed Jesus's polymorphous body was composed of celestial substance, rather like the gods as Epicurus understood them, or as Caspar Schwenkfeld[36] understood the incarnation of Christ. There is no reason at all that Marcionites should not have believed themselves to be consuming the body of Christ in the sense they defined it. May we not even see this understanding implied in 12:13, where it is assumed that even tongue-speaking, prophesying Gnostic adepts would "drink of the same spirit" as their coreligionists?

Verse 34 enjoins a policy of tolerance on nonessentials, matters where the Paulinist communities had no word of Paul. One might have expected the epistle to end right here, but eventually other issues became so controversial that Paul's guidance had to be fabricated anew to deal with them; hence the following chapters. Thus, verse 34 is exactly like John 20:30-31, intended as a conclusion, ignored but left intact by a later continuator.

12

¹Now concerning pneumatics, brothers, I do not want you to continue in ignorance. ²You recall how, when you were gentiles, you were led by circuitous paths to worship mute idols. Yes, it is easy to be led astray in spiritual matters. ³Thus I reveal to you: no one speaking by impetus of the Spirit of God says, "Jesus be damned!" and no one can say, "O Lord Jesus!" except by impetus of the Holy Spirit. ⁴Now there are varieties of charismas, but the same Spirit. ⁵And there are different ways to serve, but the same Lord. ⁶And there are different inner empowerments, but the same God energizing all of them in everyone. ⁷But to each one there is given the appropriate display of the Spirit for the greatest benefit. ⁸For to one there is given by the Spirit a saying of esoteric wisdom, and to another a saying of gnosis according to the same Spirit. ⁹To another there is given faith by the same Spirit and to another the charisma of healing powers, ¹⁰to another the working of miracles, to another prophecy, and to another the discernment of spirits, to another varieties of tongues, and to another to provide the sense of tongues-utterances. ¹¹And one and the same Spirit energizes all these things, assigning them appropriately to each as he decides best. ¹²For just as the body is one and yet has many members, but all the members of the body, while many, yet compose one body, so also is Christ. ¹³For in truth we all were baptized in one Spirit into one body, whether Jews or Greeks, whether slaves or free, and we were all given one Spirit to drink.

¹⁴For indeed, the body is not one member but many. ¹⁵If the foot should say, "Because I am not a hand, I might as well leave the body!" it would not for that reason be excluded from the body! ¹⁶And if the ear should say, "Because I am not an eye, I might as well leave the body!" that would not make it excluded from the body! ¹⁷If the whole body were one big eye, where would the hearing be? If all the organs were for hearing, where would the sense of smell be? ¹⁸But in fact, God has arranged the members in the body precisely as he wished. ¹⁹And if the whole thing were one member, what sort of body would that be? ²⁰But now there are indeed many members,

but one body. ²¹The eye cannot say to the hand, "I do not require your services!" Nor can the head say to the feet, "Who needs you? Be on your way!" ²²But the members of the body which seem lackluster turn out to be all the more necessary. ²³And members of the body that we think best to conceal, we clothe with greater splendor, designing artful garments to cover them, and the less attractive parts of the body wind up much more attractive! ²⁴The attractive members of the body, on the other hand, require no special adornment. But God designed the body so as to provide more abundant honor to the members lacking it, ²⁵to avoid schism in the body, and so that the members should look out for one another. ²⁶Should one member suffer, all the rest suffer with it; should one member feel delight, all the members rejoice with it.

²⁷You constitute a body, Christ's, each one of you a member. ²⁸And God has appointed some in the church, firstly, as apostles, secondly prophets, thirdly teachers, then miracle workers, then charismas of healing, helps, administration, varieties of tongues. ²⁹Is everyone an apostle? Is everyone a prophet? A teacher? Does everyone work miracles? Or have healing charisma? Does everyone speak in tongues? Or interpret them? Of course not! ³¹Just be sure you zealously seek the greater charismas. And yet, I must needs show you a more excellent way.

13

¹If I speak in human tongues and those of angels, but I have not love, I am merely making noise, like a trumpet blast or a crashing cymbal. ²If I have the mantel of prophecy and know all mysteries and all gnosis, and if I have complete faith so as to be able to uproot mountains at a word, but I have not love, I am nothing. ³And if I donate all my possessions, and if I deliver up my body to be burnt, but I have not love, I gain no heavenly reward by it.

⁴Love endures much; how kind is love! Never jealous, love thinks of others first, knows no conceit, ⁵throws no tantrums, has no selfish interest to pursue, turns the cheek, keeps no record of wrongs done, ⁶takes no pleasure in evil works, delighting in true deeds; ⁷it wipes the slate clean, assumes you are telling the truth, never gives up hope of you, withstands all opposition.

[8]Love never runs out, unlike prophecies, which God shall abolish, or tongues, which he shall still, or gnosis which he shall forbid. [9]Thus for now we know but fragments, we prophesy but hints. But whenever the perfect version of a thing appears, the imperfect intimations are cast aside. [11]When I was an infant, I spoke as an infant naturally does. I thought like infants do. I made childish judgments. So having attained manhood, I put an end to all childishness. As yet, we still see the truth a distorted way, spoken in riddles; then we will see it face to face. For now, my gnosis is but partial; then I shall know as fully as God knows me. When all else fails, faith, hope, and love still stand, and chief among them is love.

14

[1]Choose love as your quest, but be zealous for the pneumatic powers and, rather than the others, that you may prophesy. [2]After all, he who speaks in an angelic tongue speaks over everyone else's heads directly to God, for no one can make sense of it, naturally, since such a one, in the grip of the Spirit, utters mysteries. [3]But the one who prophesies constructively to fellow mortals speaks words of encouragement and consolation. [4]To be sure, the one who speaks in an angelic tongue edifies himself, but the one who prophesies edifies the whole assembly. [5]It is not that I love speaking in tongues less, but that I love prophecy more! I want you all to speak in tongues, but only in order for you to prophesy once your utterance is interpreted. Prophesying is a higher task than speaking in tongues, unless one interprets, in order that the congregation may be fortified.

[6]Just imagine, brothers, if I arrive among you speaking in tongues: how am I doing you any favor unless I speak to you by way of revelation or of gnosis or of prophecy or of teaching? [7]If inanimate objects like pipe or harp produced indistinguishable sounds, how could anyone tell which tune was being played? [8]Indeed, if a trumpet gives forth an indefinite sound, who will take it as a signal to prepare for battle? [9]In the same way, unless you give a clear communication through your tongue, how can anyone tell what you are saying? You will seem to be speaking into the wind! [10]Who knows how many voices there may be in this world, yet not one of them is without meaning. [11]But if I happen not to know the import of what is said,

I remain a foreigner to the speaker, and the speaker remains a foreigner to me.

[12]So in your case, since you are such zealots for the spiritual, strive to increase your proficiency in such a way as to fortify the congregation. [13]Thus the one who speaks in an angelic tongue, let him pray to be able also to interpret. [14]For if I pray in an angelic tongue, my spirit prays, but my mind lies fallow. [15]So what am I to do? Of course, I shall pray with the spirit, and I will also pray with the mind. I will sing in the spirit, and I will sing also with the mind. [16]Otherwise, when you bless God in the spirit, how is anyone who finds himself suddenly relegated to the place of the uninitiated supposed to say "amen!"? He has no idea what you are saying! [17]Indeed, you are giving thanks right enough, but he is not fortified. [18]I give thanks to God, I speak in tongues more than all of you. [19]But in the congregation, I would rather speak five good words with my mind in order to instruct others than ten thousand words in an angelic tongue.

[20]Brothers, you should be naïve only as regards malice, not in your judgment. In that, you should be mature! [21]In the Torah it is written, "'In alien speech and by alien lips I will speak to this people, and thus they will not hear me,' says Adonai." [22]Just so, the effect of tongues is not to provoke belief, but to provoke unbelief. Prophecy, on the other hand, provokes not unbelief but belief. [23]Accordingly, if the whole congregation assembles and all speak in tongues, and some uninitiated or unbelievers enter, will they not at once conclude that you are raving mad? [24]But if all prophesy and some unbeliever or uninitiated person enters, he is convicted by all, condemned by all, [25]the secrets of his heart become manifest, and thus, falling prostrate, he will worship God, declaring that without doubt God is present among you.

[26]So brothers, how should it be from now on? Whenever you gather together, follow this pattern: each one has a psalm, a teaching, a revelation, an angelic tongue, an interpretation. Let everything be done constructively. [27]If anyone perhaps speaks in an angelic tongue, let there be two or at most three, and each in turn, [28]and have someone interpret. But if there is no interpreter present, let him keep silent in the meeting and let him speak only to himself and to God. [29]And have two or three prophets speak, [30]and have the rest pass

judgment. But if a revelation strikes someone else as he sits there, let the first speaker defer to him and fall silent. [31]For you can all prophesy one by one, in order that all may learn and all may be encouraged. [32]And surely the spirits of prophets are obedient to prophets! [33]For God is never the God of confusion, but always of peace.

As in all the congregations of the saints, [34]*let the women be silent while in the congregations, for they are forbidden to speak, but let them submit, as the law also says.* [35]*But if they want to learn anything, let them question their own husbands at home, for it is disgraceful for a woman to speak in public.* [36]Do you think divinely inspired speech begins and ends with you? [37]If anyone deems himself a prophet or a pneumatic, then let him prove it and admit that what I write to you is a commandment of the Lord. [38]But if anyone claims he does not know that for a fact, dismiss him as an ignoramus, and no gnostic.

[39]In sum, then, my brothers, be zealous to prophesy, and do not forbid speaking in tongues. [40]Let everything be done becomingly and with decorum.

In chapters 12 through 14, we have, in effect, a self-contained essay that might be called Concerning Pneumatics. As is well known, the word *pneumatikon* could denote "spiritual gifts or manifestations" or "spiritual persons" such as the pneumatics envisioned already in 1 Corinthians 3:1. Good arguments attend either choice, and ultimately it matters little. However, I opt tentatively for the latter, since the discussion seems to deal with spiritual elitists more than with their gifts.

Jean Hering argues[37] that chapters 12-14 democratically address all Corinthians, seeing all Christians, not just a Gnostic elite, as spiritually endowed. In one sense he is correct, but it seems to me the goal is to level the field, to extinguish the privileges of the Gnostic pneumatics in the congregation and to exalt the ungifted by redefining mundane duties as equally spiritual. Thus, all become "pneumatics." The point is not really to lift up more people, but rather to bring down the high flyers. There can be no "stronger brethren" once weakness has been exalted as strength, where strength is redefined as weakness according to the manipulative euphemisms of Orwellian piety.

The author of Concerning Pneumatics takes a dim view, which he can scarcely disguise, of phenomena like glossolalia. I would hazard that 1 Corinthians 12:2, the invocation of the readers' pagan past, registers this disdain rather than recalling the biographies of real or imagined Corinthian readers. The point is much the same as Didymus of Alexandria's characterization of Montanus as having begun as a castrated devotee of Attis and Cybele, so as to dismiss his prophetic ecstasies as a hangover from the days of genital-chopping fanaticism. Again, one thinks of Protestant charges that Romanist Mariolatry is but a thinly-veiled retention of pagan Isis-worship.

Schmithals[38] is certainly correct in understanding the shocking 1 Corinthians 12:3 as a disapproving reference to the practice of Gnostics who underscored their preference for the Christ-Spirit over the human Jesus (merely the channeler of the former) by ritually cursing the fleshly Jesus. Origen already understood that such a practice, still familiar in his own day from the blasphemous rites of the Ophite Gnostics, underlies the passage: "They do not admit anyone into their meeting unless he has first pronounced curses against Jesus" (*Contra Celsum* VI:28). "There is a certain sect which does not admit a convert unless he pronounces anathemas on Jesus; and that sect is worthy of the name which it has chosen; for it is the sect of the so-called Ophites, who utter blasphemous words in praise of the serpent" (Catena fragm. 47 in I Corinthians xii.3). *Ophos* is Greek for "serpent."

Hans Conzelmann[39] thinks Schmithals is wrong and that no one was actually saying "Jesus be damned!" Origen merely means, according to Conzelmann, that to interpret Jesus as the embodiment of the wisdom-imparting serpent is *tantamount* to cursing him. But in my view, Schmithals has the better of the argument, and the Ophites no doubt deemed Christ, not Jesus, the avatar of the Promethean serpent. Yea, hath Origen said what Conzelmann ascribes to him? I think not. Conzelmann misreads both Origen and 1 Corinthians, all in the interest of his inexplicable tendency to adhere as closely as possible to conventional Pauline exegesis. But no matter what Origen said or thought, Schmithals is still correct. Conzelmann's own suggestion is a desperate one: Paul merely wanted to formulate a poetic parallelism, so he created the "anathema Jesus" blasphemy as an antithetically parallel member matching "Jesus is Lord." Who can countenance such a view, which requires Paul to fabricate an offensive, even an unthinkable, sacrilege merely as a stylistic flourish?

Adolf Schlatter[40] thought that the "anathema Jesus" envisioned here was the ritual denunciation of Jesus as a deceiver, which echoed in Jewish synagogues. Never mind that this theory requires an anachronistic anticipation of the malediction on heretics, dualists, and Nasoreans that Jews added to the Eighteen Benedictions ca. 80-90 CE. It is hardly likely that Paul should invoke it here: in what sense could it be considered a parallel, even an antithetical one, to the salvific confession of the Lord Jesus? The synagogue ritual cursed Christians, not Jesus.

Others have imagined that the afflatus of the Spirit in effect ignited Turret's Syndrome among some unfortunate Corinthians who found themselves barking out curses on Jesus. Such is the exegesis of desperation. Schmithals's view, by contrast, only seems "fantastic" (Conzelmann)[41] if one confusedly ascribes the outrageousness of the practice described by this interpretation to the interpretation itself. And that is what Conzelmann is doing.

Here, as elsewhere, Schmithals's reconstruction of the Corinthian Gnostic subtext, while quite persuasive, seems to undermine his belief in the Pauline authorship of the Corinthian letter, or rather, letter-fragments. Some critics dismiss Schmithals's interpretations because the Gnostic parallels he adduces are attested only in the second century, too late for Paul. His reply, not unreasonably, is that if the cases are convincingly parallel (and protesting about the date does not make them less so), we ought to admit that the Corinthian references now *become* the earliest attestations. If that were the only alternative, Schmithals would have to take the prize. But there is a third alternative: the parallels are genuine, but the historical connection cannot be ignored. Thus, *the text is not Pauline.* It is closer in time to the period of second-century Gnosticism than to Paul. The occurrence in 1 Corinthians 12:3 of a Gnostic repudiation of Jesus *as a creedal shibboleth* (and, a la Conzelmann, the juxtaposition to "Jesus is Lord" at least indicates that much) is a prime example.

At the risk of complicating a complex matter further, let me note that the identification of the historical Paul with Simon Magus would in some measure obviate these difficulties, since it would mean a first-century Paul-Simon would already have been a Gnostic, making Gnosticism as early as Schmithals places it. But we still cannot be sure all the features of Gnosticism on display in 1 Corinthians would have blossomed quite that early. Baptism for the dead (see below), for instance, is attested not for Simonians but for Marcionites and others. The real problem with Schmithals's view, in my opinion, is that he makes Paul an opponent of Gnosticism, since he attributes to him what I regard as later Marcionite and Catholic verses.

We may place "Concerning Pneumatics" in the late first or early second century. It is during this period, as all agree, that the consolidating power of emerging Catholicism was encroaching on and extinguishing the blaze of loose-cannon prophets and itinerate apostles of whom we read in the *Didache*, where they are already held in some suspicion. And we will shortly see how the present text, Concerning Pneumatics, fits precisely into the same historical trajectory.

We find an important clue to the intention of the rest of the chapter when we consider the way exegetes from the staid Protestant denominations, made uneasy by Pentecostals and Charismatics, have read the passage. The thrust of the argument is to co-opt pneumatics and to accuse them of elitism. Thus it proceeds from the side of the so-called natural men (1 Cor. 2:14), not from the pneumatics, who are perceived from outside as troublemakers and boat-rockers.

The group dynamics of the situation are drawn acutely beginning in 12:15-16. The dejected *psuchikoi*, keenly aware of their lack of rare spiritual powers, wallow in self-reproach: "Because I am not a hand, I am not of the body ... Because I am not an eye, I am not of the body." By contrast, we hear the imagined self-satisfaction of the pneumatic elite in verse 21, "I have no need of you." While this attitude mirrors that of later Christians who fancied themselves members of a true, invisible church of the regenerate, it may be doubted whether the Gnostic spiritual ones thus disdained their ungifted brethren.

For one thing, everything we know about Gnostics from their own writings (the Nag Hammadi texts) suggests they viewed themselves in a way that is analogous with the Buddhist bodhisattvas, obliged by their degree of illumination to seek to raise the *psuchikoi* up to their own level. Remember, Valentinus did not curse Jesus. Instead, he taught that the crucifixion of Jesus provided a Plan B salvation for the *psuchikoi*. Those who cursed the fleshly Jesus could not have held Valentinus's particular tourist-class soteriology, but they may have held out their own brand of hope toward their unenlightened brethren.

Also, why would these pneumatics linger among the ranks of the *psuchikoi* in the same congregation (as Gnostics still did in Irenaeus' time, to his consternation), unless it was to win others to their cause? One observes the same dynamic among charismatics and fundamentalists who remain members of staid churches today, where by their own account they cannot possibly derive spiritual nourishment. They remain behind only to treat the congregation as a mission field. Thus, the pneumatics cannot have regarded their unenlightened co-religionists as having been beyond redemption.

Similarly, if we look at the motive of modern glossolalists who linger in boring mainstream congregations, it is to shepherd their ungifted brethren into the experience they themselves so cherish. There is no obvious reason to suppose ancient glossolalists would have had a different attitude.

We also possess a modern analogy to the elitism slander, which was aimed at those who thought themselves charismatically endowed. Today, it is the representatives of staid denominations like the Baptists, Presbyterians, and Lutherans who seek to vilify charismatic revivalists in their own ranks as conceited elitists. It is a case of drawing the worst possible inferences from the other fellow's doctrine. Protestants assume Catholics must abuse the sacrament of penance by sinning heedlessly on Saturday night, all the while planning on cynically confessing it all the next morning. Believers in the doctrine of hell professed not to be able to fathom how Universalists, discounting hell, would not yield to every temptation. In the same way, the ancient Gnostics were derided as sexual libertines, though the Nag Hammadi texts provide absolutely no evidence of such practices. If anything, Gnostics drew from their flesh negation the opposite inference of asceticism.

Note the structure of the argument in chapter 12. We have an initial list of charismatic gifts: the utterance of wisdom (*sophia*), the utterance of knowledge (*gnosis*), faith (if that is how *pistis*, a key term in Gnostic epistemology, ought to be translated here), gifts of healing, workings of miracles, prophecy, distinguishing spirits, varieties of tongues, interpretation of tongues (12:8-10). This list represents the Gnostic repertoire. Then follows the simile of the body and how feet are as important as hands, ears as eyes, naturals as much as spirituals. Then comes a second list which includes the endowments of both categories of church members: *apostles*, prophets, *teachers*, miracles, gifts of healing, *helps*, *administrations*, varieties of tongues (12:28). The four italicized terms are distinctly non-charismatic. *Apostles* are accredited leaders (though the term could be used otherwise, as in the *Didache*), as witness the battle over credentials already in Acts 1:21-22 and 1 Corinthians 9:1. *Teachers* have command of the faith that prophecy threatens to undermine. *Helps* and *administrations*—the church treasurer and the organizer of pot luck suppers are every bit as important as the bearer of living revelation. It seems so only from the standpoint of the one who really esteems the pot luck supper above prophecy, the one who does not want to see the boat rocked. It is the voice of the herd condemned by Nietzsche, not that of the prophetic superman. The same thinking leads today's educators to tell children that all participants in the game are winners, oblivious that no one can excel when the playing field is leveled.

I beg leave for the moment to pass over chapter 13, which I regard as an interpolation into Concerning Pneumatics. It represents a later stage of opinion on the same topic than what is apparent in chapter 14.

The clearest mark of the late, anti-charismatic origin of Concerning Pneumatics is its utter failure to grasp the nature and intent of charismatic worship. Just as Luke betrays his late, nascent Catholic coloring by his misunderstanding or reinterpretation of glossolalia (ecstatic gibberish) in Acts 2, as if it were a missionary miracle of xenoglossia (the supernatural ability to speak foreign languages), the writer of Concerning Pneumatics has misunderstood the function of glossolalia and reinterpreted prophecy in a tendentious Protestantizing way.

For our author, as for institutional churchmen from the second century onward, inspired speech is that which "is profitable for teaching, for reproof, for correction, for instruction in righteousness" (2 Tim. 3:16). It must therefore, he thinks, be intelligible, propositional revelation. Prophecy, he imagines, is rational discourse, while tongues is worthless pyrotechnics unless it is rendered into intelligible speech. Protestant exegetes who interpret Corinthian prophecy as an exposition of salvation history, preaching of the gospel, and so on, are viewing the passage in accord with the intent of the author, but both alike are mistaking the nature of prophecy as the original prophets and ecstatics experienced it. I believe that, in the eyes of those whom the writer of Concerning Pneumatics sought to regulate, prophecy was, along with glossolalia, a subset of ecstatic speech, as in 1 Samuel 10:9-12, not the other way around ("tongues plus interpretation equals prophecy"). It was not some imagined content, but the mode of oracular delivery that marked it as the word of God. The reason an interloper in the house of the prophets might fall to his knees, feeling cut to his heart with the penetrating presence of God (1 Cor. 14:24-25), was the same as caused Saul to succumb to the prophetic afflatus. And what is that?

In Peter L. Berger and Thomas V. Luckmann's[42] terms, the ecstatics will have created a "finite province of meaning," a small bubble reality of the Kingdom of God on earth. This they will have achieved by means of glossolalia, prophecy, and accusations of demonic possession, implied in the distinguishing of spirits and explicit in Pentecostal churches the world over. The gifted will have entered upon a trance state, collectively shared, which creates the effect for them, as for the bystanders, of an alternate world, a zone of sacred space come to earth. The outsider stumbling onto the spectacle might indeed imagine himself to have wandered into the local insane asylum (1 Cor. 14:23). But he might just as well find he has staggered into the presence of God (1 Cor. 14:25-26). It wouldn't matter whether all within are speaking in tongues or prophesying, and it is very doubtful one could tell the difference. It was the spiritual predisposition of the observer that made him think he heard either prophecy or madness (Acts 2:11-13; 2 Cor. 2:15-16).

When the writer of Concerning Pneumatics imagines that glossolalic utterances are merely half-prophecies, when he thinks glossolalia cannot edify until it is made intelligible, when he thinks one can and should stifle the impulse to speak in tongues or to prophesy (three at most, one by one, etc.), he shows he has not the faintest acquaintance with the genuine life of a charismatic community. The actual *Sitz-im-Leben* of charismatic utterance has been mapped by Felicitas D. Goodman.[43] Her participant-observer research lays bare the logic of charismatic worship: all or most must speak in tongues in order to conjure the alternate reality in which, as the men of Qumran knew (*Community Rule* 1QSa 2:3-11), the angels attend one's worship and one may sing in their heavenly dialects (1 Cor. 13:1; *Testament of Job* 48:3; 49:2; 50:1). In such a hothouse atmosphere, the content of the prophecy matters as little as the gist of the Latin Mass did in the numinous pre-Vatican II Catholic liturgy.

Thus, it mattered not if a number of prophets spoke forth their revelations all at once. It was better if they did! To imagine that they should stand in line so that everyone could consider each one's sermonette in turn is preposterous, as is the notion that one must await the interpretation of glossolalia before it can be considered edifying. By contrast, whoever wrote 1 Corinthians 2:12-14 understood glossolalic prophecy: "And we did not receive the spirit of the cosmos, but the Spirit that comes from God so we may grasp the secrets freely given us by God, the very secrets we relate not in terms of learned rhetoric but of that taught by the Spirit, conveying spiritual matters to those who have the spirit. But the natural man can make nothing of the truths of the Spirit of God since to him they appear nonsense. Indeed, he is simply incapable of grasping them, for they can be understood only by means of the Spirit." This writer would not have troubled himself or his readers to await some interpreter to perform the impossible task of making the secrets of God available to the *psuchikoi*. This writer understood that the deep things of God were made known precisely in words suited to angels, not in human speech. These things will be foolishness to the natural man. Were he to stumble into the midst of glossolalic oracles, he might indeed think them mad because only fellow pneumatics could appraise their revelations correctly.

Pentecostal exegesis has labored mightily to make sense of the oddity that *all* in a congregation may be able to speak in tongues (1 Cor. 14:5,18, 23), though not that all necessarily should, and the assumption implicit in the rhetorical questions of 1 Corinthians 12:29-30 that only *some* have the ability. The solution, on my reading, is simple. The rhetorical questions of chapter 12 are an ostensible *description* with the force of a *prescription*. When the writer of 1 Timothy 2:12 says that Paul permits no woman to teach, do we have a description of Paul's apostolic practice? No, rather it is an attempt to change the reader's previous practice that *did* allow women to teach. The pseudepigraphical use of Paul's name and authority is the instrument to effect this change. The reader is to have the same reaction King Josiah did when he heard the provisions of the newly minted Deuteronomy: You mean *this* is the way Moses wanted it? We'd better change things fast! In the same way, another pseudo-Paul here argues in one place that all must not exercise the ability (which he grants they have) to speak in tongues and in another place discourages the practice by implying that many of the glossolalists must be fakes, since God has appointed only a few genuine ones. The consistency of the two otherwise mismatched arguments is that they both strive for the same conclusion, just by different routes. The contradiction would make no sense in a description of the historical situation in Corinth, but as a rhetorical strategy it is perfectly understandable.

But there are more indicators of a post-apostolic origin of Concerning Pneumatics. The writer envisions people walking into a church building:[44] "*in the church* I desire to speak five words with my mind that I may instruct others" (14:19). Are we in the midst of frontier, apostolic Christianity here? Not likely.

In 14:11 glossolalia is compared with the crude and unintelligible grunting of the barbarians, the bearded savages beyond the pale of civilization. We find the same comparison in another late church manual, the Gospel of Matthew. Matthew 6:7 interrupts its own context to warn Jewish Christians and gentile proselytes to Jewish Christianity not to "say *batta*" (usually paraphrased as "vain repetition") when they pray, as the superstitious pagans do. Again, we think most naturally of the orthodox critics of the Montanists, so utterly without sympathy for ecstatic spirituality that they equated prophecy with demonic possession. It was probably the foreign speech of Phrygia, where the movement originated, that led to its being dubbed "the Phrygian heresy." Sounds strange? Must be heresy!

Verse 14:37 sets forth the claim of the written word, ostensibly of the apostles, to take precedence over the unstable voice of living prophecy. One may think himself a prophet or pneumatic, but this must be judged as sheer self-delusion if he does not recognize the supervening authority of "the things which I write." Such a one is not "recognized" (verse 38), implying a credentialed authority alien to an ostensible 50 CE Corinthian setting.

We can tell chapter 13 is an insertion, not only from the manifest interruption of the adjacent discussion, but also from the occurrence of redactional seams. The interpolator broke off the original text after 12:31, "but earnestly desire the greater gifts." Having inserted chapter 13, he has paraphrased 12:31 in the form we find in 14:1, "yet earnestly desire spiritual gifts, but especially that you may prophesy," prophecy being, of course, the greatest available gift. The paraphrased version restores the hook from which chapter 14 originally depended. And the content of chapter 13 clashes with that of the adjacent chapters as well. Whereas chapters 12 and 14 seek merely to domesticate glossolalia and prophecy, the author of chapter 13 has had a belly-full. For him the time of prophecy and tongues is over and done with.

It is important to remind ourselves of the present-day reference of apocalyptic predictions despite the future tense in which they are cast. This is why the pseudonymity of apocalypses is integral to the genre. The ostensible author is a prophet from the past who foresaw the intended readers' day. This is true of whole books such as Daniel and of smaller apocalypses such as Mark 13; 1 Timothy 4:1-5; 2 Peter 3. The point is always a warning of the crucial hour at which the reader *now* stands. In the same way, when the author of 1 Corinthians 13 predicts that tongues and prophecy will pass away, he means the reader to understand that Paul's prediction has now come true. As he once allegedly warned the Corinthians, the Gnostic gifts of prophecy, gnosis, and glossolalia have now yielded to something far more excellent: love.

Reformed and Dispensationalist exegetes have always understood this, but their position was difficult since they took the letter to be genuinely Pauline with a future reference. Merrill F. Unger,[45] for instance, argued that what was "perfect" in 13:10 was the the completed canon of New Testament scripture, as if Paul could have had such a thing in mind. A specific reference to the canon would place the chapter, the interpolation, even later than I am willing to place it. But it seems to me that he is basically correct: a stable scripture or rule of faith, under the hermeneutical control of church and seminary authorities, is better, for the interests of those authorities, than the unpredictable voice of prophecy. The writer warns that only the immature will dally with the nursery baubles of glossolalia and prophecy. With this addition, Concerning Pneumatics has arrived at the door-slamming position the Paulinist author of 1 Thessalonians 5:19-21 warned against, "Do not snuff out the fire of the spirit. I mean, do not dismiss prophecies out of hand, but weigh them all, heeding the genuine ones, but repudiating every one that smacks of evil."

Again, it is not just the logic of the chapter that marks it as late. Note the reference to self-immolation performed as a grandstanding stunt (13:3), recalling the death of Peregrinus as recounted by Lucian (*The Passing of Peregrinus*) in the second century.

Verse 2 seems to be a gloss on 12:9's inclusion of faith as a gift of the spirit. If faith is the common possession of all believers, as well as the sole requirement for salvation in Paulinist Christianity, in what sense can it be a gift for some? Verse 13:2 supposes, by reference to the Synoptic tradition (in itself a mark of late date), that it is a special type of miracle-working faith (Mark 11:23; Matt. 21:21). We can thus trace within the section 1 Corinthians 12-14 an evolution of institutional reactions to charismatic prophecy, beginning with an attempt to domesticate it, ending with an attempt to abolish it.

15

¹Now I inform you, brothers, of the news with which I evangelized you, the same that you welcomed, in which tradition you stand, ²the one by which you are saved, providing you hold firmly to what I said when I evangelized you—unless, perhaps, it was all some mistake? ³*For I handed on to you, first and foremost, what I received the same way: that Christ died on account of our sins, as we know from the scriptures; ⁴and that he was buried; and that he has been raised on the third day, as we know from the scriptures; ⁵and that he was seen by Cephas, then by the Twelve. ⁶After that, he was seen by over five hundred brothers at once, of whom the greatest number linger even now, though some fell asleep; ⁷after that, he was seen by James, then by all the apostles.*

⁸And finally, appearing even as to the Ektroma, he was seen by me, too. ⁹For I am least of the apostles, unworthy even to be considered an apostle because I persecuted the congregation of God. ¹⁰But by the mercy of God, I have such status as I do occupy. Nor was his mercy toward me a futile gesture, for as it turned out, I labored more fruitfully than all the rest put together. Well, of course, not I myself, but the charisma of God with which I was equipped. ¹¹Thus, whether it was I myself or them, this is what we alike proclaim, and this is what you believed.

¹²But if Christ is proclaimed as having been resurrected, how is that some among you say there is no resurrection of dead people? ¹³So if it is true that there is no resurrection of dead people, then Christ has not been raised either. ¹⁴And if Christ has not been raised, then our preaching is a sham, and so is your faith. ¹⁵And we are then exposed as false witnesses about God because we testified about God, that he raised Christ, whom it turns out he did not raise if, after all, no dead will rise. ¹⁶For if dead persons are not raised, Christ has not been raised either. ¹⁷And if Christ has not been raised, then your faith is superfluous: you still languish in your sins. ¹⁸Then, too, those who have fallen asleep in death, holding fast their faith in Christ, have simply perished. ¹⁹If we have placed our hopes on Christ only for the duration of this earthly life, we are the most miserable of fools! ²⁰But as it happens, Christ has been raised from the dead, the first of those fallen asleep to ripen for harvest!

²¹For since it was through a single individual that death arrived, it was fitting that a resurrection of dead people arrived through one single individual, too. ²²For just as in Adam's wake all die, so in Christ's wake shall all be restored to life. ²³But let each rise in his proper order! Christ ripens first, then those who belong to him once he appears, ²⁴then the end, whenever he may hand over royal authority to God, his Father, namely, whenever he may declare an end to all the archons, authorities and powers. ²⁵For he must wield authority while he is occupied in subduing all his enemies. ²⁶The last such enemy to be eliminated is death, which he will vanquish by raising those who are his. For he has subjected, yea, trampled, everything; hence it must be soon. ²⁷But when it says that "all things have been subjected to him," it is obvious that "all" does not include the one who did the subjecting! ²⁸Thus once all things are subject to him,

then the Son himself will likewise subject himself to the One who subjected all else to him in order that God may be all in all.

[29]Otherwise, those who are baptized vicariously for the dead will find they have wasted their time. If the dead are not to be raised, what is the point of being baptized on their behalf? [30]And why would we risk danger every hour of the day? [31]I die each day, as you boast about me, brothers, a boast which I have earned by my years in Christ's service. [32]If, as they say, I contested with wild beasts in Ephesus, what have I gained by it? If the dead are never to be raised—well, then, let us eat, drink, and be merry! Life is short!

[33]Don't let yourselves be led off the path! Corrupt associations ruin good habits. [34]Sober up! Return to righteousness and stop sinning! For some among you are oblivious of God, which I point out to shame you.

[35]"But," someone is sure to object, "how are the dead raised? And what sort of body do they return with?" [36]You fool! The common seed you sow does not come to life unless it dies first! And the seed you sow, [37]it does not already have its eventual form as you sow it but is only a bare grain, perhaps of wheat or of some other variety. [38]But God then supplies a body for it, as he determined long ago, and he assigned each seed its own mature form. [39]All flesh need not be the same to count as flesh; rather, there is one kind for human beings, another sort of animal flesh, another sort of flesh for birds, another for fish. [40]Similarly, there are heavenly "bodies" and earthly "bodies," but the splendor of the heavenly bodies is quite different from that of their earthly counterparts. [41]The sun shines in its own fashion, as does the moon, and so the stars. Star differs even from star in magnitude. [42]And it is the same with the resurrection of the dead. One is sown in decay, raised up undecaying. [43]One is planted in shameful condition, raised up glorious! It is buried inert but raised powerful! [44]One is sowed a natural body; it is raised a pneumatic body. It stands to reason: if there is a natural body, there must also be a pneumatic one. [45]It says just this in scripture: "the primordial human being, Adam, became a living nature; the Adam at the end of time became a vivifying spirit." [46]But the pneumatic body does not come first, rather the natural, and the pneumatic after that. [47]The first human being was formed out of the earth, earthy in character; the second human

being comes out of heaven. [48]As with the clay homunculus, so will it be with the creatures of clay, and as it is with the ethereal one, so will it be with the ethereal ones [49]And as we displayed the image of the clay homunculus, so we shall display the image of the ethereal one. [50]Mark my words, brothers: flesh and blood are incapable of attaining the divine realm after death, no more than the decaying can, upon death, be made undecayed. [51]Behold, I reveal to you a mystery hitherto unguessed! Not all of us shall fall asleep in death, but all of us shall nonetheless be transformed—[52]in a moment, in the blink of an eye, at the last note of the trumpet. For a trumpet will blow, and the dead will be raised up undecayed. And we, too, shall be transformed. [53]For this body of decay must needs assume immunity from decay and this mortal body must assume immortality. [54]And when this decaying body shall clothe itself in freedom from decay, when this mortal body shall don immortality, then that saying from scripture will come true, namely, "Death was consumed by victory. [55]O Death, where is your much-vaunted victory? Where, O death, your barb?" [56]Well, of course, the barb in Death's scorpion-tale is sin, and what makes it fatal is the Torah. [57]But thank God, he has granted us, rather than our opponent, Death, the victory through our Lord Jesus-Christ. [58]In view of this, my beloved brothers, stand firm, immovable, becoming ever more productive in the Lord's service, mindful that your labor for the Lord is not futile, as it would be if there were no resurrection.

As in 11:23, we have to suspect that what follows in chapter 15 is not really a piece of previous instruction of which Paul is reminding his readers. Rather, it is a technique for lending a false historical patina to a new piece of information. Isn't he *now* informing them, rather than *reminding* them of something which he had told them long ago? The strange wording bespeaks a fictive recollection, the first-time announcement of something for which a venerable Pauline pedigree is sought long after the fact. Similarly, the list of resurrection appearances (3-11) has been interpolated into its present context. One can unpack its tradition-history fairly easily; the tree rings are still visible. As Arthur Drews,[46] G. A. Wells,[47] Winsome Munro,[48] J. C. O'Neill,[49] and others have suggested, verses 3-11 constitute an interpolated piece of apologetics for the resurrection, using several earlier bits and pieces. R. Joseph Hoffmann[50] rejects only verses 5-8 as an interpolation. J. M. Robertson, followed by L. Gordon Rylands,[51] saw that 1 Corinthians 15:3-11 was an interpolation. Thomas Whittaker avers thus: "J. W. Straatman ... in his *Critical Studies on the First Epistle* (1863-65) treated xi. 23-28 and xv.3-11 as interpolations of the second century."[52] "In so far as xi.23-25 and xv.3-7 indicate a formula of communion and a closed list of appearances of the risen Lord, we are brought in contact with pieces which we cannot suppose to have existed in 57-58, not to think of 52-53, the assumed date of Paul's teaching at Corinth."[53]

As Adolf Harnack[54] saw long ago, the parallel references to "Cephas and the Twelve" and "James and all the apostles" must originally have been rival credential claims, one making Peter the prince of apostles, the other nominating James. The redundancy of "the Twelve" and "the apostles" is the result of combining the two slogans in a subsequent ecumenical truce. They are not supposed to be two different groups.

The business about the half-thousand witnesses to the resurrection must post-date the Gospels, since it is impossible for such a memory or tradition (if such it were) to have gone unmentioned for so long and so widely. It must be even later than the rest of the list of appearances. It refers in an abbreviated manner to an episode told at greater length in the Latin *Gospel of Nicodemus* and Greek *Acts of Pilate*, where we learn that the 500 were Roman troops guarding the tomb of Jesus. In the second Greek form, chapter 12, we read, "'Lest, therefore, his disciples should steal him by night, and lead the people astray by such deceit, order his tomb to be guarded.' Pilate therefore, upon this, gave them five hundred soldiers, who also sat round the sepulchre so as to guard it, after having put seals upon the stone of the tomb" (Roberts-Donaldson trans.). Shortly, of course, they have a front row seat at the resurrection. Two chapters later, they witness the ascension, too.

The notion of James as a believer in Jesus already at the time of Easter is a second-century product, occurring also in the Gospel of Luke and implied in the Lukan redaction of Mark 3:31-35 in Luke 8:19-21, as well as in the *Gospel according to the Hebrews*. Other sources (Mark 3:21, 31-35; John 7:5) had James indifferent or hostile to Jesus.

No New Testament source has him first hostile, then converted by a resurrection appearance; that is a post-biblical harmonization.

The afterthought addition of Paul to the list of resurrection witnesses seeks to define his not-quite apostolic status in the same terms used by Acts. He is associated with the Twelve yet subordinate to them. Where resurrection appearances are concerned, he barely makes it under the wire.

It has become virtually a dogma among conservative apologists that the historical Paul received this canonical list of appearances at the earliest possible date, his first post-conversion visit to Jerusalem, and that the list must have been compiled by the eyewitnesses named in it. The utter arbitrariness of this speculation never seems to occur to the apologists. They have assimilated the 1 Corinthians 15:3-11 list to the legend of the Apostles' Creed, implicitly borrowing the myth that each apostle contributed one article to the list.

As to the various intriguing tidbits in the text, if we do not try to "naturalize them" (Jonathan Culler),[55] to whittle them down to some tamer notion already familiar to us, we get some interesting results. Verse 8 sums up the Gnostic myth of the Primordial Light Man, of whom Jesus Christ was believed to be a kind of reincarnation, showing himself to the wondering eyes of the demiurge, the Gnostic Creator, who coveted his spiritual substance and contrived to steal it to give life and order to his inert creation. This demiurge was a defective and malicious bastard offspring of the fallen Sophia (wisdom). Against the will of the Godhead, she brought him forth, and he was called the Ektroma, the Abortus. Here the risen Christ is said to have appeared to him again in triumph.[56] I suspect, however, that the interpolator no longer understood the original reference any more than modern readers do.

Verse 10 offers a portrayal of Paul squarely in accord with that of Acts. There Paul is not an apostle even though his gospel harvest appears far greater than the number of converts the Twelve have amassed. Not an independent conduit of Christ's revelation, according to Acts, Paul had to be catechized by predecessors like Ananias and Barnabas; likewise, here in verse 3, unnamed predecessors are said to have passed on the resurrection gospel to him. What a different tale is told in Galatians 1:11-12!

Here we reach the end of the first of three unrelated sections of the chapter. This one has presented evidence for the resurrection of Jesus. We arrive at a second topic, and a different source, with verses 12-20. When the author demands to know, "Then how can some of you [the latter-day factions] say there is no resurrection?" we have an interpolated section originally aimed at Epicureans and based on Acts 17 where Paul confronts Epicureans who, we know, laughed at the resurrection. That is the belief 1 Corinthians attacks here: not a Gnostic reinterpretation of resurrection, but plain mortalism. The key is the reference to "battling wild beasts in Ephesus," which, as Abraham J. Malherbe[57] says, is a well-attested figure of speech for "debating with Epicureans," which Paul is shown doing in Acts 17:18. Likewise, in Titus 1:12 "beasts" denotes hedonists. However, the writer here no longer understands the idiom and imagines Paul to have been tossed into an arena with literal leopards, lions, and bears as in the *Acts of Paul*.

Verses 21-58 embark on a third subject: Marcionite engagement with Gnostics who rejected an eschatological resurrection as superfluous, given the purely spiritual resurrection occurring in water baptism. By contrast, our Marcionite author argues for the future replacement of the fleshly corpse with a heavenly body like Jesus had throughout his earthly sojourn. It will be a celestial one, not a body of flesh. Notice the negative role of the Law as the catalyst for death.

But why does 1 Corinthians 15 propound a clearly Gnostic idea of the resurrection body, yet argue against Gnostic belief that there would be no future resurrection? By now we can make a pretty good guess. It sounds like latter-day disappointment with the promised spiritual transformation in which the baptismal resurrection should have been issued. The results were mediocre, and so the transformation was deferred once again to the future, although it will be a pneumatic resurrection when it finally happens. In fact, according to verse 28, it will result in mystic nondualism. Precisely insofar as all beings are distinct from God, or seem so to themselves, they are "at enmity" with God and must be reconciled or subjugated. The result will be absolute unity and bliss. First Corinthians 13 predicted a final vision of truth comparable to seeing face-to-face what one had hitherto only glimpsed in a cloudy mirror. Well, whose image does one usually see in a mirror? One's own. And this is the way it will look at the eschaton: "God will be All-in-All" (verse 28).

Commentators fall all over one another in their eager efforts to explain that Paul did not mean to legitimize proxy baptism for the unsaved dead in verse 29. John Chrysostom describes the Marcionite ritual of baptism for the dead: "For if one of their catechumens dies, they conceal a living person beneath the bier of the departed, approach the corpse, talk with the dead person, and ask him whether he intended to receive baptism. Thereupon the person who is concealed, speaking from beneath for the other who does not answer, avers that he did indeed plan to be baptized, and then they baptize him for the departed one." Epiphanius of Salamis tells of the rite as practiced among the Cerinthians: "When some of them die before being baptized, others are baptized in place of them, in their name, so that when they rise in the resurrection they may not have to pay the penalty of not having received baptism and become subject to the authority of the one who made the world." As Schmithals[58] notes, such practices surely form the context for the statement in 1 Corinthians 15:29.

Verses 33-34 are an inept gloss added by someone who misunderstood the point of verse 32, a *reductio ad absurdum*. No one was actually getting drunk or proposing it.

Verse 45 presents a minor puzzle. The second part of the verse, "the last Adam became a life-giving spirit," is not to be found in the ostensible source, Genesis 2:7. It may come from some lost Gnostic rewrite of Genesis, the like of which we have several in Nag Hammadi. Or more likely, the writer is quoting from memory and assuming that an inference he has long ago drawn from the text was explicit there. The basic idea sounds Zoroastrian, reminiscent of the Saoshyant, or "Benefactor," an eschatological descendant of Zoroaster whom some say is a reincarnation of the Primal Man Gayomard, who will finally come to earth to enliven the dead for judgment and salvation. In any case, we should recognize here the same move we see in *Third Corinthians*: the retrojection into Paul's ministry of a later dogma. As *Third Corinthians* has him defend the virgin birth, 1 Corinthians 15 has him defend an end-time resurrection.

Many see in verse 47 a dissent from the Philonic and Valentinian notion that our earthly bodies are poor copies of a heavenly image or prototype of perfect humanity. Commentators assure us that, while Philo believed a celestial Adam prototype came first, and that God used him as the blueprint to create the earthly Adam and his progeny, Paul believed that the celestial Adam came into being only as of the resurrection (Christ's and ours). That seems not to be the point; rather, he means that we bear first the one image, then the other. We start off as earthly copies of the first physical Adam and wind up copying a superior model. Undoubtedly the author believed in a Primordial Light Man, but his point is that it was not *manifest on earth* until the resurrection, and so it will be with the redeemed. How much more sense does this understanding of a *doxa* (glory) body of Christ make, once we realize we are reading a Marcionite text: Marcion, remember, believed that Jesus had worn a body of celestial substance all along, though some became aware of it only as of Easter? Thus, to bear the image of the first Adam, the one clothed in carnal flesh, is death, while to bear the image of the eschatological Adam, the Marcionite Jesus Chrestus, is life.

In verse 48 we pick back up the distinction between "heavenly bodies" and "earthly bodies" from verse 40. Also, the soteriology in this verse sounds Gnostic: only the pneumatics will be saved. As in the Mystery Religions, salvation is nothing but the mystical transformation of the individual through sacramental initiation which quickens an inner spark of divine nature and fans it gradually into flame 'til, at death, the inner glory-nature subsumes the outward husk, and one ascends to heaven.[59] It is still orthodox in Eastern Christianity, where the doctrine is called *theosis*, "deification." Verse 48 seems to imply that the pneumatics will thus be saved, an impossibility for mere *psuchikoi*, "natural men." The key difference between the soteriology described here and that of the Mystery Cults, which it so closely resembles, is that, ideally, mere *gnosis*, without ritual means of grace, is expected to be sufficient. The more this purity is compromised by the resort to rituals and magic formulae, the more Gnosticism becomes another Mystery religion.

Verse 52 is a rare piece of self-conscious doctrinal innovation, an admission that the eschaton will not arrive quickly enough that all alive in Paul's generation should live to see it. What we have here is precisely equivalent to the spurious Gospel predictions (Matt. 24:48; 25:5), ascribed to Jesus, of a *delay* in his own announced timetable! I tell you, he says, it will happen before this generation passes. *And* I tell you it *won't*: it will be delayed. Well, which is it? Of course a subsequent corrector is posing as Jesus before the fact. And here another is posing as Paul. The actual intended audience, as opposed to the fictive "Corinthian" narratees, can be imagined heaving a sigh of relief that those who died before the Parousia were not necessarily lost after all. If only they had read this letter from Paul as soon as it was received! What a tragedy that it had been lost in the interval!

First Corinthians 15 has thus been cobbled together as a digest, a topical Bible of clashing materials about resurrection: first, a demonstration that Jesus rose, as if that were the point in contention. Then an attempted rebuttal of an Epicurean-style denial of life after death. Then comes a discourse on the nature of the resurrection body. The discussion goes from the unthinkability of denying resurrection, given the unacceptable implications, to an argument from natural and astronomical analogies to defend the notion of a resurrection of the body that need not entail the revival of mortal flesh. As Rylands[60] points out, in all this, one would never get a hint that a writer who must resort to such discourse had himself settled the issue by directly beholding a man raised from the dead. Clearly, it is all speculation and theory, not the work of a witness to the resurrected Jesus.

16

[1]Now concerning the collection for the saints, you are to do as I urged the congregations in Galatia to do. [2]On the first day of each week, let each of you keep aside some amount, as God has prospered him, so we need not organize the collection once I get there. [3]And when I get there, whomever you approve for the task, I will send them with the appropriate epistles to carry your gift to Jerusalem. [4]And if it looks opportune for me to go, too, they shall accompany me. [5]And I will come to you whenever I pass through Macedonia. For I mean to pass through Macedonia, too, and I may even stay with you, or even spend the winter there so you may send me off rested and fully provisioned when I go. [7]I do not want to see you only in passing, for I am hoping to remain with you some time, if the

Lord permits. [8]But I will remain in Ephesus till Pentecost, [9]because a great opportunity for effective work has opened wide for me there, and typically in such situations, there are many opponents requiring my attention.

[10]Now if Timothy comes, give him no reason to be intimidated among you, for he does the Lord's work the same as I do. [11]So don't anyone there think they can disregard him. But give him a happy send-off on his way to me, for I am awaiting him with the brothers.

[12]Now concerning Apollo the brother, I strongly urged him to come to you with the brothers, but he was not wholly convinced that he should come. Rest assured, he will come when he has the opportunity.

[13]Keep guard! Stand fast in the faith! Be men! Be strong! [14]Let everything you do be done in love.

[15]*So I plead with you, brothers, about the household of Stephanas: you know them as the first converts in Achaia, and how they have devoted themselves to the service of the saints.* [16]*Submit yourselves to the authority of them and to everyone working and laboring with them.* [17]At present, I rejoice at the arrival of Stephanas and of Fortunatus and of Achaicus, *who have made up in some measure for your not being here.* [18]For they have refreshed my spirit as they do yours. Be sure to acknowledge such as these. [19]The congregations of the province of Asia greet you. Aquila and Prisca, along with the assembly meeting in their house, send fondest greetings to you all. [20]Greet all the brothers. Greet one another with a ritual kiss.

[21]I greet you in my own handwriting.

[22]If anyone does not truly love the Lord, excommunicate him! *Maranatha!* [23]May the favor of the Lord Jesus be with you. [24]I send all of you my love in connection with Christ-Jesus!

Verse 1 might naturally be taken as a reference to the collection Paul organized for the needs of the Jerusalem pillars and their community, a tribute imposed on him in Galatians 2:10 in return for apostolic recognition. But that is certainly not a necessary inference, and the text may simply be referring to charitable relief generally.

Verses 17-18 offer us a pedigree, forged after the fact by the leadership of a particular Paulinist faction or school still powerful for many years and claiming descent from Paul. It must be remembered that there were rival claims to be the official first convert in any particular city. In Philippi, was it Lydia (Acts 16), or was it Frontina, as the *Acts of Paul* reports? These were claims to authority in the church of the writers' day, especially as it was the "household," a kind of dynasty, of Stephanas, not merely Stephanas himself, that was recommended. And if Paul's missionary efforts are being officially suppressed in favor of Catholic replacement founders (fictive, of course, as in chapter 6 of the present book), that is all the more reason for the Paulinist succession line ("household") of Stephanas ("I belong to Paul!") to reassert their claim by writing a letter, or part of one, like this.

We encounter old friends in 16:19: Aquila and Prisca or Priscilla. We know them from Acts 18, likewise Apollo. Hermann Detering[61] suggests that Apollo(s) was none other than Marcion's successor Apelles and that he is responsible for later epistles. We have already seen how the Clementine *Recognitions* presents this Aquila as an erstwhile disciple of Simon Magus, who later turned to follow Peter. Well, this opens the interesting possibility that the Acts 18:1-4 scene in which Priscilla and Aquila take Apollo aside and correct his doctrine by a few tweaks might reflect the fact that, from the Marcionite perspective, Apelles, Marcion's disciple, had in later years strayed a bit from Marcionite orthodoxy. It makes it appear that he was finally brought back into the fold by the Simonian Aquila and the prophesying virgin Philumene, whose revelations and instruction Apelles is known to have sought. It is tempting also to identify this Priscilla with the Montanist prophetess Priscilla.

Verse 21 offers us, ostensibly, a real Pauline autograph to conclude the epistle. This should have been self-evident and would not have required description. It is described only because it is fictive. One is supposed to believe the autograph was there in the original, and that, since this is a later copy of it, the distinctive signature would not stand out from the handwriting of the copyist. It had to be described.

Toward the end, what is the implication of liturgical rubrics to conclude an ostensible epistle? That is what we have in verse 22: *anathema* is Greek for "damned," a liturgical fossil borrowed from Judaism, where heretics were ritually cursed in synagogue prayers, a practice instituted some thirty or forty years after Paul's death. Obviously, this fact removes the letter from the ostensible lifetime of Paul. Many think this is a piece of eucharistic liturgy, warning away the lukewarm from partaking unworthily, as in 11:27-29. *Maranatha* is Aramaic for "Our Lord comes!" or "Our Lord, come!" Again, this would make sense as part of the eucharistic liturgy: after warning away the lukewarm and hypocrites, the celebrant invokes the presence of the Lord in the eucharist, anticipating the eschatological Parousia of Christ. The inclusion of apparent liturgical rubrics in the text of the epistle implies that the writer regards Pauline writings as scripture and wants this one included in that canon and thus read liturgically.

NOTES

[1]Thomas Whittaker, *The Origins of Christianity, with an Outline of Van Manen's Analysis of the Pauline Literature* (London: Watts, 1933), 186-187.

[2]Kenneth Cragg, *The House of Islam.* Religious Life of Man Series (Encino and Belmont, CA: Dickenson Publishing, 2nd ed., 1975), 38: "Epistles, on a Quranic view, can never be revelation, since they travel horizontally: they do not 'come down.'"

[3]Marc Edmund Jones, *Occult Philosophy* (Stanwood, WA: Sabian Publishing Society and Shambhala Publications, 1948), 223-230.

[4]Of Jesus, the *Ascension of Isaiah*, trans. Robert H. Charles, rev. J.M.T. Barton, has this to say: "For Beliar was especially furious with Isaiah because of his vision ... and because it was through him that the going forth of the Beloved from the seventh heaven had been made known, and his transformation, and his descent to earth, and the likeness into which he would be transformed (that is the likeness of a man)" (3:13). "He will indeed descend into the world in the last days – the Lord who will be called Christ after he has descended and become like you in form; and they will think he is flesh and a man" (9:13). Hedley F. D. Sparks, *The Apocryphal Old Testament* (Oxford: Clarendon Press, 1984), 789, 803.

Of Simon Magus, Irenaeus relates that "he had descended, transforming himself and being made like to the Powers and Principalities and Angels; so that he appeared to men as a man, although he was not a man; and was thought to have suffered in Judaea, although he did not really suffer" (*Contra Haeresis* I. xxiii.4).

⁵Ernst Käsemann, *Perspectives on Paul*, trans. Margaret Kohl (Philadelphia: Fortress Press, 1971), 2-3; cf. Theodore J. Weeden, *Mark: Traditions in Conflict* (Philadelphia: Fortress Press, 1971). Many of the Corinthian conflicts make sense when we view the Corinthians as pneumatics or enthusiasts occupying the extreme end of the range, walking already by sight (or so they believe), with Paul curbing enthusiasm since we still occupy, at least outwardly, the old age.

⁶Arthur Mandel, *The Militant Messiah or the Flight from the Ghetto: The Story of Jacob Frank and the Frankist Movement* (Atlantic Highlands, NJ: A Peter Bergman Book, Humanities Press, 1979), chapter 9, "Ritual Sex," 39-43. Peter Worsley, *The Trumpet Shall Sound: A Study of "Cargo" Cults in Melanesia* (New York: Schocken Books, 2nd ed., 1968), 109, 150-51, 167, 202, 250-51. See also John L. Brooke, *The Refiner's Fire: The Making of Mormon Cosmology, 1644-1844* (New York: Cambridge University Press, 1994), 56.

⁷Worsley, *Trumpet Shall Sound*, 23, 52-53, 103, 107, 116-17.

⁸Ibid., 141; Stephen Fuchs, *Rebellious Prophets: A Study of Messianic Movements in Indian Religions* (New York: Asia House Publishing, 1965), 29-30, 32, 41, 96, 98, 123, 149, 220.

⁹"Rabbi Chalafta, the son of Dosa, of the village of Chananya, said, "When ten people sit together and occupy themselves with the Torah, the Shechinah abides among them, as it is said, God standeth in the congregation of the godly." Joseph H. Hertz, trans. *Sayings of the Fathers or Pirke Aboth, the Hebrew Text, with a New English Translation and a Commentary* (New York: Behrman House, 1945), 53.

¹⁰Mary Douglas, *Natural Symbols: Explorations in Cosmology* (New York: Pantheon Books, 1982), 58-61.

¹¹J. Duncan M. Derrett, "Law in the New Testament: The Parable of the Unjust Judge," *New Testament Studies* 18 (1971-1972), 178-191.

¹²H. Achelis, "Agapetae," In *Encyclopaedia of Religion and Ethics*, eds. James Hastings, John A. Selbie, and Louis H. Gray (New York: Scribner's, 1980.); Peter Brown, *The Body and Society: Men, Women, and Sexual Renunciation in Early Christianity* (New York: Columbia University Press,1988). Susanna Elm, *"Virgins of God": The Making of Asceticism in Late Antiquity*, Oxford Classical Monographs (NY: Oxford University Press, 1994); Dyan Elliott, *Spiritual Marriage: Sexual Abstinence in Medieval Wedlock* (Princeton: Princeton University Press, 1993).

¹³"But, speaking frankly, to long for the transcendent when you are in your wife's arms is, to put it mildly, a lack of taste" (Dietrich Bonhoeffer, *Letters and Papers from Prison*, ed. Eberhard Bethge, trans. Reginald H. Fuller [New York: Macmillan, 1962], 113).

¹⁴Heinrich August Wilhelm Meyer, *Critical and Exegetical Handbook to the Epistles to the Corinthians*, trans. D. Douglas Bannerman, rev. William P. Dickson (NY: Funk & Wagnalls, 1890), 156; Hans Conzelmann, *First Corinthians: A Commentary on the First Epistle to the Corinthians*, trans. James W. Leitch, Hermeneia Series (Philadelphia: Fortress Press, 1975), 120; Jean Hering, *The First Epistle of Saint Paul to the Corinthians*, trans. A. W. Heathcote and P. J. Allcock (London: Epworth Press, 1962), 52. F. F. Bruce, *The New Testament Documents: Are They Reliable?* 5th ed. (Grand Rapids: Eerdmans, 1960), 78; Günther Bornkamm, *Paul*, trans. D.M.G. Stalker (New York: Harper & Row, 1971), 110, 183.

¹⁵F. C. Baur, cited in Meyer, *Critical Handbook*, Werner Kramer, *Christ, Lord, Son of God*, Studies in Biblical Theology No. 50, trans. Brian Hardy (Naperville: Alec R. Allenson, 1966), 160; G. A. Wells, *The Jesus of the Early Christians: A Study in Christian Origins* (London: Pemberton Books, 1971), 133-34. Of course, one might venture to say that Wells's view is just as apologetically motivated as Bruce's, just apologetics for the opposite view. Bruce wants to secure a historical Jesus known to Paul, while this is exactly what Wells seeks to discredit. But this should not discredit either man's opinion. Each scholar is naturally inquiring after a plausible reading of the same data to see how far he may take his paradigm. The test is whether the exegesis may be "replicated" by other researchers. That is, does either reading strike others as plausible or as strained, special pleading? It is for each reader to decide.

¹⁶Plutarch, "Marriage Counsel," Precept 19. In *On Love, the Family, and the Good Life: Selected Essays of Plutarch*, trans. Moses Hadas (New York: New American Library/Mentor Books, 1957), 85.

¹⁷Ernst Käsemann, "Ministry and Community in the New Testament," in Käsemann, *Essays on New Testament Themes*, Studies in Biblical Theology No. 41, trans. W. J. Montague (London: SCM Press, 1964), 71; John Howard Yoder, *The Politics of Jesus* (Grand Rapids: Eerdmans, 1972), chapter 9, "Revolutionary Subordination," 163-92. Winsome Munro, *Authority in Paul and Peter: The Identification of a Pastoral Stratum in the Pauline Corpus and 1 Peter*, Society for New Testament Studies Monograph Series 45 (New York: Cambridge University Press, 1983), 3-6, 95.

¹⁸Heinrich Zimmer, *Philosophies of India*, ed. Joseph Campbell (New

York: Meridian Books/World Publishing, 1961), Section III, "The Philosophy of Duty," 151-77.

[19]Albert Schweitzer, *The Quest of the Historical Jesus: A Critical Study of Its Progress from Reimarus to Wrede*, trans. W. Montgomery (New York: Macmillan, 1961), 366; Schweitzer, *The Kingdom of God and Primitive Christianity*, trans. L. A. Garrard (New York: Seabury Press, 1968), 81-88.

[20]Josephus, *Antiquities of the Jews*, 18.1.5, Whiston trans. (London: Ward, Lock & Co., n.d.), 471.

[21]L. Gordon Rylands, *A Critical Analysis of the Four Chief Pauline Epistles: Romans, First and Second Corinthians, and Galatians* (London: Watts, 1929), 182.

[22]Fuchs, 116.

[23]Richard Reitzenstein, *Hellenistic Mystery-Religions: Their Basic Ideas and Significance*, trans. John E. Steely, Pittsburgh Theological Monographs Series 15 (Pittsburgh: Pickwick Press, 1978), 149: "for the period which alone is under consideration here, in procedures and perspectives in which Christianity is in agreement with several different pagan mystery-religions, the priority is probably to be credited to the latter. A borrowing of cultic *terms* from Christianity by paganism is more difficult to conceive; here the burden of proof always falls on the person who would assert the priority of Christianity ... By way of justification I may add only that most of the Christian authors probably knew something of pagan literature, while only very few of the pagan writers would have known anything of Christian literature, and that in general conversion from paganism to Christianity was more common than conversion from Christianity to paganism."

[24]Frederick Sontag, *Sun Myung Moon and the Unification Church* (New York: Abingdon Press, 1977), 185-86; Sami Nasi Makarem, *The Druze Faith* (Delmar, New York: Caravan Books, 1974), 100-01: Sufi mystic Al-Hallaj publicly announced, "I am the Truth," and was crucified and beheaded. "Being unprepared for this knowledge, those who heard him speak in such a way accused him of blasphemy ... He [had] caused his executioners to commit the sin of murder and to do injustice to the truth itself." Also see Reynold A. Nicholson, *The Mystics of Islam* (1914; London and Boston: Routledge and Kegan Paul, 1975), 151-52; Edward Sell, *The Faith of Islam* (London: SPCK, 1907), 117: "A system of religious reservation is a fundamental part of the system in its mystical developments, whilst all Shi'ahs may lawfully practice 'taqiya,' or religious compromise in their daily lives. It thus becomes impossible to place dependence on what a Shi'ah may profess, as pious frauds are legalised by his system of religion."

[25]Philip R. Amidon, trans. & ed., *The* Panarion *of St. Epiphanius, Bishop of Salamis: Selected Passages* (New York: Oxford University Press, 1990), 103-104.

[26]*Origen: Contra Celsum*, trans. Henry Chadwick (New York: Cambridge University Press, 1965), 117.

[27]Willem Christiaan Van Manen, "Paul," *Encyclopaedia Biblica*, ed. T. K. Cheyne and J. Sutherland Black (New York: Macmillan, 1914), cols. 3628-29.

[28]I am sorry to disagree with Schmithals, who cannot see any reference to the angelic sex predators. See my "Amorous Archons in Eden and Corinth," *Journal of Unification Studies* 2, 1998, 19-34. Of course, Schmithals would recoil in loathing at the whole approach of this book.

[29]Rylands, *Critical Analysis*, 117.

[30]Ibid., 118.

[31]Alfred Loisy, *The Birth of the Christian Religion*, trans. L. P. Jacks (London: George Allen & Unwin, 1948), 244.

[32]Hertz, *Sayings of the Fathers*, 12-15.

[33]Loisy, *Birth of the Christian Religion*, 245, speaks of "the vision of the institution of the Supper which Paul professes to have had." Jeremias prefers to understand the language as implying a pre-Pauline liturgical stream: "Paul was passing on an established liturgical formula (1 Cor. 11.23, *Parelabon*)" (Joachim Jeremias, *The Eucharistic Words of Jesus*, trans. Arnold Ehrhardt [Oxford: Basil Blackwell, 1955], 108). Hyam Maccoby vindicates Loisy's theory in Maccoby, *Paul and Hellenism* (London/Philadelphia: SCM/Trinity Press International, 1991), 91-93. Of course, one may say that the eucharistic material is actually a product of tradition but has been fictively ascribed to a Pauline vision by later Paulinists who wanted to deny any dependence by their apostle on his predecessors.

[34]Loisy, *Birth of the Christian Religion*, 245-46.

[35]Walter Schmithals, *Gnosticism in Corinth*, trans. John E. Steely (New York: Abingdon Press, 1971), 254-55. Schmithals takes 1 Corinthians, despite its jigsaw state, to be the work of Paul, albeit stitched back together like the Frankenstein monster. Is that not a bit too early for such Gnosticism? It is significant that the one clear parallel he draws is from the second-century Ignatian *Epistle to the Smyrnaeans*.

[36]Caspar Schwenckfeld, *An Answer to Luther's Malediction*, trans. George Huntston Williams, in George H. Williams and Angel M. Mergal, eds., *Spiritual and Anabaptist Writers*, Library of Christian Classics, Ichthus Edition (Philadelphia: Westminster Press, 1957), 180.

[37]Hering, *First Epistle*, 122-55.

[38] Schmithals, *Gnosticism in Corinth*, 124-29.

[39]Conzelmann, *First Corinthians*, 205.

[40]Schlatter, cited in ibid., 204.

[41]Ibid., 205.

[42]Peter L. Berger and Thomas Luckmann, *The Social Construction of Reality: A Treatise in the Sociology of Knowledge* (Garden City: Doubleday Anchor Books, 1967), 25.

[43]Felicitas D. Goodman, *Speaking in Tongues: A Cross-Cultural Study of Glossolalia* (Chicago: University of Chicago Press, 1972), chapter 3, "Altered States of Consciousness," 58-86. Also see Goodman, *Ecstasy, Ritual, and Alternate Reality: Religion in a Pluralistic World* (Bloomington and Indianapolis: Indiana University Press, 1988), 34-40.

[44]Darrell J. Doughty, class lecture.

[45]Merrill F. Unger, *New Testament Teaching on Tongues* (Grand Rapids: Kregel Publications, 1971), 93-94.

[46]Arthur Drews, *The Christ Myth*, trans. C. Delisle Burns. Westminster College-Oxford: Classics in the Study of Religion (1910; Amherst: Prometheus Books, 98), 170.

[47]Wells, *Jesus of the Early Christians*, 137-38, 149.

[48]Munro, *Authority in Paul and Peter*, 204.

[49]J. C. O'Neill, *The Recovery of Paul's Letter to the Galatians* (London: SPCK, 1972), 27.

[50]R. Joseph Hoffmann, *Marcion: On the Restitution of Christianity: An Essay on the Development of Radical Paulinist Theology in the Second Century*, AAR Academy Series 46 (Chico: Scholars Press, 1984), 131.

[51]Rylands, *Critical Analysis*, 184-87.

[52]Whittaker, *Origins of Christianity*, 172.

[53]Ibid, 195-96.

[54]Adolf von Harnack, "Die Verklärungsgeschichte Jesu. Der Bericht des Paulus (1 Kor 15, 3 ff.) und die Beiden Christusvisionen des Petrus," in *Sitzungsberichte der Preussischen Akademie der Wissenschaften* (Berlin: Walter de Gruyter, 1922), 62-80.

[55]Jonathan Culler, *Structuralist Poetics: Structuralism, Linguistics, and the Study of Literature* (Ithaca: Cornell University Press, 1975), 134-41.

[56]Rylands, *Critical Analysis*, 185-86.

[57]Abraham J. Malherbe, *Paul and the Popular Philosophers* (Minneapolis: Fortress Press, 1989), Chapter 6, "The Beasts at Ephesus," 79-90.

[58]Schmithals, *Gnosticism in Corinth*, 257.

[59]Reitzenstein, *Hellenistic Mystery-Religions*, 46; chapter XVI, "Paul as a Pneumatic," 426-500.

[60]Rylands, *Critical Analysis* notes : "A writer who could, and did, appeal to the evidence of eyewitnesses in support of so momentous an event would not immediately afterwards feel it necessary to endeavour to establish it by an abstract, and indeed, hypothetical argument" (186).

[61]Hermann Detering, "The Falsified Paul: Early Christianity in the Twilight," *Journal of Higher Criticism*, vol. 10, no. 22 (Fall, 2003), 121.

2 Corinthians

Second Corinthians seems to have shared the sad fate of the Gospel of John, in that both look to have been reassembled from a pile of fragments or reshuffled pages and not very successfully. Thus, it falls to popular readers to scratch their heads as they read and to scholars to try to put Humpty Dumpty back together again. Most scholars agree so far, but not as to which puzzle piece should go where in the grand scheme of things and not on whether all or most of the material is authentically Pauline. But I rejoice to count myself among the minority following the Dutch Radical Critics. I reject the Pauline authorship of every word.

Most of 2 Corinthians is probably taken from a pair of letters that had been composed to counteract a Catholicizing program of extracting a number of churches from the heretical Pauline sphere of influence. Second Corinthians paints Paul as having taken aim at rivals who were poaching among his converts, moving in to undermine his work after he has moved on when they should be striking out with pioneer evangelism efforts in new territories. But as Willem van Manen points out, the perspective here is retrospective: the labors of Paul are in the past, over and done. The writer looks back on them, marking out the boundaries of the Pauline mission field like the Deuteronomic historian mapping out ancestral lots of the tribes of Israel. Looking beneath the pseudonymous surface, we find the argument is aimed at posthumous attempts to supplant the legacy of Pauline congregations by proposing new foundation legends about Peter or John founding this or that Pauline congregation.

The first letter is thought to have consisted of 10:1-13:9a; 2:1-6:13; 7:2-4; 13:9b-14. Presumably the brusque opening, "Paul," was thought fitting, as if Paul were so upset and the message so urgent that he decided to skip the usual pleasantries. The second letter consisted of 1:1-2:13; 7:5-16. It expresses relief for the happy resolution of the conflict on display in the first letter. The two were most likely circulated together from the start, like an epistolary novel.

Chapters 8 and 9, as L. Gordon Rylands in his book, *A Critical Analysis of the Four Chief Pauline Epistles* (1929), argues, would seem to have been a pair of independent fund-raising letters, written probably by two different people. Chapter 9 looks to be earlier than chapter 8. The short section 6:14-7:1 has no connection to its context. Probably whoever pieced 2 Corinthians together found this material on the back of a re-used scrap and just kept copying front to back, then moved on to the next sheet.

1

¹Paul, an apostle of Christ by the will of God, and Timothy, the brother, to the congregation of God situated in Corinth, along with all the saints in Achaia.

²Grace to you and peace from God our Father and from our Lord Jesus-Christ.

The salutation immediately marks the basic letter as Marcionite, as witness the stress on God as Father, something we have long since learned to take for granted but which is not necessarily the most obvious Christian nomenclature.

³Blessed be our Lord Jesus-Christ's God and Father. All acts of

mercy are his children, and he is the God of all comfort, [4]the one who comforts us every time we are afflicted, showing us how to console others who are undergoing every affliction, using the lessons of comfort we have learned from God who played the Paraclete to us. Because as we find ourselves experiencing more and more the sufferings of Christ, we feel proportionately more of the consolation that comes through Christ. [6]So whether we are afflicted for the sake of your comfort and healing or whether we are comforted for the sake of your comfort, energizing your endurance of the same sufferings that we ourselves endure, [7]either way our hope is firm regarding you, knowing that, just as you have joined us in sharing the sufferings, so you will share in the comfort to follow.

[8]I do not want you to remain uninformed about our afflictions in Asia Minor: we were burdened entirely beyond our power to endure so that we had given up hope of surviving. [9]But we felt inside us the announcement of the death sentence in order that we might learn no longer to place our reliance on ourselves but on God, who can always raise the dead if it comes to that! [10]He rescued us from our great death-trap, and he will rescue yet again. In him we have placed our hopes that he will rescue even now, [11]as long as you cooperate in prayer so that thanks may be rendered by many for the gift granted at the request of so many.

Here already is another characteristic of Marcionite Christianity: an inspirational view of suffering. When we suffer, the writer assures us, it is only to equip us to comfort others. While any theist might appreciate such a perspective, it is especially apropos to Marcionites, who rejected the notion of God the Father *punishing* anyone through suffering. Gordon Rylands[1] asks why the description of the apostle's sufferings in 2 Corinthians is so vague, without definite references. Surely the reason is that it is like the Lament Psalms[2] in the Old Testament, designed for any reader to identify with, filling in his or her own name and suffering. It is part of the Marcionite theodicy.

[12]For when we come to the Judgment, this will be our boast, and the testimony of our conscience, too: that in this world we have behaved in holiness and in sincerity before God, not by mere mor-

tal wisdom, but in God's favor—and more especially, in our dealings with you. [13]For we write you nothing beyond the plain sense that you read and perceive, and I hope you will perceive me fully, [14]just as you already perceived part of the truth from us, because you will boast about us, as we will you, on the day of the Lord Jesus.

[15]And in this confidence, I had first resolved to come to you so that you might enjoy a second favor, [16]and by way of you I would have passed on into Macedonia, and again from Macedonia, I would have come to you, and by way of you, I would have headed for Judea. [17]So was this plan the product of fickleness on my part? Or do I make my resolutions by some cynical calculus, retreating into ambiguity and equivocal speech? [18]No, as God himself is faithful, I swear our promise to you is not equivocal. [19]For there was nothing equivocal about the Son of God, Christ-Jesus, the one preached among you by me and Silvanus and Timothy. No, in him there was only a clear affirmation. [20]For however many promises of God there are, all of them receive their confirmation in him, which is also why it is through him that we pronounce the amen as we worship God. [21]But God is the one who fortifies us and you and has anointed us [22]even with the Holy Spirit, having thus both set his stamp on us and provided us the down payment in our hearts.

[23]Now on my life, as God is my witness, I came no more to Corinth in order to spare you. [24]It is not that we domineer your faith, but rather, we are colleagues that you ought to rejoice to see since it is by the faith we promote that you stand firm.

The Paulinist writer finds himself forced to defend his beloved apostle against an enduring grudge over his having left the Corinthian congregation in the lurch when they required his presence. Apparently, Paul's latter-day defenders have sought to remove the onus from their hero by reinterpreting some passages of his earlier epistles—authentic or not, who knows? But this has only led to the accusation that in addition to being unreliable, Paul was also equivocal and double-tongued. On the other side of it, the letter explains the long absence of epistolary guidance from Paul, something unavoidable since these epistles were written long after the fact in order to be rediscovered like Deuteronomy or the Book of Mormon. Why are these letters coming to light only now if they were really by Paul? We know the answer.

The "promises of God" (verse 20) are not Old Testament prophecies fulfilled in the coming of Jesus Christ, for Marcionites did not believe in the prophecies. In light of what immediately follows, we are to think of promises to Christians of spiritual endowment (see Acts 1:8; 2:38-39) that were not fulfilled. Verse 22 suggests that Corinthian expectations about charismatic experiences were exaggerated. They *did* receive a down payment of the Spirit, but not the whole thing all at once, as they had been led to expect, all in the style of all evangelistic sloganeering. This is the language of accommodation by a second-generation religious movement when enthusiasm has gradually sputtered out. The process of churchification, the community's backsliding from sectarian zeal into complacency, is not yet complete since normalcy is still considered inadequate. Frostbite has not conquered yet, as was beginning to happen in Ephesus (Rev. 2:4) and prevailed in Sardis (Rev. 3:1) and Laodicea (Rev. 3:15-17). In the heyday of the early church, as pastors still like to preach, no one would have thought it appropriate to speak of a mere down payment or "first fruits" of the Spirit. Nor would the Gnostic adepts, whose case was discussed in 1 Corinthians 12-14, think so. They were "already reigning as kings" (1 Cor. 4:8), even as is claimed by the health-and-wealth-gospel braggarts of today's TV churches.[3]

2

[1]But I resolved this within myself: not to come to you again grieving. [2]After all, if I cause you to grieve, who is left to cheer me up? It would have been you, but then I would have saddened you instead! [3]And I wrote you about my change of plans so as to avoid coming and being made to grieve by those who ought to make me rejoice since I expect that you all share my joy. [4]Indeed, I wrote to you out of great affliction and with much inner anxiety, blinking away the tears. My point was not to grieve you but to let you know of the love I have for you, even more than before! [5]For if anyone has offended, it is not so much me he has offended but, at least in part, all of you as well, not to overburden you with my own hurt feelings. [6]It is enough for such

an offender that he receive the punishment rendered by the majority, [7]and then it is up to you to forgive and to comfort such a person so that he not be consumed by excessive self-reproach. [8]Thus I urge you to reaffirm your love for him, [9]and this in fact is precisely why I wrote, as a test to determine whether you are completely obedient. [10]Now anyone you forgive of any sin, I also forgive. For indeed, what I have forgiven, if I have forgiven anything, it is for your sake and in Christ's place, [11]so we may avoid being made fools of by the accuser, for we are well acquainted with his tricks.

[12]But coming to Troas on a mission for Christ, a door of opportunity having been opened there by the Lord, [13]still I had no inner peace when I failed to find my brother Titus there, so I bade them farewell and left for Macedonia.

Verse 5 reminds us of Luke 12:41, "Lord, are you telling this parable for us or for everyone?" It offers a wink to intended readers, an audience both later and wider than the ostensible Corinthians. The point of the passage, the writer hints, is not that the historical Paul may have suffered some offense, though that is the narrative motivation for Paul having avoided Corinth, but for the writer using Paul's persona to tell them how to deal with congregational offenders in general in their own time.

Compare 2:10 with Matthew 16:19, 18:18; John 20:23. Paul bequeaths his judicial authority to his successors. He is the vicar of Christ and, more to the point, so are they. All this is part and parcel of a second-century dispute (see chapter 6 of this book) over whether those who trace their succession to the now heretical Paul will retain ecclesiastical power or whether they will lose it to the lately named *faux* successors of other apostles like John, with whom an increasingly powerful Catholic behemoth seeks to replace Paul's legacy.

In 2:5-11 the writer seeks to lessen the severity of the excommunication procedure laid down in 1 Corinthians 5:3-5 where an offender was to be consigned to Satan, who would see to his death. This is important as a mark of Marcionite origin and further mitigation of punishment by those who had abandoned the angry Jehovah.

Verses 9, 10, and 15 imply a scenario in which the indecisive Corinthians were terrified by the threat of *en masse* excommunica-

tion, which Paul might have announced when he departed in a huff
because of an embarrassing encounter with some member who had
sinned (cf. Mark 6:11). In the implied back-story, they lacked the
backbone to second Paul's judgment. Once he had widened the
scope of the excommunication to include them, they thought better
of their actions. Just whom did the writer think Paul could have confronted? We will see a bit further on.

3

[1]Oh no! Are we starting to commend ourselves again? Surely we
do not need reference letters either to you from other congregations
we served or from you to others we hope to enter, as some apparently
do? [2]You yourselves are all the credential we need. You are engraved
on our hearts for all to read, as everyone knows. [3]It is thus plain that
you are an epistle from Christ, delivered by us, one written not with
ink but by the Spirit of the true God, not on stony tablets, but on
tablets that are fleshy hearts.

[4]And we have such confidence before God thanks to Christ. [5]It
is not from our own resources that we are competent, as if we could
ascribe anything to our own merit. No, our competence comes from
God, [6]the one who also made us competent as servants of a new covenant, not one of letter but one of spirit. After all, the letter kills,
but the spirit vivifies. [7]Now if the ministry of death, having been
engraved in letters in stone, was glorious to the extent that the sons
of Israel could not stand to look upon Moses's face because of its
radiance as it faded away, [8]how much greater glory will mark the ministry of the Spirit? [9]For if the ministry of condemnation was marked
by glory, the ministry of vindication increases in splendor much more.
[10]For indeed, the thing not hitherto glorified has been made splendid in this respect because of this superabundance of glory. [11]For if
the covenant that was fading away shone with glory, how much more
brilliant will the one be that remains in force? [12]With a prospect like
this, naturally we speak with great boldness, [13]unlike Moses, who
placed a veil over his face to prevent the sons of Israel seeing the
end of his fading halo. [14]But their thoughts became obtuse, for even
today the same veil obscures the reading of the Old Testament so it
is not revealed to them that that covenant is being rendered obso-

lete by Christ. [15]Even today whenever Moses is being read, a veil shrouds their heart; [16]"but whenever he turns to Adonai, the veil is removed." [17]So "Adonai" refers to the Spirit, and wherever the Spirit of Adonai is, there is freedom. [18]But we all, faces unveiled, look upon the splendor of Adonai in a mirror, witnessing our own metamorphosis into the same image, from splendor to splendor even as a spirit from Adonai.

4

[1]Because of this, having this ministry by the mercy of God, we will not give up; [2]on the contrary, we have repudiated underhanded and shameful methods, not conducting ourselves with craftiness, nor diluting the message of God, as is the policy of some we could name, but commending ourselves to every human conscience and in the sight of God by the simple expedient of setting forth the truth. [3]If, however, there is anything secret about our message, it is because it remains invisible to those who are lost. [4]In their case, the God of this world has blinded the thoughts of the unbelievers to prevent the dawning of the enlightenment of the news of the splendor of Christ, who is the image of God. [5]For it is not ourselves that we promote, but Christ-Jesus as Lord and ourselves as your slaves on account of Jesus.

This section is pure Marcionism. The use of the Exodus narrative should not surprise us, for the Marcionite author's point is to contrast Moses with Paul, the covenant of death with the covenant of life. This is no proof-text but rather one of Marcion's famous antitheses. The Marcionite writer uses the Jewish scripture in much the same way it is employed by the Nag Hammadi Gnostic writers in a satirical deconstruction. In Exodus 34:29-35, Moses is said to have veiled his face so as not to frighten the Israelites with his numinous radiance. By contrast, 2 Corinthians has it that Moses knew his face would quickly lose its splendor, just as his two-bit covenant would, so he hid his face to make people think it still shone after it had faded! And this notion of the Mosaic covenant being simply "a covenant of death," well, no Jew would refer to it this way. Verse 18 anticipates a divinizing metamorphosis of the illuminati into conformity with their own primordial images or prototypes in the mind of

God. This is, of course, heavily redolent of Valentinian Gnosticism. The disdainful reference (4:2) to some who dilute the true message sounds like a reference to non-Marcionite Christians who confuse the two covenants and their deities. Why would they do this? The demiurge, the Creator God of this world, namely Jehovah, has blinded their minds.

[6]Because God, the one who said, "Out of darkness, light shall shine!" is also the one who ignited in our hearts the enlightenment of knowing the splendor of God shining from the face of Christ.

[7]And we carry this treasure in brittle ceramic vessels in order that the surpassing power may be God's, not ours. [8]We are being afflicted in every possible way, but not held back; mired in problems, yet not despairing; [9]persecuted by human beings, but not abandoned by God; being thrown down, but not destroyed; [10]ever carrying around in the body the dying of Jesus, in order that the life of Jesus may be equally seen in our body. [11]For we, the living, are always being delivered up to death because of Jesus in order that the life of Jesus might be manifested against the background of our dying flesh. [12]So then, death is consuming us while life is energizing you. [13]And having the same disposition of faith as the scriptural writer who said, "I believed; therefore I spoke," we both believe and therefore speak, [14]confident that the one who raised the Lord Jesus will also raise us along with Jesus and will present us with you as our boast on that day. [15]For everything we do is for your sake so that the favor done to the greater number may cause thanksgiving to increase with greater worship rendered to God. [16]That is why we do not give up; but if, as does happen, our exterior selves are being worn down, still our inner selves are being renewed every day. [17]For the current trifling affliction in the long run generates for us an unimaginable deposit of divine splendor many times as large. [18]Thus we are not occupied with visible reality but with the invisible, for the visible realities are fleeting, while the invisible ones endure the ages.

Verse 6 must be a Catholic interpolation. The sole point of the verse seems to be to identify this saving God with the Old Testament deity. It appears here precisely because of the great concentration of Marcionite matter preceding it, so as to neutralize it. Similarly, 4:13,

386 | The Amazing Colossal Apostle

another Catholic gloss, seeks to identify the faith described by the epistle with that of Old Testament writers. That seems to be the one and only point of adding such Old Testament garnish. As of verse 16, however, we are back to Gnosticizing Paulinism, with an overt reference to the mystery soteriology of gradual inner transformation, set in motion by initiation.

5

[1]For instance, we know that if the tent we dwell in on earth is destroyed, we have a building from God to look forward to, a house not constructed by human hands, but abiding the ages in the skies. [2]For indeed, in this one we groan, urgently anxious to don our dwelling place from the sky, [3]if indeed the alternative is finding ourselves naked spirits. [4]To be sure, being yet in this tent, we groan with our burdens, but what we want is not to slough off bodily form but to put on a new one so that the mortal may be swallowed up by the life. [5]Now he who has prepared us for this great transition is God, who has provided the down-payment of the Spirit. [6]Thus, ever rejoicing and mindful that, as long as we are at home in the body, we are homesick for the Lord, [7]we live by faith, not according to appearances. [8]That way we maintain good cheer amid danger and deem it a happy prospect to depart the home of the body and come home to the Lord.

Where but in Valentinian Gnosticism (which may be the origin of the section 5:1-8) do we find a conceptuality that would make sense of this business of having spiritual bodies already extant and awaiting the elect in heaven? Compare this saying from the *Gospel of Thomas*: "The images are manifest to human perception, while the Light which is within them is hidden in the image of the Light of the Father. But he will manifest himself, and then it is his image that will be overshadowed by his Light" (saying 83). For the present, I take this to mean we see human forms made in the image and likeness of God, the divine light itself concealed within the material human body. The body allows a glimpse of inner light but obscures it more than reveals it. One day the divine light will shine forth unobstructed from the resurrection body. Again, "When you see your likeness in a mirror you rejoice. But when you see your images which came into being before you, which neither die nor are visible to the eye, you will be overwhelmed!" (saying 84). These are the bodies described in 2 Corinthians 5:1-2.

⁹And this is why our ambition is to earn his approval, whether at home or away. ¹⁰For none of us can avoid full disclosure before the judgment throne of Christ in order that each may receive due recompense for the deeds done in this life, either good or worthless.

¹¹Therefore, in godly fear, we do not hesitate to persuade people to repent. We stand thus transparent before God's sight and, I should hope, before you in all good conscience. ¹²We are not thus commending ourselves to you, only giving you the opportunity to brag about us, ready to reply to those who brag about appearances, not about the heart. ¹³If we are carried away in spiritual ecstasy, it is between us and God; if we speak rationally, it is for your benefit.

¹⁴The self-giving love of Christ compels us, since our understanding is as follows: one died on behalf of all, which means that all died; ¹⁵and he died on behalf of all in order that those who live may henceforth live no more for themselves but for him who died on their behalf and was raised. ¹⁶Thus from now on, we evaluate no one according to fleshly appearances. Even if we once took Christ for a being of flesh, we know better now. ¹⁷So provided anyone is in the mode of Christ, there is a new creation: the archaic creation has passed away and, behold, the new has appeared. ¹⁸And all this is from God, the one who reconciled us to himself through Christ and has assigned us the administration of this reconciliation: ¹⁹the news that, by Christ, God was reconciling the world to himself, not counting up their legal trespasses as evidence against them, and planting in us the message of reconciliation. ²⁰Therefore we are ambassadors for Christ as if it were God himself pleading with you through us. We plead with our hearers on Christ's behalf, "Be reconciled to God! The one who was innocent of sin, he was turned into sin on our behalf, in order that by means of him we might become the righteousness of God."

Verse 5:10 mentions a coming judgment of works but not of persons, therefore not going beyond 1 Corinthians 3:13-15 where the value of one's works, not one's eternal destiny, is decided. But 5:14-15 sounds like a correction to the motivation given for preaching in verses 10 and 11. A Marcionite reader thought it strange that fear of eschatological judgment should form any part of Paul's motivation, so he sought to correct the impression by having Paul motivated instead by Christ's sacrifice of love.

Typically, the view of scholars who do not relish the prospect of finding docetism in the Pauline epistles is that the phrase in 5:16 implies that Paul no longer wanted to make a worldly appraisal of Christ as a failed rebel or prophet. But the point seems to have to do with the peculiarity of his death, which cannot have had the effect it did, culminating in resurrection, if it had been a body of mortal flesh. Christ had to have been something else, not something more *in addition* to that. Accordingly, Marcion taught that Jesus had a celestial body that suffered in some way in payment for the manumission of Jehovah's creatures, freeing them to become the children of Jesus's Father instead.

Verse 5:17 tells us that the old world created by the Old Testament deity has become obsolete, replaced by the new, *exclusively spiritual* world of the Father. In 5:18, we learn that God did not hold our sins against us. Why not? For the very good reason that they were not committed against him! Our business with our Creator is done. The death of Jesus is understood to have paid the debt of our sins against the Creator. After that, the Creator had no further reason to detain us in his kingdom.

6

[1]As colleagues, therefore, we now urge you, do not let your initial welcome of God's favor turn out to be in vain! [2]For he says, "At a crucial time I heard your plea, and in the day of deliverance I helped you." Well, this is a crucial time! Today is a day of deliverance!

[3]Providing no occasion for anyone to be alienated in anything we do so as to keep our ministry free of blame, [4]we commend ourselves as servants of God in everything: in patient endurance, afflictions, tight spots, predicaments, floggings, [5]prisons, riots, labors, vigils, fastings, [6]purity, knowledge, long-suffering, kindness, the Holy Spirit, non-hypocritical love, [7]the utterance of truth, and the power of God, with the weapons of righteousness in the right hand and the left, through glory and dishonor, bad report as deceivers and good report as truth-

ful, [9]being unknown yet notorious, dying and alive. As being punished and yet not to death, [10]constantly grieved but rejoicing, beggars making many rich, and having nothing yet being heirs of all things.

[11]We have been free in our speech to you, O Corinthians! Our hearts have only opened wider to you. [12]You are not estranged from us; you are estranged from your own affections. [13]But for the same requital, I say as to beloved children, open yourselves wide to us as well.

In 6:1, 3-13 and 7:2-4, we find another character defense of Paul in the interest of maintaining Achaia in the Pauline sphere of influence. Verse 6:2 appears to be a cosmetic quote by a Catholic interpolator. It serves no other purpose and breaks the continuity of thought.

[14]Do not be mismated with unbelievers, for what can righteousness and lawlessness possibly share in common? Or what mutual association can light have with darkness? [15]And what peace can be negotiated between Christ and Beliar? Or what business does a believer have with an unbeliever? [16]And what ecumenical union can be effected between a shrine of God and idols? For we are a shrine of the true God, as God said, "I will take up residence among them and I will walk among them. [17]So come out from among them and be distinct, says Adonai, and do not touch any ritually unclean food. Then I will welcome you, and I will be like a Father to you, and you shall be sons and daughters to me, says Adonai Shaddai."

7

[1]Since we have these promises, brothers, let us purify ourselves from all pollution of flesh and of spirit, perfecting consecration in the fear of God.

The section from 6:14 through 7:1, as virtually all scholars recognize, is out of place here. Not only does the subject matter change abruptly, but the beginning and end are neatly set off with redactional seams at 6:13 and 7:2, one a paraphrase of the other in duplicating the peg on which the original continuation had depended. The fragment, despite its brevity, is easy to place. It stems from the Qumran environment of the Dead Sea Scrolls, the Essene matrix of John the Baptist, Simon, Dositheus, and the Mandaeans.[4]

²*Open up to us!* We did no one wrong, we injured no one, cheated no one. ³I say this not to condemn you; on the contrary, have I not already made it clear that you are so close to our hearts that we would as soon die for you as live for you? ⁴True, I dare much in speaking to you, but equally, I brag much about you. I have been filled with comfort, I overflow with joy amid all our affliction.

⁵For indeed when we arrived in Macedonia, our flesh had had no rest, but was being afflicted in every possible manner: struggles outside, fears inside. ⁶But God, the one who comforts the downcast, comforted us by the arrival of Titus. ⁷And not only by the fact of his presence but also by the comfort he himself had received in respect of you. He reported to us your urgent longing, your bitter self-reproach, your jealousy for my sake, so as to make me rejoice all the more. ⁸Because if, in fact, I had grieved you by my epistle, I do not regret it. If indeed I did regret it, I see that that epistle, though it grieved you, did so only briefly; ⁹I rejoice, not to have grieved you, but that you were grieved to the point of repenting. For you were grieved in a godly fashion in order that you might not suffer any loss from us. ¹⁰For godly grief effects a repentance that no one will regret: that which leads to salvation. But worldly grief results in death. ¹¹Is that not clear in your own case? What earnestness it produced in you! What, but defense of me? What, but vexation on my behalf? What, but fear of God? What, but eager desire for reconciliation? What, but jealousy for my good name! What, but vengeance on my offender? In every respect, you have cleared yourselves in this matter. ¹²If indeed I then wrote to you, it was not for the sake of the one who did wrong, nor for the sake of the one who was wronged, but rather so that your earnestness on our behalf might become clear to you before God. ¹³That is why we found it comforting. But speaking of our comfort, we rejoiced all the more over the joy of Titus, whose spirit has been refreshed by all of you, ¹⁴because whatever I have said bragging about you to him, I was put to shame in nothing. Rather, just as we spoke truly in everything we said to you, the bragging I did to Titus about you turned out to be true. ¹⁵And his affection for you is great, as he calls to mind everyone's obedience, as you welcomed him with fear and trembling. ¹⁶I rejoice that I can be completely confident in you.

Commentators differ as to what bitter altercation may be referred to here. Did Paul insist the congregation excommunicate a notorious sinner and they sided with the sinner instead? And now things have turned around? If so, was the excommunicated man the same as the man who was involved with his stepmother from 1 Corinthians 5:1-5? For my part, I cannot help seeing here yet another reflection of the confrontation between Paul and Peter, glimpsed also in Galatians 2:11-14; Acts 8:18-24; 13:8-12; and the Clementine *Homilies* 3.19:4-6. In some sources we see variations on the theme, the Spouter of Lies confronting the Teacher of Righteousness, Simon Magus confronting Dositheus, Paul disagreeing with Simon Peter, Simon Magus against Simon Peter, Saul versus Elymas. Such contests are variously set in, or associated with, Antioch, Samaria, Cyprus, Damascus (possibly a symbolic reference to Qumran, home of the Damascus Covenant), and Rome, so why not in Corinth as well? In fact, it would fit quite well with a pro-Cephas party (1 Cor. 1:12) resisting the preaching of Paul. Could this be true? Could 2 Corinthians 7:11-12 and its context refer to the notorious confrontation between Paul and Peter? Why not? It is worth considering the possibility that it spilled over from Jerusalem to Corinth.

8

[1]Now we make known to you, brothers, the divine favor shown to the congregations of Macedonia, [2]how in the very crucible of affliction their abundance of joy and depth of poverty combined to produce a fortune in liberal generosity, [3]how, according to their resources, even beyond their resources, on their own initiative [4]they begged us the favor of assisting in the service to the saints, [5]and as we could never have expected, they gave themselves first to the Lord and then to us by the will of God, asking us to plead with Titus to complete what he had previously begun, extending this favor to you, too. [7]But just as you are rich in everything, in faith, in inspired utterance, in gnosis, and in all diligence, and in our love for you, see that you may be equally rich in this charisma. [8]I do not pretend to command you, but to measure the reality of your love in comparison with the diligence of others. [9]You are aware of the gratuitous kindness of our Lord Jesus, how on your account, though being rich, he impov-

erished himself in order that you, by means of his poverty, might become rich. ¹⁰So I give an opinion in this matter: this is expedient for you ¹¹to bring to completion, from what resources you have, the task you were the first to resolve and to do already a year ago and to do it with the zeal you had then. ¹²For if the eagerness is already present, whatever one has is acceptable, no matter how little. ¹³For the goal is not that others should be relieved at the cost of your distress, but that by way of equality, ¹⁴at the present time your abundance might supply their lack in order that their abundance may one day supply your want so that equality might prevail. ¹⁵As it is written: "He who gathered much did not have too much, and he who gathered little had no less." ¹⁶But thank God for placing the same diligence on your behalf in the heart of Titus, for indeed he welcomed the Macedonians' request, and being more diligent on his own initiative, he went out to you. ¹⁸And we sent with him _____, the brother whose work preaching the news is praised throughout the congregations. ¹⁹Not only this, but I have also sent our traveling companion, _____, elected by the congregations, to administer this gift to the glory of our common Lord, as we are eager to avoid any possibility of anyone finding anything questionable in our administration of this bounty. ²¹For we are concerned for propriety not only before God but in the sight of other people. ²²And we sent with them our brother, _____, whose diligence we proved many times over in many tasks, and now all the more diligent for his confidence in you. ²³Whether you ask of Titus, my partner and colleague on your behalf, or our brothers, delegates of the congregations, they seek only the glory of Christ. ²⁴Therefore, demonstrate in the presence of the congregations they represent both the evidence of your love and of our bragging about you.

9

¹Now concerning the ministry to the saints, it is superfluous for me to write anything to you, ²for I know your zeal, of which I brag about you to the Macedonians, "Achaia has made preparations a year ago!" And your zeal prompted most to emulate you. ³And I have sent with this letter the brothers, just to make sure our bragging about you is not exposed as empty in this respect, that I said

you were prepared; [4]so if I arrive with the Macedonians and find you unprepared, we should both be embarrassed, not to mention you, in the confidence we had. [5]This is why I thought it needful to urge the brothers to come to you in advance so as to arrange beforehand the blessing that you promised, so it might actually be a blessing and not something you feel begrudged to give on the spot. [6]And remember this: the one who sows stingily will also reap a stingy harvest, and the one sowing blessing on blessing will also reap appropriately. [7]Each one should give as he has resolved conscientiously, not grudgingly or under pressure, for God loves a cheerful giver. [8]And God is able to cause all fortune to increase for you in order that, always having your own self-sufficiency in everything, you may increase in every good deed, [9]as it is written: "He scattered, he gave to the poor, his reputation for righteousness will last forever." [10]Now the one providing seed for the sower will both supply bread for food and increase the harvest of your righteousness [11]so that in every way you will grow rich in liberality, which results through us as your couriers in thanksgiving to God! [12]Because the ministration of this service not only supplies the needs of the saints but also increases manyfold the thanks rendered God. [13]This ministry will glorify God, demonstrating to the saints your submission, by confession of faith, to the news of God, as well as the liberality of the fellowship of the gentiles to them and to all people, [14]with them praying poignantly for you on account of the excelling favor of God upon you. [15]Thank God for his indescribable gift!

As L. Gordon Rylands[5] pointed out, though the more recent Hans Dieter Betz nowadays gets the credit,[6] chapters 8 and 9 look like they were originally a pair of fundraising letters, chapter 9 probably being the earlier one. If we may take "the saints" (8:44; 9:1, 12) for whom these funds are collected to be identical to "the saints" for whom Paul agreed to raise funds in Galatians 2:10, these letters look like instruments to that end. It would make sense for Paul to have written them, but it makes no less sense to view them through the lens of a post-Paul setting. I take them to be Catholic writings (note the Old Testament proof-texts) seeking to reconcile Jewish and gentile Christians by means of seeking a kind of tribute to the former from the more numerous latter, and this in the name of Paul.

10

[1]Now I, Paul—myself—beseech you by the meekness and the gentleness of Christ, I who am so humble among you in person but so fierce on paper! [2]Now I beg you: don't make it necessary for me to act in person with the boldness with which I plan to be daring toward some who consider us to be behaving by mere mortal standards. [3]For though we live in the flesh, we wage war not in a worldly manner, [4]for the weapons of our warfare are not material but derive from God their power to overthrow fortress mentalities, turning aside the rapier of argument, and demolishing [5]every Babel tower raised up against true knowledge of God, taking prisoner every scheme to convert it forcibly to obey Christ [6]and standing ready to avenge all disobedience once your obedience is secured.

Most scholars believe chapter 10 was originally the beginning of a separate epistle, perhaps even of the "severe letter" for which Paul was half-apologizing in 7:8 and that had shaken them up. That may be, but the scenario envisioned is fictive. The emphatic claim to be Paul, as always in such cases, indicates that the writer is not who he pretends to be. It is a staple of pseudepigrapha.[7]

[7]You look no deeper than the surface of things. If anyone has satisfied himself that he belongs to Christ, then he had better take another look and see that if he belongs to Christ, so do we. [8]For even if I do brag more than usual about our authority, which the Lord gave to fortify you, not to demolish you, I shall not wind up ashamed of what I said [9]for fear of frightening you through the epistles. [10]"Oh, his epistles," he says, "are weighty and powerful, to be sure, but his presence in person is weak and his oratory contemptible." [11]Well, let such a person remember this: what we are in word in epistles while absent, we will also be in person and in action! [12]Oh, we would never presume to class ourselves or to compare ourselves with some who commend themselves; but they, measuring themselves only among themselves and comparing themselves only with themselves, naturally do not understand. [13]But on the other hand, we will not boast without any measure, but rather according to the measure of that yardstick which God measured out and apportioned to us, demarcating our sphere of activity as far as you. [14]For we do not overreach

our proper bounds as if our territory did not reach as far as you, for we came all the way to you in our preaching the news of Christ, [15]not bragging disproportionately over others' accomplishments but expecting that, as your faith matures, we will be more appreciated by you, according to our assignment there until finally you appreciate us fully. [16]We aim to preach the news in the regions beyond you, not to brag of things already accomplished in someone else's domain. [17]No, "If anyone wants to brag, let him extol the greatness of Adonai." [18]For it is not the one who commends himself that is approved, but the one whom the Lord commends.

First, one can hardly help noticing that there is already a collection of Pauline epistles (verses 9-11)! If such a reference marks 2 Peter as a pseudepigraph (3:16), it surely denotes the same thing here. And what is the point of this one? The nub of the issue appears in verses 12-16. As we have often had occasion to observe, the overriding concern is to safeguard the Pauline sphere of influence in the second generation. It is not so much as if the historical Paul were in danger of being deserted by his many converts. Rather, the danger is that Pauline communities in the second century (Marcionite churches and Gnostic and encratite groups) may succumb to the blandishments of Catholicism to co-opt and subsume them by getting them to acquiesce in a program of historical revisionism, ascribing the origins of such churches to some other "safe" apostolic name. Verse 17, with its cosmetic Old Testament citation, must be a late addition by a Catholic redactor.

11

[1]I ask you to permit me a little bit of foolishness. No, really, permit me! [2]For I am jealous for you with a godly jealousy. I betrothed you to one husband, hoping to present a pure virgin to Christ. [3]But now I fear that perhaps somehow, as the serpent seduced Eve by his cleverness, your minds may have been seduced from the simple purity of Christ. [4]For indeed, if someone arrives and proclaims another savior whom we did not proclaim, or if you receive a different spirit that you did not receive or a different preaching from the one you originally welcomed, you have not the slightest trouble putting up with him.

This passage might have issued from a Catholic as easily as from a Marcionite or Gnostic point of view. It is not uncommon in the history of Christianity, after all, for one denomination to accuse another of revisionism of such an exaggerated degree as to constitute another gospel. Verse 3 might tend toward a Catholic author because the emphasis is placed not just on correctness but on purity. That might imply criticism of Gnostic myth-spinners who make a relatively uncomplicated doctrine pointlessly elaborate. On the other hand, anyone might consider any sort of revision proposed by another party as corruption of a pure original, even if the revision were toward streamlining and simplification. A Gnostic might say a Catholic had spoiled the pristine faith. We cannot, I think, be sure to whom we should credit this piece of text, but we still need to ask if there are any nuances, any subtleties that might nudge us in one direction or another. I think there are.

What would it mean to preach "another Jesus"? Above I have translated "another savior" since "Jesus" means "salvation," but let us stick with the literal text and take the bull by the horns. "Another Jesus" could imply a false view of Jesus, as in 2 Corinthians itself over in 5:16, but even there it is put in terms of the one Jesus versus a heretical understanding of him. The passages in 1 John 2:22; 4:1-3 reject rival ("heretical") Christologies. The first seems to take aim at what Bart Ehrman[8] calls separationism, the doctrine that the human Jesus was the channeler for the Christ-Spirit, a view also excoriated in 1 Corinthians 12:3. The second condemns docetism, the belief that Jesus did not come into the world in genuine flesh like ordinary mortals. In both cases, the complaint is about departures from the one, acknowledged Jesus of Christianity. However, both of these authors go on to say that anyone espousing such heresies is not "confessing Christ," "confessing the Son." So, what do we come up with?

It seems natural to me to consider whether "another Jesus" might actually denote another character, another historical figure sharing the name or role of Jesus. There certainly were enough of them. Just as the Synoptic apocalypse (Mark 13 and parallels) warns its readers not to conflate their Jesus Christ with other prophets and messiahs active before and during the Roman siege of Jerusalem (Mark 13:5-

6, 21-23), I would suggest that 2 Corinthians 11:4 warns its readers not to conflate their Jesus Christ with another man or god. In both cases, it is a matter of locking the barn door after the horse has gotten out. For many reasons explained elsewhere, I believe the Jesus who died for sins and rose from the dead was one of the Mystery Religion saviors well known to Jews, such as Attis, Dionysus, Hercules, Osiris, or Tammuz. His worshippers eventually began invoking him under an honorific epithet Jesus ("savior") and finally obscured and replaced the original name, just as happened with the Vedic god Rudra.[9] So terrifying was Rudra's power that one dared not speak his name lightly. His devotees came to call him Siva ("the auspicious one"), and this finally became his name. Or think of the Hebrew Tetragrammaton, which we think was once pronounced "Yahve." So sacred did this name become that no one would pronounce it, and all would substitute the slightly less numinous "Adonai," or Lord. Even so, the dying and rising savior was originally ahistorical. In this context, Christ ("the anointed one") denoted the one who was resurrected, referring to how Isis anointed the slain Osiris with oil, raising him from the dead.[10] It would have had no connection to Jewish messianism at first.

At some point, this Jesus mystery cult linked up with a Syrian and Alexandrian Gnosticism, which posited the primordial sacrifice of the Light Man, whose essence thenceforth enlivened at least some of the human race. This Light Man, a heavenly Adam or Anthropos, was identified with Jesus. Then Jesus was historicized, re-imagined as a human being who had appeared in recent times in order to found an institutional church with an orthodox party line and credentialed successors who alone possessed the truth. No such institutional consolidation would have been possible had Jesus remained a mysterious figure from the dawn of time, appearing in dreams and visions to all and sundry. No, there had to have been a historical figure upon whom one could hang the mantle of founder. It was the only way to pull rank over others who, like Simon Magus, claimed to have received teachings and authorization through subjective visions.[11]

As I mentioned in chapter 5, the historicizing transformation of Jesus from pure myth to human-like legend,[12] like the lion-slaying Hercules replacing the sun god, was largely a matter of rewriting

Old Testament episodes from the Septuagint, substituting Jesus for
Moses, David, Elijah, Elisha, Jonah, and others. Another major source
was Josephus. In *Deconstructing Jesus*, I theorized[13] that the Passion
narrative of the gospel of Jesus was based on the story of the doom-
saying prophet Jesus ben Ananias (*Jewish War*, 6.5.11).

> There was one Jesus, the son of Ananus, a plebeian and a husband-
> man, who, four years before the war began, and at a time when
> the city was in very great peace and prosperity, came to that feast
> whereon it is our custom for every one to make tabernacles to God
> in the temple, began on a sudden to cry aloud, "A voice from the
> east, a voice from the west, a voice from the four winds, a voice
> against Jerusalem and the holy house, a voice against the bride-
> grooms and the brides, and a voice against this whole people!" This
> was his cry, as he went about by day and by night, in all the lanes
> of the city. However, certain of the most eminent among the pop-
> ulace had great indignation at this dire cry of his, and took up the
> man, and gave him a great number of severe stripes; yet did not
> he either say any thing for himself, or any thing peculiar to those
> that chastised him, but still went on with the same words which he
> cried before. Hereupon our rulers, supposing, as the case proved to
> be, that this was a sort of divine fury in the man, brought him to
> the Roman procurator, where he was whipped till his bones were
> laid bare; yet he did not make any supplication for himself, nor
> shed any tears, but turning his voice to the most lamentable tone
> possible, at every stroke of the whip his answer was, "Woe, woe to
> Jerusalem!" And when Albinus (for he was then our procurator)
> asked him, Who he was? and whence he came? and why he uttered
> such words? he made no manner of reply to what he said, but still
> did not leave off his melancholy ditty, till Albinus took him to be a
> madman, and dismissed him. Now, during all the time that passed
> before the war began, this man did not go near any of the citizens,
> nor was seen by them while he said so; but he every day uttered
> these lamentable words, as if it were his premeditated vow, "Woe,
> woe to Jerusalem!" Nor did he give ill words to any of those that
> beat him every day, nor good words to those that gave him food;
> but this was his reply to all men, and indeed no other than a melan-
> choly presage of what was to come. This cry of his was the loudest

at the festivals; and he continued this ditty for seven years and five months, without growing hoarse, or being tired therewith, until the very time that he saw his presage in earnest fulfilled in our siege, when it ceased; for as he was going round upon the wall, he cried out with his utmost force, "Woe, woe to the city again, and to the people, and to the holy house!" And just as he added at the last, "Woe, woe to myself also!" there came a stone out of one of the engines, and smote him, and killed him immediately; and as he was uttering the very same presages he gave up the ghost.

Theodore J. Weeden[14] has vindicated this thesis and made it his own, drawing attention to the parallels in Josephus's account of this prophetic Jesus who died in 62 CE after he was hauled before the Sanhedrin, then the Roman procurator, for interrogation. When asked, "Where are you from?" Jesus ben Ananias refused to open his mouth, even though he was flogged. He continued to prophesy Jerusalem's doom until he was killed by a Roman catapult. I think Jesus ben Ananias is a pretty good candidate for "another Jesus." As the historicized savior was beginning to get off the ground, the Marcionites probably resisted the development of a biographical narrative, but eventually they joined in the process, as we saw in chapter 7, in helping fashion a Jesus after their own conception. In harmonizing the mythical, heavenly, primordial savior with the narrativized Jesus, docetism had its origin, as I suggest. It was a way of accepting the narrative while continuing steadfast in the belief that the real Jesus had never come to earth at all. When *this* piece of theology in turn became narrativized, what we got was the peculiar business about Jesus leaving no footprints in the sand, appearing simultaneously to different disciples in different forms, and having a phantom body no hand could touch.

What I have in mind is closely analogous to Mark's process, as envisioned by Wrede,[15] of using narrative to harmonize two primitive Christologies. Since Jesus's Parousia, originally conceived as his first appearance as messiah, had been delayed interminably, some decided he must have already become the messiah at the time of his resurrection. Others went on to give messianic color to a public career beginning with a baptism. Mark managed to harmonize the two Christologies with the notion that Jesus had indeed become messiah at his baptism but that Jesus kept this under wraps till Easter, which made it easy to understand why some supposed it was only as of Easter that Jesus entered into his messianic office. Mark, according to Wrede, narrativized the harmonization itself, making a theory into a story, having Jesus speak of and even prove his messianic dignity throughout his ministry, yet try his best to keep it a secret till the resurrection. I am picturing a similar redaction-by-narrativization: harmonizing an unhistorical Jesus with a Jesus narrative: a Jesus who seemed to be there but was not.

Now, what does 2 Corinthians 11:4 mean when it refers to "a different Spirit"? I think we have a hint of its meaning in a Marcionite passage from Luke 9:51-56:

> And it came about that, as the days to his assumption into the sky were counting down, he set an unswerving course for Jerusalem, and he sent messengers in advance of him. And on their journey they entered into a village of Samaritans, to prepare for his arrival. And they withdrew their welcome once they heard his destination was Jerusalem. And the disciples Jacob and John, seeing this, said, "Lord, do you want us to call down fire from the sky to destroy them just as Elijah dealt with Samaritans?" But turning, he rebuked them saying, *"You don't realize which spirit you belong to! For a man's task is to save human lives, not to destroy them!"* And they journeyed into another village.

The italicized phrase occurs in some manuscripts and not others. Thus, it may not be the original reading. That doesn't matter. Even if it is not original, a Marcionite scribe must have added this sentence repudiating the notion of divine judgment, and my point is the same. "A different spirit" is the spirit of divine judgment, that of the angry Jehovah, not of the Father of all mercies. It is an explicit rejoinder to the story in 2 Kings 1:9-14, in which Elijah invokes fire from heaven to barbecue the Samaritan troops sent to arrest him. It is, in other words, another Marcionite antithesis.

Finally, the "different gospel" seems to connect up perfectly with the clearly Marcionite Galatians 1:6-9:

> I am astonished that already this soon you are detaching yourselves from the one who called you by the favor of Christ, embracing a different message of salvation, which in fact is not another,

only that there are some bothering you and intent on perverting the news of Christ. As for that, even if we or some angel from heaven should proclaim to you some message of salvation besides the one we proclaimed to you, let him be excommunicated! Let me just repeat that for emphasis. If anyone proclaims a message of salvation beside the one you first welcomed, let him be excommunicated!

Why look farther than Galatians for the possible referent of 2 Corinthians 11:4?

[5]For I estimate that in no respect do I fall short of the super-apostles. [6]But if in truth I am unskilled in speech, yet I am not so in gnosis, but have instead been completely transparent in our dealings with you.

[7]Or did my sin lie in humbling myself so you could be exalted, because I evangelized you with the news of God free of charge? [8]No, I robbed the other congregations, accepting their wages so I could serve you. [9]When present with you and in need, I was a burden to no one, for the brothers arriving from Macedonia supplied my needs; and in every respect I kept from becoming a burden to you, and so I will remain. [10]As the truth of Christ is in me, I swear no one will deprive me of this boast in the regions of Achaia. [11]Why? Because I do not love you? God knows I do! [12]But what I do, I will keep right on doing, in order to prevent anyone boasting that they practice the same as us. [13]For these are pseudo-apostles, charlatans, masquerading as apostles of Christ. [14]And that should surprise no one: for the accuser himself masquerades as an angel of light. [15]Thus, it is no great surprise if his servants, too, masquerade as servants of righteousness. Their ultimate fate will be as their deeds deserve.

Debate continues over whether the "super-apostles," soon to come in for a drubbing as apostles of Satan, are the Jerusalem pillars. True, nothing really stands in the way of such a conclusion, as little love seems to have been lost between the parties. But neither is there a compelling reason to make this assumption. After all, the number of apostles was as yet unrestricted, even in the second century.[16] The Pauline epistles, outside the very late patch at 1 Corinthians 15:3-11, do not yet know of any twelve and do not mind calling other individuals apostles, including Apollo, Andronicus, and Junia (1 Cor. 4:6, 9; Rom. 16:7). The super-apostles seem to be unnamed competitors such as we find in the *Didache*, 3 John, and Acts 19:13-16. The real point of contention, as we have so often seen, is the red-hot issue of later episcopal jurisdiction, with invisible claimants jockeying for apostolic clout by connecting themselves to prestigious apostolic founders and replacing existing foundational legends with new ones. In this case, the latter-day partisans of Paul's camp (Marcionites, Gnostics, encratites) must have resisted the imposition of these apostolic pedigrees that would have subsumed their churches under the Catholic umbrella.

Verse 14 is an interesting hint that the writer does not yet know the full version of the myth of an originally virtuous Lucifer ("light bearer") turning into a wicked Satan. Here, by contrast, the splendid, radiant angel is a disguise adopted by an already evil Satan for his own schemes.

[16]Again I say, let no one think me foolish. But if you do, at least indulge me so I may do a little bragging. [17]What I am saying, I say not as an apostle of the Lord, but as if I were a jester in this pose of bragging. [18]Since it seems a popular sport, why shouldn't I, too, take a turn? [19]Being so wise, surely you can afford to be patient with fools! [20]In fact, you are patient with anyone who enslaves you, who makes a meal of you, who takes you in, who exalts himself, who slaps you in the face. [21]I am ashamed to admit that indeed we were too weak for that. But in whatever way anyone dares, I say I too will dare! [22]What, are they Hebrews? Me too! Israelites, are they? Me too! Seed of Abraham, are they? Me too! [23]Are they servants of Christ? Please keep in mind, I am speaking as if I have lost my mind. I am more of one! I can point to more numerous labors, far more imprisonments, excessive whippings, and being on the verge of death many times! [24]Let's see: from the Jews I received the thirty-nine lashes on five different occasions, [25]three times I was caned by Romans; once I was stoned; three times shipwrecked, [26]spending a night and a day adrift; many times on the road in danger from robbers, flash floods, my race, the gentiles, in the city, in the wilderness, at sea; in danger from false

brothers, [27]in labor and hardship, passing many vigils, in famine and drought, often fasting, cold and naked. [28]Apart from outward circumstances, there are the daily conspiracies against me, the burden of anxiety for all the congregations. [29]For who among them is weak, and I am not weak? Who is offended and I do not feel his anguish? [30]If one has to brag, I choose to brag about my weaknesses. [31]This one may be hard to believe, but the God and Father of our Lord Jesus, the one who will be eulogized throughout the ages, he knows I am not lying. [32]In Damascus the ethnarch serving King Aretas posted guards around the city, looking to apprehend me, [33]and I was lowered in a basket through a window in the city wall and escaped his grasp.

The implied picture of Paul is that of an indefatigable superman whom nothing can stop! This is part and parcel of the Pauline legend. While some interpreters[17] point to this list as evidence of a Pauline gospel of suffering, marking out, so to speak, the path of the bodhisattva, it seems rather to be an extravagant score sheet of the achievements of an unstoppable Hercules, busy at his labors. Far from forming a contrast with the bragging of the Cadillac-driving super-apostles, Paul here unveils an *aretalogy* or list of heroic feats to rival any miracle résumé they might have fabricated to gain approbation from the gullible. This is precisely the same sort of letter of recommendation[18] he has earlier repudiated in principle (2 Cor. 3:1)! He writes it on his own behalf. On the other hand, maybe we are dealing with either two different Paulinist authors or a single author who recognizes that Paul should deny such accolades (as in 12:1 below) but, as a devotee of Paul, cannot resist supplying them and never sees the inconsistency.

12

[1]Surely it is inadvisable for me to boast, unless perhaps on another's behalf, so I will go on to visions and revelations from the Lord. [2]I know a man caught up by Christ some fourteen years ago—whether bodily I do not know, or out of the body I do not know, only God knows—to the third heaven. [3]And I know such a man, whether bodily or apart from the body I do not know, I tell you, only God knows—he was caught up into the Paradise and there heard unutterable utterances which human beings are forbidden to speak. [5]On behalf of such

a one, I will readily brag, but not on my own behalf except for my weaknesses. [6]For should I wish to brag, it would be no foolishness; for I would be telling the truth. But I will spare you so that no one forms an opinion of me based on anything but what he sees of me or hears from me.

[7]To prevent me from becoming swell-headed over the super-abundance of revelations vouchsafed me, a thorn in the flesh was given me, an angel of the accuser to pummel me, to prevent my self-inflation. [8]I pleaded with the Lord three times about this, to call him off. [9]And he said to me, "My charisma is sufficient for you, for my power is perfected in weakness." In that case, I will all the more gladly brag about my weaknesses, in order that the power of Christ may eclipse me. [10]That is why I am delighted with weaknesses, with insults, with tight spots, with persecutions and difficulties, all on behalf of Christ, for whenever I am weak, then I am mighty!

Let us call this the third-heaven apocalypse. Are we to understand, despite verse 5, that Paul is the one who ascended to the third heaven after all? Is he talking about himself? Not necessarily. Paul is often ascribed revelations, inside and outside the canon, but the revelations alluded to in verse 7 need not have anything to do with those of the ascended man. If Paul is intended, then why the third-person reference? Perhaps, for the moment, the pseudepigraphist drops his pose, feeling himself unworthy of impersonating Paul in such an exalted condition. The situation is strikingly similar to that underlying Mark 8:38, "For whoever is ashamed of me and my words in this adulterous and sinful generation, of him will the one like a Son of Man be ashamed when he comes in his Father's splendor with the holy angels." Suddenly the speaker retreats to representing Christ without pretending to be him. It may be the same here, the writer being unable to completely erase the line between himself and the one in whose name he speaks: Paul.

The scene is imagined as taking place entirely in the third heaven before the enthroned Christ. Paul finds himself under attack by a punishing angel, reflecting the overarching biblical role of the adversary as the tester of God's servants. The apostle cries out thrice in rapid succession, begging for deliverance, as Jesus himself does in Gethsemane, and Paul is vouchsafed a lesson about where true strength lies. He learns that true discipleship lies not in conjuring miracles but in sharing the sufferings of Christ.[19]

Notice how the writer intimates that he had never shared this account of a visionary ascent to heaven before. "Paul" does so now only because his readers have forced it out of him by comparing him unfavorably with the super-apostles with whom they are so infatuated. This implies that Paul previously had not been known as a visionary. It was the need to keep him and his authority current in the marketplace that led his admirers to fabricate these visions for him, making them like or better than the ones claimed by the super-apostles, probably on their behalf by their episcopal heirs.

Paul's journey to heaven was, in that respect, like Jesus's transfiguration: no one had heard of such a thing until the debate demanded it. Skeptical scribes demanded to know how the Christian Jesus could qualify as the Messiah when Elijah had not made his appearance first. Christians answered that Elijah had indeed appeared—figuratively, as John the Baptist—and when that lead balloon failed to gain altitude, they claimed that Elijah had, after all, returned *in person* but only to an elite audience of four people, not in full view of the public.[20] Even Christians blinked at this! Why had they never heard of such a thing? Because, er, Jesus said to keep mum about it till further notice. That's the ticket. In the same way, Paul here becomes a visionary after the fact. He had to, to keep his legacy current.

[11]What a fool I have become! But it is your fault. For I should be getting commended by you. For I came short of the super-apostles in no respect, even if, as they say, I am nothing! [12]Indeed, the authenticating signs of an apostle were performed among you in all patience, both by signs and wonders and works of power. [13]So in what respect were you deprived, compared to the other congregations, except that I made myself a burden to none of you? Well, forgive me this wrong! [14]Behold, this third time I am ready to come to you, nor will I burden you, for I am not interested in your money but in you! For it is not the children who should store up money to care for their parents, but the parents who are obliged to provide for their children. [15]And as for me, I am quite ready to spend and to be spent out on behalf of

your souls. If I love you all the more, am I to be loved the less? [16]Be that as it may, the fact is, I did not burden you. But perhaps I was crafty and took you in by deceit! [17]There was no one whom I sent to you [18]through whom I cheated you, was there? I persuaded Titus and have now sent him along with the other brother—Titus hasn't cheated you, has he? And didn't we behave in the same spirit? Didn't we walk in the same path?

[19]Again, you no doubt think we are on the defensive. But we speak before God and in the voice of Christ. And all of it, my beloved, is aimed at building you up. [20]For I am afraid that when I come, I will not find you as I would like to and you will not find me as you would like to see me—that strife, jealousy, old angers, rivalries, bad-mouthing, whisper campaigns, inflated egos, and brawls may erupt again, [21]that when I come, my God may humiliate me before you and I shall have to mourn over many of the ones who previously sinned and neglected to repent of the impurity and whore-mongering and perversion which they practiced.

The Pauline legend grows: Paul performed miracles! Back in 1 Corinthians 1:22-23, he was depicted as apologizing for not having miracles he could point to, either his or Jesus's, to satisfy the requests of those who would trade their faith for them. But in 12:12, Paul is said to have dispensed them like bottles of medicine-show elixir. We may suppose that, again, his fans have updated his resume, though not in such detail as we find in Acts, much less in the *Acts of Paul*. Notice that the writer, ostensibly Paul, does not use the active voice. He does not say, "I performed wonders." Why not? The writer is too used to thinking of another, the historical Paul, doing these things. It would be interesting to know what miracles the writer had in mind: Paul healing with his handkerchief, baptizing a lion, or other feats in the repertoire of Simon Magus, perhaps? In verses 13-19, our Pauline apologist once again bristles against those who would denigrate Paul's reputation and appropriate his sphere of influence.

13

[1]This third time, I am coming to you. "By the testimony of two or three witnesses shall every word be corroborated." [2]I have said before and now say in advance while yet absent, as I did while pres-

ent on my second visit, to those who sinned before and to everyone else that if I do decide to come again, I will show no mercy, [3]since you require evidence that Christ is speaking in me, he who is by no means weak toward you but powerful in you. [4]To be sure, he was crucified by token of weakness, but he lives by the power of God. For indeed, we are weak as sharing in the death of him, but we shall live with him by the power of God exercised upon you. [5]Test yourselves, whether you are firm in the faith; prove yourselves! Don't you perceive that Jesus-Christ is in you—unless you are counterfeits? [6]But I hope you will know that we are no counterfeits [7]Even now we pray to God that you will do no evil, and not because it would reflect badly on us, but simply in order that you may do the good, whether we are counterfeits or not. [8]For we are incapable of any action against the truth, only on behalf of the truth. [9]We rejoice whenever we are weak and you are powerful; we have no desire to feel superior at your expense. We also pray for your restoration to us. [10]For this reason, while absent, I write these things, so that when I get there, I may not have to deal severely with the authority which, after all, the Lord gave me, not to tear you down, but to build you up.

[11]As for everything else, brothers, rejoice, reconcile yourselves, encourage one another, come to agreement—and the blessings of the God of love and of peace will be with you. [12]Greet one another with a ritual kiss.

[13]All the saints greet you. [14]May the favor of the Lord, Jesus-Christ, and the love of God and the visitation of the Holy Spirit be with all of you.

Verse 1 doesn't fit with the rest of the epistle. What would three visits by the same man have to do with the witness of three different men? It looks like a blundering attempt to insert something from the Old Testament (Deut. 17:6), meaning it would be a Catholic insertion.

At stake in verses 3-5 are, again, rival claims of apostolic patronage or lineage to bolster the claims of authority in the late first or early second century. On what basis would this or that congregation be held in higher regard than another? Imagine the prestige a church would enjoy if it were discovered that Paul had written an epistle to it. Just as the writer of 1 Corinthians 2:1 forswears rhetoric at the outset of his use of it, so this writer rejects the need for letters of recommendation even as he writes one!

Throughout 2 Corinthians, but especially here at the end, there is a strange wrangling over the delay of Paul's promised return. It has prompted a crisis of faith, a doubting of God's promises which, despite mortal reckoning, are always sure (2 Cor. 1:15-2:1). Then we pass on to threats of investigative judgment on that day when Paul shall make what sounds like an eschatological return. "I ask that when I am present I may not [have to] be bold with the confidence with which I propose to be courageous against some" (10:2). He writes that "we are ready to punish all disobedience, whenever your obedience is complete" (10:6). "I am afraid … that when I come, my God may humiliate me before you and I shall have to mourn over many of the ones who previously sinned and neglected to repent of the impurity and whore-mongering and perversion which they practiced" (12:20-21). Here we catch echoes of the baleful diagnoses of the Son of God, whose eyes are like a flame of fire as he catalogues sins for which his recalcitrant churches will receive judgment when he, too, comes again: "I have against you that you tolerate the woman Jezebel … [who] leads my bondservants astray, so that they commit immorality and eat things sacrificed to idols. And I gave her time to repent; and she does not" (Rev. 2:20-21).

And as for Paul's fears of being humiliated upon his Parousia in Corinth, in having to confront those who have betrayed him, we must think of the chagrin anticipated for the Son of Man, who will turn away from many in shame when he returns (Mark 8:38): "Of him will the son of man be ashamed." Paul says this is the third time for him to visit the Corinthians. "I have said before and now say in advance while yet absent, as I did while present on my second visit, to those who sinned before and to everyone else that if I do decide to come again, I will show no mercy" (2 Cor. 13:1-2). One recalls here the same tones sounding forth from Revelation 21:12, "Behold, *I am coming* quickly, and my reward is with me, to render to every man as his work is." Compare this to Amos 1:6, "For three transgressions of Gaza, and for four, *I will not relent!* … I will turn my hand against Ekron; and the remnant of the Philistines shall perish!"

In the meantime, Paul is represented among his communities by the circulation of his "lost," pseudonymous epistles, whose writers function in a manner analogous to the *Bab*s ("gates") of the Hidden Imams of the Shi'ites, providing inspired guidance to the faithful in the name of the apostle of God, upon whose revelation they wait. It may seem far-fetched to suggest that Paulinists expected a second coming of the Apostle Paul, but think again of his legend as we read it in the *Acts of Paul*, where Paul's earthly sojourn culminates in an empty tomb and an ascension to heaven! I suggest that a second coming was by this point almost inevitable for the Pauline faith.

NOTES

[1]L. Gordon Rylands, *A Critical Analysis of the Four Chief Pauline Epistles: Romans, First and Second Corinthians, and Galatians* (London: Watts, 1929), 209.

[2]Hermann Gunkel, *An Introduction to Psalms: The Genres of the Religious Lyric of Israel*, trans. James D. Nogalski, Mercer Library of Biblical Studies (Macon: Mercer University Press, 1998), 121-98; Sigmund Mowinckel, *The Psalms in Israel's Worship*, trans. Dafydd R. Ap-Thomas (Nashville: Abingdon Press, 1962), 2:1-25.

[3]Gordon D. Fee, *The Disease of the Health and Wealth Gospels* (Costa Mesa: Word for Today, 1979).

[4]Joseph A. Fitzmyer, "Qumran and the Interpolated Paragraph in 2 Cor. 6:14-7:1," *Catholic Biblical Quarterly* 23 (1961): 271-80; rpt. Fitzmyer, *Essays on the Semitic Background of the New Testament*, Sources for Biblical Study 5 (Missoula: Society of Biblical Literature, 1974), 187-204.

[5]Rylands, *Critical Analysis*, 236-43.

[6]Hans Dieter Betz, *Second Corinthians 8 and 9: Commentary on Two Administrative Letters of the Apostle Paul*, Hermeneia Series (Minneapolis: Augsburg Fortress Press, 1985).

[7]Other examples include Dan. 7:15, 28; 8:1, 15, 27; 9:2; 10:2, 7; 12:5; Rev. 1:9; 22:8, 16; *Prot. Jas.* 25:1; *Inf. Gos. Thom.* 1:1; *Apoc. Pet.* 2; *Gos. Pet.* 60; *4 Ezra* 2:33, 42; 3:1; Tob. 1:3; *Ap. John* 1:19; *Thom. Con.* 1:2; *1 En.* 25:1; *Apoc. Zeph.* B:7; *2 Bar.* 6:1; 8:3; 10:5; 11:1; 13:1; 35:1; 44:1; 77:1; *3 Bar.* 1:3,

7; 4:1; 5:1; 7:1; 9:1; 16:5; *Apoc. Abr.* 1:2, 4; 6:1; *T. Levi* 2:1; *T. Sol.* 1:3, 5; 2:1, 5, 9; 5:6, 13; 6:9, 10, 12; 7:1, 7; 8:5, 12; 9:5; 10:10; 12:4; 13:3, 5, 6; 14:8; 15:13; 18:41; 19:1; 20:5, 18; 22:6, 17; 23:4; 25:8.

[8]Bart Ehrman, *The Orthodox Corruption of Scripture: The Effect of Early Christological Controversies on the Text of the New Testament* (NY: Oxford University Press, 1993), 119-20.

[9]Mahadev Chakravarti, *The Concept of Rudra-Siva through the Ages*, 2d. rev. ed. (Dehli: Motilal Banarsidass Publishers, 1994), 28.

[10]Gerald Massey, *The Historical Jesus and the Mythical Christ: Or Natural Genesis and Typology of Equinoctial Christolatry* (Brooklyn: A & B Books, 1992), 98-99.

[11]Arthur Drews, *The Christ Myth*, trans. C. Delisle Burns, Westminster College-Oxford Classics in the Study of Religion (1910; Amherst: Prometheus Books, 1998), 271-72.

[12]Jaan Puhvel, *Comparative Mythology* (Baltimore: Johns Hopkins University Press, 1987), 2.

[13]Robert M. Price, *Deconstructing Jesus* (Amherst: Prometheus Books, 2000), 242-44.

[14]Theodore J. Weeden, "The Two Jesuses," *Forum: A Journal of the Foundations and Facets of Western Culture*, vol. 6, no. 2 (Fall 2003).

[15]William Wrede, *The Messianic Secret*, trans. J.C.G. Greig, Library of Theological Translations (Cambridge: James Clarke, 1971), 11-149.

[16]Thomas Whittaker, *The Origins of Christianity: With an Outline of Van Manen's Analysis of the Pauline Literature* (London: Watts, 1933), 158-59.

[17]Dennis R. MacDonald, "Apocryphal and Canonical Narratives about Paul," in *Paul and the Legacies of Paul*, ed. William S. Babcock (Dallas: Southern Methodist University Press, 1990), 55-69.

[18]Dieter Georgi, *The Opponents of Paul in Second Corinthians*, trans. Harold Attridge, et al. (Philadelphia: Fortress Press, 1986), 243-44.

[19]Robert M. Price, "Punished in Paradise: An Exegetical Theory on 2 Corinthians12:1-10," *Journal for the Study of the New Testament*, vol. 2, no. 7 (Jan. 1980): 33-40.

[20]David Friedrich Strauss, *The Life of Jesus Critically Examined*, trans. George Eliot, Lives of Jesus Series (Philadelphia: Fortress Press, 1972), 540-45.

12.

Galatians

Numerous contradictions and anachronisms in Galatians imply that the work is multi-layered, having gone through the hands of various redactors, and that even the original nucleus was pseudepigraphical. Following Van Manen, I take Marcion as the author, partly because of the striking comment of Tertullian in *Against Marcion* that *Marcion nactus epistolam Pauli ad Galatas:* "Marcion has discovered Paul's Epistle to the Galatians" (5.3.1). Tertullian later adds that "Marcion, discovering the Epistle of Paul to the Galatians," uses it to "destroy the character of these Gospels which are published as genuine and under the names of the apostles" (4.3.1). If we take the word *discover* in its literal sense, these comments could imply that no one had seen the epistle before and that, like Hilkiah who discovered Deuteronomy (2 Kgs. 22:8-13) or Joseph Smith who discovered the Book of Mormon, Marcion wrote the core of Galatians (chapters 3-6), and posed as Paul to an audience of early followers who were beginning to yield to the propaganda of Catholicizing Christianity. It is the Catholic devotion to the Torah that Marcion combats, not necessarily the attachment to the Hebrew Bible that a Jewish Christian might hold. The first two chapters are later additions by Marcionites who wanted to counter the story of Paul in Acts, where Paul has been co-opted by Catholic Christianity.[1]

1

[1]Paul, an apostle, not sent from any human authority, neither by human beings, but by Jesus-Christ and God the Father, the one who has raised him from the dead, [2]and with me, all the brothers, to the congregations of Galatia:

[3]May you enjoy the favor and the protection of God our Father and the Lord Jesus-Christ, [4]the one who has given himself for the sake of our sins, so he might rescue us out of the present *evil* age in accordance with the will of our God and Father, [5]to whom all worship is due throughout ages multiplied by ages. Amen.

[6]I am astonished that already this soon you are detaching yourselves from the one who called you by the favor of Christ, embracing a different message of salvation, [7]which in fact is not another; only that there are some bothering you and intent on perverting the news of Christ. [8]As for that, even if we or some angel from heaven should proclaim to you some message of salvation besides the one we proclaimed to you, let him be excommunicated! [9]Let me just repeat that for emphasis. If anyone proclaims a message of salvation beside the one you first welcomed, let him be excommunicated!

[10]Is that blunt enough for you? Am I ingratiating myself with my audience now or am I calling down God? Or am I mincing words to flatter men? For if I were still concerned to meet the expectations of mere mortals, I would have chosen some other task than being a slave of Christ. [11]For I am letting you know, brothers, that the news preached by me is not human in origin, [12]for it was not from human beings that I received it, nor was I instructed in it; on the contrary, it was revealed by Jesus-Christ. [13]*You are acquainted with my actions while I belonged to Judaism, how I went to insane lengths persecuting God's community and laid it waste,* [14]*and progressed in Jewish religion beyond many contemporaries in my race, being many times over a zealot for my ancestral traditions.* [15]And yet, when God, who had watched over me since my umbilical cord was cut, [16]thought it choice irony to reveal his Son to me, and called me by his favor in order for me to proclaim him among the nations, I paused not to consult with flesh and blood,

¹⁷neither did I go up at once to Jerusalem to the apostles previous to me. No, I took off for Arabia, and went back to Damascus. ¹⁸*It was only after three years that I went up to Jerusalem to consult with Cephas and remained with him fifteen days. ¹⁹But I did not so much as see any of the other apostles, except for James the Lord's brother.* ²⁰Now in this recounting, I swear before God: I am not lying! ²¹From there I went into the regions of Syria and Cilicia. ²²*And still I remained known only by reputation to the congregations in Christ of Judea.* ²⁴*Never having seen me in person,* ²³*they only heard rumors: "The one who persecuted us now preaches the very religion he was then intent on destroying!"* ²⁵*And they worshipped God on account of my case.*

Jerome tells us that Marcion's text at 1:1 originally credited Jesus's resurrection to Jesus himself and not to the Father or anyone else. John C. O'Neill[2] has argued that the manuscript miniscule 1955 preserves the correct reading of 1:4, "from this present [prevailing] *aion,*" omitting the word *evil.* The point is, then, that the Father rescued us from the Demiurge Creator, which is synonymous with the aion. A Catholic scribe, understandably oblivious of the point, glossed it, adding *evil* at the margin. But subsequent scribes were not quite sure where the word belonged, bequeathing us several different word orders and combinations, some of them even adding words. These are the telltale tracks of copyists in trying to assimilate a word that was originally alien to the text. Thus nearly perished an important and forthright assertion of Marcionite theology.

It should be noted that Van Manen omitted verses 4, 8-9, taking them to be subsequent additions. I am not so sure that this is a necessary inference. The verses make good Marcionite sense to me. In 1:9 the author raises the hypothetical possibility of some heavenly visitant appearing to the Galatians and imparting a new gospel, something that had happened to Zoroaster when the archangel Vohu Manah appeared to him and that would happen to John on Patmos, to Elchasai, to Muhammad, and Joseph Smith. How overwhelming such a vision must be! It is superhuman in origin and character, or seems to be, but here the author's point is that it is by definition sub-divine! It may be higher than the human imagination in origin and yet still below the level of divine truth. Truly divine revelation, by contrast, according to "Paul," must stem directly from God. We read again and again of how Paul's gospel came directly by means of divine revelation, not from an angel. Of course, the intended contrast is not merely hypothetical because the author soon explains that there is a rival gospel, however ill-deserving the name, and that it is under no circumstances to be accepted in exchange for the original Pauline gospel. Did any Galatian seer claim to have received a gospel from an angel? We cannot know. The invocation of that possibility anticipates the Simonian claim that the Mosaic Torah was from angels, not from God (Gal. 3:19-20). Thus, the recent Judaizing gospel circulating in Galatia must also be the creation of angels.

"For I am letting you know, brothers, that the news preached by me is not human in origin, for it was not from human beings that I received it, nor was I instructed in it; on the contrary, it was revealed by Jesus-Christ" (1:11-12). Here we are to think of Ananias of Damascus, Paul's preceptor in Acts 9:17-19. Strikingly, the Paul-versus-Peter debate continued to escalate to the point where Peter's tutelage under the historical Jesus was no longer deemed enough. He, like Paul, must have received the revelation about Jesus directly from the Father, not from any mortal agency—even from Jesus. This is how the story grew from Mark 8:30 to Matthew 16:16-18.[3]

As Bruno Bauer and J. C. O'Neill[4] noticed, use of the term "Judaism" in 1:13-14 is anachronistic, presupposing the historic division between the two religions, which would not have been possible to conceptualize in Paul's day. The word was used in the first century to offset Judaism from paganism but was not yet utilized vis-à-vis Christianity. Thus, O'Neill brackets verses 13-14 as an interpolation, also because he thinks the passage veers off the train of argument. The problem is not so serious if we start out admitting that the whole epistle is post-Pauline. Thus, I would not excise it.

Again, Galatians 1:15-17, 21-25 contradicts Acts 9:26-27. The writer of the epistle seeks to set the record straight by insisting that Paul, an independent apostle, needed no initiation, no confirmation, no orientation from any human authorities, which is why he sought none. Rather than make a bee-line for Jerusalem, as is implied in Acts, he went to Arabia to pursue his own ends. From thence, he traveled *back* to Damascus, then on to Syria and his native Cilicia.

No Jerusalem authorities controlled his itinerary. He was under no orders. He had not so much as shown his face in Jerusalem, contradicting both Acts 9 and the interpolated Galatians 1:18-20. To be sure, his story was being noised about among the Judean Christians, but none of them could claim to have seen him. This also means, as others[5] have pointed out, that Paul cannot have been persecuting Christians in Palestine or else he would have been known by sight there. Since Damascus, to which he is said to be *returning,* was not previously mentioned, our author must have derived it from Acts 9 as Paul's point of departure for his post-conversion travels.[6]

In Tertullian's treatise *Against Marcion,* he does not mention the visit to Jerusalem (Galatians 1:18-20), which implies that probably Marcion had not mentioned it either, again marking it as an interpolation.[7] Someone must have inserted the passage precisely to abet the notion rejected here, that Paul went to Jerusalem to submit himself to the twelve as soon as he was able to go. Had these verses been available to Tertullian, who was arguing against Pauline independence, there is no way he would have skipped an opportunity to appeal to them; they cannot yet have formed part of the Galatians text. The word *again* was added to 2:1, at the same time verses 18-20 were inserted, by way of harmonization. Tertullian mentioned the visit of 2:1-10 only as *the* visit, not as a *second* visit.

We have a crucial admission in 1:22-24, that the whole notion of Paul the persecutor was the product of popular rumor. In all probability, the notion is an unwitting distortion of the Ebionite claim that Paul, as an anti-Torah Christian, opposed the true Christian religion—theirs. In a later time, when few remembered the sectarian divisions of an earlier generation, this version was misunderstood as if Paul, not yet a Christian in any sense, had physically persecuted believers in Christianity *per se.*

2

[1]Then, after an interval of fourteen years, I went up to Jerusalem *again* with Bar-Nabas, taking along Titus, too. [2]And I went up, summoned by a revelation. And I laid out before them the news as I proclaim it among the nations, in private session with those of great repute, for fear I might have been running off course. [3]But my com-

panion Titus, a Greek, was not compelled to be circumcised. He was willing to go along with it voluntarily as a concession. [4]But on account of the pseudo-brothers who had sneaked into the session in order to spy on our freedom from the Torah that we gentiles have in Christ, thinking they would enslave us, [5]we yielded to them in submission but for an hour *in order to preserve the news for you.* [6]But as for those esteemed to be something great—what they were then makes no difference to me now; God is impressed by no man's clout—those of repute added no proviso to me. [7]*On the contrary! Once they saw how I had been entrusted by God with the news for the uncircumcised, just as Peter was for the circumcised,* [8]*the one energizing Peter for an apostolate to the circumcised energizing me also, but to the nations,* [9]*and acknowledging the favor shown me by God, James and Cephas and John, the ones reputed to be pillars, offered to me and to Bar-Nabas the good right hand of partnership, dividing the territory: we would henceforth go to the nations, they to the circumcised,*[10]except that we should not forget the poor, the very thing I was eager to do in any case!

[11]But when Cephas arrived in Antioch, I stood up to him publicly, because he was blatantly out of line. [12]For before a certain party arrived from James, he used to dine with the gentiles, but when this one arrived, he stood down, segregating himself, fearing the circumcision faction. [13]And the rest of the Jews played hypocrite along with him so that even Bar-Nabas was led astray by their hypocrisy. [14]But as soon as I noticed they were not walking the straight path of the news, I said to Cephas in front of everyone: "If you, being a Jew, nonetheless live like a gentile, where do you get off forcing the gentiles to Judaize? [15]Physically, we are Jews, not sinners from the nations, [16]and since we know that a person is not accepted as righteous by virtue of deeds of Torah, but by belief in Christ-Jesus—even we believed in Christ-Jesus in order that we might be counted righteous by token of belief in Christ and not by deeds of Torah because no human being will ever be counted righteous by deeds of Torah. [17]But if, in the very effort to be counted righteous through Christ, we were found to be sinners no better than the gentiles, does that make Christ a facilitator of sin? Never! [18]But if I start to rebuild the very things I demolished, this is what makes me a transgressor. [19]For it was by means of the Torah that I died relative to the Torah, escaping its grasp so I

might live relative to God. I have been crucified alongside Christ. I live no more, but Christ now inhabits my body; as a result, what I now undergo in the flesh I endure by the belief in *the Son of* God loving me and giving himself up on my behalf. [21]I for one do not presume to turn my nose up at the mercy of God: for if it is really through the Torah that salvation comes, then Christ's death is moot!"

Whereas Acts 15:22 has the Antioch congregation delegating Paul and Barnabas to visit Jerusalem in order to settle a dispute over the need for circumcision and Torah-fidelity for salvation, Galatians 2:2 tells a different story: "And I went up, *summoned by a revelation.*" In other words, they were summoned by unmediated divine revelation, just as when Paul received his apostolic commission, directly from the Almighty, most definitely *not* at the behest of any human authority.

"And I laid out before them the news as I proclaim it among the nations, in private session with those of great repute, afraid I might be wasting my time." This represents Paul-Louis Couchoud's translation: not that Paul feared he had been preaching falsehood, which an authoritative ruling of the apostolic magisterium would shortly banish or confirm, but rather that he feared his very mission to Jerusalem would prove to be a counterproductive mistake.[8]

We find in this passage a retrojection of Marcion's visit to Rome to set forth his doctrine and join the church leadership there. Obviously, at the time, he took seriously the reputation of that church for authority, disdaining it only after they rejected his doctrine. Hermann Detering says:

> If, as seems likely, Marcion created what would become the New Testament Paul as a messenger for his own ideas, he almost certainly used biographical material from his *own life*, particularly the power struggle he waged with the collective in Rome. Marcion, like "Paul," alone knew the truth, a mystery made manifest to him by revelation.... To give his theology added "authority" it had to be back-projected into an earlier "apostolic age."[9]

In the same way, Muhammad very often in the Koran retells the stories of ancient prophets, including those of Moses, Abraham, and Noah, in terms modeled quite closely upon himself and his conflicts.

As is well known, textual variants make it hard to tell whether the author means that Paul *did* or did *not* yield to the demands of the circumcision faction by way of momentary compromise (Gal. 2:5), forfeiting a battle to win the larger war. I take it that he is supposed to have made the compromise, and that this is the way the author of Galatians 1-2 tries to explain an embarrassing point in the Acts narrative, the circumcision of the half-Jewish Timothy (Acts 16:1-3). The author of Acts explains it in the same terms as the Apostolic Decree, owing to concern for Jewish-Christian sensibilities (15:21; 16:3). Galatians mentions the episode too, albeit cagily: "My companion Titus, a Greek, was not compelled to be circumcised. He was willing to go along with it voluntarily as a concession" (Gal. 2:3). As William O. Walker Jr. observes, the identities of Titus and Timothy seem to have been confused here, and not for the first time.[10] My version spells out what I think is intended but passed over in artful ambiguity.

How far Paul's esteem for the Jerusalem leaders, or shall we say Marcion's esteem for the Roman leaders, has fallen! In Galatians 2:6 they are merely said to be supposedly something great, pretty much the same disdainful phrase that characterizes Simon Magus in Acts 8:9—not coincidentally, since in Acts we see the other side of this very argument.

As Walker[11] points out, verses 7-9 must be an interpolation, since they rudely interrupt the sequence of verses 6 and 10 where the original meant to say that the pillars imposed no condition upon Paul and Barnabas except for the relief collection. Note that the interpolator slips and calls Cephas "Peter," his more familiar name, whereas in the rest of the discussion he is Cephas. The interpolated passage partakes of the Catholic remodeling of Peter to make him just like Paul, a missionary to the gentiles. We find the same tendency at work already in Acts 10, and that account is presupposed in Galatians 2. But Galatians 2:9 goes way beyond that to divide the *whole world* between the two missionary apostles! Here we are in the realm of legend pure and simple.

The stipulated collection of alms for the Jerusalem poor (*ebionim*, 2:10), which is to say the Jerusalem saints generally, for whom Paul is depicted in the epistles as having raised money in his churches, is a fictive version of Marcion's own initial gift of a large sum to the Roman church,[12] which they refunded after deciding he was a heretic. Its refusal is echoed in Acts (8:18-24; 21:20-26; 24:17-18) and Romans (15:16, 30). But the real point of mentioning that the collection was the *only* proviso stipulated by the pillars is to exclude the so-called Apostolic Decree issued by the same group in Acts 15:23-29. That document promulgates a compromise by which gentile Christians need not trouble themselves to keep all the measures of the Torah, which would entail adopting an alien lifestyle. Rather, gentile Christians only need live by the much more modest Tetralogue: no eating blood, no eating strangled animals, no eating the meat offered to idols, no temple prostitution or perhaps consanguineous marriage. These seem to be concessions to sensitivities of observant Jews and Jewish Christians (Acts 15:21). The author of Galatians 1-2 evidently viewed such a compromise as beneath Paul and thus would have nothing to do with it. Yet, his own subsequent narrative makes more sense on the assumption that the Tetralogue was accepted.[13] On the other hand, Van Manen judged verse 10 to be an interpolation, presumably because he thought the writer would never countenance Paul accepting *any* stipulations from the pillars, as this would appear to compromise his independence.

Who constituted the embassy to Antioch, "a certain party" which "arrived from James" (Gal. 2:12-13)? Who else but delegates sent round to check on the implementation of the Jerusalem Decree (Acts 15:30-32)? They did not like what they found, for Jews and gentiles were freely mixing at common tables, eating non-kosher food. They would have been doing this based on Peter's conviction, expressed in Acts (10:12-15; 11:3) after his vision of a sailcloth sheet filled with a bevy of nonkosher creatures and an angelic voice commanding him to butcher them and eat. God, the angel says, has declared the creatures kosher. This change facilitated gentile evangelism, which seems to commence with Peter's preaching to Cornelius's household, not with Paul's evangelism. It is not that any of this actually happened, of course, only that Galatians takes the account for granted and refutes it.

In what way had Cephas "lived like a gentile" (2:14)? By eating the same food as the gentile Christians of Antioch. In what way

420 | The Amazing Colossal Apostle

was the chastened Cephas "Judaizing the gentiles" (2:14)? Why, by so hastily, once James's envoys arrived, imposing on the Antioch gentile brethren the stipulations of the Jerusalem Decree of Acts 15, which in turn imposed a few basic Jewish kosher laws. In those deliberations, remember, Peter was shown to have preferred total gentile freedom (Acts 15:10-11) but in the end acquiesced to James. Thus, as long as the cat was away, the mice in Antioch, including Cephas, were happy to play, disregarding kosher laws altogether. It was only once the embassy from James arrived that Cephas and Barnabas felt compelled to snap to and obey the party line.[14]

The speech Galatians has Paul fire off spontaneously at Cephas during a segregated church supper has a great deal in common with the speech of Peter to the Jerusalem Council in Acts 15, especially the cardinal principle that even as Jews, the Christians know that it is faith, not Torah observance, that guarantees salvation (cf. Acts 15:11; Gal. 2:15-16). In the writer's mind, even to impose the relatively innocent Tetralogue is letting the camel's nose back under the tent flap. The Torah is being readmitted piecemeal, and when all the way in, it will neutralize the death of Christ: what could have been the point of it if nothing has really changed? This assertion makes the most sense, I think, in a Marcionite framework, where it is a question of an old, ineffective order being replaced by a new, effective one. In this view, the Marcionite text would have lacked verses 16-17.

Galatians 2:16 seems burdened with redundant statements to the effect that faith in Christ suffices to save, not works of the Law. But Gordon Rylands says that the particular instance in 16a ("no one will be justified by works of the law, but by faith in Jesus Christ") is intended to mean, "No one will be justified by works of the law except through Jesus Christ," inculcating a synthesis of Christ and Torah. Thus, it is revealed as a Catholicizing interpolation.

3

[1]O senseless Galatians! Who is it who has cast a spell on you? The crucifixion of Jesus-Christ was plainly demonstrated from scripture before your eyes. [2]This is the only question I want you to answer me: Did you experience the onrush of the Spirit by performing deeds of Torah? Or by hearing about faith? [3]Are you so obtuse that, having

started with the Spirit, you are now seeking perfection by deeds of the flesh? [4]Did you endure so much for nothing? [5]That is, if it was in vain! So the one who supplies the Spirit to you, performing powerful works among you—does he do it in response to deeds of Torah or to hearing about faith? [6]Just as Abraham believed God's promise and it was reckoned as merit to him, [7]know this: the ones marked by faith, these are sons of Abraham. [8]And scripture, foreseeing that God would count the nations righteous by virtue of their faith, pre-evangelized Abraham: "In you all the nations will be blessed." [9]So it is those marked by faith who are eulogized with the believing Abraham.

[10]For as many as are marked by deeds of Torah labor under a curse, for it is written: "Cursed is everyone who does not persist in performing all the things written in the scroll of the Torah." [11]So it is clear that no one is counted righteous, as far as God is concerned, by keeping the Torah, because "the righteous one shall live by faith." [12]And the Torah has nothing to do with faith; rather, "the one who performs them shall live by them." [13]Christ bought our freedom from the Torah's curse, becoming a curse on our behalf, as we know from Scripture: "Cursed is everyone hanging from a tree," in order that the blessing of Abraham might extend to the nations by Jesus Christ, so we gentiles might receive the promise of the Spirit through the faith. [15]Brothers, let me speak in human terms: even in the case of a covenant between mere mortals, no one has the liberty to abrogate or to add to it unilaterally. [16]So to Abraham the promises were spoken, and to his seed. It does not say "to his seeds," as if intending many descendants, but as intending a single one. [17]So I say this: the Torah, which came into being after four hundred and thirty years, does not abrogate a covenant previously ratified by God, and so abolish the promise. [18]For if what one inherits is conditional upon obeying laws, it is no longer a promise at all. But God gave the inheritance to Abraham by promise.

[19]Then what is the point of the Torah? It was added for the sake of transgressions, to deal with them until the seed should arrive to whom the promise had been made. It was promulgated by angels at the hand of a go-between. [20]Everyone knows there is no use for a go-between to represent a single individual, but God is one individual. [21]Is the Torah therefore opposed to the promises *of God?* Never! For

if a law was given that could make one alive, salvation would indeed have come by means of law; [22]but scripture consigns all to sin in order for the promise realized by belief in Jesus-Christ to be made to those who believe. [23]But before faith arrived, we were guarded under the Torah, being preserved for the faith that was about to be revealed. [24]Thus the Torah has become a schoolmaster for us to prepare us to graduate to Christ in order that we might be accepted as righteous by virtue of faith; [25]but faith having arrived, we are out from under the schoolmaster's jurisdiction. [26]For you are all mature sons of God by token of believing in Christ-Jesus and thus have no need for the Torah. [27]For each one of you who was baptized into Christ, you have assumed the likeness of Christ: there can no longer be any Jew nor Greek; there can be no slave or free; there can be no male and female, for you are all identical in Christ-Jesus. [29]But if you belong to Christ, then you are a descendant of Abraham, heirs by the provisions of the promise.

Here we pass to the original Epistle to the Galatians as "discovered" by Marcion of Pontus, just as Joseph Smith "discovered" the Book of Mormon. This passage, 3:1-24, reads naturally as a Marcionite attempt to separate the Torah as an alien factor, a monkey-wrench cast into the works, from the plan of salvation based on promise and the proper response to it: faith. Where it veers off from Catholicism is that the pedagogue who took us bruisingly in hand until faith came is the demiurge, and it does not say he and the Torah were added into the picture by God. *Just the opposite.* The Law could not have been God's idea, but rather an invention of the angels. Here is the seed form of the Marcionite doctrine of the Torah, given to the world not by the God of Jesus Christ but rather by lesser spiritual entities. In classical Jewish statements of the doctrine, the Law was given by the Hebrew God.[15] Here the Law is the creation of angels, those in charge of the elements (4:3), who are described in great detail in *First Enoch* 60:11-22, where they are said to dispense the rain, the snow, and so on as needed. To identify them with the Torah was not arbitrary, in view of the promises of good weather and lush crops if Israel kept the Torah (Deut. 28:11-12, 22-23).

We read Marcion's statement here of his doctrine that the Torah stemmed from inferior powers. We are encountering it in its earliest form, still heavily influenced by the Simonian understanding of the Torah, created and imposed by the angels of the Epinoia, the fallen First Thought. According to Irenaeus (*Against Heresies*, 1.23:3), "Simon Magus said that men are saved by grace and not by just [righteous] works. For actions are not just by nature, but by accident; according as they were laid down by the angels who made the world, and who desired by commandments of this kind to bring men into servitude to themselves."

Simonian influence is also discernible in the treatment of Abraham as proof and precedent that salvation lies outside the Torah. This must have been the main argument of the missionary who persuaded King Izates of Adiabene, Abraham's ancient region, to embrace Judaism without circumcision.[16] Which deity did Marcion mean to picture in portraying the promise to Abraham and his spiritual progeny? I should think he intends to show the one who was to be revealed as the Father of Jesus Christ. Granted, Abraham would not have known the difference, and Marcion would not have supposed he would, since it was only as of the advent of Jesus that mankind was told of the Alien God. Jerome and Tertullian both attested that Marcion omitted verses 6-9 and 15-25 and changed verse 14, "that in Christ Jesus the blessing of Abraham might come upon the gentiles, that we might receive the promise of the Spirit through faith," to "that we might receive the blessing of the Spirit through faith." Obviously, this was to omit all reference to Abraham, but I suspect we may be at the mercy of the subsequent scribes who were more Marcionite than Marcion, who no longer understood the importance of Abraham. Scholars from Adolph von Harnack[17] onward have warned us that we may not have Marcion's own text in the patristic accounts, but rather that of his disciples.

One wonders how the same writer can identify as a gentile (3:13; cf. 2:4) and Jew (3:24) in the same chapter, but Marcion's tutelage was in Catholic Christianity, which mixed the Torah of Judaism with the revelation of Jesus Christ. Where he does seem to pose as a Jew, it is part of his literary pose as Paul. He is inconsistent.

If we look closely at the Old Testament quotations, we find that nearly all of them characterize the purpose of the Torah *on its own terms.* The Torah is not part of the plan of salvation, as syncretist Christians who mix Christianity with Judaism imagine. Look at *its own* stipulations, he seems to be saying. Where does it promise anyone eternal life in return for avoiding shellfish? It must be in this sense that the Torah does not nullify divine promises, even as it leaves its adherents, in Marcion's view, holding the bag. It is a different deity who promises to save believers by pure faith. The Torah was the work of the archon and his angels who govern this world.

In verse 3:27 we find the root insight of early Christian encratism, including Marcionism, in its emphasis on the celibacy gospel. Sex was the original sin, from which all others stemmed, for the reason that it resulted from the androgynous Adam dividing into male and female. Subsequent sins begat new divisions (rich and poor, slave and free), and further sex acts produced new nations (Greek and Jew, barbarian and Scythian). However, baptism into Christ, the Second Adam, restores the baptized to a version of the primordial oneness of the androgynous Adam before the fall.[18] Again, Van Manen cut verse 27 prematurely, failing to see how snugly it fits into Marcionite ethics.

4

[1]But let me point out, for as long as the heir remains an infant, even though he were lord of all existence, he is no different from a slave, [2]under guardians and stewards until the term his father set at first. [3]It was the same with us: when we were infants, we had been indentured to the spirits who control the elements of this cosmos; but when time was almost full, God sent out his son, who became an infant born of womankind, becoming a Jew under the dominion of the Torah, [5]in order that he might buy the freedom of those under the dominion of the Torah so we could receive adoption as sons. [6]And since you are sons, God sent out the Spirit of his Son into our hearts, crying, "*Abba*! Father!" [7]Thus you are no longer a slave but a son, and if a son, also an heir just as God planned.

[8]But back then, not knowing God, you were enslaved to those who by nature are not gods. [9]But now, knowing God, or better, being known by God, what are you doing turning back to the weak and destitute elemental spirits whose slaves you want to be all over again?

¹⁰You keep holy days and months of fasting and penitential seasons and canonical calendars! ¹¹You are scaring me! Have I put in all that work with you for nothing?

¹²Become like I am, brothers, I beg you. For I am just like you! I bear no grudge, for you never did me wrong, ¹³and you remember how it was on account of weakness of the flesh that I first preached the news to you, yet you did not disdain my difficulties in the flesh, nor did you disdain me, but instead you welcomed me as an angel of God, namely, as Christ-Jesus. ¹⁴So what has become of your blessing me? ¹⁵For I swear on your behalf that, if it had been possible, you would have gouged out your own eyes and given them to me! ¹⁶So have I now become the Enemy by speaking the truth to you? ¹⁷They are zealous for you, to be sure, but not to the good, for they wish to isolate you ¹⁸to the end that you may focus your zeal on them. Well, it is always a good thing to be zealous, provided the zeal is for something good and not just when I am present with you, ¹⁹my children, for whom I am undergoing the labor pains all over again till Christ gestates within you. ²⁰How I wanted to be there with you now so I might change my tone because I don't know what to make of you.

²¹Tell me this, those who want to be under the dominion of the Torah: don't you realize what the Torah says? ²²For it is written that Abraham had two sons, one from the concubine and one from the free woman. ²³But the one from the concubine has been born according to the flesh and the one from the free woman miraculously, according to the promise. ²⁴These things are to be allegorized as follows: these stand for two covenants, one indeed issuing from Mount Sinai, issuing in slavery, which is Hagar. ²⁵Hagar is in turn Mount Sinai in Arabia and corresponds to today's Jerusalem, for she is a slave along with her children. ²⁶But the Jerusalem in heaven above is free, she who is the mother of us all. ²⁷For it is written,

> "Be glad, O barren one!
> She who bears not, break forth!
> And shout, she who is without labor!
> For many are the children of the desolate,
> Rather than her who has a husband!" (Isa. 54:1)

²⁸But you, brothers, are children by the promise, like Isaac. ²⁹And

just as back then the one born in the fleshly manner persecuted the one born spiritually, it is the same now. ³⁰But what does scripture say? "Throw out the concubine and that son of hers! For there is no way the son of the concubine shall be a co-heir with the son" of the free woman. ³¹And we, brothers, are not children of some concubine, but of the free woman.

The writer knows of the rhetoric his opponents aim at him in his absence: "So have I now become the Enemy?" (4:16). This was the epithet for Paul among Torah-Christians who viewed him virtually as the Antichrist. In Matthew 13:28, counterfeit believers like the Torah-free Paulinists are sown like weeds in the field by the Enemy. And who says Paul is now the Enemy? Is this the recollection of a later writer or is Marcion addressing his very real, immediate foes? Surely the latter, represented by Catholics who insisted on retaining the Old Testament as Christian scripture. Verse 10 tells us they were Judaizing Christians who kept certain holy days and food regulations, reminding us that in so doing, they worshipped not the true God, but the much inferior angels of the demiurge.

The writer focuses on the coming of Jesus into the time stream as the one whom God sent to assume the burden imposed on humanity by the oppressive angels, to take it from our shoulders onto his own. The expression in 4:4, which reads literally, "born of a woman, born under law," is a Catholic gloss intended to refute the Marcionite belief that Jesus descended fully grown from heaven. Otherwise, why mention it at all? Only in this case could it be remotely appropriate to affirm the most elementary fact about a person: he was born! Someone is denying it, so it is no longer uncontroversial. Not surprisingly, patristic commentators tell us that Marcion lacked verses 1-2. His version lacked verse 7 as well, and this cannot be because he omitted it since it fits Marcionite theology perfectly.

Jesus came, according to 4:5, "in order that he might buy the freedom of those under the dominion of the Torah so we could receive adoption as sons." Adoption is the major element of the Marcionite doctrine of redemption. The Father of Jesus Christ adopts as his own children the creatures of the Hebrew God. Since they are not his own, human beings can only be taken on as orphans into the household of the Unknown Father. This can happen only if Jesus manumits them from slavery to their Creator, who is their rightful owner. In no other Christian salvation scheme does the notion of redemption (manumission of slaves for money) make as much sense, as the history of post-Marcionite theories of salvation has amply demonstrated.[19]

In verses 21-31, Marcion offers an allegory of the Genesis story of Abraham, Hagar, and Sarah, only he does so in a manner reminiscent of the Nag Hammadi Gnostic texts.[20] He turns the text against itself, undermining the privilege of Judaism and Israel, making the scripture incriminate and condemn the religion it is supposed to uphold. Jews, with their legal covenant, are not really Isaac's seed but Ishmael's because the covenant of the Torah was promulgated from a mountain in Arabia, Mount Sinai, not from Jerusalem. The author undertakes a move similar to that of the Koran wherein Isaac and Ishmael are effectively reversed, and Ishmael, progenitor of the Arabs, is made Abraham's chief heir. The point of theologizing on the basis of Abraham is to circumvent and to relativize the Mosaic Torah. Galatians seems to be saying that contemporary Jews are not free, not heavenly, nor heirs of the promise of freedom. Spiritual sons of Hagar and heirs to an Arabian covenant, they are slaves like her and her son. How are Christians true miracle children such as the Torah makes Isaac? They are spiritually born, and they shun sexual reproduction. Thus, the encratite praise for Sarah precisely as the *barren* woman who nonetheless has innumerable spiritual offspring reflects the blessedness of those who remain celibate. The woman in bondage serves as breeding stock for the world-creating demiurge, creating more slaves for him.

According to Ephrem the Syrian (*Commentary on the Epistles of Paul*), the Marcionite text current in his day lacked verses 25 and 27-30. I would guess this was because Marcionites could not imagine their Paul quoting Jewish scripture even though in these passages the scripture is quoted *against itself*. It was one of Marcion's famous antitheses. The filler material in verse 26 comes from Ephesians 1:21, which was also Marcionite territory, as we will see in our next chapter. In explaining Galatians, Ephrem noted that the biblical stories are "allegorized: for these are two covenants; one indeed from Mount Sinai unto the synagogue of the Jews, according to [the] law, [which] generates unto bondage." The other stands "above all powers" and is the true "mother of us," according to his apt summary.[21]

5

[1]It was to live in freedom that Christ liberated us; so stand firm and don't allow yourselves to be lassoed and placed back under the yoke of slavery! [2]Behold! I, Paul, say to you, if you are circumcised, Christ will do you no good! [3]And I testify again to every human being who embraces circumcision, he is henceforth obliged to perform all the commandments of the Torah! [4]You who are deemed righteous by Torah observance, you were released from the fellowship of Christ; you pitched headlong from the path of divine favor! [5]For the Spirit moves us to anxiously anticipate the prospect of vindication—by faith. [6]For as far as Christ-Jesus is concerned, neither circumcision makes any difference, nor lack of circumcision, but only faith as it operates through love. [7]You were well on your way. Who held you back? Who made you so reluctant to be persuaded by truth? [8]This persuasion does not come from the one who calls you. [9]It takes only a little yeast to contaminate the whole lump of dough. [10]I have confidence in the Lord that you will think nothing else. But the one who is confusing you shall bear responsibility for it, no matter what his status. [11]As for me, brothers, if I still preach circumcision, why am I still being persecuted? Because then the scandal of the cross would be nullified. [12]I only wish that those who are upsetting you might chop themselves off!

[13]You were called to be free, brothers—just do not let that freedom become a pretext for the flesh; but motivated by love, serve one another as slaves. [14]For the whole of the Torah has been epitomized in a single maxim, namely, "You shall love your neighbor as yourself." [15]But if you bite and consume one another, watch out! You will be destroyed by one another. [16]Now I say, "Set your sail to the Spirit and you will never act upon carnal lust." [17]For the flesh lusts against the Spirit and the Spirit contests against the flesh, for the two are locked in stalemate, and thus it is your own preference that tips the balance, resulting in your act. [18]But if you are led by the Spirit, you are not under the dominion of Torah. [19]So the works of the flesh are obvious enough. They include prostitution, impurity, lewd acts, [20]idol

worship, sorcery, alienation, discord, jealousy, grudges, rivalries, divisions, sectarianism, [21]envy, drunken binges, orgies, and such things, of which I forewarn you, as I did before: those who practice such things will not arrive after death in the world of God. [22]But the harvest of the Spirit is love, joy, peace, long-suffering, kindness, goodness, fidelity, [23]meekness, self-mastery; no law is required to regulate these. [24]Now those who belong to Christ-Jesus crucified the flesh with the attendant passions and lusts. [25]If we live in the power of the Spirit, then let us behave in the newness of the Spirit. [26]Let us not seek empty glory, the one provoking, the other envying.

It is easy to multiply examples of biblical pseudepigraphists, inside and outside the canon, revealing themselves by their emphatic self-reference in "I, so-and-so" statements. It shows how ill at ease the author is in pretending to be the other person. Because of this discomfort, the writer overcompensates, claiming to be himself, which the person he imitates would not think of doing. This is what we find in verse 2. Then in verse 21, our pseudepigraphist, presumably Marcion, finds himself confusing the actual scene before him with the one he has envisioned for Paul, warning about things that are happening in the here and now. Since Paul would have *forewarned* his readers, the forger stumbles further by adding, "I forewarn you, as I did before." It is the same as the pseudonymous writer of 2 Peter 3:2, who loses track of his pretended narratees, who are all long dead, and instead reminds the actual, second-century readers of a prediction made long ago by "your apostles," forgetting that he was posing as one of them!

We receive the impression in verses 2-3 that the proponents of the Torah have not pressed for a complete conversion to Judaism. Against this, Marcion suggests that circumcision stands for entire Torah-observance. Once you have rid yourself of the pagan foreskin, you are committed to all 612 of the other commandments. In for a penny, in for a pound. This is what he means by saying that the whole lump of dough is soon permeated by a pinch of leaven: the circumcision will, or should, lead to complete Torah-observance, at least if one wants to be consistent. I cannot help suspecting that the circumcision advocates had urged the simple rite as a token gesture (see 6:13 below). It was the minimum they deemed appropriate for a gentile who wanted to consider himself a son of Abraham.

After all, if Abraham is the model here, what does circumcision properly denote? Does it signify faith in the promise or faith in the Law? It must be faith in the promise. One can well imagine the opponents urging the sort of pre-Torah approach, as we find in Romans 4, then closing in on circumcision as the seal of Abrahamic faith generally, not as a sign of submission to the Torah. But Paul, or Marcion, is in danger of losing at his own game here! Who in the early church can we imagine advocating such a piecemeal approach to the Torah, demanding that Christians acknowledge its importance as scripture but not requiring that one actually *keep* its provisions? Why, of course, Catholic Christianity taught exactly this.

Then how could detractors of Paul claim he imposed circumcision as something that was sufficient unto itself, not the beginning of complete Judaization (v. 11)? Interestingly, they make Paul a champion of their own policy, which was to follow Christian conversion with Jewish circumcision, period. The reference must be to the incident, whatever it may have been, underlying Acts 16:3, where Paul is said to have circumcised the half-Greek, half-Jewish Timothy to mollify local Jews or Jewish Christians.[22] Whereas the later Marcionite author of chapters 1-2 admits it happened, but confusing Timothy with Titus, Marcion himself, author of chapters 3-6, denies the report outright. For him, Paul could not have done it, hence he did not do it. He felt that such feather-smoothing hardly became Paul, who would not have minded enduring the necessary persecution his refusal to circumcise Timothy would have sparked.

In verses 13-25, we have a perfect statement of Marcionite ethics: the flesh inspires evil, sensual behavior, while the divine Spirit produces only a fine harvest of noble deeds and motives. Strangely, from any other standpoint than the Marcionite, the Law is linked to fleshly lusts. It all makes sense to Marcion: the flesh produces the acts the Torah prohibits, so to put the shoe on the other foot, the Law controls the explosive nature of the flesh which is otherwise about to burst forth in a lascivious lava flow. The flesh must be the origin of both carnal behavior and the Law prohibiting it, while the Spirit cannot give rise to law because it does not produce the acts the Law rides herd on. Let us rid ourselves of the harmonization that the flesh is good, except as seduced due to its fallen nature, and simply read what the text says. It denigrates the flesh itself, the material body, the bag of rotting meat created by the demiurge. If Marcion is indeed the author, the word *encrateia* ("self-control," 22-23) probably refers to celibacy, for which the word was code in anti-sexual encratite sects.

6

[1]Brothers, if it should happen that an individual succumbs to some transgression, it is up to you spiritual ones to win back such a one in a spirit of meekness, mindful all the while of how liable to temptation you are yourself. [2]Shoulder one another's burdens, and that way you will keep the law of Christ. [3]For if anyone imagines himself to be something great when in fact he is nothing, he is kidding himself. [4]But let each man point to the quality of his work as proof, and then he will have sufficient reason to brag with reference to himself alone, leaving anyone else out of consideration; [5]for in the judgment, each will have to carry his own load. [6]And let each one who receives catechism in the doctrine of Christ share all worldly necessities with the one catechizing him.

[7]Don't kid yourselves: no one makes a fool of God! For whatever an individual sows, one will reap the same thing. The one who begets physical offspring only supplies more victims to death and corruption. But the one sowing for the Spirit will reap from the Spirit agelong life. [9]And let us not give up hope of reward in doing good deeds; for in good time we shall reap if we do not give up. [10]So then, in the time we have, let us do good to everyone, and most of all to the household of faith.

[11]Notice what large letters I have hand-written!

[12]All those who wish to cultivate a reputation on fleshly terms, these people compel you to be circumcised, only to avoid incurring the persecution that the cross of Christ must bring. [13]For it is not as if those who are being circumcised keep the Torah themselves; they only want you to be circumcised so they may brag that they were able to get you to do it! [14]But as for me, may I never brag except about the cross of our Lord Jesus-Christ, through which the world has been

crucified relative to me just as surely as I have been crucified relative to the world. ¹⁵For neither circumcision nor lack of circumcision means anything; all that matters is a new creation. ¹⁶And as many as are willing to live by this rule, peace be upon them, and mercy on the Israel of God!

¹⁷From here on in, let no one bother me, for I bear in my body the very stigmata of Christ.

¹⁸May the favor of our Lord Jesus Christ be with your spirit, brothers. Amen

A Marcionite context makes better sense for the origin and meaning of the term "law of Christ" (v. 2) than any other hitherto proposed. It must be intended as the antithesis to the Law of Moses. In fact, is it not already tantamount to Marcion's call for a Christian canon to replace the Jewish one?

In verse 5, I believe we have a Catholic gloss, an attempt to correct the position in verse 2 which says we may mutually lighten our burdens. Verse 5 warns, to the contrary, each must bear his *own load* and so face the Day of Judgment alone, which is quite a different scenario!

Given the real possibility that Marcion is the author of our epistle, we must not ignore the distinct likelihood that "sowing seed unto the flesh" (6:8) refers to physical, sexual begetting, which will only supply more hostages to the Creator.

Ostensibly a mark of authenticity, the detail about the distinctive signature in 6:11 is actually proof of the reverse. If Paul had really signed the letter thus, it would be self-evident to the reader. Paul would not need to describe what he had done had his signature been visible for all to see. But the text masquerades as a subsequent copy of a Pauline letter written decades before. No autograph ever appeared on it. The wording draws attention to something only a second-generation reader—that is, of what is supposed to be a later copy—would need to have pointed out for him. "[S]ometimes, in diary novels, for example—even the physical appearance of a narration and the very practice of narration are commented on."²³ Our pseudepigraphist prepared the way for this with his reference to the apostle's eye troubles in 4:15, which is no coincidence.

NOTES

[1]John Knox, *Marcion and the New Testament: An Essay in the Early History of the Canon* (Chicago: University of Chicago Press, 1942); Joseph B. Tyson, *Marcion and Luke-Acts: A Defining Struggle* (Columbia: University of South Carolina Press, 2006); Frank R. McGuire, "Galatians as a Reply to Acts," *Journal of Higher Criticism* 10 (Spring 2003): 161-72.

[2]J. C. O'Neill, *The Recovery of Paul's Letter to the Galatians* (London: SPCK, 1972), 19-20.

[3]Alfred Loisy, *The Birth of the Christian Religion*, trans. L. P. Jacks (London: George Allen & Unwin, 1948), 101.

[4]O'Neill, *Recovery of Paul's Letter*, 25.

[5]Loisy, *Birth of the Christian Religion*, 119; Ernst Haenchen, *The Acts of the Apostles: A Commentary*, trans. Bernard Noble and Gerald Shinn, rev. Robin M. Wilson (Philadelphia: Westminster Press, 1971), 297-98.

[6] L. Gordon Rylands, *A Critical Analysis of the Four Chief Pauline Epistles: Romans, First and Second Corinthians, and Galatians* (London: Watts, 1929), 352.

[7]Frank McGuire, "The Posthumous Clash between Peter and Paul," *Journal of Higher Criticism* 9 (Fall 2002): 164.

[8]Daniel Jon Mahar, "English Reconstruction and Translation of Marcion's Version of 'To the Galatians,'" online at *Ouroboros: The Gnostic Ring*. Rylands, *Critical Analysis*, 322-323, thinks it is inconceivable that our author, given his general thrust, would permit Paul to wonder if he had been wrong in his preaching all these years or that Paul would acquiesce to the verdict of any human board of inquiry (cf. 1 Cor. 4:3). Hans Hübner, *Law in Paul's Thought: A Contribution to the Development of Pauline Theology*, trans. James C. G. Greig, Studies of the New Testament and Its World (Edinburgh: T. and T. Clark, 1984), has no qualms about positing such a querulous and cowardly Paul. Hübner seeks to harmonize the relativization of the Torah in Galatians 3:19-20 (an invention of angels) with that of Romans (a Zen koan to lead the seeker to despair of his own efforts). To put it a bit more bluntly, Hübner thinks James considered what Paul had said in Galatians heresy, so Paul back-pedaled, substituting a safer view of the Torah in Romans, a draft of which he mailed off to James, hoping to smooth the latter's feathers and make Jerusalem's gracious acceptance of his gentile collection more likely (60-65). Oh what a tangled web we weave when we determine to preserve Pauline authorship of everything at all costs! Notice how Hübner has reca-

pitulated the early Catholicizing agenda: he has subordinated Paul to James in order to paper over differences in the early church. Thus does theological history repeat itself.

[9]Hermann Detering, "The Falsified Paul: Early Christianity in the Twilight," *Journal of Higher Criticism* 10 (Fall, 2003): 93-94.

[10]William O. Walker Jr., "The Timothy-Titus Problem Reconsidered," *Expository Times*, vol. 92, no. 8 (May 1981): 231-35.

[11]William O. Walker Jr., "Galatians 2:7b-8 as a Non-Pauline Interpolation," *Catholic Biblical Quarterly*, vol. 65, no. 4 (Oct. 2003): 568-87.

[12]Detering, "Falsified Paul." On the collection and tribute, see Dieter Georgi, *Remembering the Poor: The History of Paul's Collection for Jerusalem*, trans. Ingrid Racz (Nashville: Abingdon Press, 1992); Keith F. Nickle, *The Collection: A Study in Paul's Strategy*, Studies in Biblical Theology No. 48 (London: SCM Press, 1966).

[13]McGuire, "Posthumous Clash," 163.

[14]That the seemingly trivial issue of table etiquette on display here is more than fortuitously linked to the broader issues of Galatians is suggested by Peter Worsley's description in *The Trumpet Shall Sound: A Study of "Cargo" Cults in Melanesia*, 2d. ed. (NY: Schocken Books, 1974), 43-44, in which he quotes anthropologists Stephen W. Reed and Jean Guiart regarding turf wars among European missionary organizations in Melanesia:

> "Spheres of influence" were gradually worked out, ... but "native adherents" of rival sects in interstitial areas frequently became "engaged in acrimonious disputes as to which sect had the right to proselytize in new regions" ... Such divergence between varieties of exposition of the gospel have not merely introduced new, and often bitter, social divisions into native communities, they have introduced moral and religious uncertainty into an already unstable situation. This is exacerbated by the divergence natives note between Christian doctrines of equality and brotherly love and actual practice. As one native of Tanna remarked: "Which way Missionary e no stop with em you long one table? Him e preach Jesus e say love one another, e preach, e no do it."

A footnote quotes the same speaker: "Why doesn't the missionary sit at the same table as us? He preaches that Jesus told us to love one another. He preaches this, but he doesn't practice it." This is a modern example of the same kind of rivalry portrayed in the New Testament between Paul and Peter: their jurisdictional dispute, the rancor, and charges of hypocrisy that erupted from Peter's aloofness among native converts at table.

[15]Neither Hyam Maccoby, *Paul and Hellenism* (London and Philadel-

phia: SCM Press and Trinity Press International, 1991), 9, nor Lloyd Gaston, *Paul and the Torah* (Vancouver: University of British Columbia Press, 1987), 37, find any evidence in "Jewish biblical or extra-biblical tradition" that Jews believed the Torah came from angels.

[16]Robert Eisenman, *James the Brother of Jesus: The Key to Unlocking the Secrets of Early Christianity and the Dead Sea Scrolls* (NY: Viking Press, 1996), 890.

[17]Adolph von Harnack, *Marcion: The Gospel of the Alien God*, trans. John E. Steely and Lyle D. Bierma (Durham, NC: Labyrinth Press, 1990), 30, believed, with his teacher Albrecht Ritschl, that Marcion's New Testament texts were shorter than the Catholic versions because they were bowdlerized. He thought Marcion's "pupils constantly made alterations in the texts—sometimes more radical than his own, sometimes more conservative—perhaps under his very eyes, but certainly after his death." I believe otherwise, that Marcion's texts were shorter because they were earlier versions and that what we have are altered texts, due to expansion by both Catholics and subsequent Marcionites.

[18]Wayne A. Meeks, "The Image of the Androgyne: Some Uses of an Image in Earliest Christianity," in Allen R. Hilton and H. Gregory Snyder, eds., *In Search of the Early Christians: Selected Essays* (New Haven: Yale University Press, 2002), 3-54. Dennis R. MacDonald, in *There Is No Male and Female: The Fate of a Dominical Saying in Paul and Gnosticism*, Harvard Dissertations in Religion No. 20 (Philadelphia: Fortress Press, 1987), discusses the background and meaning of this saying in great detail. He believes Paul is citing a baptismal formula, as attested in the *Gospel according to the Egyptians*. It seems more logical to me that the saying originated in the liturgy and then found its way onto the lips of Jesus, much as numerous other items preserved in a pre-Jesus form in the epistles did. Think of "Abba, Father," as one example.

[19]See the discussion of ransom and redemption in Washington Gladden, *How Much Is Left of the Old Doctrines? A Book for the People* (Boston and New York: Houghton Mifflin, 1899), 176-179.

[20]Maccoby, *Paul and Hellenism*, 49.

[21]John J. Clabeaux, *A Lost Edition of the Letters of Paul: A Reassessment of the Text of the Pauline Corpus Attested by Marcion*, Catholic Biblical Quarterly Monograph Series No. 21 (Washington, D. C.: Catholic Biblical Association of America, 1989), 3.

[22]Detering, "Falsified Paul," 103, 124-25.

[23]Gerald Prince, *Narratology: The Form and Function of Narrative* (Berlin: Walter de Gruyter and Company, 1982), 34.

13.

Laodiceans and Ephesians

Ancient writers relate that Marcion's canon included a Pauline epistle to the people of Laodicea. Tertullian thought this was most likely Marcion's version of what we call Ephesians. After all, some manuscripts do not specify any destination or recipient, which in this case later scribes might have filled in conjecturally as "Ephesians." We also know that the Marcionite version lacked some of the words and passages familiar to us from the canonical version. I find myself persuaded by John Knox,[1] R. Joseph Hoffmann,[2] and Joseph B. Tyson[3] that the Marcionite version was earlier and that the more familiar version is a Catholicized redaction. In this, I follow Hoffmann's conjectures about what was added, placing a few suspected passages in brackets in this presentation.

Edgar J. Goodspeed[4] demonstrated, via a kind of Synoptic relationships chart, how the epistle makes the most sense as an introduction to a collection of epistles. Indeed, it explicitly refers to the texts that follow it (3:3-4). The content is based mainly upon Colossians but adds an elaborate mosaic of passages quoted or paraphrased from the collected epistles except for the Pastorals, which were written later to oppose Marcionism. It connects the quotes and paraphrases in long sentences that are the result of a cut-and-paste method of composition, and this is the reason the text sounds Pauline and, at the same time, strangely non-Pauline. The content is Pauline but the redactional form is not. For the reader's convenience, I have listed the component source texts by verse at the bottom of each page.[5]

To summarize, the epistle would have been composed as a preface by the first collector of the Pauline Corpus. Goodspeed, followed by Knox,[6] nominated the freed slave Onesimus for this honor (see Col. 4:9; Philm. 10; Ign. *Eph.* 1:3; 2:1; 6:2), as we saw in chapter 3. But Walter Bauer[7] and F. C. Burkitt[8] considered Marcion the most likely candidate since he is the first person we know of who had a collection of the epistles and a pressing reason for collecting them. However, I fear this is, once again, a confusion of Marcion's achievements with others who came later and acted in his name. If we make Marcion the author of the first version of Galatians 3-6, then we have to credit Laodiceans to some later Marcionite who had the whole collection ready at hand. I think the epistle was still in the works in Marcion's day, in different versions in Gnostic, Catholicizing, and Marcionite circles.

Hoffmann and Winsome Munro[9] see the second half of traditional Ephesians (chapters 4-6) as heavily interpolated, with harmonizing, Catholicizing material added to it. I see in these chapters a second letter that was added as a Catholic appendix because it served as a rejoinder to the original Marcionite Laodiceans. The Catholic author saw, as one can hardly help seeing, how the original writer mined Pauline texts as the building blocks for his own epistle. The Catholic author continued the same procedure through chapters 4-6 but couldn't maintain the long, contrived sentence structure, which he gradually abandoned. Likewise, he decided to use the rest of Colossians, which the Laodicean writer had merely cut off, as the basis to write his own continuation. I cannot get past the form-critical consideration: surely 3:20-21 is intended as the closing of an epistle. All admit that the Gospel of John must have concluded with 20:30-31, making chapter 21 an appendix. Similarly, Romans tries to conclude at 11:36, then again at 15:32, and yet again at 16:27, all because scribes could not leave well enough alone. So I say that whatever follows Ephesians 3:20-21 must not have belonged to the original letter. Chapters 4-6 were at first a separate letter, or at least they certainly seem to open like one. I have supplied the name Paul, underlining the parallel between Ephesians 4:1 with 2 Corinthians 10:1, the beginning of a separate Pauline epistle subsequently joined to other Corinthian letters and letter-fragments. But no name would have been necessary, as witness Hebrews, 1 John, and others. The absence of a name made it easier for some subsequent scribe to join the Catholicizing Ephesians with its original counterpart, the Marcionite Laodiceans. Catholicizing the interpolations into Laodiceans cemented the union. The conflation process would have been pretty much the same as that which produced our familiar versions of 2 Corinthians, 1 and 2 Thessalonians, and Philippians, according to Walter Schmithals.[10]

1

[1]Paul, apostle of Christ-Jesus by the will of God, to the saints *at Ephesus*, believers in Christ-Jesus: [2]May the favor and protection of God our Father and the Lord Jesus-Christ be with you.

[3]May the God and Father of our Lord Jesus-Christ dwell in bliss, he who has endowed us with every spiritual blessing in the celestial spheres by virtue of our incorporation in Christ, [4]just as he selected us before the creation of the world for us to be holy and flawless in his sight, [5]in his love predestining us for adoption as sons for himself, through Jesus-Christ, according to the decided preference of his will, [6]to the end that all might extol the splendor of his favor, with

---

1:2. Col. 1:1-2
1:3. Cor. 1:3; Rom. 1:11b
1:4. Col. 3:12b; 1 Cor. 1:27a, 22b; 2 Thess. 2:13b
1:5. Rom. 8:29; Gal. 4:5b; 3:26; Phil. 2:13
1:6. Phil. 1:11b; Rom. 5:15b; 2 Cor. 9:14b, 15

which he favored us, insofar as we are joined to the one he loved, *⁷the one by whom we have received release through his blood, the forgiveness of trespasses*, the index of the abundance of his favor, ⁸which he lavished upon us in the form of all manner of wisdom, both esoteric and practical, ⁹disclosing to us the hitherto unsuspected design, which delighted him and which he silently resolved ¹⁰to administer in the pleroma of the times, to subsume the All in Christ, including what is in the concentric heavens and what is on the earth, ¹¹in whom also we were selected as his inheritance, thus predestined in accord with the universal design that operates by the judgment of his will, ¹²to the end that we should be a cause for extolling his splendor, those who had already placed our hopes on Christ; ¹³in whom you believed once you heard the message of truth, the news of your salvation, and in whom, as you believed, you were marked with the stamp of the promised Holy Spirit, ¹⁴a down payment on our eventual inheritance till the full purchase of the goods, so his splendor may be extolled!

¹⁵Therefore, I too, since I heard of the faith in the Lord Jesus that had appeared among you, and your love to all the saints, ¹⁶have never stopped rendering thanks on your behalf, making mention of you in my prayers, ¹⁷that the God of our Lord Jesus-Christ, the glorious Father, may grant you a spirit of esoteric wisdom and revelation with full knowledge of him, ¹⁸the eyes of your mind being enlight-

1:7. Col. 1:20b; 1:14b; Rom. 5:9b; 3:25, 26a; 2 Cor. 5:19b; Rom. 2:4a; 11:33b
1:8. Col. 1:9b; Rom. 5:15b
1:9. Col. 1:27a; 1 Cor. 2:7; Phil. 2:13b; Rom. 16:25b-26a
1:10. Col. 1:25b; 1:20; Gal. 4:4a; Rom. 13:9b; 1 Cor. 15:27
1:11. Col. 1:12b; Rom. 8:30a; 8:28b; 1 Cor. 12:6b; Phil. 2:13
1:12. Rom. 9:23-24; Phil. 1:11b; Rom. 8:30c
1:13. Col. 1:5b-6a; 2 Cor. 6:7a; Rom. 1:16b; 10:14b; 1 Cor. 1:22; Gal. 3:14b
1:14. Col. 1:12b; 1:14a; Rom. 8:23b; 1 Thess. 5:9b; Phil. 1:11b
1:15. Col. 1:9a; Phil. 5
1:16. Col. 1:9; Phil. 1:3-4a; Phlm. 4; Rom. 1:9a, 10a
1:17. Col. 1:3; 2 Cor. 11:31a; Rom. 6:4b; 16:25b; 2 Cor. 1:3b; 1 Cor. 2:8b; 2:10a
1:18. Col. 1:12b, 26b-27; 2 Cor. 4:4b; Rom. 9:23a; 1:21b

ened so you may know the nature of the goal he has called you to, the wealth of the splendor of his bequest to the saints [19]and the unimaginable greatness of the power he wields on our behalf—for us who have believed—appropriate to the energizing might of his strength, [20]which he exercised toward Christ when he raised him from the dead, enthroning him at his right in the heavenly spheres [21]far above all archons, authorities, powers, lordships, and every divine name invoked not only in this age but even in the one to come, [22]and subjugated all things under his feet, and bestowed upon him rule over all for the benefit of the church, [23]which is his body, the pleroma of the one who permeates all things.

2

[1]And you, *then dead in your trespasses and sins,* [2]the way you behaved, following the fashion of this age of the world, dictated by the archon of the authority of the air, the spirit now energizing those who are disobedient, [3]in whose company we too used to busy ourselves back then, with the lusts of our flesh, carrying out the wishes and the understandings of the flesh and thus intrinsically targets of wrath like the rest; [4]but God, who is rich in mercy, because of his great love with which he loved us, [5]*even with us dead in trespasses, vivified us along with Christ—and by his favor you have been saved—*[6]and he co-raised us and co-enthroned us in the heavenly spheres in Christ-Jesus, [7]in order that he might make of us a lasting monument

---

1:19. Col. 1:11a; 2 Cor. 9:14b; Phil. 3:10b, 21b; Rom. 3:22b
1:20. Col. 1:29b; 3:1b; 1 Cor. 6:14; Phil. 2:9-10; Rom. 8:34
1:21. Col. 2:10b; 1 Cor. 15:24b
1:22. Col. 1:18a; Rom. 12:5a; 11:36a; 1 Cor. 15:28b
2:1. Col. 2:13a; Rom. 6:11b
2:2. Gal. 3:19-20; 4:3; Col. 2:13-15; Col. 3:7a; 1:13a; Rom. 12:2a; 1 Cor. 2:12b; 2 Thess. 2:3b, 4a, 7a, 13b; Rom. 15:31a
2:3. Col. 3:6b-7; 1:21; 3:6b; 2 Cor. 1:12b; Rom. 15:14b; Gal. 5:16, 24; Rom. 8:7; Gal. 5:19; 2:15a; 1 Thess. 5:9a
2:4. Rom. 11:32b-33a; 5:8; 2 Thess. 2:16b
2:5. Col. 2:13a; Rom. 3:24a
2:6. Col. 2:12b; 3:1, 3
2:7. Rom. 9:23a; 2:4a; Col. 1:4b

for ages to come of the unimaginable wealth of the favor he showed us in Christ-Jesus. [8]For it is by his favor that you have been saved through faith, and such salvation is not your own doing: it is the gift of God. [9]It comes not by virtue of deeds, *otherwise someone might brag.* [10]For we are his achievement, created by initiation into Christ-Jesus *for good deeds, which God had already scheduled for us to perform.* [11]So remember how, when you were physically gentiles, those dismissed as "the uncircumcision" by those who flattered themselves "the circumcision" due to an operation performed by hand, [12]you were then without Christ, long alienated from the commonwealth of Israel, completely outside of the covenants of promise, bereft of hope for salvation and wandering without God in the world. [13]But now, grafted into Christ-Jesus, you, then remote, were brought near *by means of the blood of Christ.* [14]For he himself is our peace accord, the one who has made both one, having demolished the middle barrier wall; [15]and having abolished in his flesh the occasion for enmity, namely the Torah of commandments and decrees, in order that he might create in himself one new man from the two, making peace, [16]and reconciling both in the one body to God by means of the cross, killing the enmity in himself; [17]upon his arrival he announced the news of peace to the ones far off and peace to those nearby; [18]because through him we both have access through the same Spirit into the presence of the Father. [19]In that case you are no longer foreigners or resident aliens, but you are fellow citizens with the saints and members of the house-

---

2:8. Rom. 3:24; 8:24; 6:23b; 3:28a
2:9. Rom. 9:32b; 1 Cor. 1:29-30a
2:10. Col. 3:9-10; 1:10a; 2 Cor. 5:17a; 9:8b
2:11. Col. 2:11; 1 Cor. 12:2a; 8:5a; Gal. 6:15; Rom. 2:28b
2:12. Col. 1:21a; Rom. 9:4; 1 Thess. 4:13b; 4:5b; Gal 4:8-9a
2:13. Col. 1:22; Gal. 3:23b
2:14. Col. 1:20b; Rom. 5:1b; Gal. 3:28c, 28a
2:15. Col. 2:14a; 1:21b; 3:9b-10a; 1:19b-20a
2:16. Col. 1:22; 1 Cor. 12:13a
2:17. Isa. 52:7b; 57:19
2:18. Rom. 5:2a; 1 Cor. 12:13a; Phil. 1:27b
2:19. Col. 3:11a; Phil. 3:20a; Gal. 6:10b

hold of God, ²⁰*built squarely on the foundation of the apostles and prophets.* Christ-Jesus himself serving as cornerstone, ²¹in whom also the building, its uncut stones being carefully fitted together, are growing into a shrine befitting the Lord, ²²in whom also you are being assembled into a spiritual dwelling for God.

3

¹For just this reason, I, Paul, the prisoner of Christ-Jesus on behalf of you gentiles—²that is, assuming you are familiar with my assigned position dispensing God's favor on your behalf, ³namely, how by way of revelation, the hidden plan was made known to me, as I have previously written briefly, ⁴from which, as you read it, you can see for yourselves my grasp of the unfolding mystery of Christ, ⁵which in previous generations had never been made known to the human race as it has now been revealed by the Spirit [to his holy apostles and prophets], ⁶that the gentiles should become joint heirs and a common body and co-sharers of the promise thanks to Christ-Jesus through the news, ⁷whose servant I became through the gift of the favor of God given me as his power energized me. ⁸To me, the least of all saints, this favor was shown, to evangelize to the nations the inscrutable riches of Christ, ⁹and finally to make manifest the administration of the providential plan previously hidden for all the

---

2:20. Col. 2:7b; 1 Cor. 3:11a; 12:28a; 3:10-11b
2:21. Col. 2:19b; 1 Cor. 3:9b; 3:16b; 3:7b; 2 Cor. 6:16b
2:22. Col. 2:7b; 1 Cor. 3:16b; Rom. 8:9
3:1. Col. 1:24a; Phlm. 1; Rom. 11:13a
3:2. Gal. 1:13a; Col. 1:25b; 1 Cor. 9:17b; Gal. 2:9b; 1 Cor. 1:4b
3:3. 1 Cor. 2:10a; Gal. 1:12; Col. 1:26a
3:4. Col. 4:16a; 1 Cor. 5:9a; Col. 1:9b; 2 Cor. 11:6b; Col. 4:3b; 1 Cor. 2:7; Rom. 16:25b
3:5. Col. 1:26b; 1 Cor. 2:8a; Rom. 16:26
3:6. Rom. 8:17b; 12:5a; Gal. 3:26-29; Rom. 4:13-14, 16-17; 2 Thess. 2:14b
3:7. Col. 1:23b, 25, 29b; Rom. 5:15b; 12:3
3:8. Col. 1:27; Gal. 1:16b; Rom. 11:33
3:9. Col. 1:25b-26; 3:3b; 1:16b; 1 Cor. 2:7; Rom. 16:25

ages from the God who created all things, [10]in order that the many-sided wisdom of God might at last be made known through the Church to the archons and to the authorities in the heavenly spheres, [11]in accord with the purpose at work in the aions, which he achieved in Christ-Jesus our Lord, [12]in whom therefore we have boldness and confident access to God through faith in him.

[13]This is why I ask you not to give up hope as you hear of my afflictions on your behalf, which are actually something for you to brag about! [14]For this reason I kneel before the Father, [15][the prototype of all fatherhood in the skies and on the earth,] [16]asking that he may give you richly, befitting the wealth of his splendor, powerful strength in the inner self through his Spirit, [17]so that Christ may live in your hearts by faith, having been firmly rooted and securely founded, [18]in order for you to have the strength to comprehend, along with the rest of the saints, Platos, Mekos, Hypsos, and Bathos, [19]and to know Christ's love that surpasses all esoteric knowledge, to the end that you may be filled to the full extent of all the pleroma of God!

[20]Now to him who is able to do superabundantly beyond anything we ask or think, thanks to the power energizing us, [21]be all worship in the church and in Christ-Jesus throughout all the generations of ages multiplied by ages! Amen!

The first anti-Marcionite interpolation we can detect is in verse

---

3:10. Col. 1:16; Rom. 8:38; 2 Cor. 8:18b; 1 Cor. 2:7
3:11. Rom. 8:28b; 1 Cor. 2:7b
3:12. Rom. 5:1b-2; 2 Cor. 3:4, 12
3:13. Col. 1:24a; 2:1; 1 Thes. 2:20a
3:14. Rom. 14:11b; Isa. 45:23; Phil. 2:10
3:15. 1 Cor. 8:5b
3:16. Col. 1:27b; Rom. 9:23a; 1 Cor. 16:13b; Rom. 15:13b, 19b; 7:22; 2 Cor. 4:16b
3:17. Col. 1:19; 2:7a; 1:23a; Rom. 8:9b; 1 Cor. 3:16b; 2 Cor. 1:22b
3:18. Rom. 8:39; 1 Cor. 2:10. And see Col. 2:2b-3; 2 Cor. 1:1b
3:19. Col. 2:2b-3; 1:9b; 2:9-10a; Rom. 8:35a
3:20. Col. 1:29b; Rom. 16:25a
3:21. Rom. 11:36b; Gal. 1:5a; 1 Cor. 6:4b, 7:17b; Col. 1:26b; Gal. 1:5b

1:7a, "the one by whom we have received release through his blood, the forgiveness of trespasses." In Marcionite soteriology, the death of Jesus was a ransom, manumitting the enslaved creatures of the demiurge, not a sacrifice for sins. The same problem occurs in 2:5 where another insertion, "even with us dead in trespasses, vivified us along with Christ—and by his favor you have been saved," attempts to correct Marcionite belief. Verse 2:1 likewise contains an anti-Marcionite interpolation, "then dead in your trespasses and sins." No one was in trouble with the Father for having transgressed the commandments of the demiurge.

Gnosticism announces itself in 1:21, based on the Colossian original, with its list of successive hierarchies of heavenly beings who rule the concentric celestial spheres and separate us from the Father. God, in turn, is found deep within the pleroma ("fullness") of light, from which all divine entities emerge and into which, in Christ, all will once again be absorbed at the last. The ruler (archon) of the power of the air (2:2) would be one of the elemental spirits or angels administering the weather, as in Galatians 4:3, 9.

A pair of insertions tries to correct the Marcionite estimation of Paul as the only apostle and to win respect for Old Testament prophets as well. First, 2:20 says the church has been "built squarely on the foundation of the apostles and prophets," then 3:5b refers to "his holy apostles and prophets." Tertullian preserves the original Marcionite reading at 3:9, according to which the saving plan of the Father was unknown to the Creator: "hidden *from* the God who created all things," namely the demiurge, not "*in* the God who created all things."

Another anti-Marcionite interpolation (3:15) tries to combine the Marcionite Father with the Jewish Creator, making the Father "the prototype of all fatherhood in the skies and on the earth." For Marcionites, the Father of Jesus Christ certainly had nothing to do with the disgusting process of human reproduction. By contrast, 3:19 is definitely Gnostic, referring to the pleroma of God, which is the Godhead itself. It contains the aions, divine beings emanating from the Unknown Father before all time. Christian Gnostics identified Christ with this pleroma. This concept of Christ is paralleled in the Lore of Creation in the Jewish Kabbalah, where the externalized image of God, *Adam Kadmon*, could not be contained in the impure light-vessels (*Kelipoth*) that were prepared for it.[11]

4

[1]I, Paul, the prisoner of the Lord, urge you to behave in a manner befitting the high calling you have received, [2]always with humility and meekness, with long-suffering, bearing with one another in love, [3]eager to maintain the unity of the Spirit in the strong tie of peace: [4]one body, one Spirit, just as you were called in one prospect to which you were summoned: [5]namely, one Lord, one confession, one rite of baptism; [6]one God and Father of all, the one who reigns over all and permeates all things equally.

[7]But to each one was given a charisma as Christ deemed appropriate. [8]That is why it says, "Ascending to the Zenith he took captive all captivity and dispensed gifts to humanity." [9]Now the phrase "he ascended"—what does that mean if he had not already descended here to the sublunar world? [10]The one thus descending is identical with the one who also ascended far above all the concentric heavens in order that he might there permeate all things. [11]And in this very process he made some into apostles, some prophets, some evangelists, some shepherds and teachers, [12]for the perfecting of the saints and the task of ministry, the building of the body of Christ, [13]until the day we all arrive together at the unity of faith and of the full knowledge of the Son of God, which will be mature adulthood as measured

---

4:1. Rom. 12:1a; Phlm. 1; 2 Cor. 10:1a; Col. 1:10a; 2 Thess. 2:12b
4:2. Col. 3:12-13a, 14-15; Phil. 2:3b; 1 Thess. 4:9b
4:3. Col. 3:15
4:4. Col. 3:15; 1 Cor. 10:17b; 12:13; Rom. 12:4a, 5a; 1 Cor. 7:20
4:6. 1 Cor. 8:6a; Rom. 11:36a; 9:5b
4:7. Rom. 12:6a; 5:15b; 1 Cor. 12:7-11
4:8. Ps. 68:18
4:9. Rom. 10:6b
4:10. Rom. 10:7
4:11. 1 Cor. 12:28a; Rom. 12:6-8b
4:12. 2 Cor. 13:9b; 12:19c; 1 Cor. 14:26b; 12:27a
4:13. Phil. 3:11; Phlm. 6; Col. 1:28b; 2:9-10a; 1 Cor. 2:6a

by the stature of the full completion of Christ, [14]in order that we may no longer be naive, blown over and spun about by every new wind-gust of teaching by the trickery of charlatans with cleverness and craftiness to deceive; [15]rather, speaking the truth with love, we may assimilate to him in every respect, him who is the chief, Christ, the head [16]from whom the whole body, as it fits together and knits itself together through every ligament and artery, each playing its proper role, makes for the growth of the body, building itself in mutual love.

[17]Therefore I say this, bearing witness in the sight of the Lord: you are no longer to behave as the nations do in the futility of their thinking, [18]having become blinded in their intellect, alienated from the life of God because of the ignorance infesting them, on account of the obtuseness of their minds, [19]who having thrown all scruples aside abandoned themselves to prostitution, to perform every kind of unclean act for money. [20]But that is not what you learned of Christ—[21]if indeed you did hear him and were taught by him the truth as it is revealed in Jesus, [22]namely, that regarding your previous behavior, you must strip off the old self, reeking of the lusts of deceit, [23]and be renewed in your mode of thinking, [24]and clothe yourself in the new self, created by God's design, fragrant with the righteousness and holiness of truth. [25]Accordingly, renouncing lying, speak the truth, each one of you, to your neighbor, because we are body parts of one another! What if the hand were on fire, if it should lie to the heart, saying, "I do not hurt"? Soon you should lack the hand!

4:14. Col. 2:8; 1 Cor. 3:1b; 14:20
4:15. Col. 1:10b, 18a; 1 Cor. 11:3b
4:16. Col. 2:19a; 1:29b; Phil. 3:21
4:17. Col. 2:4; Gal. 5:3a; Col. 3:7
4:18. Col. 1:21a; Rom. 10:3a; 11:25b
4:19. Col. 3:5b; Rom. 1:24a; 2 Cor. 12:21b
4:20. Col. 2:6
4:21. Col. 2:7; 2 Cor. 11:10a; Rom. 9:1a
4:22. Col. 3:8a, 9b; Rom. 13:12b
4:23. Col. 2:18b; Rom. 12:2b; Gal. 3:27b
4:24. Col. 3:10; Gal. 3:27b; Rom. 12:5
4:25. Col. 3:8a, 9a; Rom. 12:5

[26]If you are angry, nonetheless do not sin; do not let the sun go down before you resolve the matter, [27]or you may open an opportunity for the Accuser. [28]Have the thief stop stealing; instead, have him use his nimble fingers at some good craft, so he may have enough, as well as some to share with the needy. [29]See to it that no corrupt speech issues from your lips, but speak if you have something constructive to say for your hearers, which will be a gift to them. [30]And do not offend the Holy Spirit of God, by whom you have been marked as belonging to God, looking forward to the day he claims you fully for his own. [31]Thus, repudiate all bitterness and anger and rage and shouting and blasphemy among you, with all the rest of the evils. [32]And be kind to one another, tender-hearted, forgiving each other as God, too, thanks to Christ, forgave you.

5

[1]Therefore, be imitators of God, like beloved children who eagerly imitate their parents. [2]And conduct yourselves with love, as Christ, too, loved you and handed himself over for our sakes, an offering and a sacrifice to produce a sweet savor satisfying to God. [3]But let no whore-mongering or impurity or greed ever be detected among you, as befits saints, [4]neither shameful acts nor moronic chatter nor off-color jokes, none of which is appropriate, but instead thanksgiving. [5]Don't be unaware of this: no whoremonger or impure person or greedy man, who is guilty of idolatry, has any share in the Kingdom

---

4:26. Col. 3:8b; 1 Cor. 15:34a; Rom. 12:19b
4:27. 2 Cor. 2:11
4:28. 1 Thess. 4:11b, 12b; Rom. 12:13a
4:29. Col. 3:8; 1 Cor. 14:26b
4:30. 1 Thess. 5:19; 2 Cor. 1:22; Rom. 8:23b
4:31. Col. 3:8
4:32. Col. 3:12-13
  5:1. Col. 3:12a; 1 Cor. 4:16b; 11:1
  5:2. Rom. 14:15b; Gal. 2:20b; Phil. 4:18b
  5:3. Col. 3:5a; 2 Cor. 12:21b; 1 Cor. 5:11b
  5:4. Col. 3:8, 18b; 2:7b; 3:17b; 1 Thess. 5:18a
  5:5. Col. 3:5b; 1 Cor. 6:9a

of Christ and of God. [6]Let no one deceive you with hollow words; it is just this sort of thing that is going to bring the ire of God down on the disobedient. [7]Therefore, do not share in their work! [8]You used to be part of the darkness; but now, as part of the Lord, you are light; so conduct yourselves as befits enlightened ones. [9]For what the light yields is all goodness and righteousness and truth, [10]demonstrating in practice what delights the Lord. [11]Have nothing to do with the sterile works of darkness, but rather go so far as to reprove them when you see someone else committing them. [12]It is degrading even to mention the shameful acts they perform behind closed doors, [13]but everything reproved by the light thereby becomes exposed for all to see, since for a thing to be made manifest means that it is illuminated. [14][This is why it says, "Get up, O sleeper! Stand up from the heap of corpses! And Christ will illuminate you."]

[15]So give close attention to your manner of behavior, not like the unwise, but the wise, [16]thereby giving new meaning to time otherwise wasted, for the days are evil. [17]Therefore do not be heedless, but discern the will of the Lord. [18]And do not get drunk on wine, which leads to dissipation; instead, be filled with the Spirit, [19]speaking to one another in psalms and hymns and inspired songs, singing and hymning from your hearts to the Lord, [20]ever giving thanks for

---

5:6. Col. 2:4b; Rom. 1:18a
5:7. 2 Cor. 6:14; 2 John 11
5:8. Rom. 2:19b; 1 Thess. 5:5
5:9. Gal. 5:22-23
5:10. Col. 3:20b; Rom. 12:2b; Phil. 4:18b
5:11. 2 Cor. 6:14b; Rom. 12:2b
5:12. Col. 3:8a; 1 Cor. 4:5
5:13. 1 Cor. 14:24b-25a; 4:5b
5:14. Isa. 51:17a; 52:1a; 26:19b
5:15. Col. 4:5; Rom. 13:13a
5:16. Col. 4:5; Gal. 1:4b
5:17. Col. 4:12b; Rom. 12:2b
5:18. Acts 2:4, 15; Rom. 13:13b
5:19. Col. 3:16b
5:20. Col. 3:17; 1 Thess. 5:18a; Phil. 1:3-4

all things to God the Father, invoking the name of our Lord Jesus-Christ, [21]submitting yourselves one to the other for fear of Christ's judgment on the proud, [22]the wives to their own husbands as if to the Lord, [23]because a husband is chief of the wife, just as Christ is chief of the church, being savior of the Body. [24]But as the church is subject to Christ, so too must wives be subject to their husbands in every matter. [25]Husbands, love your wives, just as Christ loved the church and handed himself over for its sake, [26]in order that he might sanctify it, cleansing it by immersion in the truth, [27]in order that he might present the church to himself radiant and rejuvenated: without age spots, wrinkles, or any such thing, but rather that it might appear holy and unblemished. [28]So it behooves husbands to love their wives like their own bodies. The one who loves his own wife loves himself since she will return his love. [29]For whoever heard of a man hating his own flesh? No, he nourishes it and cherishes it—just as Christ did the church, [30]because we are all alike members of his Body. [31]"For this cause a man shall leave father and mother and shall by joined to his wife, and the two shall become one flesh." [32]This mystery is profound, but I am speaking of Christ and the church. [33]Nonetheless, it applies also to each one of you: let each one love his wife as himself, and let the wife fear her husband.

6

[1]Children, obey your parents if they are believers in the Lord, for this is right. [2]"Honor your father and mother," which was the first

---

5:21. Gal. 5:13b; Phil. 2:3b
5:22. Col. 3:18
5:23. 1 Cor. 11:3b; Col. 1:18
5:25. Col. 3:19; Gal. 2:20b
5:26. 1 Cor. 6:11b
5:27. Col. 1:22b; 2 Cor. 11:2b
5:28. Col. 3:19a; 1 Cor. 7:3-4
5:30. 1 Cor. 6:15a; Rom. 12:5
5:31. Gen. 2:24
5:33. Col. 3:18a; 1 Cor. 7:2b
 6:1. Col. 3:20

commandment with a promise attached: [3]"so it may go well with you and you may extend your time on earth." [4]And fathers, do not provoke your children to rebellion, but nurture them in the discipline and admonition of the Lord. [5]Slaves, obey your masters in this world with fear and trembling, with single-minded devotion, as you do Christ, [6]not merely to seem to be serving while the master is watching, like those who curry favor, but as slaves of Christ, doing God's will from the soul, [7]with good humor, serving as slaves to the Lord, not merely to mortals, mindful that each one, whatever good deed he does, he will be repaid by the Lord, whether slave or free. [9]And masters, do the same toward them, thinking twice before threatening, mindful that both their master and yours watches from the sky and he is not impressed by any mortal rank.

[10]Finally, draw power from the Lord and from the might of his strength. [11]Don the complete armor of God to equip yourselves to stand unvanquished against the methods of the Accuser, [12]for our conflict is not with flesh-and-blood enemies, but against the archons, against the authorities, against the cosmocrators of the darkness that surrounds us, against the spiritual entities of evil in the heavenly spheres! [13]That is why you must put on the complete suit of divine armor, in order that you may not be vanquished on the day evil attacks, and having taken every precaution, to stand with head unbowed! [14]So stand fast, latching the belt of truth and putting on

---

6:3. Exod. 20:12
6:4. Col. 3:21; 1 Cor. 4:14b
6:5. Col. 3:22a
6:6. Col. 3:22b, 24b
6:7. Col. 3:22c-25a
6:8. Gal. 3:28b; 1 Cor. 12:13b
6:9. Col. 4:1; Rom. 2:11
6:10. Col. 1:11a; Phil. 4:13; 2 Thess. 1:9b
6:11. Rom. 13:12b; 1 Cor. 16:13; 2 Cor. 2:11
6:12. Col. 1:16b; Rom. 8:38b; 2 Cor. 10:3-4
6:13. Col. 3:12a; 4:12b
6:14. Isa. 11:5; 59:17; 1 Thess. 5:8b

the breastplate of righteousness, [15]your feet shod with readiness to announce the news of peace; [16]and most important, taking up the shield of faith and having been fully equipped, you will be able to extinguish all the flame-tipped darts of the Accuser. [17]And take the helmet of salvation and the sword of the Spirit, which is the command of God. [18]This you may do through all prayer and petition, praying on every occasion in the ecstasy of the Spirit and keeping vigil with every bit of perseverance and petitioning on behalf of the saints, [19]as well as on my behalf, that I may be given effective speech when I open my mouth, boldly making known the hidden plan of the news, [20]on behalf of which I serve as ambassador, albeit chained, in order that I may indeed speak it boldly as my position requires.

[21]But so as to keep you apprised of my affairs, what I am up to, I have dispatched Tychicus, beloved brother and faithful servant in the Lord's work, [22]whom I sent you for this specific purpose: for you to learn about us and comfort your hearts.

[23]Peace to the brothers and love, with faith, from God the Father and the Lord Jesus-Christ. [24]May divine favor visit all who love our Lord Jesus-Christ with integrity.

In verse 4:6, the reference to "one God" refutes the doctrine of the Marcionites that posits two Gods (1:17; 2:2; 3:9-12). If the Catholic writer seeks to reduce the number of deities, he equally wants to expand the number of apostles (4:11). Marcionism is subtly dismissed as a fad without merit in 4:14 and the author is just as intent, despite some vagueness, in 4:31 when he mentions blasphemy. Can

---

6:15. Isa. 52:7b
6:17. 1 Thess. 5:8c; Isa. 59:17
6:18. Col. 4:2a; 1 Thess. 5:17, 18a
6:19. Luke 21:14-15; Col. 4:3b-4; 2:15b; Rom. 15:30b; Phil. 1:20b; 2 Thess. 2:2b
6:20. Acts 28:20b; Col. 4:3-4; 2 Cor. 5:20a; Phlm. 9b
6:21. Col. 2:1a; 4:7-8
6:22. Col. 4:7-8
6:23. 2 Thess. 1:2
6:24. Col. 4:18b; 1 Cor. 16:22-24; 15:42b

he have thought his readers might be casually maligning God? No, of course, he refers to the unwitting but real blasphemy of the Marcionites who deny the identification of the Christian God with the Hebrew Jehovah.

Notice that our Catholic writer is at home with the language of sacrifice (5:2), which was alien to Marcionites but re-applied allegorically to Jesus by Catholics. He does not hesitate to quote Jewish scripture (4:8; 5:14, 31; 6:3, 17), and already in 2:17 he may have inserted an anti-Marcionite verse. The Catholic response was to allegorize the Old Testament and make it seem to teach Christianity. An excellent example greets us in 5:32, where the union of man and woman in Genesis 2:24 is said to really be about the union of Christ and the church, much as Rabbinic allegory abstracted the spicy Song of Solomon to make it an unlikely paean to Jehovah's love for Israel.

NOTES

[1] John Knox, *Marcion and the New Testament: An Essay in the Early History of the Canon* (Chicago: University of Chicago Press, 1942).

[2] R. Joseph Hoffmann, *Marcion: On the Restitution of Christianity: An Essay on the Development of Radical Paulinist Theology in the Second Century*, AAR Academy Series 46 (Chico: Scholars Press, 1984).

[3] Joseph B. Tyson, *Marcion and Luke-Acts: A Defining Struggle* (Columbia: University of South Carolina Press, 2006).

[4] Edgar J. Goodspeed, *The Key to Ephesians: A Provocative Solution to a Problem in the Pauline Literature* (Chicago: University of Chicago Press, 1956).

[5] "While this man [the author of Ephesians] shows, by what he says, that he has much in common with Paul, his way of saying it shows that, when he is actually composing a sentence, his mind works in a very different way from Paul's" (Percy N. Harrison, "The Author of Ephesians," in *Studia Evangelica*, ed. Frank L. Cross, Second International Congress on New Testament Studies at Christ Church (Berlin: Akademie-Verlag, 1964), 2:598.

454 | The Amazing Colossal Apostle

[6]John Knox, *Philemon among the Letters of Paul: A New View of Its Place and Importance*, rev. ed. (1935; NY: Abingdon Press, 1959), 107.

[7]Walter Bauer, *Orthodoxy and Heresy in Earliest Christianity*, eds. and trans. Robert Kraft and Gerhard Krodel, et al. (Philadelphia: Fortress Press, 1971), 221.

[8]Francis C. Burkitt, *The Gospel History and Its Transmission* (1906; Edinburgh: T. and T. Clark, 1925), 318-19.

[9]Winsome Munro, *Authority in Paul and Peter: The Identification of a Pastoral Stratum in the Pauline Corpus and 1 Peter*, Society for New Testament Studies Monograph Series 45 (NY: Cambridge University Press, 1983), 37.

[10]Walter Schmithals, *Paul and the Gnostics*, trans. John E. Steely (NY: Abingdon Press, 1972).

[11]Gershom G. Scholem, "Isaac Luria and His School," in Scholem, *Major Trends in Jewish Mysticism*, trans. George Lichtheim (NY: Schocken Books, 1973), 244-86, esp. 265-69: "Superficially at least, [Luria's cosmogonic speculations] resemble the myths through which Basilides, Valentinus, or Mani tried to describe the cosmic drama, with the difference that they are vastly more complicated than these Gnostical systems" (269). Hugh J. Schonfield describes parallels to the Kabbalah in Ephesians in "The Christology of Paul," in Schonfield, *Those Incredible Christians* (NY: Bantam Books, 1968), 242-58. The Kabbalah does not posit the creation of the material world by an inferior demiurge, but the Gnostic and Kabbalistic paths run parallel when we get to the shattering of the *Kelipoth*, the shards of which formed the material world in which the projected sparks of divine light (the Shekinah) are scattered, and from which they must be re-gathered. The material world winds up, here too, as the result of an intra-divine catastrophe, and the divine photons are scattered as the result of the Fall of the Adam Kadmon, who plays pretty much the actantial role of the Gnostic demiurge. There is, accordingly, only a slight reshuffling of the mythemes.

14.

Philippians

Two great New Testament scholars, Günther Bornkamm[1] and
Walter Schmithals,[2] independently concluded that Philippians must
be a compilation of three earlier letter fragments. Both scholars
ascribed all the fragments to the historical Paul. I do not, but I do
accept Bornkamm's and Schmithals's division of the epistle into its
component parts, Epistles A, B, and C.

Epistle A (4:10-23) is only a bit longer than most genuine letters in antiquity, unlike, say, Romans or 1 Corinthians, both of which
dwarf real letters from the period. The composite letter to Philippi
seems to be a self-congratulatory piece written by and on behalf of
the Philippian church. Note the praise of the congregation at the
expense of Thessalonika and other Macedonian church sites. Thus
does a later generation of Philippian bishops affirm and defend the
superior clout of their church. More specifically, the writer wants to
secure the episcopal line of succession of Epaphroditus, imagined
or remembered here as a close colleague of Paul himself. Let it be
gratefully noted, however, that even so utilitarian and political a
letter as this contributes a gem of spiritual counsel that has become
something of a Christian mantra ever since: the Christianized Epicureanism of verses 4:11-13.

Epistle B appears in two parts, from the beginning of chapter 1 through chapter 2 and the first verse of chapter 3, with an added portion at 4:4-7. It is difficult to tell whether 1:1 is an integral part of the original letter or whether it represents the redactional frame imposed on the whole mess by a Catholic redactor. Note the anachronistic reference to bishops and deacons, as in the similarly late and spurious Pastoral Epistles. Epistle C is made up of the balance of the canonical book, from verse 3:2 through 4:3, then mopping up at 4:8-9.

1

[1]Paul and Timothy, slaves of Christ-Jesus, to all the saints of Christ-Jesus located in Philippi, with bishops and deacons. [2]May the favor and protection of God our Father and the Lord, Jesus-Christ, be extended to you!

[3]I thank my God every time I think of you, [4]always praying joyfully every time I pray for all of you, [5]on account of your partnership in the work of the news from the day we met right on till the present, [6]confident of just this: the one who has initiated a good work in you will bring it to completion until the Day of Christ-Jesus. [7]And it is right for me to think so about all of you because I carry you in my heart, whether I am imprisoned or active in the defense and the corroboration of the news, all of you being partners in my mission. [8]I swear before God how poignantly I long for you all with the compassion of Christ-Jesus. [9]And this I pray: that your love may increase even more and yet more as you reach full realization and complete perception, [10]so you may choose wisely from the various options before you in order for you to be sincere and impeccable on the Day of Christ, [11]having been filled with the fruit of righteousness by means of Jesus-Christ, that God may be worshipped and praised all the more.

[12]So then, brothers, I want you to understand that the things that have befallen me actually tend toward the advancement of the news! [13]The fact that my imprisonment stems from the cause of Christ has become evident throughout the entire praetorium and to everyone else, [14]and the greater number of the brothers find that my impris-

onment has only encouraged them to speak the message of God with greater daring. [15]It is true, some preach Christ because they envy me and want to compete with me, but others do so out of sincere motives. [16]These latter preach because of their love for me, knowing that I have been called on at present to defend the news before Caesar. [17]Those others announce Christ out of a desire to imitate me, not from pure motives, aiming to frustrate me, stuck in prison, as they think. [18]What is the sum of it? Motives notwithstanding, Christ is nonetheless being announced, and this is music to my ears, so I intend to keep right on rejoicing over it!

In 1:15-18 we come upon the occasion for the epistle: factionalism in the post-Pauline church at Philippi. There is strife between the author's Catholicized Paulinism and some other version, whose preachers this author absurdly charges with insincerity, saying they are just trying to make trouble for him. Picture the situation as implied here: Paul is in jail, and the same fate awaits those who may dare replace him in preaching the gospel. Certain Pauline enemies voluntarily take on the onus of his preaching—risking life and limb as he has done—to get his goat, just to make the authorities more irritated with him! It is ludicrous. Certainly the rivals were sincere in their faith and in their disagreements with the Catholic Paulinist who is using Paul's name here. I am guessing they were anti-martyrdom Gnostics,[3] from whom, however, the Kenosis hymn of 2:6-11 has been borrowed. The rancor may have had something to do with the disagreement between the two women, Euodia and Syntyche, referred to in verse 4:2 of Letter C.

[19]For I know that the ultimate outcome will be my deliverance, thanks to your prayers and the aid of the Spirit of Jesus-Christ, [20]which is exactly what I eagerly expect and count on, that I will never wind up disappointed, but that with all appropriate boldness, as ever, even now Christ will be manifested all the more in my case, whether through a verdict of life or of death. [21]For to me, living is Christ, and dying is only gain! [22]But if my fate is to continue in the flesh, this spells for me fruitful labor, so I cannot tell which outcome would be preferable. [23]Yes, I am caught between the two, having the

desire to abandon this life and to be with Christ, since this is by all accounts much the better, [24]but your need for me to remain in the flesh would seem to outweigh that consideration. [25]Yes, in view of that, I am quite sure I shall after all remain here and continue working with all of you so your faith may continue to mature and you to rejoice [26]so that you may have all the more reason to brag on me in gratitude to Christ-Jesus on account of my return to you!

The sentiment of 1:25 is strikingly parallel to the Mahayana Buddhist doctrine of the bodhisattvas, holy persons whose deeds have earned them their own passage into Nirvana but who linger on the threshold, concerned to aid lesser mortals in their own quests for salvation.[4] Of course, there is a closer, more familiar parallel than this: the Christian saints,[5] whose ranks the blessed apostle appears to be on the verge of joining by means of a particularly close shave. This portrayal introduces Paul's Hamlet-like stage deliberations over whether to go to his heavenly reward or to continue on for the good of his converts. The passage drips with poignant irony based on the fact that the writer knows the reader knows Paul's imprisonment will end in execution. Paul does, however, "continue with them" by means of pseudepigraphical letters like this one. This language hints at a "second coming of Paul" doctrine akin to that of Shi'ite Mahdism, where a vanished imam is expected to return someday to the faithful but in the meantime communicates with them by means of sporadic messages from self-appointed "babs" ("gates") to the Hidden Imam.[6] The Philippian epistles also function like the prophecies of the Risen Christ in early Christian congregations. They were intended to keep new generations in touch with the past, although they served to obscure the original figure behind a screen of pious accretions.

[27]Just see that you behave in a manner worthy of the news in order that, whether I come and see you in person or remain absent and only hear a report of you, you may stand undaunted in one spirit, pitching in together with a single soul in the faith of the news, [28]and not being in any way intimidated by those who oppose you. That will spell out to them the promise of their own destruction but of

your deliverance, and this at the hand of God, [29]because thus you will be seen to carry out the role assigned you on Christ's behalf: not merely to believe in him but also to suffer on his account, [30]which is of course the very same contest in which you once saw me engaged and hear me engaged in now.

2

[1]Assuming there is any encouragement to be had in the bosom of Christ, any consolation offered by love, any fellowship of spirit, any gestures of compassion or pity, [2]then won't you make my joy complete by all thinking the same thing, having the same love, being one in soul, sharing the same goal, [3]doing nothing from rivalry or grandstanding, but humbly treating each other as more important than yourselves, [4]not preoccupied with your own welfare, but concerned with the good of others as well? [5]Let there flourish among you the thinking of Christ-Jesus,

> [6]Who, disposed in the very form of a god,
>> thought ill of seizing equality with God,
> [7]but cast himself into the emptiness,
>> donning the form of a slave to the archons,
>> taking on the outer likeness of humanity,
>> to be seen clothed in mortal fashion,
> [8]he humbled himself,
>> becoming obedient to the point of death, death by
>> crucifixion.
> [9]Which is why God super-exalted him,
>> and granted him the name ranking above all others,
> [10]so hearing the name "Jesus,"
>> everyone should bend the knee,
>> all angels and men,
>> and imprisoned spirits alike.
> [11]And every tongue should acknowledge the Lordship
>> of Jesus-Christ
>> as they worship God the Father.

Our Catholic pseudepigraphist or redactor has incorporated in 2:6-11 what virtually all scholars recognize as a hymn fragment. It is archaic compared to the surrounding Catholic text, whose author no longer grasps the meaning of it. For as F. C. Baur[7] saw, the hymn clearly embodies Gnostic mythology. In it, an unnamed savior ventures forth from the pleroma of divine light into the *Kenoma*, which is the empty void outside the Godhead. In doing this he is reversing the fall of Sophia, the last of the divine aions emitted from the Godhead. Sophia had longed to look into the mysteries of the Father, which were so far distant from her. In her Pandora-like hubris, she gave birth to the bungling demiurge, the Gnostic Creator of a miserable world of disgusting matter. But the savior secretly penetrates the world of the evil archons, the angels who rule the planetary spheres, to come to earth and take on the illusory semblance of human flesh. At death, his saving mission accomplished, he returns triumphantly to the pleroma and receives the titular name of Jesus, which means "salvation."

As P. L. Couchoud[8] recognized, the hymn predates the process of re-conceiving the god Jesus as a historical figure since "Jesus" becomes his name *only after his earthly mission is complete*. Those who first sang this hymn never thought of a man named Jesus traveling the roads of Galilee, teaching and casting out demons, much less getting crucified on earth at a Roman governor's order. What the Catholic redactor appreciates about the hymn, the self-sacrifice of Christ on others' behalf, is there, but he has missed the cosmic-theological framework. He recognizes the basic pattern of descent and ascent,[9] but the Gnostic elements go right over his head.

[12]So then, my beloved ones, as you always obeyed, and not only in my presence, but now all the more in my absence, work on your salvation for yourselves with deadly seriousness, [13]seeing it is God who is energizing you with both the will and the energy to do what pleases him. [14]Carry out your duties without complaining and rationalizing, [15]so you may wind up blameless and having harmed no one, irreproachable children of God in the midst of a crooked and perverted generation, among whom you shine out like stars in the night sky, [16]holding high the standard of the message of life. All this will be fodder for my bragging on the day of Christ, when it will be seen that I did not waste the time and effort I spent on you.

As elsewhere in the epistle, Paul's absence (2:12) is really due to his death in the distant past and not, as the pretense of pseudonymity would have it, a geographical separation during his lifetime. This verse also secures the Catholic identification of Letter B: Protestants have always feared to recognize what the verse urges upon them, which is the risky business of seeing about one's own salvation, without the blithe complacency of resting in the finished work of Christ. Here is one of the clearest instances of what Käsemann called nascent Catholicism.[10]

[17]But if it should happen that I must yield up my life, I will rejoice since it will be a libation offered up with the sacrifice of your faith in divine worship, and I rejoice with all of you, [18]since I know you too will rejoice along with me.

In 2:17 we recognize a piece of "Paulology," in which the death of the apostle is seen as a kind of secondary sacrifice alongside that of Christ himself. We will be seeing more of this in Colossians. Eventually this kind of thinking will be applied across the board to all Catholic saints and martyrs.

[19]But I am confident the Lord Jesus will allow me shortly to dispatch Timothy to you so I may be cheered at the news of you. [20]For I have no colleague to compare to Timothy! He will be genuinely concerned about your affairs. [21]As for the rest of them, they seek only their own advancement, and not that of the news of Christ-Jesus; [22]but his sterling character is known to you—as a child attends his father, he attended me in the work of the news. [23]Therefore, I hope to send him the moment I see how things will turn out with me. [24]But I trust in the Lord that I, too, will be able to come before long.
[25]And yet I thought it needful to send Epaphroditus back to you, my brother and colleague and fellow soldier and your apostle sent to meet my needs, [26]since he missed you all so and was disturbed because you heard he was ill. [27]He was indeed ill, at death's door, but God had mercy on him, and not just on him, but on me also: otherwise I should have suffered grief upon grief. [28]Thus I sent him all the more eagerly so that, seeing him, you might rejoice and I may be less grieved. [29]Therefore, welcome him in the name of the Lord and hold

people like him in honor, [30]because he hovered on the brink of death for the sake of the work of Christ, putting his life at risk in order to make up the service to me that you felt you owed me.

3

[1]Finally, my brothers, rejoice in the Lord! To write the same things to you again is no burden to me, but it is salutary for you.

[2]Look out for the Cynics, beware the workers of evil, watch out for the mutilators! [3]Remember, it is we who are the circumcision, those who worship not by the flesh, but by the Spirit of God and by making Christ-Jesus our boast, not placing confidence in the carving of the flesh, [4]even though I myself have just as much reason to have confidence in the flesh. If anyone else thinks to place confidence in fleshly criteria, I have more! [5]Circumcised on the eighth day, sprung from the race of Israel, the tribe of Benjamin, a Hebrew born of Hebrews and thus no proselyte, a Pharisee in my approach to the Torah; [6]as for zeal, persecuting the church, as to righteousness measured by the Torah, impeccable. [7]But what I once considered profit, I now reckon loss on account of Christ.

[8]No, furthermore, I write off everything as a loss for the sake of the superiority of knowing Christ-Jesus, my Lord, for whose sake I suffered the loss of everything and consider it all mere dung in order that, unencumbered, I might reach Christ.

In 3:2b-8 we have a Catholic Judaizing of Paul, an attempt to bring him into the Old Testament, or "Judeo-Christian," orbit, exactly as in Acts 22:3; 23:6. Remember, part of Paul's legacy comes from Simon Magus, a Samaritan who never upheld Jewish Torah-observance. Simon believed the Law was an elaborate con-game perpetrated on mankind by devious angels. Our Catholic author supplies Paul with Jewish credentials and then at once flushes them away. Why such an improbable juxtaposition? It is precisely what we ought to expect from Catholic Christianity. The Jewish Torah was not to be cut off from the canon since Judaism was the parent of Christianity in the providence of the Creator. But with the coming of Christ, Judaism was virtually demoted to the status of a false religion, all within the same epistolary passages. The Old Testament scriptures are interpreted in terms of allegorical ventriloquism, as if the Torah taught Catholic Christianity.[11] The nascent Catholics made a bold move to both co-opt Judaism and condemn it, which was like buying a junk car in order to scavenge for parts.

[9]And be found with him, not having my salvation by the Torah but rather by belief in Christ, the salvation that comes from God based on belief: [10]to know him, to experience the miracle of his resurrection, and to share his sufferings—following the example of his death, [11]hoping that I may somehow make it as far as the upraising of the dead. [12]Not that I have already received it or have already been perfected, but I follow his footsteps on the chance that I may grab hold of his coattails as I myself was grasped by Christ-Jesus.
[13]Brothers, I do not consider myself to have grasped the prize yet, but I keep one thing in view: forgetting whatever lies behind me, I press on to that which lies ahead of me, [14]the finish line toward which I race for the heavenward summons of God through Christ-Jesus. [15]Therefore, as many as are perfect, let us think this, and if you think anything else, God will reveal to you the wisdom of what I am saying. [16]At any rate, whatever level we have attained, let us at least live up to that.

The second-century Catholic character of the letter is evident from the self-abnegating humility of the writer (3:9-14). If he is lucky, his efforts may win him salvation, and he hopes he may have what it takes to achieve the resurrection. Once again the reader is anticipated as understanding that Paul would shortly attain the martyr's perfection at the hands of Nero's executioner. Even so, the focus is on the saint's anxious efforts at persevering. Other Pauline writings evidence a firm assurance of salvation based on the finished work of the Redeemer. Here we see that we have turned a corner to early Catholicism. We might as well be reading this:

Once when a person who anxiously wavered between hope and fear was one day overcome with sadness, he prostrated himself in prayer in the church before a certain altar, and debated these things within himself, saying, "O, if I did but know that I should persevere on and on!" All at once he heard within himself the divine answer: "And what would you do if you knew this? Do now what you would then do, and you will be safe enough." (Thomas á Kempis, *Imitation of Christ*, 1.25.2)[12]

True, as 3:9 has it, deeds of Torah will not save one's soul, but there the writer has in mind ceremonial regulations, which had become passé. Nothing here says that good moral deeds are not still required.

[17]Undertake together to imitate me, brothers, and those who do behave this way, mark them well in the same way you have us for an example. [18]This is necessary because there are many of whom I often warned you, and do so again now, weeping, who are foes of the cross of Christ, [19]whose fate is destruction, whose god is their own stomach, and who are proudest of their shame—those who are worldly-minded. [20]As for us, our citizenship is in the skies, whence we also expect a savior, the Lord, Jesus-Christ, [21]who will change the form of our humiliating body to conform to his own light-body, something easy for him, given his energizing ability to subdue all things to himself.

4

[1]So then, my brothers, whom I love and long to see again, my joy and greatest achievement—in this way stand firm in the faith of the Lord! [2]I beg Euodia and I beg Syntyche to come to one mind in fellowship with the Lord. [3]And I beg you, too, loyal Syzygus, help them who fought at my side in the work of the news with both Clement and the rest of my colleagues, whose names, though they are now long dead, are enshrined in the Book of Life.

The reference to the mytheme of a heavenly book hints that the names in 4:2-3 are ideal, not those of real persons. This is especially evident in the case of "Syzygus," which seems intended as a proper name but is unattested elsewhere. As Peter Carls[13] argues, all four allegorical names are derived from themes that are prominent in Philippians itself and are intended to function like the character names in Bunyan's *Pilgrim's Progress*. Euodia denotes the "good way," the Pauline path that readers are urged to emulate (3:17). Syntyche means a "joyful union," to which Paul likewise urges readers (4:2). Syzygus means "yoke-fellow," which embodies the function of mediation and makes the fictive Syzygus a figure whose identity equals his narrative function. [14] Clement's name elicits peace, signifying the harmonious condition of "forbearance" and "patience" referred to in verse 4:5. The names, then, are those of imaginary members of the founding generation of the Philippian church of Paul's day, not of actual forbears of the readers.

[4]Rejoice in your faith in the Lord always! Let me repeat that: rejoice! [5]Let your patience with others be an example to them. The coming of the Lord is near! [6]There is no need to be apprehensive, just see that in every matter you inform God of your requests by prayer and petition, not neglecting thanksgiving. [7]This way, the peace of God, justified by no earthly calculation, will garrison your hearts and minds in the strength of Christ-Jesus.

[8]Finally, brothers, whatever is true, whatever is serious, whatever is just, whatever pure, lovable, well-regarded, as long as there is anything noble or praiseworthy about it, [9]occupy yourselves with such as this. The habits you learned and appreciated and listened to and remarked in me, adopt for your own and you may be sure the God who brings peace of mind will remain with you.

Verse 8 shows just how far we have come from the early days of Christian sectarianism when Christians believed they had some revolutionary ethic to preach. No new revelation of the truth needed here! Christians are satisfied with living up to the standards of conventional morality. Everyone knows what is right—let's just try to do it!

[10]My gratitude to the Lord was great indeed when I saw that at last you had renewed your concern for me. Of course, I know the thought is not new, only the opportunity. [11]Nor do I speak thus from deprivation, for I have long since learned how to get along fine no matter the conditions. [12]I know how to be humbled one day and to prosper the next!

Do Christians cherish an ethic of radical discipleship? Not here. Verses 11-12 embody popular Epicureanism with its counsel of moderation and contentment. The lodestar of Epicureanism was pleasure, in the refined sense of "the absence of pain from the body and turmoil from the soul." Pleasure was the chief good, but expectations were low. As long as one kept an even keel, anything especially pleasing was just icing on the cake. Otherwise one was asking for constant disappointment and frustration. It is hard to see how a Christian commitment is supposed to add anything to this. Christianity has accommodated itself to the surrounding society to which it once judged itself superior.

[12]In anything and in everything, I know the secret of interchangeably being filled and being hungry, to welcome abundance and lack equally. [13]I can do anything, given the one who empowers me! [14]But don't mistake me: you did well in coming to my aid in my time of affliction. [15]Know this, too, Philippians: in the beginning of my service to the news when I came out from Macedonia, not one congregation entered into partnership in the matter of giving and receiving except you alone. [16]Why, in Thessalonica you sent aid for my needs not once but twice! [17]It is not the gift I seek, but I seek the increase of merit in your heavenly account. [18]But I have everything and prosper! [19]I have been filled by what Epaphroditus brought from you, which rises fragrant and appetizing from the altar as a sacrifice to God. In return, my God will satisfy every need of yours abundantly from his treasury of favor in celestial splendor, thanks to Christ-Jesus. [20]Let worship redound to our God and Father throughout ages multiplied by ages! Amen.

At first we might view what is said here as a position on the financial compensation of Christian workers, opposed to that which is on display in 1 Corinthians 9:15-18, but that is not the issue here. The real point is to memorialize the Philippian congregation à la Matthew 10:40-42, glorifying the writer's own church for having bankrolled Paul's apostolic labors and so deserving a share of the credit. We are witnessing typical second-century jockeying for clout among churches (bishoprics, really) via apostolic name-dropping.

[21]Greet every saint consecrated to Christ-Jesus. The brothers visiting me greet you. [22]All the saints greet you, most of all the ones in Caesar's household. [23]May you continue to enjoy the favor of the Lord Jesus-Christ in your spirit.

Christians belonging to the household of Caesar? This is not how we usually think of early Christianity, ostensibly a religion of the downtrodden, as in 1 Corinthians 1:26 and Luke 6:20-26. But perhaps the reference is to slaves.

NOTES

[1]Günther Bornkamm, *Paul*, trans. D.M.G. Stalker (NY: Harper & Row, 1971), 246-47.

[2]Walter Schmithals, *Paul and the Gnostics*, trans. John E. Steely (NY: Abingdon Press, 1972), 67-81.

[3]Elaine Pagels, *The Gnostic Gospels* (NY: Random House, 1979), chap. 4, "The Passion of Christ and the Persecution of Christians," 70-101. Keep in mind that the Gnostic doctrine of dissimulation allowed them to renege and swear off the Christian faith, then start preaching again when the coast was clear, all with a sense of sporting bravado not unlike the character Mr. Cheeky from Monty Python: "No ... no ... crucifixion really. Just pulling your leg" (Graham Chapman, et al., *Monty Python's Life of Brian (of Nazareth)* [NY: Ace Books, 1979], 140).

[4]Har Dayal, *The Bodhisattva Doctrine in Buddhist Sanskrit Literature* (1932; NY: Samuel Weiser, 1978).

[5]Peter Brown, *The Cult of the Saints: Its Rise and Function in Latin Christianity*, Haskell Lectures on History of Religions, New Series No. 2 (Chicago: University of Chicago Press, 1981).

[6]Edward Sell, *The Faith of Islam* (London: SPCK, 1907), 149.

[7]Ferdinand Christian Baur, *Paul, the Apostle of Jesus Christ: His Life and Work, His Epistles and Doctrine*, trans. A. Menzies (London: Williams and Norgate, 1876), 2:45-52.

[8]Paul-Louis Couchoud, "The Historicity of Jesus: A Reply to Alfred Loisy," *Hibbert Journal*, vol. 37, no. 2 (1938): 193-214.

[9]Reginald H. Fuller, *The Foundations of New Testament Christology* (NY: Scribner's Sons, 1965), 243-47.

[10]Ernst Käsemann, "Paul and Early Catholicism," trans. Wilfred F. Bunge, in Käsemann, *New Testament Questions of Today* (Philadelphia: Fortress Press,

1979), 236-51; see also Norman Perrin, *The New Testament, an Introduction: Proclamation and Paranesis, Myth and History* (NY: Harcourt Brace Jovanovich, 1974), "The Characteristics of Emergent Catholicism," 268-75.

[11]Robert M. Grant, *A Short History of the Interpretation of the Bible*, rev. ed. (NY: Macmillan, 1963), chap. 8, "The Authoritative Interpretation," 102-15; Randel Helms, *Gospel Fictions* (Buffalo: Prometheus Books, 1988), 18: "By a remarkably creative [feat] of interpretation, the Jewish scriptures (especially in Greek translation) became a book that had never exited before, the *Old* Testament, a book no longer about Israel but about Israel's hope, the Messiah, Jesus."

[12]Thomas à Kempis, *Imitation of Christ for Protestant Followers of Jesus*, trans. Albert J. Nevins (Huntington, IN: Our Sunday Visitor, 1973), 51.

[13]Peter Carls, "Identifying Syzygus, Euodia, and Syntyche, Philippians 4:2f," *Journal of Higher Criticism* 8 (Fall 2001): 161-82.

[14]Tzvetan Todorov, *The Poetics of Prose*, trans. Richard Howard (Ithaca: Cornell University Press, 1977), chap. 5, "Narrative-Men," 66-79.

15.

Colossians

This epistle is Gnostic, pure and simple. Commentators have for many years sought to rescue the text from saying what it plainly says by cramming the epistle into a procrustean bed which allows canonical authors to use heretical terminology and conceptuality in an ironic sense, turning it against their opponents to whom it rightly belongs.[1] This would have to count as the most muddying, confusing tactic ever seen in the polemical arena. The rejoinder would not be far enough away from the heresy it attacks, and the reader would find himself within the Gnostic frame of reference with no clearly marked exit door. I call it the "irony dodge."

One hears over and over like an apologetical mantra that Colossians rebuts Gnosticism by claiming that in Jesus Christ the pleroma of the Godhead resides bodily.[2] This is supposed to be a *refutation* of Gnosticism and not an assertion of it? Well, Gnosticism is supposed to make the Christ aion merely one entity in a long chain of them, like one among many angels. But Colossians assigns him supremacy among divine entities so that all are contained in him. But at most, such apologists have only shown Colossian Gnostics making a slight adjustment (if we can even call it that!) ascribing greater centrality to the Christ aion. Wouldn't Gnostics think the Christ aion had attained a new degree of dignity in view of his saving mission? Furthermore, if you could ask the epistle's author if he accepted that the pleromatic godhead to which he refers is bodily present in Jesus, would the writer reply that, no, he was just "borrowing the Gnostics' conceptualization in order to turn it against them," that he does not believe in a divine fullness one way or the other? There is no reason to think he would. If so, he would effectively be teaching Gnosticism in his very attempt to refute it. Was the writer that stupid? That cynical? It becomes obvious how arbitrary and contrived it is to say what apologists say, so let's stop saying it.

1

[1]Paul, an apostle of Christ-Jesus, by the command of God, and Timothy, the brother, [2]to the saints and faithful brothers in Christ in Colosse: May the favor and protection of God the Father extend to you.

We are prone to take the phrase "God the Father" (1:2) for granted, forgetting that such things are not mentioned for nothing in these ancient, polemical documents. No, the reference sounds Marcionite or Valentinian, a specification to avoid confusion with God the Creator, the Hebrew God.

[3]As we pray, we always give thanks for you to God, the Father of our Lord, Jesus-Christ, [4]having heard of your belief in Jesus-Christ and the love you have for all the saints [5]because of the sure prospect of heavenly reward amassed for you in the skies, which you heard about in the message of truth of the news [6]that came to you, just as it continues to bear fruit and to expand in the whole world, just as also in you, from the day you first heard of and experienced the favor of God for real, [7]as you learned from Epaphras, our beloved fellow-slave, who is a loyal servant of Christ on your behalf, [8]who also has demonstrated to us your Spirit-inspired love.
[9]That, too, is why, ever since the day we heard of your faith, we

have been praying unceasingly for you, asking for you to be filled with the sure knowledge of his will, possessing all wisdom and spiritual understanding, [10]so as to behave worthily of the Lord, pleasing him in all you do, evidencing every sort of good deed and ever increasing in the sure knowledge of God, [11]being equipped with every ability from the abundance of his glorious might, to provide you with all necessary endurance and long-suffering, joyfully [12]rendering thanks to the Father, who made you fit to share the portion of the saints in the pleroma of light, [13]who rescued us out of the authority of darkness and translated us over into the kingdom of his beloved Son, [14]thanks to whom we have redemption, the forgiveness of sins:

Who is the Authority of Darkness in 1:13? Not the devil, but the Creator God. Here is Gnosticism: the stern Old Testament Jehovah has become the Prince of Darkness from whom the kindly Father has rescued us. One doubts that even Marcion would go so far as this.

[15]Who is an image of the invisible God,
First-born of all creation,
[16]For in him all things were created,
In the skies and on the earth,
The visible and the invisible,
Whether thrones, or dominions,
Or archons or authorities,
All things have been created through him and for him.
[17]And he is prior to all things,
And all things consist in him,
[18]And he is the head of the body, the church,
Who is the beginning,
First-born from the dead,
In order that he may rank first in everything,
[19]For in him the whole pleroma was delighted to dwell
    bodily,
[20]And through him to reconcile all things to himself,
Making peace through him,
By means of the blood of his cross,
Whether they dwell on the earth or in the skies.

Colossians 1:15-20, an ancient hymn lyric, presents a compressed recital of the Gnostic myth. Johannes Weiss called it "the Pauline speculative gnosis."[3] We might call it Christosophy. The demiurge, identified as the Authority of Darkness in verse 13, created his own material counterfeit of the pleromatic world of God. He stole the light substance of the Primal Man, the firstborn of creation, and used it as *spermatikoi Logoi* ("seeds of the Logos"), analogous to DNA, to vivify and regulate the material creation. But the Father dispatched the Christ-aion, mysteriously identical with the dispersed Light-Man, in the name of the pleromatic entities to recover the light, enlightening those humans who contain a divine spark and preparing them to return to the world of light after death. His own death at the hands of the unsuspecting powers had the effect of defeating them and canceling the force of the Torah. The Law was a device of the angelic principalities and powers, intended to keep humanity in thrall, though it did keep some order among the otherwise chaotic creatures of the demiurge (2:14-15). No one who believed in the vanilla soteriology of Catholic Christianity would have described the plan of salvation in such dangerously suggestive terms. To deny the Gnostic character of this material is like a Creationist insisting that an archaeopteryx skeleton is simply that of a bird.

[21]And you then were alienated and hostile in mind on account of your evil deeds, [22]but now reconciled in his flesh-body through its death, which was to make you presentable, holy, blameless, irreproachable, [23]which you will be if indeed you persevere in the faith, having been grounded, steadfast and not susceptible of being budged from the sure prospect of the news that you heard proclaimed throughout all creation under the sky, of which I, Paul, became a servant.

The pseudonymous character of the epistle should be evident if only from 1:6, 23, where the Pauline gospel is said to have permeated *the world*. Could the historical Paul in the middle of the first century imagine that the Christian faith had spread throughout the world? This phrase surely intends no less than the Roman Empire, probably also the Parthian Empire. Not only that, but in verse 23 the writer *claims to be* Paul, something the genuine article would never think of doing. The pseudonymous writer thinks of little else than convincing the reader he is what he is not, *affirming* what the genuine author would take for granted.

²⁴Now I rejoice over my sufferings on your behalf, and I fill up what remained lacking from the afflictions of Christ in my flesh on behalf of his body, namely the Church, of which I became a servant, by the terms of the stewardship God assigned me for you: to fulfill the promise of God.

By the time Colossians was written, Paul had become, like Jesus, an atoning savior. Faith in Paul's atoning suffering meets us explicitly in Colossians 1:24: "Now I rejoice over my sufferings on your behalf, and I fill up what remained lacking from the afflictions of Christ in my flesh on behalf of his body, namely the Church." Note the tripartite parallelism here:

1. I rejoice in my sufferings for your sake.
2. In my flesh I share suffering on behalf of his body.
3. I do so for the church, filling up what is lacking in Christ's sufferings.

My suspicion is that someone has subsequently added the phrase "which is the Church," to soften an even more jolting statement in which "his body" meant precisely the crucified body of Jesus. But even as it presently stands in a Christian-Gnostic-Paulinist text, we can see with inescapable clarity how Paul's sufferings complement and fulfill those of Christ on behalf of the elect. The development here is parallel to the growth of Marian soteriology in medieval Catholicism, whereby the sorrows of the Virgin Mary were believed to atone for sin. Mary and Paul alike had their own cults of devotion. Paul's may have existed before it was Christianized and could have developed alongside pro-orthodox soteriology after the two sects merged. This is another of those headache-inducing texts that no one would ever have written had he held orthodox beliefs about the atonement. In the many contrived attempts to make the text mean something more amenable, the redactors simply rewrote the verse to say what they *wished* it had said instead of what it *actually* said.

Do we have any solid evidence that some congregations revered Paul, not Jesus, as their savior? Even in 1 Corinthians 1:13 and Colossians 1:24, the Paulinist soteriology is qualified, overlaid with Christian coloring. But there is one major piece of evidence portraying Paul, rather than Jesus, as the redeemer of souls. That is the Nag Hammadi *Revelation of Paul* (see chapter 4), in which we witness the apostle's ascent into heaven, where he withstands an attack of the demiurge's minions and is sent back to earth as the one to redeem the elect. In the entire text, the name of Jesus *does not appear a single time*! Paul is not said to be a herald for Jesus's gospel. No, it is *Paul* who is said to redeem souls in his own right. The document must have been produced by people who cherished Paul and venerated him as their redeemer, a sect that would have abstained from any credo other than "I am of Paul."

[26]The secret plan, hidden from the aions and from the divine emanations, but now revealed to his saints, [27]to whom God decided to display among the nations the extent of the wealth of the splendor of this secret plan: Christ in you, the prospect of sharing divine glory! [28]Him we announce, warning everyone and teaching everyone very wisely, so as to present every individual perfect in union with Christ. [29]For this, too, I labor, battling mightily thanks to the energy of him who energizes me.

The same contrast observed here in 1:26, of that between the ignorance of supramundane powers and the revelation to humble mortals, occurs in the Gnostic section 1 Corinthians 2:6-10. In fully developed Gnosticism, the knowledge of God was shared within the pleroma and its aions, being hidden only from the last of them, Lady Sophia, whose desire to know led to her Fall.

2

[1]For I want you to know how great a battle I wage on your behalf and for those in Laodicea, and as many as have never seen my face in person, [2]in order to comfort their hearts, since we are united in love and in the full assurance that understanding brings, so we may know the full scope of the mystery of God, namely Christ, [3]in whom is hidden all the wealth of wisdom and gnosis.

That there are people among Paul's audience who have never

seen him face to face (2:1) may be a wink to the reader in subtle acknowledgment of the fact that the historical individual is long gone. In the next passage, verse 5 seems to be a clever admission that the historical Paul is physically absent from the earth, having died some time past.

Christ is said, in verse 2:3, to be the living repository of all wisdom and knowledge. Of what sort? Is he a walking encyclopedia with a photographic memory? If he were available, might we ask him the order and length of the reigns of all the Caesars? Would he know how to cure diphtheria? The recipe for pepperoni pizza? Would his wisdom consist of a carpenter's know-how? Would he possess Machiavellian political savvy? Etiquette? Positive thinking? Of course, 2:3 refers not to earthly matters but to ultra-mortal, esoteric knowledge. Gnostic wisdom (*sophia*) has the same implications. To experience Christ in the mysterious bridal chamber sacrament of the Gnostics was to experience *gnosis*. Such, at any rate, was the hype, however disappointing the actual moment might have been.

[4]I say this to prevent anyone cleverly deceiving you with fine-sounding rhetoric. [5]For if, as in fact, I am absent physically, yet in the spirit I am with you, rejoicing at the sight of the proper order and the firmness of your belief in Christ.

[6]Therefore, in the same way you welcomed Christ-Jesus the Lord, walk in his way, [7]having been rooted and being built up in your new identity, confirmed in the belief you were taught, inclined to ever greater thanksgiving. [8]Watch out that no one deceives you by using philosophy and empty lies from mere human tradition stemming from the elemental spirits of the cosmos, not from Christ.

There is an important parallel between the Marcionite Epistle to the Galatians and this Gnostic Epistle to the Colossians. Galatians 1:8 warns against some hypothetical revelation of a rival gospel at the hands of an angel. I believe the same warning occurs in Colossians in an only slightly different idiom in verse 2:8. One should not heed philosophy or tradition that stems from elemental spirits, meaning the angels in charge of the weather, synecdoche (a part standing for the whole) for their rule of the material world which they created. Who is worshipping angels? Why would one do that? The wretches mentioned in 2:18 are worshipping them *unwittingly* in that those who keep the Torah are said to keep the commandments of angels and the traditions of archons without realizing it. They imagine that these rules come from God.

[9]For in him all the pleroma of the Godhead dwells bodily, [10]and being in him, you are likewise filled, him being the Head over all archons and authorities. [11]In him, too, you were circumcised with a circumcision not performed by hand, via the wholesale cutting off of the body of flesh, that is, the circumcision of Christ, [12]being buried along with him in baptism, and raised along with him through faith in the vivifying of God, who raised him from the dead, [13]you yourselves being dead in trespasses and in the uncircumcision of your flesh-existence whence he vivified you along with him, forgiving you all your trespasses, [14]expunging the handwritten ordinances which incriminated us; and he has taken it out of the way, nailing them as the posted accusation to the cross. [15]Stripping the archons and the authorities naked, he publicly exposed them, parading them as captives in the cross.

In verses 14-15, as in 1 Corinthians 2:6-10, the death of Christ is accomplished by heavenly entities with no reference to either historical individuals or worldly circumstances. The original pre-Christian Gnostic myth located the death of the Primal Man of Light at the beginning of all things when the archons attacked and dismembered him in order to use his substance to give life and order to the material creation. That is a variation of the Rig-Vedic hymn of the self-sacrifice of the Primal Man Purusha, whose sundered members formed the cosmos, the human race, and the gods. The Zoroastrian version has the Primal Man Gayomard being split in two, giving rise to the human race. The scattered sparks would have been redeemed and re-gathered simply by the gradual process of re-awakening the Gnostic elite as they recognized their own divine nature and destiny and then returned to the pleroma after death.

But in order to settle disputes over rival credentials and authority claims, Gnostics and other Christians thought it best to posit a historical founder to whom an appeal might be made. This meant updating the myth, fictively turning it into recent history. For this purpose, the Primal Man's death at the hands of the archons had to be combined with the saving mission of the Redeemer. The Redeemer was thus identified with the Primal Man as sort of a second coming. The destruction of the Primal Man was brought down to earth (Rom. 10:6b) in the crucifixion of Christ at the hands of the Romans. The slaying of the Man of Light was already understood to have given life to the world by virtue of having enlivened the inert creations of the demiurge. Now it became the instrument of salvation in another sense. Valentinian Gnosticism, which was derived, according to Valentinus, from Paul's teachings through his disciple Theodas, held that the death of Jesus availed the lower-tier *psuchikoi*, or natural ones, while the teaching and ministry of the Christ-Spirit, whom Jesus channeled, was sufficient to save the Gnostic illuminati.

[16]So don't let anyone condemn you in dietary matters or for not observing feasts or new moon celebrations or Sabbaths, [17]all this being no more than a charade pointing to things to come, Christ being the reality. [18]Let no one deprive you of your rights by an appeal to self-abasement and the worship of angels, blundering into matters someone has hallucinated, his head being filled with the phantoms of his own imagination, [19]out of touch with the head, from whom the whole body, being nourished and knitted together by means of its various joints and ligaments, will grow with God's green thumb. [20]So if you have died with Christ as far as the elemental spirits are concerned, why are you, like those native to the cosmos, living by decrees? [21]"Do not touch, nor taste, nor handle." [22]These all pertain to things destined to perish as they are used, and they stem from man-made commandments and teachings. [23]Such things, it is true, have a reputation for wisdom by way of self-imposed devotions, self-abnegation and severity toward the body, but they have no merit as they merely satisfy the cravings of the flesh in their own, more subtle, way.

We know from the Nag Hammadi texts that by far most Gnostics were flesh-hating ascetics like those presupposed in verses 21-23. On the other hand, it was possible to slide from asceticism to libertinism once one believed one had transcended traditional moral-social values. How interesting that while conventional kosher regulations are presented here as a species of asceticism, verse 22 offers a rationale for exactly the opposite: the kind of libertinism set forth in 1 Corinthians 6:12-13 whereby food and other bodily occupations are said to be ephemeral and thus morally irrelevant.

3

¹So then, if you have been raised along with Christ, seek the things above where Christ is seated to the right of God. ²Concentrate on the things above, not those on the earth. ³Remember, you died and your life is now hidden away with Christ inside God, ⁴and whenever Christ is revealed to the world, only then will you too be revealed in divine splendor.

As Bultmann and others have noted, Colossians seems to embrace Gnostic realized eschatology, the notion that the end-time events have already occurred in symbolic form, especially through baptism. Romans 8:11 envisions only the believer's death with Christ as accomplished in baptism, with his or her resurrection still a future prospect, scheduled to coincide with the Parousia, or second coming, of Christ. Colossians 3:1-4 crosses this line, inculcating a sort of Gnostic perfectionism like that discussed in 1 John. Second Timothy 2:18 seems to be referring to the same doctrine.

⁵So amputate your members on the earth: prostitution, impurity, passions, illicit desire, and covetousness—which amounts to idolatry. ⁶It is because of these things the wrath of God is on its way. ⁷Indeed, this is how you used to behave when you lived this way. ⁸But now cleanse your mouths of all rage, anger, malice, blasphemy, and abuse. ⁹Do not lie to one another since you have stripped off the old self with his duplicitous ways. ¹⁰Having donned the new self, being renewed by means of enlightenment in the image of the one who created it, where "Jew" and "Greek" have no place, neither "circumcision nor uncircumcision," nor "Barbarian" or "Scythian," "slave" or "free," but Christ is all and is in all alike. ¹²So as the chosen of God, holy and beloved, attire yourselves in the depths of compassion, kindness, humility, meekness, long-suffering, ¹³giv-

ing one another the benefit of the doubt, forgiving each other if anyone has a gripe against another; indeed, just as the Lord forgave you,
you do the same. [14]And above all, love. That is the seal of perfection.
[15]And allow the peace of Christ to hold sway in your hearts. To such
harmony you were summoned as members of a single body. And be
thankful. [16]Let the message of Christ dwell in you lavishly, teaching
and exhorting each other with complete wisdom, singing psalms and
hymns and spirit-inspired songs, singing to God with inspiration in
your hearts. [17]In fact, whatever you do in word or deed in your common worship, do everything invoking the name of the Lord Jesus,
giving thanks to God, the Father, through him.

[18][*Now wives, be subordinate to your husbands, as is befitting in the
household of the Lord. [19]You husbands, love your wives and do not be dis-
agreeable with them. [20]Children, obey your parents in everything, for this
is what pleases the Lord. [21]Fathers, see that you do not provoke your children or they may become discouraged. [22]Slaves, obey your mortal masters
in everything, not just when they are watching to curry their favor, but in
undivided devotion, fearing the reprisals of the Lord. [23]Whatever you do,
work as if for the Lord, not for men, [24]mindful that you will receive from
the Lord your inheritance as a reward. It is the Lord Christ whom you
serve. [25]The one who did wrong will receive back what he did wrong; there
is no preferential treatment.*]

4

[[1]*Masters, supply your slaves with a just and equal wage, knowing that
you are not without a master of your own in heaven.*] [2]Continue vigilant and thankful in prayer, [3]also praying together on our behalf that
God may open a door of opportunity for us to speak of the mystery
of Christ, on account of which I have been chained up, [4]that I may
make it known as behooves me as an apostle. [5]*Behave wisely when it
comes to outsiders, using the time to the best advantage.* [6]Let your speech
always be graceful, seasoned and salted, so you will know the appropriate way to answer each individual.

Winsome Munro[4] makes 3:18-4:1, 5 part of the Pastoral Stratum,
added to Catholicize, sanitize, and domesticate the Pauline letter
canon. Though Ephesians is largely based on Colossians, here the
influence appears to be in the opposite direction, the Pastoral redac-

tor having brought Ephesians 4:28-29; 5:21-6:9 into Colossians as a summarized interpolation.

⁷Tychicus will fill you in on all my affairs, that beloved brother, faithful servant and fellow-slave in the Lord's service, ⁸whom I dispatched to you for no other purpose than to inform you of the news about us, and that he might comfort your hearts. ⁹I sent him with Onesimus, that loyal and beloved brother, who is one of your own. They will tell you everything.

¹⁰Aristarchus, my fellow-prisoner, greets you, as does Mark, the cousin of Bar-Nabas, about whom you will have received word: if he comes to you, welcome him. ¹¹So does Jesus, the one called Justus. They are my only colleagues from the ranks of the circumcised in the work of the kingdom of God, and a great comfort to me. ¹²Epaphras, one of your own, greets you, a slave of Christ-Jesus, always struggling in prayer on your behalf for you to stand perfect and fully confident of the will of God. ¹³For I can vouch for him, that he endures much anguish for you and those in Laodicea and in Hierapolis. ¹⁴Luke, the beloved physician, greets you, and so does Demas. ¹⁵Greet the brothers in Laodicea, as well as Nymphas and the congregation meeting at her house. ¹⁶And once you are done reading this epistle, see that it is read also in the congregation of the Laodiceans and also that you read the one borrowed from Laodicea. ¹⁷And tell Archippus, "Remember the service rendered you for the Lord's sake, to pay it back."

¹⁸My handwritten greeting: Paul. Remember my chains. Remain in God's favor!

The mention of an autograph in 4:18 is a dead giveaway as to authorship since the actual presence of a signature would obviate the need for calling attention to it. As it stands, the pseudepigraphist meant to imply that, had you been reading the non-existent original version, you would have beheld Paul's own handwriting, perforce absent from subsequent copies. The actual, pseudonymous original poses as one of those copies.

NOTES

[1]Ralph P. Martin, *Colossians: The Church's Lord and the Christian's Ministry* (London: Paternoster Press, 1972), 48: "Perhaps this Greek term for 'fulness' (*pleroma*) was the heretics' word, which Paul boldly appropriates to his own ends." See also Willi Marxsen, *Introduction to the New Testament*, trans. Geoffrey Buswell (Philadelphia: Fortress Press, 1974), 182: "The terminology of the heretics is adopted, but their standpoint is not refuted ... but merely Christianized." Alfred Wikenhauser, *New Testament Introduction*, trans. Joseph Cunningham (NY: Herder and Herder, 1958), 417, reads: "Paul is here combating new opponents whose vocabulary he uses freely in his polemic." Günther Bornkamm, "The Heresy of Colossians," trans. Fred O. Francis and Wayne A. Meeks, in *Conflict at Colosse: A Problem in the Interpretation of Early Christianity, Illustrated by Selected Modern Studies,* Sources for Biblical Study 4 (Missoula: Society of Biblical Literature and Scholars Press, 1975), 129, adds that Paul "breaks through the gnostic dualism, even though he makes use of the language of gnosis."

[2]Wikenhauser, *New Testament Introduction*, 416; Martin, *Colossians: The Church's Lord*, 40.

[3]Johannes Weiss, *Earliest Christianity: A History of the Period AD 30-150*, trans. Paul Stevens Kramer (NY: Harper & Row Torchbooks, 1959), 2:484.

[4]Winsome Munro, *Authority in Paul and Peter: The Identification of a Pastoral Stratum in the Pauline Corpus and 1 Peter*, Society for New Testament Studies Monograph Series 45 (NY: Cambridge University Press, 1983), 35-37.

16.

Thessalonians

The issues of authorship, authenticity, and source criticism in the two Thessalonian epistles are so intertwined that I judge it better to present the usual introductory material following the first epistle as a bridge between them. Suffice it to say that in terms of overall typography, each epistle can be divided into two earlier letters, following the analysis of Walter Schmithals. I have put Letter A, in each case, in a Roman font and Letter B in *italics*. The Pastoral Stratum in both, as delineated by Winsome Munro, is in {fancy brackets}.

1

¹Paul and Silvanus and Timothy, to the congregation of Thessalonians in the care of God the Father and the Lord Jesus-Christ. May you know God's favor and protection.

²We always give thanks to God about you all, making mention of you in our prayers, never ³neglecting your faithful work, your labor of love, and your endurance in the prospect of the coming of our Lord, Jesus-Christ, ⁴all before the eyes of our God and Father, mindful, brothers beloved of God, of your having been chosen, ⁵because our news connected with you, not in mere verbiage, but in power and in the Holy Spirit and strong certainty. {You know what sort of peo-

ple we were among you, inspired by you. [6]And you became emulators of us and of the Lord, welcoming the message in the midst of affliction,} albeit with great joy inspired by the Holy Spirit, {[7]so that you became a model to all those in Macedonia and Achaia who believed.} [8]For you were a sounding board for the message of the Lord not only throughout Macedonia and Achaia, but your faith towards God has circulated everywhere, [9]so that we need not say anything: they themselves relate the tale of our reception among you and how you turned to God from the idols, henceforth to serve a God living and true, [10]and to await his Son from the skies, whom he raised from the dead: Jesus, our deliverer from the wrath to come.

2

{[1]You yourselves know, brothers, that our reception among you was not fruitless; [2]rather, having previously suffered and been insulted in Philippi, we were bold in the zeal of our God to speak the news of God to you despite great struggles.} [3]For our exhortations did not stem from error or impure motives or wily deceit as some then charged, [4]but we speak as we have been authorized by God to be entrusted with the news, not to ingratiate ourselves with our hearers, but to please God who tests our hearts. [5]For neither then did we employ flattery, as you can attest, nor did we use Christ as a pretext to despoil you, as God is our witness, [6]nor did we seek the adulation of the crowd, neither from you nor from others, [7]though as apostles of Christ we might well have thrown our weight around. [8]So cherishing you, we were delighted to impart to you not only the news of God, but our own selves because you had become dear to us. [9]For you remember, brothers, our labor and toil, working night and day so as not to be a burden to any one of you, proclaiming to you the news of God. [10]You and God are witnesses of how piously and righteously and irreproachably we behaved toward you who believed, [11]just as you know how we encouraged and consoled each one of you as a father with his own children, [12]testifying that you ought to behave worthily of God, who called you to share his kingdom and his splendor. {[13]We render thanks to God without stopping, that having welcomed the message of God once you heard it from us, you welcomed it not as some human scheme but as the message of God, which it really is, and which energizes you who believe. ¹⁴For you became imitators, brothers, of God's congregations located in Judea, safe in the bosom of Christ, because you, too, endured the same things at the hands of your compatriots as they did from the Jews, ¹⁵those who both killed the Lord Jesus and the prophets and chased us out, who are not pleasing to God and who set themselves against all mankind, ¹⁶obstructing our efforts to speak to the nations in order that they may be saved, ever in this way filling up their sins. But the wrath of God caught up with them at last.}

¹⁷But we, brothers, being bereaved of you, even for the span of a single hour, in person, though not in heart, were all the more eager with great desire to see your face. ¹⁸Thus we wanted to come to you, indeed I, Paul, not once but twice, but the adversary prevented us. ¹⁹For what is the basis for our hope, our joy, the achievement we brag about to our Lord Jesus when he arrives? What else but you? ²⁰For you are our pride and joy.

3

¹This is why, when we could bear the suspense no longer, we were quite happy to be left alone in Athens, ²and we sent Timothy, our brother and colleague for God in the news of Christ, to fortify you and encourage you in your faith so that no one might drop out because of these afflictions. For you yourselves know this is what we were destined for. ⁴For even when we were with you, we already said to you that we were about to be afflicted, as indeed it happened, as you know. ⁵Thus, no longer able to bear the suspense, I sent to find out the state of your faith, hoping the tempter had not somehow tempted you successfully, rendering our labor a loss. ⁶But now, with Timothy arriving and announcing to us the news of your faith and love, and that you have us in fond memory always, longing to see us just as we long for you, ⁷we were thus comforted about you, by your faith, as to all our distress and affliction, ⁸because now we feel alive again if you are standing firm in your commitment to the Lord. ⁹How can we render adequate thanks to God over you, given all the joy with which we rejoice over you before our God, ¹⁰vehemently petitioning night and day to be able to see your face and adjust any shortcomings in your faith?

¹¹So may our God and Father himself, and our Lord Jesus, direct our steps to you. ¹²And may the Lord make you increase and overflow with love for one another and for everyone, just as we also love you, ¹³so to fortify

*your hearts impeccable in sanctity before our God and Father at the coming
of our Lord Jesus with all his saints.*

4

{[1]Finally, brothers, we bid you and exhort you in the name of the
Lord Jesus that you conduct yourselves ever more perfectly in the
way that is pleasing to God, as you learned it from us, as of course
you already do.}

{[2]For you recall the commandments we gave you through the
authority of the Lord Jesus. [3]For God's will for you is simply this:
your sanctification in that you abstain from prostitution, [4]that each
one of you be able to control his own bodily vessel in sanctity and
honor, [5]not in the grip of passion and lust like the heathen who do
not know God, [6]nor to transgress and defraud his brother in this matter because the Lord is the avenger in all such cases, just as we told
you earlier and solemnly testified. [7]For God did not summon us to a
life of impurity, but to live in sanctity. [8]Thus whoever laughs off this
advice is rejecting not human opinion but rather God, who gives his
Holy Spirit to you.}

{[9]Now concerning brotherly love, it is superfluous to write to
you, for you yourselves are already taught by God spontaneously to
love one another; [10]for indeed you manifest it to all the brothers in
Macedonia. We only encourage you, brothers, to increase love even
more, [11]and to make a real effort to be quiet and to mind your own
business and to undertake honest labor, as we enjoined you, [12]in
order that you may conduct yourselves appropriately relative to those
outside and so you will lack nothing.}

[13]Now we do not want you to be ignorant, brothers, concerning those asleep, so you do not mourn like others who are bereft
of hope.[14]For if we believe that Jesus died and rose again, it stands
to reason that God will also bring with Jesus those who have fallen
asleep on account of him. [15]For we say this to you by a revelation
from the Lord: we who live to see the arrival of the Lord may by
no means get ahead of the sleepers. [16]Because the Lord himself will
come down from the sky with a shout of command from the voice of
an archangel sounding God's trumpet, and the dead who repose in
Christ will be the first to rise again. [17]Then we who live and remain

shall find ourselves snatched up together with them aboard clouds to meet with the Lord in the upper air, and there we will remain with the Lord forever! ¹⁸So comfort each other with these words whenever one of you dies.

5

¹So concerning the signs of the times, brothers, it is superfluous to write to you, ²for you know full well that the Day of the Lord—like a thief in the night, so it comes! ³Just when they are reassuring themselves: "Peace and security," at that moment destruction overtakes them like the labor pains of a pregnant woman. And there will be no escape. ⁴But you, brothers, are not shrouded in darkness, that the day should surprise you like a thief. ⁵For you are all sons of the light and sons of the day. We do not belong to the night, nor to the darkness, ⁶thus let us not remain comatose like everyone else; rather, let us stay clear-headed and vigilant. ⁷For the sleeper sleeps at night and the drunkard drinks by night. ⁸But since we belong to the day, let us snap out of it, donning a breastplate of faith and love and for a helmet the prospect of salvation, ⁹because God did not destine us to suffer his wrath, but to attain salvation through the arrival of our Lord Jesus-Christ, ¹⁰the one who died on our behalf in order that, whether we remain awake or we fall asleep in death, we may ultimately live with him. ¹¹Therefore, comfort one another and fortify each other, as of course you do.

{¹²Now we ask you, brothers, to acknowledge those who do the work among you and who distinguish themselves in the service of the Lord and exhort you, ¹³and to esteem them most highly in love because of their work. Be at peace among yourselves. ¹⁴And we exhort you, brothers, to reprove the lazy, encourage the timid, support the weak, and be long-suffering with everyone. ¹⁵See that no one recompenses another evil for evil, but always follow the path of benevolence toward one another and toward everyone else as well.} ¹⁶Rejoice always, ¹⁷pray constantly, ¹⁸giving thanks in whatever circumstances. For this is the plan of God for you, being in the fold of Christ-Jesus.

¹⁹Do not snuff out the fire of the Spirit. ²⁰I mean, do not dismiss prophecies out of hand, ²¹but weigh them all, {heeding the genuine ones, ²²but repudiating every one that smacks of evil.}

²³And may the God of peace himself sanctify you completely, and may your whole spirit, soul, and body be kept blameless for the arrival of our Lord, Jesus-Christ. ²⁴The one who summons you to this is faithful: he will see to it.

²⁵Brothers, you pray for us, too. ²⁶Greet all the brothers with a ritual kiss. ²⁷I command you in the name of the Lord to have this epistle read to all the brothers.

²⁸May the favor of our Lord Jesus-Christ be with you.

First Thessalonians appears, according to the analysis of Walter Schmithals,[1] to be a compilation of two short letters. According to the analysis of Winsome Munro,[2] these letters suffered the further addition of Pastoral material meant to facilitate the Catholic acceptance of the epistles. But if we are to attempt to place 1 Thessalonians along the developmental timeline, there is reason to make the original document already Catholic, though friendly to Paul as retooled in Acts. Munro makes 1:5c-6a, 7; 2:1-2, 13-16; 4:1-12; 5:12-15, 21b-22 part of the Pastoral Stratum.

Letter A (1:1-5a, 6b, 8-10; 4:13-18; 5:1-11, 16-21a, 23-28) is an attempt to cope with the dangers of prophecy (5:20), once highly valued and still esteemed in some circles contemporary with the letter but increasingly perceived as a threat to rock the boat. Clearly some prophet has introduced an apocalyptic revelation that the Thessalonian pseudepigraphist does not much like. So what he does is not to mount a counter-prophecy, which must result in stalemate or factional schism, but to undercut the new prophecy with an allegedly old letter from Paul, the venerable founder. According to this letter, Paul had already addressed these issues, though the Thessalonians may have forgotten that he did so.

What was the new, heretical revelation? First, it seems to have presupposed Christian mortalism. The only hope of eternal life was for believers to stick it out through tribulation and trial and to live long enough to see the eschatological coming of Jesus Christ. Of course, such an attitude implies belief in a very near Parousia, which most would be expected to live to see. Perhaps this revelation was an oracle from the heavenly Christ that made its way into our Gospels: "Whoever endures to the end will be saved." Against this, our pseudo-Pauline writer affirms that Christians need not despair over their newly deceased members. They will see them again when Christ returns. In fact, they will ascend to meet Christ ahead of those who are still alive at the time.

Second, the offensive prophetic teaching would seem to have been chiliastic, envisioning Jesus coming to the earth and establishing a Jewish messianic kingdom here. Such news would be totally irrelevant to Paulinists, who do not even seem to realize that *Christos* was a royal title rather than a surname.[3] The author's distaste for Jews and Jewish theocracy is implied in his gloating in 2:15 (Letter B). In contrast to Jewish chiliasm, the Thessalonian writer expects Jesus to descend from heaven—although not so far as to actually make it to the earth. The elect will rise up to meet their Lord in the air and live there forever with him on that exalted plane. This is part of the trajectory of de-apocalypticizing the Christian faith. It is one step away from saying that righteous Christians will meet their Lord in heaven when they die, with no real importance attached to any final, earthly consummation. We have not quite reached that stage yet, for the readers are warned that the Parousia is on the agenda: it will occur any time now, or at least, it *may* happen. Such a state of constant, but not very intense, expectation is already a second-generation watering down of apocalyptic zeal. At first, Christians believed Christ would come very quickly. That hope failed to materialize, and in the wake of the disappointment, we begin to hear urgings, as here, not to give up hope, to stay awake, implying that the time has grown long and it is difficult to remain alert.

Does not the Pauline correction itself pretend to be prophetic in origin? "For we say this to you by a revelation from the Lord" (4:15). No, Paul is quoting Old Testament scripture, as befits a church that is becoming disillusioned with living prophecy and is tending toward sacred writings:

> For, behold, *the Lord comes* forth out of his place, and *will come down*, and will go upon the high places of the earth. (Mic. 1:3, LXX)

> *And the sounds of the trumpet were waxing very much louder.* Moses spoke, and God answered him with a voice. And *the Lord came down* upon Mount Sinai on the top of the mountain; and the Lord called

Moses to the top of the mountain, and Moses went up. (Exod. 19:19-20, LXX)

And *the Lord descended* in a cloud, and stood near him there, and called the name of the Lord. (Exod. 34:5, LXX)

And *the Lord came down* in a cloud, and spoke to him, and took of the spirit that was upon him, and put it upon the seventy men who were elders; and when the spirit rested upon them, they prophesied and ceased. (Num. 11:25, LXX)

For thus said the Lord to me, "As a lion would roar, or a lion's whelp over prey which he has taken, and *cry* over it, *until the mountains are filled with his voice,* and the animals are awe-struck and tremble at the fierceness of his wrath: so *the Lord of hosts shall descend* to fight upon the mount Sion, even upon her mountains." (Isa. 31:4, LXX)

The use of Jewish scripture in this fashion underscores the Catholic nature of 1 Thessalonians. Marcionites and Gnostics would have made no such use of the Jewish Bible. Still, the presence of such scriptural influence would not have been sufficient for Marcionites to exclude these letters from their *Apostolicon* because they are not clearly presented as scripture citations. There was room to interpret the Pauline text as the result of private revelation, just as many readers assume today.

As F. C. Baur[4] noted long ago, the urging to read the text in public (5:25) is oddly superfluous given that the epistle was written to the whole church anyway. The real agenda is to seek inclusion of this spurious letter among the accepted list of Pauline epistles read week by week in the Marcionite churches. "Treat this like the Pauline letters you already have, okay?"

The main concern of Letter B (2:13-20; 3:1-13; 4:1) is to recall, or to create, the good old days of the Pauline ministry in founding the Thessalonian congregation. It was a great time. Paul was breathlessly eager for them to do well and, indeed, could hardly sleep for wanting to hear from them again. The point of all this is to reinforce the Thessalonians' pride in a Pauline foundation and doctrinal legacy in a time when some Catholics followed an alternative strategy of writing off Paul as the property of Gnostics and heretics (see chapter 6). Letter B wants to vindicate Paul as the founder and to sanitize his doctrinal legacy. The material from the Pastoral stratum, of which there is quite a bit, constitutes a second attempt to reinforce the same point, this time by providing an explicit character-witness defense against other Catholics who thought the Thessalonians would be better off without the Pauline albatross around their necks. We can see the same sort of double treatment of John the Baptist among late first-century Christians. Should they vilify him as the fountainhead of heresy, the preceptor of Simon Magus and Dositheus? Or should they co-opt him and sanitize him, making him the advance man for Jesus?

From 2:15 it is at least clear that our author is no Jew. It is impossible to imagine a Jew, especially a sectarian Jew who regards his sect as the true Israel, speaking of Jews in this manner. It reeks of typical Hellenistic anti-Semitism, denouncing Jews as haters of the human race.[5] The odious remark is just what history leads us to expect from the early Catholic churches: the Christ-killers are receiving their due. And 2:16 is certainly a reference to the fall of Jerusalem in CE 70, if not actually to the defeat of the Bar-Kochba rebellion in CE 136. My guess is that the real and intended reference is to the Bar-Kochba defeat, recent in the pseudepigraphist's own time, but that it is cleverly left ambiguous so one may assume the reference is to the 70 CE defeat, closer to Paul's death.

In verse 2:18, our author protests too much, referring to himself by name as Paul, which is unnatural for a genuine first-person writer but common throughout the Pseudepigrapha.[6] There are also borrowings from other epistles. In fact, one of the first things to alert Darrell J. Doughty to the composite nature of the epistles generally was the presence of underlying sources, something we would not expect in a personal, spontaneous composition. An analogy would be a line from Woody Allen's *Crimes and Misdemeanors* where a spurned lover admits to cribbing portions of his love letter from James Joyce: "You probably wondered why all the references to Dublin." When we compare 1 Thessalonians 3:1-8 with 2 Corinthians 2:12-13; 7:5-7, it is difficult to know which passage is modeled on the other, but one is dependent on the other.

In the Gospels, sometimes the device of making Jesus speak the thoughts the evangelist wants to communicate to us is so overt that the narrative veil wears thin. One of these instances is in Luke 24:44: "These are my words which I said to you *while I was still with you*, that all things which are written of me in the Law of Moses and the Prophets and the Psalms must be fulfilled." Ostensibly Jesus must be understood to mean, "when I journeyed with you and kept company with you, before recent developments," but it is clear that Jesus is no longer present on earth, in history, and that Luke is putting his own words in Jesus's mouth. Compare this to Luke 24:6 where the angel is made to say, "Remember how he spoke to you while he was still in Galilee, saying …?" Occasionally we find the same sort of thing in the Pauline corpus, and it is at the very least a mark of pseudonymous authorship: "Surely you remember how I used to tell you these things while I was still with you?" (2 Thess. 2:5). In this case, the pseudonymous character is also noticeable from the anachronism of Paul referring to the "traditions" he inaugurated (2:15). That is just like the spurious 2 Peter referring to predictions made by Peter long ago, the author forgetting his literary pose *as Peter* (2 Pet. 3:2-4). Similarly, in 2 Corinthians we read, "When present with you and in need, I was a burden to no one, for the brothers arriving from Macedonia supplied my needs" (11:9). Compare these words with those of the already exalted Son of Man in Matthew 25:35, "I was hungry and you gave me to eat; I was thirsty and you gave me drink; I was a stranger and you invited me in." In 1 Thessalonians 3:4, we encounter an equally suspicious claim: "For even when we were with you, we already said to you that we were about to be afflicted, as indeed it happened, as you know."

2 Thessalonians

1

[1]Paul and Silvanus and Timothy, to the congregation of Thessalonians in the care of God our Father and the Lord, Jesus-Christ. [2]May you enjoy the favor and protection of God the Father and the Lord, Jesus-Christ.

[3]We are obliged to give thanks to God constantly for you, brothers, as is only fitting, because your faith grows abundantly and your love, each for all the rest, increases, [4]so that we ourselves brag about

you in God's congregations for your perseverance and faithfulness amid your persecutions and the afflictions you endure, [5]clear evidence of the righteous judgment of God, that you may be counted worthy of the kingdom of God for which indeed you suffer, [6]since it is just for God to recompense affliction to those now afflicting you, [7]and to you who are being afflicted, surcease, along with us, when the Lord Jesus is revealed from heaven with his mighty angels [8]in blazing fire, dealing out full vengeance to those who want nothing to do with God and to those refusing to bow to the news of our Lord Jesus. [9]They will pay the penalty of being forever shut out from the presence of the Lord and from the splendor of his might, [10]whenever he comes to be worshipped by his saints and to be marveled at by all who have believed, because our testimony to you met with belief. [11]For this reason we indeed pray always for you, that our God may judge you as having lived up to his calling and may powerfully fulfill in you every pleasing good deed and faithful deed, [12]so the name of our Lord Jesus may be well spoken of, thanks to you, and that you in turn may receive his blessing and approval, the favor of our God and Lord, Jesus-Christ.

2

[1]*Now we ask you, brothers, when it comes to the arrival of our Lord, Jesus-Christ, and our being gathered together to him, [2]not to be too easily confused nor disturbed, neither through some prophecy, nor through some saying, nor through some epistle allegedly from us, to the effect that the Day of the Lord is immediately at hand. [3]Let no one deceive you in any such way because it will not arrive until once the apostasy comes and the Man of Lawlessness is revealed, the Son of Perdition, [4]the one setting himself against and making himself supreme over all that is called God or that is worshipped so that he enthrones himself in the temple of God, presenting himself as a god. [5]Surely you remember how I used to tell you these things while I was still with you? [6]And you know what is now restraining him so that he may be revealed only at his destined time. [7]For the unseen plan of lawlessness proceeds apace, but there is one restraining it right now till it is taken out of the way. [8]And then the Lawless One will be revealed, whom the Lord will destroy by no more than a breath and reduce him to nothing by the epiphany of his coming, [9]that one who appears, energized by the adversary with all possible miracles and signs and deceptive wonders [10]and with every wicked*

*deceit for those who are perishing because they neglected to welcome the love
of the truth which would have saved them. [11]Since the truth was not to their
liking, God sends them a powerful error, making them believe the lie, [12]in
order that all who did not believe the truth but preferred unrighteousness
may be judged.*

*[13]We are obliged always to thank God on your account, brothers beloved
of the Lord, because God chose you as the first to become ripe unto salvation
by the sanctification of the Spirit and belief in the truth, [14]to which also he
summoned you through our preaching, so you could attain to the splendor of
our Lord, Jesus-Christ.*

{[15]So then, brothers, stand firm and hold fast the traditions you
were taught, whether in person or in an epistle from us.} *[16]And our
Lord, Jesus-Christ himself, and God our Father, the one who loved us and
by his favor gave us comfort for the ages and a firm hope, [17]may he comfort
your hearts and reinforce you as those whose every word and deed are good.*

3

*[1]Finally, brothers, pray for us, that the message of the Lord may race unhin-
dered and be praised as it was among you, [2]and that we may be delivered
from perverse and evil people, for not everyone holds the faith. [3]But the
Lord is faithful: he will fortify you and guard you against the wicked.* {[4]And
we are sure about you, thanks to the Lord, that you do the things we
urge and will continue to do them. [5]And may the Lord direct your
hearts to the love of God and the patience of Christ.}

{[6]Now we urge you, brothers, in the name of the Lord Jesus-
Christ, to shun any brother who behaves lazily, not according to the
tradition you received from us. [7]For you yourselves know how it is
necessary to emulate us because we were not idle among you, [8]nor
took free food from anyone, but rather worked with labor and strug-
gled night and day so as not to be a burden to any one of you. [9]Not
that we do not have the authority to receive compensation, but we
refrain in order to set an example for you to imitate us. [10]For even
when we were with you, we urged you, "If anyone refuses to work,
then let him not eat either." [11]We hear there are some among you
who behave lazily, working at nothing but being busybodies, [12]and
such people we command and exhort in the name of the Lord, Jesus-
Christ, to work quietly and eat the bread they earn for themselves.}

{^{13}As for you, brothers, do not grow discouraged when your good deeds seem to come to nothing. ^{14}And if anyone refuses to obey our command in this epistle, take note of him and refuse to have anything to do with him in the hope that he may feel due shame. ^{15}And yet do not treat him with hostility, but admonish him as a brother.}

^{16}And may the Lord of peace himself grant you his protection always in every circumstance. May the Lord be with you all! ^{17}I, Paul, pen this greeting with my own hand. This is the mark of genuineness in every letter actually written by me. It is my handwriting. ^{18}May the favor of our Lord, Jesus Christ, remain with all of you.

Letter A (1:1-12, 16) is a letter of congratulation and encouragement for the persecuted Thessalonian congregation which seems to be a model of virtue. It would make the most sense coming from a contemporary, but as a pseudepigraph it may be best understood as a kind of aretalogy for the congregation, a letter of commendation on its behalf. The point of such a credential would be to secure the clout of this church, especially its bishops in succeeding generations, through the authority of the apostolic name on the letter. It is worth noting that the author retains belief in an imminent Parousia. He expects that the persecutions his readers are undergoing will be cut short soon by the vengeance of the savior from heaven. This makes Letter A *more* apocalyptic, more urgently eschatological, than 1 Thessalonians though scholars usually regard 1 Thessalonians as the more apocalyptic of the two.

The Pastoral Stratum in Letter A (3:6-15) has quite a different concern. It would make sense to read it as a rebuke of an eschatological work stoppage, part of an interim ethic that assumes all worldly preoccupations should be suspended in favor of the freedom of the birds of the air and the lilies of the field. Many or most scholars interpret it in that way.[7] It is an educated guess, for the history of millenarian movements, including the Cargo Cults of Melanesia, offers numerous examples of believers leaving their nets and toll booths to follow an apocalyptic seer into an imagined immediate future. That is what Albert Schweitzer[8] pictured the disciples of Jesus doing: abandoning worldly preoccupations to prepare, with him, for the Eschaton. But in light of the invocation of the Pauline example which immediately follows in 3:7-8, an example of free-gospel preaching, paying one's own way, and not being a holy freeloader, I feel sure the point is exactly parallel to that in the *Didache* 11-12:

> Let every apostle who comes to you be received as the Lord. But he shall not remain more than one day; or two days, if there's a need. But if he remains three days, he is a false prophet. And when the apostle goes away, let him take nothing but bread until he lodges. If he asks for money, he is a false prophet ... But whoever says in the Spirit, Give me money, or something else, you shall not listen to him. ... If he who comes is a wayfarer, assist him as far as you are able; but he shall not remain with you more than two or three days, if need be. But if he wants to stay with you, and is an artisan, let him work and eat. But if he has no trade, according to your under-standing, see to it that, as a Christian, he shall not live with you idle. But if he wills not to do so, he is a Christ-monger. Watch that you keep away from such. (Roberts-Donaldson translation)

Letter B (2:1-14, 16-17; 3:1-3) is taken up with eschatology. It tries to mitigate dangerous apocalyptic enthusiasm recently enflamed by either a spurious Pauline letter or a Pauline oracle. Scholars usu-ally point the finger at 1 Thessalonians with its prediction of the Par-ousia and the raising of the dead. But as we have seen, that text only warns readers, complacent because of the long delay of the end, not to lose hope or to slack off, on the off-chance that Christ might come at an unexpected time and catch them by surprise. By contrast, it is 2 Thessalonians which lists the last remaining signs of the end, soon to be fulfilled. Beyond this, we must recognize in 2 Thessalonians a declension from radical, realized eschatology. Our author objects to the recent preaching that the Day of the Lord has come. This procla-mation implies, as we saw in chapter 8, that faith had become sight, though in a demythologized way: one had to have faith in order to see that the kingdom of God had come (John 3:3). One had to eschew the childish hopes of technicolor upheavals and cataclysms, since the true kingdom has dawned *within* (Luke 17:20-21; *Gos. Thom.*, saying 51). This was the way the kingdom of the Mahdi had dawned accord-ing to the Bab in nineteenth-century Iran.[9] No miracles except faith and illumination. Such was the faith of the Johannine community:[10]

"The hour is coming, nay, now is!" (5:25). But history goes on unaffected in any discernible way. The coming of the kingdom appears to be no different from the fallen age it ostensibly replaced, and so sight retreats to faith. The initial hope is, paradoxically, renewed *as* hope once believers admit the kingdom is back where it belongs: in the future. That is the retreat from realized to future eschatology we see in 1 Thessalonians.

In chapter 7, I argued that Catholic tradition, once it had decided to co-opt Paulinism by sanitizing the Pauline legacy, including the Pauline epistles, set about taking all the previous vilification of the historical Paul and projecting it onto a monstrous double, Simon the Sorcerer. Simon Magus was thus the evil twin that Catholics had inherited from Jewish Ebionite Christians before they thought it better to make a good Catholic of him. This meant retroactively portraying him (as in Acts) as an observant Jew, so as to counteract the Marcionite Paul who would cut loose the Jewish Old Testament. Well, we are seeing the same thing here. That is perhaps the only way to explain a puzzle in the text: Jewish Christians characterized Paul himself in precisely the terms found in 2 Thessalonians 2:3: an Antichrist who prompted a great apostasy from the Torah, hence the Man of *Lawlessness*. As per verse 4 immediately following, he was even arrested in the temple for profaning it (Acts 21:27-30), which might be construed as the Abomination of Desolation. Again, Jewish Christians had vilified Paul in exactly the terms of 2:8-11. Paul had performed "the signs of an apostle" (2 Cor. 12:12), here construed as "lying wonders," and so led people astray into a Torah-free gospel (Acts 21:20b-21). What Catholic hagiographers have done is to take the portrait of Paul the Enemy and divide off his Mr. Hyde side as the Antichrist.

Second Thessalonians 2:5 again reflects Luke 24:44 and John 16:4b. "When I was with you," Paul writes, hinting that he is gone and that the pseudonymous writer is looking back on a time before Paul's death. While these teachings are said to be old and forgotten, they are actually new with this letter. The writer tries to retroject his teachings into the foundational age of the church by having Paul "remind" the readers that he had taught it all long before. And, as W. C. Van Manen pointed out, it is a gross anachronism for Paul to be referring to venerable traditions delivered by him to the church (2:15; 3:6), as if in the distant past when Paul founded the church. No, this is the language of a later Paulinist for whom they *are* hoary traditions, and he is posing as the apostle who originated them.

NOTES

[1]Walter Schmithals, *Paul and the Gnostics*, trans. John E. Steely (NY: Abingdon Press, 1972), 133, 194-95.

[2]Winsome Munro, *Authority in Paul and Peter: The Identification of a Pastoral Stratum in the Pauline Corpus and I Peter,* Society for New Testament Studies Monograph Series 45 (NY: Cambridge University Press, 1983), 82-92.

[3]Werner Kramer, *Christ: Lord, Son of God,* Studies in Biblical Theology No. 50, trans. Brian Hardy (Naperville: Alec R. Allenson, 1966), 212-13.

[4]Ferdinand Christian Baur, *Paul, the Apostle of Jesus Christ: His Life and Work, His Epistles and Doctrine,* trans. Allan Menzies (London: Williams and Norgate, 1876), 2:95-96.

[5]Ibid., 87.

[6]*Prot. Jas.* 25:1; *Inf. Gos. Thom.* 1:1; *Apoc. Pet.* 2; *Gos. Pet.* 60; *4 Ezra* 2:33, 42; 3:1; *Ap. John* 1:19; *Thom. Cont.* 1:2; *1 En.* 25:1; *Apoc. Zeph.* B:7; *2 Bar.* 6:1; 8:3; 10:5; 11:1; 13:1; 35:1; 44:1; 77:1; *3 Bar.* 1:3, 7; 4:1; 5:1; 7:1; 9:1; 16:5; *Apoc. Ab.* 1:2, 4; 6:1; *T. Levi* 2:1; *T. Sol.* 1:3, 5; 2:1, 5, 9; 5:6, 13; 6:9, 10, 12; 7:1, 7; 8:5, 12; 9:5; 10:10; 12:4; 13:3, 5, 6; 14:8; 15:13; 18:41; 19:1; 20:5, 18; 22:6, 17; 23:4; 25:8; also Dan. 7:15, 28; 8:1, 15, 27; 9:2; 10:2, 7; 12:5; Rev. 1:9; 22:8, 16; Tob 1:3.

[7]Alfred Wikenhauser, *New Testament Introduction*, trans. Joseph Cunningham (NY: Herder and Herder, 1958), 367: "Though he does not link the excitement about the Parousia with the idleness, it is natural to assume that the two phenomena are related"; Herbert T. Andrews, "I and II Thessalonians," in *A Commentary on the Bible,* eds. Arthur S. Peake and A. J. Grieve (London: T. C. and E. C. Jack, 1929), 880: "Under the influence of the Parousia hope, some Thessalonian Christians abandoned their ordinary occupations and claimed the right to be supported by the Church."

[8]Albert Schweitzer, *The Kingdom of God and Primitive Christianity*, trans. L. A. Garrard (NY: Seabury Press, 1968), 97-98: "Jesus even considers that with the Kingdom so close at hand, the earning of one's living has lost its justification. Concern about the necessities of life should now be left entirely to God."

[9]The Bab (Ali Muhammad) inaugurated his new dispensation without miracles, and his disciple and successor, Hussein Ali (Baha'u'llah), composed a lucid and elaborate apologetic treatise urging Muslims not to make the same mistake as in times past when people rejected Jesus and Muhammad, taking literally their metaphors of apocalyptic prophecy. See his *Kitab-i-Iqans* ("Book of Certitude"), trans. Shoghi Effendi (1862; Wilmette, IL: Baha'i Publishing Trust, 1974).

[10]Robert Tomson Fortna, *The Fourth Gospel and Its Predecessor: From Narrative Source to Present Gospel* (Philadelphia: Fortress Press, 1988): "The Gospel explicitly presents the work of Jesus as the already consummated end" (286); "It matters not that he is unlike the political savior so widely awaited, that the world is not radically changed. He has come, and that is eschaton enough" (287); "Consequently, there is no role to be played by a Messiah returning to earth in glory" (289).

17.

The Letter to Philemon

For traditional scholars, the letter (and it is a letter, not a treatise-length epistle) poses few problems. It appears to have been written by the aging, imprisoned apostle to his old friend in the faith, Philemon, a mover and shaker in the church at Colosse. It seems that one Onesimus, a slave in Philemon's household, has absconded with some funds and hit the road. Paul offers the slave a familiar face and perhaps salve for his wounded conscience. Onesimus is suddenly interested in Christianity. This is plausible, since people turn to religion when they are in a tight spot: the Chuck Colson Syndrome, if you will. In the meantime, Paul has taken advantage of Onesimus's willingness to run errands for him but is now sending the slave home to face the music. If Onesimus remains any longer, Paul might be accused of harboring a slave. The instruction to return to Philemon will test Onesimus's faith because his master could have him executed for desertion. Perhaps Onesimus's embrace of Christianity will mitigate his master's wrath. Beyond that, Paul wants Philemon to set Onesimus free and send him back to serve as Paul's assistant. Will he?

1

[1]Paul, a prisoner of Christ-Jesus and Timothy, the brother, to Philemon, our beloved colleague, and to Apphia, the sister, and to

Archippus, our fellow-soldier, and to the congregation at your house. [3]May the favor and protection of God our Father and the Lord, Jesus-Christ, attend you.

[4]I thank my God, always making mention of you in my prayers, hearing of the love you have for all the saints and the faith you have toward the Lord Jesus, so that the sharing of your faith may become effective for Christ by a full knowledge of all that is good in us. [7]For I had great joy and consolation from your love, because the hearts of the saints have been refreshed by you, brother. [8]Which is why, having great boldness in the authority assigned me by Christ to command you to do the right thing, [9]for love's sake, I should rather plead, simply as an old man named Paul, and now also a prisoner for Christ-Jesus. [10]It is concerning my child, begotten in my imprisonment, Onesimus, that I plead. Formerly, to be sure, he was useless to you, but now quite useful both to you and to me. [12]I have herewith sent him back to you, even my own heart. [13]I deliberated, then decided to keep him in order that he might serve me on your behalf in my imprisonment for the news, [14]but I thought it best not to do anything without your say so, not wanting your good deed to be forced, but rather, voluntary. [15]And perhaps this is why in the providence of God he was separated from you for an hour, in order that you might welcome him back forever, [16]no longer as a slave but as more than a slave, as a beloved brother, especially to me, but much more to you, both from natural affection and in the fellowship of the Lord. [17]If therefore you have taken me as a partner, welcome him as you would me. [18]And if he wronged you or owes anything, charge it to my account. [19]I, Paul, have written with my own hand: "I will repay it." [20]Yes, brother, may I have help from you in the Lord's service?

[21]I wrote to you confident of your obedience, knowing that you will do more than I have said in so many words. [22]And while you're at it, fix up a place for me to stay, for I hope, in answer to your prayers, to be restored to you.

[23]Greetings from Epaphras, my fellow prisoner in the cause of Christ-Jesus, [24]Mark, Aristarchus, Demas, Luke, my colleagues. [25]May the favor of the Lord, Jesus-Christ, be with your spirit.

It is scarcely so simple as to assume the letter is authentic. We do not, after all, have a window into the apostle's life and ministry. For an author to assert his identity as Paul does is, as we have seen, a good indication that the text was probably not written by him. Also, this letter, though parasitic upon Colossians, forgets that Paul had no acquaintances there (Col. 2:1) and lists several church members as his old friends in verse 2. Finally, as W. C. van Manen[1] pointed out, Philemon bears a startlingly close resemblance to a certain well-known letter from Pliny Secundus to Sabianus:

> The freedman of yours with whom you said you were angry has been to me, flung himself at my feet, and clung to me as if I were you. He begged my help with many tears, though he left a good deal unsaid; in short, he convinced me of his genuine penitence. I believe he has reformed, because he realizes he did wrong. You are angry, I know, and I know too that your anger was deserved, but mercy wins most praise when there was just cause for anger. You loved the man once, and I hope you will love him again, but it is sufficient for the moment if you allow yourself to be appeased. You can always be angry again if he deserves it, and will have more excuse if you were once placated. Make some concession to his youth, his tears, and your own kind heart, and do not torment him or yourself any longer—anger can only be a torment to your gentle self.
>
> I'm afraid you will think I am using pressure, not persuasion, if I add my prayers to his—but this is what I shall do, and all the more freely and fully because I have given the man a very severe scolding and warned him firmly that I will never make such a request again. This was because he deserved a fright, and is not intended for your ears; for maybe I *shall* make another request and obtain it, as long as it is nothing unsuitable for me to ask and you to grant.

Why would someone fabricate a similar letter in the name of Paul? Edgar J. Goodspeed's theory, which was elaborated by John Knox,[2] was that Onesimus, freed and forgiven as per Paul's request, became a bishop in Ephesus, the one mentioned in Ignatius's *Epistle to the Ephesians:*

> I received, therefore, your whole multitude in the name of God,

504 | The Amazing Colossal Apostle

through Onesimus, a man of inexpressible love, and your bishop in the flesh, whom I pray you by Jesus Christ to love, and that you would all seek to be like him. And blessed be He who has granted unto you, being worthy, to obtain such an excellent bishop.

Goodspeed and Knox reasoned that it was his gratitude to Paul that led Onesimus to collect the Pauline epistles. Bishop Onesimus naturally possessed a copy of the otherwise obscure letter to which he owed so much, and he made sure it was included. But Stephan Hermann Huller[3] turns the theory of Goodspeed and Knox on its head. Huller says that Philemon is a pseudepigraph intended to beef up the authority of Bishop Onesimus by linking him fictively with Paul. This would mean, of course, that the Letter to Philemon stems from Catholic Christianity.

NOTES

[1]Willem C. van Manen, "Epistle to Philemon," *Encyclopaedia Biblica*, eds. Thomas K. Cheyne and John Sutherland Black (New York: Macmillan, 1914), cols. 3693-97.

[2]John Knox, *Philemon among the Letters of Paul: A New View of Its Place and Importance*, rev. ed. (1935; Nashville: Abingdon Press, 1959), 107.

[3]Stephan Huller, "Against Polycarp," online at *Stephan Huller's Observations*, www.bibliobloglibrary.com/p/32157.

18.

The Pastoral Epistles

The Pastoral Epistles are traditionally so called because they have so much to do with Church life and governance. Two of them may even be called Church manuals, albeit wearing a thin veil of avuncular epistles from the aging Paul to young Timothy and Titus, his preferred successors and delegates in Ephesus and Crete. These were the first of the thirteen epistles bearing Paul's name to be recognized as spurious products of a later generation. Likewise, they are the most commonly so regarded. Many scholars who hang on to genuine Pauline authorship for all the other epistles are willing to let these go. The arguments are too many and too strong, so no real rejoinder can be offered that is not at once recognized as special pleading.

Sufficient to rule out Pauline authorship would be the argument of vocabulary. In all three of these texts, there is a common pool of recurring words which seldom occur in the rest of the Pauline epistles, if at all. Many of these words do not occur anywhere else in the New Testament, while some are shared mainly with Luke and Acts, giving rise to various theories of common authorship or redaction.[1] To be specific, the Pastorals contain a total of 902 unique words, 54 of which are proper names, leaving 848; of these, 306 (36%) do not occur in the other ten epistles and 175 do not appear elsewhere in the New Testament at all, outside of the Pastoral trio. Percy N. Harrison,[2] whose statistics I gratefully reproduce here, calculates how, of these unique words ("hapax legomena" in literary criticism), 1 Timothy features 96, which works out to about 15 on each page; 2 Timothy has 60, or 13 per page; and Titus comes in with 43, or 16 to a page. So what? Well, compare that with Romans, which has its own hapaxes, but only 4 per page, the same as First Corinthians, Galatians, 1 Thessalonians, and little Philemon, while the other epistles have about the same number: 3 hapaxes in 2 Thessalonians; 5 in Ephesians; and 6 each in Colossians, 2 Corinthians, and Philippians. Something is drastically suspicious here if we are to credit all these writings to a single author.

Looking at it another way, 1 Timothy has a vocabulary of only 529 words. Of that reservoir, 173 words occur elsewhere in the New Testament but not in any other Pauline epistle outside of the Pastorals. That counts for about one-third of the vocabulary, or 27 words per page! Second Timothy, with 413 different words, has 114 that occur in the New Testament outside the ten Pauline letters. That's 24 per page. With Titus, it's 81 non-Pauline words out of 293, or 30 per page. By contrast, Romans has 261 words shared with other New Testament books but not with other epistles, or 10 per page. To summarize, the Pastorals don't sound enough like Paul to be credible. That is true whether one contrasts them with a single historical Paul or a Pauline School with its own in-group lingo and technical vocabulary.

Some desperate adherents to Pauline authorship for the Pastorals suggest that the vocabulary statistics would be different if we bracketed the various poetic, hymnic, and catechetical fragments such as 1 Timothy 3:16; 6:15-16; 2 Timothy 2; 19; Titus 1:12, and the quasi-creedal "faithful sayings" in 1 Timothy (1:15a; 2:15; 4:9-10), 2 Timothy (2:11-13), and Titus (3:4-8).[3] Without such materials, the argument goes, the ratio of typical versus atypical vocabulary would be less pronounced. But that is only to squeeze the pillow here to have it plump up elsewhere: one then has to ask just why there is such a concentration of unusual patches and pieces in the Pastorals.[4] We are not dealing with a confident author who has his own things to say. Instead, we are reading an impersonator who has to employ considerable filler to sound suitably impressive.

Most damning for Pauline authorship, however, is that there is a large number of words which, while unparalleled elsewhere in the Pauline corpus, occur fulsomely in the second-century writings called the Apostolic Fathers (*Didache, Barnabas, 1 Clement, 2 Clement, Diognetus, Ignatius*). Of course, this means that the Pastorals belong to this later period. They are very likely the work of Bishop Polycarp of Smyrna. And it is not just a matter of favorite nouns, verbs, and adjectives. The use of conjunctions, particles, pronouns, and other minor features varies widely from their usage in the earlier Paulines while they are consistent among the Pastorals themselves. This is the sort of literary fingerprint that does not change, no matter how a writer's mood, circumstances, subject matter, or writing scene may vary over the years.

The overall religious conceptuality is different. In Romans and the other *Hauptbriefe*, one gains the impression that faith in Christ is an existential posture of risk, appropriate to the dawn of a new sectarian movement. Such a movement survives its first generation only if it can instill a solid emotional commitment and a changed life for each adherent. But in subsequent generations, people tend to relax and view faith as belief in the articles of a creed. Actually, faith tends to run out of gas and becomes a more respectable piety, and that is what we find in the Pastorals.

Again, the self-understanding of the Christian in the world is quite different in the Pastorals. In earlier Pauline letters, the typical Christian is a rebel, an outcast, someone persecuted for his allegiance to "another king, Jesus." But in the Pastorals, the goal of Christian families and churches is to live in peace and quiet, happily praying for the emperor and the stability of his regime. Christian values are re-assimilating those of the world outside. No longer interested in turning the world upside down, Christians are more concerned that fanatics not embarrass the church before outsiders. Within the church, sacramental ordination is replacing charismatic gifts that were once freely distributed, week by week. Where once there could be female apostles, now women are not allowed to teach or to hold any position of authority. The primitive sectarian egalitarianism has disappeared. Spirit-inspired wanderers, itinerant charismatics who once commanded hushed audiences with prophetic bulletins from the heavenly Christ, are now suspected of being freeloaders and charlatans.[5] Growing families have less and less interest in the itinerates' tales of heroism, how they left their families and possessions behind. Only the shrinking ranks of consecrated widows and virgins, paid a stipend by the Church for their shrinking ministerial chores, give the itinerant apostles much of a hearing, being fellow ascetics whose influence is similarly passing. Bishops have become the new successors of the apostles. Apostolicity, then, has been re-routed into established offices in ecclesiastical organizations. Can one read 1 Corinthians and come away with the impression that the community was organized into boards of bishops, deacons, elders, and widows? We are in a different world in the Pastorals, one in which the chief goal is the inter-generational transmission (2 Tim. 2:1) of the tradition, which is to say the apostolic succession of bishops.

Some apologists, with their heliotropism toward conservative positions, counter that the offices of bishops and elders were ready to hand out even on the first day of early Christianity. After all, the Dead Sea Scrolls community had them.[6] This misses the point. It is not that no one had heard of institutional structures until the late first century. No, it is that religious groups evolve from early sectarianism, egalitarianism, and freewheeling worship (as described in 1 Corinthians 12) to later, ossifying institutions with creeds to protect, and with officially credentialed clergy to do the protecting. It is not that there were no bishops in Paul's day; they had them over at Qumran, all right. It's just that, given the stage of social development likely for the historical Paul's day, Christianity would not yet have adopted such offices.

If the Pastorals seem at home linguistically and ecclesiastically in a later world than we envision for Paul, they are equally alien to what can be pieced together of his biography and career, whether we accept the rather schematized outline of three missionary journeys in Acts or stick to references interior to the other epistles. There does not seem to be room for the itinerary of Paul implied in the Pastorals. They fit better into the chronology of the apocryphal *Acts of Paul*. Finally, we should note that the traditional order of 1 Timothy, 2 Timothy, and Titus is arbitrary and does not seem to reflect the probable order of writing. In fact, it seems to be just the reverse.

Titus

1

[1]Paul, a slave of God and an apostle of Jesus-Christ, as the elect of God believe him to be, and according to the full knowledge of religious truth, [2]in hopes of age-long life, which God, who cannot lie, promised before the ages of time, [3]but in his own time he made manifest his message in a proclamation with which I was entrusted by the command of our Savior, God, [4]to Titus, a true child by virtue of a common faith. May the favor and protection of God the Father and Christ-Jesus our Savior be with you.

[5]You may be wondering why I left you in Crete. It was so you might organize what was still undone and appoint elders in each city as per my instructions.

The completely artificial, literary character of what we are reading is evident already. Titus has to be told how to organize the churches in Crete only now? Why didn't Paul go over this at the time? Surely he would have. Was he rushing to make a last-minute connection? No, here we see the pseudonymous author writing above the head of the fictive recipient, Titus, to reach latter-day readers, church officials whom Titus symbolizes. It is just like the numerous occasions in the Gospels when the Jesus character speaks ostensibly to the uncomprehending disciples but actually to the readers.

[6]Whoever is irreproachable, not remarried if a widower, has believing children, and not liable to accusations of promiscuity or wild conduct. [7]For a bishop is obliged to be irreproachable, as befits an administrator put in charge by God, not self-centered, not irritable, no drunken brawler, not looking to enrich himself.

Was there a real danger that Titus would just pick someone off the street to serve as bishop? Why stipulate that a high and mighty Christian bishop should not be marked by gross vices that would have gotten someone excommunicated if we were reading 1 Corinthians? We are very far indeed from the initial period of Christian sectarianism.

[8]But hospitable, a lover of the good, prudent, just, pious, celibate, [9]holding fast the reliable message according to the standard teaching in order that he may be able both to exhort on the basis of wholesome teaching and to convince the objectors.
[10]For there are many non-conformists, empty talkers and deceivers, especially those of the circumcision faction, [11]whose mouths must be shut, who throw whole households into confusion, teaching things they should never say, and all for crass profit. [12]A certain one of them, a prophet of their own, said it well: "Cretans are always liars, vicious beasts, idle gluttons."

Who is being quoted here? It is part of a poem attributed to the legendary miracle worker Epimenides, the other half of which is quoted in Acts 17:28—and no coincidence, that. It is one of many indications that Titus (like 2 Timothy) is the work of the author of Acts.

[13]This witness is true, which is why you will need to rebuke them harshly if they are ever to be healthy in the faith, [14]ignoring Jewish myths and man-made commandments that twist the truth.

In Titus 1:14 the author seems to oppose Marcionism but nonetheless to share a gentile antipathy toward Jewish beliefs and customs. That is just what we expect from a Catholic author. The casual reference to the Jewish law in 3:9 shows how very far we are from the polemics over the Torah that preoccupied the earlier period. It has already become, as it is for us, a theological museum piece.

[15]On the contrary, to the pure in heart, all things are pure, but to those who are defiled and unbelieving, nothing can be pure since both their minds and their consciences have been permanently defiled. [16]Oh, they claim they know God, but by their actions they repudiate him, being abominations unto the Lord, disobedient to his commandments, and hypocrites when it comes to good deeds.

2

[1]But as for you, speak the things conducive to wholesome teaching. [2]Older men ought to be sober, sombre, prudent, sound in faith, in love, in endurance. [3]Elderly women, similarly, ought to behave reverently—not slanderers, nor addicted to a lot of wine, teachers of what is good, [4]that is, instructing the younger women to love their husbands and their children, [5]prudent, pure, doing their housework, good, obedient to their husbands; otherwise the message of God may be libeled because of their bad examples.

Why such banalities as we find in Titus 2:5? To us, these instructions seem so tame, it is hard to understand their inclusion. Really, what husband requires to be reminded to love his wife? What wife does not know she is better off loving her husband if she can? But things are not exactly as they first appear. As Dennis MacDonald has shown, the author means to invoke Paul's name against radical Paulinists, who advocated apocalyptic, egalitarian, anti-family, celibate, vegetarian doctrines such as Gnosticism, Encratism, Montanism, and Marcionism. Thrusting aside sectarian egalitarianism, the Pastoral writer (Polycarp) wants to get back to the values of a settled society as quickly as possible.[7]

[6]In the same way, urge the younger fellows to be prudent [7]about everything, providing in your own case a good example of behavior, demonstrating in your teaching the qualities of being incorrupt-

ible, of gravity, [8]of healthy, admirable speech, in order that anyone opposed to us may be embarrassed, at a loss to say anything bad about us. [9]Slaves are to be obedient to their various masters in every matter, to be courteous and never to talk back, [10]not pilfering, but examples of complete reliability, all in order to make the teaching of our Savior, God, more attractive in every way.

[11]For the saving favor of God was shown to all humanity, [12]instructing us that, repudiating impiety and worldly passions, we might live prudently, righteously, and piously in this present age, [13]anticipating the blissful prospect of the epiphany of the splendor of our great God and Savior Christ-Jesus, who gave himself on our behalf that he might ransom us from all lawlessness and purify a people for himself to possess, one eager for good deeds. [15]Speak this sort of thing and exhort and rebuke with all due authority; leave no room through indecisiveness for anyone to have contempt for you.

3

[1]Remind them to be law-abiding citizens, obedient to rulers and authorities, prepared for every good deed, [2]blaspheming no one, avoiding brawls, being patient with others, demonstrating unobtrusiveness to everyone. [3]For once, we too were unthinking, disobedient, completely deceived by and enslaved to various lusts and pleasures, living in evil and envy, hateful and hating each other. [4]But "when the kindness and philanthropy of our Savior God appeared, [5]he saved us, not by any righteousness of ours, but by token of his mercy through the regenerating bath and the renewal of the Holy Spirit which he richly lavished upon us through Jesus-Christ our Savior, [7]in order that, having been accepted by his favor, we might become heirs awaiting the prospect of age-long life." [8]The saying is trustworthy, and I want you to make confident affirmation of these things so those who have believed in God may not leave it at that but keep on doing good deeds. These words are good and beneficial. [9]But waste no time on carping objections and genealogical credentials, discord and arguments over the Jewish law, for these do no one any good, being entirely moot. [10]Mark a quarrelsome man and avoid him after you have rebuked him once, then twice, [11]at which point you can be sure he is just being stubborn and doing what he himself knows is wrong.

¹²Whenever I get around to sending Artemas or Tychicus to relieve you, hurry and come join me in Nicopolis, where I have decided to pass the winter. ¹³Outfit Zenas the lawyer and Apollo for the next stage of their journey so they may be fully provisioned, ¹⁴and see to it that our people also learn to keep up their contributions for such needs, so the work may bear fruit.

¹⁵All those with me greet you. Greet the ones who love us in a common faith. May God's favor be with you all.

The Epistle to Titus is a miniature Church manual, not unlike the *Didache* or even the later *Apostolic Constitutions*. As we will see, 2 Timothy performs a rather different function. It is a Pauline Testament, the imagined reflections of a great man on his deathbed. This was an important genre of Jewish and Greek hagiography. The latest and greatest teaching of Socrates is imparted to his disciples in Plato's *Crito,* just before Socrates dies. The parting thoughts of the Jewish tribal patriarchs are fictively preserved in the *Testaments of the Twelve Patriarchs.* There are also testaments ascribed to Abraham, Isaac, and Jacob. The Last Supper discourses of John 13-16 also qualify.

2 Timothy

1

¹Paul, an apostle of Christ-Jesus by the decision of God, to make known the promise of life available in Christ-Jesus, ²to Timothy, beloved child. May you enjoy favor, mercy, and protection from God our Father and Christ-Jesus our Lord.

³I give thanks to God, whom I worship as my forefathers did, with a clear conscience, as I remember you without fail in my prayers night and day, ⁴longing to see you, reminded of your tears at our parting, so that I may be filled with joy. ⁵I recall your sincere faith, which dwelt first in your grandmother Lois and in your mother Eunice, and now, I am convinced, in you as well.

Timothy is pictured as a third-generation Christian. How likely is that, if he was a contemporary of the apostle Paul?

⁶And this is why I remind you to fan into flame that gift of God

that is in you through the imposition of my hands. [7]For God did not give us a spirit of cowardice, but rather of power, of love, and of temperance. [8]So do not be ashamed of our testimony to the Lord or of me, his prisoner, but be ready to suffer adversity for the news, drawing upon the power of God, [9]the one who has saved us and called us to a holy vocation—not as our deeds deserved, but on the sole basis of his plan and the favor shown us in Christ-Jesus long ages ago [10]but made manifest now through the epiphany of our Savior Christ-Jesus, on the one hand canceling death, on the other bringing into view life and freedom from decay through the news, [11]for which I was appointed herald and apostle and teacher, [12]and for which cause, too, I am suffering all these things. Nonetheless, I am not ashamed, as if I had made some terrible mistake, for I know who it is I have believed, and I am fully convinced he is able to safeguard the deposit I have left with him against that day when full payment will be mine. [13]Use a model of wholesome words which you heard from me that bespeaks faith and love shared in Christ-Jesus. [14]Guard the good deposit by means of the Holy Spirit dwelling inside us.

[15]You know how all those in Asia broke with me, including Phygelus and Hermogenes. [16]May the Lord show mercy on the household of Onesiphorus because he frequently refreshed me and was not ashamed to be associated with a prisoner, [17]but coming to Rome, he tirelessly searched for me till he found me. [18]May the Lord grant that he find mercy on that day! And the service he rendered me in Ephesus, you know very well.

The scattering of the Pauline sheep described in 2 Timothy 1:15 and 4:10 does not reflect any actual abandonment of the apostle by his fair-weather friends. There is a very different issue at stake here once we recognize the text as a pseudepigraph. As "predicted" in Acts 20:29-30, Asia was overrun with Paulinist heretics: Gnostics, Encratites, and Marcionites. One Catholic reaction was to write off Paul, along with the sectarians who claimed descent from him, saying "They can have him!" Instead, they promoted the legend of John, the son of Zebedee, as the substitute apostle to Ephesus (see chapter 6). But Acts 19:1-7 rejects this strategy and follows the same plan as the author's successors Irenaeus and Tertullian, re-shaping

Paul as a bona fide Catholic, accepting him as the apostle to Asia but separating him from the Paulinist heretics. Just so, 2 Timothy blames post-Pauline heretical developments on people who deemed themselves Paul's pupils but who broke with him at the last. On the surface level, the picture is similar to that of Jesus's arrest at Gethsemane: the disciples flee and are scattered. But the real point here is to imply that Paul's breakaway disciples would have been misusing his name to promote their own heresies. It is the same as in 1 John 2:19: "They went out from us, but they were not our true representatives; had they truly belonged to our fellowship they would have stuck with us, but this has happened in order to make clear that they do not represent us." Think of the division of Alexander's empire after his death. Are Paul's lieutenants scrambling to divide up his sphere of influence, promoting themselves as his successors in various areas of his activity? This bad-mouthing of Paul's colleagues, who are mentioned favorably in other epistles, must reflect a later schism or schisms within the Paulinist movement.

2

[1]You, therefore, my child, be empowered by the charisma that is to be had in Christ-Jesus, [2]and whatever you heard from me through many witnesses, entrust these words to faithful persons who will be competent to teach others, as well.

Here is the doctrine of apostolic succession and orthodox tradition in a nutshell. The stipulation is that the clergy, for whom Timothy stands, must adhere to what is taught by the collective of elders and bishops, without transmitting private thoughts, precisely as in 2 Peter 1:20-21 where we are warned that the sacred truth is never the product of an individual's speculation or interpretation. No, it must be approved as part of the party line. We are in the same territory with Irenaeus's disdain for the Gnostics who vied with one another in concocting ever new and more outlandish revelations. Note the similarity to what is said by the same author, I think, in Luke 1:2, namely that he and his readers are latter-day heirs, but at how distant a remove from the supposed witnesses of the original gospel teaching is not clear.

³Shoulder your share of suffering as a good soldier of Christ-Jesus: ⁴No soldier on active duty involves himself with concerns of civilian life, because he wants to win the approval of his recruiter. ⁵And no wrestler wins the championship unless he follows the rules. ⁶It is only right that the hard-working farmer be the first to enjoy the fruits. ⁷Consider what I am saying, for the Lord will make everything clear to you. ⁸Always have in mind Jesus-Christ, raised from the dead, sprung from David's line, as in the news I proclaim, ⁹in the service of which I endure adversity to the point of being chained up like a criminal—not that the message of God has been confined.

¹⁰This is why I endure everything, on account of the chosen ones, in order that they, too, may attain to salvation in union with Christ-Jesus, with age-enduring splendor. ¹¹The saying is trustworthy: "If we died with him, we shall live with him, too. ¹²If we persevere, we shall reign with him, too. If we deny him, he will deny us, too. ¹³Our faith may fail, but his faithfulness endures, for he cannot contradict himself." ¹⁴You remind them of these things, soberly testifying before God, urging them to avoid verbal battles which do no one any good but undermine the faith of those who listen. ¹⁵Be anxious to present yourself for approval before God as a workman proud of his labor, plowing a straight furrow with the message of truth.

See the Lukan addition to the Q original that reads, "No one who puts his hand to the plow and looks back is fit for the kingdom of God" (Luke 9:62). Why is this? Because if you start turning around to look back instead of keeping your eyes straight ahead, you will veer off course and not plow a straight furrow. I think we are reading the advice of the same author in both passages.

¹⁶But steer clear of profane and empty jabbering, for these lead to ever greater impiety. ¹⁷And such words will eat away like a cancer. Hymenaeus and Philetus are a case in point. ¹⁸They shot wide of the truth by teaching that the resurrection has already come, overturning some people's faith. ¹⁹However, the firm foundation of God stands and will not be overturned. It bears this seal: "The Lord knows which ones are his" and "Let every one who invokes the name of the Lord repudiate unrighteousness."

²⁰Now in a large house you will find not only vessels of gold and silver but wooden and ceramic ones, too. There is the best dinnerware as well as the chamber pot. ²¹If anyone purifies himself out of the latter category, he will become one of the former, having been sanctified, suitable for the master's table, prepared for every noble use. ²²Even so, run away from the lusts of youth, but run after righteousness, faith, love, and peace, along with all who invoke the Lord from a pure heart. ²³But refuse to waste time with moronic and uninformed questions, knowing that they lead only to arguments, ²⁴and it is unbecoming for the Lord's slave to be argumentative, but he ought rather to be gentle toward everyone, able to teach, tolerant, ²⁵instructing without defensiveness those who oppose you on the chance God may grant them a change of mind, to know the full truth, ²⁶that they may snap out of it and extricate themselves from the accuser's net, having been snared by him according to his scheme.

3

¹And you know this: how in the last days, dangerous crises will be at hand; ²for people will be self-absorbed, lovers of money, braggarts, conceited, blasphemers, disobedient to parents, ingrates, unholy, ³sociopaths, pitiless, slanderers, promiscuous, wild, haters of the good, ⁴traducers, impetuous, ego-inflated, lovers of pleasure rather than lovers of God, ⁵having the veneer of godliness but denying its power. Avoid people like this! ⁶For it is people of this ilk who sneak into houses and captivate frivolous women who are burdened with sins and led by various lusts, ⁷always disciples, yet never arriving at any definite conclusions about the truth. ⁸Now in just the same way that Jannes and Jambres opposed Moses, so too, these oppose the truth, people with corrupt minds, disqualified for the faith. ⁹But they will advance no farther, for their nonsense will be too obvious to everyone, just as the old magicians' hokum was publicly refuted. ¹⁰But you have closely followed my teaching, behavior, determination, faith, long-suffering, love, endurance, ¹¹and the persecutions and sufferings that befell me at Antioch, at Iconium, and at Lystra, what persecutions I endured, and out of all of them the Lord delivered me. ¹²And indeed, all those who want to live piously in the faith of Christ-Jesus will be persecuted. ¹³But evil-doers and charlatan

magicians will only get worse in the last days, deceiving others and finally believing their own lies. [14]But you make sure you continue in the teachings you learned and have been assured of, remembering those from whom you learned them [15]and that from infancy you have known the holy scriptures which are able to educate you about salvation through belief in Christ-Jesus. [16]Every passage of scripture is the very exhalation of God, advantageous for teaching, for reproving, for correcting, for schooling in righteousness, [17]in order that the servant of God may be equipped for every good deed that may be required of him.

Does 2 Timothy 3:16-17 state the obvious? Not if the author is a Catholic contending against certain theological rivals who make crucial distinctions between sections or levels of scripture. Our author repudiates the Marcionite/Gnostic rejection of the Old Testament as a non-Christian book. The specification of "every scripture" implies awareness of the Valentinian theory that while some texts had been inspired by God, others were added by Moses and still others by his appointed elders and thus had different levels of authority.

> First, you must learn that the entire Law contained in the Pentateuch of Moses was not ordained by one legislator—I mean, not by God alone, [but] some commandments are Moses', and some were given by other men. The words of the Savior teach us this triple division. The first part must be attributed to God alone, and his legislation; the second to Moses—not in the sense that God legislates through him, but in the sense that Moses gave some legislation under the influence of his own ideas; and the third to the elders of the people, who seem to have ordained some commandments of their own at the beginning. (Ptolemy to Flora, in Epiphanius, *Panarion*, 33)[8]

4

[1]I bear sober witness before God and Christ-Jesus, who is ready to judge the living and the dead, by his epiphany and his kingship: [2]you are to preach the message, attending to it when convenient as well as when inconvenient. Reprove, upbraid, encourage, all the while showing great patience and teaching the better way.

³For there will come a time when one's hearers will not put up with the wholesome teaching but, moved by their own lusts, will collect innumerable teachers of various doctrines who will entice their ears. ⁴On the one hand, their ear will recoil from the truth, and on the other, they will gravitate to myths. ⁵But you remain clear-headed amid all this confusion, endure adversity, do the work of the evangelist, fulfill your obligation to the ministry. ⁶For I am already spent, and the time of my departure has overtaken me. ⁷In retrospect, I have fought a good battle, I have reached the finish line, I have held onto the faith. ⁸What now remains for me is the crown of salvation which the Lord, the righteous judge, will bestow on me on that day and not only on me, but also on all those who cherished the prospect of his epiphany.

⁹Make every effort to come and join me as soon as you can. ¹⁰For Demas abandoned me, preferring this present age, and went to Thessalonica, Crescens to Galatia, Titus to Dalmatia. ¹¹Luke is the only one left with me. Find Mark and bring him with you. ¹²I sent Tychicus to Ephesus. ¹³When you come, be sure to bring the cloak I loaned to Carpus in Troas and the scrolls, too, especially the parchments.

The name Carpus hints at the pseudonymous author Polycarpus, whose scroll the reader is perusing right now. The cloak might also be an unintended hint at the veiled pseudonymity of the letter.

¹⁴Alexander, the coppersmith, sent much trouble my way. The Lord will see he gets his due reward. ¹⁵But watch out for him, for he powerfully opposed our message. ¹⁶At my first defense, no one stood beside me, but everyone abandoned me. May it not be counted against them. ¹⁷But the Lord stood with me and empowered me in order that through me the destined proclamation might be fulfilled and all the nations might hear the news, and I was delivered out of the very mouth of the lion. ¹⁸The Lord will deliver me from every evil deed plotted against me and will see me safely to his heavenly realm. To him be all worship throughout ages multiplied by ages! Amen.

Paul is, of course, safely ensconced in the heavenly realm by the time this letter sees the light of day.

¹⁹Greet Prisca and Aquila and the household of Onesiphorus. ²⁰Erastus stayed behind in Corinth, but I left Trophimus sick in Miletus. ²¹Make every effort to come to me before winter makes travel so difficult. Greetings from Eubulus and Pudens and Linus and Claudia and all the brothers.

²²May the Lord fortify your spirit. May his favor accompany you.

In Philemon we read of Onesimus seeking out Paul in prison. Now we read of Onesiphorus, a different individual, seeking him out in the same place to render comfort and aid while Paul is incarcerated. Both names mean "beneficial," signifying that they fill a narrative purpose rather than being the names of actual individuals.

1 Timothy

1

¹Paul, an apostle of Christ-Jesus by the command of God our Savior and of Christ-Jesus, our hope. ²To Timothy, a true child by virtue of a common faith. May you enjoy favor, mercy, and protection from God the Father and Christ-Jesus our Lord.

³As you recall, I urged you to stay behind in Ephesus as I left for Macedonia so you might command certain individuals to stop teaching heterodoxy ⁴nor to give attention to myths and to endless genealogies which only lead to speculations rather than facilitating the faithful administration of God's favor.

Friedrich Schleiermacher[9] demonstrated that whoever wrote 1 Timothy did not write 2 Timothy and Titus. Instead, 1 Timothy combines elements from the other Pastorals the same way 2 Peter borrows from 1 Peter and Jude. Though Schleiermacher still considered 2 Timothy and Titus to be genuinely Pauline, he relied on the same sort of argument used today to show the non-Pauline authorship of all three Pastoral Epistles. What he noticed was that in cases where the author of 1 Timothy borrowed words and phrases verbatim from Titus and 2 Timothy, the author misunderstood the meaning in its original context. For instance, Titus had in mind the false doctrines of "the circumcision party" when the author wrote about "myths" and "genealogies" (1:14; 3:9), but in 1 Timothy the author is imagining some sort of esoterica employed by false teachers to impress and confuse their patsies (1:4). When 1 Timothy 1:8-10 lifts the business about "teaching the law" from Titus 1:14-15, the author no longer understands that the reference is to the Torah. He sounds more like a Rotarian than a Lutheran.

[5]The goal of such commands is love from a pure heart, a good conscience, and nonhypocritical faith, [6]goals which some, misjudging their aim, have failed to reach, veering off course toward empty talk, [7]desiring to be teachers of the law, but neither realizing what they are saying nor understanding the matters they pontificate about. [8]Of course, we know that law is good as long as one uses it lawfully, [9]remembering that laws are not laid down to govern righteous people but the lawless and hellions, the impious and sinners, the unholy and the profane, murderers of fathers, of mothers, of husbands, [10]prostitutes, men who lie with men, child prostitute recruiters, liars and perjurers, and those who practice anything else opposed to wholesome teaching, [11]stemming from the news of the splendor of the God who ever abides in bliss, with which I was entrusted.

[12]I give thanks to the one who empowers me, Christ-Jesus our Lord, because he decided I was trustworthy and placed me in his service, [13]despite my previously having been a blasphemer, a persecutor, and filled with overweening pride. But I managed to get mercy because, being ignorant, I acted in unbelief. [14]And our Lord's favor overflowed in the form of faith in Christ-Jesus and love for him. [15]The saying is trustworthy and deserves universal acceptance: "Christ-Jesus entered the world to save sinners," of whom I am number one; [16]but it was just because of this that I obtained mercy, in order that in my case, as the worst, Jesus-Christ might demonstrate the full extent of his long-suffering, to serve as an example for those coming to believe in him for age-long life. [17]Now to the King of the Eons, unchanging, invisible, solely God, be honor and worship unto ages multiplied by ages! Amen.

[18]I command you this, child Timothy, according to the prophecies once uttered about you, that encouraged by them you may wage a good war, [19]armed with faith and a good conscience, which some have thrown aside and made of their faith a shipwreck. [20]I am

thinking of Hymenaeus and Alexander, whom I had to consign to the adversary so they may learn the hard way not to blaspheme.

2

[1]Therefore, I urge, first of all, that petitions be made, prayers, intercessions, thanksgivings, [2]on behalf of all people, on behalf of kings and all those in positions of prominence, in order that we may lead a tranquil and quiet life in all piety and gravity. [3]This is a fine and approved thing in the sight of our Savior, God, [4]who only wants all humanity to be saved and to arrive at a full realization of the truth. [5]For there is one God and also one mediator between God and humankind, a man, Christ-Jesus, [6]the one who has given himself as a ransom on behalf of all, the martyrdom at just the proper moment.

The affirmation of monotheism in 2:5, which one might have thought could be taken for granted by this time, is a shot at Marcionism with its two deities, Hebrew and Christian, not at pagan polytheism.

[7]Of all this I was appointed herald and apostle—I speak the truth and do not lie!—a teacher of the nations about faith and truth. [8]Therefore, I want the husbands in every place to pray, lifting up pious hands without anger or second thoughts. [9]In the same way, I want wives to pray dressed with modesty and sobriety, not with gold or pearls plaited into their hair or wearing expensive clothing, [10]but with such adornment as befits women claiming to be reverent, that is, good deeds. [11]Let a wife learn in silence and complete submission. [12]But I do not permit woman to claim to have created man, but to keep silent. [13]For Adam was not the one deceived, but it is the woman who, having been deceived, has fallen into transgression. [15]But "she will yet be saved through child-bearing as long as they remain steadfast in faith and love and sanctification with proper sobriety."

3

[1]This saying is trustworthy. If anyone aspires to the office of bishop, it is a worthy task he seeks. [2]Thus it is incumbent on a bishop

to be irreproachable, not remarried if a widower, temperate, prudent, well-organized, hospitable, a good teacher, [3]not a wine-lover, not violent, but patient, given neither to arguments nor to greed, [4]governing his own household well, having his children in subjection with proper seriousness. [5]If someone does not know how to govern his own household, how will he take care of a congregation of God? [6]Let him not be a neophyte, or he may become swell-headed and repeat the accuser's error. [7]And it is needful that he have a good reputation among those outside, or he may become embroiled in some scandal and be snared by the accuser.

[8]In the same way, it behooves deacons to be dour, not fork-tongued, not addicted to too much wine, not preoccupied with crass profit, [9]holding to the mystery of the faith without reservations. [10]And make sure these are given an initial probationary period; then if they do turn out to be irreproachable, let them serve. [11]Their wives, too, need to be dour, not slanderers, sober, and altogether reliable. [12]Let deacons not remarry if widowers, aptly governing their children and their own households. [13]For those who have served well acquire a good position for themselves, as well as great authority in the religion of Christ-Jesus. [14]I write you these things because, though I hope to come to you shortly, [15]in case I am delayed, I want you to know what behavior is appropriate in the household of God. It is the congregation of the true God, pillar and bulwark of the truth. [16]And admittedly, the mystery of piety is great:

> Whose epiphany was in flesh,
> Vindicated by the Spirit,
> Seen by angels,
> Proclaimed among nations,
> Believed in the world,
> Assumed in glory.

Here is a portion of a creedal formula or possibly a hymn lyric, two genres that are characteristic of the later period of doctrinal consolidation. Notice that it views the universal proclamation of the Christian message as already accomplished! Can Paul possibly have written this? If we envision the historical Paul *quoting* such a text, it makes the anachronism even worse.

4

[1]Now the Spirit says verbatim, "In the last times, some will apostatize from the faith, heeding misleading prophecies and demonic teachings [2]from lying hypocrites whose crimes are branded on their consciences to the point of moral insensitivity." [3]For example, they forbid marriage, command abstinence from foods that God created for believers and those who know the truth to share in with thankful hearts. [4]For every creation of God is good, and nothing is to be placed off limits if it is welcomed with thanksgiving, [5]for it has been rendered holy by means of the command of God and prayer.

Here the author ascribes vegetarianism and celibacy to the devil, taking aim at Gnostic, Marcionite, and Encratite asceticism, which was rampant in Asia Minor.

[6]By assuring the brothers of these things, you will be a good servant of Christ-Jesus, nourished by the trustworthy sayings and the fine teaching which you have followed. [7]But pay no mind to pagan myths or old wives' tales. Train yourself in piety. [8]For though bodily training is worthwhile, its value in the scheme of things is small. But piety is advantageous in every area of life, being full of promise for the present life as well as the coming one. [9]The saying is trustworthy and deserves everyone's acceptance: [10]for this we labor and strive because "we have set our hope on a living God who is the savior of all humanity, mostly of believers." [11]Command and teach these things. [12]Give no one room to disregard you for your youth, but become a model for believers in speech, in conduct, in love, in faith, in purity. [13]Until I arrive, see to the public reading of scripture, to exhortation, to teaching. [14]Do not take for granted the charisma within you, which was imparted to you by means of prophecy with the imposition of hands by the council of elders.

Second Timothy 1:6 recalls Timothy's ordination at the hands of Paul himself, but in 1 Timothy 4:14 the ordination is credited to the presbyters collectively. Why? The author of 1 Timothy wanted to distribute Paul's authority among his imagined successors in the same manner that what is ascribed to Peter in Matthew 18:18 is distributed more broadly in Matthew 16:17-19.[10]

[15]Give attention to these matters; immerse yourself in them, and your progress will be plain to all. [16]Pay close attention to your own sanctification and the teaching: persevere in them. By so doing, you will save yourself and your hearers.

5

[1]Do not presume to reprimand one of the elders, but exhort him as you would a father, younger men as brothers, [2]older women as mothers, younger women as sisters in strict purity. [3]Support the genuine widows. [4]But if any widow has children or grandchildren, let them learn to show piety first of all toward their own household and to return the favor of their parents' care: this is what God approves. [5]By a "genuine widow," I mean one who has been left alone, who has cast her hope on God and perseveres in the assigned petitions and prayers night and day. [6]But the "widow" who is promiscuous is one of the living dead. [7]And you must speak out on this so they may be free from scandal. [8]But if anyone does not provide for his own relatives, and especially his immediate family, he has in effect denied the faith and is worse than an outright unbeliever. [9]Let a woman be enrolled among the widows only if she is no younger than sixty years of age, having never remarried, [10]with a reputation for good deeds such as bringing up children, giving hospitality to strangers, washing the feet of the itinerant holy men, relieving the afflicted, actively following up every opportunity to do good. [11]But refuse to enroll younger women as widows, for sooner or later they will grow restive, unfaithful to Christ, and they will want to get married, [12]incurring judgment because they violated their original pledge. [13]And in the meantime they learn the ways of idleness, making the rounds of the houses, and become not only idle but also gossips, attending to others' business, speaking of things that are not their responsibility. [14]I would rather have these younger women marry, bear children, take charge of a household so they will avoid giving any excuse for our critics to reproach us. [15]It is too late for some, who have already turned off the path to follow the adversary.

[16]If any consecrated woman has celibate women living with her, let her provide for them rather than letting the congregation bear the financial burden, in order that it may provide for the literal widows.

1 Timothy updates the ecclesiastical rules from the earlier Pastorals. Some of the features of Church organization and government on display in 1 Timothy imply a later stage of institutional development than that reached in 2 Timothy and Titus. Titus 1:5-9 deals only with bishops, but 1 Timothy 5:4-16 has a separate order of deacons, not to mention a stipendiary order of consecrated widows.

[17]Let the elders who govern well be considered worthy of double compensation, especially those engaged in speech and teaching. [18]For the scripture says: "You shall not muzzle the ox while he is treading out the grain" and "The workman is worthy of his wage." [19]Do not credit any accusation against an elder unless two or three witnesses confirm it. [20]Those who are found to be guilty, you must publicly rebuke so as to instill fear in the others. [21]I solemnly command you in the sight of God and Christ-Jesus and the chosen angels that you follow this procedure without partiality, doing nothing out of favoritism. [22]Do not ordain anyone prematurely or you will be liable for his mistakes.

Keep yourself pure. [23]No longer drink only water, but have a little wine for the sake of your nervous stomach. [24]The sins of some people are evident early on, leading them to judgment, but some indeed come to light only later. [25]In the same way, good deeds are evident right up front, but those that are not cannot remain hidden forever.

The urging to drink a bit of wine sounds like mitigation of asceticism, specifically teetotalism, characteristic of the encratites and Gnostics.

6

[1]Let all those who bear the yoke of slavery consider their masters worthy of all honor; otherwise the name of God and the teaching may be blasphemed. [2]And those who have believers for masters, let them not despise them because they are brothers, but rather let them slave for them precisely because the ones receiving their good service are believers and thus should be beloved.

Teach and exhort all this. [3]If anyone teaches heterodoxy and does not agree to the wholesome sayings of our Lord, Jesus-Christ, and to the edifying teaching, [4]he is a windbag who understands nothing but is obsessed with questions and verbal battles which yield only envy, discord, blasphemies, suspicions, evil, in short, the pointless disputes of people with corrupt minds, bereft of the truth, viewing piety as one more money-making gimmick. [6]In fact, piety with self-sufficiency is a great profit, [7]for we have brought nothing into the world, and we will be carrying nothing out of it! [8]As long as we have food and clothing, we will be satisfied. [9]But those who make it their goal to be rich fall into temptation and snares and many foolish and harmful lusts which cause people to sink into the quicksand of ruin and destruction. [10]For the love of money is a root of all manner of evils, and some who have yearned for it have drifted away from the faith and been feathered with the shafts of many sorrows. [11]But you, O man of God, flee from these things; pursue righteousness, piety, faith, love, perseverance, a slow temper. [12]Fight the noble fight of the faith, grab hold of the prize of age-long life, to which you were summoned and concerning which you affirmed the noble confession before many witnesses. [13]I command you in the sight of God, the one who gives life to all creatures, and Christ-Jesus, the one who witnessed to the noble confession in the presence of Pontius Pilatus, to keep this command without reproach until the epiphany of our Lord, Jesus-Christ, [15]which the blessed and sole potentate, the king of kings and lord of lords, will signal at its own appointed time, the only possessor of immortality, dwelling at the center of unapproachable light, whom no mortal has beheld or ever may behold, to whom be honor and sovereignty throughout the ages! Amen.

[17]Command those who have worldly wealth not to be snobbish, nor to set their hopes for the future on uncertain riches but on that God who lavishly offers us all creation to enjoy. [18]Command them to practice benevolence, to be rich in good deeds, to be ready to donate, willing to share, [19]amassing for themselves a good foundation for the future in order that they may grab hold of age-long life.

[20]O Timothy, guard the precious deposit, recoiling from profane and empty jabbering and the *Antitheses* of the falsely labeled "gnosis," [21]for some who profess it have shot wide of the faith. May God's favor be with you.

Here, in verse 6:20, the author actually mentions Marcion's tract *Antitheses*, which contrasted the Jewish scriptures unfavorably with the Pauline letters. True, the author confuses Marcionism with Gnosticism, but this is not uncommon even among scholars today.

Both Titus and 2 Timothy mention a missionary, Tychicus, who does not appear in 1 Timothy. Nor does 1 Timothy update readers on the status of Apollo, Claudia, Luke, Mark, or the eleven other individuals from Titus and 2 Timothy. Why would two of these letters engage in name dropping and 1 Timothy does not? I think it would be for the same reason Matthew omitted most of Mark's denigrating references to Jesus's disciples. Remember that in 2 Timothy we saw Paul's companions fleeing like rats from a sinking ship—like the disciples fleeing their master in Gethsemane. All but one of Paul's disciples had abandoned him at the time of his earlier trial, according to 2 Timothy 4:16, Luke being the only one standing by his side on the eve of the next trial. Everyone else suddenly remembered some pressing obligation elsewhere, including Demas, Crescens, Titus, and Erastus (2 Tim. 4:10, 20). In 1 Timothy, we might be witnessing an attempt to rehabilitate the reputations of people who were said to have been part of Paul's circle, also explaining why Timothy was chosen over Titus as the fictive recipient of the epistle. Titus was said to have been elsewhere (4:10), while Timothy was on his way back (4:9). Otherwise we would be reading 2 Titus.

In 2 Timothy we were told about Moses's Egyptian rivals, the sorcerers Jannes and Jambres (3:8), who are absent from 1 Timothy, and not by accident. It looks to me like we are seeing here a tendency to expunge non-canonical material. In precisely the same way, 2 Peter borrows much from Jude, often word for word, but the author of 2 Peter chopped away Jude's references to *1 Enoch* and the *Assumption of Moses*. Such canon anxiety is a sign of late composition.

Earlier on, I hypothesized that when Marcion wrote in the epistles, or when his successors wrote for him, they seemed to be unacquainted with any Gospel, including the Ur-Lukas. On the other hand, there is ample evidence that, once the Gospels, and Gospel material generally, began to be composed, there was major input from the Marcionites. The traditional picture of Marcion choosing one among several extant Gospels confuses the picture, attributing to

Marcion himself what his lieutenants must have done a bit later. But here in the Pastorals we find epistles which are very likely the products of a writer such as Polycarp who knew of the Gospels and was, in all probability, the ecclesiastical redactor of both John and Luke. Yet Titus and 2 Timothy evidence no more acquaintance with the Gospels than Romans does. Does this not give the lie to the notion that an epistle writer who knew Gospel traditions must have used them and that hence the epistles were early compositions?

Apologists argue that the writers of the epistles knew the Jesus traditions without explicitly mentioning them. There was something about the epistle genre that excluded any recognizable or explicit citation of Gospel material. I cannot figure out what it is about the epistle genre that would have excluded quoting from Jesus. It remains impossible to deny that the epistolarians would have had frequent occasion to quote sayings of the Lord Jesus to settle issues of concern to them. The discussion of circumcision in Romans 3:1-2 might have made good use of Jesus's remark in *Thomas* 53. Those who discussed the gentile mission in Romans 4:9-12; 9:22-30, and Ephesians 2:11-22 would have referred to the Great Commission in Matthew 28:18-20 if they had ever heard of it. In Romans 14 and Colossians 2:16-17, 20-23, the writer discusses the dietary laws but makes no mention of what Jesus supposedly said on the topic in Mark 7:14-19 and Luke 10:7-8. On the ticklish matter of paying Roman taxes, how could you not settle the issue by appealing to Mark 12:13-17? Is celibacy the issue in 1 Corinthians 7? Why not invoke Jesus, as reported in Matthew 19:12? Controversy over glossolalia in 1 Corinthians 12-14? Try quoting Matthew 6:7. Indeed, it is not too much to say that the Gospels replaced the epistles for this very reason: dominical sayings and precedents, like the hadith of Muhammad, trump everything else.

But apologists are nonetheless accidentally close to the truth. Since the Gospel tradition did not yet exist when the Pauline corpus was written, the fact is that by the time Polycarp got around to writing pastiche epistles, the genre did in fact exclude Jesus-material by default. So if Polycarp wanted his pastiches to sound like real Pauline epistles, he had to leave aside many juicy Gospel bits. Note the progression: 1 Corinthians has a few elements of Gospel-like material (7:10, 25; 11:23-25; 14:37) that seem, however, to be prophetic oracles vouchsafed to Paul in visions and auditions (cf. 2 Cor. 12:8-9). In 1 Thessalonians 4:15, we see an appeal to "the word of the Lord," likely in reference to prophetic scripture such as Isaiah 31:4. But things change when we come to 1 Timothy, written even later than Titus and 2 Timothy. 1 Timothy 5:18 ascribes the saying, "The laborer deserves his wages," to scripture, which means the author already regards Luke as canonical.[11] Again, 1 Timothy 6:13 explicitly refers to the Gospel of John's trial scene with Jesus before Pilate (18:33-38). Concerned, for the sake of what had become genre convention, to exclude such references to the Gospels, the epistolarian does his best but in the end cannot leave them out altogether. So I would say the Pastorals, pastiches of earlier Pauline epistles (especially 1 Timothy, a pastiche of two pastiches) constitute the exception that proves the rule.

NOTES

[1] I find Stephen G. Wilson, *Luke and the Pastoral Epistles* (London: SPCK, 1979), pretty convincing on common authorship.

[2] Percy N. Harrison, *The Problem of the Pastoral Epistles* (NY: Oxford University Press, 1921).

[3] George W. Knight III, *The Faithful Sayings in the Pastoral Epistles*, Baker Biblical Monographs (Grand Rapids: Baker Book House, 1979).

[4] Though he is speaking of Colossians, Norman Perrin's comment applies perfectly to the Pastorals too: "These linguistic factors could be due to pseudonymity, in part difference from and in part deliberate imitation of genuine Pauline vocabulary and style. Or they could be due to a deliberate use [by Paul] of the opponents' vocabulary and to the very extensive use in this letter of traditional material—hymns, confessions, lists of virtues, household codes, and the like. [Thus] it can be argued that this accounts for the non-Pauline language and style. If this is the case, the non-Pauline language and style are not indications of pseudonymity. But then it could be retorted that such an extensive use of traditional material is itself non-Pauline" (*The New Testament: An Introduction* [NY: Harcourt Brace Jovanovich, 1974), 121.

⁵Stevan L. Davies, *The Revolt of the Widows: The Social World of the Apocryphal Acts* (Carbondale: Southern Illinois University Press, 1980), 35-42. See also Hans von Campenhausen, *Ecclesiastical Authority and Spiritual Power in the Church of the First Three Centuries*, trans. J. A. Baker (Stanford: Stanford University Press, 1969), chapter 8, "Prophets and Teachers in the Second Century," 70-212.

⁶Edwin M. Yamauchi, *The Stones and the Scriptures* (Philadelphia: Lippincott, 1972), 138-39. He is seeking to telescope the sect-to-church evolution as traced, famously albeit broadly, by Rudolf Sohm, *Outlines of Church History*, trans. May Sinclair (London: Macmillan, 1931), 19-20, 32-36. There is just something about evolution that conservatives can't stomach. For them, everything has to have appeared all at once on a platter like the head of John the Baptist.

⁷Dennis R. MacDonald, *The Legend and the Apostle: The Battle for Paul in Story and Canon* (Philadelphia: Fortress Press, 1982).

⁸Ptolemy was a Valentinian Gnostic. The letter comes by way of Epiphanius, the bishop of Salamis in the late fourth century.

⁹Friedrich Schleiermacher, *Über den sogenannten ersten Brief des Paulos an den Timotheos: Ein kritisches Sendschreiben an J. C. Gass* ["Concerning the So-called First Letter of Paul to Timothy: A Critical Open Letter to J. C. Gass"] (Berlin: Realbuchhandlung, 1807), available in *Friedrich Schleiermacher's Sämmtliche Werke* (Berlin: G. Reimer, 1864), 2:221-320.

¹⁰Arlo J. Nau, *Peter in Matthew: Discipleship, Diplomacy, and Dispraise* (Collegeville: Liturgical Press, 1992), 26, 97, 112, 120, 131.

¹¹In David Trobisch's *First Edition of the New Testament* (NY: Oxford University Press, 2000) and follow-up article, "Who Published the New Testament?" *Free Inquiry*, vol. 28, no. 1 (Dec. 2007/Jan. 2008): 30-33, he demonstrated to my satisfaction that it was Polycarp of Smyrna who put together the canon of the Old and New Testaments that Christians use today. He expanded some New Testament books and wrote others in their entirety (Acts, Titus, 2 Timothy). Based on Schleiermacher's analysis, I would posit that a disciple of Polycarp wrote 1 Timothy, which his master then added to the canon.

A CANTICLE FOR PAUL

If New Testament scholars, at least those who retain any Christian faith, were to lose Paul, they wouldn't know what to do! To whom could they appeal for a true vision of God and his purposes for mankind? Could they turn to the author of the Epistle to the Hebrews? Jude? Not likely. Here at the end of this exploration of the amazing colossal Paul, who looms so large over the religious landscape, it is worth asking whether and in what sense we have retained a useful Paul.

Following Hermann Detering, I identify Paul as having some connection to the historical figure of Simon Magus. F. C. Baur saw the tie between the two, but he took the Simon character to be a polemical evil twin or "monstrous double" of Paul. Detering saw that Paul was a mystification of the historical Simon Magus, that Marcion was not merely the collector of the Pauline letter corpus but even the writer of some of those epistles. I differ from Detering in two respects. First, just as some scholars have admitted that we cannot tell the difference between Marcion's own scripture texts and those of subsequent Marcionites, I contend that we have long erred in ascribing to the Pontic Lion the work of his disciples in penning and collecting epistles and in the writing and choosing of Gospels. Marcion had as yet no Gospel text, though soon his followers would join in the broader process of composing Jesus stories and sayings. Marcion cannot have written all the letters ascribed to Paul, since some are Gnostic, not Marcionite, and others like Galatians 1-2 supplement his own and threaten to obscure the originals. As the old heresiologists averred, I think Marcion may have been Simon's disciple, at least a Simonian if Marcion was not himself a companion of the Magus.

The Pauline epistles began, most of them, as fragments by Simon (part of Romans), Marcion (the third through sixth chapters of Galatians and the basic draft of Ephesians), and Valentinian Gnostics (Colossians, parts of 1 Corinthians, at least). Some few began as Catholic documents, while nearly all were interpolated by Polycarp, the ecclesiastical redactor who domesticated John (as Bultmann saw it), Luke (as per John Knox), and 1 Peter, then composed Titus and 2 Timothy. The result is that in the end we stand, almost uncomprehendingly, before a pile of literary scraps. Like researchers studying the Dead Sea Scrolls, magnifying glass in one hand and pincers in the other, we are doing our darnedest to lend some order to a pile of flaking puzzle pieces.

Some readers, if they have lasted this long, may be tempted to snicker that I am sadly unable to comprehend what seems gloriously clear to them. In which case I ask, why can mainstream Pauline scholars not agree on any one supposed center of Pauline theology? Why is there virtually no agreement among commentators on even so basic an issue as whether the apostle wanted Christians to obey the Torah's commandments or not? I will never forget the experience of reading numerous Pauline translations and seven major commentaries, cover to cover, and discovering a collision of readings of these "authoritative texts" forming the ostensible bedrock of Protestant theology—key scriptures that allegedly give guidance to an otherwise clueless human race.

Is it possible that the materials, to which we have reduced the Pauline epistles, can function as a binding canon for Protestants? I don't think so. Repositories of opposing opinions, like the Upani-shads, are commentaries, not coherent treatises after being rewrit-ten, corrected, revised, and redacted. There is no authority there, for there is no author. Brilliant exegetes may find ways of tracing some meandering line of thought from one ill-matched pericope to the next, but what will they really be doing? Not thinking the inspired thoughts of the Apostle Paul after him, but rather, if they are lucky, discerning the contrivances ancient scribes employed to lend some semblance of continuity to the texts. They will be ingeniously harmonizing (as they have already been doing, with-out admitting it to themselves) diverse and contradictory compos-ite documents. And there will be no way to tell whether the order they find is one imposed in ancient days by scribes who arranged the letter fragments this way or that, or a new and artificial theo-logical framework they themselves are imposing on the texts today. The latter is a head start toward abstracting the texts into a Pauline theology which, if they were honest, they would admit they prefer over a confusing collection of old texts anyway.

Protestantism is based on Martin Luther, and Luther's theol-ogy is based on Paul, but Paul stands based on nothing at all. Paul does not have a unitary voice, is not a single author whose implied opinions might be synthesized and parroted. He is not even a single historical figure. He is certainly not a divine apostle who received his gospel, not from man nor through men, but directly from God one climactic day on his way to Damascus. That story, as we saw, is pure fiction, based on 2 Maccabees and Euripides's *Bacchae*.

No author, no authority, only texts—and finally not even texts but fragments. All we can do, it seems to me, is read them for what they have to say, or seem to be saying, and let them strike us as they may. Very likely, many of them will open our eyes to interesting new possibilities, may unveil responsibilities we tried our best to for-get we had. Some will edify and some will challenge, and it will no doubt prove to have been well worth reading them, but we cannot hide behind the artificial figure of Paul with his "apostolic authority." We are used to hearing fundamentalists appropriate Paul's mantle to thunder dogmas and whisper pieties unattested in the texts. Today we witness the same spectacle in politically correct New Testament scholars with their own Pauline ventriloquist dummies issuing screeds against American imperialism and capitalism. The role of the Pauline texts in these endeavors is like that of the grocery list in Walter M. Miller Jr.'s novel, *A Canticle for Liebowitz*, in which survivors of a nuclear holocaust venerate the only cryptic text surviving from the pre-bomb era.

One cannot help thinking it is all quite as cynical and manipulative as any self-appointed Grand Inquisitor's work ever was. Like the scams of television preachers, it is a shameless use of the Bible for ulterior ends. Like the pseudepigraphists of old, today's Paul-quoters usurp authority for themselves. Inevitably one must suspect they do it because they lack confidence that their ideas, carefully attributed to Paul, will convince anyone unless ramrodded home with his backing. But the amazing colossal apostle to whose sky-filling authority they appeal turns out to be no more real than the radioactive giant in the old science fiction movie, *The Amazing Colossal Man*: it was all just a trick of the light with cheap special effects.

INDEX

Abgarus of Edessa, 118, 119, 202

Abu-bekr, first caliph, 54

Achtemeier, Paul J., 182

Acts of Andrew, xv, 145, 165

Acts of the Apostles, 4-5, 7, 23n41, 36, 41n2, 104, 106, 137, 406, 414, 418; date of composition, 37, 56, 67; exorcism, 178; harmonization of competing traditions, 41n2, 142, 174, 177, 180, 182-83, 288-89, 419-20; invents twelve apostles, 139, 402; prescriptions for belief and living, 321, 323, 363; quo vadis episode, 162; story of Paul, 1-3, 9-12, 36, 65-66, 82-83, 94, 140, 173-74, 179-80, 256, 290, 391, 419; sources, 13-14, 16-17, 20n9, 22n26, 140-41; Titus as author, 510; written by "Luke," xiv, 56-57, 65; written by Polycarp, 125. *See also* Catholicism; Polycarp

Acts of John, 153-54, 157, 160, 175, 180-82, 184n10; docetic view of Jesus, 93, 147, 150-52, 160, 165, 334

Acts of Paul, xv, 36, 38, 89, 102-06, 161, 165, 368; borrows from *Third Corinthians*, 117, 119-23, 125, 153; early composition, 114; encratic, 104, 108, 112, 326; no references to epistles, 63, 90, 106, 116; popular in second century, 103-04; references Gospels, 106; rejects docetism, 153, 409

Acts of Paul and Thecla, 103-05, 295, 319

Acts of Peter, xv, 96, 150-51, 153, 157-58, 160, 165

Acts of Peter and Paul, 154

Acts of Philip, 145

Acts of Pilate, 361

Acts of Thomas, xv, 145-47, 150-54, 157-59, 163-65; Thomas sold into slavery, 163. *See also* Thomas, *Gospel of*

Acts Seminar, xiii-xiv

Adam (biblical), 114, 133, 265-66, 338-39, 358-59, 364-65; androgynous, 424; Adamas, 134-35, 155, 231, 397; Ancient of Days, 98;

537

513, 528; anti-Semitism, 16, 35, 305, 313, 489; Jewish Christianity, xiv, 14, 16, 36-37, 53, 72, 77, 94-95, 105, 195, 254-55, 258-59, 261, 263-64; 269, 289, 293, 296n3, 297n3, 323, 355, 414-16, 418-22, 429-30, 497; Hellenized, vii, xiv, 36, 105, 132, 186, 214, 259, 296n3, 282-83, 286, 296n3; Levitical sacrifices, 282, 297, 313-14; literature, 22n27, 23n33, 90, 133, 434n15; Marcion's view of, 427; Sanhedrin, 2, 12, 16, 399. *See also* circumcision; Ebionites; Essenes; Heliodorus; Mandaeans (Jewish Gnostics); Midrash; Mishnah; Nazoreans (Jewish Christians); Nazirites, Jewish ascetics; Philo of Alexandria

Judas Iscariot, 31, 141

Jude, 99, 116, 520, 528, 533; references to *1 Enoch* removed, 528; non-Pauline epistle, 29

Junia(s), female apostle, 5, 294, 402

kabbalism, 16; *Sefer Refuot,* 14

Kant, Immanuel, 83

Käsemann, Ernst, 58, 68, 136, 242-43, 250, 311, 313

Kenosis Hymn, 16, 23n39, 28, 95, 336

King of Kings, 55

Kirby, Jack (cartoonist Jacob Kurtzberg), 28

Klijn, A.F.J., 129n31

Knox, John, 52, 64-65, 67-68, 120,

193, 437-38, 534. *See also Marcion and the New Testament*

Koran, 54, 82, 127n12, 168n20, 302, 369n2, 417, 427

Kuhn, Thomas S., 38-39

Lake, Kirsopp, 60-61, 86n40

Laodiceans, 437-39; futility of nationalism, 447; Jews and gentiles should unite, 443; one god, 452-53; whoremongering, 448-49. *See also* Ephesians; Jesus; Marcionism; Romans

The Legend and the Apostle, 77

legends, xiv-xvi, 2-3, 5-6, 9, 20n9, 118-19, 131-37, 141, 146, 153-56, 167n5, 174-75, 254, 293, 329, 362, 402, 418-19, 454n11, 515; artistic license, 3, 314, 397-99; exaggeration, 6-7, 14, 16-18, 22n28, 31, 182, 330, 403, 405-06, 418; fictitious names, 141, 162, 184n9, 301, 312, 378, 464-65; structuralism, 142-46. *See also* history; maenads; Pentheus

Letter of Lentulus, 119

Leucius, disciple of John, 146, 182

Levi-Strauss, Claude, 142-44

Lewis, Bernard, 173

Lewis, C. S., 40

Life of Appolinus of Tyana, 192

Lightfoot, Robert H., 61

Lindemann, Andreas, 64, 90, 102, 127n15

Lohfink, Gerhard, 3

Lohse, Eduard, 57

of virgins and widows, 110-12,
114-15, 146-47, 152, 288, 320,
324-25, 368, 508, 525-26; Paul's
view of, 337-38, 347, 355; prophets, 11, 59, 114, 337-38, 368;
reproduction, 143, 150, 320-22,
339, 425-27, 432; veneration of
Mary, 319, 348, 424, 473. *See also*
Junia; legends; Lydia, first convert in Philippi; Maria, Jewish
convert; oracles; Phoebe, female
deacon; Priscilla, missionary; sexuality; Sophia, mother of demiurge; Thecla, convert

Worsley, Peter, 241, 245, 250-51,
434n14

Yamauchi, Edwin M., 531n6

Zaehner, Robert C., 127n12
Zakkai, Johannon ben, 78
Zeller, Edward, 2, 231
Zoroastrianism, 97, 127n12, 216,
364, 413, 476
Zuntz, Günther, 60, 74, 76, 78